THE GIANT BOOK
OF
QUESTIONS
AND
ANSWERS

THE GIANT BOOK
OF
QUESTIONS
AND
ANSWERS

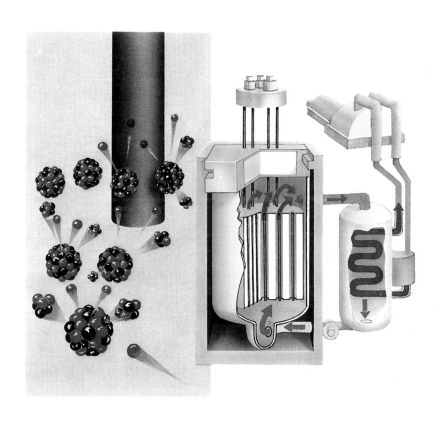

COLOUR
LIBRARY
BOOKS

General Editor
Lesley Firth

Contributors
Neil Ardley
Beverley Birch
Brenda Clarke
Jean Cooke
David Lambert
Mark Lambert
Christopher Maynard
James Muirden
Christopher Pick
Theodore Rowland-Entwistle
Jenny Vaughan
Brian Williams
Jill Wright

Illustrators
Bob Bampton, Mark Bergin,
Norma Burgin, Jeffrey Burn,
Paul Crompton, Geraint Derbyshire,
Jim Dugdale, Dave Etchell & John Ridyard,
Oliver Frey, Jerry Hoare,
John James, Ron Jobson,
Charlotte Kennedy, Jerry Malone,
Tony Payne, Bernard Robinson,
Mike Roffe, Chris Ryley, Mike Saunders,
Trevor Scobie, Tammy Wong, Michael Youens

CLB 2257

Published in 1988 by Colour Library Books Limited,
Godalming Business Centre,
Catteshall Lane,
Godalming, Surrey

The material in this book has previously been
published by Kingfisher Books Limited in six
separate volumes: *Why is It?*, *How Does it Work?*, (1983),
What is it?, *Where is it?*, (1984), *When did it
Happen?*, *Who Were They?* (1985).

Printed in Italy

ISBN 0 86283 680 8

CONTENTS

PLANET EARTH

▶ WHEN WAS THE EARTH
FORMED?

The oldest rocks found so far are thought to be about 3850 million years old – so the Earth had a solid crust by then. Some meteorites and pieces of Moon rock are probably 4600 million years old, so scientists now think that the Earth and other parts of our Solar System were formed about 4600 million years ago.

As scientists have studied the Earth's rocks more, they have decided on an earlier and earlier date for the Earth's formation. In the 17th century, Archbishop Ussher dated the Earth's creation to 4004 BC. By the 19th century, geologists thought the Earth might be 100 million years old. During this century, scientists have discovered that many rocks contain radioactive elements which gradually decay over long periods of time. With special equipment, the rate of decay can be measured.

Early attempts to measure the age of the Earth with the help of radioactive elements in rocks put its formation at 2000 million years ago. Today scientists believe it is more than twice as old. They base their estimates on tests made on samples of very old rocks from remote areas such as Greenland, and also on Moon rock and meteorites.

▶ WHEN WAS THE
SAHARA DESERT
COVERED BY ICE?

Geologists have found evidence of glaciation in the bedrock of the Algerian desert. This suggests that the Sahara was covered by ice about 450 million years ago. Further studies suggest that when this happened the area was situated near the South Pole.

The shape and position of the continents on our globe have not always been the same. The Earth's crust is broken into many giant 'plates' which are slowly moving. As they move, they carry the continents with them. Some plates contain whole continents, such as Australia. Some plates contain parts of the present continents.

About 200 million years ago, in Triassic times, there was one supercontinent called Pangaea. This has since broken apart. Pangaea was formed when separate continental plates drifted together.

The history of the continents before the formation of Pangaea is still rather uncertain. But evidence from rocks, especially rock magnetism, shows that 450 million years ago, in Ordovician times, today's Sahara lay at the South Pole. The Equator ran diagonally across today's North America.

▶ WHEN DID THE OLD
WORLD AND THE NEW
WORLD SEPARATE?

The continents of the Old World (Europe, Asia and Africa) and the New World (North and South America) have been slowly drifting on the surface of the Earth since our planet became solid. About 200 million years ago they were joined together in Pangaea. Then the Atlantic opened up, separating the Americas from Africa and Europe. The Americas drifted westwards to join Asia for a time.

Since Jurassic times, the Atlantic Ocean has opened up very slowly. In the last 150 million years, it has changed from a broad rift valley to a wide ocean. Samples of rocks and sediments from the ocean floor enable geologists to date the different parts of the Atlantic and work out the average rate of movement of the continents.

The South Atlantic formed first, as the southern continents split apart. Then North America separated from Europe and drifted towards eastern Asia. Land which now forms both Alaska in North America and the Chukchi Peninsula of Siberia joined on to the rest of Siberia.

During the Pleistocene Ice Ages there were many changes of sea level, forming the Bering Strait. At present, Alaska and Siberia are separated by this narrow, shallow sea.

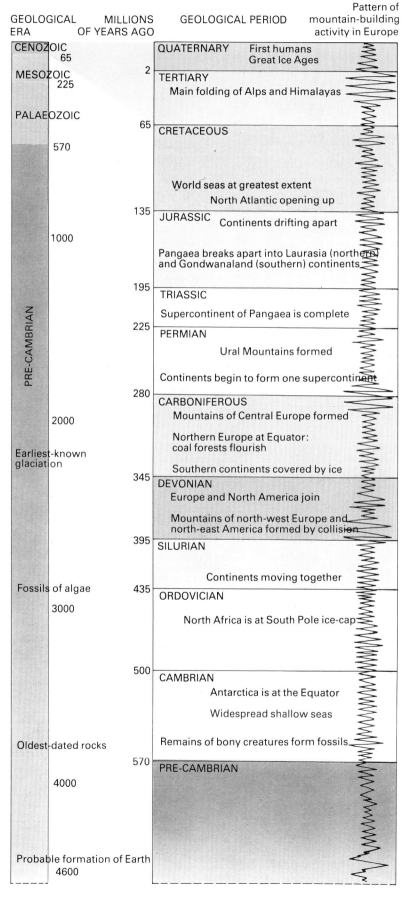

GEOLOGICAL ERA	MILLIONS OF YEARS AGO	GEOLOGICAL PERIOD	Pattern of mountain-building activity in Europe
CENOZOIC	65	QUATERNARY First humans Great Ice Ages	
MESOZOIC	2	TERTIARY Main folding of Alps and Himalayas	
	225		
PALAEOZOIC			
	65	CRETACEOUS	
	570		
		World seas at greatest extent North Atlantic opening up	
	135	JURASSIC Continents drifting apart	
	1000		
		Pangaea breaks apart into Laurasia (northern) and Gondwanaland (southern) continents	
	195	TRIASSIC	
		Supercontinent of Pangaea is complete	
	225	PERMIAN	
		Ural Mountains formed	
		Continents begin to form one supercontinent	
	280	CARBONIFEROUS Mountains of Central Europe formed	
	2000	Northern Europe at Equator: coal forests flourish	
Earliest-known glaciation		Southern continents covered by ice	
	345	DEVONIAN Europe and North America join	
		Mountains of north-west Europe and north-east America formed by collision	
	395	SILURIAN	
		Continents moving together	
Fossils of algae	435	ORDOVICIAN	
	3000	North Africa is at South Pole ice-cap	
	500	CAMBRIAN	
		Antarctica is at the Equator	
		Widespread shallow seas	
Oldest-dated rocks		Remains of bony creatures form fossils	
	570	PRE-CAMBRIAN	
	4000		
Probable formation of Earth	4600		

(In ERA column: PRE-CAMBRIAN spans the Palaeozoic through to the formation of Earth)

The Alps are made mainly of rock layers which were uplifted and folded about 25 million years ago.

The Alps are part of a series of fold mountains stretching through southern Europe and the Middle East to the Himalayas and other mountains of Asia. They are the result of the movement of the continents since the break-up of the supercontinent Pangaea.
Africa and Eurasia drifted eastwards and rotated towards each other. Sediments in the ocean floor between these continents were compressed, folded, faulted and uplifted. The uplift was much faster than erosion, so great mountains formed.

Six million years ago the Mediterranean Sea was a dry valley. Boreholes made in many places beneath the present sea have revealed a layer of salt hundreds of metres thick.

The climate around the present Mediterranean must have been much hotter and drier in Tertiary times, about six million years ago. Few rivers flowed, and water must have evaporated quickly. A mountain range across the Strait of Gibraltar kept out the waters of the Atlantic Ocean. Geologists think that this mountain dam was breached about five and a half million years ago. Salt water poured in, flooding the present Mediterranean.

▼ WHEN DID PEOPLE
DISCOVER THAT THE
EARTH IS ROUND?

**The ancient Greeks
discovered that the Earth is
round. Pythagoras (582–507
BC) described the Earth as a
sphere.**

The Greeks studied the
shadow of the Earth and Moon
during eclipses. They believed
a sphere to be the perfect
shape, so thought that all
heavenly bodies, and the
universe itself, must be
spherical. In 350 BC, Aristotle
argued that the Earth is round.

Although the Greeks were
right about the Earth's shape,
most of them believed that it
was at the centre of the
universe. About 280 BC,
Aristarchus said that the Sun is
at the centre, but his ideas
were ignored for 1500 years.

When the Roman Empire
broke up, Greek ideas were
condemned by the Church or
forgotten. Christians were told
that the Earth is flat. But the
Arabs kept Greek ideas alive
through their translations, and
later medieval scholars and
map makers rediscovered that
the Earth is round.

▼ WHEN DID SEA CHARTS
COME INTO USE?

**The earliest record of a sea-
chart dates from 1270, when
Louis IX of France studied a
chart on board a Genoese
ship during the Eighth
Crusade.**

The earliest navigators kept
close to land or drifted with
ocean currents. Once the
compass was used, ships could
sail more directly from one
port to another. The Chinese
and Arabs may have used sea-
charts before Europeans, but
none survive.

From about 1200,
compasses and rudders were
used on European ships.
Navigators used *portolani* –
books which listed ports,
landmarks, distances and
navigation advice. Later,
charts were added to these
books. The Genoese were great
sailors and compiled the
oldest-known *portolani* and
charts. Other countries copied
them. By 1354 sea-charts were
more common. The chart
shown here dates from 1548. It
shows the Mediterranean and
part of the Atlantic.

◄ WHEN WERE THE FIRST
MAPS MADE?

**Simple sketch-maps were
probably drawn before people
could write, so maps may be
older than written history.
The oldest surviving map was
drawn on a Babylonian clay
tablet about 2300 BC.**

An ancient map was found at
Gar-Sur, nearly 400 kilometres
north of Babylon. It shows
mountains and a river
(probably the Euphrates)
flowing through a delta.

The ancient Egyptians drew
maps to record land
boundaries. But scientific
map-making began with the
Greeks who worked out the
size and shape of the Earth.

The Greek geographer
Claudius Ptolemy, shown
here, drew maps of the whole
world. In his famous work
Geographia, he discussed
globes, map projections and
principles of map-making.
Arab geographers translated
Ptolemy's writings, and in
1405 a Latin translation was
made. For several centuries
many new maps were based on
this.

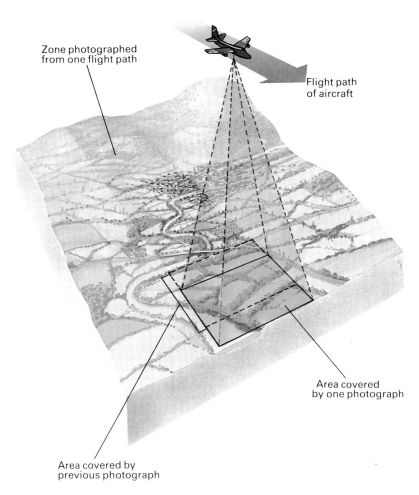

Zone photographed
from one flight path

Flight path
of aircraft

Area covered
by one photograph

Area covered by
previous photograph

**The first aerial photographs
were taken from a balloon
above Paris in 1858. The
photographer and balloonist
was Gaspard Felix
Tournachon, who was also
known as Nadar.**

These first air photographs of
Paris were used to help with
map-making. Experiments
continued with balloons and
kites, but it was not until
World War I that aerial
photography became really
useful for reconnaisance
mapping. As better lenses,
cameras and planes were made
after 1918, many more air
photographs were taken.
During World War II, vast
areas of the world were
mapped from air photographs.
    Modern air photographs are
taken with a 60 per cent
overlap, as shown in the
diagram. When pairs of
photographs are viewed
stereoscopically, the land
appears in 3-D and contours
can be plotted. Satellites are
also used for aerial
photography.

**The first collection of maps
to be called an atlas was
published by Gerardus
Mercator in 1585. The
picture shows the title page
from one of these books.**

Until printing was invented,
maps were hand-made and
very expensive. In 1477, a
Latin version of Ptolemy's
Geographia was printed.
    Abraham Ortelius of
Antwerp produced the first
modern type of atlas in 1570.

It had 70 maps. At the same
time, Gerardus Mercator was
working on a series of volumes
in which he planned to
describe the creation and
history of the world. He
named it after the Greek god
Atlas because he symbolized
the study of heaven and earth.
    Part one of Mercator's atlas
was a list of important dates
and events up to the year 1568.
The maps were not published
until 1585. They included
world maps drawn on a map-
projection which is still named
after Mercator.

▼WHEN DID CROP ROTATION BEGIN IN EUROPE?

All crops take goodness out of the soil, but some crops are able to put goodness back into it. Farmers can improve their soil with manures and fertilizers; by resting the soil for a fallow year; and by growing different kinds of crops after each other in the same fields.

Variations of the medieval three-field system (top diagram) have been used in Europe for over 2000 years. In the three-field system, large fields are divided into strips which are cultivated by different farmers. Every year, two fields are cultivated and the third is left fallow. Today, modern fertilizers make a fallow year unnecessary.

A new system which cut out the fallow year was probably first used in the Netherlands in the 15th century. Fodder crops were grown on the land, instead of using a fallow year. In this way, farmers could cultivate all the land all the time, though they did not then know that many fodder crops put nitrogen back into the soil. Plants need nitrogen to grow properly.

In 17th-century England, pioneers of new farming methods introduced the Norfolk four-course rotation (lower diagram). In this system, cereal crops such as wheat and barley alternate with clover and root crops. Cereal crops take a lot of goodness out of the soil, but clover puts nitrogen back into the soil. Even with modern fertilizers, farmers still use crop rotation.

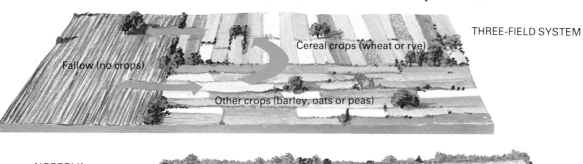

THREE-FIELD SYSTEM

Fallow (no crops)

Cereal crops (wheat or rye)

Other crops (barley, oats or peas)

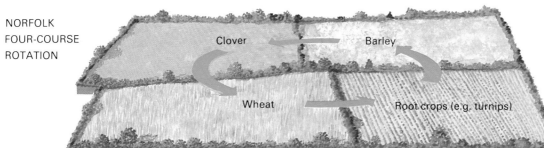

NORFOLK FOUR-COURSE ROTATION

Clover

Barley

Wheat

Root crops (e.g. turnips)

Sugar beet   Sugar cane

◄WHEN WAS SUGAR INTRODUCED TO EUROPE?

The sugar we eat is refined from either sugar cane (a tropical grass) or sugar beet (a temperate root crop).

Sugar-making may have started in India about 3000 BC. Alexander the Great took samples home to Greece.

The Arabs learned about sugar-making from India. By the 8th century, Arabs were growing cane and making sugar in Spain and France.

Christopher Columbus took sugar cane from Europe to the West Indies in 1493. Gradually, sugar plantations were established in many parts of the New World. The sugar trade across the Atlantic became very important.

At the beginning of the 19th century, Europe could not get sugar supplies from America because of the Napoleonic Wars. By then, a few people had proved that sugar could be obtained from certain kinds of beet. Napoleon encouraged the growth and refining of beet sugar in Europe.

▶ WHY DOES THE SUN RISE IN THE EAST?

Our Earth is rotating on its axis from west to east. As we travel eastwards on the rotating Earth, we pass into the zone of light where we can see the Sun. So we see the Sun first in the east in the morning.

Work it out for yourself with a globe and a torch. Shine the torch on the globe to represent sunlight, as in the diagram. Fix a model person, such as a little doll or a toy soldier, on to the globe so that it stands on the country where you live.

Now rotate your globe gently from west to east (see arrow on diagram). Watch the model pass from dark to light and light to dark. It is dawn as the model approaches the zone of light, and it will face east to see the Sun. It is evening as it passes into the zone of darkness and the Sun sets in the west.

▲ WHY DO WE HAVE DAY AND NIGHT?

At any one time, half the Earth is facing towards the Sun and is in its light. The other half is shaded from the Sun, experiencing night. The Earth rotates on its axis once in 24 hours. During that time, the place where you live turns into the sunlight for part of the time (day) and then shadow (night).

The Earth's axis is an imaginary line joining the North and South Poles. This diagram shows the Earth in December. Notice how the axis is tilted. The South Pole is tilted towards the Sun (shown here by a torch) and it is summer in the southern hemisphere. Imagine the globe spinning: it would be light all the time in the Antarctic.

Towards the North Pole the days are short and in the Arctic it is night all the time. In June, the North Pole would be tilted towards the Sun and the Antarctic would be in the dark.

▶ WHY DO WE HAVE SEASONS?

In one year the Earth travels right round the Sun. The diagram shows the Earth at four different times of the year. Notice how the axis remains tilted at the same angle. First one hemisphere, then the other, is tilted towards the Sun.

In June, when the northern hemisphere is tilted towards the Sun, it is summer in Europe, Asia and North America. The Sun is overhead at the Tropic of Cancer. It is then winter in the southern hemisphere.

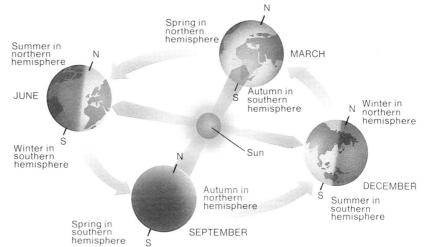

Six months later, in December, the southern hemisphere is tilted towards the Sun. So it is summer at Christmas-time in Australia, but it is winter in Europe.

The Sun is overhead at the Tropic of Capricorn. In March and September the Sun is overhead at the Equator. Both hemispheres are enjoying either autumn or spring.

WHY ARE FOSSILS IMPORTANT TO GEOLOGISTS?

Fossils of the same kind help geologists to put different kinds of rocks in the same age-group. Fossils also give information about the conditions that existed when they were alive. And similar fossils in different places have helped in the study of continental drift.

The fossils most useful to geologists are of plants and animals which originally lived in a wide variety of places, but only for a fairly short period of time. These are called index fossils. They prove that the rocks in which they are now found were all formed at about the same time.

Fossils of plants and animals that were very sensitive to their environment also tell us about the kind of conditions existing when the rocks were formed. Identical fossils of plants and animals which could not get across water have been found on opposite sides of oceans. This means that such areas were once joined before the continents drifted apart.

WHY DID THE DINOSAURS DIE OUT SO SUDDENLY?

Dinosaurs became extinct about 65 million years ago, at the end of Cretaceous times. They had existed for 130 million years. No one knows for sure why they died out.

Many other types of animals died out at about the same time as the dinosaurs, including flying reptiles, sea reptiles and the sea creatures called ammonites. But a few reptiles did survive from that time and still exist today, such as crocodiles, turtles and tortoises, lizards and snakes.

There are many theories to explain why the dinosaurs died out, including changes of climate and vegetation, cold winters, and new parasites and diseases. Volcanic dust, meteorites, and even mammals eating all the dinosaur eggs, have also been suggested. But the question remains an unsolved mystery.

WHY DO SOME ROCKS CONTAIN FOSSILS AND NOT OTHERS?

Some rocks are too old to have fossils. Other rocks were too hot when formed.

The three groups of rocks are igneous, sedimentary and metamorphic. Igneous rocks, such as lava and granite, are made from molten material which cooled down. No plant or animal could survive such heat, so there are no fossils.

Sedimentary rocks are made from material which was deposited in water or on land and many contain fossils. Some, such as coal and some limestones, are made almost entirely of fossils. Others, like sandstone, contain some fossils.

Metamorphic rocks have been changed by intense heat or pressure. Marble is a changed form of limestone, for example. Any fossils in them will have been changed beyond recognition.

Sandstone (sedimentary rock) with fossil

Granite (igneous rock)

▶ WHY ARE THERE COAL SEAMS IN THE ANTARCTIC?

Coal is a rock made of the fossil remains of plants. The icy Antarctic has very few plants now, but when these coal seams were formed, there must have been plenty of plants. So the climate then must have been a lot warmer.

The coal seams of the Antarctic were formed in Permian times, about 250 million years ago. Modern theories of continental drift explain why Antarctica was much warmer then.

The maps below show where the continents could have been at different times in the past. In Permian times, Antarctica was probably part of the great continent called Pangaea. It was then at a much warmer latitude than now. When this huge continent split, Antarctica was part of Gondwanaland. When Gondwanaland split up, Antarctica slowly moved to the South Pole.

▶ WHY DO THE CONTINENTS MOVE ABOUT?

The crust of the Earth is a relatively thin layer. Scientists believe it is divided into huge sections called 'plates'. These are moved very slowly by convection currents inside the Earth.

The scientist Alfred Wegener suggested in 1915 that the continents might have moved. He had noticed that their shapes fit together like a jigsaw. His theory was called 'continental drift'.

These maps show the possible movement of the continents in the past. From a study of earthquakes and sea-floor spreading, scientists think that the continents and oceans are on the rigid plates into which the Earth's crust is divided. They can move because the rocks of the mantle (immediately below the crust) are moving.

Mantle rocks are not liquid, but 'gooey' like thick tar. Convection currents rise from the core, up through the mantle and spread out, moving the crustal plates like rafts.

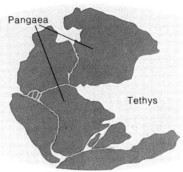

Pangaea

Tethys

200 million years ago

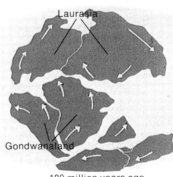

Laurasia

Gondwanaland

180 million years ago

65 million years ago

◀ WHY HAVE SOME SEAS DISAPPEARED?

Small seas can be filled up by sediments brought in by rivers. Large shallow seas can also be partly filled with sediments, and their floors pushed up by earth movements.

An inland sea such as the Caspian is filling up quickly. Old maps show that it was much larger a few hundred years ago. Larger seas, like the Mediterranean and North Sea, can also fill up as sediments are carried in, and their sea floor may be pushed up by earth movements. Most of the sedimentary rocks found on dry land were originally laid down in seas that have long disappeared.

These maps show the pattern the continents may have formed in the past. Notice how the movements of the continents altered the shape of the oceans, such as Tethys.

Scientists believe that at the moment the Pacific is slowly getting smaller and the Atlantic wider. The Red Sea seems to be widening and may one day become a great ocean.

Ash

Lava

Rising magma

◀ WHY DO VOLCANOES
ERUPT?

The lava of volcanoes is molten rock, most of which rises from the Earth's mantle. It is called magma. Some magma rises straight to the surface. Some is stored in a magma chamber in the crust, where the gases collect and help to drive the magma out.

The upper part of the mantle, under the Earth's crust, is nearly molten, or liquid. A slight rise in temperature or drop in pressure will make this magma melt. Because it is lighter than the rocks around it, the magma rises.

Magma contains several gases, including water vapour, carbon dioxide, sulphur dioxide and hydrogen sulphide. Bubbles of gas expand near the surface and drive the magma out as an eruption. Some gases burn as they reach the air and heat up the lava. Volcanic eruptions vary from place to place, mainly according to how fluid or gaseous the lava is.

▶ WHY DO EARTHQUAKES AND VOLCANOES OCCUR ONLY IN SOME PARTS OF THE WORLD?

The map shows where earthquakes have happened and where volcanoes have erupted. Both occur near the edges of the Earth's crustal plates.

The zones of volcanic and earthquake activity happen near the edges of the crustal plates. These are slowly moving together or apart. For instance, one zone encircles the Pacific. Here, the floor of the Pacific is being pushed down under the continents. This gradual movement of the Pacific plates against the continental plates causes earthquakes. The rocks of the sea floor are drawn deep down and heated up, and become the lava for volcanoes.

Another zone is the Mediterranean, where the African plate is pushing against Europe. One of the zones of greatest volcanic activity is the Atlantic, where new lava is added as Europe and America drift apart.

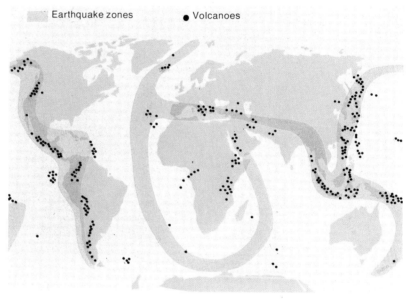

Earthquake zones ● Volcanoes

▲ WHY DO EARTHQUAKES OCCUR?

Earthquakes occur on deep faults in the Earth's crust. When the rocks suddenly move, shock waves are sent out in all directions. The movement is felt as an earthquake.

Many major faults in the crust are moving very slowly all the time. When the strain becomes too great the rocks suddenly move, causing an earthquake. The actual location of this movement is called the focus. This may be near the Earth's surface or deep in the crust. The place on the surface right above the focus is called the epicentre. Here the effects of the earthquake are felt first.

Scientists know why earthquakes happen and where they happen. The problem is to predict when they will happen. Delicate instruments can detect minor movements on a known fault which may build up into a major earthquake. But it is impossible to forecast an earthquake, or prevent it from happening.

**All geysers occur in areas
of volcanic activity, but
not all volcanic areas have
geysers. They only occur
where water can soak
through cracks in the
rocks and collect under-
ground.**

Here the water is heated
under pressure, and as it
starts to bubble out there
is a sudden gush of steam
and hot water high into the
air.

A geyser seems to work in a
similar way to a pressure
cooker. The higher the
pressure, the hotter the water
has to be to boil. Water deep
underground in a volcanic
area is super-heated before it
reaches boiling point. When it
boils, bubbles of steam rise,
expand and push some water
out at the surface. This
reduces pressure below and
lowers its boiling point. The
super-heated steam and water
is pushed out as a powerful
jet. When enough water has
seeped back and heated up,
the process starts again.

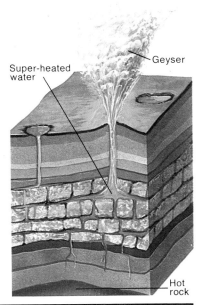

Super-heated water

Geyser

Hot rock

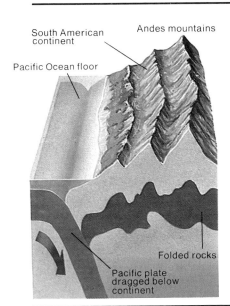

South American continent

Andes mountains

Pacific Ocean floor

Folded rocks

Pacific plate dragged below continent

**The highest mountains of
the world are found in
long ranges, like the
Himalayas, the Andes and
Rockies, the Alps and
Pyrenees.**

There are also great
mountain ranges beneath
the oceans, such as the
Mid-Atlantic Ridge. All
these mountain ranges are
close to the edges of the
great crustal plates, where
one plate is pushing
against another.

The diagram shows how the
Andes are being formed. Part
of the Pacific Ocean floor is
being pushed under South
America. Earthquakes and
volcanoes result. And the
rocks at the edge of South
America are being folded and
faulted and pushed up to form
a great mountain range.
Similar movements are
happening along the western
edge of North America.

Mountain ranges in other
parts of the world have
formed as two continents have
moved closer together, such
as Africa towards Europe.

**As you climb up a high
mountain the air gets
thinner and colder. You
may think you are getting
nearer the Sun, but a
kilometre is nothing when
the Sun is 150 million kilometres away! In fact, the
Sun heats the Earth, and it
is the Earth that heats the
air.**

The Sun's energy that reaches
the Earth's surface and heats

Permanent snow

High alpine plants

Pastures

Coniferous trees

Deciduous trees

it up arrives as shortwave
radiation. This is easily
absorbed by the air. There is
more air to absorb this heat
near the Earth's surface than
higher up. So the higher you

go, the colder it gets.

This has an effect on the
vegetation that will grow at
different altitudes in
mountain areas, as the
diagram shows.

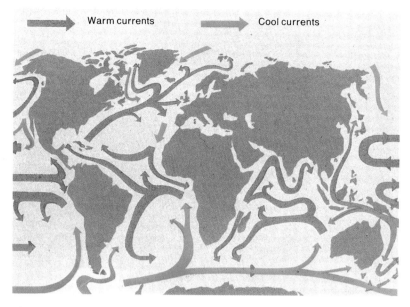

Warm currents → Cool currents →

◀ WHY DO OCEAN
CURRENTS OCCUR?

The main reason is winds. Prevailing winds blow the water at the surface of the oceans. But winds blow across land as well as sea. The ocean currents they cause do not stop or pile up against the land! So counter-currents develop.

Ocean currents are important because they move water from warm to cold areas, and from cold to warm areas. Currents that move away from the Equator are warm currents. Those that move towards the Equator are cool currents.

A cool current like the Labrador current, which flows from the Arctic to the Atlantic, may carry icebergs into the trans-Atlantic shipping lanes. A warm current like the Gulf Stream, which flows from the Caribbean to the north Atlantic, keeps ports in Norway free of ice all year.

Where these two currents mix, plankton flourish and fog is common in the famous fishing area of the New-foundland Banks.

▲ WHY IS SEA WATER SALTY?

Sea water contains many minerals. They have all been washed out of the land and carried to the sea by rivers or glaciers. When sea water evaporates, these minerals remain in the sea and become more concentrated.

Salt (sodium chloride) makes up about 85 per cent of all the minerals in sea water. The saltiness of deep-sea water is fairly constant, but near the surface it varies from place to place. Saltiness is low where lots of fresh water is added from rivers and where there is little evaporation. The Baltic is one of the least salty seas. The Red Sea has few rivers and a lot of evaporation, and so is very salty. The saltiest seas are inland. The Dead Sea is the saltiest sea on Earth.

Salt can be made in hot countries by collecting sea water in shallow ponds and leaving the water to evaporate. The salt is left behind. But it is very difficult to make sea water fresh.

▶ WHY DO THE TIDES RISE AND FALL?

The water in the oceans is held close to the Earth by gravity. But the Moon and Sun also have some 'pull' on the Earth. The Moon's gravity affects water in the oceans. The sea is 'pulled' slightly towards the Moon, causing a bulge, or high tide. On the opposite side, the sea is pushed away, causing a second bulge.

High tides occur twice in about 25 hours. This is because at the same time as the Earth is rotating on its axis, the Moon is travelling round the Earth (every $27\frac{1}{2}$ days). So high tide is usually about one hour later every day.

The height of the tide varies. In the open ocean, the difference between high and low tide (the tidal range) is less than a metre. In an enclosed sea like the Mediterranean, it is much less, 30 centimetres. But where sea water is funnelled into a narrow bay or channel, the tidal range can be very high.

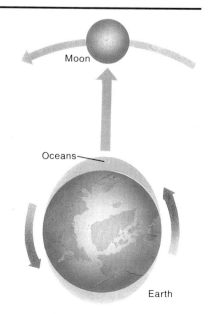

Moon

Oceans

Earth

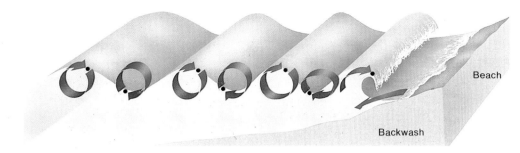

Arrows show movement of a water particle on the sea's surface

▲ WHY DO WAVES BREAK?

Winds cause waves, which form far out to sea. The wind pushes the water particles, which move round and round. Near the coast, where the sea is shallower, the sea bed interferes with the movement of the water. Then the top of the wave breaks on to the beach.

Waves have length as well as height. Wave length is the distance between one wave crest and the next. When the sea is shallower than half the wave length, the waves change. They drag on the sea bed and slow down. Then the crests crowd together.

On a gently sloping beach the crests often spill over and make a lot of surf. When the slope of the beach is steeper, the waves plunge on to the beach. They often have a strong backwash.

▲ WHY DO RIPPLE MARKS APPEAR ON SANDY BEACHES?

Both wind and waves affect the sand on the beach, causing ripples.

Ripples on sandhills are formed and move in a similar way to sand dunes. The ripples lie at right-angles to the wind and are very small. Wind blows the sand grains up the gentler face and they fall down the steeper downwind face.

Low tide ripples are formed by the gentle movement of small waves. Even with a very shallow sea and a gently sloping beach, the wind can form tiny waves. They work in the same way as larger waves but with much less power. However, they can mould the sand over which they pass. If the power of the waves increases, the ripples will be smoothed out.

▼ WHY DO SEAS SOMETIMES ERODE THE LAND?

The sea is very powerful, and attacks the land with waves, with stones and rocks in the waves, and with air compressed by the waves.

Erosion is at its most powerful when three conditions are combined: when the tide is high, the sea is rough, and the wind is on-shore. Waves can attack beaches, sand dunes and cliffs. The waves hurl stones picked up from the shore at the land. The waves also compress air in gaps and cracks in the rocks and force them apart.

A cliff face is only as strong as its weakest part. When the cracks are attacked, the other parts become weakened. Cliffs are undercut by the waves, as the diagram shows, and then cliff-falls occur.

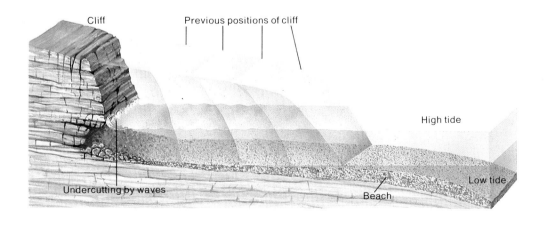

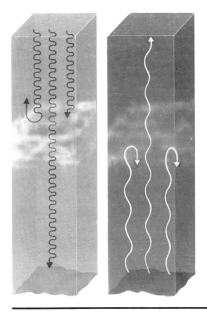

◀ WHY ARE CLOUDY NIGHTS WARMER THAN CLEAR, STAR-LIT NIGHTS?

Our Earth is heated by the Sun. Clouds act like a blanket, so a cloudy day will stop some of the Sun's heat from reaching the Earth. But a cloudy night will stop the Earth's warmth escaping.

The left-hand diagram shows daytime, when the Sun warms the Earth. Clouds stop some of the Sun's heat (shown as red arrows) reaching the Earth. The right-hand diagram shows night-time, when there is no heat from the Sun. The Earth has warmed up during the day, and the clouds stop some of the Earth's heat (shown by white arrows) from escaping.

When there are no clouds, more of the Sun's heat reaches the Earth during the day. But during a clear night more of the Earth's heat is lost, so it can get very cold. In deserts it is hardly ever cloudy. Because of this, the days are hot but the nights can become very cold.

▶ WHY DO WINDS BLOW?

The Sun's heat warms the air and makes it move. This movement is called a wind.

Different parts of the Earth receive different amounts of heat, as shown in the top picture. Near the Equator, the Sun is overhead and heats the Earth intensely. Nearer the poles, the Sun's rays strike the Earth at a low angle so the heat is not so intense.

A lot of the Earth's heat is reflected back into space, by the atmosphere, clouds, dust in the air and by water, snow and ice. So some parts of the Earth are warm and some are cold.

Warm air tends to rise and creates areas of low pressure. Cold air tends to sink and creates areas of high pressure. As warm air rises, cold air flows in and replaces it. The greater the pressure difference, the stronger the wind blows.

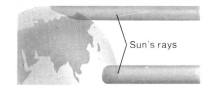

Sun's rays

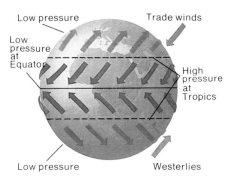

Low pressure / Low pressure at Equator / Low pressure — Trade winds / High pressure at Tropics / Westerlies

◀ WHY DO WEATHER SYSTEMS HAVE A CIRCULAR PATTERN OF WINDS?

Winds blow in a curved pattern because the Earth spins, or rotates.

If the Earth stayed still, the winds would blow straight from an area of high pressure to an area of low pressure. But because the Earth is spinning so fast, winds swirl across the surface in a curved pattern.

In the northern hemisphere, winds blow into an area of low pressure in an anticlockwise direction. In this satellite picture, the winds are swirling anti-clockwise, so this low-pressure system, or depression, must be in the northern hemisphere. A cyclone or hurricane shows the same swirling movement, but the pressure is very low and the winds are strong.

An area of high pressure is called an anticyclone. Winds blow out from an anticyclone. They move out in a clockwise direction in the northern hemisphere.

▼ WHY DO CLOUDS FORM?

A cloud is made up of tiny droplets of water or ice. When a cloud forms, the invisible water vapour in the air condenses into visible droplets of water.

All air contains water vapour. Warm air can hold more water vapour than cold air. If the air cools down, it cannot hold so much water vapour, and it turns into tiny droplets of water. You can see this happen when the hot steam from a kettle cools down in your kitchen. A lot of the water vapour turns into a cloud of water droplets.

Air cools down when it rises, because the higher in the atmosphere it goes, the cooler it gets. In the diagram below, the picture on the left shows air rising on a hot day above a city. The air rises and cools, and the water vapour condenses into droplets to form clouds. Towering clouds more than ten kilometres high can form in less than an hour on a very hot day.

Air rising over mountains (bottom right) will cool, and clouds will form. Clouds also form when warm, moist air rises over a layer of cold air.

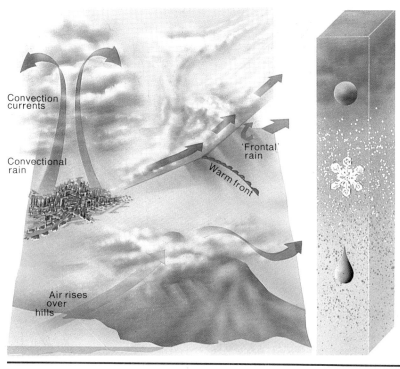

Convection currents

Convectional rain

'Frontal' rain

Warm front

Air rises over hills

◀ WHAT MAKES IT RAIN?

When it rains, the tiny water droplets in a cloud form bigger drops which fall to Earth. No one knows exactly why this happens.

One theory about rain is that tiny water droplets stick together round something solid near the top of a cloud. This could be a speck of dust or an ice crystal. The larger, heavier drop of water then falls through the cloud, picking up more tiny droplets on the way. A raindrop may seem tiny, but it is several thousand times bigger than when it began as a tiny droplet.

▶ WHAT CAUSES FOG?

The cause of fog and cloud is the same, because fog is cloud at ground level. When damp air near the ground cools enough for the water vapour to condense into droplets of water, then fog and mist occur.

Air near the ground can cool for several reasons. If the surface of the Earth is especially cold, it will cool the air above it. If the air above a cold surface is almost still, then as it cools the water vapour will condense and fog will form. This can happen over a glacier, or over land which is cooling down quickly during a clear winter night (see top diagram). It can also happen over a cold sea. Sea fogs are common at San Francisco, in California, because there is a cold sea current near the coast.

Cold air is heavy and tends to sink. So fog may form on the cold tops of hills and mountains, and roll down into the valleys (see bottom diagram).

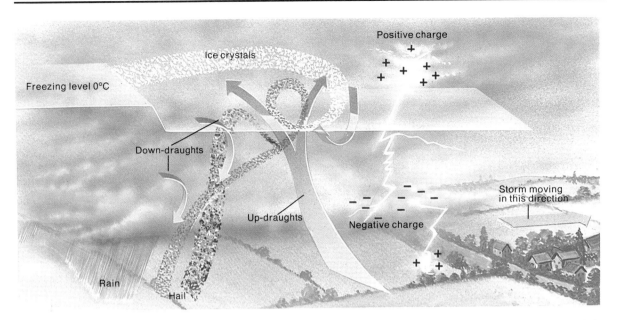

Positive charge

Ice crystals

Freezing level 0°C

Down-draughts

Up-draughts

Negative charge

Storm moving in this direction

Rain

Hail

▲ WHY DOES THUNDER ALWAYS FOLLOW LIGHTNING?

Lightning is a huge spark of electricity. Thunder is the sound made by the air as it is suddenly heated up by the lightning. They both happen at the same time. But light travels faster than sound, so we see the lightning first and then hear the thunder.

Thunder is caused when lightning heats up the molecules of air along its path. The heated molecules expand, collide with cooler molecules and set up sound waves.

Light travels very quickly, at about 300,000 kilometres per second. Sound is slower, travelling about 20 kilometres per minute. We see the flash almost as it happens, but we hear the sound afterwards.

The closer the storm, the closer together the flash and the thunder. Count the seconds between the lightning flash and the thunder. Divide this number by three to find out how many kilometres away the storm is.

▲ WHY DOES LIGHTNING OFTEN STRIKE TREES?

When lightning flashes from a cloud to Earth it takes the easiest path. It is always attracted to the highest point in an area, which is often a tree.

A storm cloud is like a giant electricity generator. The positive charge is at the top of the cloud and the negative charge at the base. Lightning is the spark between the two: first within a cloud, then from cloud to cloud, and then from cloud to Earth.

A lightning flash begins with a downward 'leader stroke'. This seeks out the easiest path to Earth. Air is very resistant to electricity and the leader stroke is attracted to the nearest high point. A single, damp tree offers a low-resistance route to Earth through the trunk.

Tall buildings also attract lightning, but fortunately they can be protected by lightning conductors. These are strips of copper (a good conductor of electricity), which offer a path for the lightning to reach the Earth.

▲ WHY DO WE SOMETIMES GET HAIL?

If you could cut a hailstone in half you would find that it is made up of lots of layers of ice. This is because a hailstone has risen high into the coldest part of the storm cloud again and again. Each time, another layer of ice freezes round it until the hailstone is so heavy that it falls to Earth.

The diagram shows a typical storm cloud. For a hailstorm, the top of the cloud must be above freezing level and there must be rapidly rising convection currents swirling up through the cloud. These carry up droplets which freeze near the top of the cloud and begin to fall. Before they reach the base of the cloud they are swept up again, and another layer of ice is added near the top of the cloud.

This process is repeated until the hailstone becomes too heavy for the up-draught to carry it higher, and it will fall to Earth. Hail from such storm clouds can form in temperate or tropical areas.

▶ WHY IS A SNOWFLAKE
MADE UP OF CRYSTALS?

**When water vapour cools,
it usually condenses into
water droplets. In very
cold air the water vapour
can condense directly into
ice crystals. These crystals
may cling together to
make a snowflake.**

Snow forms in a completely
different way from hail. There
is no freezing then thawing
process, and no great up-
draughts in a snow cloud. The
temperature of the cloud is

important. It must be cold
enough for ice crystals to form
straight from water vapour.

The shape of snow crystals
varies according to the temperature and humidity of both
the air in which they form and
the air through which they
fall. So it is not surprising that
no two crystals are alike.
'Dry' snow falls in very cold,
dry conditions. It has very
small crystals and blows into
snowdrifts easily. 'Wet' snow
forms when the air is very
moist and warm enough for
the crystals to bond together.

▲ WHY DO HURRICANES
CAUSE SO MUCH DAMAGE?

**Hurricanes (also called
typhoons or cyclones) are
spiralling winds that can**

**blow at 250 to 350 kilo-
metres per hour. They
start over a warm sea,
absorb lots of moisture
and hurtle towards the
land. A hurricane can**

**measure 400 kilometres
across. It can uproot trees,
destroy buildings and fling
cars about.**

The centre of a hurricane is
called the 'eye'. It can be 40
kilometres across and is
relatively calm. Around it
swirl the hurricane winds.
They are strongest nearest the
eye. These winds circle round
and rise up high in the
atmosphere. Ocean water is
drawn up into the eye,
causing great storm surges
and very high tides when it
reaches the coast.

▶ WHY DO WE SEE
RAINBOWS?

**When sunlight passes
through raindrops it is
slightly bent. Sunlight is a
mixture of colours. The
raindrops bend some
colours more than others,
so they are separated out
to make the colours of the
rainbow.**

Light rays travel in a straight
line, but they do change
direction when they pass
through substances of
different density, for example

from air to water. Have you
noticed that if you look down
at a drinking straw in a glass
of water it appears bent? This
bending is called refraction.
Raindrops refract sunlight.

Sunlight has to pass
through raindrops at a low
angle for the colours to show
as a semicircular bow. This is
why you see rainbows most
often after showers in the
early morning or late evening,
and not at midday. From an
aircraft or a mountain top you
can sometimes see a rainbow
below you as a complete
circle.

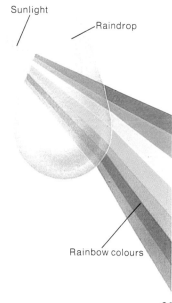

Sunlight

Raindrop

Rainbow colours

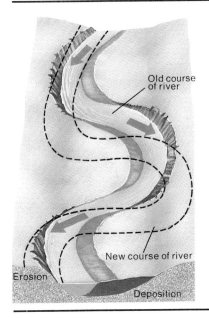

Old course of river

New course of river

Erosion

Deposition

◀ WHY DO RIVER
MEANDERS CHANGE THEIR
SHAPE?

The diagram shows that river currents hit the outside bend of a meander, where erosion occurs. On the inside of the bend, mud and sand are deposited. The two act together and change the shape of the meander.

Imagine you are in a canoe on the river. The current rushes you towards the outside of the meander. You paddle fast and just avoid hitting the bank. Then the current pushes you towards the other bank.

The current is constantly hitting the outside bank of a meander, undercutting it. When the river is in flood, it will wear away, or erode, the outside bank more quickly. The water will erode more powerfully when sand grains and pebbles are carried along.

One question remains: how did the meander begin? The slightest eddy will start a small bend in the river's flow. Once it has started, a meander gets bigger every year.

▶ WHY DO SOME RIVERS HAVE DELTAS?

A delta is shaped like a triangle, which is also the Greek letter D, called 'Delta'. A river delta is caused by deposits at the mouth of a river.

A river forms a delta if it transports more silt to its mouth than can be removed by waves, currents or tides. So deltas in lakes are very common. The Mediterranean Sea has a very small tidal range, so big rivers like the Nile (seen here from space) and the Rhône have very big deltas. Deltas are less common on rivers that flow to oceans and tidal seas.

When a river reaches the sea or a lake, the flow of water suddenly slows down. Still water cannot hold so much silt, and the river channel becomes blocked by deposits. The water spills over on both sides of the old channel. Soon the two new channels will be blocked, and the water will find new routes. So a delta has many water channels and is constantly changing.

◀ WHY DO LAKES SOMETIMES DISAPPEAR?

Lots of lakes have vanished. Some have been filled up, the water of others has flowed away, and other lakes in very hot countries have simply dried up.

Lakes can be filled up with material brought down by rivers. Deltas in a lake can eventually fill up the whole lake, which becomes an almost flat plain. Lakes in glaciated areas often vanish in this way.

Secondly, the outlet from the lake can be worn away so that the point at which the lake flows out is lowered. The lake will drain away, leaving dry land. Earth movements and volcanic activity can also make new outlets for lakes.

Some lakes dry up because of evaporation. Less water is being brought into the lake by rivers than is evaporating in the heat. After a series of wet years, Lake Eyre in Australia is a huge lake, but after several dry years it vanishes!

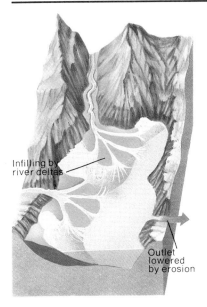

Infilling by river deltas

Outlet lowered by erosion

A glacier is like a great river of ice. Glaciers appear when more snow falls than melts every year. The snow collects, squeezing the lower layers hard. It turns to ice and forms a glacier.

Glaciers appear only in cold climates where there is snow all year round. This is either in high latitudes (the Arctic or Antarctic) or at high altitudes (in mountains). Glaciers often appear first on the shady side of a mountain. There are more glaciers on the north-facing shady slopes of the Alps than on the sunny southern side.

Most glaciers today are left over from the last Ice Age. In the last two million years there have been five glaciations. Ice-sheets spread from mountain areas and from the Arctic to cover most of Europe. This happened when the climate was much colder than now. No one knows why the climate changed from warm to cold so many times.

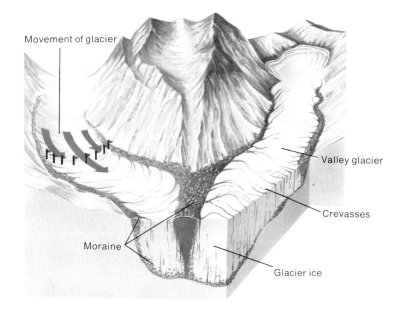

All the time snow is being added at the top, the glacier will move forward under its own weight.

Glacier ice is under such pressure that the crystals melt slightly and can slip easily. The rate of movement will vary according to the slope of the valley, the thickness of the glacier, the roughness of the valley bottom and the temperature.

Movement can be observed by putting a line of stakes across a glacier. Those at the centre of the glacier move faster than those at the side. The differences in the rate of movement within a glacier create huge gaps or crevasses.

Rocks and stones (moraine) fall on to a glacier and are picked up by the ice at the bottom of a glacier. It is able to deepen and widen old river valleys by scraping the bottom like sandpaper and by plucking material out like pincers. The valley floors are deepened and flattened, and become U-shaped.

Ice-sheets alter a landscape in very different ways from valley glaciers. They deposit moraine consisting of clay, sand and gravel.

Look at an atlas map of Finland or north-east Canada. There are thousands of lakes. These are examples of areas with very old hard rocks which have been eroded by ice-sheets. The material that is eroded is deposited on

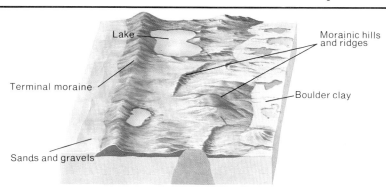

lower land where the ice-sheet is moving slowly or melting. In much of Great Britain and northern Europe, the lowland is a plain of boulder clay (clay with boulders) left by ice-sheets. They leave a landscape of low hills and hollows filled with lakes. At the edge of ice-sheets, great piles of rocks, gravels and sand are deposited. These make heath-covered hills such as the Lüneburg Heath in Germany.

23

▶ WHY ARE SOME SOILS
FERTILE?

**A fertile soil is rich in
humus, bacteria and
minerals. It also has
enough water and a good
texture.**

The rock beneath soil is
important. Permeable rocks,
such as sandstone, make the
soil light and dry.
Impermeable rocks, like clay,
cause heavy waterlogged soils.
Very limey (alkaline) soils are
bad for some plants. Broken-
down rock fragments provide
the minerals which plants
need.

Climate and natural
vegetation are also important.
Plants need organic matter.
Humus is made by soil
bacteria which decompose, or
rot, vegetation. They work
best in a warm, airy soil,
where there is plenty of leaf
mould or grass. Water is very
important in the right
amount. Too much causes
waterlogging or 'leaching',
where the goodness is washed
away through the soil. Too
much evaporation can bring
salts to the surface.

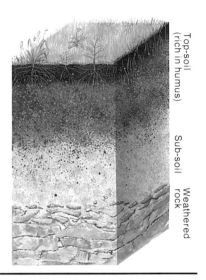

Top-soil
(rich in humus)

Sub-soil

Weathered
rock

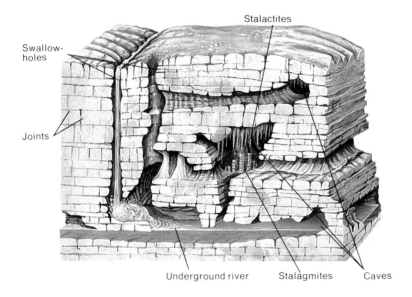

Swallow-
holes

Joints

Stalactites

Underground river   Stalagmites   Caves

▲ WHY DO UNDERGROUND
CAVES OCCUR?

**The most spectacular
caves are found in lime-
stone. They are caused by
rainwater and rivers dis-
solving the stone.**

Caves in limestone are caused
by water in two ways. Rainwater can dissolve the
limestone and cracks are
gradually enlarged to form
caves. Also, underground
rivers can erode the
limestone. Many caves have
rivers in them, or evidence of
old, dry river beds. Some
caves are made spectacular
because of limestone deposits
known as stalactites and
stalagmites.

There are also caves in
basalt rocks. These form
when molten lava cools on the
surface, but underneath it is
still hot enough to flow away
downhill. Caves remain when
the lava has cooled down.

At the coast there are caves
formed by the erosive power
of the sea. With changes in sea
level, they are sometimes
found high above the present
beach.

◀ WHY IS LIMESTONE
DIFFERENT FROM OTHER
ROCKS?

**There are different kinds
of limestone, all of which
are sedimentary rocks.
They are made of the fossil
remains of sea creatures.
You can see if rock is limestone by adding a drop of
weak acid. Limestone will
fizz and a little will
dissolve.**

In some limestone you can see
the fossils of many shellfish.
Other limestones are formed
from corals which were living
in warm seas millions of years
ago. Some limestones were
made chemically from
calcium carbonate. Chalk is a
soft type of limestone made
from the remains of sea
creatures.

All limestones are
permeable. This means that
water can pass through joints
and cracks. All limestones will
dissolve in rainwater, which is
a weak acid. Some cracks
become swallow-holes
through which rivers vanish.
Underground, water is continually dissolving the limestone and creating new caves.

◀ WHY DOES SOIL EROSION OCCUR?

Soil can be eroded, or worn away, by wind or by water. It occurs most often when a light soil is bare and dry and when there are strong winds or sudden heavy rainstorms.

Soil erosion is usually caused by bad farming. If a big field of light soil is ploughed, harrowed and left bare in dry weather, a strong wind will blow the topsoil away. Too many animals, such as goats, grazing on a semi-desert area, will eat plants and even roots and leave the soil bare. Then the wind will blow the topsoil away.

Water can cause as much damage as wind. Heavy rain or floods washing across bare earth can take the topsoil with it. Gully erosion is even more serious in some places. If a farmer ploughs down instead of across a slope, the furrows form little ditches down which rainwater can flow. In a sudden heavy storm, these ditches become rivers and dig deep channels.

▶ WHY DO SAND DUNES MOVE ACROSS DESERTS?

Only about one-fifth of hot deserts are covered with sand. Strong winds often blow in deserts. Because deserts are dry and do not have any vegetation, loose sand can be driven along by the wind. The constant movement of sand from one side of a dune to the other moves the dune.

The diagram shows the wind blowing across an area of crescent-shaped dunes called

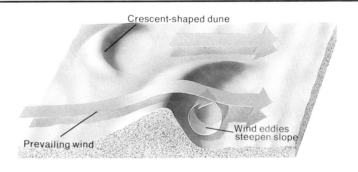

Crescent-shaped dune

Prevailing wind

Wind eddies steepen slope

'barchans'. The sand grains are blown up the gentle windward slope. They then fall over the crest and roll down the steep leeward slope. This slope stays steep because of wind eddies. The lower ends of the dune move faster, and are curved round by the wind in a crescent shape.

In other places, there may be long ridges of dunes, parallel to the wind direction, called 'seif' dunes.

◀ WHY ARE SOME DESERTS GETTING BIGGER?

Deserts are probably getting bigger because there is less rain. Also, strong winds move sand further out to cover the neighbouring land. Bad farming has also led to the soil being worn away, causing deserts.

Deserts have not always been the same size as now. There are prehistoric cave paintings of giraffes and elephants in the middle of the Sahara, and the Romans grew wheat in north Africa. The amount of rainfall in the Sahara and other deserts has probably changed. A small change can reduce the amount of vegetation and dry up rivers.

Very dry, hot winds can kill plants and move sand dunes. Dunes have overwhelmed villages and farms. Soil will blow away if land is over-grazed or ploughed up. Too many wells and pumps lower the level of water under-ground. This also affects the soil and makes irrigation more difficult.

25

The oldest piece of rock that has been dated is a piece of gneiss from the Ameralik Fiord in western Greenland. It is about 3800 million years old.

Gneiss is a metamorphic rock – one that has been changed by heat and pressure. It is one of many ancient rocks that form Greenland and the neighbouring Canadian Shield. These rocks are the ancient base of the North American continent. The samples were dated by measuring the rate of change of tiny amounts of radioactive rubidium and strontium in the rock.

It is significant that the oldest rocks have been found on a land area. For it shows how long-lasting the lighter rocks of the continents are. In contrast, the oldest known rocks of the ocean floors are only 200 million years old. It is beneath the oceans that the Earth's crust is being created and destroyed.

The Colorado Desert in the south-west of the USA has layers of rock which have formed over a period of about 1600 million years. The River Colorado and its tributaries have sliced through these layers in the Grand Canyon and other nearby canyons.

The Grand Canyon area is the only place on Earth where geologists can study so many layers of undisturbed rock and an almost perfect sequence of fossils.

The 'Granite Gorge' at the bottom of the Grand Canyon is cut into the rocks that form the base of most of North America. These ancient rocks were formed about 1700 million years ago. They are buried beneath horizontal layers of rocks. At the bottom of the pile is the Tapeats Sandstone, 570 million years old. At the top of the pile, on the rim of the Canyon, is the Kaibab Limestone, about 270 million years old. Layers of more recent rocks have been eroded from the top of the Grand Canyon.

The rocks of the top of the Grand Canyon form the base of Zion Canyon. This canyon is cut into sandstones that are 150 to 200 million years old. The youngest rocks in Zion Canyon form the base of Bryce Canyon where 60 million-year old shales, sandstones and limestones have been eroded into countless spires. The youngest rocks of the Colorado Plateau are at Brian Head, the plateau's highest point, and are only 37 million years old.

WHERE DO CRYSTALS FORM?

Crystals form either where a solution has evaporated slowly or where molten rock has cooled slowly beneath the surface. The best crystals are those which have the space and the time to form slowly.

You can make salt crystals by leaving seawater (or a strong salt solution) undisturbed to evaporate slowly.

Where a hot mineral solution forces its way into cracks in rocks, and then cools down very slowly, crystals may grow in any spaces left as the solution cools and shrinks. You may find beautiful crystals of quartz or calcite in rocks that have been veined with mineral solutions millions of years ago. Igneous rocks are formed from a variety of molten minerals which cool to form rocks. If the hot rock cools very slowly, the minerals will grow large. Granite is a rock which cooled deep in the Earth's crust. If you look at a granite sample you can see crystals of quartz and feldspar.

WHERE ARE THE BEST PLACES TO LOOK FOR GOLD?

Gold is found in mineral veins in rocks, or in gravels which have been washed away from areas where gold-bearing rocks have been eroded. Prospectors may pan the gravel in streams for grains of gold, as shown in the photograph.

Gold is sometimes found with quartz veins where extremely hot solutions containing molten gold have cooled in cracks and joints in the rocks. Rich veins have been found in areas of recent volcanic activity, earthquakes and mountain-building, such as the mountains on the western edge of the American continents. Famous gold rushes took place in Alaska, California and the Andes, and in 1980 a rich new find was made in the Chilean Andes.

Placer deposits are those washed down with river gravels or moved by ice. Much of South Africa's gold comes from mines reaching down to ancient gravels which formed a rock called conglomerate.

WHERE ARE DIAMONDS FOUND?

Diamonds were formed deep underground in conditions of intense heat and pressure. The pictures show an uncut diamond and one that has been cut and polished.

Artificial diamonds can be made in factories. Pure carbon is baked under great pressure to over 1400°C. Natural diamonds probably formed under similar conditions.

Diamonds are thought to have been formed millions of years ago from carbon which was caught up in molten rock deep in the Earth's crust. This molten rock reached the surface in a few places in the form of tube-like 'pipes'. As it cooled, it turned into a rock called kimberlite. Kimberlite pipes are mined for diamonds in South Africa, Tanzania and Siberia. But many diamonds come from the gravels of rivers which once eroded away kimberlite pipes. Such diamonds are found in many parts of Africa, India, Indonesia, Brazil, Australia and the USSR.

▼ WHERE IS THE WORLD'S
GREATEST MOUNTAIN
RANGE?

The greatest mountain range on land is the Himalaya-Karakoram Range to the north of India. It has most of the world's highest peaks.

The Andes of South America are a longer but lower mountain range. There are also great mountain ranges beneath the oceans, the longest of which stretches from the Gulf of Aden to the Gulf of California.

'Himalaya' means 'abode of snow' in Sanskrit, an ancient Indian language. This great mountain range stretches about 2500 kilometres from east to west and 80 to 150 kilometres from north to south. Seventy-nine peaks are over 7500 metres high.

The Himalayas were formed in the last 35 million years at the boundary of two crustal plates, the Indian Plate and the Eurasian Plate. When the edges of these two crustal plates collided, they crumpled to form a great mountain range.

▼ WHERE IS THE LARGEST
ACTIVE VOLCANO?

The highest active volcanoes on land are in the Andes, in South America. But even larger volcanoes rise from the floor of the Pacific Ocean and form the islands of Hawaii.

Mauna Loa, on Hawaii, is probably the largest active volcano in the world. It rises 4170 metres above sea level, but its base is 5180 metres below sea level. This base is roughly oval in shape: 119 kilometres long and 85 kilometres across. So a colossal amount of volcanic material forms this mountain.

The lava from Hawaiian volcanoes (shown here) is very liquid and flows for long distances. Mauna Loa erupts about every 3½ years. Kilauea Crater, south-east of the main volcano, is filled with a red-hot lava lake called Halemaumau, 'The Fire Pit'.

Volcanoes in the Andes reach higher above sea level than Mauna Loa. Ojos del Salada, on the border of Argentina and Chile, is 6885 metres high.

▲ WHERE IS THE WORLD'S
HIGHEST MOUNTAIN?

Mount Everest is the highest mountain on land: 8848 metres high. It is in the Himalayas, on the border of Nepal and Tibet.

The height of Mount Everest was discovered in 1852. It was named after Sir George Everest, the Surveyor-General of India at the time. It is called *Sagarmatha* in Nepalese and *Miti Guti Chapu Long-na* in Tibetan.

Like the other high peaks of the Himalayas, Everest is snow-covered all year. Avalanches are common and glaciers fill the valleys. These present great difficulties to climbers, who also face low temperatures, high winds and lack of oxygen.

Although the top of Everest is the highest point of the Earth's surface, it is not the tallest mountain when measured from base to peak. Mauna Kea on Hawaii is a total of 10,023 metres tall – only 4205 metres above sea level but its base is 5818 metres below the Pacific.

**The photograph shows
Surtsey, an island off the
coast of Iceland that was
born in a flurry of steam and
boiling sea in November
1963. It is just one of many
thousands of islands that are
volcanoes. Vulcano, an
Italian island rising from the
Mediterranean Sea, gave its
name to all volcanoes.**

The mid-Atlantic Ridge is a
string of volcanoes down the
middle of the Atlantic Ocean.
These volcanoes often erupt as
new material is added to the
Earth's crust. The ridge rises
above sea level in Iceland,
where there are many active
volcanoes, lava flows, geysers
and hot springs. Tristan da
Cunha is another volcano on
the same ridge, but far away in
the South Atlantic.

The Pacific has many island

volcanoes. An arc-shaped
pattern of volcanic islands is
found near many of the deep-
sea trenches, such as the
Aleutian Islands. Other
volcanoes rise from the ocean
floor above 'hot spots' beneath
the Earth's crust. Examples
include the Hawaiian Islands
in the Pacific and the Azores in
the Atlantic.

**The biggest explosion in
history happened in 1883
when the island of Krakatoa,
in Indonesia, was blown to
bits. In 1815, another
Indonesian volcano,
Tambora, produced the
most matter discharged in
any known eruption.**

Krakatoa was an island in the
Sunda Straits between
Sumatra and Java. Before 1883
it covered 47 square

kilometres. The eruption of 27
August 1883 woke people in
Australia and India, 3000
kilometres away. Rocks were
hurled 55 kilometres up into
the atmosphere and volcanic
dust fell on places over 5000
kilometres away. Tidal waves
caused as much damage and
more deaths than the eruption
itself. For three years after
Krakatoa exploded, the fine
dust in the upper atmosphere
cooled the weather and caused
amazing sunsets in Europe.

Today, a small volcano is
growing in the remains of the
old volcano.

Mount Vesuvius rises above the Bay of Naples in southern Italy. In AD 79 this volcano erupted and buried Pompeii, Herculaneum and other Roman towns.

Mount Vesuvius had been dormant for 800 years. Few people realized that it was a volcano, and those who did thought it was extinct. Fine towns were built on the Bay of Naples, and the rich soil on the slopes of Vesuvius was farmed. Then, on 24 August 79 AD Mount Vesuvius suddenly erupted. Gases trapped inside built up such pressure that tonnes of lava, pumice and ash were blown out.

For three days Pompeii was bombarded with pumice and ash. About 16,000 people died. But the ash preserved minute details of Roman life for archaeologists.

Nearby Herculaneum was buried under 13 metres of boiling mud. Vesuvius was blown apart in the eruption. But part of the wall of the old crater still exists.

When the world's volcanoes are plotted on a map, the Pacific Ocean appears surrounded by a ring of fiery volcanic activity.

Around the Pacific Ocean there are many active volcanoes. Some of the world's highest volcanoes are in the Andes and the mountains of Central America. Other volcanoes are found in the mountains of the western USA and Alaska. The Aleutians are a chain of volcanic islands. There are more active volcanoes in the Kamchatka Peninsula of the USSR, and in Japan, Papua-New Guinea and New Zealand. In addition, huge volcanoes rise from the Pacific Ocean floor to form Hawaii and other islands.

Most of the volcanoes that ring the Pacific are found quite near the deep sea trenches at the edge of the ocean. They are caused by the destruction of the Pacific Ocean Plate as it disappears beneath the surrounding continental plates.

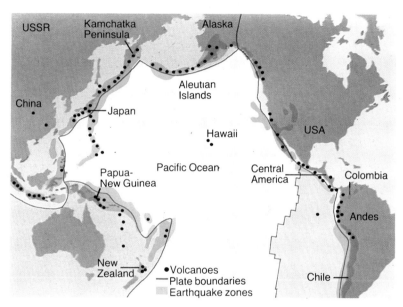

The strongest earthquakes so far this century have occurred in Colombia (in 1906); San Francisco, USA (1906); China (1920 and 1976); Japan (1923); Assam, India (1950); Kamchatka, USSR (1952); Aleutians (1957); Chile (1960); Alaska (1964).

Earthquakes are usually measured on a scale devised by Charles Richter in 1954. Since 1977, the biggest quakes have been recorded on the Kanamori scale. On this new scale, the strongest earthquake this century occurred at Lebu, in Chile on 22 May 1960. It measured 9.5 on the Kanamori scale. A 300-kilometre long stretch of the coast sank two metres into the Pacific. Shock waves were felt round the Earth for two weeks.

Many serious earthquakes have occurred around the Pacific Ocean. Like volcanoes, they are caused by movement at the edges of crustal plates.

► WHERE DOES MUD BOIL?

Boiling mud is one of the side-effects of volcanic activity. Hot water and gases from beneath the surface bubble through the mud, so that it looks like a pan of boiling porridge!

Boiling mud is found in a number of volcanic areas of the world. Volcanic gases such as sulphur, which create the heat and boiling effect, usually give the mud an evil smell. But the associated minerals are thought to promote healing, so

mud pools are often health centres.

People visit the Italian island of Vulcano to be coated in hot, smelly mud as a cure for rheumatism. Similar healing centres thrive near the hot mud pools and springs of the volcanic plateau in North Island, New Zealand.

Boiling mud is still found where volcanoes have been inactive for centuries, such as on the West Indian island of St Lucia. This shows that heat is still coming from deep down, and volcanic activity is not dead.

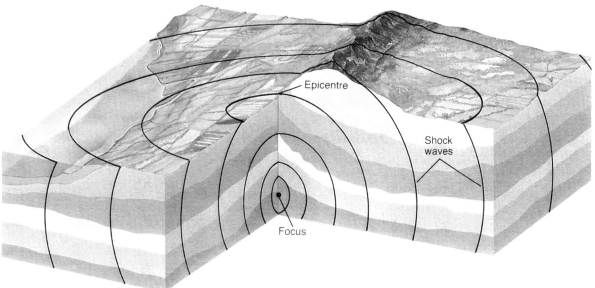

Epicentre

Shock waves

Focus

▲ WHERE IS THE EPICENTRE OF AN EARTHQUAKE?

The epicentre of an earthquake is the point on the Earth's surface immediately above the place where the movement of the Earth's crust has caused shock waves.

Earthquakes occur where rock layers are moving against one another on a fault line. Sudden release of the tension sends out shock waves (called seismic waves) in all directions. The point from which the seismic

waves radiate is called the focus. As the diagram shows, the epicentre is at the Earth's surface above the focus.

The depth of an earthquake is the distance between the focus and the epicentre. Seismologists (people who study earthquakes) classify earthquakes as shallow if the focus is less than 50 kilometres beneath the epicentre, and deep if the focus is more than 200 kilometres below.

As the epicentre is the closest point to the focus, it feels the shocks first and usually suffers the most

damage. Surface waves radiate out from the epicentre and damage surrounding areas.

Deep earthquakes are felt over great distances. The 1897 earthquake in Assam, northern India, was one of the deepest on record. Tremors were felt in Rome, Strasbourg and Edinburgh.

Shallow earthquakes may cause great damage near the epicentre but are less noticeable farther away. The 1960 earthquake at Agadir, Morocco, flattened the city centre, yet a kilometre away there was little damage.

▲ WHERE ARE THE WORLD'S HOTTEST PLACES?

The highest shade temperature on record is 58°C in September 1922 at Al'Aziziyah in the Sahara Desert in Libya. Nearly as hot was the 56.7°C recorded in Death Valley in the USA, in July 1913.

You might expect the hottest places to be on the Equator. Although equatorial lands are hot all year, they are also very cloudy. The hot deserts are near the Tropics where the sun is overhead in mid-summer. Because there is very little rain, there is very little cloud, so it is sunny and hot all day.

The eastern Sahara has more sunshine than anywhere else: sunshine has been recorded for 4300 hours in a year. That is an average of 11 hours 47 minutes per day. So it is not surprising that the highest temperature on record occurred in the Sahara.

The picture shows Death Valley, where temperatures up to 50°C in summer are not unusual. This is also a desert area.

▲ WHERE ARE THE WORLD'S COLDEST PLACES?

The coldest temperatures are recorded in winter in Antarctica. In July 1983, Russian scientists measured a new record low of −89.2°C.

Until modern weather stations were set up in Antarctica, the coldest temperatures were recorded in Siberia: −68°C was recorded at Verkhoyansk in 1892. Verkhoyansk holds the record for experiencing the greatest temperature range: from a coldest winter temperature of −68°C to a hottest summer temperature of 36.7°C.

The Arctic 'cold pole' is some way from the North Pole because of the surrounding Arctic Ocean. Seas have a moderating effect on the climate of coastal areas. Verkhoyansk is inland from the Arctic Ocean, and a long way from any other sea. The huge land-mass of Eurasia heats up quickly in summer to give surprisingly high temperatures even in the far north, but it loses its heat quickly in winter.

▲ WHERE DOES FROST COME FROM?

Frost is small crystals of ice which cling to any surface such as twigs, blades of grass or windows. It forms when the temperature is low enough for water vapour in the air to condense as ice instead of as water droplets.

The air around us always contains some water vapour. Cold air can hold less water vapour than warm air. At the end of a warm day the air will cool down. If the air is moist and still, some of the water vapour will condense as mist or dew. If the temperature falls below freezing, ice crystals will form instead of water droplets. A coating of ice crystals is called frost.

Frost is especially likely on a clear calm night. If there is no cloud cover to act as a blanket over the surface of the Earth, heat will radiate back into the atmosphere very quickly, and temperatures will fall fast. Because cold air tends to sink, frost may occur in hollows and valley bottoms and not on the hill slopes above.

Very high rainfall occurs when warm, moist winds are forced to rise. As the air cools, the water vapour condenses as rain.

Cherrapunji clings to a hillside in Assam, in north-east India. It faces the full force of the monsoon winds as they sweep north from the Indian Ocean in July. As the warm, wet winds rise towards the Himalayas, torrential rain falls for a few weeks. The photograph shows dense rain-forest in Assam.

The Hawaiian mountains are wet all year. They are in the path of the North-East Trade Winds which pick up moisture from the vast Pacific Ocean. This causes the record rainfall on Mount Wai-'ale-'ale. It has 350 rainy days a year, and has the highest average annual rainfall: 11,455 millimetres.

▲ WHERE ARE THE WETTEST PLACES ON EARTH?

Cherrapunji, in India, holds the record for the most rain in one month: 9299 millimetres in July 1861. It also had the most rain in a year: 26,461 millimetres in the year up to 31 July 1861. Mount Wai-'ale-'ale in Hawaii has the most rainy days (350 a year), and the highest average annual rainfall.

▲ WHERE IS THE DRIEST PLACE ON EARTH?

The photograph shows the Atacama Desert in northern Chile, where the first rain for 400 years fell in 1971. All deserts are dry, but the Atacama is the driest.

The Atacama Desert is hemmed in between the Pacific Ocean and the Andes mountains. The Andes shut out all winds from the east. Like the other hot deserts of the world, the Atacama lies astride one of the Tropics where air pressure is high. The air descends and is therefore warm and dry. There is little cloud, so the sunny days are intensely hot but the starry nights can be cold.

The Atacama Desert is exceptionally dry, but rainfall is very low in all desert areas. Cairo, in the eastern Sahara, averages 28 millimetres a year. Bahrain, on the edge of the Arabian Desert has 81 millimetres. But average rainfall figures for deserts can be confusing: there may be heavy storms on a few days in some years, and almost continuous drought in others.

Not all the dry parts of the Earth are also hot. Large areas of Central Asia are sheltered by mountains from any rain-bearing winds. Yet deserts such as the Gobi are very cold in winter. The Polar lands are also very dry – although the moisture that does fall accumulates as snow.

35

▼ WHERE ARE THE WORLD'S LONGEST GLACIERS?

Eight of the world's ten longest glaciers are in Antarctica. The longest is the Lambert-Fisher Ice Passage, which has a total length of 515 kilometres.

Petermanns Glacier in Greenland is the largest glacier in the northern hemisphere, and extends 40 kilometres out to sea.

The largest glaciers are fed with ice from the great ice sheets covering Antarctica and Greenland. Greenland has the fastest-moving glacier: the Quarayaq advances at 20-24 metres a day.

Spectacular glaciers are found elsewhere in the world. The longest Himalayan glacier is the Siachen (76 kilometres long) in the Karakoram Range. Also in the Himalayas, the Hispar and Biafo Glaciers join to form an ice passage 122 kilometres long.

Among the world's twenty longest glaciers are those in North America (in Alaska), Asia (in the Pamirs), in New Zealand and in the Alps.

▼ WHERE ARE THE WORLD'S BIGGEST EXPANSES OF ICE?

Just over 10 per cent of the land surface of the world is permanently covered by ice. Most of the world's ice (87 per cent) is in Antarctica. The Arctic has 12.5 per cent (mainly covering Greenland), and the rest is found in the glaciers which exist on every continent.

Antarctica is covered almost completely by the world's

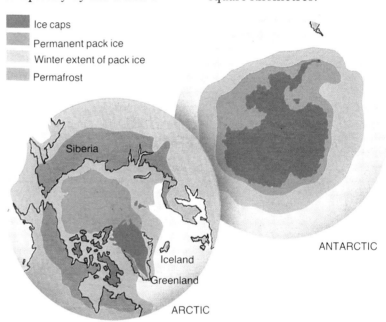

Ice caps
Permanent pack ice
Winter extent of pack ice
Permafrost

Siberia

Iceland

Greenland

ARCTIC

ANTARCTIC

largest ice sheet and only a few edges of the shore are exposed. In all, there are 13,600,000 square kilometres of ice. The thickest ice recorded was 4776 metres in depth.

The North Pole is an ocean area, and the largest area of land ice is on Greenland where the ice sheet covers 1,700,000 square kilometres. It is about 3000 metres thick at its centre.

The total amount of ice outside the Polar regions is very small. The largest expanse is in Iceland: 8800 square kilometres.

▲ WHERE IS PERMAFROST FOUND?

Permafrost is permanently frozen ground. It is found beneath permanent ice and snow. It is also found in large areas around the Arctic Ocean where the snow melts in summer but only the top few centimetres of the soil thaw.

Permafrost covers the whole of Antarctica. In the Arctic, permafrost is shallowest near the coast and deepest inland where the weather is coldest.

Permafrost 1370 metres deep has been found in Siberia.

In summer, when the snow melts and the topsoil thaws, water cannot drain into the frozen ground below. The whole surface is marshy.

It is difficult to build on permafrost. Heated buildings have to be insulated from the ground beneath, else they defrost the soil and sink into the mud. Permafrost is also a great hindrance to oil-drilling and mining. But it has preserved the remains of ancient animals, such as woolly mammoths.

▼ WHERE ARE THE BIGGEST ICEBERGS FOUND?

The icebergs with the biggest area are the tabular icebergs that break away from Antarctica. The largest ever seen was over 31,000 square kilometres (bigger than Belgium). The tallest icebergs break away from Greenland. The tallest ever seen was 167 metres above the water.

The iceberg with the largest area was seen in the South Pacific in 1956. The huge icebergs in this area have broken away from the Ross Ice Shelf. There, the Antarctic ice sheet extends out over the sea in an ice shelf as large as France. Its ice cliffs tower up to 50 metres above the sea. Along its 650 kilometre front it cracks with the rise and fall of the tide. Enormous icebergs break loose and float northwards into the Pacific.

The very tall Arctic icebergs are especially dangerous as eight-ninths of the ice is hidden beneath the sea.

ARCTIC ICEBERGS

TABULAR ICEBERGS

▲ WHERE DO ICEBERGS MELT?

Icebergs gradually melt as they float away from the Polar lands. But how long it takes will depend on the size of the iceberg and the temperature of the sea.

Melting icebergs have been seen very close to tropical waters. In 1935, an Arctic iceberg was recorded at latitude 28½°N in the North Atlantic. And in 1894 a ship recorded an iceberg in the Atlantic at latitude 26½°S.

As icebergs drift away from the Polar regions they are melted by the sun and by warmer water. Waves and rain erode them further. An iceberg may actually break apart while drifting, and if this disturbs its balance it may roll over. As an iceberg melts, the rocks in the ice sink to the sea bed.

Cold ocean currents carry icebergs far away from their point of origin. When the cold Labrador Current continues further south than usual, it brings Arctic icebergs into the busy North Atlantic shipping route.

▼ WHERE ARE CREVASSES FOUND?

Crevasses are cracks in the ice of glaciers and ice sheets. They are often quite narrow, but extremely deep and dangerous, especially if hidden by a thin crust of frozen snow.

The great mass of ice in a glacier or ice sheet moves slowly downhill. But the surface layers are always rigid and brittle. Different parts of a glacier move at different rates: the surface moves faster than the base, and the centre of the surface moves faster than the sides.

The different rates of flow create tensions in the ice and cause cracks in the surface layers. Whenever a glacier flows round a bend or over a hump, or changes its speed for some other reason, crevasses and pressure ridges form.

At the head of a mountain glacier there is an especially deep crevasse called the Bergschrund. This forms where the glacier ice is pulling away from the permanent snow on the mountain slope.

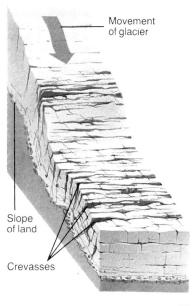

Movement of glacier

Slope of land

Crevasses

▼ WHERE IS THE GREATEST
OCEAN CURRENT?

▼ WHERE ARE THE
DOLDRUMS?

▼ WHERE IS THE GULF
STREAM?

The greatest ocean current is the West Wind Drift (also called the Antarctic Circumpolar Current). Its cold waters originate near the Antarctic and encircle that continent. The current is driven along by strong Westerly Winds.

The West Wind Drift varies in width from 200 to 300 kilometres. Its surface flow is less than one kilometre an hour. Measurements made in Drake Passage, where the current is squeezed between South America and Antarctica, recorded a flow of water at 270 million cubic metres per second – three times the greatest flow of the Gulf Stream.

The West Wind Drift is driven along by the strong Westerly Winds of the southern hemisphere. These are called the Roaring Forties because they blow at latitudes 40°-50°S. There are few land obstacles this far south to either wind or ocean current. Here there are some of the roughest seas and fiercest gales.

The Doldrums is a name given by early sailors to a zone at the Equator where winds are often light, their direction uncertain and where sailing ships were often becalmed.

For sailors in sailing ships, the Doldrums were a great contrast to the Trade Winds which blow steadily in the zone between the Tropics and the Equator. The North-East and South-East Trade Winds converge on the Equator where pressure is low and the air rises.

Because the air rises at the Equator there is plenty of rain. Sudden squalls and thunderstorms occur frequently, even though, in general, winds blow along the surface lightly. Sailing in such conditions is difficult because the boat is not carried along in any particular direction.

The exact location of the Doldrums moves with the seasons. In June they are about 5° north of the Equator, and in December they are about 5° south.

The Gulf Stream is a warm ocean current which begins in the Gulf of Mexico and flows across the North Atlantic towards Europe.

The Gulf Stream bursts into the Atlantic through the Straits of Florida, between the USA and Cuba. It flows close to the coast of America as far as Cape Hatteras and then continues north-east towards Europe. In the open ocean it is driven along by the Westerly Winds.

The Gulf Stream is a meandering current about 100 kilometres wide. Its average speed is less than one kilometre an hour. To the north of the Gulf Stream there is a very sudden change to cold water. And as it is only a surface current, the water temperature cools rapidly below 350 metres.

The warm water of the Gulf Stream is vital to northern Europe. Ports are ice-free and the weather is warm enough for farming much further north in Europe than in eastern Canada on the opposite side of the Atlantic.

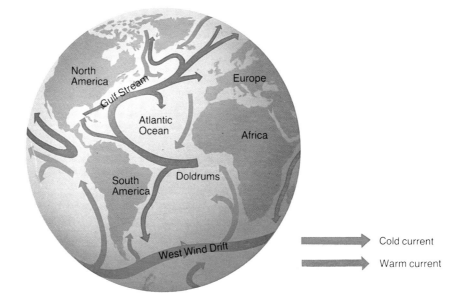

North America · Gulf Stream · Europe · Atlantic Ocean · Africa · South America · Doldrums · West Wind Drift

Cold current
Warm current

'Abyss' usually means the lowest depth of the oceans. The abyssal plain is the deep ocean floor. As the diagram shows, it lies nearly 4000 metres beneath the ocean surface. Large areas are almost flat and featureless. The abyssal plain has been called 'the smoothest surface on Earth'. But in places the plain is broken up by deep chasms and sea mountains.

The abyssal plain covers about two-thirds of the ocean floor. It begins at the foot of the steep continental slope. Here, sediments have slumped off the slope and been dumped by muddy currents. Away from the continental slope, the layer of sediments on the abyssal plain thins out and its slope becomes almost level.

Features such as under-sea volcanoes and deep ocean trenches break up the flat surface of the abyssal plain. These occur at the margins of crustal plates. There are also isolated sea-mounts, only a few of which reach the surface to form islands.

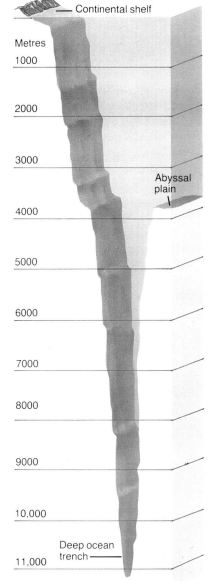

Continental shelf

Metres
1000
2000
3000
Abyssal plain
4000
5000
6000
7000
8000
9000
10,000
Deep ocean trench
11,000

The deepest part of the ocean was found in 1951 by the survey ship *Challenger*. Echo-soundings showed that part of the Mariana Trench, south of Japan, is 10,900 metres deep. In 1960 the US Navy bathyscaphe *Trieste* descended to the bottom of the Challenger Deep.

The Mariana Trench is one of many deep-sea trenches around the edges of the Pacific Ocean. These V-shaped trenches are parallel to a continent or line of islands.

A deep-sea trench plunges down from the abyssal plain. It may be 50-100 kilometres wide at the top, but only a few kilometres wide at the bottom. Most are found in the Pacific, but they also occur in the Caribbean, the South Atlantic and the Indian Ocean.

Deep-sea trenches mark places where the ocean floor is being subducted beneath a continental plate. Scientists are studying sediments in the deep trenches, which might one day be used for dumping dangerous waste materials.

The Dead Sea, on the borders of Israel and Jordan, is the world's saltiest sea. It is over ten times saltier than the average ocean.

The Dead Sea has no exit. Most of its water comes from the north, in the River Jordan. Mineral springs at the bottom of the Dead Sea, and around its shores, add to the salts in the water. The climate is very hot and dry, so an enormous amount of water is lost by evaporation. Salts in the water are therefore very concentrated. They are extracted in large evaporation pans. The picture shows natural salt deposits in the Dead Sea.

The shores of the Dead Sea are the lowest exposed point on the Earth's surface: 393 metres below sea level.

To the south is the Red Sea, the saltiest part of the open sea. Here, too, the salt is concentrated because so much water evaporates in the hot sun and so little is added from the surrounding desert.

▼ WHERE IS THE LARGEST
ARCHIPELAGO?

An archipelago is a sea studded with islands. The word was first used for the Aegean Sea with its many Greek islands. The largest archipelago is in South-East Asia where thousands of islands make up the countries of Indonesia, eastern Malaysia and the Philippines.

The country of Indonesia is made up of over 13,000 islands of which about 3000 are inhabited. The islands stretch over 5000 kilometres from west of the Malay Peninsula to New Guinea. Many of the islands in Indonesia are volcanoes. They form a great arc to the north of a deep-sea trench called the Java Trench.

Indonesia shares two of its islands with two other countries. Eastern Malaysia is part of the island of Borneo, and Papua-New Guinea shares an island with West Irian.

There are over 7000 islands in the Philippines, although more than 90 per cent of the land area consists of just the eleven largest islands.

▼ WHERE DO TIDAL BORES
OCCUR?

A tidal bore is a high wave which travels up an estuary as the tide comes in. Such bores are only found where there is a big tidal range and a funnel-shaped estuary.

As the tide rises in a river estuary, it is held back by the shallow water and the out-flowing river current. This causes the water to pile up and move up the river like a large breaking wave.

The most remarkable bore is on the River Ch'ient'ang'kian which flows into the Bay of Hangchow (Hangzhou) in China. Each spring tide, the bore is 7.5 metres high, and travels at 24 kilometres an hour. It can be heard coming 22 kilometres away!

The tidal bore with the greatest volume flows up the Canal do Norte, the main exit of the River Amazon. One of the fastest tidal bores flows up the River Hooghly, which is a branch of the River Ganges.

In contrast the tidal bore on the River Severn in England is only just over a metre high.

▲ WHERE ARE THE
WORLD'S HIGHEST TIDES?

The greatest rise and fall of the tide is recorded in the Bay of Fundy, between New Brunswick and Nova Scotia provinces in eastern Canada. The average spring tide range is 14.5 metres, though tidal ranges of up to 16.3 metres are recorded.

The tides of the Atlantic Ocean are funnelled into the narrow Bay of Fundy to produce the largest tidal range. This enormous range creates a tidal bore in the bay, even though it is not the estuary of a major river. The tidal flow enriches the marine life in the water, and the Bay is a haven for wading birds.

In Europe, the Rance estuary in northern France has a large tidal range. It is the site of the world's first tidal power station.

Unexpected high tides can cause great damage. They are usually the result of tidal surges, caused by very high winds and low air pressure at the same time as the expected high tide.

▼ WHERE IS THE LONGEST
REEF IN THE WORLD?

The Great Barrier Reef, off the north-east coast of Australia, is the world's longest coral reef. It stretches for over 2000 kilometres from near Papua to the centre of the Queensland coast.

Coral reefs can only form in tropical seas where the water is warm and shallow enough for the coral polyps to flourish. Like many other reefs, the Great Barrier Reef plunges into water which is too deep for corals to survive today. But sea level was probably much lower in the past when the reef first began to form.

The Great Barrier Reef lies between 45 and 65 kilometres off the Australian coast. In the north it is only 15-20 kilometres wide, but in the south the reef area extends up to 325 kilometres out to sea. There are only about ten safe passages through the reef, so it is a perilous area to navigate.

More than 340 varieties of coral have been identified on the reef. They present an incredible array of colours and shapes and are the homes of many beautiful fish and other sea creatures. Recently, parts of the reef have been destroyed by the Crown of Thorns starfish which sucks the living polyps off the hard coral skeletons.

▼ WHERE ARE FIORDS
FOUND?

Fiords are long, narrow, steep-sided inlets of the sea. They were made by glaciers which deepened the valleys along which they flowed. After the glaciers disappeared, their U-shaped valleys were flooded by the sea to form fiords.

Fiords are found on mountainous coasts which have been eroded by glaciers. The fiords of Norway are famous and are among the longest in the world. Sogne Fiord is 183 kilometres long from the open sea to the head of Lusterfiord. Its average width is 4.75 kilometres. Like most fiords, it is exceptionally deep, but becomes shallower towards the coast. At its deepest point, Sogne Fiord is 1245 metres deep.

Even longer is the Nordvest Fiord arm of Scoresby Sound in eastern Greenland. This fiord is 313 kilometres long.

Fiords are also found along the coast of Iceland, the Pacific coast of Canada and Alaska, in southern Chile and in South Island, New Zealand. The picture shows a village at the head of a Norwegian fiord.

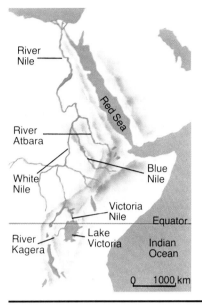

◄ WHICH IS THE LONGEST RIVER?

The three longest rivers in the world are the Nile in Africa: 6670 kilometres long; the Amazon in South America: 6448 kilometres; and the Mississippi-Missouri in North America: 5970 kilometres.

Different experts give different lengths for these great rivers. This is because it is not easy to say exactly where a river begins and where it ends. All have many tributaries, and there are many channels in their deltas.

Does the Nile begin in Lake Victoria, as some books say? The furthest source of the Nile is the Luvironzo in Burundi, which flows into the Kagera and then into Lake Victoria.

The furthest source of the Amazon was discovered in Peru in 1953. But where does the river end? The Canal do Norte is usually classed as the main exit. But the Rio Para is also navigable, and if this counts as an exit, then the Amazon is 6750 kilometres long.

► WHICH IS THE LARGEST RIVER?

The River Amazon is larger than the River Nile. The Amazon drains nearly twice as big an area. It contains far more water, and boats can travel much farther upstream.

The two major tributaries of the Nile, the White Nile and the Blue Nile, begin in areas with quite high rainfall. But for most of its course the Nile flows through desert where little water is added and a lot of water evaporates. Consequently, the flow of the Nile is very low for a major river: an average discharge of 3120 cubic metres per second. All the world's major rivers, except the Murray-Darling in Australia, have a greater flow.

The River Amazon carries a greater volume of water than any other river: its average discharge is 180,000 cubic metres per second. Its many long tributaries drain an area of over seven million square kilometres, most of which receives heavy rain all year through.

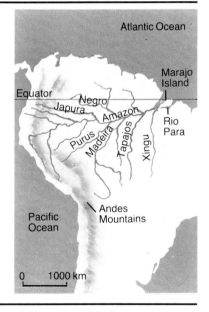

◄ WHERE ARE THE HIGHEST WATERFALLS?

The highest falls in the world are the Angel Falls on the Carrao River, a tributary of the Caroni River, in Venezuela, South America. The total fall of water is 979 metres; the longest single drop is 807 metres.

The Angel Falls are one of several very high waterfalls in this part of Venezuela, most of which are unmeasured and unnamed. They occur where rivers flow over the edge of a high, steep-sided plateau.

The Angel Falls have long been known to the local Indians who call them Cherun-Meru. Europeans first saw them in 1910. They were then re-discovered in 1937 by an American pilot named Jimmy Angel who crash-landed nearby.

The world's second highest falls are the Tugela Falls in Natal, South Africa. The Tugela River drops 947 metres at the falls. In Norway, the Utigard Falls carry water from the melting Jostedal Glacier 800 metres into Nesdal.

Some of the world's worst floods have occurred when the Hwang-ho River in China has burst its banks. Floods in 1931 killed over 3,500,000 people.

Hwang-ho means 'Yellow River' and it is the muddiest river in the world. It flows for 4800 kilometres through northern China and carries over 1500 million tonnes of silt. About a quarter of this silt is dumped near the mouth of the river, to raise the river bed and alter the course of the river channel. For thousands of years dykes have been built to prevent flooding but when the dykes burst disaster occurs.

The main flood season is from July to September, when most of the rain falls. But there are problems in spring-time too, when the southern part of the river thaws while the great loop to the north is still iced up. Sluice gates on the Hwang-ho, like those shown in the picture, are now used for flood-control and irrigation.

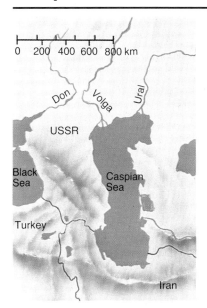

The world's largest lake is the Caspian Sea, between Iran and the USSR. Although it is called a sea, it is not connected with the oceans, but is a very large inland lake. Its total area is 371,800 square kilometres.

The surface of the Caspian Sea is 28 metres below sea level, and the deepest point of the lake is a further 980 metres down.

The Volga and Ural rivers both flow into the Caspian. No river flows out. The lake is in a desert area, so a lot of water evaporates and the water is very salty. As more river water is used for irrigation and industry, so less water reaches the Caspian. The world's largest lake is getting smaller.

The largest fresh-water lake is Lake Superior, between the USA and Canada. It covers 82,350 square kilometres. Lake Superior does have an exit: into Lake Huron and the other Great Lakes and then to the Atlantic via the St Lawrence River.

The highest lake in the world is an unnamed glacial lake near Mount Everest which lies at 5880 metres above sea level. Tibet's largest lake, Nam Tso is 4578 metres above sea level. The world's highest navigable lake is Lake Titicaca (shown here), on the border of Peru and Bolivia. It is 3811 metres above sea level and is navigated by lake steamers.

The total area of Lake Titicaca is about 8300 square kilometres, and its maximum depth is 370 metres. The lake receives water from several mountain rivers of the Andes. Its water drains south to Lake Poopo, and then disappears into the dry *altiplano* (high plain).

The land around Lake Titicaca is bleak and treeless. Llamas and vicunas graze on the coarse grass. Totoro reeds grow in the lake and are used by the local Indians to make reed fishing-boats, houses and even the islands on which they live.

WHERE IS THE BIGGEST CAVE?

The largest single cavern in the world is the Sarawak Chamber, in Sarawak, Eastern Malaysia. It was discovered in 1980.

The largest cave system in the world is under the Mammoth Cave National Park in the US state of Kentucky.

Sarawak is part of Eastern Malaysia and is on the island of Borneo in South-East Asia. The Sarawak Chamber is under the Gunung Mulu National Park. It was surveyed in 1980 and found to be 700 metres long, an average of 300 metres wide, and at least 70 metres high.

At Mammoth Cave National Park (see photograph), there is a maze of caves and passageways at different levels. The Mammoth Cave system itself is 307.5 kilometres long. Only four kilometres from the entrance to Mammoth Caves is the entrance to Flint Ridge Caves. In 1972, Mrs P. Crowther found an underground route linking the two systems.

WHERE IS THE DEEPEST CAVE?

The deepest cave found so far is the Gouffre Jean Bernard Cave in the French Alps. In 1982, a team of French cavers reached 1494 metres below the surface.

On a five-day expedition in 1982, the Groupe Speleo Vulcain set a new world depth record for cavers. Their route down included a dive through a sump 40 metres long which led them into a new series of descending passages. The final cave was measured as 1494 metres deep.

France has other very deep caves. The Gouffre Berger Caves near Grenoble are 1.1 kilometres deep. Gouffre de la Pierre Saint-Martin in the Pyrenees is now known to be 1350 metres deep.

Snezhnaya Cave in the USSR is now claimed to be the second deepest cave. Explorers have reached 1350 metres down. They could feel a current of air coming through the rubble at the bottom, and hope to find another passage descending even further.

WHERE ARE THE LARGEST STALACTITES AND STALAGMITES?

Stalactites hang down from cave roofs. The largest is in Spain. Stalagmites grow up from cave floors. The largest is in France.

Stalactites and stalagmites grow in caves where water saturated with calcium carbonate drips from the cave roof. The deposits build up very slowly, so large formations have probably been undisturbed for thousands of years.

The largest stalactite is a wall-supported column which hangs down 59 metres from the roof of the Cueva de Nerja, east of Malaga in Spain. The huge cave was discovered in 1959 by a shepherd boy looking for his ball. It is now an underground auditorium for concerts and ballets.

The longest free-hanging stalactite hangs down seven metres in the *Poll an Ionain* cave in County Clare, Ireland.

La Grande Stalagmite in Aven Armand cave in France is the world's tallest. It stands 29 metres high.

► WHERE ARE THE
LARGEST SAND DUNES?

The highest measured sand dunes are found in central Algeria, in the Sahara Desert. They stand up to 430 metres high.

Only about a tenth of the Sahara Desert is covered with wind-blown sand. The rest is gravel plains, plateaus and mountains. Most of the sand is found in 25 large sand-seas, called ergs. These are quite distinct from the surrounding sand-free desert.

The highest dunes are found in the sand-sea of Isaouane-n-Tifernine to the north of the Hoggar mountains. The Sahara's largest area of sand dunes is the Grand Erg Oriental, on the border of Algeria and Tunisia. This sand-sea covers about 518,000 square kilometres.

The world's largest area of sand dunes is Rub'-al-Khali, 'the Empty Quarter', in the Arabian Desert. It covers about 650,000 square kilometres of southern Saudi Arabia. The central sand mountains rise to 250 metres.

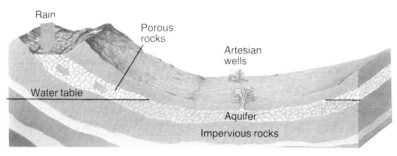

Rain
Porous rocks
Artesian wells
Water table
Aquifer
Impervious rocks

▲ WHERE IS ARTESIAN
WATER FOUND?

Artesian water is underground water which rises to the surface under natural pressure. The name comes from Artois in France, where many wells have been dug to reach artesian water in the underlying chalk.

The diagram shows how an artesian basin can form. Rain falling on the higher land can flow through the layers of porous rocks. Beneath the low land, the porous rocks are sandwiched between impervious layers. The water-bearing layer is called an aquifer.

In the lowland, a well dug through the top impervious layer will reach the aquifer below. Because the water table (the top of the underground water) is higher than the top of the well, the water will gush to the surface under its own pressure.

The Great Artesian Basin of Australia is the world's largest.

◄ WHERE ARE DESERTS
BEING CREATED?

On the edges of some of the Earth's natural deserts, the environment is being upset by poor farming methods and mismanagement.

Semi-desert areas have fragile soils and difficult climates. Several good years are often followed by several bad years. In the good years, farmers may extend the cultivated areas, or increase their flocks and herds, and dig more wells. But in a series of dry years crops fail, animals exhaust the pasture, the bare soil is eroded, and many wells dry up. Such problems created the 'dust bowl' in the USA in the 1930s, and extended the Sahara in the 1970s.

The problem of finding enough fuel for cooking has denuded large areas of semi-desert of all trees and bushes. This makes the soil more prone to erosion. Some areas have been transformed by large irrigation schemes, but poor water management can harm the soil. Then, large areas may revert to desert.

▶ WHERE HAS LAND
RECLAMATION DOUBLED
THE SIZE OF A COUNTRY?

The Netherlands is one of the smallest countries in Europe. Yet half its land area is the result of reclaiming land from marshes, lakes and sea.

The Netherlands lies in the delta area formed by the Rivers Rhine, Meuse (Maas) and Scheldt. Most of the land is below 30 metres, and half the total area below high tide level.

The areas of reclaimed land are called polders. They are surrounded by dykes (banks) to keep out flood-water, and criss-crossed by drainage ditches. The water was once removed by wind pumps, but diesel pumps are used now.

Major modern reclamation schemes include the Zuider Zee and Delta Projects. The Zuider Zee was closed off from the North Sea by a 32-kilometre-long dam in 1932. The former bay was transformed into the freshwater Lake Ijssel and 2260 square kilometres of new land in five huge polders. The Delta Project involved damming all but two exits of the Rhine, Maas and Scheldt. This scheme protects land from floods and created a freshwater reservoir and 150 square kilometres of new land.

▶ WHERE IS THE REMOTEST
PLACE ON EARTH?

Only a fifth of the Earth's land surface is densely populated, so there are still plenty of remote places. The remotest inhabited land is Tristan da Cunha, a volcanic island in the South Atlantic. The nearest inhabited land is over 2000 kilometres away.

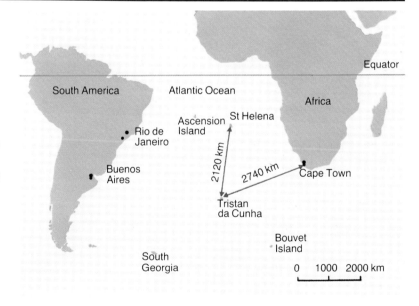

Four-fifths of the Earth's land surface is too dry, too cold, too mountainous or too densely forested to support many people. The most sparsely populated continent is Antarctica, which has no permanent settlement. The most sparsely populated country is Greenland.

The remotest island is Bouvet Island, an uninhabited Norwegian dependency in the South Atlantic. The nearest land is 1700 kilometres away, and that is the uninhabited coast of Antarctica.

The remotest inhabited island, Tristan da Cunha, covers just 98 square kilometres. Its nearest inhabited land is the island of St Helena, 2120 kilometres to the north-east.

In 1961 Tristan da Cunha erupted and all its inhabitants were evacuated, but they returned in 1963. Although the island looks lonely, they are happy there. Loneliness is often worse in great cities than in remote places.

▲ WHERE IS THE LARGEST ARTIFICIAL LAKE?

▲ WHERE IS THE BIGGEST MAN-MADE HOLE ON EARTH?

▲ WHERE DOES ACID RAIN OCCUR?

The artificial lake with the greatest area is Lake Volta in Ghana, West Africa. The Bratsk Reservoir on the Angara River in the USSR holds the greatest volume of water in an artificial lake.

In 1965, the Akosombo Dam was completed across the River Volta. The dam is built at the southern end of a gorge, and produces hydro-electric power.

Lake Volta began to build up behind the dam in the valley of the River Volta and its main headwaters, the Black Volta and the White Volta. Altogether the lake now covers 8482 square kilometres and its shoreline is 7250 kilometres long. Villagers had to move from the flooded area to the new shoreline, where they began a fishing industry.

Lake Volta is large but fairly shallow. In places, the remains of flooded forests stick out of the water. Its total volume is 148 cubic kilometres – compared to 169.25 cubic kilometres for the USSR's Bratsk Reservoir.

The largest modern quarry, excavated by machine, is Bingham Canyon Copper Mine, shown here, in Utah in the USA. It covers 7.2 square kilometres and is 774 metres deep.
The 'Big Hole' of Kimberley in South Africa is an old diamond mine which was dug out last century by thousands of miners working with only picks and shovels. It is about 500 metres in diameter and nearly 400 metres deep.

In 1871 diamonds were found on a farm which became the site of Kimberley Mine. By 1872 more than 3500 men claimed patches of land where they could dig for diamonds. As they dug out the pipe of kimberlite rock, they made a huge hole. Over 25 million tonnes of rock were dug out, yielding about three tonnes of diamonds.

Open mining stopped when rock falls became too frequent. The mine closed in 1915 and is now half full of water.

All rain is very slightly acid, but over the industrial areas of North America and Europe the rain is more acid because it absorbs waste gases which pollute the atmosphere.

Rainwater reacts with the carbon dioxide in the air to become a very dilute carbonic acid. This weak acid can dissolve limestone, which is an alkaline rock.

Rain can also react with the waste gases emitted into the air by factories, power stations and cars. Such gases may be carried great distances by winds and then fall as dilute sulphuric acid and nitric acid, often on areas far away from the source of pollution. This is called acid rain because its acidity is artificially high.

Acid rain increases the erosion of rocks and building materials, especially limestone. Lakes and streams are slowly poisoned, threatening wildlife. The face of the statue shown in the photograph above has been eaten away by acid rain.

◄ WHERE IS RICE GROWN?

Rice provides food for more people than any other cereal crop in the world. It is the basic food crop in much of southern and eastern Asia.

Rice needs hot weather and plenty of water. The water may come from heavy rain, such as the monsoon rains of Asia, or from irrigation. Rice needs flat land, because the water level in the fields must be carefully controlled. Many hillsides in Asia are terraced to get enough flat land. Some terraces are hundreds of years old.

The seedlings are grown in a 'nursery' bed and then transplanted to the flooded paddyfields. After four to five months the rice is ready for harvest and the water is released.

Rice is now grown in many hot, wet parts of the world apart from Asia. Mechanized rice-fields in the USA and southern Europe grow rice for export. Rice is also an important food crop in Egypt, West Africa, Madagascar and parts of South America.

▶ WHERE DOES COTTON COME FROM?

The cotton thread we sew with or weave into cloth is spun from fibres in the cotton boll. This is the seed pod of the cotton plant.

The cotton bush is an annual plant. It grows quickly and flowers, then small green seedpods develop. The seeds inside the cotton boll are surrounded by a mass of fine hairs. When the boll is ripe, it bursts open and the soft white cotton can be picked.

Once the cotton crop is harvested, it has to be ginned. This process separates the cotton fibre from the seeds so that the fibres can be cleaned, carded and spun.

Cotton was a major crop in south-eastern USA. Many Africans were imported as slaves to work on the cotton plantations. The USA still produces nearly a fifth of the world's cotton. Egypt and Sudan also export cotton. It is important too in parts of East Africa, India and Pakistan, China and parts of South America.

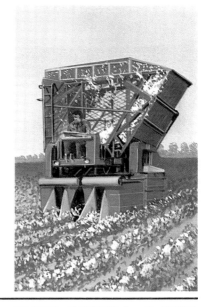

▶ WHERE IS TEA GROWN?

The tea we drink is made from the crushed leaves of an evergreen bush which grows in hot, damp climates. It seems to thrive at quite high altitudes, up to 2300 metres, in tropical areas.

Tea was first brought to Europe from China. As the drink became fashionable, plantations of tea bushes were planted by the Dutch in Indonesia and by the British in India and Sri Lanka. Now tea plantations are also found in Japan, in East Africa and on hillsides in Georgia in the USSR.

The tea plant needs a warm climate with plenty of moisture and a rich, well-drained soil. On tea plantations, the bush is pruned to a maximum height of 1.5 metres so it is easy to pick. The young leaves at the tops of the stems are picked. These are taken to a factory on the plantation where they are spread out to wither. They are then rolled and left to ferment. Heating and drying seals in the flavour and the tea is packed for export.

▶ WHERE DOES RUBBER COME FROM?

Natural rubber is made from latex, which is found under the bark of the rubber tree. This tree is a native of the Amazon rain forest and grows in hot, wet equatorial conditions.

Amazon Indians first collected latex from trees to make a type of rubber. Goodyear discovered how to harden rubber in 1842. When bicycles and cars became popular there was a great demand for rubber and the Amazon became a boom area.

The rubber tree was introduced to South-East Asia via London's botanical gardens at Kew. Plantations in Malaysia and Indonesia have supplied much of the world's rubber. Smaller amounts come from Zaire and West Africa.

The bark of the rubber tree is cut and the latex oozes into a cup fixed by the rubber tapper. The latex is then smoked and vulcanized to make rubber.

Nowadays, much of our rubber is synthetic and is a by-product of oil.

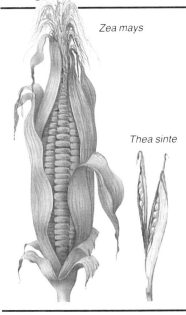

Zea mays

Thea sinte

◀ WHERE WAS MAIZE FIRST GROWN?

Maize is an important cereal crop which is now grown in many parts of the world which have hot summers. It is a native of the Americas, and was an important food crop for many Indian tribes before Europeans arrived.

The origin of the modern maize plant (*Zea mays*) is still a mystery. It is an annual plant which now depends on humans for planting. It may be related to *Thea sinte*, a grass which grows in Mexico and whose cobs look very like miniature corn cobs. This plant can reproduce in the wild.

It is possible to cross *Thea sinte* with maize to develop fatter cobs. These look very like corn cobs found by archaeologists in New Mexico which may be 2000 years old.

For the early European settlers in America, 'Indian corn' was often a life-saver. Most American maize is now used as cattle food, but some is eaten as sweetcorn or turned into cornflakes or flour.

◀ WHERE DOES COCOA COME FROM?

Cocoa is made from the beans which develop in the large pod of the cacao tree. Cocoa was drunk by the Aztecs of Central America before Europeans arrived. The cacao tree is still grown in hot, wet areas of Central and South America, but most of the world's cocoa now comes from West Africa.

The tropical cacao tree grows in hot, wet, forested areas near the Equator. Large pods, 15-35 centimetres long, grow directly out of its branches and trunk. Each pod contains 30-40 beans. The beans are fermented and dried, and then exported for processing into cocoa and chocolate.

The Spanish *conquistadores* liked the bitter cocoa drink they found in Central America, and by the 17th century other Europeans had developed a taste for cocoa. It was the British and French who introduced cacao trees to West Africa, which is now the world's principal cocoa-producing region.

49

WHERE IS MONUMENT VALLEY?

Monument Valley is part of the Colorado Plateau, in the dry south-west of the USA. The towers, columns and castle-like masses of rock are completely natural monuments.

The rocks of Monument Valley are mainly sandstones with some other sedimentary rocks. These rocks were pushed into an upfold or anticline. As this happened, the layers were stretched and weakened. Faults developed at the edges of the area. Lakes filled the faulted area, and rivers flowed along weaknesses in the rocks. As the rocks were uplifted the river deepened their valleys.

Over millions of years, many metres of rock have been eroded away. More resistant rocks have been left standing as columns and as islands of rock called 'buttes'. The toppled remains of columns litter the floor. Today, the climate is desert and the area is dry, but wind and flash-floods continue to erode the area.

WHERE IS THERE SNOW NEAR THE EQUATOR?

Snow lies on the ground all year in places where the temperature is low enough to prevent it melting completely. Although it is hot at sea level at the Equator, it can get very cold indeed at the top of high mountains. Some Equatorial mountains are high enough to have permanent snow and ice, such as Mount Kilimanjaro in East Africa and the peaks of the Andes in Ecuador.

Mount Kilimanjaro is a volcano rising high above the East African plains on the borders of Kenya and Tanzania. The highest point is 5894 metres above sea level.

The place where permanent snow begins is called the snowline. The height of the snowline depends on the temperature and the amount of snow falling. Near the Poles, the snowline is at ground level. At latitude 40° the snowline is at 2500-5000 metres depending on the dryness of the climate. At the Equator, the snowline i a little over 5000 metres.

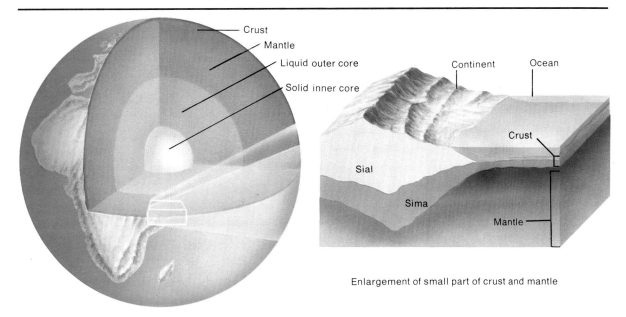

Crust
Mantle
Liquid outer core
Solid inner core

Continent   Ocean

Crust

Sial

Sima

Mantle

Enlargement of small part of crust and mantle

▲ WHAT SHAPE IS THE EARTH?

Our planet is not a perfect sphere. It is slightly flattened at the poles, and even the Equator is not an exact circle.

New information from satellites has agreed with measurements made on the surface of the Earth. So scientists now have more details of the Earth's shape.

The Earth's circumference at the Equator is 40,075.03 kilometres and its circumference through the Poles is 40,007.89 kilometres. Its diameter at the Equator is 12,756.28 kilometres and its diameter at the Poles is 12,713.51 kilometres.

The variations are because of flattening at the Poles and bulging at the Equator. This is partly the result of the fact that the Earth spins so fast. The Equator itself is slightly oval: its longest diameter is 159 metres longer than its shortest diameter! The South Pole is 45 metres nearer the centre of the Earth than the North Pole.

▲ WHAT IS THE EARTH MADE OF?

From studying earthquakes and the Earth's gravity, scientists know that the Earth is made of a number of layers.

The Earth's crust is the thinnest zone of all. It varies in thickness from five kilometres under parts of the oceans to 40 kilometres under the continents. The rocks of the continents are lighter than the rocks of the ocean floors, but all are rich in silicon.

The top layer of the mantle may be rigid, but the rest consists of molten rocks which are slowly moving. The rocks of the different layers of the mantle are rich in magnesium and iron silicates.

About 2900 kilometres beneath the Earth's surface is the divide between the mantle and the core. The outer core is probably liquid, while the inner core is solid. The rocks of the core are probably 90 per cent iron with some nickel, similar to many meteorites.

▲ WHAT IS THE CRUST LIKE BENEATH THE CONTINENTS AND OCEANS?

The rocks of the continents vary but on average they are much less dense than the rocks of the ocean floor. The rocks under the oceans also continue deep beneath the rocks of the continents.

The rocks of the continents are mostly granite, or are made from sediments which come from granite. They are rich in silicon and aluminium. All the rocks of the continents are grouped together as *sial*.

The rocks beneath the deep oceans are very like basalt. They are rich in silicon and magnesium, and are grouped together as *sima*.

The Earth's crust consists of a layer of sima above the mantle. The continents are huge 'rafts' of sial floating in the sima. So it is possible for the continents to move apart or together (continental drift) and to move up and down (isostacy).

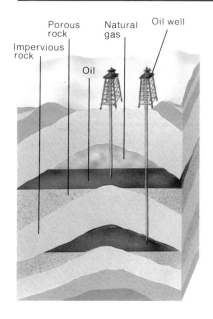

Porous rock   Natural gas   Oil well
Impervious rock
Oil

▲ WHAT ARE OIL AND NATURAL GAS?

Oil and natural gas are fossil fuels. They formed from the remains of tiny plants and animals which once lived in tropical seas. They were changed by chemical processes into gases and liquids.

Oil and natural gas formed from different kinds of microscopic plant and animal remains, at different depths in the Earth, at different temperatures, and over different periods of time.

Oil varies in type from a very light oil to thick, black bitumen. Natural gas also varies in type and quality. Different types of oil may be mixed at refineries, which produce paraffin, petroleum, diesel oil and chemicals.

As the diagram shows, oil and gas collect in porous rocks (rocks which allow liquids to soak through). They are trapped between impervious rocks (which will not allow liquids to pass through). Some oil wells pump oil from a huge area. Others tap only a small area and soon run dry.

▼ WHAT IS A FOSSIL?

A fossil is the remains of an animal or a plant preserved in the rocks.

There are many ways in which plants and animals that lived hundreds of millions of years ago have been preserved. A few fossils are the hard parts of animals or plants, such as dinosaur bones or sharks' teeth. These remains sank to the bottom of seas and were trapped in the sediments, which now form layers of rock.

▲ WHAT IS COAL?

Coal is a rock which can be burned as a fuel. It is called a 'fossil fuel' because it formed from the remains of trees and plants millions of years ago. Imprints of these plants can be found on some lumps of coal.

Coal is usually found in layers (called seams) of different thicknesses sandwiched between other rocks which formed at the same time. This suggests that dead vegetation

Many fossils are moulds or casts. The remains of living things slowly dissolved as they lay buried in sediments. Their exact shape was preserved in the rocks that formed. Minerals or sediments took the place of their remains to form a cast. Some ancient trees were 'petrified' as the decaying logs were gradually replaced by minerals dissolved in water.

Interesting details can be fossilized, too. Footprints, once made on mud which then dried out, may be uncovered.

Fossil leaf imprint on coal

collected in swamps. This was buried by mud and silt. Then new swamp forests grew and eventually they too were buried. These layers of vegetation, mud and silt eventually became coal seams between sandstone and clay.

The oldest known coal seams are about 360 million years old. Then coal is found in rocks of all different ages until less than 70 million years ago. The most valuable coal in Europe and North America is found in Carboniferous rocks formed 265 to 290 million years ago.

A mineral is a single substance that is formed naturally. Different samples of the same mineral usually look similar and react in the same way when they are tested. Rocks are made up of different minerals.

There are over 3000 different minerals known today. Each one has its own chemical formula. Mineralogists group minerals into 'families' such as micas, feldspars, quartz and calcites.

All minerals (except mercury) are solids, though they melt under enormous heat and pressure. As they cool down again, most minerals can form crystals. Some minerals make up the common rocks of the Earth's surface. Some rare minerals are valuable (such as gold and diamonds).

Collectors identify minerals by their crystal shape, their hardness, the way they break, and the colour of the mark they make when scratching a white surface.

Mica

Quartz

Feldspar

Calcite

The majority of minerals found in the rocks of the Earth's crust are silicates.

The Earth's crust is made up of different kinds of rocks. Igneous rocks formed as molten lava cooled down. Most sedimentary rocks formed from accumulations of minerals which were weathered out of igneous rocks. Sometimes the minerals in these rocks can be seen quite easily, for example in granite and in gritstone. Sometimes the minerals can only be seen under a microscope. In either case, most of the minerals you will see are silicates.

The silicates are a large group of minerals, all of which contain silica and oxygen. The commonest silicate families are feldspars (about 60 per cent of rock-forming minerals), amphiboles and pyroxenes (about 17 per cent), quartz (about 12 per cent) and micas (about 4 per cent).

Rocks are used as building materials because they resist weathering. Usually such rocks are hard and often they are beautiful too. Rocks that are easily quarried and shaped for building are especially important. Softer rocks such as clay and sand are dug up and made into harder building materials such as bricks and concrete.

Many old buildings are built of local stone or bricks. When transport was difficult, only the richest people could afford to import special stone.

Now that stone can be transported easily, modern buildings may be made with rocks from far away. Building materials made from clay, limestone, sand and gravel are the most common.

Impressive buildings are often built or faced with hard-wearing rocks such as meta-morphic rocks. These have been naturally hardened by heat and pressure. They include marble and slate.

Earthquakes strike without warning. They are heard first as a great rumble. Strong earthquakes cause enormous damage in built-up areas.

Buildings collapse, and fractured pipes and cables cause fires. Rescue services are hampered by lack of communications. Landslides may increase the damage, and cause flooding. *Tsunami*, or tidal waves, may devastate the coast, and also do great damage thousands of kilometres away.

Earthquakes are most violent at a point on the Earth's surface immediately above the place where the Earth's crust has moved.

The most destructive earthquakes are 'shallow focus'. These are earthquakes that begin less than 60 kilometres beneath the surface. Sometimes the land at the surface is cracked and displaced after an earthquake.

Several thousand earthquakes are recorded by seismographs every year.

Volcanoes can be classed as active, dormant (sleeping) or extinct. Active volcanoes vary in shape.

Fluid lava usually wells up fairly slowly, giving plenty of time for any gases to escape. Such volcanic eruptions are peaceful, but the fluid lava may flow long distances to form a very large volcano with a gently sloping dome.

Thicker lava traps gas bubbles which may burst at the surface and send up a shower of lava and volcanic 'bombs'. These explosive eruptions make a lot of ash and form steep-sided cinder cones which often have a beautifully symmetrical shape.

Really thick lava hardly flows at all. It is squeezed out of the volcano like toothpaste from a tube. Sometimes such lava forms a volcanic plug. Gases build up inside, and may eventually make the whole volcano explode.

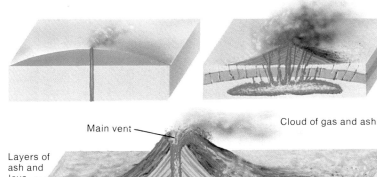

Quiet shield volcano — Explosive volcano

Main vent · Cloud of gas and ash · Layers of ash and lava · Secondary vent · Lava

Eruptions vary according to the type of magma produced. Besides the burning lava, ash and gas may affect large areas. An eruption may cause earthquakes and landslides. A violent eruption may destroy land, or may bring a new island to the surface.

The recent eruptions of Mount St Helens in the north-west USA have been recorded in great detail by scientists. When eruptions began in 1980, an earthquake triggered off a landslide. Immediately, a blast of hot gases and steam flattened forests up to 27 kilometres away. Blast after blast sent ash and rocks high into the air.

Valleys were buried, and people and animals choked to death. Floods and mudflows did more damage. A great ash storm, with lightning, turned daylight to night 140 kilometres away. Towns were choked with ash, and beautiful sunsets followed.

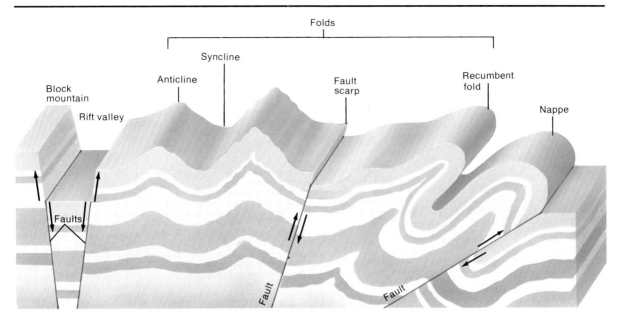

▲ WHAT DIFFERENT KINDS OF MOUNTAIN ARE THERE?

The three main types of mountain are volcanoes, fold mountains and block (or faulted) mountains.

Volcanoes are the only mountains formed from new material added to the Earth's surface.

Fold mountains are formed when great areas of sedimentary rocks are pushed together. The rocks are folded, crushed and pushed up to make mountain ranges such as the Alps and the Jura. Such ranges probably formed when continents moved against one another, or against part of the ocean floor.

Block mountains are formed when great areas of rocks are faulted, and some areas are pushed up between the faults. Rift valleys (formed when an area slips down between faults) often occur with block mountains. For example, the Vosges and the Black Forest are block mountains on either side of the Rhine rift valley.

▲ WHAT DO GEOLOGISTS MEAN BY 'FOLDING'?

Most rocks may seem very hard. But when pressure is applied from one or both sides, layers of rock can be bent into folds.

If you push this page gently towards the centre of the book it will arch up into an 'upfold'. Moderate pressure produces gentle folds in rocks. Upfolds are called anticlines and downfolds are called synclines. Uneven pressure produces folds with one side steeper than the other. These are called asymmetrical folds.

Intense pressure can crumple the rocks, producing dramatic folds and faults so that one part of a fold may be pushed over another.

Folds can sometimes be seen on mountainsides or cliff-faces. They vary greatly in size and are formed very slowly.

The pressure needed to create folds probably comes from the movement of parts of the Earth's crust against each other.

▲ WHAT DO GEOLOGISTS MEAN BY 'FAULTS'?

Faults are great cracks through layers of rocks. Pressure on the cracks causes movement, which is felt as an earthquake. This usually results in the rock layers being displaced on each side of the fault.

Faults cross strata (layers) of different kinds of rock. They are caused by enormous pressure pushing or pulling the rock strata, which break under the great stress. Faults are often found with folds.

Areas of rock may shift up or down on each side of the fault. This may cause a fault scarp in the landscape, but often faults are hardly visible.

Movement along a fault can be quite small-scale and you may see faults in road-cuttings or cliffs. There can also be large-scale movements, such as along the faults on either side of the Great Rift Valley. This stretches for 4800 kilometres through parts of the Middle East and eastern Africa.

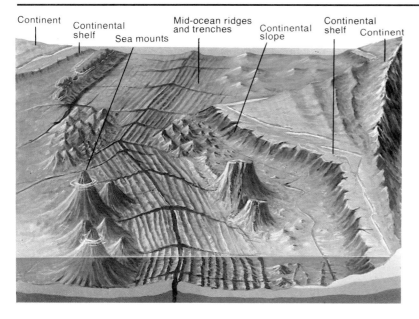

Continent | Continental shelf | Sea mounts | Mid-ocean ridges and trenches | Continental slope | Continental shelf | Continent

◄ WHAT DOES THE SEA BED LOOK LIKE?

◄ WHAT DOES THE SEA BED LOOK LIKE?

The sea bed has cliffs, plateaus, canyons, volcanoes, mountain ranges and deep trenches.

Echo-sounders, underwater cameras, manned and unmanned submersibles are helping oceanographers know more about the sea bed.

There are three main zones. The continental shelf slopes gently away from the beaches surrounding dry land. At a depth of about 180 metres, it suddenly ends at the steep continental slope. This huge cliff around the continents is gashed with deep gorges and sediments pile up at its foot.

The deep ocean floor begins at the bottom of the continental slope. Submerged volcanoes rise up in places. Some reach the surface, as at Hawaii and the Canary Islands. Mountain ranges such as the Mid-Atlantic Ridge are far longer than any mountain ranges on land. There are also deep, narrow trenches such as Challenger Deep, the lowest place on Earth.

▲ WHAT IS THE CONTINENTAL SHELF?

The continental shelf is the true edge of the continents. All round the continents, the sea floor slopes gently away from present-day beaches. Where the depth of the sea is about 180 metres, this gentle slope ends abruptly at the steep continental slope.

The width of the continental shelf varies enormously, for example, around South America. There is hardly any continental shelf off the coast of Chile. The steep slope of the Andes is matched by a steep drop into the ocean depths. But off Argentina the continental shelf stretches far into the Atlantic, east of the Falkland Islands.

The continental shelf is valuable. The shallow waters are often rich in fish. Sands and gravels accumulating as sediments on the sea floor are dredged up in some places. Sometimes they include minerals such as gold and diamonds.

◄ WHAT ARE SPRING AND NEAP TIDES?

Spring tide

Full Moon | Earth | New Moon | Sun

Neap tide | Quarter Moon | Earth | Quarter Moon | Sun

Arrows show pull of gravity on oceans

Spring tides have the greatest tidal range, with the highest high tides and the lowest low tides. Neap tides have the least tidal range. Tides are partly caused by the Moon, and are related to its phases. Each type of tide occurs twice in every lunar month (28 days).

The water of the oceans is kept on the Earth's surface by the pull of the Earth's gravity. But it does respond to the pull of gravity of the Moon and the Sun. The Moon orbits the Earth in one lunar month. Near Full Moon and New Moon, the pull of gravity of the Sun and Moon are in the same direction (top diagram), causing particularly high and low spring tides.

When the pull of the Sun and the Moon are in different directions (lower diagram), neap tides occur. They coincide with the Moon's first and last quarters.

▶ WHAT IS A 'TSUNAMI'?

Tsunami is a Japanese word meaning 'over-flowing' (*tsu*) 'wave' (*nami*). A tsunami is caused by earthquake shocks.

Shock-waves from an earthquake affect the sea floor as well as the land. A major earthquake can make the sea floor rise and fall and create huge sea waves. If these reach coasts, they swamp large areas and cause great damage.

At sea, *tsunamis* have long wavelengths. The distance from one wave crest to the next may be 200 kilometres. They travel quickly, at up to 800 kilometres an hour. Where the sea bed gets shallower, they slow down but become higher. From the land, people may see the sea withdraw a long way, then rush up in a series of giant waves.

In the 1755 earthquake at Lisbon, Portugal, the harbour was emptied of water. Then waves 17 metres high added to the devastation already caused by the earthquake.

▶ WHAT ARE ICEBERGS?

Icebergs are huge lumps of ice which have broken away from ice sheets and glaciers and drift in the sea. When ice floats in water, only about a ninth shows above the surface. The rest is hidden beneath the water, and may damage ships.

In the northern hemisphere, icebergs come from the Greenland ice sheet. The world's tallest iceberg, 167 metres high, was sighted off western Greenland in 1958.

The largest icebergs are found in the southern hemisphere and come from Antarctica. The largest ever recorded was 335 kilometres long and 97 kilometres wide (31,000 square kilometres in area). It was measured in the South Pacific in 1956.

Icebergs may break from a glacier and fall into the sea. Usually, icebergs form from a glacier which extends into the sea. Waves, tides and floating movement of the ice cause huge pieces of ice to break off and float away.

Tip of iceberg above ocean

▶ WHAT IS A RAISED BEACH?

The photograph seems to show a beach with boats drawn up on the sand. But there is rock instead of sea! In fact, this beach is raised above high-tide mark. Either the land has risen or the sea-level has dropped.

A change of sea-level sounds the simplest answer, but the world's ice is still slowly melting, so sea-level ought to be getting higher, not lower.

But ice is a key to the answer. Sea-level has changed a great deal in the past million years as the amount of ice has increased and decreased. Some high-level beaches were formed when the climate was warmer. Sea-level was higher than it is now because there was little ice in the world.

Other raised beaches result from changes in land-level. The great weight of ice during the Ice Age pushed parts of the continents down. As the ice melted, the sea-level rose quickly, but the land-level rose more slowly.

▶ WHAT IS THE ATMOS-
PHERE MADE OF?

The atmosphere is the air which surrounds the planet Earth. The gases in the air allow plants, animals and humans to live. The dampness and movement of the air near the Earth cause our weather. The atmosphere also shields us from the Sun's harmful rays and from falling meteorites.

Air is made up of many gases. The most common are nitrogen (78%) and oxygen (21%). There are small amounts of other gases, including argon, water vapour and carbon dioxide.

The atmosphere is held round the Earth by gravity. Its pressure, temperature and composition vary according to the distance away from the Earth's surface. It can be divided into four layers.

The troposphere is about 18 kilometres thick over the Equator and about 8 kilometres thick over the Poles. It has 80% of the Earth's atmosphere. Air pressure, temperature and humidity (dampness) are greatest near the surface.

Above the troposphere is the stratosphere which reaches to 80 kilometres above the surface. The ozone layer filters out some of the Sun's harmful ultraviolet rays.

Beyond the stratosphere is the ionosphere. It helps to transmit radio waves, and meteoroids burn up in its layers.

About 500 kilometres above the earth's surface comes the exosphere. This has very little air and merges into outer space.

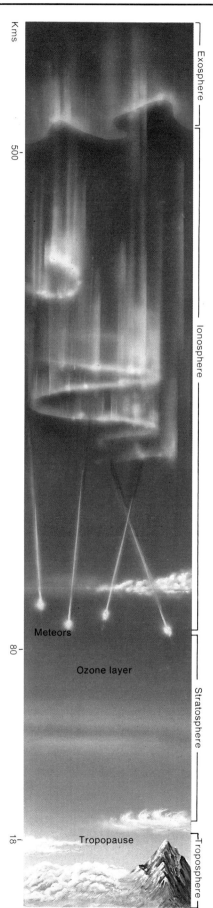

Kms

500

80

18

Exosphere

Ionosphere

Meteors

Ozone layer

Stratosphere

Troposphere

Tropopause

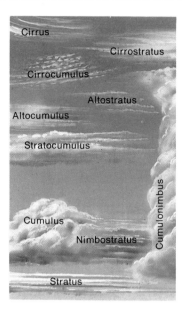

Cirrus

Cirrostratus

Cirrocumulus

Altostratus

Altocumulus

Stratocumulus

Cumulonimbus

Cumulus

Nimbostratus

Stratus

▲ WHAT KINDS OF
CLOUDS CAN WE SEE?

Clouds are made of millions of tiny water droplets or ice crystals suspended in the air. They are named according to their shape and height.

Air cools when it rises. When air rises slowly over a large area, layers (strata) of clouds form. Cirrostratus is a thin, almost transparent layer of cloud at a high level. Altostratus is a thicker layer of cloud at high level. Nimbostratus forms at a lower level, while stratus clouds are layers within 500 metres of the Earth's surface.

When air rises rapidly, it produces puffy clouds. These are called cumulus clouds. At a high level they are called altocumulus. When they join together they form stratocumulus. Cumulonimbus are great, towering thunder clouds.

A third type of cloud is cirrus, wisps of cloud high in the sky. Because of their shape, they are sometimes nick-named 'mares' tails'.

▲ WHAT IS THE DIFFER-
ENCE BETWEEN A HURRI-
CANE AND A TORNADO?

Hurricanes and tornadoes are violent storms with whirling winds. A tornado covers a much smaller area than a hurricane, but it is often more violent.

The huge swirling mass of cloud which rotates round the calm 'eye' of a hurricane may be over 400 kilometres across. The spiralling winds may reach 15 to 20 kilometres up into the atmosphere. Hurricanes form over warm oceans and gradually die out when they reach land.

A tornado is a violent twisting funnel of cloud which extends down to land from a large storm cloud. It may be only 50 to 500 metres wide, but it rushes across land at speeds of 30 to 65 kilometres an hour.

Winds in a tornado can be even more violent than in a hurricane. They twist up the funnel at speeds up to 650 kilometres an hour and cause a trail of damage along the tornado's narrow path.

▼ WHAT DO 'HIGH' AND
'LOW' MEAN ON A WEATHER
MAP?

Air pressure varies at different parts of the Earth's surface. Areas of high air pressure are marked 'high' on weather maps. Areas of low air pressure are marked 'low'. Air, like water, can flow and it is a rule that winds always blow from high to low.

Areas of high pressure are sometimes called 'anti-cyclones'. Air presses down and flows gently outwards from an anticyclone. Such 'highs' often indicate clear skies and fine, dry weather. But anticyclones can also bring foggy weather.

Winds blow into areas of low pressure, which are sometimes called 'depressions' 'Lows' usually indicate unsettled weather with wind and rain. Deep depressions, with very low pressure, usually bring gales and storms and very high tides.

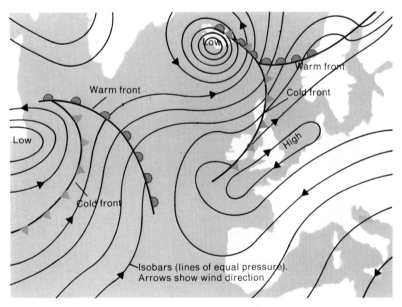

Isobars (lines of equal pressure). Arrows show wind direction

▲ WHAT ARE 'FRONTS' ON
WEATHER MAPS?

A 'front' is the dividing line between two different kinds of air. The different kinds of air will not mix easily, and usually one kind of air is pushing over or under the other.

'Fronts' are often found on weather maps of Western Europe because this area has varied types of air. Polar air pushing down from the north is cold. Some is cold and damp, some is cold and dry.

Tropical air pushing up from the south may be warm and moist, or warm and dry.

A body of air with similar temperatures and humidity (dampness) is called an air mass. The dividing line between two air masses is called a 'front'. A 'warm front' is where warm air is advancing. It rises over the colder air. A 'cold front' is where cold air is advancing: it pushes under the warm air. So on each front the warm air is rising. It cools and condenses and the result is clouds and rain or snow.

▼ WHAT ARE JET
STREAMS?

**Jet streams are strong
winds which blow from
west to east high above the
Earth's surface. If high-
flying aircraft are
travelling eastwards, jet
streams can enable them
to travel faster.**

Jet streams encircle the Earth
at 10 to 15 kilometres above
the surface. They blow in
definite zones at about 250
kilometres an hour.

Usually there are two jet
streams in each hemisphere:
the sub-tropical jet stream
and, nearer the Poles, the
polar-front jet stream. They
are strongest in winter and
early spring. Jet streams may
be marked by a line of clouds,
as shown in the photograph.

The position and strength
of the jet streams affect the
weather in a complex way.
The polar-front jet stream
influences the number and the
route of the fronts which give
much of Europe its varied
weather. The movement of
the sub-tropical jet stream
influences the monsoon in
Asia.

▼ WHAT IS THE MONSOON?

**'Monsoon' means season.
This word is used for the
season of heavy rain which
occurs in some parts of the
world, especially in
southern and eastern Asia.
This rainy season begins
suddenly when winds
from the sea sweep across
the land.**

The maps show India, which
has a monsoon climate. From
April to June the weather gets
hotter and hotter, and the air
is very dry. Winds blow

Rainfall June–Oct
Winds in July

Rainfall Nov–April
Winds in January

Millimetres
of rain

Over 1800
1000–1800
500–1000
250–500
120–250
25–120
Under 25

outwards from the land.

In June or July, the
monsoon bursts. The day
when the rain will begin can
be forecast. Then, winds
begin to blow from the sea,
bringing with them much-
needed rain.

About 1700 millimetres of
rain fall between June and
September, and only another
100 millimetres in all the rest
of the year. By September
only a few showers fall in
most parts of India. A
pleasantly cool, dry season
takes over. Once again, the
winds blow from land to sea.

▲ WHAT EFFECT DOES THE
SEA HAVE ON CLIMATE?

**Winds blowing from sea to
land usually bring
moisture. Places near the
sea have a less extreme
climate than inland.
Warm and cold ocean
currents also affect the
temperature of winds.**

Air blowing over a fairly
warm sea quickly becomes
saturated with moisture. If it
rises and cools as it reaches
land, much of the moisture
will fall as rain near the coast.

High land which faces winds
from the sea has a very high
rainfall.

Places near the sea are often
cooler in summer than places
inland. This is because the
moving ocean absorbs the
Sun's heat slowly in summer.
But it is slow to lose its heat in
winter, and the sea helps to
keep coastal areas warmer
than inland areas. Compare
the average temperatures of
London and Irkutsk, USSR,
which are on almost the same
latitude: London: January
4°C; July 18°C. Irkutsk:
January −21°C; July 18°C.

▼ WHAT HAPPENS TO ALL
THE WATER THAT FALLS TO
EARTH?

Rain or snow falls on to the land and flows off in rivers or glaciers, or soaks in as underground water. Eventually the water reaches the sea. Water is evaporated from the sea to form clouds, from which rain falls on to the Earth.

This process is called the water cycle. Each part of the cycle depends on other parts, involving water as a liquid, a solid (ice) and a gas (water vapour).

Water is absorbed into the air over the land as well as the sea. It comes from lakes and rivers, wet soil and from plants. Water vapour condenses and returns to the land and sea in many different forms: dew, fog and hail, as well as rain and snow. Most falls over the sea, but about a quarter falls over land. Almost half that does reach the land evaporates soon after falling. The rest flows back to the sea. Water is constantly recycled in this way.

▲ WHAT IS SPECIAL ABOUT
THE MEDITERRANEAN
CLIMATE?

Places near the Mediterranean Sea have hot, dry summers. Most of their rainfall comes in the warm winter months. This climate is the only one which has its rain at the coolest time of the year.

A similar climate to the Mediterranean occurs in parts of California (USA), central Chile, south-west Australia and near Cape Town (South Africa).

All these places are on the west side of continents. In the winter they receive rain from westerly winds. All these areas are also close to deserts. In summer they share the high pressure found over deserts and have hot, dry weather. Plants native to these areas are adapted to survive long, hot droughts.

This change of season is caused by a shift in the world's wind pattern each year as the Sun is overhead at the Tropic of Cancer in June and the Tropic of Capricorn in December.

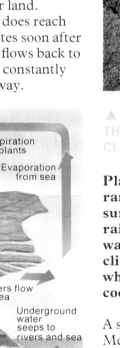

▲ WHERE DOES YOUR TAP
WATER COME FROM?

We break into the water cycle to obtain our water. Then we purify it and send it through pipes to our homes.

Rainwater can be collected from the roof and stored in tanks. In some places water is pumped out of rivers or lakes and piped to homes. Elsewhere, the water we use comes from underground springs or boreholes. It is pumped up from permeable rocks such as chalk, limestone and sandstone in which water can collect.

But in most large cities there is not enough surface water or underground water for everyone. Water may be brought from other parts of the country where there is more rain or fewer people. Valleys in wet, hilly areas may be dammed for water storage. Near large towns, water may be stored in huge reservoirs.

In a few parts of the world, sea water is turned into fresh water (desalination), but this is a very expensive process.

▼ WHAT IS THE DIFFERENCE BETWEEN WEATHERING AND EROSION?

'Weathering' is the breaking up of rocks by sun or frost, for example. 'Erosion' is the shaping of the Earth's surface by wind or water.

When rocks are exposed to the atmosphere, they are affected by its temperature and moisture. 'Mechanical weathering' occurs when water in the rocks freezes and cracks the rocks. Constant heating and cooling splits the surface of some rocks, too.

'Chemical weathering' rots rocks. Rainwater reacts with some minerals to dissolve the rocks or change them chemically. Weathering may be speeded up by plant roots and burrowing animals.

Rock pieces broken by weathering are moved by rivers, glaciers, the sea or the wind. Wind and water erode most when they contain particles of rock. For instance, sand carried by desert winds may chisel rocks into strange shapes.

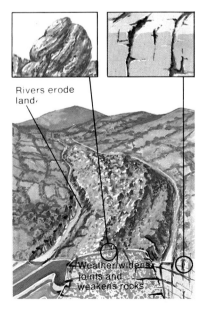

Rivers erode land.

Weather widens joints and weakens rocks

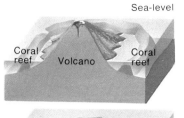
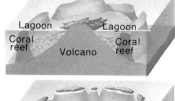
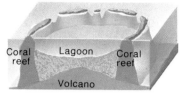

Sea-level

Coral reef — Volcano — Coral reef

Lagoon — Lagoon — Coral reef — Volcano — Coral reef

Coral reef — Lagoon — Coral reef — Volcano

▲ WHAT IS AN ATOLL?

An atoll is a coral reef which forms an almost complete circle around a lagoon.

The coral polyp is a tiny sea-creature which lives in a shell. New coral polyps grow on the shells of dead ones, eventually forming a great mass of coral. Corals live in fairly shallow water (up to 45 metres deep) that is warm (over 18°C) and clear. In ideal conditions large coral reefs may form.

The circular coral reefs of most atolls reach deep down into water where no coral can grow. As the diagrams show, they may once have been reefs in shallow water surrounding a volcano. As the island sinks, or the sea-level changes, the coral continues to grow. The original island disappears far below the lagoon, and the reef forms an atoll.

There are many atolls in the Pacific and Indian Oceans, where conditions are ideal for corals to flourish. Volcanic islands, some with coral reefs, are also found today.

▲ WHAT ARE STALACTITES AND STALAGMITES?

Both these features are found in limestone caves. They are formed from a rock which is sometimes called 'dripstone'. Stalactites are columns of dripstone hanging down from the ceiling. Stalagmites rise from the floor.

The word 'dripstone' gives a clue to the formation of stalactites and stalagmites.

Limestone is mainly made of calcium carbonate. When rainwater seeps through cracks in this rock it reacts with the calcium carbonate and gradually dissolves it. So water dripping from a cave roof is saturated with calcium carbonate and other minerals. As each drip hangs for a while, some water is evaporated, leaving a tiny deposit of calcium carbonate on the cave roof. Very slowly, these deposits grow to form stalactites.

Drips reaching the floor of the cave gradually form stalagmites. Natural pillars occur when stalactites and stalagmites join.

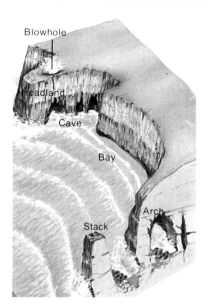

Blowhole

Headland

Cave

Bay

Arch

Stack

▲ WHAT HAPPENS WHEN
THE SEA ATTACKS THE
BASE OF A CLIFF?

**Great waves hurling water
and stones at a cliff are an
awesome sight. The sea
undercuts cliffs, causing
cliff falls and features
such as caves, arches, bays
and headlands.**

The effects of the sea's action
differ according to the
geology of the coast. Soft
rocks wear away more quickly
than hard rocks. The dip of
the strata (rock layers) helps
or hinders erosion. Faults and
folds create weaknesses which
the sea attacks.

Often, a notch can be seen
in a cliff near high-tide level
where the sea has battered the
cliff. As this notch deepens,
the cliff above will fall. The
sea carves out bays in areas of
weak rocks. Harder rocks are
left extending out as
headlands.

Cracks in even the hardest
rocks are widened and
deepened and may become
caves. In a headland, caves
may meet to form an arch.
When an arch collapses, part
of it is left as a stack.

▲ HOW IS NEW LAND
CREATED BY THE SEA?

**The sea can build as well
as destroy. When
conditions are right, the
sea can build sand dunes.
Mud may collect on the
sheltered side of sand and
shingle ridges. Marshes
grow and gradually new
land develops.**

The sea can create areas of
dunes. Sand pushed up a
beach may be blown into sand
dunes. Long-rooted grasses
start to grow and 'fix' the
dunes. More and more plants
grow, creating an area of sand
hills.

Tides and currents can
move sand or shingle along a
beach. Sometimes sand or
shingle spits are formed.
Water protected by such
features is quite still, and
sediments in the water sink to
the bottom.

Gradually the water gets
shallower, and more and more
mud is exposed at low tide.
Salt-loving marsh plants start
to grow and trap more mud.
Muddy creeks develop,
channelling the outgoing tide.

▼ WHAT IS THE
DIFFERENCE BETWEEN
SAND GRAINS ON A BEACH
AND IN A DESERT?

**In a desert, the sand grains
are blown about and keep
knocking each other. So
they become rounded. In
rivers and the sea, sand
grains do not collide so
often, so they are less
rounded.**

Sand mainly consists of grains
of quartz, but other minerals
may be present. All these
minerals have been weathered
out of rocks.

When handfuls of desert
sand and of beach sand are
studied under the microscope,
they look different. Sand
grains from the desert
(bottom) are mostly quartz.
River and sea sand (top) often
include softer minerals such
as mica.

The rounded desert sand
grains are all about the same
size and look 'frosted' instead
of shiny after countless
collisions with each other in
the wind. Sand grains in
rivers and the sea have been
'cushioned' by water and are
more varied in shape and size.

63

An avalanche is a mass of snow which comes loose from a mountainside and hurtles down a steep slope towards the valley below.

Avalanches occur wherever there are high mountains, open slopes and heavy snow. Many avalanches occur each winter, but only a small number cause death and destruction. Avalanches vary in type. Some are formed of loose snow, and others consist of huge snow-slabs.

Changes of temperature and wind can cause avalanches. Changes in the depth, pressure and humidity of the snow itself can allow one layer to slide over another. Late winter is the worst time for avalanches, when there is plenty of snow but warmer weather starts a thaw.

Sometimes explosives are used to make small avalanches which prevent larger ones. Walls, snow-fences and snow-bridges are built on hillsides to break up avalanches. Planting trees on slopes helps to keep the snow stable.

Rivers can erode the land and deposit eroded material further down-stream.

In the upper part of its course, the river flows down steep slopes. Rocks are bounced along by the water and help to erode the river bed. A deep V-shaped valley is formed.

On the lower land, the river meanders. Powerful river currents undercut the outside of the meanders and deposit sand and mud on the inside of meanders. This widens the valley.

At times of flood the river can cause great damage to low-lying land, and its course may be straightened. Old meanders are cut off to form oxbow lakes.

Near its mouth, the river flows over a broad flood-plain, where it deposits eroded material. If the river flows into a lake or sea with little or no tide then its silt is dumped to form a delta.

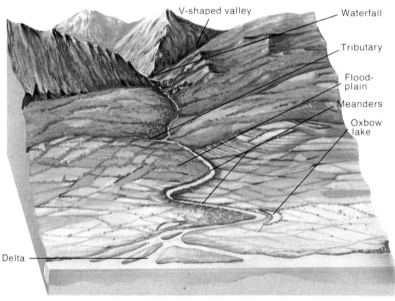

V-shaped valley
Waterfall
Tributary
Flood-plain
Meanders
Oxbow lake
Delta

Heavy and prolonged rain can flood large areas. Many parts of the world receive almost all their rain from heavy storms during a short wet season.

The rocks of an area may help to cause floods. Impermeable rocks and large built-up areas cause the rain to run off the land very quickly. Streams and rivers may overflow and flood the surrounding land. Permeable rocks soak up the water.

When snow that has collected through the winter suddenly melts, there can be widespread flooding. Parts of Siberia are flooded every spring when the snow in the south melts while the mouths of the north-flowing rivers are still blocked by ice.

Very high tides can flood land, especially if there are strong winds. The low-lying country of Bangladesh suffers terrible floods when cyclones (hurricanes) cause exceptionally high tides.

WHAT HAPPENED DURING THE ICE AGE?

During the last million years, large parts of northern Europe and North America have been covered by ice. There was not just one cold period when the ice sheets advanced; there were many.

The periods of ice advances are called 'glacials'. Snow accumulated, and glaciers and ice sheets extended over large areas. As these advanced, land was eroded and the sea-level was lower. There was much more sea ice and more ice-bergs than now.

In the interglacials much of the ice melted. Moraine and other glacial deposits were dumped over large areas. Melt-water left spreads of sand and gravel. The courses of rivers were often altered. Sea-level changed, flooding large areas.

Elsewhere in the world the pattern of ocean currents, winds and climate also changed with each glacial and interglacial.

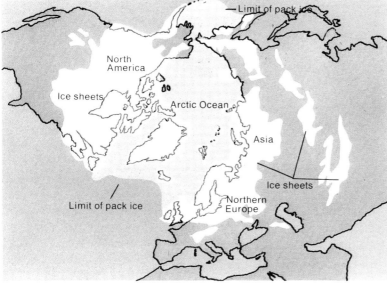

WHAT WOULD HAPPEN IF ALL THE WORLD'S ICE MELTED?

If all the ice in the world melted, new land would be revealed in the Arctic and Antarctic and in some high mountains. But large areas of the world would be flooded as sea-level rose.

Sea-level has changed in the past during glacials and inter-glacials, so it may change in the future. The depth of ice in parts of Greenland and Antarctica has now been measured, so scientists can estimate the amount of water stored there.

If all the world's ice melted, sea-level would rise by at least 65 metres. The coastline of Europe would change dramatically. Areas of low land would be flooded, including the whole of Denmark and the Netherlands. Many major cities would be drowned, including great capitals such as London, Dublin, Paris, Rome and Helsinki.

WHAT ARE THE CHANCES OF ANOTHER ICE AGE?

No one knows, partly because scientists still do not understand why an Ice Age begins.

Some geologists point out that, in the past, the warm interglacials lasted about 10,000 years, and our climate has been as warm for that long already. Some climatologists say that the Earth's warmth is about the same now as 90,000 years ago when a sudden cooling probably occurred.

Historians know that Europe's climate has varied. Northern Europe was warmer and less stormy in Roman and Viking times. Between 1550 and 1880 there was a 'Little Ice Age' when winters were colder than they are now.

Some ecologists believe humans could create an Ice Age. All the dust and fumes we add to the air could reduce the Sun's heat. Others argue that as we burn so much fuel, and chop down forests, we increase the carbon dioxide in the air. This could trap more of the Sun's heat.

▶ HOW DO SATELLITE PICTURES TELL US ABOUT EARTH?

A lot of satellites are circling our globe. Some send back photographs, such as those used in weather forecasting. Others send back images using visible light and infra-red light. Computers can turn these into pictures of the Earth.

The *Landsat* carries a special scanner which senses the light and heat reflected from the Earth below. Information is relayed back to special ground-receiving stations and converted into pictures like the one shown here.

From *Landsat* pictures we can study the land use of any part of the Earth. Floods can be predicted and pollution warnings given. Because heat differences are measured, warm and cold sea-currents can be mapped. Pictures from *Landsat's* infra-red readings can be processed to show the health of growing crops, the effects of drought or types of surface rock.

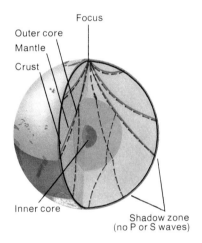

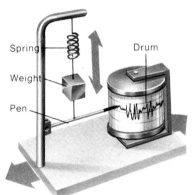

Red arrows show direction of movement caused by a seismic wave

▲ HOW CAN SCIENTISTS 'SEE' INSIDE THE EARTH?

Scientists tell us that the inside of the Earth is in layers: the crust, the mantle, the outer core and the inner core. Evidence for these has come from seismology, the study of earthquakes.

Seismographs record three different kinds of earthquake waves. Primary (P) waves travel fastest and can pass through solids, liquids or gases. Secondary (S) waves travel through solids only. Long (L) waves are slowest of all as they only travel along the surface. Long waves do most damage.

Geologists are especially interested in P and S waves. Their speed and path change with the density of the rocks. P waves speed up in the mantle, slow down in the outer core, and speed up again in the inner core. S waves will not pass through the outer core. This suggests it is like a liquid. The waves change direction as they pass from one layer to another.

◀ HOW ARE EARTHQUAKES MEASURED?

Earthquakes cause *seismic* waves to travel through the Earth. These are recorded on a seismograph. Scales are used to measure their intensity. The Richter Scale measures the strength of an earthquake. The higher the number, the more severe the earthquake.

The seismograph is firmly embedded in a masonry column which reaches down to solid rock. The weight is attached to the support by a tie-wire or spring. Attached to this weight is either a pen or a beam of light which makes a mark on paper covering the rotating drum. When an earthquake occurs, the weight stays still, while the rest of the seismograph moves.

The trace that is made on the paper round the drum records several kinds of shock waves. The time difference between the waves is noted. It is possible to work out how far away and how severe the earthquake is.

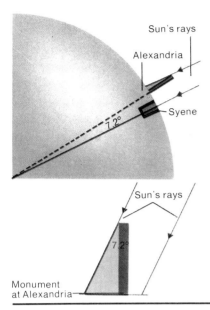

◄ HOW CAN PEOPLE
MEASURE THE EARTH?

The science of measuring the Earth is called geodesy. When people realized that the Earth is round, they were able to measure it by using their knowledge of circles and angles (geometry). Nowadays, geodimeters can measure long distances very accurately, by using light rays.

The diagram shows how, in about 250 B.C., Eratosthenes measured the Earth's circumference. At noon in midsummer, the Sun shone straight down a well at Syene, near Aswan in Egypt. At the same time in Alexandria, a monument showed that the Sun made an angle of 7.2°. Using geometry, Eratosthenes knew that the angle at the centre of the Earth would be the same. He calculated that the Earth's circumference was 46,300 kilometres.

Eratosthenes was not far out. In fact the distance round the equator is 40,076 kilometres.

► HOW ARE DIFFERENT
KINDS OF ROCK FORMED?

Geologists put the rocks of the Earth's surface into three main groups: igneous (meaning 'fire-formed'), sedimentary (made from sediments) and metamorphic (meaning 'transformed').

The first rocks of the Earth's crust were igneous, made from molten material which cooled down. These rocks were eroded, and the particles were deposited as sediments in the sea or on land. These became sedimentary rocks. Rocks that were subjected to great heat and pressure were transformed into metamorphic rocks.

Rocks are still being formed today. The Earth's surface is being worn away by rivers, which carry mud and sand to the sea where sediments build up. They are squeezed and cemented into rocks such as clay and sandstone. Rocks move downwards at the edges of crustal plates and are metamorphosed, or changed. Igneous rocks rise to the surface from volcanoes.

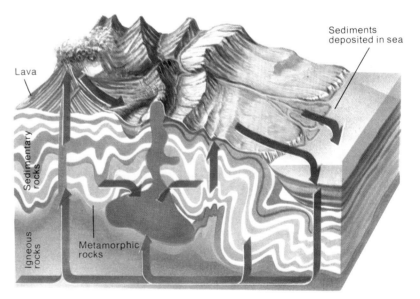

◄ HOW CAN WE MEASURE
THE AGE OF ROCKS?

From a study of the rock layers (strata) and of any fossils they contain, geologists can work out the order in which rocks were formed, but not their age. Normally, the lowest strata are the oldest. The age of some rocks can be worked out by measuring the decay of their radio-active elements.

Radioactive elements gradually change into different elements. For example, uranium gradually changes into lead. This rate of change can be measured. Rock samples can be analyzed to see how the radioactive elements have changed, and this gives some idea of their age.

Radioactive elements like Uranium-238 and Potassium-40 take hundreds of millions of years to decay. Tiny amounts are found in igneous rocks and can be used to date some Pre-Cambrian rocks. Fossils of the last few million years can be dated using Carbon-14.

PLANTS AND ANIMALS

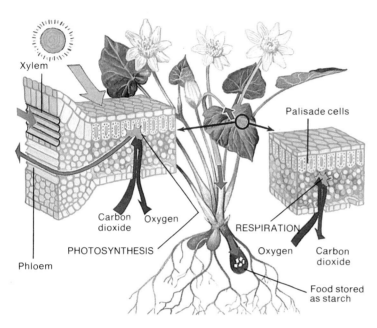

**Plants make food by
photosynthesis. Using
light energy, carbon
dioxide and water, they
build up food sugars.**

Photosynthesis relies on the
green pigment chlorophyll,
which captures the Sun's light
energy. It is contained in tiny
structures called chloroplasts.
These are most numerous in
the upper (palisade) layer of
cells in each leaf.
 Chlorophyll converts light
energy into chemical energy,
which fuels the chemical
reactions of photosynthesis.
Carbon dioxide, taken from
the air, and water are used to
build up sugar, which is
carried to other parts of the
plant by the phloem tissue of
the vascular bundles. It is
stored in the form of starch.

**Plants take in oxygen.
They use it to break down
food sugars, releasing
energy and carbon
dioxide. This process is
called respiration.**

The process of respiration is
basically the opposite of
photosynthesis. The sugars
that the plant built up during
photosynthesis are broken
down again, using oxygen,
into carbon dioxide and
water. The energy released in
the process is used for other
activities of the plant, such as
growth and reproduction.
 Respiration takes place in
tiny cell structures called
mitochondria. About 40 per
cent of the energy stored in
the food sugar is converted
into chemical energy. The
rest is lost as heat.

**A seed begins to germinate
when water soaks through
the hard seed coat. The
seed swells and starts to
grow a root and a stem.**

As germination begins, the
young root, or radicle, grows
from the seed first. As it
grows the young stem, or
plumule, develops.
 The young seedling is
nourished by food reserves, or
endosperm, which in many
seeds is contained in the seed
leaves, or cotyledons. Sometimes, as in sunflower seeds,
the growing stem carries the
cotyledons above the ground.
There they turn green and
carry on photosynthesis until
the first true leaves develop.
In other seeds, such as broad
beans (shown here), the
cotyledons remain under-
ground.

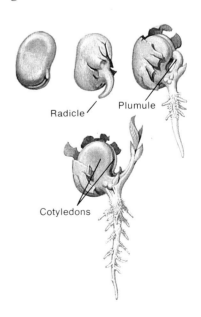

68

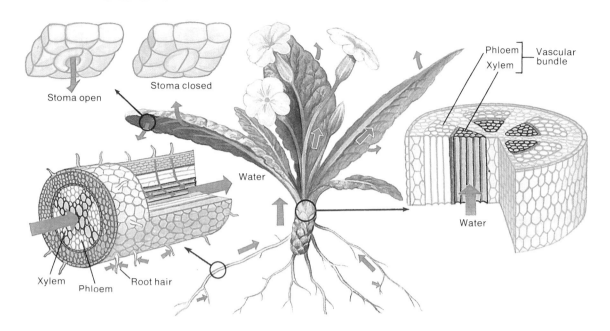

Stoma open

Stoma closed

Xylem

Phloem

Root hair

Water

Phloem

Xylem

Vascular bundle

Water

▲ HOW DO PLANTS GET WATER?

Plants take water from the soil. Fine roots and root hairs collect the water, which passes on to other root cells.

The roots of a plant have two functions. First, they anchor the plant firmly in the ground. Second, they seek out and take up the water that is so essential for the plant.

Plants have several different kinds of root system. Some spread out horizontally near the surface. Others go down deep into the soil.

The plant takes in water near the tips of the finest roots and through root hairs. These are single, long cells that grow out from the root surface. From these cells it is drawn into the inner cells of the root. Finally, it enters the conducting tissue at the centre of the root.

The conducting tissue is called the xylem. It forms a star-shaped column up the middle of the root. Water passes up the xylem to the stem.

▲ HOW DOES WATER TRAVEL UP THE STEM?

Water travels to the leaves up the xylem, or conducting tissue, of the stem. In a green-stemmed plant, the xylem vessels are contained in a number of bundles, known as vascular bundles.

Water-conducting xylem vessels are non-living, tube-like cells. They are open at both ends and many cells are joined together to form long conducting tubes that run the whole way up the plant.

It was once thought that water was pumped up the stem, either by the roots or by living cells in the stem. However, this has been shown to be impossible. Scientists now believe that the water is drawn up the stem from above. Water molecules exert an enormous pulling force on each other. Evaporation of water from the leaves, or transpiration, creates a partial vacuum. Water from the leaf veins moves in to fill this vacuum. As it does so, it draws more water up.

▲ WHAT IS TRANSPIRATION?

Transpiration is loss of water from the leaves. Water evaporates from the leaf cells and diffuses out through tiny pores called stomata.

Losing water by evaporation from its leaves helps to keep a plant cool. On a hot day a large tree can reduce its temperature by several degrees. But in the process it loses several hundred gallons of water. More importantly, transpiration causes the plant to take up water from the soil, bringing minerals with it.

The rate at which a plant transpires varies according to the outside conditions. On hot, dry days plants transpire very quickly. Dry winds also increase the transpiration rate. On cool days, and when the air is moist, plants transpire more slowly.

The rate of transpiration can also be controlled by the stomata. When there is little water available in the soil and the plant is nearly wilting, the stomata close.

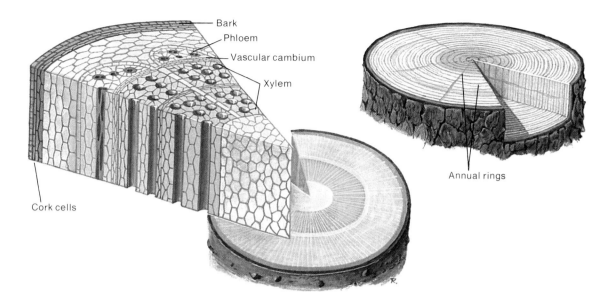

Bark
Phloem
Vascular cambium
Xylem
Cork cells
Annual rings

HOW IS WOOD FORMED?

The wood of a tree is its water-conducting tissue, or xylem. Each year more wood is added and the trunk becomes thicker.

The vascular bundles of a young shoot are arranged in a ring. Each bundle contains phloem and xylem and, between them, a layer of cells called the vascular cambium. The cells of the cambium are able to divide and produce new xylem and phloem.

A stem starts to become woody as cambium develops in between the bundles. At the same time it produces new xylem tissue, which forms a cylinder inside the stem.

Each year the cambium produces more xylem and the woody shoot increases in thickness. The xylem cells are tough and have greatly thickened walls, which gives the shoot strength.

In older branches and the main trunk of a tree the wood in the centre becomes blocked up. Water conduction is left to the outer wood, or sap-wood, while the central core provides immense strength.

HOW CAN YOU TELL THE AGE OF A TREE?

If you look at a tree stump you will see a series of rings. Each one represents one year's growth. So by counting the rings you can find the age of the tree.

A tree grows only during the spring and summer. In spring the cambium produces large xylem cells. But gradually, as summer passes, the new xylem cells become smaller. In late summer or early autumn growth stops until the next spring, when large cells are produced again. The difference between small, late summer cells and large spring cells shows up clearly as a growth ring. And the number of growth rings therefore shows how many seasons have passed since the tree first began to grow.

The cambium also produces new phloem cells each year. But, unlike xylem cells, they do not form growth rings. Phloem cells are soft and thin-walled. As each year's new phloem develops, the old phloem is crushed and becomes part of the bark.

HOW IS BARK FORMED?

As a young shoot becomes woody on the inside, bark forms on the outside. Bark is composed of non-living, waterproof cells.

As wood is laid down inside a shoot, a layer of cells near the outside begins to divide and produce 'cork' cells. The walls of these cells soon become heavily thickened with a waterproof substance. The cells die and form bark.

Over the years the bark is constantly added to from the inside. So as the diameter of the twig, branch or trunk increases, the waterproof barrier is maintained. But the outer bark often splits and cracks or becomes flaky.

Bark gives a tree protection against the weather and sudden temperature changes. It contains substances that repel insects and it resists fire. Bark often has commercial uses. True cork comes from the bark of the Mediterranean cork oak. The drug quinine comes from the bark of cinchona trees and cinnamon comes from the bark of the cinnamon tree.

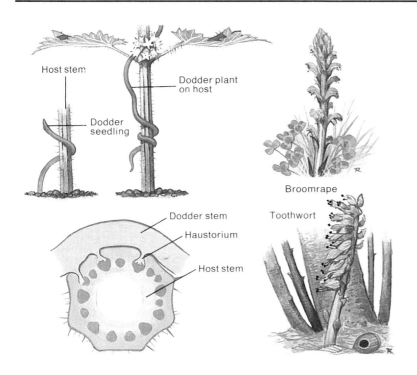

Host stem

Dodder plant
on host

Dodder
seedling

Dodder stem

Haustorium

Host stem

Broomrape

Toothwort

▲ HOW DO PARASITIC
PLANTS GET THEIR FOOD?

**Parasitic plants depend
entirely on their hosts for
their nourishment. They
have no green leaves and
so cannot photosynthesize**

**food. Instead they bore
into the tissues of other
plants and take the food
they need.**

Parasitic plants are those that
live on other plants without
giving any benefit to their

hosts in any way. In some
cases, parasites cause harm to
their hosts.

Dodders are one of the
largest groups of parasitic
plants. They have long,
twining red or yellow stems,
with tiny scale-like leaves.
Most dodders live off small
plants, such as nettles or
gorse, but some are parasites
of trees. A young dodder
seedling quickly twines round
a host plant, and buries its
suckers (haustoria) into it in
as many places as it can.

Broomrapes and toothworts
are also common parasites.
Broomrapes attack such
plants as clover and daisies,
while toothworts are parasites
of trees, such as hazel. Both of
these parasites attack the roots
of their hosts.

One of the most extra-
ordinary parasites is *Rafflesia*.
Its huge flower, the largest in
the world, is the only visible
part of the plant. The
remainder consists of threads
buried in the host's roots.

▶ WHY DOES MISTLETOE
GROW ON TREES?

**Mistletoe grows high up in
the branches of trees to be
as near to the light as
possible. To help it
survive, it takes the water
it needs from the sapwood
of its host tree.**

The mistletoe plant is a
partial parasite. It can be
found on several kinds of tree,
such as apple, hawthorn,
willow, poplar and lime. It is
not a total parasite because it
has green leaves and makes its
own food by photosynthesis.
But it does take water and
nutrients from its host.

Mistletoe seeds are spread
by birds, which feed on the
white berries. The sticky

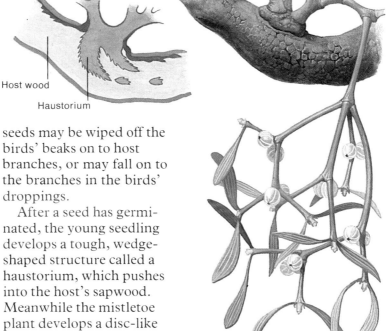

Host wood

Haustorium

seeds may be wiped off the
birds' beaks on to host
branches, or may fall on to
the branches in the birds'
droppings.

After a seed has germi-
nated, the young seedling
develops a tough, wedge-
shaped structure called a
haustorium, which pushes
into the host's sapwood.
Meanwhile the mistletoe
plant develops a disc-like
structure that clamps onto the
outside of the branch.

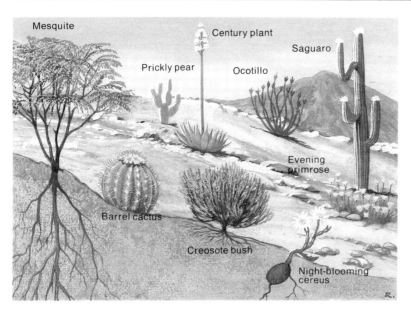

A number of desert plants avoid drought altogether. Their seeds only germinate after rain.

During dry periods the seeds of many desert plants lie dormant in the ground. But after a rainstorm they quickly germinate, flower and die.

In North America, dry valleys may suddenly be covered with the blooms of the California poppy and evening primrose.

Another way of surviving drought is to store water. Many desert plants store water in their stems and leaves.

A great deal of water can be stored in fleshy leaves and stems. After a rainstorm, a barrel cactus may double its diameter. To cut down loss of water due to transpiration, cacti have no leaves. Instead, they have spines, which also serve to keep away animals.

Desert plants that store water in their leaves are also common. The century plant has a rosette of tough, sharply pointed leaves. Pebble plants have a pair of fleshy leaves that look like pebbles.

Many desert shrubs, such as ocotillo, shed their leaves in times of drought, growing new ones when the rains return. Prickly pear cacti and chollas sometimes shed the ends of their stems.

The root systems of desert plants are also important. Cacti have shallow roots, but they spread out over a wide area. The root tips of a saguaro may be as far as 15 metres from the stem. Mesquite, on the other hand, has very deep roots that can reach over 30 metres down to find water.

The creosote bush is an unusual desert plant. Its leaves shrivel up in dry conditions, but they revive again after rain. Creosote bushes defend their water-collecting territory. Their roots give out poisons that prevent other plants, even their own seedlings, from growing too close.

Alpine plants are mostly small and they often have coverings of hair.

Alpine plants have to survive biting cold winds, low rainfall and poor soil. Generally, alpines are small and low-growing. For example, the leaves of the alpine aster are all close to the ground. Many alpines are ground-hugging cushion plants.

Generating warmth is important. The temperature

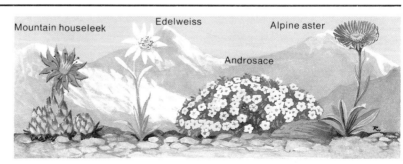

inside a cushion plant is often much higher than the outside temperature. Some alpines, such as gentians, generate their own warmth, which allows them to grow beneath the snow in spring.

Some alpines are covered in hair; edelweiss is a well-known example. This not only keeps the plant warm but also helps to protect the plant from strong sunlight and to conserve water. Several alpines, such as houseleeks, store water in fleshy leaves.

HOW DO SALT-MARSH PLANTS SURVIVE?

Salt water kills most flowering plants. But salt-marsh plants have special adaptations that enable them to tolerate these conditions.

A salt-marsh occurs where a river deposits mud along the banks of an estuary. A number of plants live in this salty mud. Others live higher up, in the drier, less salty regions of the salt-marsh.

Salt water usually draws water out of plants, which die as a result. But salt-marsh plants have unusually high amounts of salt in their cells. So they can actually take in water from sea water. Many salt-marsh plants store water in fleshy leaves or stems.

The most salt-tolerant plant is glasswort, which can stand being completely covered at high tide. Higher up the salt-marsh are plants such as seablite, sea aster and common salt-marsh grass. On the drier ground are such plants as salt-marsh rush, sea lavender and sea milkwort.

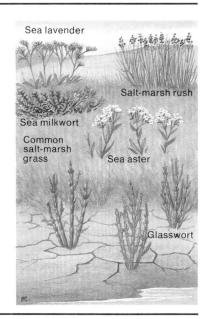

Sea lavender
Salt-marsh rush
Sea milkwort
Common salt-marsh grass
Sea aster
Glasswort

Hawthorn
Gorse
Bramble
Nettle

HOW DO SOME PLANTS STING AND SCRATCH?

Some plants defend themselves against plant-eating animals. Plant defences include thorns, spines, prickles and stings.

Picking thistles or holly can be a painful business. The edges of their leaves are armed with sharp spines. Gorse and cacti go even further; their leaves are modified into spines. Plants such as blackthorn, hawthorn and acacia, defend themselves with thorns. These are formed from modified twigs. The prickles of roses and brambles also grow on the stems. They are produced by the outer layer, or epidermis.

Some plants, such as comfrey, bugloss and prickly pear cacti, produce tiny bristles that cause intense irritation. Others have stinging hairs. A nettle sting consists of a hollow hair with a hard bead on the end. When it is touched, the bead breaks off. The hair pierces the skin and poison is pumped in.

HOW DO CLIMBING PLANTS HOLD ON?

Climbing plants climb by using tendrils, hooks or suckers. Or they may just coil round other plants.

Most plants put a lot of energy into growing strong stems in order to reach the light. Climbing plants save this energy and use the stems of other plants for support.

The prickles of roses and brambles enable them to cling on and ramble up and over other plants. Ivy grows up trees and buildings by putting out tough, penetrating aerial roots. Some climbers, such as bindweeds and honeysuckle, coil round their hosts.

Other plants have special grasping organs. Some vetches, for example, have tendrils at the ends of their leaves. Other plants, such as gourds and many vines, have long tendrils that grow out of their stems.

Old man's beard and other species of clematis grasp hold of supports by coiling their leaf-stalks. Virginia creepers have tendrils with sticky pads.

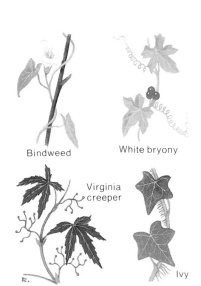

Bindweed
White bryony
Virginia creeper
Ivy

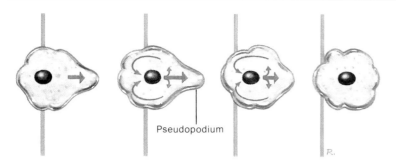

Pseudopodium

▲ HOW DOES AN AMOEBA MOVE?

An amoeba moves by first putting out a *pseudopodium*, or 'false foot'. Then the rest of the animal's body follows on behind it.

The main part of an amoeba's body is made of a grainy liquid called endoplasm. Outside this, just inside the outer membrane, there is a thin layer of clear, jelly-like material called ectoplasm.

When an amoeba starts to move, the ectoplasm becomes liquid at a certain point and the animal starts to put out a pseudopodium. A stream of endoplasm moves up the centre of the animal into the pseudopodium. There it spreads out and becomes firmer, adding to the ectoplasm at the sides. At the rear end the opposite happens so that the whole animal moves towards the pseudopodium.

We still do not know what causes the endoplasm to stream forward. But scientists think that the 'rear' end of the animal contracts and squeezes the animal forward.

▲ HOW DO BIRDS FLY?

When a bird flaps its wings through the air, it produces lift, like the wings of an aircraft. At the same time it produces forward thrust, which in an aircraft is produced by the propellers or jet engines.

In cross-section, a bird's wing is shaped in a similar way to the wing of an aircraft. It is slightly curved so that air passes more rapidly over the upper surface than over the lower one. This produces lift.

In flight the downstroke of the wing is the power stroke. The wing beats downwards and forwards and the inner part of the wing produces lift. The outer part of the wing, which has large flight feathers, produces even more lift and forward thrust. As the wing comes down, the flight feathers twist and curl upwards to act like propellers.

▶ HOW DO SNAKES MOVE?

Some snakes move in a series of leaps, using a movement like a concertina. Others pass waves down their bodies and others use the scales on their bellies. Sidewinding snakes move in a series of steps.

On rough ground most snakes move by passing waves of muscle movement down their bodies. The waves push against stones and other objects (2).

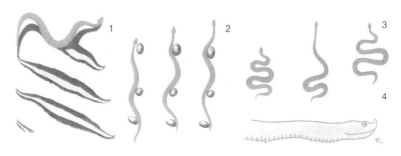

On smoother ground, a snake may move in a concertina fashion. The snake draws its body up into a series of bends. Then, keeping the tail region firmly on the ground, it throws its head and body forwards (3).

Some snakes can move in a straight line. Waves of muscle movement pass down the snake's belly (4).

Sidewinding snakes are usually found in the desert. They move over the sand in a series of sideways steps (1).

► HOW DOES A
PARAMECIUM MOVE?

Cilia

A paramecium swims through the water using its tiny hairs, or *cilia*, as 'oars'. It swims in a cork-screw fashion and finds its way by trial and error.

The body of a paramecium is covered in diagonal rows of tiny hairs. The animal swims by beating these hairs, or cilia, backwards and forwards. When it is swimming forwards, each cilium beats just after the one in front. This gives the impression of waves travelling down the animal.

Because the rows of cilia run diagonally across the body, the paramecium rotates as it swims. At the same time it travels in a spiral path through the water. It can swim over 500 times its own length (one third of a milli-metre) in one minute.

When a paramecium meets an object blocking its way, it reverses, changes its angle of approach slightly and tries again.

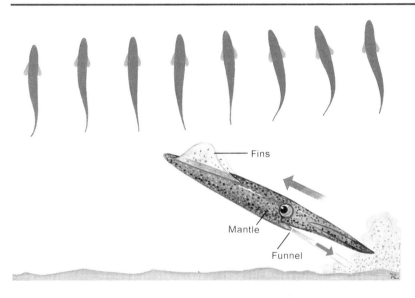

Fins

Mantle

Funnel

▲ HOW DOES A SQUID
SWIM?

A squid swims by using jet propulsion. It squirts water out of its funnel and can move extremely fast.

On the underside of a squid there is a large chamber called the mantle cavity. It is surrounded by a muscular wall known as the mantle. The mantle cavity opens towards the animal's head and situated in the opening there is a short funnel.

The squid draws water into the mantle cavity through the opening. The mantle then closes against the funnel and contracts, or shrinks, forcing the water out through the funnel. The squid then moves in the opposite direction.

The funnel can be pointed either forwards or backwards, depending on which way the squid wants to go. The animal steers by means of its two fins.

Squid have highly stream-lined bodies and can push water out through their funnels with great force. As a result, they are very fast swimmers.

◄ HOW DO FISHES SWIM?

A fish swims by causing its muscles to contract, or shorten, all the way down its body. These push against the water and the fish moves forward.

When a fish swims, each part of its body moves from side to side. The contracting movement of the muscles travels in waves, which pass from the front to the rear of the fish. Many fishes also have a large tail to give them more forward thrust.

Most fishes control steering and braking with the front, or pectoral fins. However, this is not always so. Unlike bony fishes, sharks and their relatives do not have swim-bladders (air-filled sacs) to keep them afloat. So they have to propel themselves not only forward but also upwards. A shark uses its front fins, together with its specially shaped tail, to produce lift.

The strange puffer fish rows itself through the water using only its pectoral and dorsal fins. The tail fin is used as a rudder.

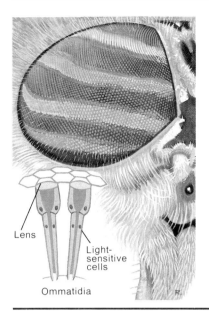

Lens

Light-sensitive cells

Ommatidia

The eye of an insect is made up of hundreds of tiny, separate units. Each one has its own lens and light-sensitive cells. Information from each unit passes to the brain, where an image is created.

The eye of an insect has many lenses, each of which directs light to its own group of light-sensitive cells. An insect's eye is therefore known as a compound eye.

The lenses lie on the surface of the eye and each one faces in a slightly different direction. Under a microscope, an insect's eye has many facets, or sides.

When the insect sees an object, it does so with several units, or *ommatidia*. But only one is actually facing the object and this is the only one that sees the image of the whole object. The surrounding ommatidia see only part of the object. This gives the insect information about the direction and shape of the object.

Cats and other animals that hunt or feed at night have specially adapted eyes. As a result they can see in very dim light.

The eyes of mammals contain two kinds of light-sensitive cells. There are cones, which provide good vision in daylight, and rods, which are sensitive to dim light. A cat has a large number of rods in its eyes.

At night a cat's eyes have enormous round pupils to let in as much light as possible. In bright light the pupils narrow to thin, vertical slits to protect the sensitive rods.

Another feature of a cat's eyes is that they are very large, so that they can let in as much light as possible. At the same time they are shaped rather like a squashed tennis ball.

Finally, a cat has a layer of reflective cells at the back of each eye. This reflects back the light that has already passed through the retina once.

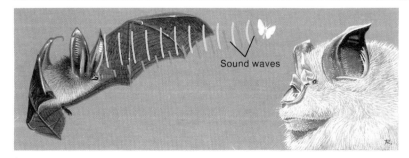

Sound waves

A bat does not have good eyesight, but is able to 'see' by sound waves. It produces a series of high-pitched squeaks which are reflected back by the objects around it.

The way in which bats find their way about is called echo-location. They produce high-pitched squeaks that humans cannot hear. Some bats, such

as the long-eared bat on the left, produce these sounds from their mouths. Others, such as the greater horseshoe bat, on the right, produce the sounds from their noses. The returning echoes are picked up by the bat's large, sensitive ears.

The bat receives information about the direction, loudness and pitch (high or low notes) of echoes returning from a flying insect. It can then work out the direction, distance and speed of the insect with amazing accuracy.

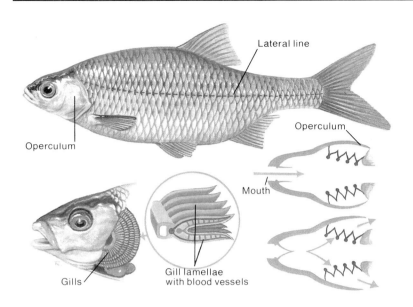

◄ HOW DO FISHES 'SEE' WITH THEIR SIDES?

A fish has a special sensory system known as the lateral line system. This seems to provide the fish with information about what is going on around it.

The lateral line system of a fish consists of a canal down each side of the body that branches into several canals over the head. Inside each canal there is a row of neuromasts (groups of sensory cells), which have hairs running into the canal. In most fishes, the canals open to the surface by a long line of pores.

It is thought that neuromasts respond to pressure changes in the water around the fish. Using its lateral line system, a fish can tell that there are other fishes near it or even moving some distance away. This is useful in helping to detect prey or enemies. And it may help fishes that swim in shoals to stay together. It is also possible that the system helps a fish to detect objects by echo-location.

HOW DO FISHES BREATHE?

A fish takes in oxygen through its gills. It causes water to flow over the gills and oxygen passes from the water into the gill blood vessels.

A fish's gills lie in two passages that lead from the back of the mouth cavity to the outside. Each of the openings to the outside is covered by a flap called the operculum.

Water is pumped over the gills. When the fish opens its mouth, the operculum is closed and the mouth cavity is expanded, drawing water in. Then the fish closes its mouth, the operculum is opened and the water is squeezed out over the gills.

The gills are supplied with many blood vessels that lie just beneath the surface of the skin. When water flows over the gills, oxygen is taken into the blood through the blood vessels and carbon dioxide is released into the water.

► HOW DOES A SPERM WHALE STAY UNDERWATER FOR LONG PERIODS?

A sperm whale can dive to a depth of about a thousand metres and may spend over an hour under-water. To achieve this it has to have very special control over its breathing and blood circulation.

In between deep dives, a sperm whale spends about ten minutes on the surface, taking between 60 and 70 breaths. With each breath it renews

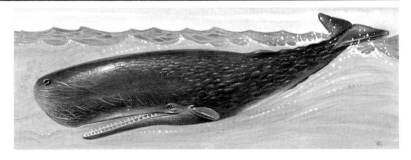

about nine tenths of the air in its lungs. (Humans only renew about a quarter of the air.) Then, with its oxygen supply renewed, it dives again.

A whale is adapted in several ways to help it to stay underwater. For example, it

stores oxygen in its muscles. While diving, its heartbeat slows down and only essential organs, such as the brain and heart, are kept fully supplied with blood. The remaining organs have their blood supply reduced or cut off.

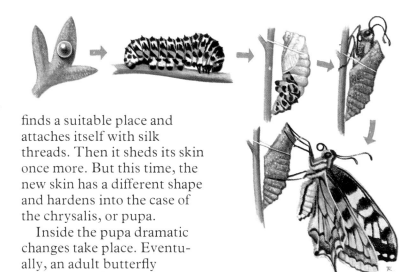

The amazing change from a caterpillar to a butterfly happens inside a chrysalis. The process is called metamorphosis, which means 'change of form'.

A caterpillar's life is spent feeding and growing. It eats large amounts of plant material. Every so often it sheds it skin, to show a larger skin underneath.

When it is fully grown, it finds a suitable place and attaches itself with silk threads. Then it sheds its skin once more. But this time, the new skin has a different shape and hardens into the case of the chrysalis, or pupa.

Inside the pupa dramatic changes take place. Eventually, an adult butterfly appears and flies away.

A tadpole becomes a frog by a series of dramatic changes. It develops lungs, grows legs, loses its tail and finally emerges from the water as a frog.

When a tadpole hatches from its egg, it has a small black body, a tail and a pair of feathery external gills. For a few days after hatching it has no mouth. It attaches itself to a leaf or a stone and feeds on the remains of its yolk.

Then it develops a mouth with a fringe of horny teeth and begins to feed by rasping off pieces of plant material. Soon afterwards it develops internal gills.

After about three months, metamorphosis, or a change of form, begins. The tadpole develops lungs and loses its internal gills. Then hind legs begin to develop and a few days later the front legs appear. The tail becomes shorter and the mouth gets bigger. Within a short time the animal has become a young frog.

A chick usually has to break out of its shell by itself. To do this, it has a horny 'egg tooth' on its beak and a 'hatching muscle' on its neck.

When it is ready to hatch, a chick starts calling from inside the egg. This helps to make a bond between it and its parents. Within a few days it starts to chip away at the inside of the shell using its egg tooth. Then, using its strong hatching muscle, it heaves part of the shell away and struggles free. The egg tooth and hatching muscle disappear after a few days. Some birds usually take only a few hours to hatch. Larger birds may take up to three days.

Many chicks are helpless when they hatch out. They are often blind, naked and can only open their mouths for food. They may remain in the nest for several weeks.

Other birds, especially those that nest on the ground, have chicks that can run within a few days.

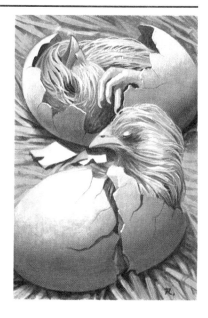

WHICH ARE THE OLDEST KNOWN ANIMALS?

The first animals probably appeared at the same time as the first plants. But the first animals that we know of for certain are worms, jellyfish and similar animals that existed over 700 million years ago.

The first animals were almost certainly single-celled types, or protozoans. But we have no fossil evidence of such animals. In turn, protozoans gave rise to simple, many-celled animals. We have no real idea of what these animals looked like.

The first fossil evidence comes from the Ediacara Hills in Australia, where there are fossil-bearing rocks over 700 million years old. The fossil animals contained in these rocks are known as the Ediacara fauna.

The picture shows reconstructions of some of the Ediacara animals. *Ediacara* and *Kimbrella* were jellyfish, and *Cyclomedusa* was one of their bottom-living relatives. Sea pens were also relatives of the jellyfish. *Spriggina* and *Dickinsonia* were worm-like animals. *Tribrachium* was a primitive relative of modern sea urchins and starfish.

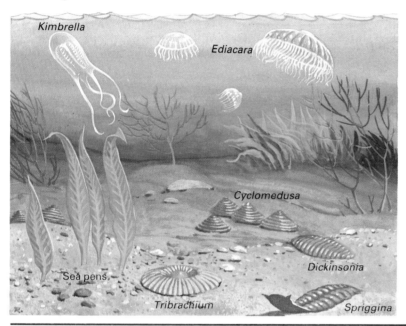

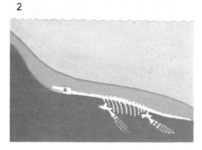

WHEN DO FOSSILS FORM?

A fossil is formed when all or part of an animal or plant becomes included in rock. Usually it is the hard parts, such as bones or shells.

Scientists believe that over 9800 million species have existed since life began. But only a small number of these (about 800,000) have left fossil remains. This is because the process of fossilization needs special conditions.

A typical fossil is formed from hard material, such as bone. When an animal dies (1), its soft parts decay rapidly (2). If the animal died in water, the bones may then become quickly buried in a sediment, such as particles of clay or limestone. As time passes, the sediment is covered by other layers of sediment and hardens into rock (3). At the same time, the tiny holes or pores in the bone may be filled with minerals from the sediment. Or the bones may dissolve and be entirely replaced by minerals. This leaves stone copies, or casts, of the original bones in moulds formed by the surrounding rock. Finally, over millions of years, the rocks may be pushed out of the sea to form land. When the rocks are eroded, the fossil bones are eventually exposed (4).

▼WHEN DID ANIMALS
WITH SHELLS APPEAR?

**The Cambrian period marks
the start of the main fossil
record. This is because about
600 million years ago animals
with hard parts (shells) began
to evolve.**

Precambrian animals were all
soft-bodied creatures and were
therefore very vulnerable to
predators. Animals that could
protect themselves with hard
shells had a great advantage.

Many animals with
limestone shells lived in the
Cambrian seas. There were
gastropod mölluscs (sea snails)
and bivalves (molluscs with
shells divided into two hinged
parts, or valves). Brachiopods,
or lamp shells, were very
common. Also there were
primitive echinoderms ('spiny
skinned' animals), which were
the ancestors of modern
starfish and sea urchins.

Other animals, too, had
developed hard outer
coverings. These were the first
arthropods (animals with
jointed limbs, e.g. crabs and
insects), among which were
the trilobites.

▲WHICH ANIMALS LIVED
IN THE ANCIENT SEAS?

**During the Cambrian,
Ordovician and Silurian
periods the seas teemed with
all kinds of invertebrate (non-
backboned) animals.**

The picture shows some of the
animals that lived in the sea
during the Ordovician period
(530–440 million years ago).
Trilobites (1) were very
common. They were between
two and 60 centimetres long.
Most of them crawled about
the sea bed, feeding on soft-
bodied creatures.

Earlier groups of animals
also spread. There were
sponges (8), jellyfish (7) and
various kinds of coral (9).
Several types of echinoderm
included cystoids (4), crinoids,
or sea lilies (5), and echinoids,
or urchins (6). Brachiopods (2)
were still common, as were
gastropod (3) and bivalve
molluscs. There was also
another mollusc group, the
nautiloids (10). These were
squid-like animals with long,
conical shells, ancestors of the
ammonites and the modern
squids and octopuses.

▼WHEN DID THE FIRST
FISHES APPEAR?

**Sometime during the
Ordovician period, the first
vertebrates (backboned
animals) evolved. These were
the jawless fishes or
ostracoderms ('shell skins').**

We do not know how the first
vertebrates evolved. But it is
possible that they arose from a
group of echinoderms.

Most ostracoderms were less
than 50 centimetres long.
Their mouths were just holes
or slits through which they
could suck water and food
particles. There were three
main groups. Cephalaspids
(e.g. *Hemicyclaspis*) were
sluggish fishes with flattened
heads that were covered by a
bony head-shield. Pteraspids
(e.g. *Pteraspis*) also had head-
shields, but these were made
up of several bony plates.

Anaspids (e.g. *Jamoytius*)
were the smallest
ostracoderms. They had no
head-shields, but many of
them had bodies covered in
thick scales. Anaspids may
have been the ancestors of
lampreys and hags, the
modern jawless fishes.

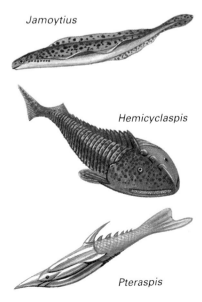

Jamoytius

Hemicyclaspis

Pteraspis

WHEN DID THE FIRST
JAWED FISHES APPEAR?

The first fishes with movable jaws appeared during the Silurian period, about 420 million years ago. But their jaws were very different from those of the sharks and bony fishes, which appeared soon afterwards.

The first jawed fishes were the placoderms ('plate skins'). Their heads were covered in heavy armour-plates and the jaws were formed from two hinged plates.

The early placoderms were fairly small. But by the Devonian period there were giants. *Dunkleosteus* was over nine metres long and it would have been possible for a human to stand inside its open jaws.

The Devonian period is often called the Age of Fishes. Jawless fishes and placoderms were both present. In addition, more advanced fishes were starting to appear. Among these were the sharks, such as *Cladoselache*, with skeletons made of cartilage. Bony fishes also appeared at this time. *Climatius* was a member of a

group known as spiny sharks, so called because there was a spine at the front edge of each fin. It is thought that spiny sharks evolved from anaspid fishes and gave rise to all the later bony fishes.

Bony fishes are divided into two main groups. The lobe-fins include the coelacanth and the extinct rhipidistians (see page 14). They get their name from the fact that their fins are supported on fleshy lobes. All other fishes belong to the ray-fins. *Cheirolepis* is the earliest known ray-fin.

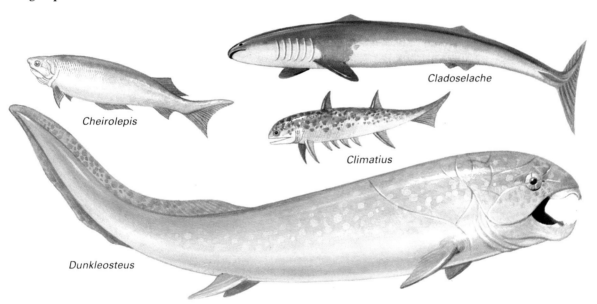

Cheirolepis

Cladoselache

Climatius

Dunkleosteus

WHERE DID PLANTS
FIRST GROW ON THE
LAND?

During the Silurian and Devonian periods the land began to be invaded. The first colonizers were plants.

Mosses and similar plants may have invaded the land during the Ordovician or early Silurian periods. But no fossil remains of such plants have been found. The earliest land plants seem to have been a group known as psilophytes. These were simple plants with

no true roots or leaves, but their stems were upright and contained water-conducting cells. The oldest known psilophyte is *Cooksonia*, fossils of which have been found in late Silurian rocks (400 million years old). *Zosterophyllum* was a Devonian psilophyte that grew stems up to 30 centimetres high.

Clubmosses also existed during the Devonian period. Plants such as *Baragwanathia* and *Drepanophycus* were the ancestors of the modern clubmosses and of the giant Carboniferous types.

Cooksonia

Zosterophyllum

Ichthyostega

Hylonomus

**The first amphibians
appeared in the late Devonian
period. They are thought to
have evolved from lobe-
finned fishes.**

During the Devonian period
there was a group of lobe-fins
known as the rhipidistians.
These fishes became extinct
about 250 million years ago,
during the Permian period.
Before they disappeared, they
probably gave rise to the
amphibians.

Rhipidistians, like other
fishes, had fins for swimming.
But their fins were supported
on fleshy lobes that could
easily have been used for
crawling. Some rhipidistians
may have been tempted to
crawl out of their ponds to feed
on the increasing amount of
plant food on land. Young,
light-bodied fish may have
found this easier than older
ones. Gradually, the more
successful crawlers developed
stronger limbs and spent more
and more time on land,
eventually giving rise to the
first true amphibians.

**The swampy forests of the
Carboniferous period were
dominated by clubmosses,
including both small and
giant kinds. In addition,
there were large numbers of
horsetails, some of which
also grew into huge trees.
Ferns, tree ferns and seed
ferns were abundant.**

The origins of the various
groups of Carboniferous plants
are uncertain. They probably

evolved from the psilophytes.
But no linking fossils have
been found.

Like modern clubmosses
and ferns, the Carboniferous
plants needed moisture to help
them produce their spores. So
they lived around swamps and
ponds, forming vast swamp
forests.

Club mosses varied in size
from small types that
resembled modern clubmosses
to huge trees over 30 metres
high, such as *Lepidodendron*,
Bothrodendron and *Sigillaria*.
On the left of the picture are
(from left to right) a

Lepidodendron, two *Sigillaria*
and a tree called *Calamites*.
This last type was a giant
horsetail. *Sphenophyllum*, a
much smaller horsetail, is
shown in the bottom-left
corner.

The Carboniferous period is
often called the Age of Ferns.
This is because there are many
fern-like fossils in coal, which
was formed at that time. There
were indeed a large number of
ferns, including tree ferns, But
many of the fossils belonged to
seed ferns. Like modern
conifers, these reproduced by
seeds rather than spores.

The dominant animals during the Carboniferous period were the amphibians.

Carboniferous amphibians belonged to two main groups. The labyrinthodonts, such as *Ichthyostega*, were fish-like animals with short, but useful, limbs. Some were large animals. *Ichthyostega* was about one metre long and others were even larger.

Lepospondyls, on the other hand, were generally smaller. Most spent all their lives in water and had small or non-existent limbs. *Ophiderpeton* was a snake-like lepospondyl.

The labyrinthodonts dominated the scene. *Eogyrinus*, one of the later types, was five metres long and lived entirely in water. It fed voraciously on fish. Competition from such giants may have caused some of the smaller amphibians to leave the water. Such animals may have developed tougher skins and given rise to the first reptiles.

The dominant group of reptiles during the Permian period were the mammal-like reptiles. Some were very strange animals with 'sails'.

The mammal-like reptiles are so called because they possessed some of the features of mammals. The earliest types were the pelycosaurs. Among these were the 'sail-backs', such as *Dimetrodon* and *Edaphosaurus*. *Dimetrodon* was a large, flesh-eating pelycosaur about 3.5 metres long. Its 'sail' may have been used to help control its body temperature. If the sail was turned sideways on to the Sun, the blood running through it heated up. If the animal needed to cool down, it would have found some shade or turned so that the front edge of the 'sail' faced the Sun.

Later mammal-like reptiles varied from huge, ferocious creatures, such as the gorgonopsian *Lycaenops*, to smaller, dog-like cynodonts. It was probably the cynodonts that gave rise to the first true mammals.

Eogyrinus
Ophiderpeton
Rhipidistians

The first reptiles evolved during the late Carboniferous period. During the Permian period (280–225 million years ago) they took over the land.

The earliest known reptile is *Hylonomus*, fossils of which have been found in late Carboniferous rocks. It measures between 20 centimetres and one metre in length, and it probably fed on insects. It seems to have made its home in old tree stumps.

Hylonomus belonged to a group known as cotylosaurs, or stem reptiles, so called because they probably gave rise to all the later reptiles. Other stem reptiles included the flesh-eating *Limnoscelis*, and its smaller relative *Labidosaurus*. The largest stem reptiles were the plant-eating pareiasaurs, such as *Scutosaurus* and *Pareiasaurus*. They were protected by an armour of bony knobs and were over three metres long. By the end of the Permian period all the stem reptiles had disappeared.

Dimetrodon

The history of life on Earth is divided into three eras. The Mesozoic, or 'middle life', era is known as the Age of Reptiles.

The geological timescale below shows the history of living things based on the ages of the rocks in which their fossil remains are found. There are three main eras. The boundaries between the eras mark the times when major changes took place. Many groups of animals became extinct at these times. Each era is divided into periods.

The Palaeozoic, or 'ancient life', era saw the evolution of the invertebrate groups, the fishes, the amphibians and the first reptiles. The Mesozoic, or 'middle life', era was dominated completely by the reptiles, which took over the land, the seas and the air. The Cenozoic, or 'new life', era saw the rise of the mammals and still continues today.

During the Triassic period there existed a group of reptiles called the thecodonts. Some of these began to run on their hind legs. Their descendants were the dinosaurs.

The thecodonts gave rise to all the ruling reptiles, or archosaurs. These included not only the dinosaurs but also the pterosaurs (flying reptiles) and crocodiles.

There were several types of thecodont. Many were crocodile-like creatures with limbs that were held out sideways. Others, however, had limbs that were placed underneath their bodies, enabling them to run more swiftly. Some of these developed large hind legs and short front legs, and began to use only their hind legs for running. From this type arose the dinosaurs, which also typically ran on their hind legs. Even those that returned to walking on all four legs tended to have larger hind legs than front legs.

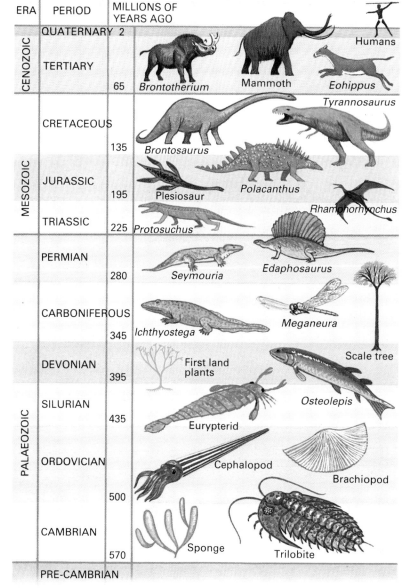

ERA	PERIOD	MILLIONS OF YEARS AGO
CENOZOIC	QUATERNARY	2
CENOZOIC	TERTIARY	65
MESOZOIC	CRETACEOUS	135
MESOZOIC	JURASSIC	195
MESOZOIC	TRIASSIC	225
PALAEOZOIC	PERMIAN	280
PALAEOZOIC	CARBONIFEROUS	345
PALAEOZOIC	DEVONIAN	395
PALAEOZOIC	SILURIAN	435
PALAEOZOIC	ORDOVICIAN	500
PALAEOZOIC	CAMBRIAN	570
	PRE-CAMBRIAN	

Brontotherium · Mammoth · Eohippus · Humans · Tyrannosaurus · Brontosaurus · Polacanthus · Plesiosaur · Rhamphorhynchus · Protosuchus · Seymouria · Edaphosaurus · Ichthyostega · Meganeura · First land plants · Scale tree · Osteolepis · Eurypterid · Cephalopod · Brachiopod · Sponge · Trilobite

Euparkeria

▼ WHICH DINOSAURS HAD LARGE PLATES?

▼ WHICH WERE THE LARGEST DINOSAURS?

▼ WHICH DINOSAURS HAD HORNS?

Among the strangest dinosaurs were the stegosaurs, which were equipped with plates.

The stegosaurs, such as *Stegosaurus*, evolved during the Jurassic period. But they were not particularly successful and many questions about them remain unanswered.

Stegosaurus is usually thought of as a plant-eater. But it had a very small head and mouth, so it would have taken *Stegosaurus* a long time to eat enough plant material to keep it alive. Some scientists think therefore that *Stegosaurus* may have lived on carrion (dead animals).

The plates are often thought of as armour. But *Stegosaurus* would still have been very vulnerable, particularly along its flanks. Another idea is that the plates may have been used to warm or cool the blood.

The spiked tail of *Stegosaurus* is another mystery. *Stegosaurus* could not have flailed the tail from side to side. So this 'weapon' does not seem to have been very useful.

The largest dinosaurs were the sauropods, such as *Brontosaurus*. But despite their size they were probably gentle animals. Their size was merely a form of defence against flesh-eating dinosaurs.

The huge size of a sauropod is hard to imagine. *Diplodocus*, the longest of them all, measured 25 metres from head to tail. It appears to have had a 'relay station' – a swelling in the spinal nerve cord – to help its brain control the rear end of its body. *Brachiosaurus*, the most massive of the sauropods, is thought to have weighed between 80 and 100 tonnes.

Sauropods appeared in the Triassic period and became very common during the Jurassic period. They were plant-eaters and probably spent their time browsing on leaves, reaching up to the highest branches. Their great size probably deterred most predators, but they may have been able to defend themselves with their powerful legs and tails.

The horned dinosaurs, or ceratopsians, appeared during the Cretaceous period. The horns and head-shields must have been useful protection against the fierce carnosaurs.

The horned dinosaurs were a very successful group that survived right to the end of the Cretaceous period. Primitive types included the relatively small *Protoceratops*. This had a head-shield, but no horn, and was about two metres long. Later types developed single horns at the front of the head-shields, and additional horns at the back.

Among the largest of the advanced ceratopsians was *Triceratops*, which was about eight metres long. The horns and head-shield almost certainly provided protection for the animal's head and neck. The horns may have been used in 'battles' between rival males. They could have locked horns and engaged in a pushing match to establish which of the two was the stronger.

Brontosaurus

Triceratops

Protoceratops

Stegosaurus

►WHICH DINOSAURS LOOKED LIKE ARMOURED TANKS?

The most heavily armoured dinosaurs were the ankylosaurs. Some of them must have been almost impossible to attack and kill.

The ankylosaurs appeared in the early Cretaceous period. They may have been descendants of the stegosaurs, which also had armour. Among the early types was *Polacanthus*. Its relatively light armour consisted of two rows of tall spiky cones down its neck and part of its back. There were also bony knobs and plates around its hips and tail.

The later ankylosaurs were all squat animals that bristled with armoured spines and knobs. *Euoplocephalus* (formerly also known as *Ankylosaurus*) was about four metres long. It was half the length of *Stegosaurus*, but weighed twice as much. The whole of the upper surface of its body was protected by closely-packed bony plates strengthened with bony knobs. Its best method of defence was probably to drop onto its belly and wait for the attacker to give up and go away. If necessary, it could probably have swung its massive club-like tail from side to side. But it probably could not swing its tail very accurately.

Ankylosaurs appear to have been fairly common during the Cretaceous period, so their armour was presumably very effective. One of the best-protected ankylosaurs was *Scolosaurus*. Its body was covered in large spines. The two largest spines were on the end of its club-like tail.

Tyrannosaurus

Euoplocephalus

Ornithomimus

Deinonychus

▲WHEN DID FLESH-EATING DINOSAURS APPEAR?

Throughout the history of the dinosaurs there were flesh-eating types. The largest and fiercest appeared in the Jurassic and Cretaceous periods.

The early flesh-eating dinosaurs, or theropods, were very similar to their thecodont ancestors. *Coelophysis* was a Triassic type that measured three metres long. It belonged to the group of lightly-built theropods called coelurosaurs. Jurassic coelurosaurs included the chicken-sized *Compsognathus* and the two-metre-long *Coelurus*.

The larger, heavier theropods are known as carnosaurs. The most massive and fearsome types existed during the Jurassic and Cretaceous periods. The largest were the Jurassic megalosaurs, such as *Megalosaurus* and *Allosaurus* and the Cretaceous tyrannosaurids, such as *Tyrannosaurus*.

Anatosaurus

Ornitholestes

Compsognathus

Deinonychus

WHICH DINOSAURS COULD RUN THE FASTEST?

The fastest dinosaurs were the ornithomimids. These were egg-eating dinosaurs that raided the nests of other dinosaurs.

The ornithomimids were a group of Cretaceous coelurosaurs. Unlike their flesh-eating relatives, they had no teeth. They appear to have fed by sucking out the contents of the eggs of other dinosaurs,

Ornithomimids had three-fingered 'hands' that were probably used for scraping away sticks or sand to find nests. They had very long hind legs and were obviously very agile. Scientists have calculated that *Ornithomimus* could have run at speeds of up to 80 kilometres an hour. However, studies of its footprints have shown that it usually travelled at less than 20 kilometres an hour. It probably used its high-speed running ability only in real emergencies.

WHICH WAS THE LARGEST FLESH-EATER?

The largest known flesh-eating land animal that has ever lived is *Tyrannosaurus*. It stood over five metres high and measured 14 metres from head to tail. Its teeth were 15 centimetres long.

Tyrannosaurus lived in North America during the late Cretaceous period. It is often thought of as one of the most terrifying animals that has ever lived. But its reputation is probably exaggerated.
  Like other carnosaurs,

Tyrannosaurus and its relatives ran on their hind legs. But tyrannosaurids had tiny front limbs that were almost useless. They relied on their massive jaws for catching prey. The hind legs of these animals were set quite far apart. As a result they probably waddled along rather slowly. Most other animals would have been able to escape fairly easily and so tyrannosaurids probably preyed on sick and wounded animals, and may have lived on carrion for much of the time. So *Tyrannosaurus* and its relatives were probably not the dominant predators.

WERE DINOSAURS WARM-BLOODED?

Mammals and birds are described as being warm-blooded animals. Reptiles are described as cold-blooded. Dinosaurs were reptiles, but some evidence indicates that they may have been warm-blooded.

A warm-blooded animal produces the heat that it needs from inside its body, and can maintain an almost constant body temperature. A cold-blooded animal, on the other

hand, relies on heat from outside its body to keep it warm. Its body temperature therefore rises and falls with the temperature of its surroundings.
  Cold-blooded animals tend to be relatively small. Many dinosaurs, however, were large. Cold-blooded animals of this size would have been rather sluggish and they would have had difficulty in regaining lost heat quickly enough. But even the largest dinosaurs appear to have been able to move fairly swiftly for quite long periods of time.

Cold-blooded animals are active during the day. At night they cannot get warm enough to move about very much. The coelurosaur *Deinonychus*, however, seems to have been a night-hunter – it had keen sight and an acute sense of smell. But to hunt at night, without the Sun's warmth, it must have been warm-blooded.
  These, and a few other pieces of evidence, indicate that dinosaurs may have been warm-blooded animals. However, we cannot be certain.

▲WHICH DINOSAURS HAD DUCK-BILLS AND CRESTS?

The hadrosaurs, or duck-billed dinosaurs, appeared in the late Cretaceous period. Some of them had extraordinary crests on their heads.

The duck-billed dinosaurs were a group of plant-eating dinosaurs that evolved from the group known as ornithopods. They were the last and most specialized members of this group.

The long, flattened tails and duck-like beaks of these dinosaurs suggest that they lived in lakes or marshes. But the bill of a hadrosaur contained many tightly-packed rows of crushing teeth that formed two grindstones. This suggests that they ate tough food. In fact there is evidence that they ate twigs and conifer needles. So hadrosaurs may have been forest browsers.

The purpose of the crests is unknown. They may have helped the animals' sense of smell. Or they may have acted as resonating chambers to increase the sound of the animals' calls.

Tanystropheus

Nothosaur

Placodont

▲WHEN DID THE FIRST SEA REPTILES APPEAR?

Reptiles are now basically land animals. Yet by the Permian period some had returned to live in water.

The first reptile to return to the sea was the Permian lizard-like animal *Mesosaurus*. It was about 70 centimetres long and had an eel-like tail and webbed feet for swimming.

During the Triassic period there were a number of sea reptiles. Placodonts were two-metre-long, heavily armoured, newt-like animals that appear to have fed on shellfish. Nothosaurs were three-metre-long amphibious reptiles with webbed feet and long necks. They were probably the ancestors of the later plesiosaurs.

One of the strangest of the early sea reptiles was *Tanystropheus*. This creature had a very long, stiff neck. It may have fed by standing in shallow water and reaching out and dipping its head in the water to catch squid and fish.

▼ WHEN DID *IGUANODON* LIVE?

***Iguanodon* was an early Cretaceous dinosaur. It belonged to the group known as ornithopods, or bird-footed dinosaurs.**

Ornithopods had existed since Triassic times. They were unspecialized, plant-eating dinosaurs that survived right through until the end of the Cretaceous period.

Iguanodon was a large ornithopod that grew to about eight metres in length and

▼ WHEN DID ICHTHYOSAURS LIVE?

Ichthyosaurs appeared in the Triassic period and were a highly successful group until the middle of the Cretaceous period.

Ichthyosaurs looked amazingly like modern dolphins. They evolved almost exactly the same streamlined shape for high-speed swimming. An ichthyosaur swam by using its fish-like tail. A dorsal fin kept the reptile upright, and the flippers on each side were used

for steering and braking.

The first ichthyosaurs fed on fish, which they caught with their sharp teeth. Later types were able to tackle ammonites and squid. Some were almost toothless.

Ichthyosaurs could not move on dry land and so had to breed in water. Fossil evidence shows that they did not lay eggs. Instead they produced live young.

Ichthyosaurs began to die out during the early Cretaceous period. Possibly, they could not compete with the plesiosaurs.

Elasmosaurus   Ichthyosaur

Short-necked plesiosaur

stood over five metres tall. Its only real specialization seems to have been its thumb, which had become a sharp spike. This may have been used as a defensive weapon against large carnosaurs.

Ornithopods, like many modern plant-eating animals, may have lived in herds. The fossil remains of a herd of *Iguanodon* have been found in Belgium. Over 30 skeletons were found together. Perhaps the herd fell into a ravine while rushing away from an attacking predator.

▲ WHEN DID PLESIOSAURS LIVE?

Plesiosaurs were sea reptiles that appeared in the late Triassic period. They flourished until the end of the Cretaceous period.

There were two main types of plesiosaur. Long-necked plesiosaurs had small heads and needle-sharp teeth. They swam through the water in the same way as modern penguins. They used their paddles as 'wings' and could twist and turn very rapidly. They fed

mostly on fish. Some of the later long-necked plesiosaurs had very long necks indeed. *Elasmosaurus* had 70 neck bones and its neck made up half of its total length of 10 metres.

Short-necked plesiosaurs had much larger heads. They were strong swimmers and could move faster over long distances than their long-necked relatives. They fed mostly on squid and ammonites, which they caught in massive jaws. The largest short-necked plesiosaurs were over 12 metres long.

▶ WHEN DID REPTILES TAKE TO THE AIR?

Flying reptiles, or pterosaurs, first appeared in the Triassic period. They probably evolved from thecodonts that took to living in trees.

The ancestors of the pterosaurs were probably thecodonts that ran on their hind legs. Some took to scrambling about in trees, and some of these developed membranes for gliding. *Podopteryx* was a Triassic reptile that had membranes stretched between its front and hind limbs. It lived in trees and could glide from one to another.

One of the most primitive pterosaurs was a creature called *Dimorphodon*, which appeared in the early Jurassic period. It had a large head, and its jaws were armed with many large teeth. Its wingspan was about 1.5 metres, but it was probably a very poor flier. Like all pterosaurs, it probably used its wings for gliding rather than flying.

Rhamphorhynchus appeared in the last Jurassic period. Its head and body were much lighter than those of *Dimorphodon* and it was better adapted for life in the air. Its tail had a diamond-shaped structure on the end. This probably acted as a stabilizer when the reptile was in flight.

The forward-pointing teeth of *Rhamphorhynchus* may have been used for spearing fish. But it is unlikely that the animal could have dived into the water, or even landed on the surface. *Rhamphorhynchus* probably caught fish by skimming along the surface of the water and dipping its beak in.

Rhamphorhynchus

Pteranodon

Dimorphodon

▲ WHICH WERE THE BIGGEST FLYING REPTILES?

The largest flying reptiles were pterodactyls such as *Pteranodon* and *Quetzalcoatlus*.

The pterodactyls were the most advanced group of pterosaurs. They had no tails, and their teeth were slender and delicate. Some had no teeth at all.

Pterodactylus was a small, sparrow-sized reptile. But *Pteranodon* and *Quetzalcoatlus* were giants. Pteranodon had a wingspan of over eight metres It glided slowly over the sea, probably catching fish by scooping them up into its huge throat sac. *Quetzalcoatlus* was even larger, with a wingspan of about ten metres. This enormous vulture-like reptile lived inland and probably lived on carrion.

Pterosaurs probably flapped their wings rather slowly and were amost certainly better gliders than fliers. On the ground they could hardly move. They probably lived on the tops of cliffs.

▼ WHEN DID THE FIRST
BIRDS APPEAR?

**The earliest-known bird is
Archaeopteryx, which lived in
the late Jurassic period.**

Birds probably evolved from
thecodont or coelurosaur
ancestors. Feathers probably
evolved from reptile scales.
Their first use would have
been in helping to keep the
animals warm.

Archaeopteryx was certainly a
bird, as it had wings and
feathers. But it also still had a
number of reptile-like
features. Its beak contained
sharp teeth, it had claws on its
wings, and its long tail had
bones down the middle.

Archaeopteryx is on its own
in the fossil record. Nothing is
known of its immediate
ancestors or descendants.
There is some evidence that
there were a few goose-like and
grebe-like birds during the
early Cretaceous period. Late
Cretaceous birds were more
widespread. They included
Ichthyornis, a tern-like bird,
and *Hesperornis*, a large,
flightless diving bird.

▼ WHEN DID THE FIRST
MAMMALS APPEAR?

**The first mammals evolved in
the Triassic period. They
were tiny shrew-like creatures
that lived on insects and other
small animals.**

Mammals evolved from a
group called the cynodonts –
one of the last groups of
mammal-like reptiles.
Mammals appeared during the
Triassic period, at the same
time as the dinosaurs were
evolving. But, while the
dinosaurs took over the world,
the mammals remained a small
and unimportant group.

During the Jurassic and
Cretaceous periods several
groups of mammals appeared.
Their fossil remains consist
mostly of teeth. The names of
the groups describe the shapes
of the teeth. Jurassic mammal
groups included the
docodonts, triconodonts and
symmetrodonts. The most
important group was the
pantotheres. By the middle of
the Cretaceous period, the
pantotheres had given rise to
the marsupials and placental
mammals.

Hesperornis

Archaeopteryx

Ichthyornis

▲ COULD
ARCHAEOPTERYX FLY?

***Archaeopteryx* does not seem
to have been built for flying.
It was probably better at
gliding and may have spent
most of its time on the
ground.**

In order to fly well, a bird
needs a large breastbone to
support the massive flight
muscles. *Archaeopteryx* had a
small, poorly developed
breastbone.

Various suggestions have
been made as to how
Archaeopteryx lived. One idea
is that it was a tree-dwelling
creature that used its claws to
scramble from branch to
branch, and could glide from
one tree to another. However,
scrambling about in trees
would soon have damaged its
feathers.

Another idea is that
Archaeopteryx lived on the
ground and used its wings to
catch prey. But it seems more
likely that *Archaeopteryx* used
its limited powers of flight to
run and take off from high
ground to escape from
predatory coelurosaurs.

**The end of the Cretaceous
period, 65 million years ago,
marks the extinction of the
dinosaurs.**

The dinosaurs and a number of
other animal groups appear to
have died out as a result of
dramatic changes in the
world's climate. But we do not
yet understand what caused
these changes.

During the Palaeocene
epoch, the last of the Jurassic
mammal groups died out.
These were the rodent-like
multituberculates, such as
Taeniolabis, which had until
this time been very successful.
Meanwhile the placental
mammals evolved rapidly. By
the middle of the Eocene
epoch there were 27 different
groups. Insectivores and
primates, such as *Plesiadapis*,
were among the first to appear.
There were also a number of
'experimental' groups that
quite soon became extinct.
Among these were the
amblypods, such as
Coryphodon.

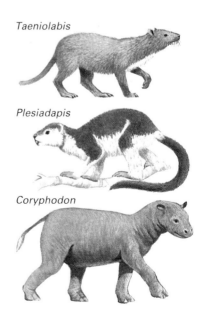

Taeniolabis

Plesiadapis

Coryphodon

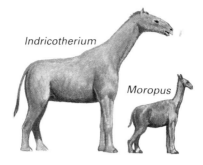

Indricotherium

Moropus

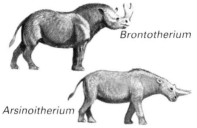

Brontotherium

Arsinoitherium

**The largest land mammal of
all time was the giant hornless
rhinoceros *Indricotherium*. It
lived in the Oligocene epoch.**

All the main animal groups
have produced giant types, and
the mammals are no exception.
Some still exist today. The
blue whale is still the largest
animal that has ever lived.

Giant mammals were
particularly common during
the Oligocene epoch. The huge
Indricotherium stood 5.5 metres
high at the shoulder, and its
head would have towered
above a modern giraffe.

Brontotheres, such as
Megacerops and *Brontotherium*,
stood 2.5 metres high or more
at the shoulder. The horse-like
animal *Moropus* was only
slightly smaller. All these
animals probably browsed on
the open plains. *Moropus* may
have dug for roots.

Arsinoitherium was a strange
two-horned animal, about the
size of a modern rhinoceros. It
lived in what is now Egypt and
may have been a relative of the
elephants and mastodons.

**Sabre-toothed cats were
probably the most formidable
of the early mammal
predators. They existed from
the Eocene to the Pleistocene
epoch.**

The sabre teeth of a sabre-
toothed cat are the greatly
enlarged canine teeth of the
upper jaw. They appear to
have evolved as stabbing
weapons for killing large
tough-skinned prey. Sabre-
toothed cats had particularly
powerful front limbs. This
suggests that they held fast
onto their prey while stabbing
it to death.

Early sabre-tooths, such as
the Oligocene cat
Hoplophoneus, had relatively
short sabre teeth. *Eusmilus* was
a leopard-sized Oligocene cat
with huge sabre teeth.
Machairodes was a lion-sized
animal that was common in
Europe during the Pliocene
epoch. The most powerful of
all the sabre-tooths was
Smilodon, which lived in North
America during the
Pleistocene epoch.

▼ WHEN DID MASTODONS AND MAMMOTHS EXIST?

Mastodons first appeared in the Oligocene epoch. During the Pliocene epoch they gave rise to the elephants and mammoths.

The earliest mastodons, such as *Palaeomastodon*, had short trunks and tusks and stood about two metres high at the shoulder. During the Miocene epoch there were three groups of mastodons. The deinotheres, or hoe-tuskers, had short, downward-pointing tusks. Short-jawed mastodons, like modern elephants, had long trunks and tusks. The American mastodon, *Mammut americanus*, lived in the tundra during the Pleistocene epoch.

Long-jawed mastodons formed the third group. One of the strangest types was the shovel-tusker, *Platybelodon*. It was from this group that the true elephants and mammoths evolved. The first known elephant is *Primelephas*, which lived in Africa during the Pliocene epoch. Mammoths also evolved in Africa, but the woolly mammoths lived in the tundra.

▼ WHEN DID THE MODERN HORSE APPEAR?

The modern horse evolved about two million years ago, during the Pliocene epoch. Its ancestry can be traced back to a dog-sized animal called *Hyracotherium*.

Hyracotherium stood about 50 centimetres high at the shoulder. It had four toes on each front foot and it fed on soft woodland plants.

In North America the descendants of *Hyracotherium* were *Orohippus* and *Epihippus*.

The Oligocene horse *Mesohippus* had three-toed front feet and stood about 60 centimetres tall. All these horses were still woodland browsers, but the grasslands were now beginning to spread. *Parahippus* and *Merychippus* both had teeth that could grind up the tough grasses. Their descendants were all grazing horses. Some remained with three toes on each foot, but others lost the two outer toes. *Pliohippus* was the first of the one-toed horses and was the ancester of *Equus*, the modern horse.

Platybelodon

American mastodon

Woolly mammoth

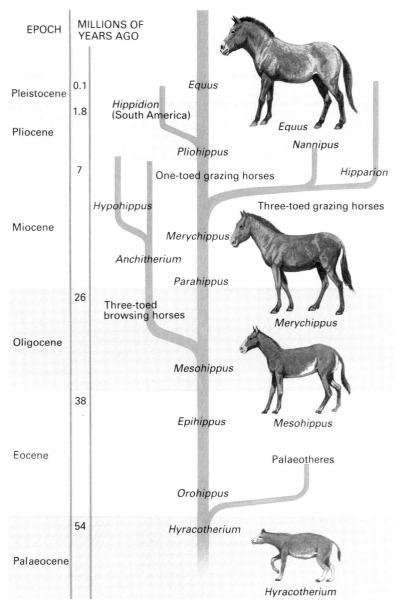

EPOCH	MILLIONS OF YEARS AGO	
Pleistocene	0.1	Equus
	1.8	Hippidion (South America)
Pliocene		Equus
		Pliohippus / Nannipus
	7	One-toed grazing horses / Hipparion
		Hypohippus / Three-toed grazing horses
Miocene		Merychippus
		Anchitherium
		Parahippus
	26	Three-toed browsing horses / Merychippus
Oligocene		Mesohippus
	38	Epihippus / Mesohippus
Eocene		Palaeotheres
		Orohippus
	54	Hyracotherium
Palaeocene		
		Hyracotherium

▼ WHAT ARE VIRUSES AND BACTERIA?

Viruses and bacteria are the smallest living things. Viruses have no cell walls and can only work properly inside the cells of other living organisms. Bacteria are larger than viruses and can exist by themselves.

A virus is made up of a protein coat wrapped around a small amount of DNA or RNA. It can reproduce itself but only when it is inside a

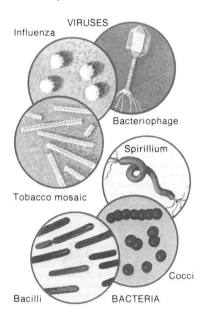

VIRUSES
Influenza
Bacteriophage
Tobacco mosaic
Spirillium
Cocci
Bacilli
BACTERIA

living cell. Viruses are therefore on the borderline between living and non-living things. When they invade cells they usually cause disease.

Bacteria are tiny, single-celled organisms. Some are round, others are rod-shaped and some even look like cork-screws.

Some bacteria cause disease but many others are useful. A large number feed by breaking down dead plant and animal matter. They release chemicals into the soil that can be used by plants.

▼ WHAT IS A PLANT?

A living thing that makes its own food by photo-synthesis is called a plant. Nearly all plants have cellulose cell walls.

Like all living things, plants feed, grow, breathe (respiration) and get rid of waste materials. They can also make certain movements and are sensitive to certain stimuli.

But what sets plants apart from animals is the fact that they make their own food by photosynthesis. For this they need the green pigment chlorophyll, which is why most plants are green.

There are, of course, some exceptions to this rule. Parasitic plants, such as dodder and broomrape, do not contain chlorophyll, but they have cellulose cell walls like normal plants.

Fungi, on the other hand, are not like other plants. In fact, they are sometimes placed in a separate group called the Protista, together with the bacteria and all single-celled living things.

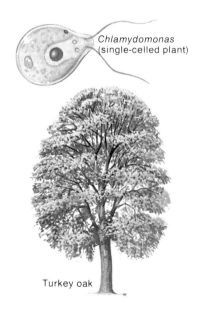

Chlamydomonas (single-celled plant)

Turkey oak

▼ WHAT IS AN ANIMAL?

An animal is a living thing that feeds by taking in organic matter. Its cell walls are usually non-rigid. Most animals can move about and have nervous systems.

An animal cannot make its own food. It has to feed on material obtained from plants or other animals.

In other ways animals are similar to plants. They grow, reproduce, breathe and get rid of waste matter. However, to

Sea anemone

Mink

obtain food, animals have to be able to reach it or draw it towards them in some way. So animals must be able to move, and animals that perform complicated movements have nervous systems to control their bodies.

It is sometimes difficult to tell the difference between an animal and a plant. For example, the single-celled organism *Euglena* has chloroplasts and is often classed as a plant. However, it can also feed in an animal-like way. So some biologists classify *Euglena* as an animal.

▼ WHAT IS EVOLUTION?

Evolution is the process of slow change that takes place in populations of animals and plants.

Very few species of animals and plants remain the same over a long period of time. Each generation may have features that are different from those of the generation before. These changes may lead to new species being formed.

Evolution has been responsible for the appearance of all modern living things. From the study of fossils, and other work, it is possible to see how some groups have evolved.

The first vertebrates (animals with backbones) to appear, about 500 million years ago, were fishes. Many groups of fishes appeared in the seas over the next 100 million years. Gradually some fishes left the water and developed as amphibians. In turn, some of these land animals evolved into reptiles, the group from which birds and mammals arose.

▼ WHAT IS NATURAL SELECTION?

Evolution has taken place over many years because of natural selection. Animals and plants that are suited to their surroundings survive. Those that cannot compete die out.

Sometimes an animal or plant accidentally develops a new characteristic. This may make it more (or less) able to survive than one that has not developed such a feature.

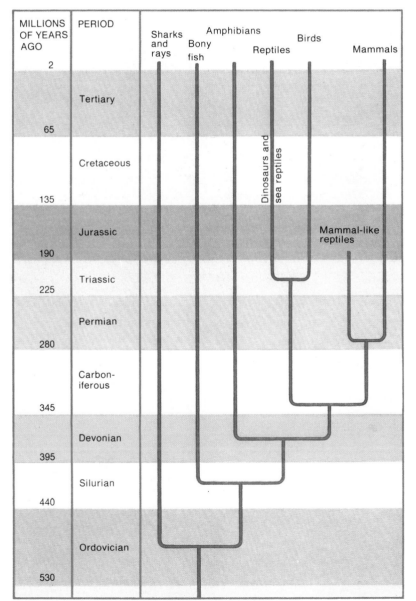

MILLIONS OF YEARS AGO	PERIOD						
2		Sharks and rays	Bony fish	Amphibians / Reptiles	Birds	Mammals	
	Tertiary						
65							
	Cretaceous			Dinosaurs and sea reptiles			
135							
	Jurassic					Mammal-like reptiles	
190							
	Triassic						
225							
	Permian						
280							
	Carbon-iferous						
345							
	Devonian						
395							
	Silurian						
440							
	Ordovician						
530							

PEPPERED MOTHS

Light, speckled form

Dark form

Peppered moths show natural selection in action today. There are two varieties of this moth, one light-coloured type and a dark type.

Before the Industrial Revolution in Great Britain, the dark moths were rare. They were easily spotted by birds as they rested on the lichen-covered bark of trees. But pollution began to kill the lichen and blacken the trees. So the dark moths became the ones that were well camouflaged and the light-coloured moths soon began to decrease in numbers.

95

Single-celled plants belong to the large group known as the algae. There are many different forms. Some can move about using whip-like flagella.

The algae are the world's simplest plants. They have no roots, stems or leaves and a large number consist of just one cell. Such plants often float freely in lakes and oceans. They form, together with tiny animals, a drifting mass called plankton.

Like other plants, algae contain chlorophyll. Many algae are therefore green, but in some the colour is hidden by other pigments.

Single-celled green algae include forms such as *Pleurococcus*, which can be found on the moist bark of trees, and pond algae such as *Euglena* and *Chlamydomonas*. Other single-celled algae include the yellow-green algae, golden algae and dinoflagellates.

Diatoms, such as *Coscinodiscus*, form the largest group. They have cell walls made of silica.

Seaweeds also belong to the plant group called the algae. They are many-celled plants.

The smallest many-celled algae include plants like the *Volvox*, which is a hollow ball of cells, and the pondweed *Spirogyra*. This consists of long strings, or filaments, of cells. The many-celled algae found in the sea are known as seaweeds.

Among the simplest green seaweeds is sea lettuce *(Ulva)*, which consists of a flat, two-layered 'leaf'. Its relative, *Enteromorpha*, has tube-like fronds. *Cladophora* is made up of long branched filaments or strands.

Brown seaweeds include the familiar wracks *(Fucus)* and kelps, or oarweeds *(Laminaria)*. Most of these are attached to rocks, but some float freely in the sea. The Sargasso Sea is named after its vast floating rafts of *Sargassum* seaweed.

Red seaweeds are usually smaller and many have complicated structures. Most live in deep water.

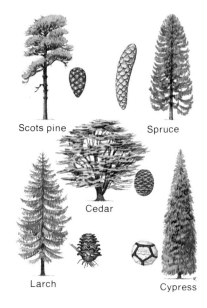

Scots pine   Spruce

Cedar

Larch   Cypress

Conifers are seed-bearing plants. But unlike flowering plants, they produce seeds in cones.

Conifers are easy to recognize. They all have leathery, needle-like or scale-like leaves and they produce cones.

Conifers include the pines, spruces, firs, larches, hemlocks, cedars, cypresses and junipers.

All these species, except the larches and the swamp cypress, are evergreen. This means that they bear leaves at all times of the year. They are able to do this because their tough leaves conserve water and do not need to be shed when water is scarce. They can also withstand wind and frost.

In fact, evergreen conifers do shed their leaves. But leaves are being grown and shed all the time. Each leaf lives for about three years.

Because conifers can stand up to harsh conditions, they can grow in places where broadleaved trees cannot. Most grow in a broad band just below the Arctic Circle.

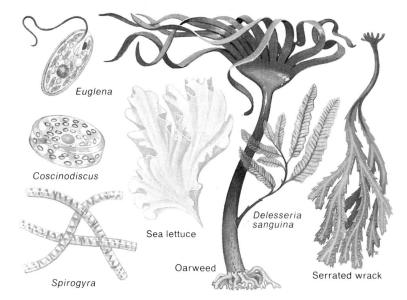

Euglena

Coscinodiscus

Sea lettuce

Delesseria sanguina

Oarweed

Serrated wrack

Spirogyra

Mosses are low-growing plants that have no true roots. Together with the liverworts, they form the plant group known as Bryophytes.

Mosses form mats or small cushions in several different places. They grow on the ground in woodlands, on the bark of trees, on moist banks, in bogs and on rocks. In fact, they grow in places where flowering plants find it difficult to grow.

A moss plant has a thin stem with a number of simple leaves attached. The plant has no roots but holds onto the ground using root-like threads called rhizoids. Most moss plants can conduct water up their stems. They reproduce by means of spores which develop in capsules.

The largest European moss is the hair moss *(Polytrichum commune)*. In damp places its stems can reach a height of 20 centimetres. The water moss *(Fontinalis antipyretica)* lives in streams and ponds. Its long straggling stems may be over 100 centimetres long.

Liverworts belong to the same plant group as mosses. Some have simple, flat plant bodies, others are more like mosses.

Liverworts dry out more easily than mosses and so are only found in damp, shady places. Those with flat plant bodies are known as thalloid liverworts. They have no stems or true leaves and they sprawl across the wet ground, clinging on with tiny rhizoids. Thalloid liverworts include such types as *Pellia*.

Over 90 per cent of liverworts are of the moss-like type, known as leafy liverworts. They have stems and thin, filmy leaves. *Lophocolea* grows on bark in dark woods.

Like mosses, liverworts reproduce by means of spores that develop inside capsules. But the liverwort capsules develop more slowly.

Most liverworts can also reproduce in another way. They grow small round or disc-shaped structures on their leaves. Each one can become a new plant.

Hart's tongue fern   Maidenhair fern

Bracken   Buckler fern

Ferns are another group of plants that make spores. But, unlike mosses and liverworts, they can live in fairly dry places.

Ferns range from smallish plants that grow in the world's temperate regions to tall, tropical tree ferns.

They are much larger than mosses for two reasons. First, their stems contain good water-conducting cells for carrying water up to their leaves. Second, adult ferns produce only spores. Their sex cells, which need moisture, develop on tiny heart-shaped structures called prothalli. These develop from spores lying on the ground.

An adult fern is anchored to the ground by an underground stem, or rhizome. Above the ground there are one or more leaves, or fronds.

Sometimes the fronds have simple shapes, like the hart's tongue fern, which has strap-like leaves. But more often fronds are divided into leaflets known as pinnae. These may be divided into smaller leaflets called pinnules.

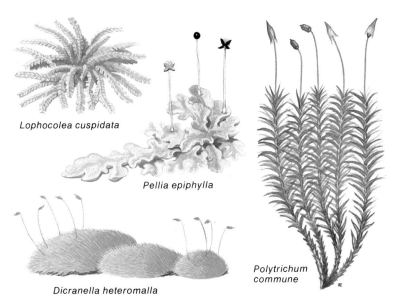

Lophocolea cuspidata

Pellia epiphylla

Dicranella heteromalla

Polytrichum commune

▶ WHAT ARE FLOWERING PLANTS?

These are plants that produce their reproductive organs in flowers. This huge group of plants includes a wide range of herbaceous (green-stemmed) plants, shrubs and trees.

Conifers and their relatives belong to the plant group known as gymnosperms. The word *gymnosperm* means 'naked seed' and these plants produce seeds that are exposed to the air.

Flowering plants, or angiosperms ('enclosed seed'), on the other hand, produce seeds that are surrounded by an ovary wall, which often develops into a fruit.

There are about 360,000 known species in the plant kingdom. Over 220,000 of these are flowering plants. They are very successful because of two important factors. First, their methods of seed formation and seed dispersal are very efficient. Second, they are a very adaptable group of plants. There are flowering plants in most of the world's environments, including deserts and high mountains.

There are two main groups of flowering plants. Monocotyledons are those with long, thin leaves with parallel veins. Their flowers almost always have three or six petals. This group includes grasses, bulb plants such as bluebells, and orchids. Only a few tropical monocotyledons, such as palm trees, are large.

Dicotyledons form a much bigger group. Their leaves are usually broad with a network of veins. Their flowers usually have four, five or many petals.

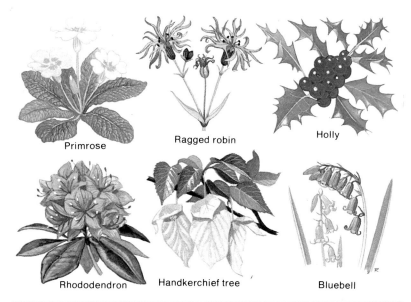

Primrose   Ragged robin   Holly

Rhododendron   Handkerchief tree   Bluebell

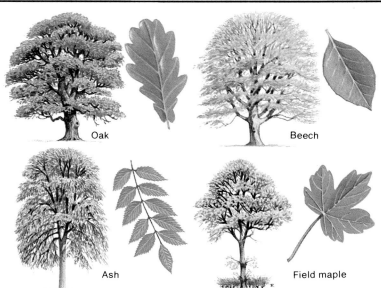

Oak   Beech

Ash   Field maple

▲ WHAT ARE DECIDUOUS TREES?

Deciduous trees lose their leaves in autumn. They are mostly the broadleaved trees of the northern hemisphere.

Winter in the northern hemisphere is too harsh for most broadleaved trees. So they let their leaves fall in autumn and survive the winter in a state of dormancy (sleep). If they did not do this, their leaves would be damaged by wind and frost. And during severe frost they would lose more water than they could take up from the ground.

Deciduous, broadleaved woodlands are found in Europe, but North America and Eastern Asia have the greatest variety of trees. In North America there are about 100 different species, including maples, magnolias, hickories and tulip trees.

European deciduous woodlands have mostly oaks, ash, beech, birch or alder. Other European trees include hornbeam, whitebeam, field maple and mountain ash, or rowan.

▼ WHICH ARE THE
LARGEST FLOWERING
PLANTS?

The world's largest plant is a Chinese wisteria.

The Chinese wisteria at Sierra Madre in California has branches over 150 metres long. It produces about one and a half million flowers each year.

Another large plant is the giant Bolivian bromeliad *Puya raymondii*. Its spikes of 8000 flowers reach ten metres high.

▲ WHICH TREES GROW THE
TALLEST?

▲ WHICH TREES LIVE THE
LONGEST?

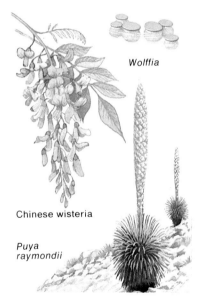

Wolffia

Chinese wisteria

Puya
raymondii

▲ WHICH ARE THE
SMALLEST FLOWERING
PLANTS?

The smallest flowering plant is the duckweed *Wolffia punctata*.

Duckweeds form large floating masses on ponds. But each plant is tiny, consisting of one or more disc-like 'leaves' with a few hanging roots.

The smallest duckweeds belong to the genus *Wolffia*. *Wolffia* plants can measure just half a millimetre across.

The world's tallest trees are found in the USA. They are the gigantic coast redwoods of California. But other trees also reach great heights.

The tallest living coast red-wood, known as 'Tallest Tree', is over 111 metres high. However, its top is dying and it probably once reached over 112 metres.

Other trees living in the same place have healthy tops and stand over 110 metres high. They may one day over-take 'Tallest Tree'.

Even taller trees may have existed in the past. A eucalyptus tree in Australia is believed to have reached 114 metres in 1880, and a Douglas fir felled in British Columbia in 1895 may have been over 127 metres high.

The world's largest trees are also found in California. They are the massive giant sequoias. The largest of these stands 85 metres high and measures over 24 metres round the trunk near its base.

The world's oldest trees are the bristlecone pines. Some are believed to be over 4500 years old.

Until the early 1900s, scientists thought that the giant sequoias were the oldest living trees. Some of them have existed for 3400 years. But the bristlecone pines of the White Mountains in California are even older.

The oldest specimen of bristlecone pine that has been recorded was 4900 years old. It was cut down in 1969. The oldest living tree, called 'Methuselah', is believed to be 4600 years old.

Bristlecone pines live in a harsh environment, 3000 metres above sea level, on bare mountain slopes. There they grow into stunted, twisted forms.

Scientists have estimated that bristlecone pines could reach an age of 5500 years. But they also suggest that giant sequoias could live for 6000 years.

▼ WHAT ARE FUNGI?

Fungi are thread-like organisms that reproduce by means of spores. Some fungi produce their spores in large fruiting bodies which we know as toad-stools, brackets, cups, puffballs and jellies.

Fungi are classed as plants, but their cell walls do not contain cellulose. Also, they do not contain the green pigment chlorophyll and cannot make their own food. They have to take their food from what is around them. Some fungi feed on dead and decaying plant or animal material.

Other fungi are parasites and take their food from living plants or animals.

The word 'fungus' usually makes us think of a toadstool. But the toadstool is only the fruiting body. The main part of the fungus is a mass of fungal threads called the mycelium. This is always hidden in the soil or wood on which the toadstool is growing.

Fungi that produce large fruiting bodies are the most advanced types. Apart from the familiar mushrooms and toadstools there are cup fungi, puffballs, jelly fungi and bracket fungi. Dry rot in houses is caused by a fungus with a large fruiting body.

But not all fungi produce large fruiting bodies. Simple fungi include moulds, mildews and parasites such as potato blight.

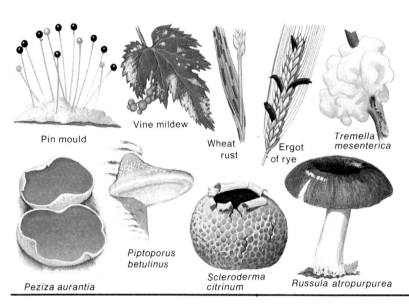

Pin mould

Vine mildew

Wheat rust

Ergot of rye

Tremella mesenterica

Piptoporus betulinus

Peziza aurantia

Scleroderma citrinum

Russula atropurpurea

Parasol mushroom

Field mushroom

Shaggy ink cap

Fairy ring champignon

Blusher

Cep

Giant puffball

Chanterelle

Oyster mushroom

Truffle

Morel

▲ WHICH FUNGI ARE GOOD TO EAT?

Field mushrooms are delicious and popular. But these are not the only kinds of fungi that are good to eat.

When field mushrooms appear in September and October, they are quite easy to recognize. But this is also true of several other kinds of edible mushrooms and toad-stools.

In fields you may find giant puffballs which are delicious when cut into 'steaks' and fried. Fairy ring champignons have a nutty taste and shaggy ink caps, which cannot be mistaken for anything else, are also good.

In woods you may be lucky enough to come across other delicious fungi. Parasol mushrooms and bright yellow chanterelles are really worth searching for. Morels are a well-known delicacy in some places. Ceps are also popular, and blushers (which *must* be cooked) are even better. Oyster mushrooms can be found growing on trees.

Truffles are a great delicacy. They are not easy to find, as they grow underground in certain beech-woods.

Never eat any toadstool that you cannot identify for certain.

Poisonous toadstools must never be eaten. Many can cause extreme illness and some can cause death.

Of all the toadstools, only a few are actually good to eat. Most are tasteless or even unpleasant. And some are poisonous and must be avoided at all costs.

The death cap and destroying angel are deadly poisonous. Eating either of these usually results in death.

Death cap

Panther cap

Destroying angel

Fly agaric

Devil's boletus

Yellow stainer

Inocybe patouillardi

Sickener
Russula emetica

The panther cap is only slightly less poisonous. Devil's boletus and the striking red and white fly agaric are also poisonous, but not usually fatal. Most species of *Inocybe* are poisonous and quite difficult to identify.

There are less harmful, but still poisonous toadstools. *Russula emetica* may cause sickness. The yellow stainer can be mistaken for a field mushroom, but its flesh stains yellow when bruised. People who eat this toadstool may develop alarming symptoms, but they always recover.

As well as edible fungi, there are others that are useful. *Penicillium* and other moulds produce antibiotic drugs, and yeasts are essential in making bread and alcoholic drinks.

In 1929 Alexander Fleming noticed that *Penicillium* mould destroyed bacteria. Some years later, scientists took the antibacterial agent from *Penicillium* and called it penicillin. Since then, antibiotic drugs have been obtained from other moulds. *Penicillium* is also used in the making of certain cheeses.

Another important group of fungi are the yeasts, which can turn sugar into ethyl alcohol and carbon dioxide. They are used in the making of alcoholic drinks.

In bread-making, yeast produces carbon dioxide bubbles, which cause the dough to rise. When the bread is cooked, the yeast dies and the alcohol evaporates.

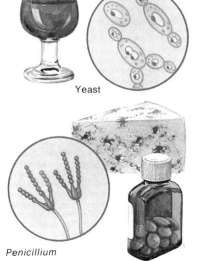

Yeast

Penicillium

A lichen is not a single plant. It consists of a fungus and an alga tightly bound together. Both plants benefit from this arrangement.

The outer layers of a lichen are made up of densely-packed fungal threads. These protect the inner layers. Nearer the centre the fungal threads are looser and surround the cells of an alga.

The alga obtains protection

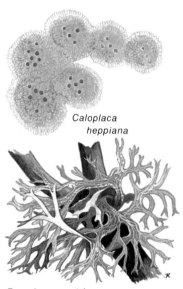

Caloplaca heppiana

Evernia prunastri

from wind, frost and sunlight. In return it supplies the fungus with food, which the alga makes by photosynthesis.

Some lichens encrust rocks, others have a leafy or shrubby appearance and can be found on trees. Lichens can reproduce themselves by producing a powdery mass of structures that contain pieces of both partners.

The fungus can also produce spores. When these are scattered, they form new lichens only if they come into contact with the right alga.

101

Single-celled animals make up the group known as protozoans. They include amoebas, *Paramecium* and the malaria parasite.

The most familiar single-celled animals are the amoebas. These are tiny, jelly-like animals that constantly change their shape. Relatives of the amoebas include the foraminiferans, which have shells, and radiolarians, which have delicate skeletons made of silica.

Some protozoans move about by using whip-like appendages called flagella. *Trypanosoma* is a flagellate that causes sleeping sickness in humans.

Other protozoans have tiny hairs known as cilia. *Paramecium* uses its cilia for swimming, while *Stentor* uses its cilia to create water currents which bring it food.

The last group of protozoans are all parasites. They include the malaria parasite *Plasmodium*.

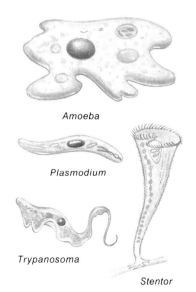

Amoeba

Plasmodium

Trypanosoma

Stentor

Jellyfish belong to the animal group known as coelenterates. This group also includes sea anemones and corals.

A typical jellyfish is a large, umbrella-like 'bag' with tentacles hanging below it. The bag keeps the animal floating in the water while the tentacles catch food.

This is the adult stage of the jellyfish, known as the medusa stage. The eggs of most jellyfish do not develop

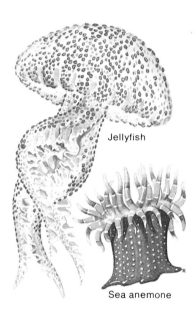

Jellyfish

Sea anemone

directly into medusae. Instead they develop first into polyps, which attach themselves to rocks or other surfaces. There they feed and grow before developing into medusae.

In other coelenterates the polyp is the adult stage and in sea anemones it is the only stage. They remain attached to rocks and their stinging tentacles seize prey.

The Portuguese man-o'-war may look like a jellyfish, but it is actually a floating colony of polyps suspended under a gas-filled bag.

Corals are closely related to sea anemones. But sea anemones are usually large and unprotected, while corals are small and protect themselves with a chalky skeleton.

The lumps of coral that can be bought in shops are only the skeletons of once-living animals. Living coral is really a skeleton covered with a fleshy mass of polyps, which are often brightly coloured.

A coral colony begins to form when a young polyp reproduces itself by budding. New polyps formed in this way also reproduce themselves, and so the colony grows.

The polyps remain connected to each other and they share the food caught by the colony. Each one produces its own part of the chalky skeleton.

Corals can be found in most seas, but the reef-forming types prefer warm, shallow water. A coral reef begins as a fringing reef along the shore of a continent or island.

HELIOPORA BLUE CORAL

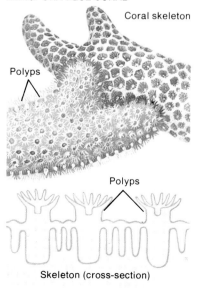

Coral skeleton

Polyps

Polyps

Skeleton (cross-section)

Flatworms are simple-bodied, flat, worm-like animals. Most are between one and ten millimetres long, but some tropical land species are much larger.

Flatworms are found in most temperate and tropical regions of the world. Some live underneath stones and leaves in freshwater streams and ponds, but most live in the sea. Some tropical kinds are brightly coloured. A few flatworms live on land and some tropical land species measure over 30 centimetres.

Flatworms are famous for being able to regenerate, or remake, parts of their bodies. In fact, if a flatworm is cut up into several pieces, each piece will grow into a new flatworm. Some flatworms even reproduce naturally by tearing themselves in half!

Flatworms are mostly free-living animals. However, some are parasites and their close relatives, which include the flukes and tapeworms, are all parasites.

Freshwater flatworm

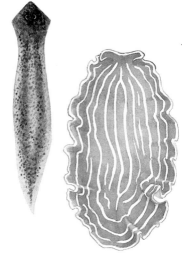

Tropical sea flatworm

Molluscs are basically animals with shells. But some, such as squids, have internal shells. Others, such as slugs and octopuses, have no shells at all.

Slugs and snails belong to the mollusc group known as gastropods. This is the largest mollusc group and also includes such animals as limpets, top shells, cowries, cone shells, brightly coloured sea slugs and sea butterflies.

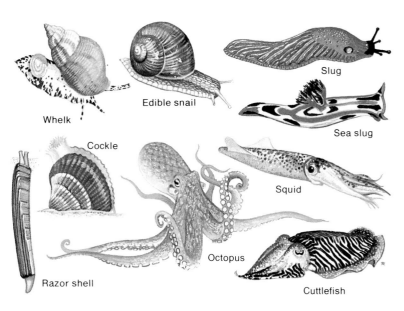

Whelk

Edible snail

Slug

Sea slug

Cockle

Razor shell

Octopus

Squid

Cuttlefish

The world's largest known squid is the Atlantic giant squid.

In 1878 an Atlantic giant squid was washed up on the shores of Newfoundland in Canada. It weighed about two tonnes and its body measured 6.1 metres. Its tentacles measured another 10.65 metres, making a total length of 16.76 metres.

Giant squid are the world's largest invertebrates (animals

The bivalves are another large group. Usually, all members of this group have a two-part shell, hinged in the middle. But different forms are adapted to different ways of life. Cockles are shallow sand burrowers, whereas sand gapers burrow deeper. Razor shells can burrow very rapidly. Mussels and oysters are attached to rocks. Scallops are swimming bivalves.

The largest molluscs are the cephalopods, such as squids, cuttlefish and octopuses.

without backbones). They feed on fish, crustaceans and smaller squid.

Giant squid probably spend most of their lives in deep water. But sometimes they may venture near the surface.

Brief sightings of these huge sea animals may have started off some of the legends about sea serpents and other monsters. According to Norse (Norwegian) legend, a *kraken* was supposed to be about two kilometres long! It was said to snatch crewmen from ships with its long tentacles.

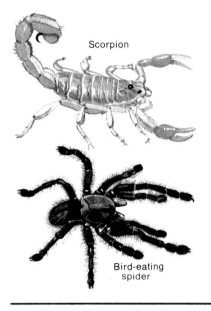

Scorpion

Bird-eating spider

◄ WHAT ARE SPIDERS AND SCORPIONS?

Spiders and scorpions belong to the group known as arachnids. They have hard outer skeletons like insects, but they have eight legs instead of six.

The arachnids are a group that includes scorpions as well as ticks, mites and harvestmen (daddy-long-legs). But spiders are the most familiar of the arachnids.

The body of a spider is divided into two separate parts and its head bears a pair of poison fangs. Many spiders build webs for catching prey but others catch prey by simply chasing it. Trapdoor spiders lie in wait in specially constructed burrows.

A scorpion carries its poison in a sting at the end of its long curving tail. Instead of poison fangs the head bears a pair of large pincers for seizing prey.

Most scorpions use their sting to kill their prey before chewing it up with their pincers. Sometimes scorpions use their sting for defence.

▶ WHICH ANIMALS ARE CRUSTACEANS?

The group known as crustaceans includes many kinds of many-legged, hard-bodied animals. The best-known of these are the lobsters, crabs, shrimps and wood-lice. Barnacles are also crustaceans.

Crustaceans are different from other arthropods (animals with hard bodies and jointed legs). They have two antennae, or feelers. In addition, they have more legs than other arthropods and their legs are often two-branched. Many crustaceans have a carapace, or shell.

Most crustaceans are tiny, sea-dwelling animals, such as brine shrimps, ostracods and barnacles. However, water fleas live in fresh water and woodlice are land dwellers.

The largest crustaceans are known as decapods (ten legs). Shrimps and prawns are swimming crustaceans. Crabs and lobsters use their legs for walking and have large pincers.

Lobster

Crab

Prawn

Woodlouse

Barnacle

Water flea *Daphnia*

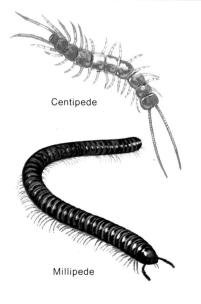

Centipede

Millipede

◄ WHAT IS THE DIFFERENCE BETWEEN CENTIPEDES AND MILLIPEDES?

Centipedes and millipedes are both arthropods. But while centipedes are flesh-eaters, millipedes live on plant material.

The name *centipede* means '100 legs' and the name *millipede* means '1000 legs'. But this is not always true. Some centipedes have as few as 30 legs and others have up to 340 legs. Millipedes usually do have more legs than centipedes, but no millipede has more than 400 legs and some have only 26 legs.

Centipedes are all fast-moving carnivores that feed on insects and other small animals. They have flattened, flexible bodies with one pair of legs on each segment.

Millipedes, on the other hand, are slow, plant-eating animals. Their bodies are usually round and the body segments are fused into double segments, each of which bears two pairs of legs.

▼ WHAT IS AN INSECT?

Insects are hard-bodied animals with six legs. Their bodies are divided into three parts and many insects have wings.

More than 85 per cent of the world's known animals are insects. About one million species have already been discovered and there may be another four million species we do not know about.

Like other arthropods, insects have hard outer skeletons and jointed legs. However, they are different from other arthropods in some ways. Their bodies are divided into three parts: head, thorax and abdomen. In addition, there are three pairs of legs on the thorax and often one or two pairs of wings.

Insects can be found in almost every habitat except the sea. Some primitive, wingless insects include springtails and bristletails.

Winged insects include dragonflies, grasshoppers, mantids, termites, bugs, moths, butterflies, true flies, ants, beetles and wasps.

▼ WHICH ARE THE LARGEST LIVING INSECTS?

The world's largest insects include the fist-sized goliath beetle and the Queen Alexandra bird-wing butterfly. This has a wingspan that would reach from the top to the bottom of this page.

The most massive living insects are the goliath beetles of Africa. They weigh up to 100 grams and can measure up to ten centimetres long. Some of the scarabs, dung beetles and the rhinoceros beetles are only slightly smaller.

The titan beetle of Brazil is one of the longhorn beetles. It grows to 15 centimetres in length and many stick insects are even longer. The world's longest insect is an Indonesian species that reaches over 30 centimetres in length.

Butterflies and moths have the largest wings and the world's largest butterfly is the Queen Alexandra birdwing butterfly of New Guinea. Females have wingspans of over 28 centimetres.

▼ WHICH WERE THE LARGEST INSECTS OF ALL?

The largest known insect lived 280 million years ago in the steamy swamp forests of the Carboni-ferous period. It is known as *Meganeura monyi*.

Insects cannot grow beyond a certain size. A human-sized insect, for example, would be impossible. It would not be able to take in enough oxygen and, in any case, its body would probably be crushed by air pressure.

Even so, some of the earliest insects were much larger than those of today. The largest were the giant dragonflies *(Meganeura)*, which had wingspans of up to 70 centimetres.

These insects could reach such a size because there were no predators in the air and they did not have to compete with other animals for food.

Today such insects would make easy prey for birds. And they would find it difficult to compete for food with all the insects, birds and mammals that feed in the trees.

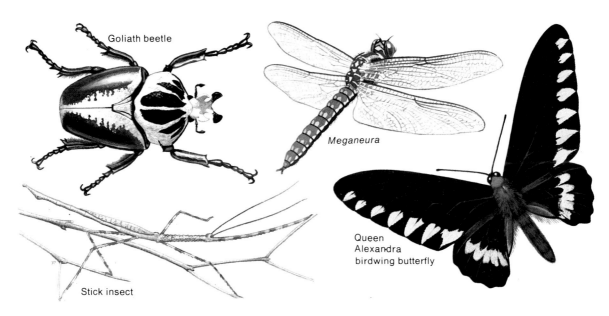

Goliath beetle

Meganeura

Queen Alexandra birdwing butterfly

Stick insect

Most insects live alone. But a few species live in groups, or colonies. Some colonies are small but others may contain millions of individuals.

Social insects include some bees, such as honey bees, and some wasps, such as the common wasp. All ants and termites are social insects.

The important fact about social insects is that all the members work for the good of the whole colony. In most colonies there are three or more different types, or castes, of individuals. Each one has a particular task to do.

There are many kinds of colonies. Wasps build complicated nests with many layers in underground chambers or in hollow trees. They use paper, which they make by mixing chewed wood with saliva.

Honey bees build nests of vertical wax sheets, or combs. Termites often build huge, mound-like nests. Many ants dig underground nests.

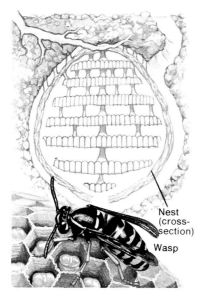

Nest (cross-section)

Wasp

In the middle of summer a beehive contains one queen, between 50,000 and 60,000 workers and a few hundred males, or drones.

Queens, workers and drones are the three castes of honey bee. A colony contains only one queen. She lays eggs and her presence controls what the other members of the colony do. Worker bees are all infertile females. Their task is to look after the colony. Drones are fertile males. They are produced only in mid- to late summer. They do no work and their only function is to mate with a queen.

After hatching from her pupa, a worker spends the first two weeks of her life tending and feeding the grubs in their cells. During the third week she helps to build new cells and repair damaged parts of the nest. She also converts nectar into honey. The next three weeks are spent collecting nectar and pollen, after which she dies.

Stories about army ants are often exaggerated. However, any animal that cannot get out of the way of a marching column of army ants will be eaten down to its skeleton in a very short time.

During the day army ants march in long columns, foraging for food as they go.

The main part of the column consists of between 80,000 and one million small workers, who carry the queen, grubs and pupae. Soldier ants are larger workers with huge heads and jaws. They act as scouts and guards for the column.

At night, the column rests and the workers link their legs to form a temporary nest for the queen and grubs.

Army ants feed mostly on other insects. But any other animal, dead or alive, that they come across is also rapidly devoured. A snake that is too full of food to move quickly will be eaten and a tethered horse stands no chance.

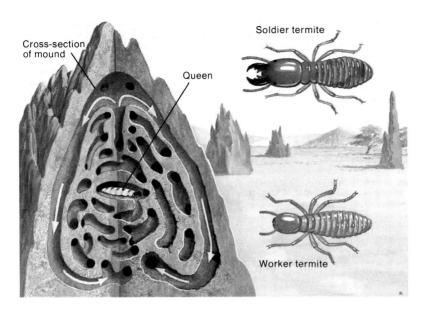

Cross-section of mound

Queen

Soldier termite

Worker termite

▲ WHAT HAPPENS INSIDE A TERMITE MOUND?

▲ WHAT ARE SOLDIERS AND WORKERS?

▼ WHAT ARE CATER-PILLARS AND NYMPHS?

Caterpillars and nymphs are both young forms of insects.

Before becoming adult, a young insect has to go through a series of growth stages. Between each stage the insect moults, or sheds its skin. At the last stage it goes through a change, or metamorphosis, to become an adult.

The young of some insects have growth stages that are similar to the adults. These forms are called nymphs. The nymphs of winged insects are like the adults. But they have wing buds instead of fully-formed wings.

Caterpillars and grubs, on the other hand, are not at all like the adult forms. Their bodies and legs are usually soft and no wings are visible. They also live and feed in a totally different way. The differences are so great that they have to have a special growth stage called the pupa, or chrysalis stage, before they can become adults.

Many termites build their nests inside huge mounds. Inside a mound is a network of tunnels and chambers where the workers look after the young.

A termite mound is begun by a new queen and her king. Later on the workers take over the task of nest-building.

The mound is built of earth and plant material cemented together with saliva and dung. The outer walls are rock hard. But the inside of the mound is like a huge sponge, with thousands of small chambers connected by tiny openings.

Ventilation shafts keep air circulating through the nest. But the atmosphere inside is warm and moist and the carbon dioxide content of the air is unusually high.

The shapes of termite mounds vary. Some are huge towers over three metres high. When land is being cleared for farming, some termite mounds are even too strong for bulldozers, and have to be destroyed by explosives.

In any termite nest there are four different castes. The king and queen produce young. Workers tend the nest and soldiers defend it.

Termites look like ants, but they are not related. Ants are close relatives of bees and wasps, whereas termites are more closely related to cockroaches. Ant workers and soldiers are all infertile females, but in a termite colony they are of both sexes.

Worker termites are the smallest but most numerous members of the colony. Their mouthparts are designed for feeding the queen and her young and for building and repairing the nest.

Soldier termites are much larger. They have huge heads and are often armed with a pair of fearsome jaws. They defend the colony from ants, which are the main enemies of termites. The soldiers of some termites have long snouts instead of jaws. These are used to squirt a sticky liquid at ants.

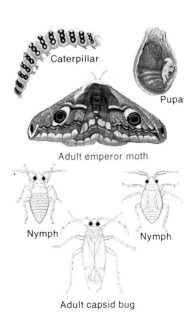

Caterpillar

Pupa

Adult emperor moth

Nymph

Nymph

Adult capsid bug

107

▼ WHAT ARE SEA URCHINS AND STARFISH?

Sea urchins and starfish belong to the group of sea animals known as echinoderms (spiny-skinned animals). This group also includes the sea lilies and sea cucumbers.

The hard shell, or test, of a sea urchin is formed from a number of chalky plates that lie in its skin. Many of these plates bear long spines.

Other echinoderms also have skeletons made of chalky

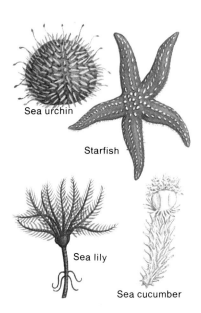

Sea urchin

Starfish

Sea lily

Sea cucumber

plates. But the plates of starfish are more loosely arranged, so they are flexible animals.

Another feature of the echinoderms is that their bodies are always based on a five-sided plan. This is most easily seen in starfish, which have five arms. But if you examine a sea urchin closely, you will see five rows of tube feet down its sides.

These tube feet are fluid-filled tubes that extend out of the body. They may be used for walking, feeding or taking in oxygen.

▼ WHAT ARE SEA SQUIRTS AND LANCELETS?

Lancelets are small fish-like creatures that live in the mud or sand of shallow water. Sea squirts are bag-like animals that live attached to rocks.

The lancelet amphioxus is about five centimetres long. It feeds by filtering particles from the water around it. Amphioxus is not a fish. Its body is different in many ways.

In particular, it does not

Sea squirts

Amphioxus

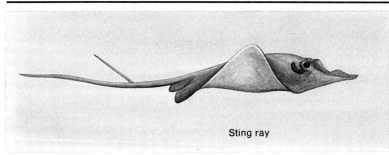

Sting ray

▲ WHAT ARE SKATES AND RAYS?

Skates and rays are fishes with flat bodies. Their skeletons are made of cartilage.

The 'wings' of a ray are formed from the flattened sides of its body and the greatly enlarged pectoral, or shoulder, fins. It swims by passing waves along its wings.

Most skates and rays feed on shrimps, shellfish and crabs, which they crush with their powerful jaws. Many of

have a true backbone. Instead it has a long, rod-like structure, or notochord, down its back. A notochord is also found in the early embryos of all vertebrates (animals with backbones). So lancelets and vertebrates are both classified in the group known as the chordates.

Sea squirts are also chordates. At first glance this seems strange because an adult sea squirt is even less like a vertebrate than a lancelet. However, the young larva of a sea squirt does have a notochord.

the smaller species hide from predators by lying camouflaged on the sea bed. A sting ray defends itself with a poison spine on its tail.

Manta rays, or devil fish, have wingspans of up to seven metres. They are harmless plankton feeders. Electric rays are carnivores. They stun their prey with their electric organs.

The shark-like sawfish uses its saw for digging up shellfish. But it will also flail its saw from side to side in a shoal of fish and then feed on the injured fish.

▼ WHAT IS A SHARK?

Sharks, like skates and rays, have skeletons made of cartilage. Most sharks are predatory and have many sharp teeth.

Sharks are closely related to the skates and rays. They are streamlined fishes designed for fast swimming.

Unlike a bony fish, a shark has no swim bladder to keep it buoyant in the water. Instead, the shape of its head, its wing-like fins and its upturned tail all help to provide lift as the shark swims. Some sharks increase their buoyancy by storing oil in their livers.

A shark's skin is covered in thousands of tiny, pointed scales. These continue into the mouth, where they are larger and form many rows of sharp teeth. These are used for holding and tearing the flesh of prey. The shark swallows pieces of prey whole.

The smallest sharks are the harmless dogfish, which scavenge for food on the sea bed. Other sharks are fierce predators.

▼ HOW DANGEROUS ARE SHARKS?

All large flesh-eating sharks may attack humans. But stories of man-eating sharks are often greatly exaggerated.

Most sharks are not really dangerous and do not always attack. But it is wise to get out of the water when a shark is nearby. Sand sharks and hammerhead sharks have been known to attack bathers. Grey reef sharks sometimes attack divers, and seafarers used to fear mackerel sharks. The great white shark sometimes grows to over ten metres long. It is a terrifying predator.

Other dangerous sharks include the porbeagle, tiger shark and the great blue shark. Makos, the fastest of all sharks, sometimes attack small boats.

Splashing the water to drive sharks away is a mistake. Sharks feed on sick or wounded prey and may mistake a human for a dying fish. Splashing only adds to this impression.

▼ WHICH IS THE LARGEST FISH OF ALL?

The world's largest fish is the whale shark. But far from being a man-eater, this fish is a completely harmless plankton feeder.

Whale sharks are found in tropical waters. Most are about 15 metres long, but a record specimen caught in 1919 was 18.5 metres long.

A whale shark feeds by sieving plankton from the water. Inside its mouth its gill arches bear a number of 'strainers', or gill rakers. These collect up plankton and small fishes from the water that passes into the fish's mouth and out through its gills.

Basking sharks are also large sharks, reaching lengths of up to 12 metres. They are plankton feeders like whale sharks, but they are found in colder waters. Their food consists of small, shrimp-like animals, fish eggs and arrow worms. During winter when food is scarce, they lose their gill rakers and stop feeding.

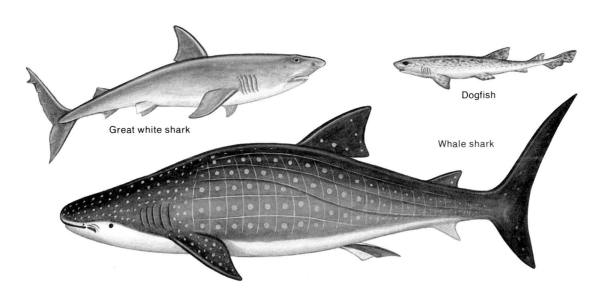

Great white shark

Dogfish

Whale shark

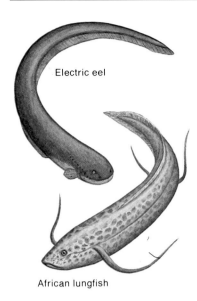

Electric eel

African lungfish

Lungfishes are able to breathe air and survive out of water.

The swim bladders of bony fishes originally evolved as simple lungs. Many early fishes lived in stagnant swamps. There was not much oxygen and so the ability to breathe air was an advantage. Most modern fishes live where there is plenty of oxygen and so do not need to breathe air.

Lungfishes have kept their lungs. Some lungfishes can survive without water in times of drought. Other fishes with lungs include bichirs, gar-pikes and the bowfin.

Some fishes, such as the catfish *Clarias*, have special gills that do not collapse in air and can take in oxygen. Another catfish, called *Hoplosternum*, gulps mouthfuls of air and takes in oxygen through the lining of its gut.

The electric eel can breathe through the lining of its mouth. So can the mud-skipper, which spends much of its time out of water.

Bony fishes have skeletons made mostly of bone rather than cartilage. They are the true masters of the world's seas and rivers.

Bony fishes have become adapted to a wide variety of lifestyles. There are at present about 18,000 species.

The body of a bony fish contains a swim bladder. This is a gas-filled bag that helps it to float at any level in the water. The body of a typical bony fish is flattened from side to side and is used in swimming.

Most bony fishes use their fins for steering and braking, although some species use their fins as oars to 'row' them through the water.

The shapes and colours of bony fishes depend on their ways of life. Predatory fishes, such as swordfish and tuna, are streamlined, fast swimmers. Flatfish are camouflaged on the sea bed, while brightly coloured fishes live around equally brightly coloured coral reefs.

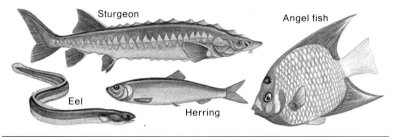

Sturgeon

Angel fish

Eel

Herring

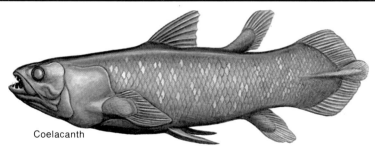

Coelacanth

The coelacanth is a 'living fossil'. It is a type of fish that has remained unchanged for millions of years.

Until 1938, scientists believed that the coelacanth had been extinct for 70 million years. Since then over 80 specimens have been caught near the Comoro Islands off the East Africa coast.

Coelacanths belong to the group of fishes known as lobe-fins, which have fins supported on fleshy lobes. This group also includes the lung-fishes and the extinct rhipidistians, which lived about 370 million years ago and were probably the ancestors of the first amphibians.

The coelacanth is something of a puzzle. Its body has unusual features. For example, it has a notochord instead of a backbone and its heart and stomach are very simple. There seems to be no reason why this fish should have survived for so long with so little change.

▼ WHAT KIND OF ANIMAL IS
A SEAHORSE?

▼ WHICH FISHES LIVE DEEP
IN THE OCEANS?

▼ WHICH FISHES CARRY
THEIR OWN LIGHTS?

These strange sea creatures, that look like the knights in a game of chess, are in fact bony fishes.

Seahorses are well named. The large heads of these fishes look amazingly like horses' heads.

Seahorses vary in size and colour, but they all have the same basic shape. When resting, a seahorse wraps its tail round a piece of seaweed.

It swims in an upright position, using its dorsal fin to drive it along. The fin vibrates very rapidly (up to 35 times a second), but the seahorse actually swims rather slowly.

Seahorses are unusual in another way – the males produce the young. A male seahorse has a pouch on its belly. During courtship, the female places her eggs into this pouch and the male then fertilizes them. When the eggs hatch out, the male, with a series of jerks, shoots the young out one by one.

Many strange fishes inhabit the Earth's deep waters. They are adapted for life in a dark world where food may be scarce.

Most sea animals live in the upper layers of the oceans. Light can easily get through and there is plenty of food.

Below 500 metres, however, in the bathypelagic zone, the water becomes darker and food is scarce. Fishes that live in this zone have become adapted to making the most of the occasional prey they can find. Viper fish, bristlemouths, hatchet fish and angler fish all have large mouths for swallowing prey rapidly.

At the bottom of the sea, in the abyssal zone, food is actually more plentiful. It consists of dead plankton and other animals.

The most common fishes of these totally dark depths are rat tails and deep-sea cods. Among the predators there are deep-sea angler fish. Gulper fish and swallowers can swallow very large prey.

Many deep-sea fishes have light-producing organs. These may help fishes to recognize their own kind and they may act as lures for prey.

Lantern fish have rows of light-producing organs down their sides which can be switched on and off. These organs may be used as a means of communication and to help lantern fish to recognize members of their own species.

At night, lantern fish rise closer to the surface to feed on small animals. Their light-producing organs may act as lures. Deep-sea angler fish have luminous lures.

Other deep-sea fishes that have light-producing organs include viperfish, bristle-mouths and hatchet fish. The organs of a hatchet fish are arranged along its belly. They appear to help to camouflage the fish. The light shining down from its belly matches the light coming from above and the fish does not appear as a dark shadow from below.

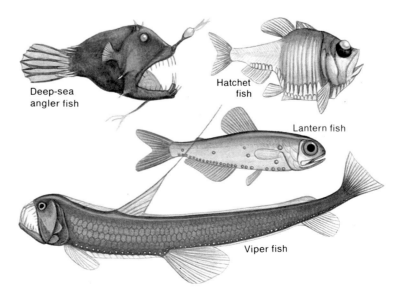

Deep-sea
angler fish

Hatchet
fish

Lantern fish

Viper fish

▼ WHAT ARE NEWTS AND SALAMANDERS?

Newts and salamanders are amphibians. They are four-legged animals with long bodies and moist skin.

A salamander has a long tail and four limbs held out sideways from its long body. Its soft, moist skin tends to lose water easily and so salamanders have to live in water or in damp places.

Salamanders lay soft eggs without shells. Usually they lay these in water to prevent them from drying out. The eggs hatch out into larvae, which use gills to obtain oxygen. After a time, a larva goes through a change, or metamorphosis. It loses its gills and other larval features to become an adult with lungs.

Most salamanders spend at least part of their lives on land. But a few never leave the water. The Mexican axolotl never even reaches true adulthood. It is able to breed while still keeping its gills and other larval features.

▼ WHAT ARE FROGS AND TOADS?

Frogs and toads form the largest group of amphibians. Some live in water, but most are land-dwellers.

Adult frogs and toads have short bodies, well-developed hind legs and no tails. Frogs are usually slender animals. They have large eyes and are extremely agile. Toads are heavier and clumsier. Land-dwelling toads often have dry skins.

Common frogs, common toads and many others are ground-dwellers that live in woods and fields. A few toads, such as the South African clawed toad and the Surinam toad, live in water all the time. Tree frogs have toe pads that enable them to climb.

The young of frogs and toads hatch out from the eggs as tadpoles, which later undergo metamorphosis to become adults. Most frogs and toads lay their eggs in water. But the male midwife toad carries the eggs in strings wrapped round his legs.

▼ WHICH ARE THE LARGEST AMPHIBIANS?

The world's largest amphibian is the Chinese giant salamander. The largest frog is the goliath frog of Africa and the largest toad is the marine toad of South America.

Giant salamanders, or hellbenders, are found in China, Japan and North America. Most are over one metre in length and some Chinese giant salamanders grow to over three and a half metres long. They are carnivorous amphibians that live in fast-flowing mountain streams.

Giant frogs, or goliath frogs, are found in tropical West Africa. Their bodies may be up to 34 centimetres long and can weigh over three kilograms. They live near waterfalls and are excellent swimmers.

The marine toad is a native amphibian of tropical South and Central America. Adults can grow to about 24 centimetres in length and may weigh up to 1300 grams.

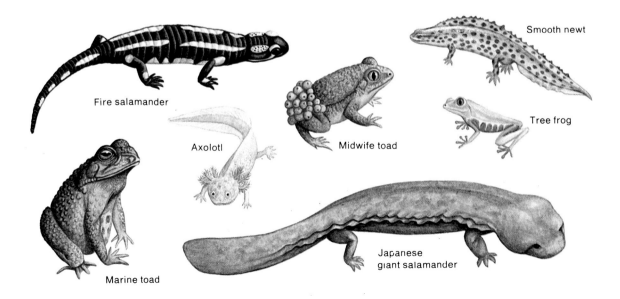

Fire salamander

Smooth newt

Axolotl

Midwife toad

Tree frog

Marine toad

Japanese giant salamander

▼ WHAT ARE TURTLES AND TORTOISES?

Turtles and tortoises are reptiles. Their bodies are encased in hard shells.

The shell of a turtle or tortoise is made up of a number of bony plates that lock together. Turtles and tortoises have no teeth, unlike most reptiles. Instead they have sharp, horny beaks.

There are two main groups of turtles. One group contains those that withdraw their heads by bending their necks

▼ WHAT ARE LIZARDS?

Lizards are long-bodied reptiles. The group includes geckos, iguanas, chameleons and skinks.

Like all reptiles, lizards have scaly skins and lay hard-shelled eggs on land. They are closely related to the snakes. But, unlike a snake, a lizard has movable eyelids and an eardrum just behind its lower jaw. And, of course, most lizards have four legs.

Almost all lizards live entirely on land. Many are

fast runners and some can run on their hind legs. The basilisk can run so fast that it is able to run across water.

Typical lizards include the common lizard and the green lizard. The most numerous lizards are the skinks, which have fat bodies. The smallest lizards are geckos. A few species measure just three and a half centimetres long.

Other groups of lizards include the agamids, the iguanas and the chameleons. Lizards without legs include the slow-worm and the worm-lizards, or amphisbaenids.

Tortoise

Turtle

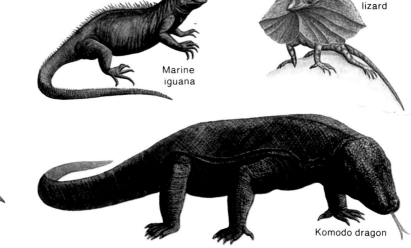

Marine iguana

Frilled lizard

Komodo dragon

sideways. All the remaining turtles and tortoises bend their necks vertically.

Tortoises are land-dwellers. They have rounded shells like domes and well-developed legs. The largest are the Galapagos tortoises, which can grow to one and a half metres long.

Most freshwater turtles spend part of their time out of water. Sea turtles, on the other hand, only leave the sea to lay eggs. They have powerful paddles that are used like 'wings' for flying through the water.

▲ WHAT IS A KOMODO DRAGON?

The Komodo dragon is the largest lizard in the world. In fact it is the largest land lizard that has ever existed.

The Komodo dragon belongs to the family of monitor lizards, several of which are large animals. Nile monitors can measure over two metres long and the Komodo dragon can be over three metres long.

Although the Komodo dragon looks like a relic of the

age of dinosaurs, it is in fact a true lizard. The only larger lizards that have ever existed were the ten-metre-long mosasaurs that lived in the seas 100 million years ago.

Komodo dragons are found only on the island of Komodo and a few other Indonesian islands. They feed on carrion but will also kill large animals.

A Komodo dragon tears off large chunks of meat and swallows them whole. It can devour a whole deer or goat in about ten minutes and then go for several days without food.

Thrush

Grey heron

Capercaillie

Goldeneye

Rhea

King penguin

Kiwi

Brown-throated spinetail swift

Peregrine falcon

◀ WHAT IS A BIRD?

Birds are warm-blooded vertebrates (animals with backbones). They have feathers to keep them warm. They walk on their hind legs and their front limbs are wings.

A bird's body is designed for flying. It is compact and light, but at the same time it is very strong. Lightness is achieved in several ways. The skull, for example, has fewer bones than the skulls of other vertebrates and the jaws are small and do not carry teeth. The larger bones of the body are hollow, reinforced inside with cross-struts. Some bones are fused together for strength.

A bird's wings are mostly made up of feathers. These are supported on the greatly lengthened bones of the 'arm' and 'hand'. The large breast bone, or sternum, has powerful wing muscles attached.

Flying uses up a large amount of oxygen. So a bird has eight air sacs that supply its lungs with a continuous stream of air.

◀ WHICH BIRDS CANNOT FLY?

Some birds, such as the ostrich and emu, have lost the ability to fly. The wings of penguins are used for swimming instead of flying.

Flightless birds are found in a number of places. The ostrich roams the African savannah and the two species of rhea live in the grasslands of South America. Emus and takahes are Australian birds. Cassowaries are also found in northern Australia and New Guinea. Kiwis live in the forests of New Zealand.

Most flightless birds live where there are few natural enemies. But they have no protection against introduced predators and human hunters.

Penguins are found in the colder regions of the southern hemisphere. They are different from other flightless birds because their wings are far from useless. They are very efficient flippers and penguins are superb swimmers.

◀ WHICH BIRDS ARE THE FASTEST FLIERS?

Swifts are among the fastest of all flying birds. Other fast fliers include peregrine falcons, swallows and homing pigeons.

The fastest known bird in level flight is the white-throated spinetail swift. It has been recorded as flying at speeds of over 170 kilometres an hour (km/h). Peregrine falcons can chase their prey in level flight at 60 km/h, but when stooping, or diving, on prey they reach much higher speeds. There are claims of stooping peregrines achieving speeds of between 290 and 350 km/h.

Other high-speed birds include buzzards, which can glide at between 110 and 130 km/h. Swallows are believed to be able to reach 160 km/h when migrating, but they do not normally fly faster than about 50 km/h.

Speeds of up to 80 km/h have been recorded for house martins and homing pigeons.

▶ WHAT IS A BIRD OF PREY?

Birds of prey are those that hunt live animals. They have sharp talons (claws) on their feet and large, hooked beaks.

Almost all birds of prey catch and kill their own food. They use their sharp talons for grasping their prey and they tear the flesh with their strong, hooked beaks.

There are over 250 species of birds of prey. They include all the eagles, hawks, kites, buzzards and falcons. Small birds of prey, such as the kestrel (one of the falcons), prey on small animals, amphibians and insects. Larger types prey on birds and larger mammals. The harpy eagle, the world's largest bird of prey, lives on monkeys, squirrels and birds.

Several birds of prey specialize in particular kinds of animal. The osprey and the African fish eagle feed only on fish. The secretary bird of South America catches only reptiles. The Everglades kite feeds on a freshwater snail.

Golden eagle

Sparrowhawk

▶ WHICH BIRDS HUNT AT NIGHT?

Almost all owls are night-hunters. They have good night vision and exceptionally good hearing.

Like birds of prey, owls have sharp talons and hooked beaks for catching and eating live animals. A few, such as the short-eared owl and the snowy owl, hunt both at night and during the day. But most owls hunt only at night.

Owls have large, forward-pointing eyes that help them to see well in the dark. But the owl uses sound to find its prey. Its ears are surrounded by small flaps of skin which help to collect sounds. The arrangement of the feathers on and around the face is also thought to help in hearing.

Most owls make their nests in trees, either in holes or in the abandoned nests of other birds. However, a few owls, such as the short-eared owl and the snowy owl, nest on the ground. The rare burrowing owl of western America makes its nest in a hole in the ground.

Tawny owl

▶ WHICH BIRD HAS THE LONGEST WINGSPAN?

Albatrosses have long, thin wings for gliding. The bird with the longest wing-span is the wandering albatross.

Wandering albatrosses soar across the southern oceans, feeding on fish and other sea animals near the surface. They cover enormous distances with very little effort.

Their long, thin wings are designed for fast gliding. Fully spread, the wings of a wandering albatross measure over three metres from wingtip to wingtip. The greatest recorded wingspan is 3.63 metres. Such wings provide only a small amount of lift. But this does not matter, as this bird lives in an area where there is almost always enough wind to provide the lift it needs.

Wandering albatrosses nest on the tops of cliffs. From there, they can usually take off from the cliff edge into upcurrents of air.

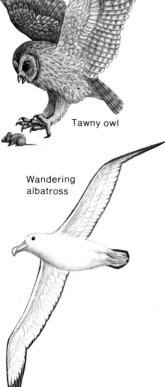

Wandering albatross

117

◀ WHICH MAMMALS LAY EGGS?

The duck-billed platypus and the five species of spiny anteaters, or echidnas, are egg-laying mammals. Together they form the group known as the monotremes.

All mammals are warm-blooded, hairy-skinned animals that feed their new-born young on milk produced by mammary glands. Most mammals nourish their developing young inside the female's body. But mono-tremes lay eggs.

The platypus lives in slow-moving rivers in western Australia. After mating, a female platypus lays two eggs in a burrow and tends them for about ten days until they hatch. Then she suckles her young with milk.

A female echidna lays her single egg into a pouch, which develops on her belly at the start of each breeding season. In about ten days the young echidna hatches and sucks milk from tufts of fur inside the pouch.

▶ WHAT ARE POUCHED MAMMALS?

Mammals that have pouches for rearing their young are known as marsupials. They are all found in South America or Australia, except one.

A young marsupial is nourished in its mother's womb by only a very simple placenta and does not stay in the womb for long. It is born in a very underdeveloped state, and continues to grow in its mother's pouch.

Australian marsupials include kangaroos, wallabies and koalas. There are also the possums, phalangers, wombats, bandicoots, the marsupial mole and the numbat, which does not have a pouch. Marsupial carnivores include the Tasmanian devil, the native-cats and marsupial mice.

South American marsupials include the water opossum and the mouse opossums, which do not have pouches. The only marsupial found in North America is the Virginia opossum.

Virginia opossum

Koala

◀ WHAT ARE PLACENTAL MAMMALS?

Placental mammals form the largest group of mammals. A female placental mammal nourishes her young for some time in her womb by means of an organ called a placenta.

Placental mammals are the most advanced type of mammals. A young placental mammal stays in its mother's womb until it is fairly well developed. The all-important placenta keeps it supplied with food and oxygen and removes the young mammal's waste material. The placenta brings the bloodstreams of the mother and young close together without the blood actually mixing.

There are 18 orders, or groups, of placental mammals. The smallest group contains just one species – the aardvark. Colugos (flying lemurs), elephant shrews and tree shrews form three other small orders. The largest is that of the rodents, with over 1600 species.

Hedgehogs, moles and shrews all belong to the mammal order Insectivora. This name means 'insect-eaters', but insects form only part of the diet of these animals.

Hedgehogs are omnivorous animals. They feed not only on insects but also on worms, snails and plant material, such as berries and acorns. Sometimes they take the eggs of wild birds.

Moles live and feed underground. They do eat insects but their main source of food is earthworms. Moles are well adapted for their underground way of life. They have large front limbs for digging and their short fur can be brushed in any direction.

Shrews are the smallest and most numerous insectivores. They feed on insects and other animals, and a shrew has to eat its own weight in food every 24 hours. Some shrews will even kill and eat rodents their own size.

Shrew

Mole

Hedgehog

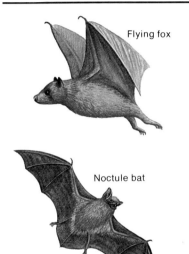

Flying fox

Noctule bat

The only true flying mammals are the bats. All bats fly at night and most feed on insects.

A bat's wing is formed from a large membrane supported by both the front and hind limbs and by four long 'fingers' of its 'hand'. Other 'flying' mammals, such as flying squirrels, can only glide, but a bat actually flies.

Most bats eat insects. They are able to find their prey and avoid obstacles in the dark by using sound waves (echo-location). A bat catches an insect in its wing membrane and then transfers it to its mouth.

However, not all bats eat insects. Vampire bats feed on the blood of large mammals. One false vampire bat preys on lizards, smaller bats, birds and mice.

Some tropical bats have extra-long tongues for drinking nectar from flowers. Others eat fruit and flowers. The best known fruit-eating bat is the flying fox.

The mammal order primates includes the lemurs and their relatives, monkeys, apes and man.

All primates have five fingers and toes and can grasp objects with their hands (and often their feet). They have good colour vision and use sight rather than smell to find food and spot predators.

The lemurs, bushbabies, tarsiers and lorises are some of the most primitive primates. Monkeys are divided into two main groups. The New World monkeys of tropical America have broad, flat noses and widely-spaced nostrils. They include the marmosets, spider monkeys, howler monkeys, capuchins and douroucoulis. Most of these have grasping tails.

Old World monkeys, such as colobuses, langurs, guenons, macaques and baboons, only use their tails for balancing.

Apes include the gibbons, the orang-utan, gorilla and chimpanzee. Apes are found only in Asia and Africa.

Mandrill

Tarsier

Red-mantled tamarin

Gorilla

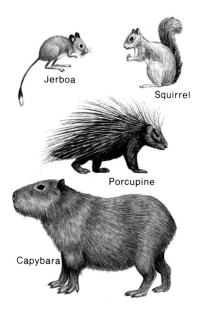

▲ WHAT ARE RODENTS?

Rodents are mammals with chisel-like incisor (cutting) teeth at the front of their jaws. These teeth grow continuously as they are worn down.

All rodents gnaw their food with their two pairs of front teeth. Between these teeth and the grinding teeth at the back of the jaw there is a gap. When a rodent is gnawing at inedible material, such as wood, it can close off its mouth by pushing its cheek folds into the gap.

Rodents are plant-eaters, although they sometimes eat snails and insects. Most use their front paws to hold their food while they eat. And most are burrowing animals.

Rodents include mice, rats, voles and tree squirrels. Also in this group are the beavers, porcupines, jerboas, kangaroo rats and ground squirrels, such as prairie dogs.

The largest rodent is the South American capybara, which is the size of a small pig. This creature lives in water, rather like a hippopotamus.

▲ WHAT IS THE DIFFERENCE BETWEEN A RABBIT AND A HARE?

Rabbits raise their young in burrows. Hares raise their young in the open.

Rabbits and hares belong to the mammal order Lagomorpha. They are like rodents because they have gnawing incisor teeth that grow continuously. But lagomorphs have four incisor teeth in their upper jaws while rodents have only two.

Rabbits build warm nests in burrows. Their young are born blind and without fur and remain in the nest for about a month. A newly-born leveret (young hare), on the other hand, has fully-opened eyes and is covered in soft fur. To begin with, young leverets are left in their 'forms', which are just depressions in the grass. But they can fend for themselves much sooner than young rabbits.

The true rabbit is a native of Europe and North Africa. Hares include the brown hare and alpine hare of Europe, and the snowshoe rabbit and jackrabbit of North America.

▼ WHAT IS AN ARMADILLO?

Armadillos are armoured mammals found in South America.

Most mammals have soft skins covered in fur or hair. They rely on their speed, or their ability to hide, to escape from predators. Armadillos, however, have developed armour for protection.

The armour consists of bony plates that cover the animal's back and sides. Some species can roll themselves into a ball. Others just pull in their feet and crouch. If attacked, they can also fight fiercely with their sharp claws.

Armadillos eat a variety of small animals, such as insects (especially ants and termites), worms and lizards. The nine-banded armadillo is the most common. It is the only one found in North America.

South American armadillos include the smaller six-banded armadillo, the rat-sized fairy armadillo and the hairy armadillo. The largest is the giant armadillo, which may be a metre long.

▼ WHAT ARE ANTEATERS AND SLOTHS?

Anteaters and sloths are relatives of the armadillos. Anteaters are ground-dwellers that feed on ants and termites. Sloths spend their lives hanging in trees.

Armadillos, anteaters and sloths make up the mammal order known as the edentates. This name means 'without teeth', but this is only true of the anteaters. Armadillos and sloths do have some teeth.

Anteaters live entirely on ants and termites. They tear open nests with their sharp claws and reach deep inside with their long tongues. Anteaters are found only in South America. The giant anteater may measure two metres from head to tail and its tongue may be 90 centimetres long.

Sloths are slow-moving inhabitants of the rain forests of South and Central America. They spend all their lives hanging upside down in trees, feeding on leaves and fruit.

Two-toed sloth

Giant anteater

▲ WHAT IS A PANGOLIN?

Pangolins are a small group of South African and Asian mammals. Most of a pangolin's body is covered in horny scales.

Pangolins form a mammal order (the Pholidota) on their own. A pangolin has overlapping scales in place of most of its fur. Only the underside of its body is hairy.

The giant pangolin and Temmink's pangolin are the largest members of the order. They can measure up to 170 centimetres, including a 70-centimetre tail.

They and the Indian pangolin are all ground-dwellers. Like anteaters they use their sharp claws and long tongues to feed on termites and ants. The remaining four species are all tree-dwellers and feed mostly on tree ants.

A pangolin's scales help to protect it from the attacks of ants and soldier termites. They can also close their nostrils and their eyes are protected by thick eyelids.

The pangolin swallows pebbles to grind up the ants in its stomach.

▲ WHAT IS AN AARDVARK?

The aardvark is an African mammal that lives mostly on termites. It looks similar to an anteater, but is not closely related to it.

The aardvark is the only member of the mammal order Tubulidentata ('tube teeth'). This order takes its name from the aardvark's peculiar and unique teeth. They have no enamel on the outside, no roots and they contain many fine tubes.

Like anteaters, the aardvark has a long nose. However, its ears are much larger than an anteater's and its nose ends in a snout, like a pig. *Aardvark* is the Afrikaans word for 'earth pig'. A fully grown aardvark can measure about 180 centimetres long from nose to tail.

Aardvarks are seldom seen. They feed at night and lead secretive lives. Like other termite-eaters, they have strong limbs, sharp claws and long tongues. They also feed on other soft-bodied insects and fruit, but they cannot digest ants.

The word *carnivore* means 'flesh-eater' and there are many carnivores in the animal kingdom. Some belong to the mammal order Carnivora.

Some of the best-known members of the Carnivora belong to the cat family. This includes the lion, tiger, leopard, cheetah and jaguar, as well as a number of smaller cats, such as the European wild cat.

The dog family includes the wolf, coyote, dingo, jackals and foxes. Hyenas belong to a separate family.

The weasel family includes the skunk, sable and mink, as well as weasels, polecats, badgers and otters. Civets, mongooses and genets belong to another family.

Other Carnivora include the seals, sea lions and the walrus. Bears and raccoons, which include coatis and the red panda, eat a great deal of plant material. The giant panda, which may be a relative of the bears, lives entirely on bamboo shoots.

The world's fastest land animal is the cheetah, which can run at speeds of up to 100 kilometres an hour. However, it cannot run very far at this speed.

Some mammals can run swiftly over fairly long distances. Pronghorn antelopes can travel at more than 55 kilometres an hour for over one and a half kilometres.

Cats, on the other hand, cannot run very far. They hunt by stalking their prey. They get as close as possible and then rush over the last few metres. Cats that hunt in open country cannot get very close to their prey, so the last rush has to be very fast. Lions, which often hunt in groups, can reach speeds of up to 65 kilometres an hour.

Cheetahs hunt alone, and can chase their prey at even higher speeds. However, if a cheetah does not catch its intended victim within a few hundred metres, it becomes exhausted and gives up.

Kodiak bears and polar bears are the largest land carnivores.

There are several examples of large carnivores in the world. The largest cat is the Siberian tiger. An adult male can measure over three metres from nose to tail and stand over one metre high at the shoulder.

The largest wild member of the dog family is the grey wolf, but there are taller and heavier breeds of domestic dog.

The bear family contains the largest carnivores. There are several races of brown bear. The fierce grizzly bear is one North American race. The Kodiak bear, on Kodiak Island off the coast of Alaska, is another. The average adult male measures about two and a half metres from head to tail and may weigh over 500 kilograms. Most polar bears are under 400 kilograms in weight. But there are claims of some weighing 800 or even 1000 kilograms.

Tiger

Coyote

Polar bear

Cheetah

Mongoose

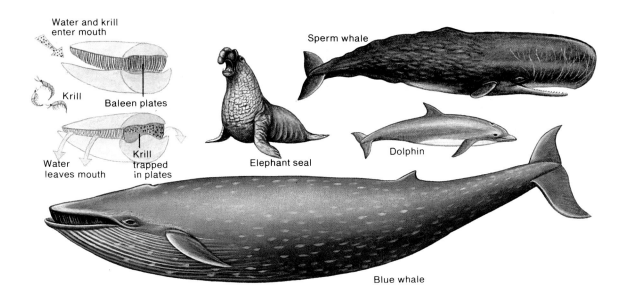

Water and krill enter mouth

Krill

Baleen plates

Water leaves mouth

Krill trapped in plates

Sperm whale

Elephant seal

Dolphin

Blue whale

Seals, dolphins and whales are all sea mammals. Seals breed on land, but dolphins and whales never leave the water.

Dolphins and whales make up the mammal order Cetacea. In spite of their fish-like appearance, they are true placental mammals.

They are well adapted for life in water. They have streamlined bodies, paddles instead of front legs and horizontal tail fins, or flukes, instead of hind legs. Instead of nostrils, a dolphin has a blow-hole on the top of its head that can be closed when the animal is underwater.

Seals and sea lions are members of the order Carnivora. Like most mammals, they are covered in fur, but this lies flat on their streamlined bodies. Their limbs have become flippers, but, unlike dolphins, they can use their front flippers for crawling. Sea lions and fur seals can also use their hind flippers for moving on land.

The largest animal that has ever lived on Earth is the blue whale. The largest specimen ever recorded was 33.58 metres long.

Most whales and dolphins are quite small animals, but a few are enormous. Land animals the size of the blue whale have never existed because they could never support the weight of their bodies. A beached whale cannot breathe because its tremendous weight prevents it from expanding its lungs. Usually the whale's mass is supported by the water around it.

The largest toothed whale is the sperm whale, so called because of the large amounts of spermaceti (a valuable oil) stored in its barrel-shaped head. Bull sperm whales can measure up to 20 metres long and weigh over 50 tonnes.

But even this large animal is dwarfed by the enormous blue whale. A female blue whale can measure over 30 metres in length and may weigh over 130 tonnes.

Toothed whales, such as dolphins and sperm whales, feed on fish and other large sea animals. Baleen, or whalebone, whales feed on tiny shrimp-like animals.

Most dolphins feed on fish, squid and cuttlefish near the surface of the sea. Killer whales feed on seals and dolphins as well as fish. Sperm whales dive deep down to feed on squid.

Despite their size, baleen whales, such as the blue whale, humpback whale, minke whale and right whales, are gentle creatures. They feed on plankton, especially the tiny shrimp-like animals called krill.

Instead of teeth, a baleen whale has a number of horny (whalebone) plates on each side of its upper jaw. These form two huge sieves. The whale takes a mouthful of water and krill and closes its mouth. It then forces the water out through the plates, leaving the krill behind.

123

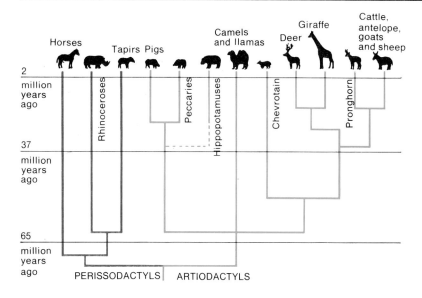

Horses
Tapirs Pigs
Camels and llamas
Deer
Giraffe
Cattle, antelope, goats and sheep

2 million years ago

Rhinoceroses

Peccaries

Hippopotamuses

Chevrotain

Pronghorn

37 million years ago

65 million years ago

PERISSODACTYLS   ARTIODACTYLS

▲ WHAT ARE HOOVED ANIMALS?

Many plant-eating mammals walk on the tips of toes that have enlarged nails, or hooves. They are often very fast runners.

The ungulates, or hooved mammals, belong to two separate mammal orders. The perissodactyls have an odd number of toes on each foot. The artiodactyls have an even number of toes on each foot.

Perissodactyls include the

horses, which walk on just one toe. Ancestors of modern horses had three toes on each foot, but most of the weight was placed on the central toe. Gradually, their descendants lost the use of the two outside toes. The central toe, with its large 'nail', became a single hoof.

Except for hippopotamuses, which have four-toed feet, modern artiodactyls have two toes and are often referred to as cloven-hooved animals. Cloven hooves provide a better grip on slippery rocks, which is why so many artiodactyls are successful mountain-dwellers.

The artiodactyls are a much larger group than the perissodactyls. There are nine families, the largest of which are the deer family and the enormous cattle family.

▼ WHICH ANIMALS ARE RELATED TO HORSES?

Horses belong to the mammal order Perissodactyla, or odd-toed ungulates. Rhinoceroses and tapirs are the other members of the order.

There is only one genus of horses *(Equus)*, of which there are seven living species. Most of the horses we see are breeds of domestic horse. They are all thought to be descended from a wild species known as the tarpan, which became extinct in the 1850s. The only

living wild species of horse is Przewalski's horse of Mongolia.

Other members of the horse family include the three species of zebra in Africa and the two wild asses of Africa and Asia. A donkey is a domesticated breed of African wild ass.

Rhinoceroses are three-toed perissodactyls with horns and tough, armour-like hides. There are five species. The white and black rhinoceroses are both found in Africa. They have two horns and are hairless. The three Asian species (Indian, Javan and Sumatran) have only one horn and have a sparse covering of hair.

Tapirs have four toes on their front feet and three toes on their hind feet. One species lives in south-east Asia. Three species live in South and Central America.

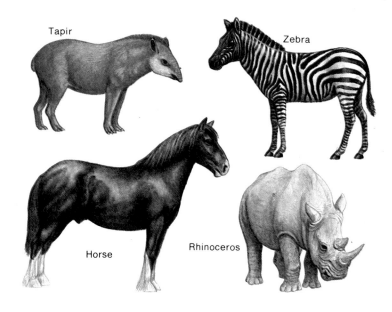

Tapir

Zebra

Horse

Rhinoceros

▶ WHICH ANIMALS HAVE HORNS?

Animals with horns include the giraffe and the okapi, members of the deer family, the pronghorn, and all cattle, antelopes, sheep and goats.

The four families of horned artiodactyls are different because of the structure of their horns.

The giraffe and okapi have simple, bony knobs covered with hair. The bony horns of deer are known as antlers and a new set grows each year. Except in reindeer, only male deer grow antlers.

Animals belonging to the huge cattle family have permanent horns that consist of a bony cone covered with a horny sheath. Often both males and females have horns.

The cattle family includes antelopes, sheep (such as the mouflon) and goats as well as bison and buffalo.

The pronghorn is the last survivor of a once large family. It sheds the horny sheaths of its horns each year.

Mouflon

Roe deer

Bison

◀ HOW MANY KINDS OF ELEPHANT ARE THERE?

The two species of elephant in the world today are the African and the Asiatic, or Indian, elephant.

Elephants are the largest living land animals and the larger of the two species is the African elephant. It can grow to a height of about three and a half metres at the shoulder and may weigh over six tonnes.

The African elephant has a less prominent, more rounded forehead than the Asiatic elephant. Its ears and tusks are larger and it has a hollow back.

An elephant's trunk is really the nose and upper lip joined together. It is a long, flexible tube which the elephant uses for carrying food and water to its mouth, dust-bathing and smelling the air.

An elephant's tusks are actually overgrown incisor teeth. They are used as weapons and for digging for water in times of drought.

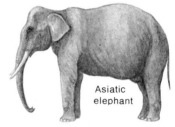

Asiatic elephant

African elephant

▶ WHAT IS A HIPPOPOTAMUS?

The hippopotamus is a distant relative of the pigs and peccaries.

The name *hippopotamus* means 'river horse'. It is a land animal, but it spends most of its time in water.

During the day it lies partly or almost totally submerged in a slow-moving river. Its eyes and ears are placed near the top of its head, so that as much of its body as possible can remain underwater. And it can close its nostrils when fully submerged.

At night hippopotamuses leave the river and follow well-worn paths to their feeding grounds. They eat grass and, like other herbivores (plant eaters), they chew it up with large grinding teeth. But hippopotamuses also have huge incisors and long, tusk-like canine teeth. Males use these for fighting.

The hippopotamus is found only in Africa. Its smaller relative, the pygmy hippopotamus, is only found in a small part of western Africa.

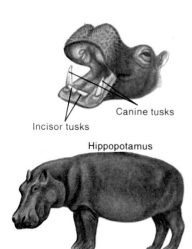

Canine tusks

Incisor tusks

Hippopotamus

▶ WHERE DO PENGUINS BREED?

All penguins live in the southern hemisphere. A number of them breed in Antarctic and sub-Antarctic areas.

Penguins spend most of their time at sea, but they all come ashore to breed. Only two, the emperor and Adélie penguins, breed on the Antarctic coast.

Emperor penguins, which are the largest penguins of all, breed in the perpetual darkness of the Antarctic winter. They gather in large 'rookeries' on the ice and do not build nests. The males incubate the eggs for two months. Adélie penguins begin nesting in September and October, during the Antarctic spring. They make nests of pebbles on the beaches.

Emperor penguin

Chinstrap penguin   Macaroni penguin   Gentoo penguin

King, macaroni, chinstrap and gentoo penguins breed on sub-Antarctic islands. The king penguin is closely related to the emperor but, like the Adélie, it breeds on stony beaches in the Antarctic spring. The male and female take turns at incubating the egg.

The remaining 11 species all breed farther north. Some, such as the rockhopper penguin, breed on Southern Ocean islands. Others are found on continental coasts.

▶ WHICH SEALS LIVE IN THE ANTARCTIC?

Only four true seals breed in Antarctic waters. They are the crabeater seal, the Weddell seal, the Ross seal and the leopard seal.

Each species of Antarctic seal has its own specialized way of life. Crabeater seals live along the coasts and feed on krill, which they filter from the water using specially adapted teeth.

Ross seals, the smallest of the Antarctic seals, are usually seen on the pack ice and seem to be strong, agile swimmers. They eat squid, fish and krill. Ross seals have been known to play with killer whales, their natural enemies, while feeding on squid.

Weddell seals live along the coasts and are the most placid of the Antarctic seals. They

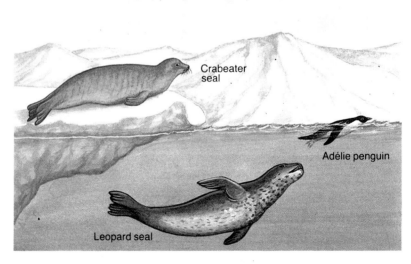

Crabeater seal

Adélie penguin

Leopard seal

feed on fish such as Antarctic cod and icefish, and are known for their diving skills. They can dive down to over 300 metres and stay submerged for over 40 minutes. Their blood and circulatory system are specially adapted for this. Ice covers their feeding areas in

winter. Weddell seals make holes in the ice so that they can come up for air.

Leopard seals are the most carnivorous of the Antarctic seals. They live along the edge of the pack ice and feed on fish, penguins and even the cubs of other seals.

Polar bear

Ringed seal

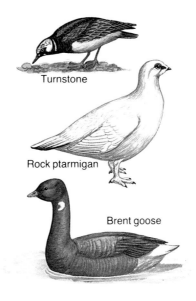

Turnstone

Rock ptarmigan

Brent goose

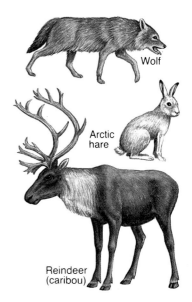

Wolf

Arctic hare

Reindeer (caribou)

▲ WHERE ARE POLAR BEARS FOUND?

▲ WHICH BIRDS NEST IN THE ARCTIC?

▲ WHERE DO CARIBOU LIVE?

Polar bears live in the snowy wastes of the Arctic. They roam for many kilometres hunting seals and other animals.

Polar bears are found farther north than any other land mammal. In winter they range across the pack ice of the Arctic Ocean. There they hunt seals, particularly ringed seals, which they capture with great skill. They also eat young walruses and stranded whales.

In spring and summer, polar bears are carried south by the ice. In the tundra they eat plant material such as lichen, moss, grass and berries. Polar bears are good swimmers, although they usually avoid large stretches of open water. They walk with ease across the ice floes because their feet have hairy, non-slip soles.

Polar bears mate in the spring and the cubs are born in December or January. The female gives birth inside a 'maternity den' dug into a bank of snow.

Over 100 types of bird nest in the Arctic in summer. Only a few remain during winter.

The Arctic summer lasts only about three months. But during this time many birds nest and rear their young.

Among the summer visitors are ducks, such as long-tailed ducks, geese, such as Brent geese, and swans. They all come to feed on the rich summer vegetation of the tundra wetlands. Insect larvae attract wading birds such as phalaropes, turnstones, knots and dunlins. Flying insects attract warblers, wheatears, fieldfares and yellowhammers. Arctic terns and skuas feed on fish.

As summer ends, many birds fly south to avoid the harsh Arctic winter. Of those that remain, the rock ptarmigan moults its brown feathers and becomes totally white. It shelters in burrows tunnelled into the snow. Other birds that spend winter in the Arctic include the snowy owl, raven, gyr falcon, peregrine falcon and the redpoll.

The caribou of North America, together with a number of other mammals, range across the tundra wastes. Reindeer are a semi-domesticated variety of caribou found in northern Europe and Asia.

Caribou and musk oxen are the large herbivores (plant-eaters) of the tundra. In summer they range across the tundra, feeding on many kinds of plants. Their main enemies are wolves and sometimes grizzly bears. Smaller carnivores (flesh-eaters) include foxes and weasels. These hunt shrews, lemmings, ground squirrels and the Arctic hare.

In winter, caribou move south and feed on reindeer moss (a type of lichen), and the twigs of trees such as birch and aspen. Musk oxen remain farther north. In the coldest weather they huddle together to keep warm.

Small mammals tunnel beneath the snow. There they are protected from the biting winds. They feed on seeds and dry grass.

127

Bighorn sheep are found in the Rocky Mountains. They, and the Rocky Mountain goats which also inhabit this region, are agile climbers.

North America has three main mountain ranges. In the east the Appalachians stretch from Labrador to Georgia. In the west there are the coastal ranges that form the Pacific Rim, and the Rocky Mountains which stretch from Alaska to Mexico.

Many animals live in these mountains. Bighorn sheep are sure-footed and scramble among the rocks with ease. Rocky Mountain goats are an American form of goat-antelope. In addition to these animals, there are mountain lions (cougars), Canadian lynxes, beavers, the hoary marmot and the jack rabbit, and many small rodents. Mule deer are found on the lower slopes.

There are also vultures such as the red-headed turkey vulture, and birds of prey such as the golden eagle, bald eagle and osprey.

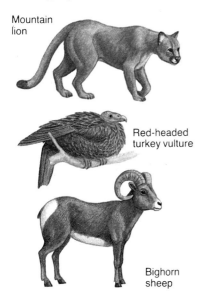

Mountain lion

Red-headed turkey vulture

Bighorn sheep

Ibexes are wild goats. The seven types of ibex are all found in the mountains of Europe, Asia and North Africa. The European species are the Spanish ibex and the Alpine ibex.

The three mountain ranges of Europe – the Carpathians, Alps and Pyrenees – are all relics of the last Ice Age. When the glaciers retreated, these mountains were left as cold 'islands' in a much warmer Europe.

Ring ouzel

Golden eagle

Ibex

Marmot

Ibexes are excellent climbers. They sometimes use their dew claws (at the back of each foot) to give them extra grip. Two other cloven-hooved mountain animals are the mouflon (a wild sheep) and the chamois (a goat-antelope).

Other alpine animals include lynxes, marmots and susliks (European ground squirrels). The Pyrenees are home to the Pyrenean desman, a water-living relative of the mole. Alpine birds include the alpine chough, ring ouzel, wallcreeper and birds of prey such as the golden eagle.

The yak is the largest of the Himalayan mammals. Wild herds live on the high plateaus of Tibet. Domesticated yak are found all over the highlands of Central Asia.

The Himalayas are home to a number of unique animals. As well as the yak there are several hooved animals such as the Tibetan wild ass, the tahr, markhor, bharal and the largest of all living sheep, the argali. The Siberian ibex is the main prey of the beautiful and rare snow leopard. Smaller animals include the alpine marmot and the high-mountain vole. The large-eared pika is unusual because it does not hibernate during the winter. Instead it lives in its burrow, feeding on hay and other dried plants gathered during the summer.

Himalayan birds include choughs, ravens and the Himalayan snow partridge. Carrion-eaters such as the lammergeier vulture, Himalayan griffon and black vulture, are common.

Lammergeier vulture

Snow leopard

Markhor

Yak

▼ WHERE DO PANDAS LIVE?

East of the Himalayas lies Szechwan, in the highlands of south-west China. High in these mountains are the bamboo thickets in which pandas live.

The valleys of Szechwan contain subtropical habitats. These change to broadleaved woodland, coniferous woodland and alpine habitats towards the snow-capped peaks of the mountains. Between 1800 and 2500 metres above sea level, the coniferous forest is broken by thickets of bamboo and rhododendron. Here the giant panda lives. It feeds on bamboo shoots and other plants, and even eats small animals occasionally.

The red, or lesser, panda is also found in this region. It too feeds on leaves and fruit, but it is not closely related to the giant panda.

Szechwan is the home of three goat-antelopes – the takin, goral and serow. There are also primitive shrews such as the mole shrew, the web-footed water shrew and the Himalayan water shrew.

▼ WHERE DO LLAMAS LIVE?

The llama is the domesticated pack animal of the High Andes in South America. Its close relatives are the alpaca, guanaco and vicuna.

The Indians of the High Andes domesticated the llama over 4000 years ago. The llama and the alpaca are thought to have been bred from the guanaco. Vicunas and guanacos have never been domesticated. All these animals are well-adapted for life where the air is thin.

Torrent duck

Spectacled bear

Llama

They have large lungs and extra red blood-cells.

The northern part of the Andes has high plains. These are home to many animals, including the spectacled bear, South American mountain tapir, and deer such as the Ecuadorian pudu and the Andean deer, or guemel.

Many birds also inhabit the High Andes. The Andean condor soars high among the peaks. The sierra finch builds its nest among the spiny leaves of puya plants, and torrent ducks live in the tumbling streams.

▼ WHERE ARE THE STRANGEST MOUNTAIN PLANTS FOUND?

Some mountainous regions have very unusual plants. In the mountains of Africa there are giant lobelias and tree groundsels. The Andes have giant lupins and bromeliads. The Chilean pine, or monkey puzzle tree, is one of the few remaining southern conifers.

Mountain plants must survive extreme cold. They are usually low-growing, creeping or cushion-forming plants. However, the giant plants of Africa and South America are extraordinary exceptions.

Giant lobelias and tree groundsels grow to about six metres in height. Their leaves are arranged so that they close up at night into 'buds'. The undersides of the leaves also have a covering of thick, felty hair to protect the 'buds' from the cold.

The giant plants of the Andes are similar. One of the most spectacular is the giant puya, *Puya raymondii*. This has a palm-like trunk, a rosette of long leaves and a tall spike of bird-pollinated flowers.

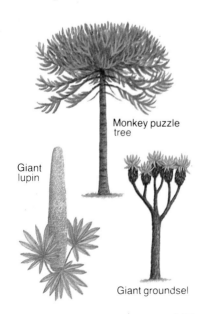

Giant lupin

Monkey puzzle tree

Giant groundsel

129

NORTH AMERICAN
BOREAL FOREST

Tengmalm's owl

Larch

Lodgepole pine

Great horned owl

Sitka spruce

Flying squirrel

Chickaree

Moose

Wolverine

Brown bear

Chipmunk

Mink

Virginia opossum

Ground squirrel

▲ WHERE DO MOST
CONIFERS GROW?

Below the tundra of the northern hemisphere there is a broad band of poor soils left behind after the last Ice Age. In these cold regions the land is mostly covered with coniferous forest.

The habitat provided by the world's northern coniferous forests is known as taiga. The North American boreal (northern) forest, which is shown above, contains trees such as white and black spruce, sitka spruce, lodgepole pine and tamarack (a larch). In wet areas a few deciduous trees, such as aspen, willow and birch, are found.

In the coniferous forest of northern Europe, the main trees are Norway spruce and Scots pine. But farther east in the Siberian taiga (shown on the opposite page) the forest becomes more varied. Here the most commonly found conifers include Siberian fir, Siberian larch, stone pine and Siberian spruce. Forest fires are common, so many areas of the Eurasian taiga are at different stages of growth. In the newly burned areas birches and aspens are the most common tree. The Eurasian taiga is the world's largest forest. It is about one third larger than the whole of the USA.

Few herbaceous (non-woody) plants grow in the taiga because it is too cold and too dark (the conifers shut out much of the light). Also, the decomposing conifer needles produce a very acid humus. Many kinds of fungi help break down the humus, and some plants do survive in clearings.

SIBERIAN TAIGA

Pine marten

Ural owl

Stone pine

Siberian tit

Goosander

Siberian fir

Siberian rubythroat

Crossbill

Varying hare

Waxwing

Northern lynx

Capercaillie

Hazel hen

Wood lemming

The northern forests provide food for many seed-eating and insect-eating birds. Hawks and owls hunt small birds and mammals.

During the summer vast swarms of aphids, mosquitoes and other insects appear in the taiga and provide food for migrant birds such as warblers. Resident insect-eaters include woodpeckers and tits.

Seed-eating birds are also very common. These include the crossbill, the Siberian jay and the pine grosbeak. Waxwings feed on berries as well as seeds. Members of the grouse family, such as the capercaillie, hazel hen and spruce grouse (in North America), feed on seeds, leaves, buds and berries.

Predatory birds include the great horned owl of North America and the Ural owl of Siberia, and a few hawks such as the goshawk. Two unusual taiga birds are the goldeneye and goosander ducks, which nest in abandoned woodpecker holes in trees.

The coniferous forests of North America and Eurasia support both herbivores and carnivores. The herbivores feed on the leaves, seeds and bark of the trees, and they are hunted by the carnivores. Similar but different species have evolved in each region.

The largest herbivore of the North American forest is the moose (known as the elk in Eurasia) which feeds on low-growing plants and the leaves

of deciduous trees. Caribou also venture into the forest during the winter.

Seed-eating mammals include ground squirrels, tree squirrels (such as the grey squirrel), the golden chipmunk, the spruce mouse and the Virginia opossum. Flying squirrels and the chickaree (an American red squirrel) feed on pine cones and toadstools as well as on the eggs and nestlings of small birds. North American tree-porcupines feed on catkins and leaves. In winter they strip the bark off trees and can cause a

lot of damage.

The carnivores of the North American forest include the wolf, brown bear, black bear, American mink and wolverine.

Similar animals are found in the Siberian taiga. Here we find the elk, the brown bear, the Siberian chipmunk, the wood lemming, the Siberian weasel, the sable and the pine marten. There are also flying squirrels, ground squirrels and tree squirrels such as the European red squirrel. The northern lynx eats hares, and the wolverine eats northern red-backed voles.

▶ WHY IS DECIDUOUS
WOODLAND SO RICH IN
WILDLIFE?

Deciduous forests contain a fine undergrowth of small trees, shrubs and herbaceous (non-woody) plants. Such a variety of plants provides food for many animals.

Deciduous forest once covered the entire northern temperate region. Today, in this region, there are only three principal areas of deciduous woodland. The most varied woodland is found in eastern Asia, which has magnolias, tulip trees, sweet gums, planes, horse chestnuts, oaks, beeches, hickories and hornbeams, to name just a few. Many of these trees also grow in the woodlands of eastern North America, although fewer species are found there. European woodlands contain only about 20 species. The main types include oak, ash, beech, hornbeam, field maple, birch and alder.

Deciduous woodland consists of several layers of vegetation. The top layer is formed by tall trees; then come smaller trees and a layer of shrubs such as holly, honeysuckle, blackthorn, elder and hazel. Below this there is a layer of herbaceous plants such as bluebell, primrose and dog's mercury. Finally there is a ground layer, consisting of mosses and other small plants.

The leaves of all these plants are much less tough than the needles of conifers, so they attract a large number of plant-eating animals. The wealth of seeds and fruits also attracts plant-eaters. In turn, many predatory animals feed on the plant-eaters.

▶ WHICH ANIMALS LIVE IN
DECIDUOUS FORESTS?

Plant-eating woodland animals range from large species such as deer to small ones such as mice and voles. Predators include foxes and weasels.

Large European herbivores include the red deer, roe deer, fallow deer and wild boar. In North America the whitetail deer, which was once almost wiped out by hunters, is now increasing in numbers.

Smaller European plant-eaters include the red squirrel, the dormouse, bank vole, wood mouse, hedgehog and rabbit. In America there are similar animals, such as the grey squirrel, eastern chipmunk, white-footed mouse and the pine vole.

The largest predators, such as the wolf, the lynx (in Europe) and the mountain lion (in North America), have almost completely disappeared from deciduous woodland. Instead, today's main predators are foxes such as the European red fox and the North American red and grey foxes. In America other predators include the bobcat, the racoon, the ring-tailed cat, the skunk, the long-tailed weasel and the short-tailed shrew. European predators include the weasel, stoat, beech marten, polecat and pine marten. Badgers feed on plant material, as well as small animals.

Invertebrate animals play a vital part in the life of deciduous woodland. Worms, beetles and ants help to break down the leaf litter into humus. Many insects are eaten by birds.

▶ WHICH BIRDS LIVE IN
DECIDUOUS FORESTS?

Enormous numbers of birds nest and feed in the world's deciduous forests. They feed on insects, seeds, berries, buds and leaves. Birds of prey feed on small birds and mammals.

A number of birds live all the year round in European deciduous woodland. Omnivorous species include the blackbird, which feeds on insects, worms and berries; the song thrush, which enjoys snails; and the jay, which eats eggs and nestlings and sometimes mice and lizards. The chaffinch feeds on small seeds and insects, as do the wren and the goldfinch. The hawfinch feeds on fruit stones and large seeds. Tits, such as the great tit and blue tit, feed mainly on insects but also eat berries and seeds. Woodpeckers search for insects under pieces of loose bark, and treecreepers dig insects out of small crevices. The wood pigeon feeds on leaves, buds and seeds.

Summer visitors include the nightingale, which feeds mainly on ground insects. The nightjar catches flying insects with its wide-open mouth. Other summer visitors include flycatchers, warblers and the turtle dove.

Woodland birds of prey include the sparrowhawk, kite and buzzard. Tawny owls hunt by night.

American woodland contains a similar range of birds. It includes several woodpeckers and the striking blue jay. Summer visitors include a number of warblers, vireos and tanagers.

EUROPEAN DECIDUOUS WOODLAND

Tawny owl

Sparrowhawk

Greater spotted woodpecker

Blue tit

Jay

Green woodpecker

Lacewing

Gall wasp

Fallow deer

Red fox

Wild boar

Roe deer

Tortoise moth

Stoat

Hedgehog

Badger

Rabbit

Dormouse

NORTH AMERICAN DECIDUOUS WOODLAND

Bobcat

Scarlet tanager

Red-headed woodpecker

Blue jay

Whitetail deer

Grey squirrel

Grey fox

Red-eyed vireo

Skunk

Eastern chipmunk

Racoon

▼ WHERE DO COYOTES LIVE?   ▼ WHERE DO PRAIRIE DOGS MAKE THEIR HOMES?   ▼ WHAT HAPPENED TO THE BISON?

The North American prairies lie between the Mississippi River and the Rocky Mountains. They are the home of a number of plant-eating animals. The coyote is one of the main predators.

The grey wolf was once common on the North American prairies, but it has largely been replaced by the smaller and highly successful coyote, or prairie wolf. The coyote's prey includes jack rabbits, cottontails, prairie dogs and other rodents. It also eats carrion (the carcasses of dead animals).

Coyotes are well-known for their 'singing'. In the evening two or three coyotes may 'sing' together – an eerie sound that has given rise to many legends.

Other predators include the mountain lion, the black-footed ferret and the American badger. The favourite food of the American badger is the prairie dog. American badgers can burrow underground with amazing speed. Unlike European badgers, they hunt by day as well as by night.

Prairie dogs are so called because of their short barking calls. They dig underground burrows in large colonies on the North American prairies. Prairie dogs are rodents belonging to the squirrel family.

Prairie dogs' colonies, or 'towns', can be very large. In 1901 one colony was estimated to cover an area 160 by 380 kilometres. It is thought to have contained about 400 million animals. Today, however, prairie-dog towns are much smaller.

Each town is divided into a number of wards. These, in turn, are divided into coteries, which form the basic family unit. Members of the same coterie groom each other and feed together, and chase off outsiders.

Prairie dogs feed on grasses and other small, fast-growing plants. They have many predators, but an alarm call from one prairie dog is enough to send all those within earshot running for their burrows. It is usually only the sick, slow or unwary that get caught.

Large herds of bison and pronghorns once roamed the North American prairies. But during the 1800s hunters almost wiped them out.

The American bison is descended from the Asian bison (now extinct) which crossed into America via the Bering land bridge that existed a million years ago. At one time there were probably about 50 million plains bison in North America, but by 1889 there were only 540 left. The rest had been slaughtered for their meat, bones or hides – and often simply for sport. However, since the bison became a protected animal, numbers have increased and there are now several thousand in national parks.

The story of the pronghorn is a similar one. About 20 million years ago, there were probably over 40 million of these animals. In the 1800s, European settlers hunted them in great numbers and by 1925 there were only about 30,000 pronghorns left. But they have now grown in number to about 400,000.

Coyote
Bison
Pronghorn
American badger
Prairie dogs

The South American pampas is the home of some unique animals. These include armadillos and the viscacha, mara and aperea.

The temperate grassland known as the pampas is found on the plains of Argentina and Uruguay. Here it is possible to travel hundreds of kilometres without seeing a tree.

There are few large herbivores. The rare pampas deer is the largest, and there are occasional herds of guanaco.

Small herbivores include a number of South America's unique range of rodents. Viscachas tunnel labyrinth-like towns underground. The mara, or Patagonian hare, digs deep burrows. This animal is also found farther south on the dry Patagonian steppe, and manages to live without drinking. Other grassland rodents include the pampas guinea-pig, or aperea, and the tuco-tuco. The aperea does not burrow. Instead it hides in tufts of grass.

Several armadillos are found in the pampas. They include the nine-banded, giant, hairy, and fairy armadillos. The giant anteater also roams the plains.

Pampas predators include the southern grey fox, the long-legged maned wolf and the rare pampas cat.

Pampas birds include the rhea, the rufous ovenbird and the burrowing owl, which is also found in the dry areas of North America. There are also some species of tinamou. These are shy, partridge-like birds that can fly, but rarely take to the air.

Grassland occurs in those parts of the world where the rainfall is low or very seasonal. Fires and grazing animals help to prevent trees from growing.

Some temperate parts of the world, especially the centres of large continents, receive most of their rain at particular times of the year. In summer such areas have dry, hot weather and in winter there is often a thick covering of snow.

Trees find it difficult to grow in these conditions and so the land is mainly covered with grasses mixed with small herbaceous plants. Fires are common during the dry season and these help to keep down the trees. Grazing animals also help to maintain temperate grassland, as they nibble off the young shoots of any trees before they can grow.

Temperate grasslands include the steppes of central Asia, the North American prairies, the South American pampas and the South African veld.

Guanaco

Rhea

Maned wolf

Pampas deer

Hairy armadillo

Rufous ovenbird

Cavy

Viscacha

▶ WHAT IS SAVANNAH?

Savannah is tropical grassland. It occurs in hot regions where rainfall is very seasonal. The best-known savannah is that of Africa.

The African savannah is a dry, dusty region for most of the year, and the rainy season lasts for only four months. The most common grass is red oat-grass, and the savannah is also dotted with acacia and baobab trees. Some areas are fairly well wooded.

▶ WHICH BIRDS LIVE IN THE SAVANNAH?

The African savannah supports huge numbers of insect-eating and seed-eating birds. Among the most notable of African birds is the ostrich.

The huge, flightless ostrich is the world's largest living bird. It feeds on fruit, seeds and small animals. The savannah is also the home of the world's heaviest flying bird, the kori bustard, which may weigh over 50 kilograms. Bustards also feed on both plant material and animals.

Oxpeckers are common on the savannah. They perch on the backs of grazing animals, and feed on ticks and other parasites. Other savannah birds include bulbuls, shrikes, marabou storks, cranes and ground hornbills. Weaver birds build elaborate hanging nests in trees, as do their close relatives, the queleas. Huge flocks of queleas can cause a lot of damage to trees.

Birds of prey include the secretary bird and lanner falcon. Several types of vulture feed on the carcasses of dead animals.

▲ WHICH SAVANNAH ANIMALS LIVE IN HERDS?

The savannah is populated with large, sometimes vast, herds of grazing hooved mammals. Zebras and wildebeests form some of the largest herds.

A lone antelope grazing on the savannah is open to attack. The chances of such an animal surviving are small. On the other hand, the members of a herd give each other some protection. They can warn each other of the presence of danger. An individual animal within a herd also stands a much greater chance of not being singled out by a predator. When a predator does attack, the milling, rushing herd may confuse it.

The most abundant hooved mammals are wildebeests, zebras, hartebeests and Thomson's gazelles. They normally live in small scattered herds, but during the calving season they gather together in larger herds for protection. At the start of the dry season they also migrate in vast herds to moister areas.

Weaver birds

Wildebeest

Ostriches

White rhino

Oxpecker

Grant's gazelle

Lion

◀ HOW DO SO MANY ANIMALS LIVE TOGETHER IN THE SAVANNAH?

If all the savannah plant-eaters grazed in the same way, they would soon run out of food. But in fact each species feeds in a different way. In some cases the feeding method of one species actually helps another.

The herbivores of the savannah do not compete with each other for food. On the grassy plains of the Serengeti National Park, zebras chew off the coarse tops of grasses before moving on to another area. They are followed by wildebeests and topis, which eat the leafy centres of the plants almost down to the ground. Finally, Thomson's gazelles eat fallen seeds and young shoots at ground level. The gazelles benefit from the feeding of the earlier, larger animals. They can find their food easily because the tall grasses have been trampled and eaten.

In more wooded areas of savannah, competition for food is avoided in a similar way. Warthogs graze and also dig for bulbs and tubers on the ground. Springboks feed mainly on grass, but other antelopes are only partial grazers. They feed on the leaves and twigs of bushes and trees as well as on grass, and each species has its own preferred type of food. Dik-diks, steinboks, Grant's gazelles, kudus, elands and white rhinos browse increasingly higher levels of the bushes and trees. The topmost branches are browsed by elephants, which often destroy whole trees, and also by giraffes.

▲ WHICH ARE THE SAVANNAH HUNTERS?

Where there are so many plant-eating animals, there are naturally a number of predators. Each species of predator has its own method of hunting.

The best-known savannah hunter is the lion, the 'King of Beasts'. Lions often hunt in groups, or prides, and it is the lionesses who usually do the work of stalking and killing the prey.

The world's fastest animal, the cheetah, is also a savannah hunter. It approaches stealthily to within 100 metres or so of its prey and then runs it down by sheer speed. The leopard, on the other hand, prefers to lie in wait in a tree or among any suitable cover. The victim is then taken with a short, powerful charge.

Other savannah predators include the wild dog, serval, bat-eared fox, civet and banded mongoose. Jackals and hyenas hunt small animals. They are also scavengers, often taking over the abandoned kills of larger predators.

The deserts of Central Asia are baked dry during the summer. But in winter they are exposed to icy air from the Arctic. Even so, many animals survive there.

The Central Asian deserts stretch from the Caspian Sea eastwards to the Gobi Desert in Mongolia. Some of the most common animals are the jerboas, of which there are a number of species. Other rodents include the desert hedgehog and long-eared hedgehog. Large mammals are more common than in other deserts. The bactrian camel lives in the Gobi Desert. Wild asses and Mongolian gazelles (the most northerly of all gazelles) also roam the deserts of Asia. Snakes and lizards are very common. One of the largest desert snakes is the lebatine viper.

A number of birds can be found in the Asian deserts, particularly in spring, when food is plentiful. They include desert warblers, desert larks, stone curlews, desert shrikes, sandgrouse and hawks.

Eared agama
Jerboa
Grey monitor
Bactrian camel

At the southern end of Death Valley in Nevada, USA, there is a series of small streams and lakes. These are the home of desert pupfish, which survive water temperatures that would kill most fish.

The streams and lakes these pupfish live in were once very

Cactus wren
Scott's oriole
Kit fox
Cottontail
Kangaroo rat
Burrowing owl
Night lizard
Western diamondback rattlesnake
Pupfish

Cacti are the most familiar of all desert plants. But they are not found in all deserts – only in those of North and South America. They help support a number of desert animals.

Pronghorns sometimes visit the desert to feed on cacti and shrubs, but most North American desert animals are much smaller. The kangaroo rat is a jumping rodent that burrows into the sandy ground and shelters in its burrow during the day. At night it comes out to feed on seeds and other plant material. It probably never drinks. Other small herbivores include the

large lakes. During the last Ice Age they covered much of what is now desert. Pupfish feed on the algae that grow in these warm waters. They can survive temperatures of just over 42°C.

The populations of the various species of pupfish were once numbered in tens of thousands. Today, however, predators and irrigation schemes have reduced their numbers.

desert cottontail, wood rat and grasshopper mouse. Desert hunters include the bobcat and the kit fox which resembles the Saharan fennec.

Amongst the many snakes and lizards are the American sidewinder, a rattlesnake, and the gila monster, one of the world's two poisonous lizards. Insect-eating birds include Scott's oriole, the cactus wren and the poor-will, which hibernates during the winter. Elf owls nest in abandoned woodpecker holes in saguaro cactus stems. The burrowing owl shares the underground homes of other animals, including, on occasions, rattlesnakes!

The world's largest desert is the Sahara Desert, which forms a broad band across North Africa. In most places the annual rainfall is less than 100 millimetres and it is one of the hottest places in the world.

Desert is often thought of as stretches of rolling sand dunes.

But, although the Sahara does contain seas of dunes (known as ergs), there are other types of desert as well. There are raised plateaus of rock known as hamadas, and large flat, stony regions known as regs.

Despite this bleak landscape, the Sahara is far from lifeless. Tough, hardy plants provide food for many insects such as beetles, grasshoppers and crickets. Even moths and butterflies appear after the occasional rainstorm. In turn, these insects are eaten by other animals such as lizards, snakes, scorpions, jerboas, gerbils, sand rats and desert hedgehogs. Larger animals include the fennec, which preys on small rodents, and the addax, a desert antelope. Desert birds include sandgrouse, larks and several species that fly in to feed on seeds and insects.

Skink

Fat sand rat

Lanner falcon

Pintail sandgrouse

Sidewinding snake

Eland

Fennec

Addax

The desert presents its inhabitants with several problems. The biggest of these are how to stay cool and how to get enough moisture. Desert animals have evolved a number of adaptations that enable them to survive.

Many desert animals have large ears, feet and tails. These are used as radiators to help get rid of excess heat. Large ears have an additional advantage. They enable their owners to hear the slightest sound in the still desert air. The hearing of the fennec, for example, is particularly keen.

Most desert animals shelter from the heat of the Sun during the day and are active only at night or in the early morning and evening. But some animals are out and about during the day. A desert locust keeps cool by turning its head towards the Sun, thus exposing the least possible area of its body to the searing heat.

Because water is scarce in the desert, animals have to make full use of the little they can get. Many desert animals do not sweat and they produce very concentrated urine and dry faeces. Large herbivores, which cannot shelter in burrows, have the greatest problem. The eland, which lives near the edge of the Sahara, manages to find some shelter and some water. But the addax and the oryx survive in the hottest areas without drinking. All their water is obtained from dew and the sparse plant-life. Few birds nest in the desert, though the sandgrouse is an exception. It flies long distances to find water, which it carries back to its nestlings by soaking its breast feathers.

Movement in sandy areas of desert is not easy. Many desert rodents are jumping rather than walking animals. The horned viper of the Sahara sidewinds across the sand and sandfish (types of skink) almost 'swim'.

▶ WHERE IS THE WORLD'S
LARGEST RAIN FOREST?

Tropical rain forest occurs in warm, moist regions near the Equator. The largest area of rain forest is the Amazon basin in South America.

Of all the world's biomes, tropical rain forests contain the greatest variety of wildlife. This is because these areas receive an enormous amount of warmth, sunlight and rain. In the wettest areas plant growth, flowering and fruiting continues throughout the year. This kind of habitat provides homes and food for ten times the number of animals found in deciduous woodland.

Five layers can be seen in tropical forest. At ground level, fungi, mosses and ferns grow in the rich leaf litter. The second layer consists of tree ferns, shrubs and lianas. Next there is a layer of young tree crowns, and above this is the thick canopy, the crowns of mature trees. The topmost layer consists of the few trees that stand above the canopy.

Tropical rain forest contains a wealth of insect life. There are countless butterflies, beetles, mantises, stick insects and crickets. Many of these have amazing forms of camouflage. Others have bright warning colours or markings that are used to startle predators.

Amphibians and reptiles are also common. In the Amazon forest arrow poison frogs, tree frogs and horned frogs prey on insects and other small animals. Snakes include the anaconda, boa constrictor and coral snakes. Lizards include the green iguana, anole and tegu.

White-eared puffbird
Harpy eagle
Topaz hummingbird
Spectacled owl
Sulphur-breasted toucan
Gold and blue macaw
Paradise jacamar
Amazon parrot
Lovely cotinga
Gold-hooded manakin
Great curassow
Common marmoset
Red-mantled tamarin
Spider monkey
Howler monkey
Bird-eating spider
Leafcutter ant

▲ WHICH KINDS OF BIRD
LIVE IN RAIN FOREST?

The canopy of any tropical rain forest provides food for a host of birds. Many feed on the nectar, fruits and seeds of the trees.

The brightly coloured birds of the Amazon forest blend with the luminous greens, reds and yellows of the flowers and foliage. Toucans, parrots, parakeets, macaws and curassows feed on the plentiful supply of fruit. Smaller fruit-eaters include manakins, cotingas and bellbirds. Insect-eaters include jacamars, puff-birds, trogons and tanagers. Hummingbirds and honeycreepers feed on nectar.

One of the strangest birds of the Amazon is the hoatzin, whose young have claws on their wings to help them scramble about the trees. One of the few birds of prey is the harpy eagle.

A similar range of birds can be found in the African rain forests. As in South America, there are a number of parrots, but in Africa hornbills take the place of toucans.

Tropical forests are inhabited by a large number of monkeys. The Amazon forest is also the home of sloths and other climbing mammals.

New World Monkeys abound in the Amazon forest. Troops of capuchins, titis, spider monkeys, woolly monkeys, squirrel monkeys, tamarins and marmosets (the smallest of all monkeys) spend their days in the forest canopy, searching for fruit, flowers and buds. Douroucoulis are the only ones that sleep during the day. Uakaris and sakis move around singly or in pairs. The largest of the South American monkeys are the howler monkeys, which set up a howling chorus just after sunrise to establish the whereabouts of rival groups.

Most of these monkeys have grasping, or prehensile, tails. This is also true of other South American forest animals, such as the Brazilian tree-porcupine, the kinkajou and the tamandua, or collared anteater. Other tree dwellers include the sloths. They hang from branches, using their huge claws, and move very slowly through the forest, feeding on leaves. Coatis are excellent climbers and eat almost anything that is edible, as does their relative the crab-eating racoon.

Rodents, such as acoushis and agoutis, forage on the forest floor, eating all kinds of plant material, especially fallen fruit and nuts. Forest hunters include the jaguar, ocelot, margay cat and tayra, a member of the weasel family.

The rain forests of Africa are the home of a number of Old World monkeys and other primates. There are also several forest antelopes.

The largest group of African monkeys are the guenons, such as the Diana monkey, the De Brazza monkey, Hamlyn's monkey and the moustached monkey. Each one of these has its own preferred forest layer. Other African forest monkeys include the colobus monkey and the drill, which is a ground-living baboon.

African forests also contain other primates, such as bushbabies and galagos, the potto and the angwantibo. In addition, there are apes – the chimpanzee and gorilla.

Hooved mammals are common in African forests. They include the okapi, bongo, water chevrotain, several duikers and giant forest hogs. Small mammals include elephant shrews, squirrels and scalytails. The forest hunters include the leopard, African golden cat, forest genet and slender mongoose.

Colobus monkey

Chimpanzee

Gorilla

Tree pangolin

Royal antelope

Bongo

Genet

Elephant shrew

Water chevrotain

Okapi

▲ WHERE DO FLYING
LEMURS LIVE?

Flying lemurs, or colugos, are found in the tropical forests of South-East Asia. These forests are also inhabited by a number of primates.

The name 'flying lemur' is misleading. This animal does not actually fly, and it is no relation of the true lemurs of Madagascar. However, flying lemurs are superb gliders and can glide from tree to tree with amazing accuracy. They have features somewhere between those of bats and insectivores, and are classified in a mammal order by themselves.

Flying lemurs are not the only gliders of these forests. There are also flying squirrels, flying frogs, flying lizards and even gliding snakes.

The Asian forests are the home of the primitive tree shrews and a number of primates. These include the tiny tarsiers and the lorises. The two main groups of monkey are the langurs and the macaques, and there are two kinds of ape – the gibbon and the orang-utan.

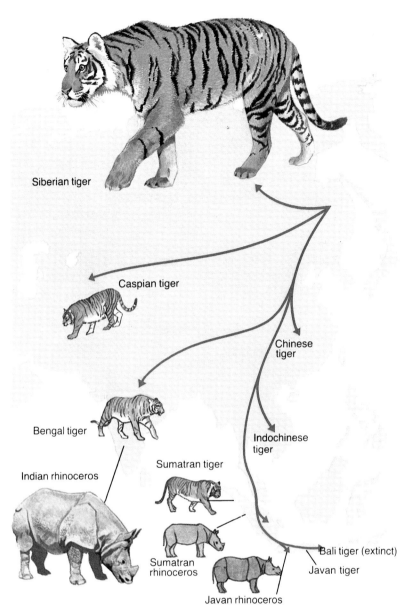

▲ WHERE DO TIGERS AND
RHINOCEROSES LIVE?

Rhinoceroses are found in Africa and South-East Asia. Tigers are found only in Asia.

Five species of rhinoceros exist today. Two of these, the black rhinoceros and the white rhinoceros, are found in Africa. Both African species have two horns.

The three one-horned species are found in India, Sumatra and Java. They are all in danger of extinction, but the most endangered is the Javan rhinoceros, which survives only in one small reserve.

The tiger is a highly adaptable animal. It originated in the cold north-east region of China. From there it spread northwards into the snowy wastes of Siberia, westwards to the Caspian Sea and southwards into the tropical rain forests of India and South-East Asia. Today naturalists recognize eight races of tiger. However, they differ only in their markings. Once all the races were widespread, but now they are all endangered.

Silvered langurs

Proboscis monkey

Mudskippers

▲ WHERE IS THE HOME OF THE ORANG-UTAN?

The orang-utan is found only in the rain forests of Sumatra and Borneo. It was once widespread throughout South-East Asia, but is now in danger of extinction because the rain forests are being cleared and young orang-utans are captured for zoos.

The name *orang-utan* means 'man of the woods'. Like humans, individual orang-utans are easy to identify by their facial features and expressions. However, the orang-utan is less closely related to humans than the chimpanzee or gorilla.

Like the gibbons, the other Asian apes, orang-utans are tree-living animals. They can swing from branch to branch or walk along branches with great ease.

Adult males live alone for most of the time. Their huge throat pouches are used to produce loud booming sounds. Females often travel about in small groups with their young. At night an orang-utan sleeps in a rough 'nest' in a tree.

▲ WHERE ARE MANGROVE FORESTS FOUND?

Mangrove swamps occur where rain forest borders the sea. Mangrove forests are found in many tropical parts of the world.

Along the coasts and estuaries of tropical rain forests, the rivers deposit a rich, fine silt which forms extensive mudflats in the tidal waters. Trees and shrubs take root in the mud. The most common tree is the mangrove. Many mangroves have stilt-like roots for support. Others have special breathing roots that stick out of the mud and take in oxygen (the mud contains very little oxygen). The tangled plant life of a mangrove swamp helps to bind the mud, and in doing so gradually reclaims new land from the sea.

Mangrove forests are extensive in South-East Asia. The forests of Borneo are the home of certain langurs, such as the dusky langur, the silver leaf monkey, the strange proboscis monkey and crab-eating macaques.

Little king bird
of paradise

Count Raggi's
bird of paradise

Greater bird of paradise

Red bird
of paradise

Wilson's bird
of paradise

◀ WHERE DO BIRDS OF
PARADISE LIVE?

**Birds of paradise are some of
the world's most colourful
and spectacular birds. Most
of the 43 species are found in
the forests of New Guinea.**

The ancestor of the bird of
paradise was probably a drab,
crow-like bird that made its
way to New Guinea from Asia.
Today, a few members of the
family are still rather drab, but
others are startlingly colourful.

As is the case with many
birds, it is the male bird of
paradise that is the most
splendid. Its bright colours
and long feathers are used to
attract a female mate. Display
techniques vary, enabling
females to recognize males of
their own species easily. Some
birds of paradise even display
upside down. After mating,
the females fly away to build
their nests and rear the young
on their own.

The feathers of these birds
were once much sought by
European hat-makers, and
thousands of birds were killed
each year. Today, however,
birds of paradise are protected.

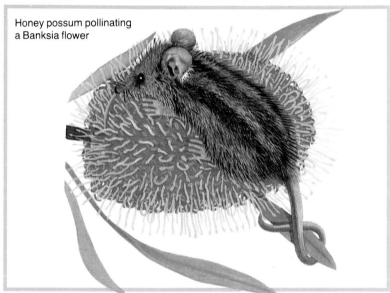

Honey possum pollinating
a Banksia flower

▲ WHERE ARE BANKSIAS
FOUND?

**The south-western corner of
Australia has a high rainfall
and luxuriant vegetation. It
is cut off from the rest of
Australia by the desert and is
the home of some unique
plants and animals. Among
these are the flowering trees
known as Banksias, and their
pollinators.**

Most brightly coloured flowers
are pollinated by insects. But
Banksia flowers are pollinated
by birds such as honeyeaters,
which visit the flowers to drink
nectar. Small marsupials such
as the honey possum also visit
these flowers. They use their
long tongues to probe deep
into the flowers. Pollen sticks
to the fur on their faces. This is
then carried to other flowers.

Other bird-pollinated plants
in this part of Australia include
certain eucalyptus trees which
are pollinated by parakeets. A
nectar-feeding parakeet has a
long tongue tipped with a
brush-like organ. The 'brush'
soaks up nectar and picks up
pollen as it is withdrawn from
the flower.

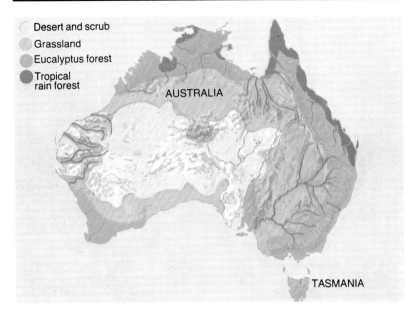

Desert and scrub
Grassland
Eucalyptus forest
Tropical rain forest

AUSTRALIA

TASMANIA

Pretty-faced wallaby

Red kangaroo

Koala

Tiger cat

Wombat

Tasmanian devil

Sugar glider

Tasmanian wolf

▲ WHAT DO MARSUPIALS EAT?

There are very few placental mammals in Australia. Instead, most Australian mammals are marsupials (pouched mammals). They occupy almost all the habitats that would normally be taken by placentals. Marsupials therefore range from peaceful grazers to fierce carnivores.

In the Americas, Europe and Asia, grassland and scrub are grazed by hooved mammals. There were no such mammals in Australia. Instead, kangaroos and wallabies became the grazers. They range from the large grey kangaroo and red kangaroo to the tiny rat kangaroo. Among this group there are also browsing forest animals, such as the tree kangaroo and the shrub wallaby.

There are no tree-living primates or rodents in Australia. Their habitats are taken by the phalangers and opossums. The cuscus, for example, is a monkey-like phalanger. Other phalangers and opossums resemble squirrels. Flying phalangers, such as the sugar glider, look exactly like flying squirrels. Most of these animals feed on plants but they also eat insects, eggs and even small birds. The koala eats the leaves of certain types of eucalyptus tree.

Rabbits and some small ground rodents have been introduced into Australia. Their marsupial equivalents, the wombat and the bandicoot, are now declining in numbers. Two other Australian ground-dwellers are the marsupial mole, which is almost identical to a placental mole, and the numbat, which is the equivalent of an anteater.

Marsupial carnivores include the dasyures, such as the tiger cat, and the eastern native cat, or quoll. These animals look more like mongooses than cats, but they are agile climbers and they stalk their prey. The so-called marsupial mice are the smallest carnivores. The largest are the Tasmanian wolf, or thylacine, and the Tasmanian devil, which eats carrion as well as live prey. Both these animals now live only in Tasmania, and the thylacine is probably extinct.

Himatione sanguinea

Vestiaria coccinea

Hemignathus procerus

Psittirostra cantans

▲ HOW MANY KINDS OF
HAWAIIAN HONEYCREEPER
ARE THERE?

**On the remote islands of
Hawaii honeycreepers have
become even more varied
than the Galapagos finches.
About 23 species evolved, of
which 14 still exist today.**

The ancestors of the Hawaiian
honeycreepers were probably
finch-like birds (possibly
tanagers) that managed to
make the 3500-kilometre
journey from North America.
The honeycreepers which
evolved from these travellers
vary in size and colouring, but
the main differences are in
their feeding habits – which
are indicated by the shapes of
their bills.

Some honeycreepers have
long, curved bills and brush-
tipped tongues for drinking
nectar. Others use their curved
bills to probe for insects.
Honeycreepers with shorter
bills use them as woodpeckers
do to chisel away at the bark of
trees to get at insects. Seed-
and fruit-eating honeycreepers
have short, stout bills like
those of finches.

▼ WHY ARE ISLAND
ANIMALS DIFFERENT FROM
OTHERS?

**New species evolve in
isolated places. Remote
islands with stable climates
provide ideal places for new
species to evolve.**

When a new island forms far
away from any large continent,
it takes time for animals to
colonize it. The few animals
that do arrive have to adapt to
their new surroundings. For
those that can adapt there are
tremendous advantages.

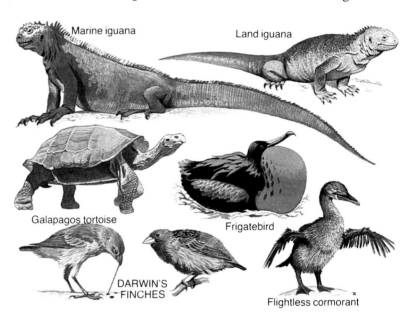

Marine iguana

Land iguana

Galapagos tortoise

Frigatebird

DARWIN'S
FINCHES

Flightless cormorant

▲ WHICH ANIMALS LIVE IN
THE GALAPAGOS ISLANDS?

**The Galapagos Islands were
formed about two million
years ago. Since that time
several unique species have
evolved there. As well as the
finches, there are giant
tortoises, marine iguanas
and flightless cormorants.**

A Galapagos giant tortoise can
measure over a metre in
length. At one time each island
had its own race of tortoise,
but during the 1600s and 1700s
visiting sailors killed them for

Unhindered by the animals
that formerly preyed on them
or competed with them for
food, they can take over all the
different types of habitat that
are so freely available.

This process is called
adaptive radiation and it can be
seen in the finches of the
Galapagos Islands. The
ancestors of these finches
probably flew in from South
America. Over a long period of
time they gave rise to the 15
different species that exist
today. Each one has evolved to
suit a particular type of habitat
and method of feeding.

food, and some races have
disappeared completely.

Iguanas probably arrived on
floating logs from South
America. Water and food are
not as easy to find on these
islands, and the iguanas
adapted in two ways. Today
there are land iguanas that feed
on fruit and cacti and marine
iguanas that feed on seaweed.

The islands provide nesting
sites for a number of sea-birds.
These include a flightless
cormorant, the Galapagos
penguin, and oceanic sea-birds
such as frigatebirds and
boobies.

146

▼ WHERE ARE MOST
FLIGHTLESS BIRDS FOUND?

Flightless birds tend to live where there are few, if any, predators. A large number of flightless birds are found in Australia and New Zealand.

One of the main advantages of being able to fly is the ability to escape from predators. However, for birds that evolved in places where there were no enemies, this ability became less necessary and many abandoned flight altogether.

Unfortunately, flightless birds are extremely vulnerable to introduced predators such as cats and foxes, and to other animals such as rats, which eat their eggs and compete with them for food. Many flightless birds have also been hunted by people. Some, such as the elephant bird of Madagascar, the moa of New Zealand, many flightless island rails, and the Mauritian dodo, are now extinct.

Several flightless birds do still exist in New Zealand. The three species of kiwi are nocturnal forest-dwellers, and

this has probably helped them to survive. The weka, one of the few remaining flightless rails, actually thrives on introduced animals: it eats rats and mice! On the other hand, the coot-like takahe (another member of the rail family) is in danger of extinction.

In Australia the common emu still exists in fairly large numbers, but it is the only survivor of several species of emu that lived there before the arrival of humans. Its close relatives, the cassowaries, are secretive forest-dwellers.

Emu

Cassowary

Weka

Kiwi

Takahe

► WHERE DO CRABS CLIMB
TREES?

Some island animals are particularly strange and unusual. The robber crabs that live on islands in the Indian and Pacific oceans are adept tree-climbers.

Crabs are usually thought of as sea creatures, but robber crabs and other land crabs are well-adapted for living on land. Although the larvae of such crabs live in the sea, an adult robber crab will drown if left in water for more than a day.

Robber crabs are expert at climbing trees. But why they do so is something of a mystery. It was once thought that they climbed coconut palms to dislodge coconuts, which they then cracked open and ate. However, a robber crab is quite unable to get inside a coconut. And, in fact, its main food is carrion: dead animal matter that is washed up on beaches. They do eat the flesh of coconuts, but only after the coconuts have been broken into by other animals. They also eat certain fruits.

147

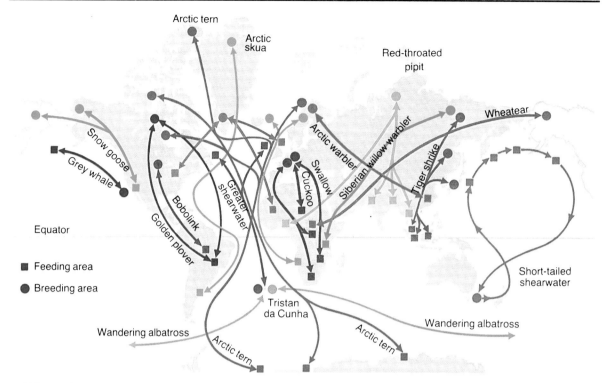

Arctic tern

Arctic skua

Red-throated pipit

Snow goose

Grey whale

Arctic warbler

Swallow

Siberian willow warbler

Cuckoo

Wheatear

Tiger shrike

Bobolink

Greater shearwater

Golden plover

Equator

■ Feeding area

● Breeding area

Tristan da Cunha

Short-tailed shearwater

Wandering albatross

Arctic tern

Arctic tern

Wandering albatross

▲ WHY DO BIRDS MIGRATE?

A migrating bird typically moves from a summer breeding area to a winter feeding area. The reasons for such migrations include the availability of food and avoiding extreme cold.

The migrations of northern birds may have started at the end of the last Ice Age. As the ice cap melted, some birds moved north in summer to take advantage of the food that became available. Each winter they retreated south again, but gradually their journeys became longer and longer.

The most northerly birds migrate south to avoid the Arctic winter. The Arctic tern covers the longest distance: it migrates all the way to the Antarctic. Farther south, the migratory birds are mostly insect-eaters that cannot find enough food in winter. Seed-eaters and omnivorous birds often remain in the same area all year.

▲ WHERE DO SHEARWATERS MIGRATE TO?

Shearwaters, or petrels, are sea-birds that breed in large colonies in the same place each year. Outside the breeding season some shearwaters make long journeys.

The Manx shearwater breeds only on certain European coasts. But during the remaining months of the year it wanders around the Atlantic Ocean. The greater shearwater breeds on the island of Tristan da Cunha between November and April, but spends July and August in the North Atlantic.

Between October and March, short-tailed shearwaters breed in thousands off the coasts of Tasmania and south-eastern Australia. But in April they begin a complete circuit of the Pacific Ocean. This migration enables them to take advantage of the abundant fish supplies of the North Pacific Ocean.

▲ WHY DO WHALES MIGRATE?

Most migratory animals breed in their northern range. But northern whales migrate south to breed in warmer waters. Southern whales migrate in the opposite direction.

The best-known whale migration is that of the California grey whale. This animal feeds all summer in the Bering Sea. Its autumn migration route follows the coast of North America to breeding lagoons off the coast of California.

Other migrating whales include the blue whale and the humpback whale. There are populations of these whales in both the northern and southern hemispheres. The northern populations move south to summer breeding grounds, and the southern populations move north. But because the seasons of the two hemispheres are different, the two populations never meet.

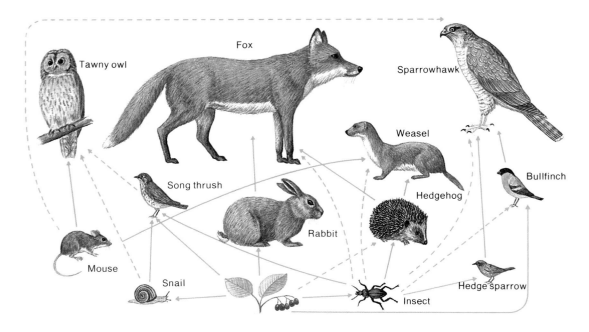

▲ WHO FEEDS ON WHAT?

Every animal and plant eats, or is eaten by, other living things. Together, a small group of living things form a food chain. Plants are eaten by plant-eating animals, which in turn are eaten by meat-eating animals. These meat-eaters may also be eaten.

A single food chain consists of a plant, a herbivore (plant-eating animal) and one or more carnivores (meat-eaters). However, a food chain rarely exists by itself. Most animals eat a variety of foods and may themselves be eaten by several predators. As a result they form part of a more complicated food web.

The illustration shows some of the animals that may be involved in a hedgerow community. The usual food eaten is shown by a solid line. Occasional food is shown by a dotted line. Plant-eaters, such as rabbits, voles, snails and insects feed on the leaves of plants. Some small mammals, birds and insects feed on the fruits and seeds. In turn, all these animals are preyed on by larger animals. At the top of the food web are the large predators, such as foxes, hawks and owls.

The chain does not really end there. Dead animals and plants are cleaned up by soil-dwellers such as earthworms, ground beetles and bacteria.

▶ WHY DO SOME PLANTS LOSE THEIR LEAVES IN AUTUMN?

A large number of trees shed their leaves in order to survive the cold during winter. They lie dormant for several months, avoiding water loss and frost damage.

In temperate regions of the world the soil is too cold during the winter months for most broadleaved trees to take up enough water. So to avoid losing water during the

Beech leaf (broadleaved)

Beech leaf in autumn

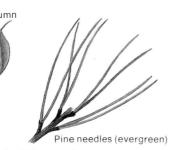

Pine needles (evergreen)

winter, these trees (known as deciduous trees) shed their leaves in autumn. Before they do so, however, the precious green chlorophyll is withdrawn. This leaves other pigments, such as yellows, oranges and reds, which give autumn leaves their familiar brilliant colours.

The evergreen trees of temperate regions are mostly conifers. They live in areas where water is scarce. They have thin, needle-like leaves that keep water loss to a minimum. So they can keep their leaves during the winter.

▶ WHAT ARE FLOWERS FOR?

Flowers produce seeds that can grow into new plants. They often have brightly coloured petals, which surround the male and female organs.

The parts of a flower all have important functions. They are held on a swollen base called the receptacle. The outer parts of the flower are green, leaf-like structures called sepals. They cover and protect the bud before the flower opens out. Inside the sepals are the petals. Brightly coloured petals attract insects or other animals to the flower.

The male organs are called stamens. Each one consists of an anther (four pollen-containing sacs) on the end of a long stalk or filament. The female organs are called carpels. Each one consists of an ovary and a pollen-receiving surface, or stigma, which is often on the end of a stalk, or style. The ovary contains one or more ovules, each of which has a female egg cell, or ovum, inside.

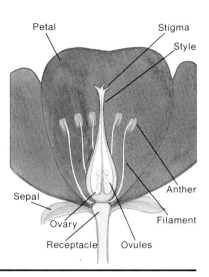

◀ WHY ARE INSECTS NECESSARY TO PLANTS?

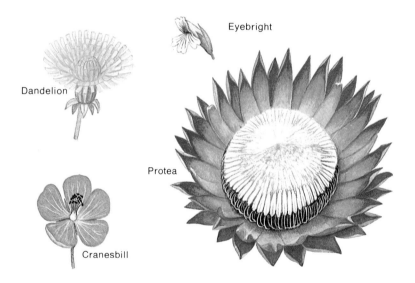

Eyebright

Dandelion

Protea

Cranesbill

▲ WHY DO FLOWERS HAVE BRIGHT COLOURS?

Transferring pollen from an anther to a stigma is called pollination. In many cases this is done by animals. To attract animals, flowers have bright colours and often produce nectar.

Several kinds of animal pollinate flowers, but the chief pollinators are insects which are attracted to the flowers by their colours and scents. Often there are lines and markings on the petals to guide insects towards the nectar (for example eyebright and cranesbill). Insect-pollinated flowers are usually blue, yellow, pink or white. However, the colours we see are not the same that insects see. To a bee, for example, red appears grey. But a bee can detect ultraviolet light. So a white or yellow flower probably looks blue to a bee.

In tropical and subtropical regions birds, bats, rodents and marsupials pollinate flowers. These flowers are often very brightly coloured. Protea, for example, is bird-pollinated.

Insects are useful to plants because they carry pollen from one flower to another. This kind of pollination produces the strongest plants.

Transferring pollen from an anther to a stigma in the same flower is called self-pollination. Transferring pollen from one flower to another is called cross-pollination. It is better for plants to be cross-pollinated, because this results in healthier offspring. Self-pollination does happen, but usually only if cross-pollination has failed.

Many insect-pollinated flowers have ingenious ways of preventing self-pollination. Sometimes the stamens and carpels ripen at different times. Some plants, such as the primrose, have more than one kind of flower in which the stamens and stigmas are in different places. Pea flowers have flaps that prevent insects from brushing pollen collected from a flower onto the stigma of the same flower.

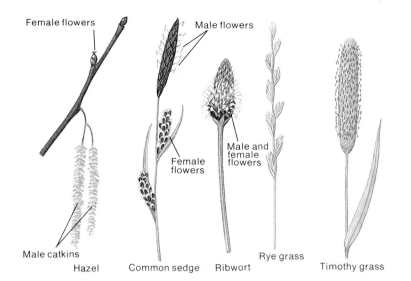

Female flowers

Male flowers

Female flowers

Male and female flowers

Male catkins

Hazel   Common sedge   Ribwort   Rye grass   Timothy grass

Wind pollination leaves a lot to chance. To make sure some pollen lands on the right stigmas, the anthers have to produce huge amounts.

A single rye flower produces about 50,000 grains of pollen and one silver birch catkin sheds over five million grains. Wind-pollinated plants produce their pollen in large stamens that hang out of the flowers. When they are ripe the anthers split open, shedding clouds of pollen into the air. Most of it is wasted, however. Only a small amount lands on the stigmas of female flowers. To increase their chances of catching pollen, female flowers often have large, feathery stigmas that act like nets.

In spite of the waste, wind pollination is very effective. Pollen is easily spread among the tall stems of grass plants that cover the ground. Wind-pollinated trees shed their pollen early in the year. At this time there are not many leaves to obstruct the pollen grains.

A number of plants are pollinated by wind. Such plants do not need large showy flowers to attract insects. Instead they have small flowers with tiny petals or none at all.

The largest group of wind-pollinated plants is the grass family. There are about 10,000 species and these include the cereals we grow for food, such as wheat, rice and maize. Grass flowers have no petals, but are protected by tiny leaf-like structures.

Other wind-pollinated plants include sedges, rushes and plantains. Some trees and shrubs are also pollinated by wind. These include hazel, birches, alders and willows. To ensure cross-pollination, these trees produce separate male and female flowers. Willows even have separate male and female trees. The male flowers are produced in bunches, known as catkins. The female flowers are produced in smaller catkins or cone-like structures.

Mosses and ferns do not produce seeds. Instead they reproduce by means of spores.

A moss plant develops sex cells amongst the leaves of its small shoots. The male cells reach female cells by swimming through the thin film of water on the leaves.

However, the fertilized female cell does not develop either into a seed or directly into a new moss plant. Instead it develops into a stalked capsule, which contains thousands of tiny spores. When the capsule is ripe, the spores are released. Each one is capable of producing at least one new moss plant. The spores of ferns develop on the leaves of the adult plant. When it lands on the ground, a spore develops into a tiny heart-shaped structure called a prothallus. This produces male and female cells. Only the tiny prothallus has to be wet. The adult fern can live in much drier conditions.

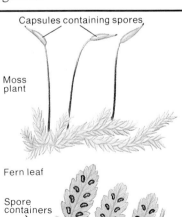

Capsules containing spores

Moss plant

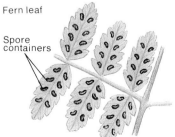

Fern leaf

Spore containers

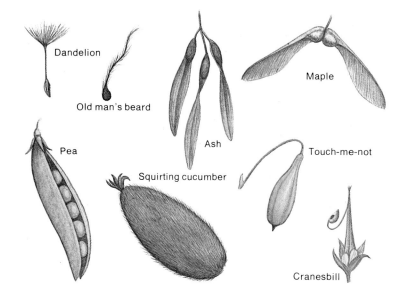

Using the wind is a useful way of spreading seeds. Some seeds are light enough by themselves. Others are helped by wings or parachute-like tufts of hair.

Many seeds are dispersed by wind, and a number of them have specially designed fruits. The fruits of dandelions, thistles and many other members of the daisy family are crowned with hairy plumes that act as parachutes. The seeds of willowherbs and willows also have plumes like this. The fruits of old man's beard have hairy 'tails' that help the wind to carry them through the air.

The most spectacular winged fruits are found on trees. A birch fruit has a pair of small wings with the seed in between. An ash fruit forms a long, aerodynamic wing with the seed at one end. Maple trees have two-seeded, double-winged fruits that spin like helicopter blades as they fall to the ground.

▲ WHICH FRUITS EXPLODE?

One way of dispersing seeds is to hurl them away from the parent plant. Several plants have fruits that burst violently.

Most exploding fruits are capsules, pods or similar structures. They gradually lose water and, when they are dry, they split apart, throwing out the seeds with some force. For example, when the fruits of cranesbills and other geraniums break open, the seeds are hurled out on the ends of spring-like fibres.

Laburnum and many other members of the pea family produce their seeds in long pods. When a laburnum pod dries out it breaks open with a loud pop. Both halves twist suddenly, flinging the seeds out.

Some exploding fruits swell up with water. Touch-me-not balsam fruits become so full that they explode at the slightest touch. The squirting cucumber shoots out its seeds in a jet of water.

▶ WHICH FRUITS ARE CARRIED BY ANIMALS?

Many plants use animals as seed-carriers. Animal-dispersed seeds include those found in juicy fruits and hooked fruits.

Animals may carry fruits a long way from the parent plant. Juicy fruits, such as those of blackberry and hawthorn, provide birds and small rodents with tempting meals. The tough seeds are eaten with the fruit, but they pass through unharmed.

Some plants produce fruits

Blackberries

Acorns

Burdock

Goosegrass

with tiny hooks on them. Goosegrass and burdock are common examples.

Some animals disperse fruits by forgetting about them! Squirrels collect and store away oak acorns and hazel nuts. During the winter

they often forget about some of their food stores.

Sometimes even insects disperse seeds. Snowdrop and sweet violet seeds are carried away by ants, who are rewarded by juice from an oily knob on each seed.

The lords and ladies plant makes sure that it is cross-pollinated. Flies are attracted by the rotten smell and fall inside the sheath. They pollinate the female flowers. Then they are showered with pollen and released.

Flies investigating the foul-smelling spike, or spadix, of the lords and ladies plant land on the inside of the green

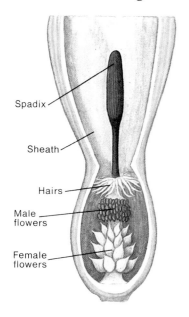

Spadix

Sheath

Hairs

Male flowers

Female flowers

Some plants can produce new plants without using flowers. They grow the new plants from their leaves or stems. Bulbs, corms and rhizomes are all kinds of stem used to produce new plants.

A bulb is a very short stem with closely-packed, fleshy food-storing leaves. New bulbs are formed in between the base of the leaves.

A corm is a swollen food-

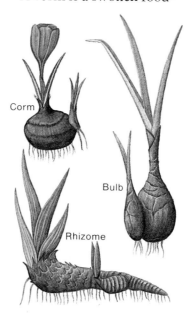

Corm

Bulb

Rhizome

Some plants attract insect pollinators in an unusual way. Instead of smelling sweetly of scent, they stink like rotting meat. This attracts pollinating flies.

One of the best known stinking flowers is that of the Malayan plant *Rafflesia*. It is also the world's largest flower and flies are attracted by its smell and its dark red-brown petals.

The African stapeliads also produce stinking flowers,

Rafflesia

sheath. This has a slippery surface and the flies slide down past a fringe of stiff, downward-pointing hairs.

The flies remain at the bottom of the trap all night. First they crawl over the female flowers, pollinating them with pollen brought from other plants. The stigmas then wither and the stamens of the male flowers ripen and burst, scattering pollen over the flies. Next morning, the slippery surface inside the sheath falls away, the downward-pointing hairs wither, and the flies escape.

storing stem. A new corm develops at the base of the flowering shoot, above the old corm, which dies.

Rhizomes are stems that grow horizontally under-ground, putting up shoots at intervals. Some plants, such as couch grass, have long, thin rhizomes. Others, such as irises, have thick rhizomes that act as food stores. Some plants, like the potato, have long thin rhizomes that swell in certain places into large tubers. These act as food stores. New shoots develop from buds on the tubers.

known as carrion flowers. Blow-flies are sometimes so convinced that a flower really is rotting meat that they lay their eggs on it. But when the maggots hatch out they die, because there is actually nothing for them to feed on.

The lords and ladies plant also attracts flies by the smell given out by the spike that sticks out of the top. One of the lords and ladies' tropical relatives stands two metres high and gives out a smell like rotten fish.

153

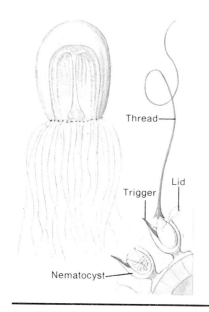

Thread

Lid

Trigger

Nematocyst

◀ WHY DO JELLYFISH STING?

All animals have their own ways of feeding. Jellyfish and their relatives, such as sea anemones, catch their prey with their tentacles. These are often armed with poisonous stings.

The tentacles of a jellyfish are covered in tiny cells called cnidoblasts. Each one produces a structure called a nematocyst. This consists of a hollow thread, a lid and a trigger hair. When a prey animal comes close, it stimulates the trigger hair. The lid flies open and the thread shoots out.

There are several different kinds of nematocyst. Some have long, barbed threads that become entangled with the prey. Others have sticky threads. And some have shorter, tougher threads that can pierce the victim. Poison is then injected through the hollow thread and the prey is paralyzed.

Once the prey is caught, the jellyfish pushes it into its mouth with its tentacles.

▶ WHAT DO LIMPETS EAT?

Limpets and many other shellfish feed on tiny seaweeds, or algae. They wander over the rocks, using a rasp-like 'tongue' to scrape off the algae as they go.

At low tide limpets can be found clinging tightly to the rocks. To make a perfect airtight fit, the limpet grinds a shallow cavity into the rock. The shell fits exactly into this cavity, and the limpet returns to this spot each time the tide goes out.

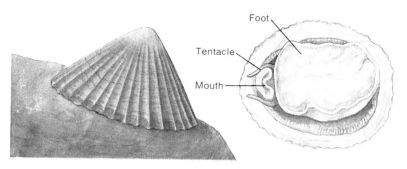

Foot

Tentacle

Mouth

At high tide, when the limpet is underwater, it leaves its base and wanders over the rock looking for food. It moves by a rippling action of its large foot. Inside its mouth is a small sac that contains a kind of rasping 'tongue' called a radula. It is a long membrane attached to the base of the sac and it has many rows of curved teeth. When the limpet feeds, it pushes the radula out of its mouth and scrapes off the tiny algae that live on the rock.

◀ WHY DOES A SPIDER BUILD A WEB?

Many spiders catch their prey in silken webs. An insect that blunders into one of these webs finds it difficult to escape.

There are two main kinds of web-building spider. Some build shapeless sheetwebs, like the familiar cobweb of the house spider. Others, such as the garden spider, build beautiful, cartwheel-like orbwebs.

A sheetweb spider builds 'trip-wires' into its web and hides, often in a silk tunnel, near the edge. An insect that lands on the web stumbles and loses its balance. Before it can fly away again, the spider rushes out and seizes it.

The webs of orbweb spiders are sticky. A small insect that flies into one of these cannot escape. Its struggles alert the spider.

Most spiders catch insects in their webs. But some large tropical spiders build webs that can trap small birds.

◀ WHY DO WASPS STING?

Wasps use their stings to kill other insects, which they feed to their grubs. They only sting people when they are annoyed or become trapped.

Adult wasps feed on nectar, fruit and tree sap. But their grubs, or larvae, feed on the bodies of other insects.

In a colony of social wasps the adult workers go out hunting. When an insect is caught it is killed by the wasp's sting. Then it is taken back to the nest and chewed up. Its juices are fed to the larvae.

Solitary wasps, such as the sand wasp shown here, also hunt and sting live food for their larvae. The prey is paralyzed and dragged back to the wasp's burrow. Then the wasp lays an egg. When the larva hatches out, it feeds on the prey's body. Most solitary wasps hunt other insects, such as caterpillars. But some tropical wasps prey on large spiders.

A wasp's sting is actually a modified egg-laying organ.

▶ WHY DO LEAFCUTTER ANTS CUT LEAVES?

Leafcutter ants are 'farmers'. They use the leaves they cut up to grow a crop of fungus, which supplies them with food.

Leafcutter ants can cut and carry pieces of leaf many times their own size. They are tropical ants that live in huge colonies. Workers cut up hundreds of plant leaves and carry the pieces back to the nest.

Inside the nest smaller workers chew up the leaves

into a kind of compost. They use this in special chambers to grow a special kind of fungus. The ants feed on the swollen juicy branches that the fungus produces. The fungus does not grow anywhere else and the ants tend it with great care. They weed out other fungi that may swamp it. They feed it with their droppings and treat it with their saliva to kill off any bacteria.

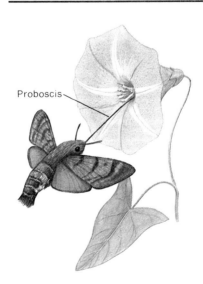

Proboscis

◀ WHICH INSECTS DRINK THROUGH STRAWS?

Many insects have 'straws' for sucking up liquids. The longest 'straws' are owned by some moths and butterflies.

Insects that suck up liquids have mouthparts that are extended into long tubes. Sucking insects include aphids, which have a sharp tube for piercing plant stems and sucking out sap. Mosquitoes pierce animal skin to suck up blood. A housefly has a tube with a sponge-like organ on the end for sucking up liquid.

The best 'straws', or proboscis, are found in insects that drink nectar from flowers. The long proboscis of a butterfly is normally kept coiled up and is extended only when in use. The convolvulus hawk moth has a proboscis 14 centimetres long for reaching deep into certain kinds of flower. One South American moth has a proboscis 30 centimetres long.

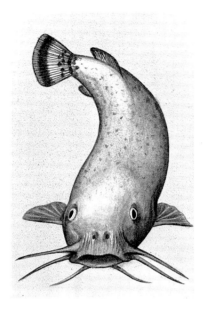

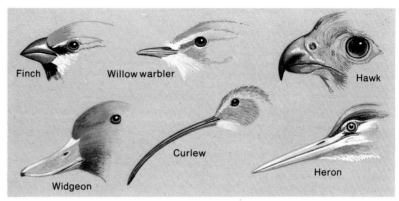

Finch Willow warbler Hawk Curlew Heron Widgeon

▲ WHICH FISHES KILL WITH ELECTRICITY?

Some fishes kill or stun their prey with electric shocks. Such fishes include the electric catfish, electric rays and the powerful electric eel.

The electric catfish (shown here) uses electrical discharges to stun and capture other fish and to warn off enemies. Its electric organ lies just under the skin and covers its body and part of the tail. A large catfish may produce 350 volts.

Electric rays are found in the warmer parts of the Atlantic Ocean. An electric ray has two separate electric organs, one on each side of the head. It catches a fish by pouncing on it, wrapping its fins around it and stunning it with electric shocks. Most electric rays produce about 50 volts.

The most powerful electric fish is the electric eel of South America. Its electric organ is in its tail and can produce 550 volts. This stuns or kills nearby fishes. Even a horse may be stunned by this eel.

▲ HOW DO BIRDS FEED?

Birds may feed on insects, seeds, fishes, plants and small animals. You can often tell which food a bird prefers by looking at its beak.

Many birds that feed in similar ways have similar beaks. Birds of prey, such as hawks, have hooked beaks for tearing flesh. Seed-eating birds, such as finches, usually have short, conical beaks.

Some birds have very specialized beaks. The flat beak of a widgeon is used for cropping grass. A heron uses its dagger-like beak for spearing fish. Long beaks (for example, the curlew) are often used for probing, either in the ground for worms or in tree bark for insects. Willow warblers and swifts are insect-eaters.

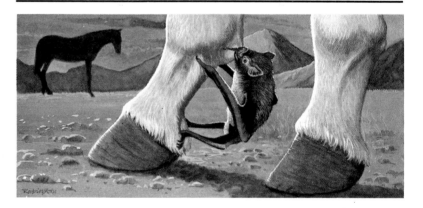

▲ DO VAMPIRES SUCK BLOOD?

Vampire bats are not the man-sized creatures seen in horror films. But these small mammals do drink the blood of other mammals, including humans.

Vampire bats are found only in Central and South America. They are small animals, no more than six to nine centimetres long.

Vampires feed at night. Common vampire bats suck the blood of mammals, such as horses and cattle. A vampire approaches its prey quietly, while the animal is asleep. With razor-sharp teeth it cuts away a small piece of skin, usually on the neck or leg of the animal. Its saliva contains a chemical that stops blood clotting. The vampire then sucks up the blood as it oozes from the wound.

Bears eat all kinds of things and most bears will eat honey when they can find it. The sun bear of southeast Asia is very fond of honey and is often called the honey bear.

Like Pooh Bear, nearly all bears are partial to a meal of honey. A bear will raid a nest of wild bees, tearing open the nest with its claws and licking out the honey with its long tongue. A sun bear will tear open a tree trunk to get at a nest inside.

Although bears belong to

the mammal order Carnivora (which means 'flesh-eaters'), they are actually omnivorous, that is, they eat all kinds of food. They like berries and other fruits and catch many kinds of small animals such as rodents, lizards, birds and insects.

A bear will even stand in a stream and catch fish, either by flipping them out on to the bank or by seizing them in the water. Some bears are experts at this.

An elephant's trunk is actually a combination of its nose and upper lip. It is used for many purposes, including feeding and drinking. Elephants acquired this useful 'tool' about 25 million years ago through evolution.

The ancestors of elephants were like large pigs. Gradually, they grew larger, but they had to develop long, sturdy legs. They also developed tusks and large, heavy heads. A heavy head cannot be carried on a long neck, so elephants need long trunks to reach their food.

An elephant uses its long, snake-like trunk for carrying food and water to its mouth and for spraying its body with water or dust. The trunk can be used very delicately – an elephant can pick up an object as small as a pea. It is also an efficient scent-detector, and elephants can often be seen with trunks raised, sniffing the scents in the air.

A giraffe's long neck and legs enable it to eat the leaves from branches that are far above the reach of other browsing animals. It can also see predators easily.

The giraffe is the world's tallest animal. An old male may reach a height of about five and a half metres. Being able to browse high in the trees and bushes is a great advantage to a giraffe. It has no competition from other browsing animals. And, as its eyes are so far above the ground, it can easily see predators long before they can get close enough to attack.

The disadvantage of long legs and a long neck is that a giraffe has to stretch a long way down to drink. However, it manages this quite well by splaying its front legs apart. A system of blood reservoirs and valves in its arteries prevents the giraffe from suffering a rush of blood to the head.

159

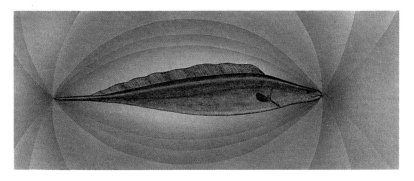

▲ WHICH FISHES 'SEE' WITH ELECTRICITY?

Some fishes that live in tropical rivers have little use for eyes because the water is too murky.

Instead they send out electric pulses and 'see' by detecting how the pulses are altered.

Fishes that navigate using electricity include the knife

fishes of Africa, Asia and South America and the Nile fish of Africa. A Nile fish has a weak electric organ on its tail. This sends out a stream of electric pulses that form an electric field around the body (shown here). The pulses are picked up by special sense organs in the fish's head. Another fish or any obstruction nearby alters the pulses and the sense organs detect the change.

With this system of electric pulses a Nile fish can 'see' behind as well as it can to the front.

▶ WHY DO SOME ANIMALS HAVE NO EYES?

Animals without eyes live in dark places, such as caves. There, because there is no light to see by, sight is useless.

There are several species of blind cave fishes around the world. Their young often begin life with normal eyes, which then become useless as the fishes grow. In some species the remains of the eyes become covered with skin. Cave fishes find their way

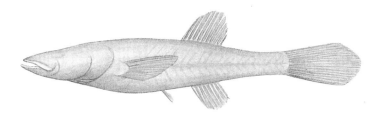

about by detecting pressure changes in the water around them. All fishes can do this, but in cave fishes the detection system is very highly developed. Some cave fishes explore their surroundings using taste buds on their lips.

Other blind cave dwellers

include a number of beetles and the olm, a blind salamander. A young olm is black and has well-developed eyes. But as it grows older, its eyes become useless and it loses its pigment, becoming pink. Olms probably find prey animals by sensing the vibrations they make.

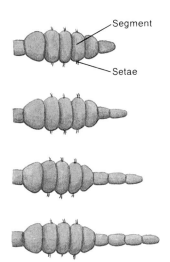

Segment

Setae

◀ HOW DOES A WORM HOLD ON?

An earthworm has no legs. But it does have tiny bristles that dig into the soil and help the worm to burrow.

On each segment of an earthworm's body there are four pairs of small bristles, or setae. When a segment shortens, it also expands and the setae are pushed outwards. When the segment lengthens, the setae are withdrawn. The setae of

several segments together give the worm a firm grip.

The setae are mainly used in burrowing through the soil. An earthworm moves forward by first shortening and expanding the segments near its head. Then these segments are lengthened, one by one, and segments farther back are shortened. So a wave of 'shortening' seems to travel down the worm. As each segment shortens, its setae grip the sides of the burrow, allowing the lengthened segments in front to push forward.

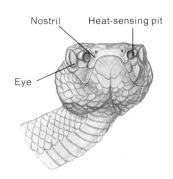

Nostril   Heat-sensing pit

Eye

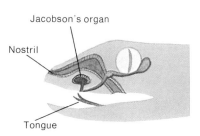

Jacobson's organ

Nostril

Tongue

A snake 'tastes' the air by using a special organ in its mouth. It uses its flickering tongue to carry a stream of air samples back to this organ.

A snake's sense of smell is helped by a pair of special organs called Jacobson's organs. These are sensory sacs that lie side by side and open into the roof of the mouth.

When the snake's forked tongue flicks out of the mouth, it picks up chemical particles from the air. Inside the mouth the tips of the tongue are pushed into the Jacobson's organs which

'taste' the chemicals.

Some snakes, such as pit vipers and rattlesnakes, can also detect heat. They have special heat-sensing pits between their eyes and nostrils.

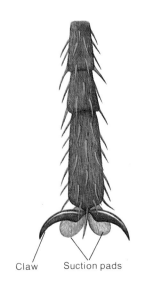

Claw   Suction pads

▲ HOW DOES A FLY WALK
UPSIDE DOWN?

A fly can walk easily up a wall or across a ceiling because it has claws and suction pads on its feet.

The legs of all arthropods (the group that includes insects, spiders and crabs) are made up of several jointed segments. On the last segment of each leg a housefly has a pair of claws and two suction pads. These enable the fly to walk across almost any surface, even upside down.

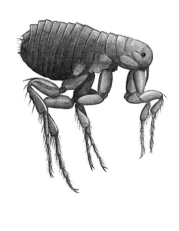

For flying a housefly has a single pair of wings. Instead of hindwings it has a pair of club-like organs, called halteres. These vibrate rapidly when the insect is flying and act like gyroscopes to keep it stable. They also enable the fly to change direction suddenly. So it can make sharp, right-angle turns in mid-flight. And they help in landing. A fly approaches a ceiling flying in a normal, upright position. At the last moment, it performs a rapid backward half-somersault and lands upside down.

◀ HOW HIGH CAN A FLEA
JUMP?

Fleas are tiny parasites with incredibly powerful hind legs. A flea can jump over a hundred times its own height. This is very useful when transferring from one animal host to another.

Fleas live in the fur or hair of animals. Their flattened bodies allow them to move between the hairs. They have no wings. Instead they have large hind legs for jumping.

A flea is less than one and a half millimetres long. But in one leap it can travel a distance of over 300 millimetres. And it can jump to a height of 190 millimetres. This is about the same as a human jumping to the top of a 65-storey office block.

To achieve this feat, a flea has very powerful hind leg muscles and tendons. In addition, the jumping apparatus of the flea has a piece of rubber-like material called resilin. When this is compressed and suddenly released, it produces a tremendous thrust.

161

▶ WHY DO SOME FISHES CLEAN OTHERS?

Cleaner fishes and their clients have an arrangement that is good for both of them. The cleaner fish gets food and the clients lose their parasites and other unwanted material. This partnership, where both sides benefit, is called a symbiosis.

A cleaner fish feeds on the tiny parasites that infest other fishes. However, it is quite a small fish and its clients may be large carnivores. To make sure that it does not get eaten, it has distinctive dark stripes. And before starting to clean, the cleaner fish makes sure that it will be accepted by performing a special kind of 'dance' in front of the client.

Often the client makes movements that show which parts of its body need cleaning. The cleaner fish then approaches and picks off parasites, dead skin and other debris from outside the clients body and inside its mouth and gills.

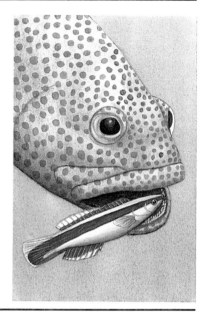

▲ WHY DO ANIMALS HIBERNATE?

Hibernation is a kind of deep winter 'sleep'. Animals hibernate to survive this cold period, when there is little or no food for them to eat.

Many animals hibernate during the winter. Some insects hide themselves away in nooks and crannies. Snails 'sleep' tucked up in their shells. Snakes, lizards, frogs and salamanders bury themselves in soil or mud.

A few birds, such as the poorwills of North America, hibernate. And a number of mammals, such as bears, hedgehogs, dormice and bats, go into a deep winter 'sleep'.

Hibernation begins as the days get shorter and the temperature drops. Mammals eat a lot of food before hibernating. They store it as fat, which their body processes use up very slowly while they are asleep.

▶ WHY DO A FISH AND A SHRIMP SHARE A HOME?

Some animals benefit each other by sharing a burrow or a nest. In the case of the *Alpheus* shrimp and the stargazer goby, the shrimp digs the burrow and the goby acts as sentry.

Alpheus shrimps dig burrows in the sand. There is usually a pair of shrimps in each burrow. They also share their home with a stargazer goby.

During the night both shrimps and goby rest in the burrow. During the day the goby places itself just outside the burrow, keeping watch for predators. The shrimps only feed when the goby is on sentry duty. As a shrimp feeds, it keeps one antenna touching the fish's tail. At the first sign of trouble, the fish flicks its tail and both animals retreat.

The goby cannot dig, so it benefits by getting a home. The shrimp's senses are not as good as the goby's, so it benefits by getting an early warning system.

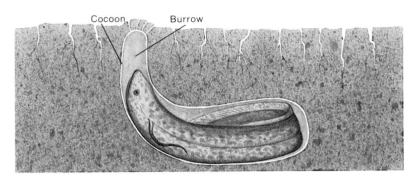

Cocoon   Burrow

In dry weather a lungfish burrows into the mud. There it survives the

drought in a state of deep 'summer sleep' called aestivation.

As their streams dry up, some lungfishes tunnel into the mud. Each lungfish makes

itself a burrow with a hole or a plug of porous mud at the top. Inside the burrow it produces a large quantity of mucus. This hardens into a cocoon that stops the fish drying up.

A lungfish usually breathes air and it continues to get air through the hole at the top of the burrow. Its body processes slow down and it lives by absorbing some of its own muscle tissue. In this way it survives until the rains return and its stream fills up again. African lungfishes have survived embedded in dried mud for over four years.

Cuckoos are parasitic birds. They lay their eggs in the nests of other birds and let the other parents, or hosts, raise their young for them. The host parents' eggs and young are thrown out of the nest.

After mating, a female cuckoo keeps watch for small birds building their nests. She selects a nest in which one or more eggs has been laid. While the parents are away, she quickly flies down,

removes one egg and replaces it with one of her own. Common cuckoos lay their eggs in the nests of such birds as reed warblers, dunnocks and meadow pipits.

The cuckoo's egg is looked after by the host parents. But after it has hatched, the young chick pushes out the remaining eggs and any other chicks that have already hatched. The young cuckoo grows rapidly and soon becomes much larger than its foster parents. But they continue to feed the monster chick.

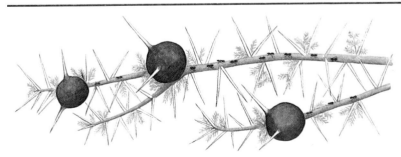

A whistling thorn has an armoury of sharp spikes to keep large, plant-eating animals away. But it also provides homes for fierce

ants, which keep off plant-eating insects.

A browsing animal that dares to try and eat the leaves of a whistling thorn is attacked by a horde of biting, stinging ants. The ants make their

homes in the large swollen bulbs that develop at the bases of the thorns. To build their nests, the ants bore into the bulbs and dig out the material inside.

The ants defend the tree from caterpillars, aphids and all other plant-eating animals. They are rewarded for defending the plant. The tips of the leaves grow small sausage-shaped 'food-bodies', which are harvested and carried away by the ants. And the leaf stalks grow special nectaries, which provide the ants with a sugary drink.

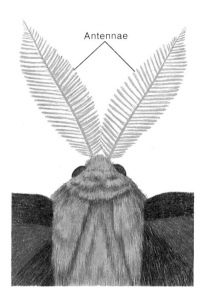

Antennae

Moths often have large, feathery antennae. Using these, a male moth can detect the scent of a female several kilometres away.

Moths are mostly night-flying insects. So sight is not very useful in finding a mate. However, they have an amazing sense of smell. A male emperor moth can detect a female 11 kilometres away upwind.

Female moths produce special chemicals to attract males. They can even 'call' to males by inflating their scent glands and producing extra scent. The scent particles drift down-wind, spreading out in a plume.

The feather-like antennae of male moths have many highly sensitive scent receptors. And the antennae are spread out to catch as many scent particles as possible. Some moths, such as the silk moths, have massive antennae that can detect even the faintest trace of a female's scent.

A queen termite is a huge egg-laying machine. All she can do is lay eggs, which she does at the rate of more than one a minute.

Termites live in large colonies. Some build huge, towering nests. At the centre of the nest lies the queen with her smaller king.

A mature queen has an enormously bloated body, up to 19 millimetres long, that

serves as an egg-producing factory. At times she can produce over 30 eggs in a minute. She cannot move and has to be fed and tended by her workers.

A termite queen starts her life as a winged reproductive female. With many other winged females and males, she flies from the nest in which she was raised. When she lands, she mates with a winged male. Their wings drop off and together they found a new colony. The queen may live for over 20 years.

A swarm of bees consists of a queen surrounded by a large number of workers and a few drones. They have left their old, over-

crowded nest to found a new colony.

In late summer a colony of bees may contain over 60,000 workers and the nest may be overcrowded. At this stage new queens are produced together with a number of fertile males, or drones.

When the first new queen emerges, she usually kills the other queen larvae. Then she flies off, pursued by a number of drones. She mates with one of them and then returns.

If the existing queen is old, she dies when the new queen returns. On the other hand, if the existing queen is still young, she leaves her over-crowded nest, usually before the new queen hatches. She takes with her a swarm of workers and drones and they found a new colony.

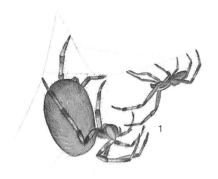

WHICH MALES MUST BEWARE?

Some spiders and insects are so ferocious that the males must be careful how they approach their much larger females.

Black widow spiders get their name from the reputation of the females. They are said to eat their mates after mating. But this may not be entirely true.

Male diadem spiders are much smaller than the females, so they do have to approach with some caution (1). If they are careless they may be mistaken for prey. Usually, however, a male mates successfully, and lives to mate again. Just occasionally, when a male is exhausted after several matings, he makes the wrong signals and is devoured (2).

Male mantids, on the other hand, stand no chance. A male approaches a female very slowly and cautiously. At the last moment he jumps onto the female and mates with her. But within a few seconds she bites his head off and proceeds to eat him.

WHY DO STICKLEBACKS CHANGE COLOUR?

A male stickleback puts on his 'wedding' colours to attract a female to his nest. He encourages her to lay her eggs, which he fertilizes and tends.

In spring, as a male stickleback begins to choose and defend a territory, his belly turns bright red. This is a warning to other males to keep out. He builds a nest of weed glued together in a shallow pit. Then his back turns bright blue to attract females.

When he has gained a female's attention, the male 'dances' under her belly and shows her the way into his nest. Once she is inside, he prods her tail to encourage her to lay eggs. After she leaves, he fertilizes the eggs.

The male tends the eggs. When they hatch, he guards the young until they can fend for themselves.

WHY DO BIRDS SING?

A bird usually sings to stake out and defend its territory or to attract a mate.

Most birds begin to sing just before dawn. They sing to advertise their presence. In spring, many birds continue to sing all day. A yellow-hammer may repeat its 'little-bit-of-bread-and-no-cheese' over a thousand times before nightfall.

Birds can vary their songs. The song of a chaffinch has six possible variations. The chaffinch has 13 other calls. These may be used to tell of such things as the location of food or a good nesting site. Many birds sound an alarm. And different alarm calls can tell other birds whether the danger is in the air, in a tree or on the ground. Jays have several different alarm calls and can sometimes signal exactly which predator is nearby.

▶ WHY DO GREBES DANCE?

Grebes and many other birds perform ritual courtship displays before mating. It is a form of 'language' that birds use to attract mates of their own species.

Courtship displays have evolved over millions of years. They make sure that males and females of different bird species do not mate. If they did they would produce sterile eggs. Courtship is a special 'language'. A bird can indicate its species, its sex, where its territory is, when it is ready to mate and where there is a possible nesting site.

Grebes have several courtship dances. One of these is the 'head-shaking ceremony', in which the birds face each other and shake their heads from side to side. After head shaking, the birds may dive down to collect weed. Then they perform a 'penguin dance', in which they rise out of the water breast to breast and sway their weed-filled beaks from side to side.

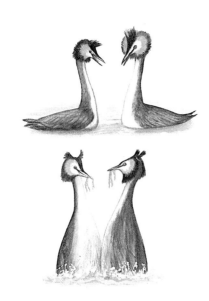

▲ WHICH BIRD IS THE GREATEST WOOER?

A male bower bird goes to great lengths to attract a mate. He builds a bower, decorates it and entices a female into it.

The satin bower bird of Australia builds his bower during the summer. Using sticks, he constructs a platform and two thick 'walls' on the ground. Sometimes he uses a 'brush' made of fibres to paint the walls with the juice of berries or a mixture of saliva and charcoal.

At one end of the bower the male decorates a display ground with brightly coloured objects. These may be feathers, flowers, insect wings, berries and even man-made objects, such as tinfoil and bottle tops.

Eventually, a female comes to the bower and the male displays and calls to her. She enters the bower and, after she has rearranged some of the twigs, the birds mate. Then the female flies away and makes her own nest in a tree.

◀ WHICH BIRDS BUILD APARTMENT BLOCKS?

Weaver birds build elaborate, cosy nests. Many weavers live in colonies, and social weavers build huge communal nests in trees.

A weaver bird builds its nest high in the trees, usually suspended from a twig to help keep predators out. Generally, the male builds the nest. He weaves grass and strips of leaf into a hollow ball with a small entrance. The baya weaver of Malaya has a very neat nest with a long, downward-pointing tube as an entrance.

The social weavers of southern Africa build huge communal nests that may measure over four and a half metres across. They share the work of building a large 'thatched roof'. Then each pair builds a flask-shaped nest underneath. The 'apartment block' may be used again and again. Some colonies may be 100 years old.

▶ WHY DO MARSUPIALS HAVE POUCHES?

Marsupials, such as kangaroos and koalas, produce their young at a very early stage of development. The young crawl into their mothers' pouches, where they continue to develop in safety.

Most mammals nourish their developing young by means of a placenta. This is an organ that forms in the mother's womb and carries food and oxygen to the young. Most marsupials have no placenta and the young are born much earlier.

A young kangaroo is born 33 days after mating. It crawls, completely unaided, up through its mother's fur and into her pouch. There it fastens onto one of the nipples.

Two days later, the mother mates again. But the development of the second offspring is delayed. It is not born until seven months later. By this time the first offspring has left the pouch and only returns to it occasionally.

Kangaroos and koalas have pouches that open to the front. Burrowing marsupials, such as bandicoots, have pouches that open to the rear, so that soil does not enter as they dig.

▶ WHY DO BEAVERS BUILD DAMS?

A family of beavers build a lodge with underwater entrances to keep out predators. And to make sure that the water stays at the right level, they construct one or more dams.

A beaver lodge is built on an island of twigs, stones and mud just above the level of the beaver pond. Over this there is a dome of sticks and grass that is carefully plastered with mud. A small area at the top is left unplastered and this provides the chamber inside with ventilation.

A lodge built in a natural pond would flood during the rainy season and have its entrances exposed during the dry season. To avoid these problems a beaver family creates its own pond by building a dam downstream. Other dams may also be built upstream and below the main

dam. The dams are built using large, felled trees, boulders and small saplings. To seal a dam, beavers use sticks, leaves and mud.

Beavers work hard on their dams, heaving every tree and boulder into place. A dam rarely fails, partly because it is constantly being repaired.

Fangs

All spiders kill their prey by injecting them with poison. But only a few spiders are actually poisonous enough to cause large animals much harm.

A spider's jaws are equipped with a powerful pair of fangs. These are used to inject venom into its prey to kill it. So, as far as prey animals (mostly insects) are concerned, all spiders are poisonous.

However, few spiders have much effect on humans. A garden spider will sometimes bite. But such a bite is, at most, only mildly painful. Even one of the huge bird-eating spiders of South America has a bite no worse than a bee sting.

A few spiders are dangerous. One of the most notorious is the black widow spider. A bite from a European black widow can cause severe illness. And in North America black widow bites have proved fatal on a few occasions.

Many antelopes, especially gazelles, leap high in the air. Sometimes they appear just to be playing. But they also leap to warn other antelopes that a predator is near.

The springbok is so called because of its ability to leap. When a grazing springbok sees a predator, it leaps suddenly into the air with its back arched and all four legs pointing straight downwards. The message is passed rapidly through the herd and soon all the animals are running and leaping away from the danger.

Impala, too, are well known for their extraordinary leaps. They may jump three and a half metres into the air. A series of leaps makes an impala look as though it is bouncing for joy. When disturbed by a predator, impala do not run in straight lines. They dodge about and leap as they go. A herd of animals moving in this way probably confuses predators.

A bee stings to defend its nest. Any animal or human that interferes with a bee colony is liable to be set upon by a horde of worker bees.

Like the sting of a wasp, a bee's sting is its egg-laying organ shaped into a needle-like tube for injecting poison. A bee's sting is equipped with tiny barbs that prevent it from coming out. When the bee flies away, the sting is often ripped out. As a result the bee soon dies.

The European honeybee is fairly mild-mannered, although its sting is painful. However, there are other more ferocious bees. The giant honeybees of Asia are dangerous and people have been stung to death. In South America a strain of very aggressive African 'killer' bee accidentally introduced in 1957 is causing a problem. 'Killer' bees have chased out the local honeybees and are spreading rapidly.

Barbed sting

DO FLYING FISHES FLY?

Flying fishes travel long distances in the air. But despite their name, they glide rather than fly.

The most common flying fish is the two-winged type, which is found in all tropical seas. It is about 25 centimetres long and its pectoral (shoulder) fins are expanded into two large wings. The largest flying fish (45 centimetres long) is a four-winged type that lives off the coast of California.

A flying fish swims through the water until it reaches a speed of about 65 kilometres an hour. Just below the surface it starts to spread its wings and leaps out of the water. Then it glides through the air. Its momentum may carry it over 130 metres.

Flying fish leave the water partly to escape underwater predators. Unfortunately, when they are in the air, they are then prey to large seabirds.

WHY DO HEDGEHOGS HAVE SPINES?

When frightened, a hedgehog curls up into a ball. Its spines give it excellent protection.

A hedgehog is born with a few rubbery prickles. Within seven weeks it has the thick coat of tough spines that will protect it for the rest of its life.

Hedgehogs mostly eat insects and other small animals. But a hedgehog will also tackle an adder. The adder finds it difficult to bite such a spiky creature. And in any case the hedgehog is immune to the adder's poison.

When a predator approaches, a hedgehog remains completely still until it has seen what the danger is. Then if really frightened, it rolls up with its head almost touching its tail. Only large carnivores, such as badgers and foxes, can penetrate this spiny ball.

Unfortunately, a hedgehog's defences also cause it a problem. It is hard to groom a skin covered in spines. As a result hedgehogs are infested with many small parasites.

WHY ARE SOME SNAKES DANGEROUS?

Many snakes are deadly. Their fangs can inject poisonous venom.

Poisonous snakes can be divided into two groups, according to the position of their fangs. Snakes with poison fangs at the back of the mouth are not usually dangerous. They have some difficulty in sinking their fangs into a human.

The most dangerous snakes have fangs at the front of the mouth. These include puff adders, cobras, pit vipers, rattlesnakes and mambas.

Although many of these snakes have bites that can be fatal, most snakes do not attack humans unless provoked. Some give a warning before attacking; puff adders hiss loudly and a rattlesnake shakes its rattle. A few, however, such as the banded krait of Asia, the king cobra and the African mambas, may attack without any provocation or warning.

▲ HOW DOES AN ANIMAL BECOME INVISIBLE?

Many animals camouflage themselves to avoid being seen. The colouring and body patterns of a camouflaged animal enable it to merge with the background.

A number of animals are brightly coloured. But in their normal surroundings, this may be a great advantage. A bright-yellow crab spider remains unseen in a yellow

flower as it waits for its prey. Other animals, such as lions, need more drab camouflage colours.

Many animals camouflage themselves to avoid being eaten. Several species of moths rest on trees, where their markings blend with the bark and lichen. Other insects may be coloured green to match leaves.

Flatfish merge with the sand and pebbles on the seabed, but some fishes have irregular outlines as well as camouflage colours.

◀ WHEN IS A TWIG NOT A TWIG?

Some animals, especially insects, not only camouflage themselves by their colouring. They also disguise themselves as twigs or leaves.

Several kinds of insects look like twigs and stems. The picture shows a swallowtail moth caterpillar. Not only does its body have a bark-like colour and texture, but the insect also tries to act like a twig.

Stick insects are slow-moving animals. Their bodies are very long and they look like the stems of the plants on which they live. Different types have colours ranging from straw to brown and green. Some can even change colour to camouflage themselves.

Some green insects look like leaves. The leaf insect of southeast Asia is related to the stick insects, but its body is flattened and has 'leaf veins'. It looks exactly like a leaf, and even has slightly 'chewed' and battered edges.

▼ WHY ARE SOME ANIMALS BRIGHTLY COLOURED?

When animals are poisonous or unpleasant to eat, they sometimes advertise the fact with their bright colouring.

Bright warning colours warn predators that an animal should be avoided. A bird soon learns to leave the unpleasant-tasting cinnabar moth, with its red and black markings. Other animals with warning colours include the

Central American poison frogs, which are used to produce poison for arrow tips, and European wasps.

Some distasteful animals copy the warning colours of others. A cinnabar moth caterpillar is as unpleasant-tasting as the adult. To make sure its predators know this, it mimics a wasp's colouring.

Harmless animals also mimic the colours of poisonous ones. For example, a hoverfly looks very much like a wasp. The hoverfly gains protection from this colouring, because birds avoid it.

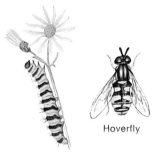

Hoverfly

Cinnabar moth caterpillar

Poison frog

▲ WHY DOES A
CHAMELEON CHANGE
COLOUR?

**Chameleons move slowly.
By changing colour to
match their surroundings,
they make it difficult for
their enemies and prey to
see them.**

The skin of a chameleon has
cells that contain coloured
pigments. Some cells contain
black pigment, others have
red or yellow pigment. By
using these pigments in
different ways, a chameleon
can change colour as it wishes,
sometimes very quickly.

A chameleon needs to be
camouflaged, or disguised,
because it may remain in one
place for a long time. When it
does move, it creeps very
slowly, so it is easy for
predators to catch it.

Chameleons feed by
remaining absolutely still
until a suitable prey comes
close enough. Then, faster
than the human eye can see,
the chameleon catapults out
its long, sticky tongue and
seizes its prey. Chameleons
usually eat insects and other
small animals.

▶ WHY DO SOME ANIMALS
HAVE FALSE EYES?

**One way of getting out of
trouble is to bluff. False
eyes can fool or startle a
would-be predator for
long enough to allow an
animal to escape.**

Several butterflies and moths
have false eyes on their hind
wings. When these are
exposed suddenly, an
approaching predator may be
startled into believing that it
is looking at a much larger
animal. By the time the
predator realizes its mistake,
the insect has flown away.
Other animals that have eye-
spots include caterpillars,
fishes and even a frog.

Some butterflies have not
only eye-spots but also false
antennae on their rear wings.
When the wings are in the

upright, closed position, the
back end of the insect appears
to be its head. A predator
trying to grab the insect goes
for a point just in front of the
'head' end and misses when
the insect flies away in the
other direction.

▼ WHY DOES A SQUID
SQUIRT INK?

**When it is alarmed, a
squid squirts a cloud of
black ink into the water.
This acts as a sort of
'smokescreen', behind
which the squid can
escape.**

Just below its head, a squid
has a small funnel. The squid
can contract its muscles and
force a jet of water through
this funnel. And, at the same
time, it can release ink into

the jet of water.

Squid can often avoid being
seen by camouflaging themselves. They are masters of
colour change and can
produce a wide variety of
patterns on their bodies.
When this fails, however, they
may escape by using jet
propulsion. At the same time,
they leave a smokescrecn of
ink behind them. In some
species, the ink forms the
shape of a squid and the
predator attacks the ink decoy
while the real squid escapes.

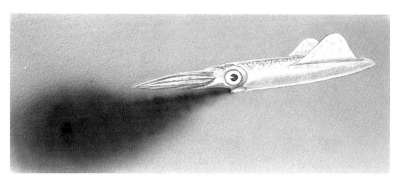

▶ WHAT KINDS OF JOINT ARE THERE?

There are four main kinds of movable joint. They are ball and socket joints, hinge joints, pivot joints and sliding joints.

Ball and socket joints are found in such places as the shoulders and hips. In this type of joint the head of a long bone fits into a socket on another bone.

Elbows and knees are hinge joints, which act like the hinge on a door. Sliding joints are found in such places as the hands and feet. A pivot joint between the first and second neck vertebrae allows the head to swivel from side to side.

Every joint is surrounded by a tough, fibrous capsule lined with a membrane. This contains a fluid that keeps the joint lubricated.

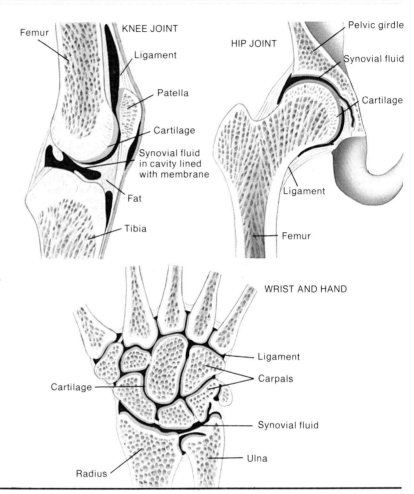

KNEE JOINT
Femur
Ligament
Patella
Cartilage
Synovial fluid in cavity lined with membrane
Fat
Tibia

HIP JOINT
Pelvic girdle
Synovial fluid
Cartilage
Ligament
Femur

WRIST AND HAND
Ligament
Carpals
Cartilage
Synovial fluid
Ulna
Radius

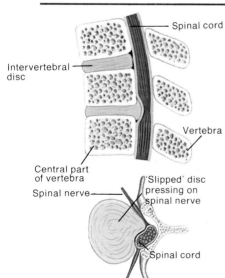

Spinal cord
Intervertebral disc
Vertebra
Central part of vertebra
Spinal nerve
'Slipped' disc pressing on spinal nerve
Spinal cord

◀ WHAT IS A SLIPPED DISC?

A so-called 'slipped disc' is a weakened cartilage in the spine that has bulged out from between its two vertebrae. It may press on a nerve and cause pain.

An intervertebral disc is a flexible pad consisting of a jelly-like core surrounded by a fibrous cover. It lies directly in between two vertebrae and acts as a shock absorber.

The weakest part of a disc is near the back. Sometimes the fibrous cover develops a crack and the jelly-like material inside bulges out. This is usually caused by putting too much strain on the back.

If the bulge is to one side, it may press on a nerve branching off the spinal cord. In this case the person will feel pain in the area supplied by the nerve, such as the leg or arm. If the bulge pushes straight back into the spinal cord itself, the person may feel pain in such places as the back, neck or chest.

▼ WHAT DOES THE
SKELETON CONSIST OF?

The human skeleton is made up of 206 bones.

The central supporting part of the skeleton is the spine, or vertebral column. This consists of 33 vertebrae.

Seven neck vertebrae support the skull, which is made up of several bones fused together. Below the neck are 12 thoracic vertebrae, which have curved projections known as ribs. All but two of these on each side are also joined to the breast-bone, or sternum. The sternum is fused to the collar bone, or clavicle. This links up with the shoulder bone, or scapula, which is linked to the arm bones.

Below the thoracic vertebrae are five large lumbar vertebrae. At the base of the spine are five fused vertebrae that form the sacrum. Four more fused vertebrae form the coccyx. The sacrum is fused to the bones of the hip girdle, to which are linked the leg bones.

◀ WHAT IS CARTILAGE?

Cartilage is a glass-like material, often called gristle. It helps to reduce friction and jarring between bones.

Cartilage is a protein fibre material. It is found in several parts of the body, such as the outer part (pinna) of the ear, the tip of the nose, the larynx and windpipe (trachea).

Cartilage is found in all movable joints, where it helps to reduce friction and acts as a shock absorber. It also makes up the discs between the vertebrae of the spine.

Cartilage has no blood supply and, unlike bone, does not repair itself when damaged. So a damaged knee cartilage may have to be removed by surgery. Some-times cartilage becomes weakened. Arthritis is partly caused by wearing away of cartilage in joints.

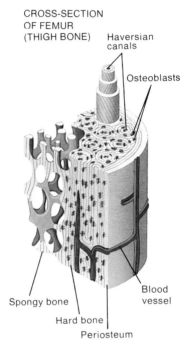

CROSS-SECTION OF FEMUR (THIGH BONE)
Haversian canals
Osteoblasts
Spongy bone
Hard bone
Periosteum
Blood vessel

Cranium
Maxilla (upper jaw)
Clavicle
Scapula
Mandible (lower jaw)
Sternum
Ribs
Humerus
Vertebrae of spine
Radius
Pelvic girdle
Ulna
Sacrum
Carpals
Coccyx
Meta carpals
Phalanges
Femur
Patella
Tibia
Fibula
Tarsals
Metatarsals
Phalanges

▲ WHAT IS BONE?

Bone is the hard material from which the parts of the skeleton are made.

A typical long bone, such as the femur, consists of a long shaft with swellings at each end. The outer part of the bone is made of hard bone and this surrounds a core of spongy bone containing air spaces. Down the middle of the shaft is a cavity, filled with a soft material known as marrow.

The outside of the bone is covered with a fibrous sheath (the periosteum), which is well supplied with blood vessels. Hard bone is made up of a number of long columns. Each one has a channel (Haversian canal) down the middle. This contains blood vessels and is surrounded by several rings of bone cells (osteoblasts), which produce the hard bone material.

Bone consists mostly of calcium, phosphorus and other minerals, which give it great strength. Bone can also be stretched. Elasticity is provided by protein fibres.

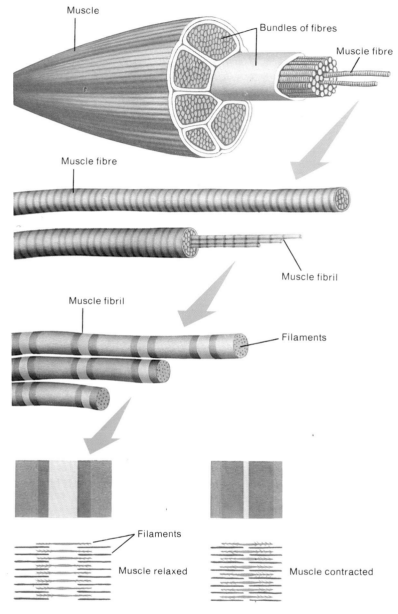

Muscle

Bundles of fibres

Muscle fibre

Muscle fibre

Muscle fibril

Muscle fibril

Filaments

Filaments

Muscle relaxed

Muscle contracted

Muscle is a living tissue that is able to contract. Many of the body's muscles are linked to the bones of the skeleton. Contraction of these muscles gives movement.

There are three types of muscle. Muscles that move bones are composed of a tissue known as striped muscle. Each major muscle consists of several bundles. Each of these is made up of a number of fibres. Each fibre consists of tiny fibrils.

Muscle fibrils have a striped appearance, which gives this type of muscle its name. The stripes are due to the presence of filaments inside the fibrils. Where filaments overlap, the fibril appears darker. The dark regions of all the fibrils in a fibre coincide. Thus the whole fibre appears to have dark stripes across it.

Muscle contraction is stimulated by nerve impulses. These cause chemical changes in the fibrils. The filaments slide over each other and the whole muscle contracts.

The second type of muscle is called smooth muscle. This consists of long cells, tapered at both ends. The action of smooth muscle is not controlled consciously. It is automatically controlled by a special part of the nervous system. Smooth muscle is found in such places as the lining of the gut and the walls of arteries.

Cardiac muscle is found only in the heart. Its structure is somewhere between that of striped muscle and smooth muscle. It can contract regularly without being stimulated by nerve impulses.

▲ WHAT CAUSES CRAMP?

Cramp is a painful spasm (continuous contraction) of a muscle. It is often caused by lack of oxygen in the muscle.

When a muscle contracts, it uses up energy. This is provided by respiration – the breakdown of sugar using oxygen with the release of carbon dioxide, water and energy.

During normal exercise the body can take in sufficient oxygen. But after a period of violent exercise the supply of oxygen may start to run out. At this point energy is supplied to the muscle by breaking down the sugar into a chemical called lactic acid. A certain amount of lactic acid can be tolerated. But if too much builds up in the muscle it causes cramp. When the exercise stops, the lactic acid diffuses out of the muscle and is broken down.

Cramp may also be caused by poor blood circulation and by swimming in cold water too soon after a meal.

▼ WHAT IS A GLAND?

A gland produces a chemical substance that is then delivered to a place outside the gland.

There are two kinds of gland. Exocrine glands have ducts leading to the outside. Sweat glands, for example, are exocrine glands that deliver sweat through coiled ducts to the surface of the skin. Digestive glands in the stomach and intestines produce digestive juices. Salivary glands produce saliva and tear glands produce the fluid that keeps the eyes moist. The liver, which is the largest gland in the body, produces bile.

Endocrine glands, or ductless glands, produce hormones. These are released directly into the bloodstream and are used to control such things as growth and reproduction. One of the most important endocrine glands is the pituitary gland, which is situated in the brain and is about the size of a pea. It produces at least nine hormones.

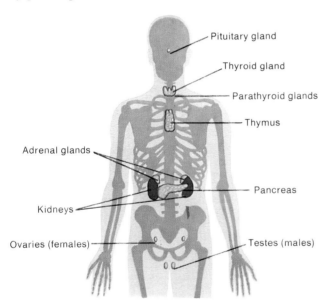

Pituitary gland

Thyroid gland

Parathyroid glands

Thymus

Adrenal glands

Pancreas

Kidneys

Ovaries (females)

Testes (males)

▲ WHAT IS A HORMONE?

A hormone is a chemical produced in one part of the body and transported in the blood to other parts.

Each hormone has an important controlling effect on the functions of a particular part of the body.

For example, the islets of Langerhans produce the hormone insulin. This controls, via the liver, the level of blood sugar in the body.

The thyroid gland produces thyroxine, which controls the rate at which chemical processes take place in the body. This gland is under the control of the pituitary gland, as are the testes and ovaries.

In males the testes produce testosterone, which controls the development of the sex organs and other male characteristics. In females the ovaries produce oestrogen, which controls female characteristics, and progesterone, which controls pregnancy.

▼ WHAT ARE TENDONS AND LIGAMENTS?

Tendons connect muscles to bones. Ligaments link the bones of a joint.

Muscles are not directly connected to bones. Instead, each end of a muscle has one or more tendons.

Some tendons are short and thick, such as the two tendons that connect the biceps muscle to the shoulder blade. Some, such as the tendons of the hand and fingers, are long and thin. They extend from the muscles in the forearm into the fingers.

Tendons can sometimes be stretched, particularly when being used in energetic sports. A sprinter, for example, may tear the Achilles tendon in the back of a heel.

A ligament is a flexible band of elastic tissue that links two bones in a joint. Ligaments cannot be stretched and a joint should not be moved beyond the point at which the ligaments are taut. If the joint is moved beyond this point, the ligament tears and the result is a sprain.

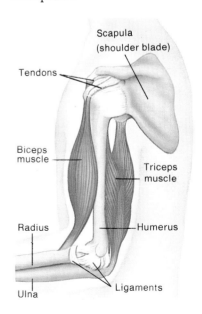

Scapula (shoulder blade)

Tendons

Biceps muscle

Triceps muscle

Radius

Humerus

Ulna

Ligaments

▼ WHAT DOES YOUR BRAIN CONSIST OF?

The brain is a mass of nerve cells and nerve fibres. Different parts of the brain have different functions.

The largest part of the human brain is the cerebrum, which consists of two cerebral hemispheres. The outer layer of each hemisphere is known as the cerebral cortex. This consists of a much-folded mass of grey matter containing 2500 million nerve cells. Many activities are controlled by this part of the brain, including voluntary, or conscious, movement, speech, hearing, sight, smell, thought and memory. These activities are each controlled by a particular part of the cortex.

Inside the cortex, the rest of the cerebral hemisphere consists of white matter, which is largely made up of nerve fibres.

Other parts of the brain have their own important functions. The corpus callosum is a band of nerve fibres that links the two cerebral hemispheres. The cerebellum helps coordinate movement and control balance. The thalamus is a relay station. It processes all sensory nerve impulses before passing them on to the cortex. The hypothalamus controls body temperature, blood pressure and the pituitary gland. The hind brain, which consists of the medulla oblongata, the pons and the cerebellum, controls the heart, lungs and digestive system.

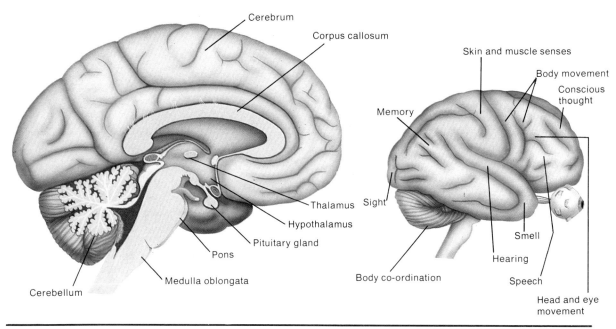

Cerebrum

Corpus callosum

Skin and muscle senses

Body movement

Conscious thought

Memory

Thalamus

Sight

Hypothalamus

Pituitary gland

Smell

Pons

Medulla oblongata

Hearing

Body co-ordination

Speech

Cerebellum

Head and eye movement

▶ WHAT IS YOUR 'FUNNY BONE'?

Your 'funny bone' is a place on the elbow where a nerve passes close to the surface. A sharp knock stimulates this nerve and the brain registers pain.

There is nothing funny about being struck on the 'funny bone'. This part of the elbow may have been given its name because people thought that it had something to do with the humerus, the bone of the upper arm. But, in fact, the humerus is not involved at all. The 'funny bone' is the knob on the back of the ulna of the forearm.

Most nerves lie well-protected in layers of muscle. However, the ulnar nerve, which runs from the hand to the spinal cord, passes over the elbow just underneath the skin. If it is struck sharply, a stream of impulses is sent to the spinal cord and the brain registers a sharp pain in the elbow. The effect may also be felt in the fingers as tingling.

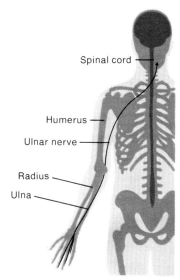

Spinal cord

Humerus

Ulnar nerve

Radius

Ulna

▼ WHAT ARE TOUCH AND PAIN?

The skin contains many sense organs sensitive to touch, pressure, pain, cold and heat. The information they send tells the brain what is happening at any point on the skin.

Pressure receptors (1) are buried deep in the skin. Touch receptors (2) are nearer the surface, as are cold (3) and heat (4) receptors. Pain receptors are simply free nerve endings (5). Some areas of skin have more sense organs than others. Touch receptors, for example, are plentiful in the fingertips, the tip of the nose and the lips.

Touching an object involves stimulating more than one type of receptor. For example, holding a glass of water involves the sensations of touch, pressure and cold. But holding a glass of water does not stimulate pain receptors. These require more extreme pressures or temperatures before they are stimulated into sending signals to the brain.

◀ WHAT IS A REFLEX ACTION?

A reflex action is one that happens without the person thinking about it.

When you reach out to pick something up, your brain is sending out a stream of instructions to your muscles. But in a reflex action the brain is not directly involved.

If you place your finger too near a lighted candle, the pain receptors in that finger send out a rapid stream of impulses, which travel to the spinal cord. From there some impulses are relayed to the brain. But before the brain can respond, impulses are sent directly from the spinal cord to your arm and shoulder muscles. These contract and you pull your hand rapidly away from the flame. Reflex actions of this kind help to protect the body from harm.

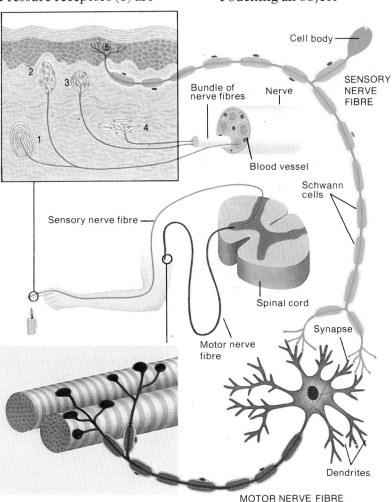

Cell body

SENSORY NERVE FIBRE

Bundle of nerve fibres

Nerve

Blood vessel

Schwann cells

Sensory nerve fibre

Spinal cord

Synapse

Motor nerve fibre

Dendrites

MOTOR NERVE FIBRE

▲ WHAT ARE NERVES?

A nerve consists of bundles of special cells that carry electrical impulses.

A nerve contains several bundles of nerve fibres, together with some blood vessels. Each fibre, or neuron, is a long cell.

Nerve impulses travel down one or more long fibres called axons. An axon is covered with a sheath (myelin sheath) produced by special cells (Schwann cells). At the tip of an axon are fine fibrils. These connect up with the next neuron by means of a junction called a synapse.

There are two main kinds of neuron. A sensory neuron carries impulses from a sense organ to the spinal cord or brain. A motor neuron carries impulses from the brain or spinal cord to an effector organ, such as a muscle.

Motor neurons have small fibres called dendrites extending from their cell bodies. They connect up to muscle fibres by means of motor end plates.

▼ WHAT ARE ARTERIES AND VEINS?

Arteries and veins are the main blood vessels of the body. Arteries carry blood from the heart to the tissues. Veins carry blood back to the heart.

Arteries and veins form a network of tubes around the body. Small blood vessels are known as arterioles and venules. The smallest vessels are called capillaries.

Arteries and veins have three-layered walls. On the inside is a layer of lining cells. Around this is a layer of smooth muscle. On the outside is connective tissue.

Arteries have thicker, more muscular walls than veins. They carry a fast-flowing stream of blood under pressure from the heart.

Veins are generally larger and more branched than arteries. They carry a slow-moving stream of blood, which is under much less pressure than arterial blood. Veins have one-way valves to prevent the blood flowing backwards.

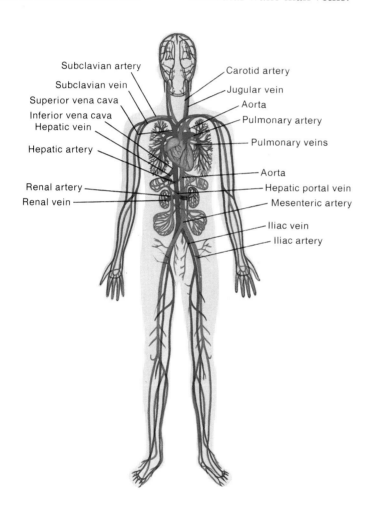

Subclavian artery
Subclavian vein
Superior vena cava
Inferior vena cava
Hepatic vein
Hepatic artery
Renal artery
Renal vein
Carotid artery
Jugular vein
Aorta
Pulmonary artery
Pulmonary veins
Aorta
Hepatic portal vein
Mesenteric artery
Iliac vein
Iliac artery

◀ WHAT IS BLOOD PRESSURE?

Blood pressure, as measured by a doctor, is the pressure of blood in a main artery.

Blood pressure is measured by an instrument called a sphygmomanometer. There are two measurements. The first is when the heart is contracting (the systolic pressure) and the other, much lower, pressure is when the heart is resting (diastolic pressure). The results are shown in millimetres of mercury. The average blood pressure of a young person is 120/80.

Blood pressure tends to increase with age and during exercise. Abnormally high blood pressure, or hypertension, may be due to disease, but there is often no easily recognizable cause. Hypertension may strain the heart or damage the kidneys.

▲ HOW DOES BLOOD CIRCULATE ROUND YOUR BODY?

The human body contains between eight and nine pints of blood. The heart pumps it round the body in less than a minute.

Blood from the body enters the right auricle of the heart through the two main veins (vena cavae). It leaves the heart from the right ventricle and passes, via the pulmonary arteries, to the lungs. There it receives oxygen. It returns back to the left auricle of the heart via the pulmonary veins.

The left ventricle then pumps the blood out through the aorta. Branches from this supply the rest of the body.

When the blood has passed through the tissues, it is collected up by the veins. All but one of the large veins return blood directly to the heart through the vena cavae. The exception is the hepatic portal vein. This collects blood from the intestine and carries it to the liver, which deals with the products of digestion.

178

► WHAT IS A BLOOD TRANSFUSION?

A blood transfusion is the injection of blood from one person (the donor, seen here) into the blood system of another person.

A blood transfusion may be given to a person with poor blood or one who has lost a lot of blood after an accident.

Usually, blood is supplied from a blood bank. This is a place where blood is stored after being collected from donors.

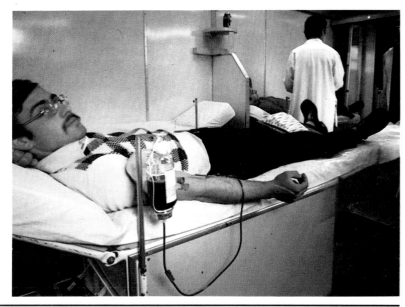

► WHAT ARE BLOOD GROUPS?

There are four main groups of blood, known as A, B, AB and O, which contain different factors. If the wrong factors are mixed then blood will clot.

A person's blood may contain two important types of factor. On the surface of the red blood cells there may be factors known as antigens, of which there are two kinds, A and B. Some people have only antigen-A and are therefore said to have blood group A. Other people have only antigen-B (blood group B). Others have both A and B antigens (blood group AB) and yet others have neither antigen (blood group O).

There may also be antibodies in the serum of the blood. Again there are two types – antibody-a and antibody-b. Antibody-a attacks antigen-A, causing damage to the red blood cells that may make them clump together. Similarly, antibody-b attacks antigen-B. So these antigens and antibodies do not occur in the same blood.

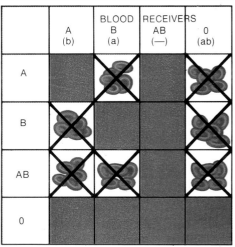

BLOOD DONORS

	A (b)	BLOOD B (a)	RECEIVERS AB (—)	O (ab)
A	No clumping	Clumping	Clumping	Clumping
B	Clumping	No clumping	No clumping	Clumping
AB	Clumping	Clumping	No clumping	Clumping
O	No clumping	No clumping	No clumping	No clumping

 No clumping (can be mixed)

 Clumping of red blood cells (donor and receiver blood must not be mixed)

However, group A blood may contain antibody-b and group B blood may contain antibody-a. Group AB blood contains neither and group O blood may contain both.

In theory, therefore, group A blood should never be mixed with group B or group AB. However, in practice the serum of a group A donor is rapidly diluted in the blood of a group AB receiver. As a result the donor's antibody-b does not have much effect on the antigen-B of the receiver.

For the same reason a person with group AB blood can receive group B blood. A person with group AB blood can therefore receive blood from any donor.

Group AB blood can only be given to a group AB receiver. In all other cases the antigens (A and B) would be attacked by the receiver's antibodies. Group O blood contains no antigens and can be given to anybody. But because group O blood contains both a and b antibodies, a group O person can only receive group O blood.

Lid of glass dish

Glass dish
Culture of bacteria
Transparent jelly

Areas in which bacteria cannot grow
Paper discs

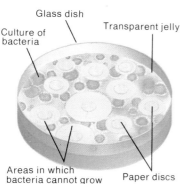

▲ WHAT IS AN ANTIBIOTIC?

An antibiotic is a drug that kills bacteria. Many antibiotics are produced from living organisms, such as fungi. There are also man-made types.

Penicillin was discovered in 1929 and was first used in 1941. Since then many other antibiotics have been discovered, some of which are man-made, or synthetic. Modern antibiotics include streptomycin, chloramphecol, ampicillin, and the tetracyclines.

Some antibiotics can cause harm if taken over a long period of time. One of the safest is still penicillin. However, the use of antibiotics has resulted in new, resistant strains of bacteria.

The illustration shows a number of antibiotics being tested for effectiveness against a particular bacterium. The paper discs are impregnated with the antibiotics. Each one is therefore surrounded by an area in which the colony of bacteria cannot grow. Those with the largest clear areas are the most effective.

◀ WHAT ARE GERMS?

A germ is a tiny living organism that causes disease.

The world's smallest living organisms include bacteria and viruses and tiny single-celled animals, or protozoa. Some of these are harmless or even useful. Others cause disease and are sometimes known as germs.

Most protozoa are harmless, but a few, such as the malaria parasite and the dysentery amoeba, are disease-causing organisms.

Harmful bacteria may cause disease themselves or they may produce poisonous waste substances. Bacterial diseases include most kinds of food poisoning, bubonic plague, diphtheria, pneumonia, scarlet fever, typhoid fever, typhus and whooping cough.

There are vast numbers of different viruses. Most cause disease. Colds, chicken pox, influenza, measles, mumps and poliomyelitis are all caused by viruses. Some types of cancer are thought to be caused by virus infection.

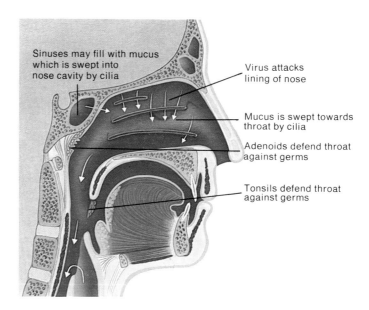

Sinuses may fill with mucus which is swept into nose cavity by cilia

Virus attacks lining of nose

Mucus is swept towards throat by cilia

Adenoids defend throat against germs

Tonsils defend throat against germs

▲ WHAT CAUSES A COLD?

The common cold is a virus disease that affects the linings of the nose, sinuses and, sometimes, the throat and bronchi.

There are large numbers of viruses that cause colds. A cold begins when infected droplets enter the nose or mouth and a virus attacks the lining of the nose or throat. Between 18 and 48 hours later the lining becomes inflamed and starts to produce mucus, resulting in a running nose.

Mucus is driven by cilia towards the throat. At the back of the throat are the adenoids and tonsils. These are lumps of lymph tissue, whose main task is to defend the throat against infection.

Despite these organs the virus often does enter the throat, which also becomes inflamed and sore. If the bronchi of the lungs become infected the result is a cough. Mucus from the throat and bronchi is driven down the oesophagus to the stomach. In time, the body's natural defences deal with the virus.

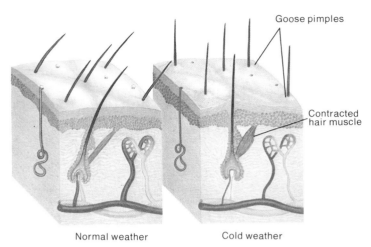

Goose pimples

Contracted
hair muscle

Normal weather   Cold weather

**When you are cold or
frightened, the hairs on
your body stand up. At the
same time, the skin
around each hair becomes
raised into a 'pimple'.
Your skin has a rough,
bristly appearance, very
much like the skin of a
plucked goose.**

All mammals are covered in
hair. This insulates the body
by trapping warm air next to
the skin. In cold weather, the
thickness of the layer of warm
air is increased by raising the
hairs. The erector muscle of
each hair automatically
contracts and the hair stands
upright. This is why a cat
looks larger on cold days.

Compared to other
mammals, we humans have
very little hair and so cannot
trap much air next to our skin.
We wear clothes instead.
Even so, our hairs do stand up
when we get cold. And as the
erector muscle of each hair
contracts, it draws together
the skin around the base of
the hair. The skin is pushed
upwards to form a 'pimple'.

**When you are cold you
need to warm up.
Shivering is a form of
movement that happens
automatically and helps to
generate heat.**

When muscles contract and
relax, they produce heat. This
is why you get hot when
running or digging in the
garden. Sometimes, however,
your body gets cold and your
muscles 'switch on' auto-
matically. They contract and
relax rapidly, producing the

movement we call shivering.
In this way they generate
some heat to help to overcome
the effects of the cold.

Sometimes shivering is not
enough to warm you up
properly. This is why you
often jump up and down and
flap your arms on cold days.
Again, the extra use of
muscles produces more heat.

Exposure to cold conditions
that chill the body can be very
dangerous, especially to old
people. They may suffer from
hypothermia, which is a kind
of drowsiness, followed by
unconsciousness and
sometimes death.

**Sweating is a vital process
for cooling you down when
you get too hot. Sweat is
produced by the sweat
glands on the surface of
the skin. There it
evaporates and cools the
body.**

Your body prefers to operate
at its normal temperature. So
when your body temperature
gets too high, such as during
strenuous exercise, you need
to lose heat. There are two
ways in which this happens.

First, the tiny blood vessels
in your skin increase in size
and fill with blood, giving you
a flushed appearance. Heat
travels from the blood to the
outside air.

When your body becomes
even hotter, your sweat glands
produce a mixture of water
and waste chemicals known as
sweat. When water
evaporates, it uses up a great
deal of heat (called latent heat
of evaporation). So as the
water in your sweat
evaporates from your skin, it
takes heat rapidly from your
body.

▲ WHY DO SOME PEOPLE HAVE BLUE EYES AND OTHERS BROWN EYES?

You inherit the colour of your eyes from your parents. Special inherited factors, known as genes, **control the colour of your eyes and other features, such as your hair colour.**

Every person carries two genes for each feature. Often, one gene dominates the other. In the case of eye colour, a brown-eye gene dominates a blue-eye gene. If a person has two brown-eye genes then he or she will have brown eyes. Similarly, the presence of two blue-eye genes means blue eyes. But if a person has one brown-eye gene and one blue-eye gene, then the brown-eye gene dominates and the eyes are brown.

But a 'hidden' blue-eye gene is not lost forever, and can be passed on. In fact, it is even possible for two brown-eyed people, both with 'hidden' blue-eye genes, to produce blue-eyed children.

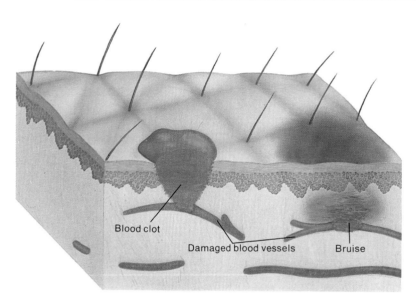

Blood clot

Damaged blood vessels

Bruise

▲ WHY DOES BLOOD CLOT?

When your skin is damaged, blood vessels near the surface are broken and you bleed. But unless the damage is severe, you do not bleed for long. Your blood contains special substances to stop the bleeding. These substances form a clot that dries into a hard scab.

Clotting of blood takes place very quickly. It begins when a substance called thrombin forms in the blood as it seeps from the wound. Thrombin is an enzyme. This is a chemical that causes a biological reaction to take place, without itself being used up in the reaction. Thrombin acts on a protein called fibrinogen and changes it to fibrin. This consists of many long fibres that become entangled with each other, trapping blood cells as they form.

Only the clear blood serum escapes, leaving behind a clot of fibrin and blood cells. This forms a protective covering over the wound.

◄ WHY DO BRUISES GO BLACK AND BLUE?

When an object strikes your body hard, the blood vessels beneath your skin may be damaged. If so, they release blood into your skin tissue, which becomes purple in colour.

The surface of your skin is relatively tough compared with the tissues beneath it. As a result, it is possible to damage these tissues without breaking the skin. Blood is released from damaged blood vessels and damaged cells also release fluid.

Often the area becomes swollen with excess fluid. When the damaged area is in a place where bone lies near the surface, such as the head or shin, the swelling has nowhere to go but outwards and a large bump appears.

The blood that enters the skin tissue shows as a purple discoloration. The blood cells break down and their contents are absorbed by the body again. While this is going on the colour of the bruise changes to brown and then yellow before it disappears.

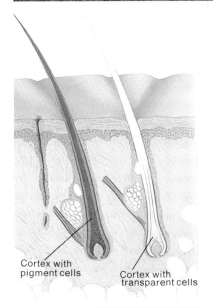

Cortex with pigment cells

Cortex with transparent cells

◀ WHY DOES HAIR GO GREY?

The colour of a person's hair is caused mainly by the presence of pigment-containing cells in each hair. In later life, some or all of the hairs grow without pigment and the colour appears grey.

The colour of a single hair is determined by cells in the hair follicle. This is the bulb-shaped structure at the hair root. These cells inject pigment granules (black, brown or yellow) into the cells of the hair cortex.

In early life, the colour of people's hair varies from black, through shades of brown and red, to fair and blonde. After a while, however, the pigment-producing cells in some hair follicles stop working. The hairs that grow from these follicles are actually colourless, but because of the refraction of light, they are seen as white. White hairs mixed with black or brown hairs give an overall grey colour to a person's hair.

▶ WHAT MAKES US CRY?

Our tear glands are constantly producing tears. Usually, they do not overflow, but gently bathe the front of our eyeballs before draining away. But sometimes, for example when we are upset, we produce tears faster than they can drain away. Then they flow down our cheeks.

The main purpose of the tears produced by our tear glands, or lacrimal glands, is to defend the eye against outside infection. They are mildly antiseptic and contain a substance that kills bacteria.

Tears are wiped over the eye regularly by blinking. This is an automatic action that occurs at least once every ten seconds. Excess tears drain away into the tear ducts and from there into the tear sac and the cavity of the nose.

Sometimes, because of pain or emotion, we produce a lot more tears than the tear ducts can cope with. When this happens, tears flow over our eyelids and down our cheeks. A blocked tear duct also causes tears to overflow.

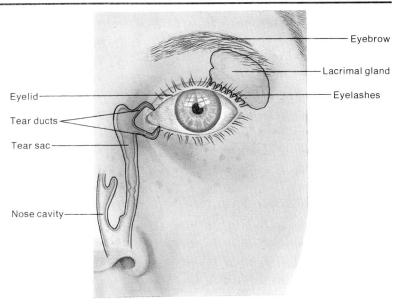

Eyelid

Tear ducts

Tear sac

Nose cavity

Eyebrow

Lacrimal gland

Eyelashes

▲ WHAT PROTECTS YOUR EYES?

Your eyes are very delicate organs that need protection. Tears kill invading germs and your eyelids, eyelashes and eyebrows help to keep out other harmful objects.

Your eyes' first line of defence are eyelashes and eyelids. Your eyelashes form two rows of stiff hairs around each eye. They help to catch and remove any large objects that come too close to your eyes.

Your eyelids are equipped with muscles so that they can close. The reflex action that makes you close your eyes helps to protect them from being injured by objects or dazzled by bright light. Any dust or dirt that does reach your eyes is removed when you blink. Your eyelids close briefly, sweeping across the front of your eyeballs.

The eyebrows form two long patches of protective hairs above your eyes. They prevent moisture from your forehead from running down into your eyes.

Foods containing iron

Foods for a balanced diet

Foods containing vitamin C

▲ WHY DO YOU NEED VITAMINS AND MINERALS?

Vitamins and minerals are present in your body in very tiny amounts. But they are very, very important to your health. Without them you would become ill.

You need only about one seven-hundredth of a gram of vitamin B_1 (thiamine) each day. But without it you would get a disease called beri-beri. Vitamin B_1 is found in bread and meat. All of the other 16 vitamins are also vital. For example, vitamin A (found in liver and carrots) is needed to help you to see in dim light. Vitamin C is especially plentiful in fresh fruit and vegetables. In olden times, lack of these foods on board ship led sailors to develop a disease called scurvy.

Minerals are also essential. You need iron (from meat, eggs and bread) in order to make the red blood pigment haemoglobin. Calcium (in milk, cheese and bread) and phosphorus (in most foods) are needed for the growth of bones and teeth.

▲ DOES IT MATTER WHAT YOU EAT?

In order to be healthy you must provide your body with the right raw materials. These are proteins, sugars, fats, vitamins and minerals. A balanced diet should include all of these.

You need energy to keep your body working. The energy value of food is measured in calories. The foods with most calories are those containing large amounts of carbo-hydrates (sugars and starches) and fats. Sugar, cereals, milk and cheese provide most of the carbohydrates and fats you need.

Proteins are also essential. An adult needs about 60 grams of protein every day to replace protein lost by wear and tear in the body. Growing children need protein to build new body tissue. Proteins are obtained from foods such as meat, fish, cheese and beans.

A balanced diet is completed by including fresh fruit and vegetables, which provide the remaining vitamins and minerals.

▲ DOES IT MATTER HOW MUCH YOU EAT?

If you do not eat enough food, you do not have enough energy to keep going. However, if you eat too much food, you do not use up all the energy it contains and it turns to unwanted fat.

The rate at which you use up energy depends on a number of things, including your age, weight and build. It also depends on what you do. For example, a man working in an office all day uses up fewer calories than a labourer on a building site. Active, growing children need a large number of calories. Old people need far fewer calories.

Ideally, therefore, everyone should eat food containing the right number of calories for their needs. Eating too much fat, carbohydrate and even protein leads to too many calories in the body. Excess calories turn to fat and so people who eat more than they need begin to become overweight. And people who are greatly overweight can suffer from poor health.

184

WHY DO WE NEED EXERCISE?

Your body is a kind of machine. And like any other machine it needs looking after to keep it working properly. Exercise keeps your muscles working well. And general fitness helps you to be healthy.

An unfit person, who takes no exercise, converts only a small amount of food into energy and may become overweight. At the same time his muscles become weak and his blood circulation may become slow.

Exercise helps to make muscles stronger and improves their tone, or readiness for action. Well-toned muscles help to keep the bones properly placed in relation to each other. So a fit person has a better posture than an unfit person and is less likely to have backache.

Muscle movement helps to speed up blood circulation. At the same time exercise helps to increase a person's depth of breathing, making it easier to take in oxygen.

WHAT IS YOUR BODY MADE OF?

Your body contains over 20 different chemical elements. The most plentiful element in the body is oxygen. Oxygen, together with hydrogen, forms water. Water makes up nearly two-thirds of your weight.

The body of an average person contains about 4.5 litres of water. It also has an amount of carbon equal to nearly 13 kilograms of coke.

Much of this carbon, together with hydrogen and oxygen, makes up fats and sugars. Carbon, hydrogen, oxygen and nitrogen form the body's vital proteins.

There are also large amounts of calcium and phosphorus. The body contains over one and a quarter kilograms of calcium and enough phosphorus to make over 2000 matches. The body also contains a couple of spoonfuls of sulphur, enough iron to make a 2.5-centimetre nail, and nearly 30 grams of other metals.

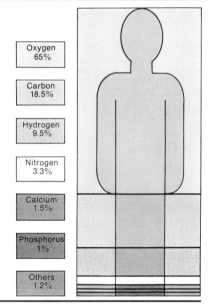

Oxygen 65%
Carbon 18.5%
Hydrogen 9.5%
Nitrogen 3.3%
Calcium 1.5%
Phosphorus 1%
Others 1.2%

WHY DO YOU NEED REST?

You spend about one-third of your life sleeping. No one knows exactly why we sleep, but it seems to be essential for the health of both the mind and body.

The amount of sleep we need depends on several things, including a person's age and what he does during the day.

A new-born baby sleeps nearly all day. It only wakes up to be fed. A young child needs about 12 hours sleep a day. An adult generally needs to sleep for about eight hours, although some people stay healthy with only two hours sleep a night.

After a period of sleep you should wake feeling rested and refreshed. Someone who goes for more than 36 hours without sleep becomes irritable and confused. If he manages to stay awake without collapsing for over 60 hours, he may begin to 'see' and 'hear' things that are not there.

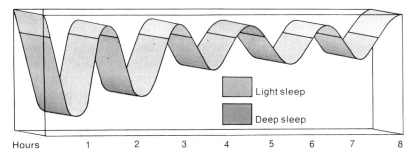

Hours 1 2 3 4 5 6 7 8

Light sleep

Deep sleep

▲ WHY DO YOU DREAM?

Sleep is an essential part of our lives (see previous page). It is a kind of unconsciousness, but we can wake fairly easily. Even though the conscious part of the mind is totally at rest, the subconscious part of the mind continues working and produces dreams.

When you fall asleep, you quickly go into a state of deep sleep. But about five times during the night you change from periods of deep sleep to periods of light sleep. And as morning approaches, the periods of light sleep become longer.

You dream during the periods of light sleep. At these times you make rapid eye movements and some body movements. If you wake up while you are dreaming, you can often remember the dream. No one really knows why we have dreams. But they appear to be an important part of sleep.

▶ WHY IS YOUR TEMPERATURE TAKEN WHEN YOU ARE ILL?

Your normal body temperature is about 37°C, or 98.4°F. An increase in temperature may be a sign of illness.

Body temperature is measured by using a clinical thermometer. This is a glass tube with a bulb containing mercury at the end. Expansion of the mercury in the bulb causes it to move up the tube. A scale on the side shows the temperature.

A person's temperature is usually taken by placing a thermometer in the mouth for about three minutes. It can also be taken by putting the thermometer in the armpit, but this may show a lower temperature.

Normal temperatures vary between 36°C and 37°C. A temperature above this is often a sign of infection. However, a high temperature is not always a sign of illness. On the other hand, a person may be very ill yet still have a normal temperature.

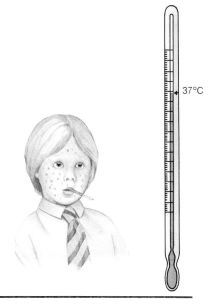

37°C

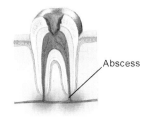

Cavity

Abscess

◀ WHY SHOULD YOU BRUSH YOUR TEETH?

Teeth have hard surfaces that seem impossible to get through. But they can be attacked and eaten away by bacteria. These tiny living organisms thrive on any food that is left on or around your teeth. So to prevent your teeth from decaying, you should brush them regularly.

Food debris on a tooth begins to form a hard material called plaque. Bacteria grow in plaque and start to eat away the enamel layer of the tooth. If this decay is not stopped, you may eventually have a cavity that reaches into the inner pulp of the tooth. Then, because nerve endings are exposed, you will have a very painful toothache. If the bacteria infect the tooth right down to the root, they then attack the bone in which the tooth is set. This causes an extremely painful abscess.

To prevent this you should brush your teeth after every meal.

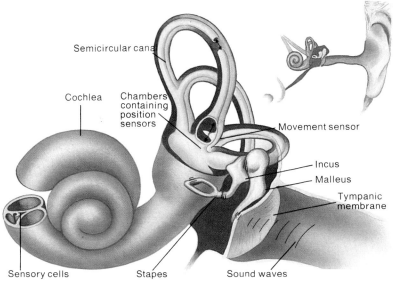

Semicircular cana

Cochlea Chambers containing position sensors

Movement sensor

Incus
Malleus
Tympanic membrane

Sensory cells   Stapes   Sound waves

◢ HOW DO YOU HEAR?

Your ears are organs that convert sound waves into nerve impulses. Sound waves are passed from the outside to the cochlea. There, sensory cells are stimulated and send nerve impulses to the brain.

Sound waves cause the tympanic membrane to vibrate. The vibrations are passed on by three small bones called the malleus, incus and stapes.

The cochlea is a long, coiled tube filled with watery liquid. Vibrations pass from the stapes to the liquid and are picked up by a membrane in the middle of the cochlea. Sensory cells in this membrane are stimulated as it vibrates.

At the tip of the cochlea the membrane responds to low notes. Farther back, nearer the stapes, it responds to higher notes. Your brain senses exactly which sensory cells are being stimulated and 'hears' the original sound.

◢ HOW DO YOU BALANCE?

The semicircular canals of your inner ear send information to your brain about the movements of your head.

Your inner ear contains three semicircular canals. Each one is set in a different plane and filled with liquid. Inside a swelling at one end of each canal there is a bunch of receptor cells. These have sensory hairs embedded in a lump of jelly-like material. When you move your head, the liquid in the semicircular canals causes the jelly-like lumps to shift and bend the sensory hairs. The receptor cells send the information to your brain.

Under the semicircular canals are two more chambers. Each of these contains another group of receptor cells with sensory hairs. But on the ends of these hairs are tiny chalky particles. These respond to gravity and the receptor cells send out information about the position of your head.

▶ HOW DO YOU TASTE AND SMELL THINGS?

Your nose and mouth contain special receptor cells. When these are stimulated by chemical molecules, they send nerve impulses to the brain.

Your tongue is covered with tiny lumps or papillae. On the sides of some papillae are small groups of cells known as taste buds. Each taste bud contains between four and 20 receptor cells with short sensory hairs. These react to molecules of food dissolved in your saliva.

Your tongue is sensitive to four main kinds of taste. Bitterness is tasted at the back of the tongue, sourness is tasted at the sides and sweetness is tasted at the front. Saltiness is tasted all over, especially at the tip.

Your smell receptors are in the roof of the nasal (nose) cavity. They have sensory hairs that branch and project into the mucus that lines the cavity. Molecules in the air dissolve in the mucus and stimulate these hairs. There are about 15 different kinds of smell receptor, and they can detect over 10,000 different smells.

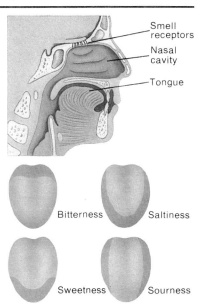

Smell receptors
Nasal cavity
Tongue

Bitterness   Saltiness

Sweetness   Sourness

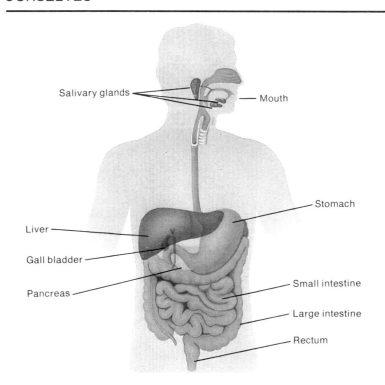

Salivary glands — Mouth

Liver
Gall bladder
Pancreas

Stomach
Small intestine
Large intestine
Rectum

**Your body digests food by
breaking down compli-
cated food chemicals into
simpler ones. Digestion
starts in the mouth and
stomach, but most takes
place in the small
intestine.**

Digestive juices contain
enzymes, which are chemicals
that help to break down food.
Digestion begins in the
mouth, where saliva mixes
with food as it is chewed.
Then the food is churned up
in the stomach for some time.

There is some digestion in
the stomach, but most
happens in the small intestine.
The churned-up food, or
chyme, leaves the stomach a
little at a time. In the small
intestine it is mixed with bile
(produced by the liver and
stored in the gall bladder) and
digestive juices from the
pancreas. Proteins, carbo-
hydrates and fats are broken
down by enzymes into simple
chemicals, which are then
absorbed into the body.

The rest of the food passes
into the large intestine. Water
is taken back into the body.
The remains, or faeces, go to
the rectum.

**The liver is the largest
gland in the body. It
receives all the food
chemicals absorbed by the
small intestine. The liver
processes many of these
chemicals.**

Your liver works in many
ways. It changes all
carbohydrates into glucose
and controls the amount of
sugar in your blood by storing
the excess as glycogen. It also
helps with the processing of
fats.

Amino acids are the
product of protein digestion,
and the body uses these to
make new proteins. But
excess amino acids cannot be
stored, and so they are broken
down by the liver into sugar
and nitrogen-containing
waste. The liver also makes
certain proteins, such as the
blood-clotting protein
fibrinogen.

The liver makes bile, a
greenish liquid which
contains the remains of blood
pigments collected by the
liver from worn-out red blood
cells. The liver also deals with
any poisons in the blood, such
as alcohol. The liver is also a
storage organ. Iron, removed
from blood pigment, is stored
here as well as several
vitamins.

**A stethoscope is a device
used for listening to
sounds inside the body.
The sounds are picked up
at the surface of the body
and transmitted along
tubes to earpieces.**

The first stethoscope was a

wooden tube invented in
1815. The modern version
was introduced in the late
1800s. Rubber tubes lead
from a disc or cone to two
earpieces. Sounds picked up
by the cone are carried by the
air in the tubes to the
earpieces. This very simple
device is still the easiest way
of listening to a person's heart
and lungs.

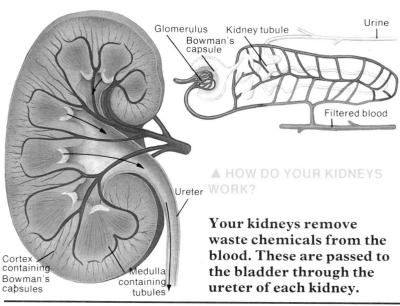

Glomerulus Kidney tubule Urine
Bowman's capsule
Filtered blood
Ureter
Cortex containing Bowman's capsules
Medulla containing tubules

▲ HOW DO YOUR KIDNEYS WORK?

Your kidneys remove waste chemicals from the blood. These are passed to the bladder through the ureter of each kidney.

A kidney consists of about two million microscopic filtering units. Each unit has a cup-shaped structure called a Bowman's capsule surrounding a tightly-bunched network of blood capillaries called a glomerulus.

Water and dissolved chemicals pass from the blood into the Bowman's capsule. Useful chemicals and over 80 per cent of the water, are taken back into the blood from the tubule. Urine, containing waste chemicals, passes into the ureter.

▶ HOW DOES A KIDNEY MACHINE WORK?

If a person's kidneys do not work properly, waste chemicals build up in the blood. A special filtering device, or kidney machine, can take the place of the kidneys. Blood is pumped over a thin membrane that allows water and waste chemicals to pass through.

A person suffering from kidney failure is linked up to a kidney machine by two tubes.

One is attached to an artery in an arm. Blood from the artery is pumped into the machine.

Inside the machine the blood passes through a long tube that is made of a thin, semi-permeable plastic membrane. Outside the membrane is a salt solution that is kept well stirred. Water and dissolved waste chemicals pass through the membrane from the blood to the salt solution. The blood is then warmed and passed back to a vein in the person's arm. The process of cleaning the blood takes several hours.

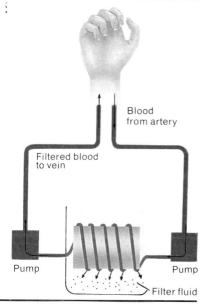

Blood from artery
Filtered blood to vein
Pump
Pump
Filter fluid

◀ HOW DO BONES MEND?

When a bone is broken, the two pieces must be held in place for several weeks so they can grow together properly. New bone material slowly forms between the pieces.

Bones may break, or fracture, in several different ways. A simple fracture is one in which the two ends remain in position, and not much damage is done to the surrounding tissue. In a compound fracture, the

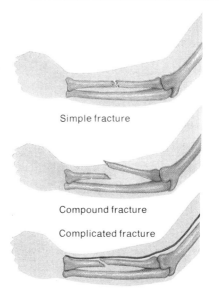

Simple fracture
Compound fracture
Complicated fracture

broken bone pierces the skin. In other kinds of fracture large blood vessels may be damaged, or the bone ends may be smashed.

The healing process begins when blood from broken blood vessels forms a clot. After a few days the broken ends of the bone become soft and the space between them fills with a sticky 'glue' which contains bone-forming cells.

After two or three weeks, new soft bone tissue has completely filled the gap between the broken ends. This slowly hardens.

As you breathe in and out, your diaphragm contracts and relaxes, increasing and decreasing the volume of your lungs.

The movement of your lungs is controlled automatically by your diaphragm. When this muscular sheet contracts, it becomes flatter. When this happens, the pressure in the chest cavity is reduced and the lungs expand, drawing in air. At the same time the rib muscles contract, lifting the ribs upwards and outwards.

Breathing out takes place when the diaphragm and rib muscles relax. The lungs shrink and force the air out. A person's lungs contain between four and six litres of air, but usually less than half a litre is breathed in and out.

Air is breathed in through the mouth and nose. It passes into the windpipe, or trachea. This divides into two bronchi, which enter the lungs and divide into a number of smaller tubes called bronchioles. These divide into even smaller

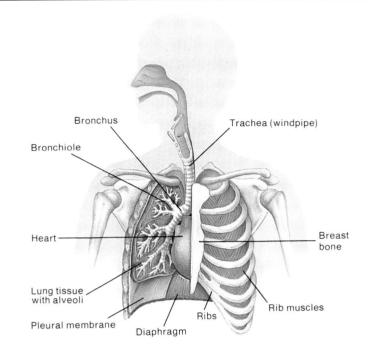

tubes, which finally end in tiny air sacs, or alveoli.

Each alveolus is surrounded by hundreds of minute blood vessels. The lining of the alveolus is very thin and is kept moist. Oxygen dissolves in the moisture and passes into the blood. Waste carbon dioxide passes from the blood into the alveoli and is breathed out.

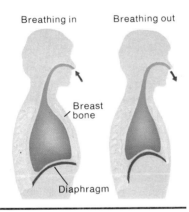

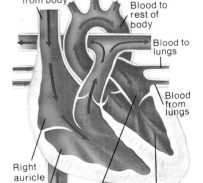

Your heart is a muscular pump divided into two parts. One part pumps blood to your lungs. The other part pumps blood to the rest of the body.

Your heart consists of four chambers: two auricles and two ventricles. The walls of these chambers are made of special muscle that contracts rhythmically. Each heartbeat has two stages. The auricles contract first, followed

quickly by the ventricles. This gives your heartbeat its familiar 'lub-dub' sound.

Between the chambers are one-way valves. These allow blood to flow through the chambers in one direction only. The right auricle receives blood from the body. As it contracts, blood flows into the right ventricle. When this contracts, it pumps the blood to the lungs.

The left auricle receives blood from the lungs and passes it to the left ventricle. This pumps blood to the rest of the body.

▶ HOW DOES A HEART-
LUNG MACHINE WORK?

This machine is used during major heart surgery. The machine pumps blood round the body, supplies the blood with oxygen and removes carbon dioxide.

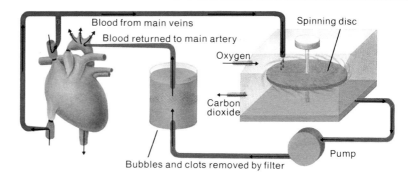

Blood from main veins
Blood returned to main artery
Spinning disc
Oxygen
Carbon dioxide
Pump
Bubbles and clots removed by filter

During a heart operation, the patient's heart cannot pump blood. And, because the chest cavity is open, the lungs cannot work either. So the main blood vessels are tied off and the patient's blood is piped into a heart-lung machine. There, oxygen is made to enter the blood. This is done either by bubbling oxygen through the blood in a bubble chamber, or (as shown here) by dripping the blood onto a spinning disc. There the blood forms a thin film into which oxygen can pass. Carbon dioxide is removed at the same time.

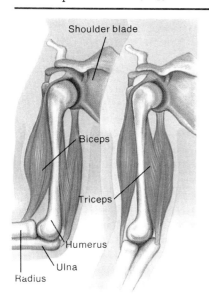

Shoulder blade
Biceps
Triceps
Humerus
Ulna
Radius

◀ HOW DO YOUR MUSCLES
WORK?

Muscles can only contract (shorten) and pull. So to move a part of your body to and fro, muscles have to act in pairs.

For every muscle that causes a particular movement, there is another muscle that causes an opposite movement. A typical example of this can be seen in the arm. To bend your arm at the elbow, you contract your biceps muscle. The top of this muscle is attached by tendons to your shoulder blade. The other end is attached to the radius bone of your forearm. When the biceps muscle contracts, your forearm is pulled towards the upper arm.

When you want to straighten your arm, your biceps muscle relaxes. But this by itself is not enough. The triceps muscle contracts, pulling on the back of the ulna bone, and the forearm swings downwards.

Other, more complicated movements involve using two opposing sets of muscles instead of just two muscles.

▶ HOW DOES A KNEE-JERK
REFLEX HAPPEN?

When someone taps you just below the knee, you cannot stop your lower leg from jerking upwards. This is because the nerve impulses travel via the spinal cord directly to the leg muscle, and are not controlled by the brain.

When the tendon just below your knee-cap is given a sharp tap, the extensor muscle of your leg is slightly stretched. This stimulates a sensory nerve, which carries a nerve impulse to your spinal cord. Here, the sensory nerve divides and part of the impulse passes to the brain, telling the brain that the knee has been struck.

However, the brain does not control the knee's response. Part of the sensory impulse is sent directly to the motor nerve of the muscle.

To counteract the original stretching, the extensor muscle contracts. But it usually over-reacts, with the result that the leg jerks upwards.

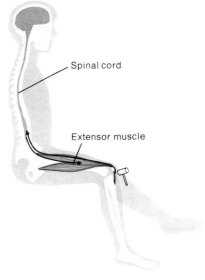

Spinal cord
Extensor muscle

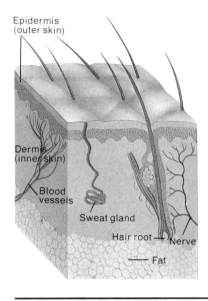

Epidermis (outer skin)
Dermis (inner skin)
Blood vessels
Sweat gland
Hair root — Nerve
— Fat

◄ WHAT IS YOUR SKIN FOR?

Your skin is a waterproof, elastic covering to your body. It helps to protect your body from damage and germs and also helps to keep your body at a constant temperature.

Your skin is a tough cushion that protects the tissues underneath. It acts as a barrier to germs and is also a sense organ, having receptors that respond to cold, heat, touch and pain. The skin makes vitamin D when exposed to sunlight and it produces hair and nails.

The skin is a waterproof body covering that prevents moisture from escaping. But moisture does escape through your sweat pores. This is particularly useful in hot conditions, as evaporating sweat cools you down. Cooling is also helped when blood vessels in the skin expand and heat is lost from the blood. In cold conditions, the surface blood vessels in the skin become narrower and help keep heat inside your body.

► WHAT ARE YOUR TEETH MADE OF?

A tooth consists of a crown above the gum and a root embedded in the bone of the jaw. A layer of hard enamel covers the crown. Under this outer enamel there is a layer of dentine surrounding the core, or pulp.

The outer layer of the crown of a tooth is made of a substance called enamel. This is the hardest substance in the body and is very resistant to wear. Inside the enamel layer is a layer of dentine. This is also hard, but not as hard as enamel. Dentine forms the roots (or just one root in the case of the front teeth), which are set into the jawbone with a layer of cement.

The inner core of the tooth is called the pulp. This contains nerve fibres and blood vessels. Nerve fibres also go through the dentine and cement layers. If the dentine is exposed by decay, painful toothache results. Cement left exposed by receding gums is also painful.

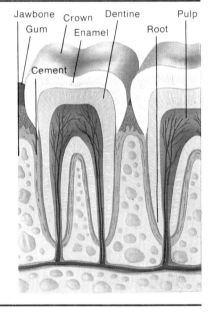

Jawbone Crown Dentine Pulp
Gum Enamel Root
Cement

◄ HOW DO YOUR TEETH WORK?

Your teeth consist of slicers, stabbers and grinders. The slicers (incisors) are at the front. Behind these are the stabbers, or canine teeth. At the back of the mouth are the grinders or molars. Children do not have as many teeth as adults.

Children have 20 teeth altogether. In each jaw there are four incisors. These are wedge-shaped teeth used for cutting off pieces of food. Behind the incisors are two pointed canine teeth, used for tearing off pieces of tough food that the incisors cannot cut. Behind the canines are four molars. These have broad, ridged crowns and are used for chewing food.

Adults have 32 teeth. They too have four incisors and two canine teeth in each jaw. But the molars they had as children have been replaced by four grinding premolars. In addition, adults have six molars at the back.

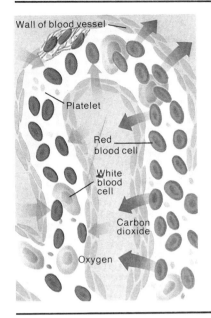

Wall of blood vessel

Platelet

Red blood cell

White blood cell

Carbon dioxide

Oxygen

◀ WHAT DOES YOUR BLOOD DO?

Blood is the vital transporting liquid of your body. It carries oxygen to all the tissues and takes carbon dioxide away to the lungs. It also carries food materials to the liver and other tissues and waste chemicals from the liver to the kidneys.

Blood consists of several kinds of cell suspended in a pale liquid called plasma. Over 55 per cent of the blood is plasma, which is mostly water. Also in the plasma are proteins, minerals, food chemicals and waste chemicals.

There are three main kinds of cell in blood. Platelets are tiny cells that help in clotting. White blood cells fight disease. Red blood cells are the vital oxygen-carrying cells. There are many millions of them in the blood. They contain the red pigment haemoglobin, which picks up oxygen at the lungs and releases it into the tissues of the body.

▶ HOW DOES YOUR BLOOD HELP FIGHT DISEASE?

White blood cells are one of your body's main defence systems. There are several kinds. Some attack and engulf germs. Others help in producing special chemicals called antibodies.

Compared with the vast number of red blood cells, there are not many white blood cells in blood, only about 9000 in each cubic millimetre.

When germs invade the body, for example through a cut, white blood cells called neutrophils rush to the wound and begin to engulf the germs. Then larger white cells called monocytes appear and engulf more germs, together with any debris. Any germs that escape are dealt with by a third kind of white cell called lymphocytes. These recognize germs as being 'foreign protein', or antigens. Then they start the production of antibodies, which are protein substances that stop germs working.

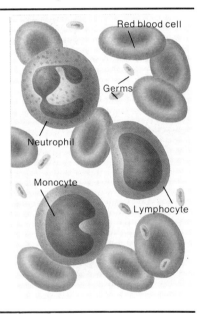

Red blood cell

Germs

Neutrophil

Monocyte

Lymphocyte

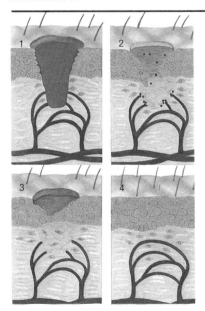

1

2

3

4

◀ HOW DOES A WOUND HEAL?

An open wound can be invaded by germs. To prevent infection, blood clots and forms a scab over the wound. New skin tissue develops beneath the scab.

When your skin is damaged, the broken blood vessels immediately become very narrow. This stops too much blood being lost and helps to keep germs out of the blood. Then substances released into the blood cause it to clot. The blood clot holds the edges of the wound together and hardens into a protective scab (1).

Meanwhile, white blood cells arrive at the wound and destroy dangerous bacteria (2). In the lower layer (the dermis) of the skin, special cells called fibroblasts move into the wound and start producing new tissue (2). In the upper layer (epidermis) the cells around the wound start to multiply and fill the gap (3). When this is nearly complete, the scab falls off (4).

193

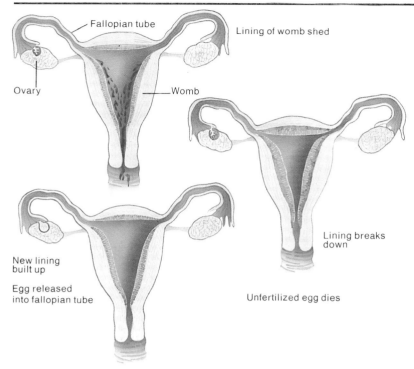

Fallopian tube

Lining of womb shed

Ovary

Womb

New lining
built up

Egg released
into fallopian tube

Lining breaks
down

Unfertilized egg dies

▲ WHAT IS THE MENSTRUAL CYCLE?

This is the cycle of changes that occur in a woman as she produces eggs. The cycle takes about four weeks. **During the first two weeks an egg develops in an ovary and is released into the womb. If it is not fertilized, it is expelled from the body with part of the womb lining.**

At the start of the menstrual cycle an egg begins to ripen in one of the two ovaries. As it ripens, hormones are released into the body. These cause the womb to increase in size and its lining to thicken, ready for the egg to develop if it is fertilized.

After about 14 days the egg is released from the ovary and the womb continues to increase in size. If the egg is not fertilized on its way to the womb, it dies within two days. About a week later the womb begins to shrink and its lining breaks down.

On the last day of the cycle the unfertilized egg and the remains of the womb lining are expelled, together with some blood. This process is called menstruation and it lasts for about five days. Menstruation begins some time between the ages of 12 and 14. It continues until the age of about 50.

▶ WHAT CAUSES TWINS?

Identical twins occur when a single fertilized egg splits into two. Both cells then develop into a baby. Non-identical twins are the result of two separate eggs being fertilized at the same time.

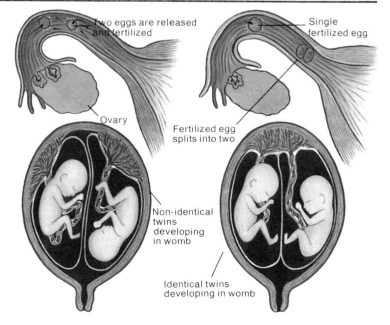

Two eggs are released and fertilized

Single fertilized egg

Ovary

Fertilized egg splits into two

Non-identical twins developing in womb

Identical twins developing in womb

If a fertilized egg splits into two, both cells start to develop in the normal way. They become implanted in the womb close together and, as a result, both developing babies share the same placenta.

Identical twins are of the same sex. They share the same features, such as hair colour, height and weight and look very much alike. Non-identical twins develop from two separate eggs fertilized at the same time. In the womb they are nourished by separate placentas. They may or may not be of the same sex and they bear no more than a family likeness to each other.

Non-identical twins are born more often than identical twins. Triplets are usually a combination of identical twins and a non-identical brother or sister.

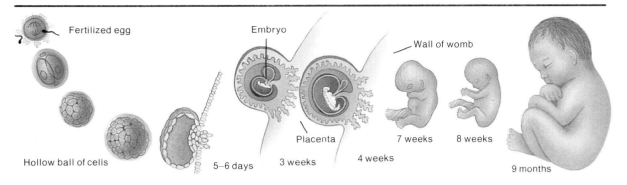

Fertilized egg

Embryo

Wall of womb

Placenta

7 weeks

8 weeks

Hollow ball of cells

5–6 days

3 weeks

4 weeks

9 months

▲ HOW DOES A BABY DEVELOP?

A baby begins life as a fertilized egg. This develops quickly into an embryo. After eight weeks it is recognizable as a human baby. It continues to grow and after nine months it is born.

After about nine days a fertilized egg has developed into a hollow ball of cells, which becomes implanted in the wall of the womb. Part of this ball, with part of the womb lining, forms the placenta. This is the organ that keeps the developing embryo supplied with food and oxygen. The major organs of the embryo,

such as the heart and brain, appear soon. After about six weeks the limbs, eyes and ears develop.

After eight weeks the baby (now called a foetus) has almost all its organs and tissues, including its nervous system, muscles and skeleton. During the next seven months all these continue to develop.

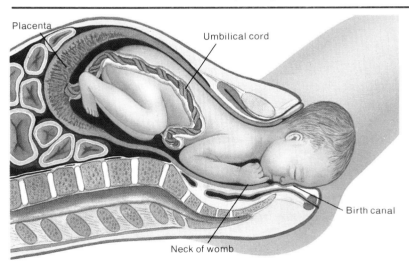

Placenta

Umbilical cord

Birth canal

Neck of womb

▲ HOW IS A BABY BORN?

When a baby is ready to be born, the mother begins labour. The muscles of the womb push the baby downwards and the neck of the womb starts to open. Eventually, the baby is pushed out.

Labour appears to start because the baby has reached the right stage of development. Labour pains are contractions of the womb. These may continue for several

hours, gradually becoming stronger and more frequent. All the time the baby's head is being pushed down, gradually stretching the neck of the womb. When the neck of the womb is fully open, the membranes around the baby break, releasing fluid (this sometimes happens earlier). Then the baby is pushed out.

Soon after it is born, the baby begins to breathe and the umbilical cord is cut. Then the afterbirth (the placenta and membranes) is also pushed out.

◀ WHAT IS A TEST-TUBE BABY?

Babies do not grow in test-tubes! A so-called 'test-tube baby' is produced by removing an egg from a woman's ovary and fertilizing it outside her body. The fertilized egg is then placed inside the womb, where it grows.

Some women cannot have children in the normal way. The woman's fallopian tubes (the tube leading from the ovaries to the womb) may be blocked, or the man's sperm may not be fertile enough.

In such cases, doctors can perform an operation to remove one of the woman's eggs. The egg is placed in a special culture material, where it is fertilized with sperm taken from the man. The fertilized egg starts to divide in the usual way. When the embryo is still just a ball of cells, it is inserted into the woman's womb. There it grows into a normal baby.

195

MEDICINE

▼ WHO WERE THE FIRST DOCTORS?

The beginnings of medicine go back to prehistoric times. But for thousands of years medicine was based largely on superstition.

We know very little about prehistoric medicine. But people must have learned a good deal about the human body as they treated wounds and broken bones. One prehistoric 'cure' for disease was the practice of trepanning. In this operation a surgeon cut a round piece of bone out of the patient's skull. Evil spirits were then supposed to come out of the hole.

Among the best of the ancient doctors were the Egyptians. By about 1500 BC they had developed a large vocabulary of special medical words and were experimenting in surgery and pharmacy.

▼ WHO IS KNOWN AS THE FATHER OF MEDICINE?

In about 400 BC the Greek physician Hippocrates (460-c.370 BC) founded the first school of medicine on the island of Cos.

Doctors at the Hippocratic school of medicine were taught that diseases were the result of parts of the body not working properly, rather than of possession by demons. But Hippocrates and his followers did not know enough about the structure of the human body. They believed that diseases were caused by an imbalance of four vital fluids, or 'humours' – blood, bile, phlegm and black bile.

Over 50 books were written by Hippocrates and other members of the school. The medical code of practice called the Hippocratic Oath also dates from this time.

▼ WHO WAS GALEN?

Galen (c.130-c.200) was one of the greatest Greek anatomists. His ideas remained popular for hundreds of years.

Galen was born in Pergamum (now in Turkey). When he was about 30 years old he became physician at the gladiatorial school there. Later he settled in Rome and began studying anatomy. He studied a number of animals but not humans.

Galen worked out an idea of how the body's physiological system worked. The body was supposed to contain spirits which ebbed and flowed through the arteries, veins and nerves. Many of Galen's ideas were wrong, as they were based on theory and old textbooks, rather than the study of human anatomy. But they remained popular until the 1500s.

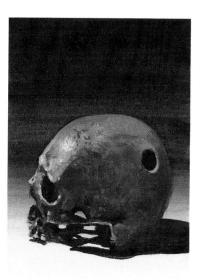

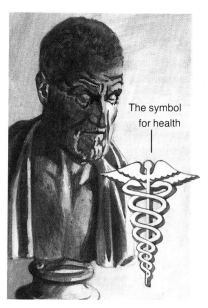

The symbol for health

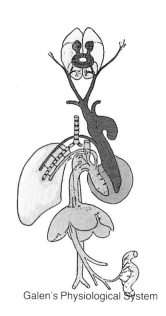

Galen's Physiological System

**Acupuncture – the use of
needles inserted in the body –
has been used in Chinese
medicine for thousands of
years.**

In the Chinese Taoist religion
order in the body depends on
two opposite states called yang
and yin. Yang is associated
with light, the Sun, the south,
masculinity and dryness. Yin
is associated with darkness, the
Moon, the north, femininity
and wetness. All illness is
thought to be an imbalance
between these two states.

Acupuncture is used to
restore the balance of yang and
yin. The needles vary from 2 to
25 centimetres in length. They
are inserted at one or more of
over 800 points lying along
certain lines on the human
body. The needles may be left
in for several hours. This form
of treatment is still used today
and surgery is often performed
using acupuncture instead of
anaesthetics.

**Paracelsus (1493-1541) was a
Swiss physician. His real
name was Theophrastus
Bombastus von Hohenheim.
He was a vain man and lived
up to his middle name. He
took the name Paracelsus
because it meant 'better than
Celsus', a popular Roman
physician.**

Paracelsus made several
important contributions to
medicine. For example he
wrote the first work on an
occupational disease – 'Miners'
sickness'. He also insisted on
cleanliness as being essential
for good health. He was the
first to use laudanum and is
sometimes called the father of
anaesthesia. One of his most
important ideas was that
alchemists should study how to
make medicines and not gold.

Paracelsus became Professor
of Medicine at Basle
University in 1527. Before
starting his first lecture he
publicly burnt books by Galen.
This emphasized his idea that
medicine should be studied by
referring to human patients
instead of just to textbooks.

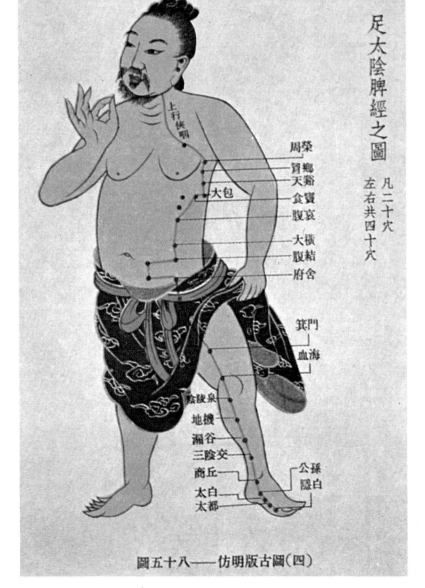

圖五十八──仿明版古圖（四）

**Ambroise Paré (1510-1590)
was a French surgeon. He
improved the practice of
surgery in several ways and
devised several ingenious
artificial limbs.**

In the 1500s surgery was not
practised by physicians.
Instead it was one of the
specialities of the haircutting
profession. As a boy Paré
started as a barber's
apprentice. In 1541 he
qualified as a barber-surgeon
and joined the army.
Eventually, he became surgeon
to the French King Henry II
and the King's three sons, who
later succeeded him.

Paré was a popular surgeon,
largely because of the
improvements he introduced.
For example he gave up the
practice of cauterizing wounds
with boiling oil. Instead he tied
off the exposed arteries and
covered the wounds with
simple dressings.

Paré devised several artificial
limbs. Among these was an
arm that could be bent at the
elbow and a hand with
moveable fingers.

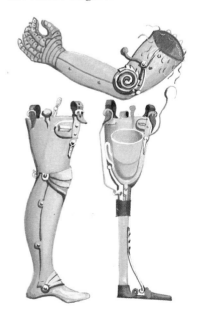

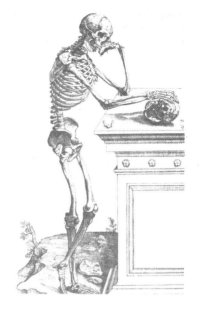

**Andreas Vesalius (1514-
1564), a Flemish physician,
made the first really accurate
studies of human anatomy.**

Galen's ideas about human
anatomy persisted throughout
the Middle Ages. This was
partly due to the fact that
anatomists did not perform
their own dissections.

The first to change this
practice was an Italian,
Mondino de Luzzi (c. 1275-
1326), who wrote the first book
devoted entirely to anatomy.
But the study of anatomy
remained much the same until
the time of Vesalius.

Vesalius taught anatomy at
several Italian universities.
Like de Luzzi, he began to do
his own dissections, mostly
because he was appalled at how
badly dissections were being
done by anatomy assistants.
After much research he wrote
one of the greatest books in the
history of science. It was called
De Corporis Humani Fabrica
('On the Structure of the
Human Body'). One of its
illustrations is shown above.

**The English doctor William
Harvey (1578-1657) was the
first to realize how blood
passes round the body.**

William Harvey spent much
time doing research on the
heart and blood vessels.
Eventually, he came to the
conclusion that Galen was
wrong. Blood did not ebb and
flow. It flowed through the
heart, veins and arteries in one
direction only. One-way valves
in the heart and veins
prevented it from flowing in
the opposite direction.

Harvey's theory relied on
the fact that there had to be a
connection between the
arteries and veins. Harvey
decided that, as both veins and
arteries divided into smaller
and smaller branches, the
connecting vessels must be too
small for the eye to see. Italian
physiologist Marcello Malpighi
(1628-1694) later proved this
with the aid of a microscope.

Harvey published his ideas
in 1628. At first they were
ridiculed, but before he died
they had become accepted.

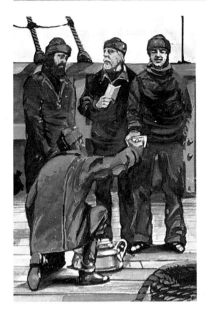

▲ WHO DISCOVERED A CURE FOR SCURVY?

▲ WHO DISCOVERED THAT GERMS CAUSE DISEASE?

The Scottish doctor James Lind (1716-1794) discovered in 1747 that eating fruit prevented scurvy.

Lind realized that scurvy only appeared when people's diet was short of fresh fruit and vegetables. He managed to convince Captain Cook, who successfully prevented scurvy onboard his ships in the 1770s. Finally, in 1795 the British Navy began to issue lime juice to sailors.

In 1866 the French chemist Louis Pasteur (1822-1895) was the first to realize that diseases are caused by tiny organisms, or germs. But this was only one of the great scientist's achievements.

Louis Pasteur was not a biologist or a physician but a chemist.

In 1854 he decided to work on the fermentation of wine and beer, showing that a living organism – yeast – was

involved. To prevent wine going sour as it aged, he introduced the idea of heating it to 120°F (49°C) to kill off the unwanted yeast cells. This technique became known as 'pasteurization', which is still used to kill germs in milk.

In 1860 Pasteur finally disproved the idea that living micro-organisms could be generated out of nothing, through the decomposition of substances. He showed that the air contains spores of already existing micro-organisms (germs), which can infect food and other materials. In 1865 he helped to save the French silk industry by detecting a tiny parasite that was attacking the silkworms and their food.

All this work eventually led Pasteur to believe that germs were the cause of disease and that they could be spread from one person to another.

In 1881 Pasteur successfully tried out a vaccine for anthrax, a fatal disease of cattle and sheep. In 1885 he managed to prevent a case of rabies. The Pasteur Institute, established in 1888 to treat rabies, is now one of the world's most famous centres of biological research.

► WHO INTRODUCED VACCINATION AGAINST SMALLPOX?

In 1796 the English doctor Edward Jenner (1749-1827) discovered that a person inoculated with cowpox could not get smallpox.

Smallpox was once one of the world's most dreaded diseases. In the 1700s one in three of those who caught it died.

However, Jenner noticed that those who got the disease mildly never caught it again. He began to think about

inoculation – but with what? At the time it was believed by country people that those who caught the mild disease cowpox never got smallpox. Jenner decided to test this. In 1786 he found a milkmaid with cowpox. He took fluid from one of her blisters and injected it into a boy. A few days later he inoculated the boy with smallpox germs. The boy didn't develop the disease.

Within a few years the practice of vaccination against smallpox became common and it has now been completely wiped out.

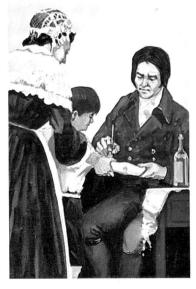

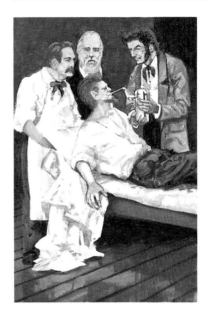

Lister's carbolic spray

▲ WHO INTRODUCED THE USE OF ANAESTHETICS?

An American dentist called William Morton (1819-1868) was the first to publicize the idea of using anaesthetics in surgery.

William Morton was not the discoverer of anaesthetics. In 1800 Humphry Davy (1778-1829) had discovered laughing gas, or nitrous oxide. In 1831 chloroform was discovered by the American chemist Samuel Guthrie (1782-1848). And the term 'anaesthetic' was first suggested by an American doctor called Oliver Wendell Holmes (1809-1894).

The first recorded use of an anaesthetic in surgery was in 1842. Crawford Long (1815-1878), another American doctor, used ether to remove a neck tumour.

In 1844 William Morton, looking for a painless way to extract teeth, began taking an interest in ether. Together with an American chemist called Charles Jackson (1805-80), he patented a process for producing anaesthesia. His first operation using ether took place in September 1846.

▲ WHO FIRST USED ANTISEPTICS IN SURGERY?

In 1865 the English surgeon Joseph Lister (1827-1912) used carbolic acid to prevent infection.

Joseph Lister qualified as a doctor in 1852. He became a surgeon and his particular interest was in amputation (removing limbs). The technique of anaesthesia had recently been introduced by William Morton and Lister was pleased that he could now perform painless operations. However, the fact that many patients died later from infection worried him.

In 1865 he learned of Pasteur's work on germs and diseases and began trying to kill germs in surgical wounds. He experimented with various chemicals and eventually found that dressings soaked in carbolic acid were effective. The first patient to be successfully treated in this way was a five-year-old boy with a fractured shin. Lister also used a carbolic spray to create an antiseptic mist round the operating table. But this was later found to be unnecessary.

▲ WHO IDENTIFIED THE BACTERIUM THAT CAUSES TUBERCULOSIS?

The German scientist Robert Koch (1843-1910) discovered the tubercle bacillus in 1883. For this work he was awarded the Nobel Prize for Medicine and Physiology in 1905.

Robert Koch began studying disease while still a country doctor living near Breslau. He looked particularly at the bacterium that causes anthrax in cattle, and succeeded in cultivating the bacterium in blood serum and studying its whole life-cycle.

Koch then moved to Berlin and, as his fame grew, developed important techniques for the study of bacteria. Among these was the now standard method of growing bacteria on agar-agar jelly. He also established rules for identifying the bacteria that cause particular diseases.

Among the many bacteria that Koch discovered, the most important were those that cause tuberculosis, cholera and bubonic plague. With Pasteur, Koch is regarded as the founder of medical bacteriology.

▲ WHO WAS SIGMUND FREUD?

▲ WHO FOUND A WAY OF PREVENTING POLIO?

▲ WHO PERFORMED THE FIRST HEART TRANSPLANT?

Sigmund Freud (1856-1939) was an Austrian psychiatrist. He was the founder of the technique called psychoanalysis and is famous for his ideas on dreams and child development.

After obtaining a degree in medicine in 1881 Freud studied the biology of the nervous system – in particular nerve cells. But he soon became more interested in the psychological aspect of the brain and learned that certain mental disorders could be helped by hypnosis.

Freud later abandoned hypnosis in favour of a technique he called 'free association' or the 'talking cure', in which patients were psychoanalysed by making them talk about incidents that had greatly affected them in their childhood and that they could not face up to. Freud also believed that dreams were able to show what was going on in the unconscious mind. In 1900 he published a book called *The Interpretation of Dreams*.

The first vaccine that successfully prevented poliomyelitis was produced by the American microbiologist Jonas Salk (1914-).

Robert Koch and others had been very successful in cultivating bacteria. But viruses were more difficult. In 1949, however, the American microbiologist John Enders (1897-) and others succeeded in growing some polio virus.

The polio virus could now be studied easily. Salk began trying to kill the virus in a way that made it unable to cause the disease but left it able to cause the production of protective antibodies. He succeeded in 1952 and two years later the vaccine was produced in large quantities.

In 1957 another American microbiologist, Albert Sabin (1906-), produced polio vaccines that contained strains of live viruses that were too feeble to actually cause polio. Mass vaccination against polio began and by 1960 the occurrence of the disease had been greatly reduced.

The world's first human heart transplant was carried out on December 3 1967 by the South African surgeon Christiaan Barnard (1922-).

Surgeons began trying to transplant organs such as kidneys and hearts in the 1940s. But the main problem was that the body's natural defence system tended to 'reject' a new organ.

This problem was eventually eased by the discovery that if the tissue types of both people were carefully matched, the person receiving the heart had a much better chance of survival. At the same time it was discovered that drugs could be used to control the body's defence system which usually rejects 'foreign bodies'.

Since Barnard's first transplant hundreds of such operations have been carried out all over the world. Even babies are now receiving new hearts. However, heart transplants are very complex operations and control drugs make patients more liable to get diseases.

THE PAST

▶ WHEN DID PEOPLE FIRST MAKE TOOLS?

The first primitive people to use tools lived in Africa about 1,800,000 years ago. Their fossil remains, and some of the tools they made, have been found at Olduvai Gorge in Tanzania.

The fossils were found by two palaeontologists (people who study fossils), Louis and Mary Leakey. The Leakeys spent most of their lives exploring fossil sites in East Africa, where their son Richard still works.

The tools the early people used were made by taking pebbles and hammering away at one edge with a second rock until bits flaked off. Stones

flaked in this way have sharp edges, and they can then be used for cutting, scraping and chopping. These early people probably used the tools to kill animals and chop up the meat.

The Leakeys gave this early type of tool-user the scientific name *Homo habilis*, which means 'handy man'. *Homo habilis* walked upright, probably stood about 1.2 metres tall, and had a powerful grip.

▲ WHEN DID THE NEANDERTHALS LIVE?

Neanderthal people lived in Europe during the last Ice Age, which began about 70,000 years ago. Remains of Neanderthal people have also been found in the Middle East and North Africa.

The first remains were found in the Neander Valley, near Düsseldorf in West Germany, in 1856. Remains have since been found in other places, including Britain, France and Italy.

Neanderthal people were short and muscular, and not much over 1.5 metres tall. They had long, low skulls, with heavy ridges over the eyes. The Neanderthals lived in caves, and used fires to keep themselves warm.

Neanderthals made stone scrapers and hand-axes, and wooden spears. They hunted large animals such as the mammoth and the woolly rhinoceros. They buried their dead.

Neanderthals disappeared about 35,000 years ago.

WHEN DID THE CRO-MAGNON PEOPLE LIVE?

WHEN DID THE CRO-MAGNON PEOPLE LIVE?

Cro-Magnon people were one of the earliest-known types of human being. The Cro-Magnons lived in Europe, **Asia and North Africa from about 35,000 years ago.**

The Cro-Magnons get their name from a cave at Les Eyzies, in south-western France, where their bones were first found. They belonged to the same species as we do, *Homo sapiens sapiens* ('very wise man').

The Cro-Magnons lived in caves, and they made the splendid prehistoric cave paintings which have been found in France and Spain. The most important of these caves are at Lascaux in France and Altamira in Spain. The Cro-Magnons lived near the mouths of their caves, but they made their paintings deep inside.

The Cro-Magnons probably came to Europe from western Asia. They stood about 1.7 metres tall, and their skeletons show that they were very like people of today.

The Cro-Magnons made better stone tools than the Neanderthals, but they seem to have been less suited than the Neanderthals to life in very cold climates. That is why they did not reach Europe during the worst of the Ice Age. But they were much cleverer than the Neanderthals.

WHEN DID PEOPLE FIRST SETTLE IN AMERICA?

WHEN DID PEOPLE FIRST SETTLE IN AMERICA?

The first people arrived in America some time between 28,000 BC and 23,000 BC. They walked there from Asia across dry land where the Bering Strait now is.

During the Ice Age great sheets of ice covered the northern part of the world. So much water was frozen into this ice that the sea-level fell. As a result, a lot of land that is now under the sea was dry.

The Bering Strait became dry on two occasions: between 28,000 BC and 23,000 BC, and again between 14,000 BC and 10,000 BC. Scientists think that

a group of people crossed during each of these periods.

The first inhabitants of America, the American Indians, are Mongoloids – that is, they are similar in type to the people of China, Japan and Siberia. The Indians of North America became farmers, or lived by gathering fruit and seeds or by hunting and fishing, as shown here.

► WHEN DID THE INDUS VALLEY CIVILIZATION FLOURISH?

The valley of the River Indus lies in Pakistan. One of the world's first civilizations grew up along its banks between 2500 BC and 1500 BC.

Like the other great early civilizations in Egypt, China and Mesopotamia, the Indus civilization grew up along a river, where there was plenty of water and good rich soil to grow crops.

There were about a hundred small towns and villages along the river bank, plus two large cities. One is called Mohenjo-Daro, a Hindu name meaning 'mound of the dead'. It lies about 450 kilometres upstream from Karachi. The other, further inland on a tributary of the Indus, is named Harappa.

The people of the Indus Valley built their cities of kiln-baked mud bricks. They laid out their streets on a grid pattern, and built brick sewers. Mohenjo-Daro had a fortified citadel, containing temples and a large granary (shown here). There was also a large public bath, possibly used for religious ceremonies.

The people of the Indus civilization had a system of weights and measures. They made objects of copper, bronze and silver, and used gold as jewellery. They were still halfway between the Stone Age and the age of metals, because they also used flint knives.

Objects made in ancient Babylonia have been found amid the ruins, showing that the Indus people engaged in long-distance trade.

Nobody knows how the Indus Valley Civilization ended. Flooding or invasion may have finished it.

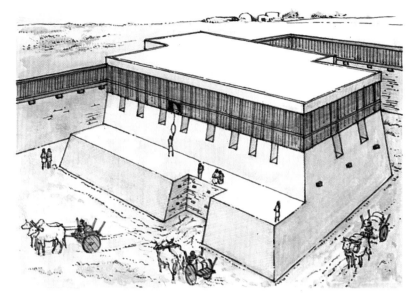

▲ WHEN DID THE FIRST DYNASTIES RULE IN CHINA?

Dynasties are ruling families. The first of these families we know of was the Shang Dynasty. It governed China from about 1500 BC to 1027 BC.

There may have been an even earlier dynasty, the Hsia. An ancient Chinese writer of history, Ssu-ma Ch'ien, referred to the Hsia, but no other traces of them have been found.

The Shang people built big cities in the flat plains near the Yellow River. Poor people lived in pits with thatched roofs over them. The richer people lived in large houses above ground. Tall earth banks surrounded the cities.

The nobles used chariots drawn by horses for hunting in peacetime and to take them into battle during war. In war each chariot carried two soldiers besides the driver.

The Shang made elaborate objects in bronze, and were also skilled sculptors. The Chou Dynasty overthrew the Shang in 1027 BC.

▼ WHEN WAS EGYPT RULED BY PHARAOHS?

The word *pharaoh* means 'great house' or 'royal palace'. The Egyptians used the term for their kings from about 1570 BC until the Romans conquered Egypt in about 30 BC.

For hundreds of years the Egyptians regarded their pharaohs not just as kings, but as gods, and supreme gods at that. An inscription to one pharaoh reads: 'Adore the king . . . he is the One who creates all.'

The pharaoh himself worshipped the Sun-god, Rê. Among his many titles was 'Son of Rê'. He was also called 'King of Upper and Lower Egypt'. Although in theory the pharaoh was all-powerful, in practice he had to abide by fixed rules and customs.

The pharaoh is usually shown, in paintings and statues, wearing a double crown (for Upper and Lower Egypt). He carries a crook and a flail as emblems of his power. Queens are usually shown much smaller. Statues were always very stylized.

▼ WHICH GODS DID THE EGYPTIANS WORSHIP?

The Egyptians had many gods. Some were local, worshipped in a particular region or city. Then there was Osiris, god of the dead, and people also worshipped the pharaoh and the Sun.

The greatest local god was Amon, god of the air, who was worshipped in the city of Thebes. Amon later became identified with the Sun-god, Rê, as Amon-Rê.

Other local gods included the cat-headed goddess Bast; Apis the bull; and Thoth, the god of learning and the Moon. Thoth was usually shown with the head of an ibis.

Osiris had the dual role of god of the dead and vegetation. His sister and wife, Isis, was regarded as 'the mother of all things'. Their son, Horus, was the god of Heaven. He is shown with a falcon's head. Setekh, the sky-god, was the brother of Osiris. Anubis, shown as a jackal or with a jackal's head, was the god of death. The pharaoh was thought to personify Horus and Osiris.

▼ WHEN DID PEOPLE FIRST WORK WITH METAL?

The oldest metal objects so far found were made of copper, before 7000 BC. They were discovered at Çayönü Tepesi in Turkey.

These copper objects were made by hammering the metal cold. The makers used what is called 'native' metal. This is metal occurring almost pure in small nuggets. Copper and gold are often found like this. The most important metal for early people was bronze. It is an alloy of copper and tin that is harder than either. The bronze stand shown here was made in Cyprus in the 1100s BC.

Metal was not widely used until people discovered how to smelt it – that is, extract it from rock by heating it in a furnace. This probably happened about 4000 BC. By the 3000s BC smiths in Mesopotamia (present-day Iraq) were making elaborate bronze objects. But they may not have been the first to do so. In Thailand, archaeologists have found a bronze spearhead dated at about 3600 BC.

Osiris   Anubis   Thoth

Work began on the Palace of Knossos in Crete about 2200 BC. Most of what is standing today was built between 1775 BC and 1580 BC.

The Palace at Knossos was one of several that have been found in Crete, and was probably the home of the Minoan kings. It was built on several floors around a central courtyard, and was full of large, airy rooms.

The walls of the main rooms were decorated with painted pictures. One is shown here. From these pictures we know that the wealthy people who lived in the palace wore fine clothes. Most of the women and men had curly black hair.

In 1450 BC a great disaster occurred which virtually ended the Minoan civilization. It was probably one of the many earthquakes which rock Crete from time to time and cause great destruction.

People from Mycenae, on the Greek mainland, lived on Crete for a time. In 1375 BC the Palace of Knossos was burned down.

▲WHEN WAS CRETE THE HOME OF A GREAT CIVILIZATION?

The great civilization in Crete flourished between about 3000 BC and 1100 BC. It is called the Minoan Civilization after its legendary king, Minos.

The civilization of Crete was forgotten for centuries. The only clue to it was a legend that every seven years the ancient Greeks had to send seven girls and seven young men as sacrifices to a terrible monster, the Minotaur, who lived in Crete.

In 1899 the archaeologist Arthur Evans found the remains of the Minoan civilization. He found that kings and nobles lived in large, luxurious palaces. Ordinary people lived in flat-roofed stone houses in small towns or villages.

The Minoans traded food in exchange for gold, silver, copper and other materials. They also made beautiful pottery.

▶WHEN WAS STONEHENGE BUILT?

Stonehenge was built in three stages. The earliest was begun about 2750 BC, and the last additions were made about 1300 BC.

Nobody knows exactly what the purpose of Stonehenge was. It was undoubtedly a religious place, but it may also have been an observatory. Some of the stones are aligned with sunrise on Midsummer Day, and with moonrise on Midwinter Day.

Late Stone-Age people

began Stonehenge by digging a huge circular ditch and bank. They also dug a ring of 56 pits, now called 'Aubrey Holes' after the 16th-century writer John Aubrey, who found them.

Between 2000 and 1700 BC, a long avenue was made between Stonehenge and the River Avon. Eighty bluestones, from Wales, were erected in a double circle. About 1700 BC, huge blocks of sandstone capped by lintels were put up. Some more bluestones were erected about 1300 BC.

**The Mycenaeans invaded
Greece from Russia in about
2000 BC. Their great city of
Mycenae flourished from
about 1450 BC to 1100 BC,
when it was destroyed by new
invaders.**

Mycenae was the home of
King Agamemnon who,
according to the poet Homer,
led the attack on Troy. For
years scholars thought
Agamemnon and his people
were legendary.

Then, in 1877, a group of
royal tombs was found just
inside the Lion Gate at
Mycenae. The tombs were
built 300 years before the time
of Agamemnon. They were
full of treasures made of gold,
silver and alabaster.

The people of Mycenae
dominated Greece for
hundreds of years, sailing
across the sea to Crete and
other islands. They were
engaged in almost constant
warfare, and they built huge
stone walls around their cities
for defence. The picture shows
the citadel at Mycenae.

**The siege of Troy, which
Homer described vividly in
his poem the *Iliad*, took place
somewhere about 1250 BC.**

Homer probably lived about
800 BC, but practically nothing
is known about him. His poem
about Troy was based on older
stories and legends, and is a
mixture of fact and fancy. The
poem is called the *Iliad*, from
another name for Troy, Ilios.
According to Homer, Troy
was besieged by a Greek army
led by Agamemnon.

The ruins of Troy were
rediscovered between 1870 and
1890 by a German, Heinrich
Schliemann, who was
fascinated by archaeology. We
now know that Troy was
destroyed and rebuilt many
times. The earliest town on the
site was probably built about
3000 BC.

The Troy of the great siege
was the seventh town to stand
on the site. Its ruins show signs
that it was plundered and set
on fire.

**The Phoenicians were traders
from about 2900 BC, but they
were at the height of their
power about 2000 years later.**

The Phoenicians lived in the
coastal regions of what are now
Syria, Lebanon and Israel.
They were the Canaanites of
the Old Testament of the
Bible. Canaan and Phoenicia
both mean 'land of purple',
and refer to the purple dye the
Phoenicians made.

The Phoenicians were
skilled craftsmen. They made
glass and metalwork, carved in
ivory and wood, and wove
cloth. Their decorative
furniture was famous. They
also dealt in timber, and in
metal ores from Spain.

The Phoenicians set up
several colonies, notably at
Cadiz in Spain, and Carthage
(near modern Tunis in
Tunisia). Their bold sailors
ventured into the Atlantic
Ocean, and traded along the
coast of West Africa and
western Europe.

The Persian Empire was founded by Cyrus the Great in 549 BC. He extended his rule over most of western Asia.

Cyrus was king of Anshan, a small principality in south-western Iran. His overlord was Astyages, King of Media. Cyrus gradually got other Persian tribes on his side, and in 553 BC he began a rebellion against the Medes. By 549 BC he had overthrown Astyages and became king.

Cyrus spent the next few years crushing opposition to his rule, and conquering the small principalities that acknowledged Media as their overlord. Cyrus called his new empire the Achaemenid Empire, after Achaemenes, an ancestor of his.

Cyrus then began a career of conquest. In turn he subdued Lydia in Asia Minor, all the lands that were dependent on Babylon, and finally Babylon itself. He was killed trying to conquer lands to the east.

The Battle of Salamis was fought between a Greek fleet and a Persian fleet in 480 BC. The Persians were heavily defeated.

For more than a hundred years the Persians tried to conquer Greece. Their first efforts failed, though they captured Cyprus and a number of Greek states in Asia Minor (modern Turkey).

In 480 BC King Xerxes of Persia began a new attack. He crossed the Hellespont (the old name for the Dardanelles) from Asia Minor into Europe, with a huge army. The army was supported by a large fleet.

Gradually the Persians drove the Greeks back, until they had to take up a defensive position on the Isthmus of Corinth. The Greek fleet sheltered in the nearby strait of Salamis. The Persian fleet attacked them there and was soundly beaten. A year later the Persian army was defeated at the Battle of Plataea, and the Persians were driven from Greece.

Darius I seized the throne of Persia in 522 BC, and ruled it until 486 BC. He is often known as Darius the Great.

Darius was not the real heir to the throne of Persia, but the son of the governor of Parthia, a Persian province. When King Cambyses of Persia died in 522 BC, civil war broke out, and the throne was taken by a man who claimed to be Cambyses' brother, Bardiya.

Darius and six Persian noblemen killed Bardiya, and Darius made himself king. He claimed that 'Bardiya' was really an imposter, but modern historians think Darius invented this story.

Darius was powerful. He soon brought his empire under control. He divided it into provinces, each ruled by a *satrap* (governor). To keep in touch with the provinces he had good roads made, along which royal messengers sped. Darius is shown here receiving tribute from his subjects.

WHEN DID THE GREEK CITY-STATES ARISE?

The early Greeks began building fortified cities as long ago as 1500 BC. These cities developed into different states because they lay in valleys that were separated by mountains.

The geography of Greece encouraged its people to be independent. Secure in its mountain-girt valley, each city developed its own way of life. People even spoke different dialects of Greek.

THE ACROPOLIS OF ATHENS

The earliest city-states were monarchies, but by about 600 BC most of the cities had got rid of their kings. Because they were small, the cities could settle major problems by a meeting of all the most important citizens. In this way, the idea of democracy (government by the people) gradually emerged.

The Greek city-states had to establish colonies if they wanted to expand. Colonies were set up in Italy, Sicily, Spain, southern France, and on the shores of the Black Sea.

In the 700s BC Sparta became the most powerful of the city-states. In the 400s the Greek cities banded together to fight off a Persian attack – the only time they ever united.

Soon afterwards Athens became the most important city. It had the finest writers, artists, sculptors and thinkers in all Greece.

Eventually Greece came under the domination of the northen state of Macedonia and its rulers Philip II and his son, Alexander the Great.

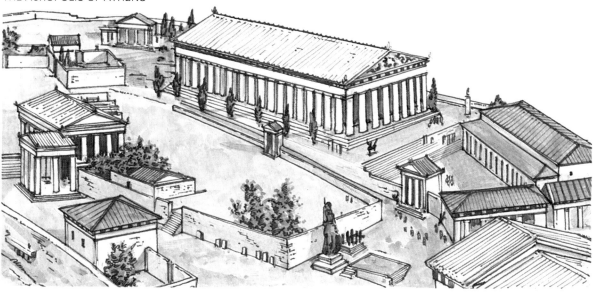

WHEN WAS THE GOLDEN AGE OF ATHENS?

Athens reached the height of its fame and influence during the rule of the statesman Pericles, from 461 to 431 BC.

Pericles was a member of a noble Athenian family. He became the leader of a popular democratic party and, in effect, head of state in 461 BC.

He was determined to make life better for the poor. When he came to power, poor people could not hold any of the offices of state because the

posts were unpaid. Pericles introduced salaries for all public officials, and allowed the common people to hold any of the state posts.

Under his leadership the Athenians also began to rebuild their city, which had been partly destroyed during wars with Persia. Many of the buildings on the Acropolis, the hilltop citadel which dominates Athens, date from the city's 'Golden Age'. They include the Parthenon, a marble temple dedicated to the goddess Athena. It was decorated with sculptures by

the great sculptor Phidias (the so-called 'Elgin Marbles').

Many great writers were active during the Golden Age. They included the playwrights Aeschylus and Sophocles, who wrote tragedies, and the comedy-writer Aristophanes. The first great historian, Herodotus, lived in the Athenian colony of Thurii.

But Pericles also involved Athens in wars. In 404 BC, after Pericles' death, Athens was defeated by Sparta.

The Byzantine Empire was founded by the Emperor Constantine I in AD 330. It was an eastern division of the Roman Empire.

The Roman Empire was divided in two by the Emperor Diocletian in 286. By the time Constantine came to the throne, the eastern part of the empire was more important than the western part.

Constantine decided to move the headquarters of the empire to the east. He built a new city as his capital, which he called Constantinople after himself. It is now Istanbul.

Constantinople was built on the site of a small town named Byzantium. The term 'Byzantine Empire' is one used by modern historians. Its people always thought of themselves as Romans.

The Byzantine Empire lasted until 1453, when Constantinople was captured by the Ottoman Turks. The picture shows a mosaic of Constantine IX, who ruled from 1042 to 1055.

Islam was founded by the prophet Muhammad, in Arabia. It spread rapidly in the years immediately after his death in AD 632.

The word Islam means 'submission', and implies the obedience of its followers to the will of God. They are called Muslims, which means 'those who submit'.

The basis of Islam is the *Koran*, a holy book. Muslims

The Islamic Empire lasted from AD 632 to 1256. It stretched from Spain to India.

After Muhammad died in 632, his friend and chief adviser Abu Bakr was elected caliph. Caliph means 'successor'. From then on, the Islamic Empire was ruled by caliphs.

Abu Bakr and his successors launched a *jihad* (holy war) to convert people to the Muslim faith. Within 12 years of

believe that the Koran contains the words of God, revealed to Muhammad by the Archangel Gabriel in a series of visions.

Muslims do not worship Muhammad, but regard him as the last in a series of major prophets which include the Old Testament prophets and Jesus.

Muhammad did not write down the words of the *Koran*. They were written down by his followers as he taught them. The Koran took its final form about 652, during the reign of the Caliph Othman.

Muhammad's death, the caliph controlled Arabia, the whole of the Middle East, including part of Persia, and all of Egypt.

By 750, Islam had spread along the North African coast. The Moors, Muslims from Morocco, had also conquered most of Spain and Portugal. The Muslims also reached western India and central Asia.

Trade and learning flourished in the Islamic Empire. Muslim merchants travelled far and wide to trade in luxuries such as silks and spices.

The wild Mongol tribes of the Asian plains were united in 1206 by a chieftain named Temujin, later called Genghis Khan.

The Mongols were nomads who wandered over the bleak countryside with their herds of horses and cattle. They lived in felt tents called *yurts*, and were skilled hunters and fierce warriors.

Temujin was born in 1162. He was a very strong man, and was a born leader. He was loyal to his friends but he punished traitors severely.

In his early years, Temujin survived many attempts to kill him by rival tribes. The Merkits were a tribe from the frozen lands further north. On one occasion, they captured Temujin's wife, Bourtai, in a night raid. But with the aid of another tribe, the Karaïts, he won her back.

Soon after, Temujin led his Mongols to victory against an attack by twice their number of Taidjuts. By this and other victories he gradually gained the respect of other tribes. More and more people came under his rule.

When he was about 40 years old, Temujin was proclaimed *Genghis Khan*, which means 'King of the Oceans'. In 1206 he was elected as Great Khan, ruler of all the Mongol peoples. He set up a code of laws, and began to train his unruly warriors into a disciplined force. Once this army was formed, Genghis Khan set out to conquer other lands.

The Mongol Empire reached its greatest extent by 1294, when it stretched from the River Danube in the west to the Pacific Ocean in the east.

Genghis Khan began his conquests with an attack on China. At first his warriors were trained only for open warfare on the plains. They had no siege engines to attack fortified towns. But they soon captured skilled Chinese soldiers and made them help.

Genghis Khan also practised 'psychological warfare'. He terrorized people into surrender with horrific tales of what would happen if they resisted the Mongols.

The Mongols broke their way through the Great Wall Of China in 1213. By 1215 Peking had surrendered, and Genghis Khan ruled over north China. He then set out for the west, and in a six-year campaign swept through Persia and Afghanistan into southern Russia.

When Genghis Khan died, his empire was divided among his four sons. One of them, Ogotai, led an army of 150,000 horsemen into Hungary and Poland in a devastating raid.

The empire was reunited later when Genghis's grandson, Kublai Khan, was elected Great Khan in 1260. He still had rivals, including his own younger brother, but he defeated them all. Kublai completed the conquest of China. He founded a new dynasty, the Yüan, which ruled China until 1368. After Kublai died, in 1294, the Mongol Empire broke up.

Vikings raided European lands and founded colonies for about 200 years up to around AD 1000.

The Vikings were pirates from Scandinavia. They were bold and skilful navigators, who sailed the European seas in their long, elegant ships. Each ship had a large, square sail, but could also be driven by oars.

At first the Vikings went in search of plunder. They often raided monasteries, where some of the greatest wealth could be found.

From 793 onwards, Vikings from Norway raided England. They began to settle there in the late 800s. Other Vikings started settlements in the Orkneys, Shetlands and Hebrides. Settlers sailed in shorter, wider ships, as shown in the picture.

Vikings attacked France and settled there. They were known as Northmen, or Normans, and gave their name to Normandy. Others reached Spain, Sicily, Italy and Russia.

The feudal system existed in Europe during the Middle Ages, from about AD 700 to the 1400s.

The term 'feudal system' is used by historians to describe a system under which a person held land in return for military or other service. The land was called a *fief*, or *feodum* in medieval Latin.

The feudal system began in the kingdom of the Franks (now France) and spread gradually over western Europe. It reached its height in the period from the 800s to the 1200s, but disappeared in the 1400s.

In its simplest form, the feudal system could be seen as a pyramid. At the top was the king. He let the great barons have lands in return for providing him with soldiers when he needed them. The barons in turn gave land to lesser lords or knights in return for their services. Peasants also held land from each lord in return for working on his land.

America was probably first sighted in about 986 by a Viking named Bjarni Herjólfsson, but the first visit was by Leif the Lucky in AD 1000.

Vikings settled in Iceland about 870. Among them was a warrior named Eric the Red, so-called for his habit of feuding and killing. Eric was exiled from Iceland for three years. He founded a settlement further west, now Greenland.

Bjarni Herjólfsson was on his way to Greenland from Iceland when he was blown off course and sighted land to the west. Eric's son, Leif Ericsson (known as Leif the Lucky) heard Bjarni's story. He decided to make a voyage to the west himself.

Leif reached the coast of Labrador and cruised south until he came to a land where wild grapes grew. He called it Vinland. Vikings later tried to settle there, but were driven away by hostile Indians.

▼ WHEN WERE
MONASTERIES FOUNDED
IN EUROPE?

**The first monasteries in
Europe were founded in Italy
and France in the AD 300s.**

The earliest Christian
monastery was founded by St
Anthony of Egypt in the
Egyptian desert in the early
300s. St Anthony himself
spent most of his life as a
hermit, in a cave.

Christians in Italy and Gaul
(as France was then called)
were inspired by St Anthony's
example. St Martin, bishop of
Tours, established an
important monastery at nearby
Marmoutier. From there,
monks travelled to take the
monastic idea to many lands.

An important step was taken
by St Benedict of Norcia in
Italy. In 529 he established a
monastery at Monte Cassino,
which still flourishes. There he
wrote his *Rule*, a code of
conduct for monks which has
been followed ever since.
Monasteries became the main
centres of learning in Europe
during the Middle Ages.

▼ WHEN WAS JAPAN
RULED BY SHOGUNS?

**The first shogun to rule Japan
was Minamoto Yoritomo in
1192. The last shogun
resigned in 1867.**

The word *shogun* means
commander-in-chief. It was
originally used in the 700s as a
purely military title. Japan was
then, as now, ruled by an
emperor, but real power was in
the hands of the Fujiwara
family, who acted as regents.

In 1160 the Taira family
seized power from the

Fujiwaras, only to be defeated
by the Minamoto family led by
Yoritomo. From then on the
shoguns acted as military
governors of Japan.

The title of shogun became
hereditary. It was held by the
Minamoto family until 1336,
when the Ashikaga family took
over. They ruled until 1573.
The Tokugawa family took
over in 1603. In 1867 several
important *daimyo* (noblemen)
banded together to overthrow
the shogun. The emperor then
took over the shogun's powers.

▲ WHEN WERE GREAT
CASTLES BUILT IN JAPAN?

**The great period of castle-
building in Japan was in the
1500s and 1600s. At that time
the country was divided into
many small states at war with
one another.**

Every local chief had a heavily
fortified home. Warriors
known as samurai fought on
horseback for their lords. But
castle-building really
developed when a warrior
named Toyotome Hideyoshi
became shogun in 1585.

Hideyoshi built a series of
castles to help him control
Japan. Each castle consisted of
a palace surrounded by
defensive walls, lookout towers
and a moat. Japanese castles
were similar to the medieval
castles of Europe, but their
central buildings were not so
heavily built as the keeps of
European castles.

Hideyoshi's successor as
shogun was Tokugawa Ieyasu.
He ended the long period of
civil war that had ravaged
Japan, and castles ceased to be
of military importance.

WHEN DID THE SWISS BECOME INDEPENDENT?

The Swiss gained their independence from the Holy Roman Empire in 1499. This was officially accepted by the Empire in 1648.

In the early Middle Ages Switzerland consisted of several cantons, or states, which formed part of the Holy Roman Empire.

Three cantons – Uri, Schwyz and Unterwalden – formed a league in 1291, but did not then claim independence. They took the name Switzerland from Schwyz. Other cantons joined them later.

Between 1315 and 1388, the Swiss defeated three attempts by Austria to subdue them. One of their earliest victories was the Battle of Margarten in 1315, shown here.

In 1499 the Swiss defeated the army of Maximilian I, the ruler of the Holy Roman Empire, and became independent. After a defeat by the French in 1515, Switzerland became a neutral country and has stayed so ever since.

WHEN WAS JOAN OF ARC BURNED AT THE STAKE?

Joan of Arc freed much of France during the Hundred Years' War. She was burned to death for heresy by the English in 1431.

Joan was a peasant girl. Her name in French is Jeanne d'Arc. She was born at Domrémy, in eastern France, in 1412. When she was 17, Joan heard voices which she said commanded her to free her country from the English, who controlled the northern half of France.

Joan went to the young king of France, Charles VII, who had not even been crowned, and demanded to lead his army. Charles agreed. Wearing armour and a sword, Joan led French forces to save the town of Orléans, which was under siege by the English. She won four other battles and saw Charles crowned at Rheims.

In 1430 Joan was captured by troops of Burgundy, who sold her to their allies, the English. They put her to death.

WHEN DID THE BLACK DEATH SWEEP ACROSS THE WORLD?

The Black Death was an outbreak of bubonic plague. It ravaged Asia and Europe between 1334 and 1351.

Bubonic plague is named after the buboes, or swellings, that appear on the bodies of its victims. It has been known at least since the days of the Romans, and possibly existed in Biblical times.

The epidemic of plague known as the Black Death started in central Asia. It was carried by fleas that lived on rats. Ships and overland trading caravans carried the plague westwards. By 1346 it had reached the Crimea. From there it was carried to Europe by ships.

The plague reached Europe in 1348. By the end of 1350 it had swept through most of Europe. The outbreak was over by the end of 1351. About one person in three died from the plague during this time. Bodies were carted away for burial by corpse-collectors.

▶ WHEN DID THE ITALIAN CITY-STATES ARISE?

The Italian city-states began to develop in the 1000s. They became independent in the late Middle Ages. Some became rich and powerful.

After the fall of the Roman Empire in 476 there was no strong central government in Italy. Lombards from Germany occupied the north. Normans from Normandy set up a kingdom in the south which included Sicily. The popes controlled the Papal States in central Italy.

From the late 900s, northern Italy became part of the Holy Roman Empire. Because the emperor lived far away in Germany, some of the cities began to gain independence.

Coastal cities with the best opportunities for trade grew rich and powerful first. Among them were Pisa, Genoa and Venice. Other important cities included Milan and Florence. Some cities were ruled by dictators, but they were often controlled by assemblies of citizens, especially the rich merchants.

▲ WHEN DID VENICE BECOME RICH?

Venice began to grow rich in the 800s. It reached the height of its wealth and power in the 1400s.

Venice (shown here) is built on a group of islands in the Adriatic Sea, off the coast of Italy. Fishermen and traders fled there in the 400s to escape from the barbarians who were raiding Italy. By the 800s they had built Venice, and were trading by sea with Constantinople and other Mediterranean cities.

Venice was ruled by a leader called a *doge*, who was elected from among the most powerful families. From 1310 onwards, however, real power was held by a group called the Council of Ten.

By the 1400s Venice controlled trade in the eastern Mediterranean. Silks and spices from the East were imported into Europe in Venetian ships. Great churches and palaces were built along the canals of Venice by rich merchants.

◀ WHEN WAS THE HANSEATIC LEAGUE FORMED?

The Hanseatic League was an association of German towns. They banded together for trade and protection in the late 1200s.

'Hanseatic' comes from an old French word, *hanse*, meaning a guild. At its height, the Hanseatic League was like a small-scale Common Market. Merchants in a number of north German towns formed a series of *hanses* for trading abroad, particularly with England and Flanders (modern Belgium).

The merchants of Hamburg and Lübeck co-operated first. They made an agreement to combat robbery in the area. They soon found that working together made them stronger than their competitors when trading in the Baltic Sea area. Almost all the larger cities on the shores of the Baltic and North seas eventually joined the League. The picture shows Hanseatic merchants discussing trade.

221

▼WHEN WAS THE
OTTOMAN EMPIRE
FOUNDED?

The Ottoman Empire was founded by the Turkish sultan Osman, who died in 1326. The Ottoman Turks take their name from him.

The Ottoman Turks came from Asia Minor, which is now known as Turkey. Until 1071, Asia Minor was part of the Byzantine Empire. Then it was conquered by Seljuk Turks.

Shortly before 1300, the Ottoman Turks began to build their empire. They were based at first in Bithynia, in the north of Asia Minor. Soon they had conquered almost all of Asia Minor. In 1345 they crossed into Europe, and by 1400 they controlled most of the Balkan peninsula, from Bulgaria to Greece.

The Ottoman Empire grew fast. Its lands stretched from North Africa to the Middle East. The Ottoman army even laid siege to Vienna, but failed to capture it. At first, the huge empire was strong, but gradually it lost much of its power.

▼WHEN WAS THE LAST
MAJOR BATTLE WITH
GALLEYS FOUGHT?

The last major battle with galleys was the Battle of Lepanto. It was fought near Greece on 7 October 1571, between a Christian fleet and a Muslim Turkish force.

In 1570 the city of Venice appealed for help to the Pope and Spain against the Turks who were attacking the Venetian colony in Cyprus.

After much argument, a Christian fleet was assembled to fight the Turks. It consisted of ships from Venice, Spain, Malta, Genoa and Savoy.

The main ships in both the Christian and Turkish fleets were galleys. These were long, slim warships driven by oars. They were easier to manoeuvre than sailing ships.

The Turkish fleet consisted of 274 galleys carrying 88,000 men. The Christian fleet had 316 galleys, including small craft, and 80,000 men. It was commanded by Don Juan of Austria. The battle lasted five hours before the Christian fleet won.

▲WHEN DID THE
OTTOMAN TURKS
CAPTURE
CONSTANTINOPLE?

Constantinople was the capital of the Byzantine Empire. The Ottoman Turks captured it in 1453.

By 1400 the Ottoman Turks had overrun all the Byzantine lands except a small area around Constantinople. The Byzantine emperor had to acknowledge the Turkish sultan as his overlord.

From 1424 onwards, Sultan Murad II was content to live at peace with the emperor. But when the sultan died in 1451 he was succeeded by Muhammad II, whose ambition was to conquer Constantinople.

Muhammad built a castle, now called Rumili Hisar, on the European shore of the Bosporus near Constantinople. With this as a base, he began to besiege the city in March 1453. The final assault (shown here) began on 25 May. In a few hours the Turks captured Constantinople. They renamed it Istanbul.

The Renaissance was a revival of learning and a change in people's ways of thinking. It began in Italy around 1300, and lasted about 300 years.

The word *Renaissance* means 'rebirth'. It was first used in the 1800s to describe this great period of change.

The Renaissance began in the Italian city of Florence (shown in the picture). One of its pioneers was the painter Giotto. Unlike other artists of his time, he painted figures that looked realistic.

Writers, led by the poet Petrarch, began to explore the almost forgotten literature of ancient Greece and Rome. Their own writings were influenced by these works.

Architects such as Filippo Brunelleschi studied Greek and Roman buildings and began to design new buildings in a similar style.

The Renaissance received an enormous boost from the invention of printing. This was the work of a German goldsmith, Johann Gutenberg of Mainz, around 1440. Before printing was invented, books were rare objects because they were copied slowly and laboriously by hand. Now more people could study new ideas.

The Renaissance spread from Italy to France in the late 1400s, and soon reached Germany, the Netherlands and Britain. It reached its peak in the 1500s, a period known as the High Renaissance. An offshoot of the Renaissance was the Reformation, the great change in religion.

Members of the Medici family were involved in politics in Florence from the early 1200s, but their real power began in 1434. It lasted until 1737.

The power and influence of the Medicis came from their great wealth. They were bankers involved in international dealings. Giovanni de'Medici (1360-1429) was probably the richest man in Italy.

Giovanni's son Cosimo rose to supreme power in 1434. Cosimo never held office, but he influenced all the decisions of the city council. Florentines later called him 'the father of his country'. Cosimo spent large sums of money on the arts, and many of the famous Renaissance artists were supported by him.

The greatest of the Medicis was Cosimo's grandson Lorenzo (1449-1492), known as 'the Magnificent'. Under his rule, Florence (seen here) became the most powerful city-state in Italy. Architects and artists worked to make it also one of the most beautiful. After Lorenzo died, the Medici had some weak rulers. The family was twice exiled and twice restored.

Three of the Medicis became pope. They included Leo X, Lorenzo's son, and Clement VII, his nephew. The third, Leo XI, was elected pope in 1605, but died 27 days later.

Two Medicis became queens of France. Catherine married Henry II, and Marie married Henry IV. Their name in France was spelt *de Médicis*.

Henry VIII and Anne Boleyn

WHEN DID THE ANGLICAN CHURCH BREAK WITH ROME?

The break between the Church in England and the Pope came with the Act of Supremacy of 1534. This named Henry VIII and his successors as Supreme Head of the Church of England.

At first the Reformation in England was not a matter of beliefs but was dictated by political reasons. The basic cause was that Henry VIII had no male heir, and his wife, Catherine of Aragon, was too old to have another child. Henry asked the Pope to annul (end) the marriage so that he could marry a younger woman, Anne Boleyn.

The Pope refused to annul the marriage. Henry felt he had no alternative but to break with Rome and have an English court grant him a divorce. This political move led to religious changes. The English, or Anglican, Church became quite separate from the Roman Catholic Church. Henry also abolished the monasteries in England.

WHEN WAS THE SOCIETY OF JESUS FOUNDED?

The Society of Jesus was founded by St Ignatius Loyola in 1534.

Loyola (shown here) was a Spanish soldier who became a priest. He and six other men formed this Roman Catholic society in Paris. It was approved by Pope Paul III in 1540.

Its members, called Jesuits, have a special interest in education and missionary work.

WHEN WAS THE MASSACRE OF ST BARTHOLOMEW'S DAY?

The massacre took place on 24 August 1572, in Paris. It spread to other cities during the next few days.

The cause of the massacre was the enmity between the Roman Catholics in France and the Protestants, known as Huguenots. A civil war between them lasted from 1562 to 1570.

Several Huguenots held high office, and many Catholics feared that they would gain too much power. Among those who feared the Huguenots most was Queen Catherine de Médicis. She was the mother of Charles IX.

In August 1572, Huguenots flocked to Paris for the wedding of one of their leaders, Henry, King of Navarre, to Catherine's daughter, Margaret. Urged by Catherine, Charles ordered the assassination of the leading Huguenots. Armed mobs began the slaughter early in the morning of St Bartholomew's Day; 5000 people were killed.

Russia was united by Ivan III, Grand Prince of Moscow, who reigned from 1462 to 1505.

Moscow was one of several Russian states when Ivan became Grand Prince in 1462. They included Lithuania, Novgorod and Pskov. To the south and east lay three Mongol states: the Crimea, Kazan and the territory of the Golden Horde.

The Golden Horde claimed overlordship over Moscow and demanded a yearly tribute. When Ivan refused to pay, the Mongols marched to attack.

Ivan faced up to the threatened onslaught. His brothers, Boris and Andrei, supported him with 20,000 men, and the Mongols retreated.

Soon afterwards, the Mongols fell out among themselves and Moscow was safe from attack. Ivan also won control of Novgorod and Pskov, thus uniting Russia. He adopted the title of *tsar*, which means 'Caesar'.

▲ WHEN WAS INDIA RULED BY THE MOGULS?

Ivan III

Ivan IV

▲ WHEN DID IVAN THE TERRIBLE RULE RUSSIA?

Ivan IV was the grandson of Ivan III. He ruled from 1533 to 1584. His brutality gave him the nickname of 'the Terrible'.

Ivan IV came to the throne at the age of three, but did not begin to rule for himself until 1547, when he was almost 17. For several years his cruelty was kept in check by his wife, but she died in 1560.

While Ivan was a boy, Russia was ruled by a council of *boyars*, the rich noblemen. Ivan decided to curb the power of the boyars and so began a reign of terror. He could not forgive the bad way in which the boyars had treated him.

Ivan formed a bodyguard of secret police, called the *oprichniki*. At his command, the oprichniki hunted down and killed all the boyars whom he suspected of treason. In 12 years more than a thousand boyars were killed. Ivan grew more mad as he grew older, and even killed his eldest son in a quarrel.

The Mogul Empire was founded in 1526 by Babur, the ruler of Kabul in Afghanistan.

Mogul is an Indian equivalent of 'Mongol'. Babur was part Mongol by birth. He is shown here with his courtiers in a garden.

Several Afghan tribes were quarrelling over the right to rule Delhi when Babur decided to intervene. He won a decisive victory at Panipat, and made himself master of Delhi and its territory.

Babur's grandson, Akbar, ruled from 1556 to 1605. He extended the Mogul Empire throughout northern India as far as Kashmir. It reached its greatest size during the reign of Aurangzeb (1658-1707). It then included almost all of present-day India, Pakistan and Bangladesh.

After that the Empire slowly declined as the British gained control. The last Mogul emperor lost power in 1858, after the Indian Mutiny.

▶WHEN WERE THE EAST
INDIA COMPANIES
FOUNDED?

**The East India companies
were trading organizations
founded in the 1600s by
European countries. The
English, French and Dutch
companies were the most
important.**

Other East India companies
were established by Austria,
Denmark, Scotland, Spain and
Sweden. Few of these lasted
long, but the Danish company
sold out to the English
company as late as 1845.

The Portuguese discovered
the sea route to India in 1497-
1499, and at first they had a
monopoly of trade with India.
The Dutch soon gained control
of the islands that now form
Indonesia, which were a rich
source of spices.

The English East India
Company was formed in 1600,
the Dutch company in 1616,
and the French company in
1664. France and England
competed for trading and
military control of India
during the 1700s. Between
1750 and 1763 France and
Britain fought each other in
India. From 1756 they fought
in Europe too, in the Seven
Years' War. After the French
were defeated, they kept only a
few bases in India.

The British soldiers in India
were in the service of the East
India Company. They were
commanded by one of the
company's officials, Robert
Clive. The Mogul emperor,
seen in the picture with Clive,
lost much of his power to the
British.

The East India Company
ruled India until the Indian
Mutiny of 1857. After that the
British government ruled India
directly.

▼WHEN DID THE THIRTY
YEARS' WAR TAKE PLACE?

**The Thirty Years' War raged
in Europe from 1618 to 1648.
It began as a religious civil
war in Germany and ended by
involving most European
countries.**

The war began as a dispute
over whether a Roman
Catholic prince or a Protestant
one should be King of
Bohemia; and also whether a
Catholic should be elected as
Holy Roman Emperor.

The Catholic contender,
Ferdinand, became both King
of Bohemia and Emperor. The
Danish king, Christian IV,
then fought on the Protestant
side but he was defeated in
1629.

The Swedish king, Gustavus
Adolphus, then entered the
war, also on the Protestant
side. He was supported by
France, whose chief minister
was the Roman Catholic
Cardinal Richelieu.

By the time peace was made,
in 1648, Germany had been
devastated and millions of
innocent people had been
killed.

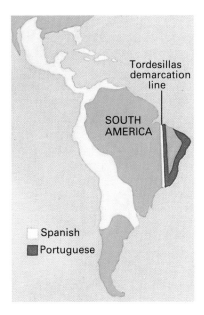

▲ WHEN DID A POPE DIVIDE UP THE WORLD?

▲ WHEN DID THE AZTECS THINK THAT GOD HAD ARRIVED ON EARTH?

▲ WHEN DID 180 MEN CONQUER AN EMPIRE?

Pope Alexander VI made the division in 1493 to prevent disputes between Spain and Portugal.

Christopher Columbus reached the West Indies in 1492. He thought that he had arrived in the outer islands of Japan, and reported this to his masters, the Spanish rulers Isabella and Ferdinand.

Ferdinand and Isabella knew that the Portuguese were already trying to reach the riches of the East by sailing eastwards around Africa. They appealed to Pope Alexander VI for a ruling that would divide the 'unknown' world fairly between Spain and Portugal.

The Pope drew an imaginary line from pole to pole, 100 leagues (556 kilometres) west of the Azores. He gave Spain rights to the west of it and Portugal rights to the east. In return, the Spanish and Portuguese had to convert the people of their new lands to Christianity. The line was later moved further west by the Treaty of Tordesillas between Spain and Portugal.

When Hernan Cortés landed in Mexico in 1519, the Aztecs thought he was their god Quetzalcoatl.

The Aztecs had a legend that Quetzalcoatl, the Feathered Serpent, had come to Earth in human form. He had a black beard and white skin. After a time he sailed away to the east. Prophets said he would come back one day, dressed in black.

Cortés lived in the Spanish colony of Cuba. Although rich, he was anxious to explore the lands that lay further west. Cortés sailed to Mexico with 11 ships and a few hundred men. He was white-faced, black-bearded, and wore black clothes. He also arrived in what the Aztec calendar called a 'One-Reed Year' – just the time that Quetzalcoatl was expected.

The Aztecs were terrified of the guns and horses that Cortés brought with him. Within two years Cortés had conquered the Aztecs and all of Mexico.

Francisco Pizarro was a Spanish soldier. He conquered the Inca Empire of Peru in 1532, with only 180 men.

Pizarro and a fellow soldier, Diego de Almagro, had already found the Peruvian empire six years earlier. They realized it was rich in gold and were determined to capture it.

Pizarro sailed from Panama in 1531 with three ships. His tiny force included his three brothers. Pizarro found the Inca Empire in a state of civil war. The emperor, Atahualpa, had been fighting his brother, Huascar, and had just captured him.

Pizarro captured Atahualpa by treachery. He asked for an enormous ransom of gold and silver which the emperor paid. While in custody, Atahualpa gave orders for his brother to be killed. Almagro and another 150 men arrived to support Pizarro. The two Spaniards accused Atahualpa of treachery, and had him strangled. Soon they were masters of Peru.

227

▼ WHICH FRENCH RULER WAS KNOWN AS THE 'SUN KING'?

Louis XIV was known as the 'Sun King' because he once danced a part with that name in a court ballet.

Louis reigned from 1643 to 1715, the longest reign of any French king. He became king when he was five years old, after the death of his father. Until 1661, France was ruled by Louis' chief minister, Cardinal Mazarin. When the cardinal died, Louis took over the throne himself.

Louis inherited a country that was weakened by foreign and civil wars. There was also rivalry among the people of his court, and his finances had been badly managed.

The young king ruled as a dictator. He believed that he had a divine right to rule. 'Only God has the right to question the conduct of kings', he said. On another occasion Louis said '*L'état, c'est moi*' ('I am the state').

Within twenty years Louis had raised France to heights of prosperity and glory. His court was the most dazzling in Europe. Louis fought four wars. As a result of these France gained Flanders (modern Belgium) and some German border-territory including Alsace and Lorraine.

Louis was a staunch Roman Catholic, and persecuted the Huguenots (French Protestants). About 400,000 of them emigrated, many to the Netherlands and to Brandenburg in Germany.

▲ WHEN WAS THE PALACE OF VERSAILLES BUILT?

The Palace of Versailles is near Paris. It was built between 1661 and 1708, on the orders of Louis XIV. Additions were built in 1756 for Louis XV. The palace is now a museum.

The picture shows Louis XIV at Versailles, with some of his courtiers. Louis had the palace built to show off the power and wealth of his court. The palace is more than 800 metres long. It consists of a vast centre section and two long wings.

There are hundreds of rooms in the palace. The most remarkable is the Hall of Mirrors, which is 73 metres long. It has windows down one side, and huge mirrors on the opposite wall.

Louis employed the finest painters, sculptors and craftsmen to decorate the palace. Formal gardens were laid out around the buildings.

In the grounds stand two smaller palaces, known as the Grand Trianon and the Petit Trianon. The Grand Trianon was built as a retreat for Louis XIV when he wanted to relax away from the court. The Petit Trianon was built by Louis XV for one of his favourites, the Comtesse du Barry.

The extravagance of Versailles caused great anger in France. People resented having to pay for the court, especially the poor peasants, who were taxed heavily. This helped to bring about the French Revolution in 1789, when Louis XVI was king.

THE PAST

Roundhead   Cavalier

WHEN DID THE ENGLISH CIVIL WAR TAKE PLACE?

The English civil war began in 1642 and lasted until 1646.

The war was between King Charles I and his Parliament. The main cause was money. Charles did not have enough money to run the government. When Parliament tried to control his income, he ruled as a dictator. So the King's power provided a second cause for conflict.

A third cause was religion. Many people, especially in Parliament, wanted a purer form of religion. They feared that Charles favoured Roman Catholicism.

The Parliamentary forces were known as 'Roundheads' because of their short hair. They defeated the Royalists, or 'Cavaliers', in four years and took Charles prisoner. They tried him for treason and executed him in 1649.

In 1650-51 Charles's son, Charles II, tried to recapture the throne but was defeated. In 1660, however, the monarchy was restored, with Charles II as king.

Peter I, known as 'the Great', modernized his backward country and made it a strong nation.

Peter became joint tsar with his half-brother, Ivan V, in 1682. Ivan was feeble-minded, so Peter became sole ruler in 1689, when he was 17.

In 1697-98 Peter made a tour of western Europe. Among his companions was his tutor. Peter travelled under the name of Bombadier Peter Mikhailov – though everyone knew perfectly well who he was.

Although he met other kings and statesmen, Peter spent a lot of time studying European technology. He even worked for a week as a carpenter in a Dutch shipyard, learning how ships were built.

On his return to Russia, Peter forced his nobles to adopt western dress and to cut off their long, shaggy beards. He built a new capital city, St Petersburg (now Leningrad), and modernized Russia's civil service.

Maria Theresa was ruler of Austria from 1740 to 1780, but she had to fight for her right to rule.

Maria Theresa was the only child of the Habsburg ruler of the Holy Roman Empire, Charles VI, who was also Archduke of Austria. Before he died, Charles named his daughter as his heir. He persuaded most of the other European rulers to agree that she should succeed him.

Many people did not like the idea of a woman ruler. France, Poland, Prussia, Sardinia and Saxony formed an alliance to seize her lands. Maria Theresa fought them off with help from Britain, Hungary and the Netherlands in the War of the Austrian Succession. She lost the province of Silesia to Prussia, but persuaded the German princes to choose her husband, Francis of Lorraine, as emperor. Maria Theresa tried to regain Silesia in the Seven Years' War of 1756-1763, but failed.

229

▶ WHEN DID THE
AMERICAN REVOLUTION
TAKE PLACE?

The American War of Independence broke out in 1775 and lasted until 1783.

The war was between Britain and its 13 North American colonies. The colonists had some independence, but the British controlled their overseas trade and their industries.

Trouble began to develop after the British defeated the French in North America, and took over their Canadian empire. The British decided that they must keep an army in North America, and taxed the colonists to pay for it.

In 1774 a Congress of 12 of the colonies agreed not to trade with Britain until the British changed their policies. The following April a British force went to seize a store of weapons held by the colonists at Concord, Massachusetts. Colonial militiamen confronted the British soldiers at dawn. Somebody fired a shot, and war began.

As the fighting went on, the colonists issued a Declaration of Independence on 4 July 1776. They decided to make a complete break with Britain.

After an American victory in 1777 at Saratoga, New York State, the French decided to enter the war against Britain. The Dutch and Spaniards also joined in the following year. In 1781 a British army surrendered at Yorktown, Virginia, and the British then agreed to peace talks. In 1783, the United States of America was recognized as an independent country. Its first president was George Washington.

Danton   Robespierre   Marat

▲ WHEN DID FRANCE
BECOME A REPUBLIC?

The first French Republic was declared on 21 September 1792. It lasted until 18 May 1804.

The French Revolution, which led to the declaration of a republic, began in 1789. It followed years of unrest that were caused by great inequalities. Peasants did not always have enough to eat. They and the middle classes paid heavy taxes, while the wealthy nobles lived in great luxury and paid little tax.

The revolution began with the storming of the Bastille, a prison in Paris. It continued with the arrest of the king, Louis XVI, and the formation of a National Convention. Among the Convention's leaders were Georges Danton, Maximilien Robespierre and Jean Marat. The Convention tried Louis for treason and had him executed. A Committee of Public Safety took over the government. In a Reign of Terror, it had thousands of its opponents put to death.

The rebellion took place in 1791 on the island of Hispaniola in the West Indies.

In 1791 Haiti was the French colony of St Domingue. It had a population of about 520,000, of whom 85 per cent were slaves. The slaves were Africans who had been imported to work on the plantations. The white plantation owners treated the slaves badly, and also the 27,000 free *mulattos* (people of mixed Black and French ancestry).

When France was torn by revolution, the oppressed peoples seized their chance to rebel. Their leader was Pierre Dominique Toussaint L'Ouverture (shown here) one of the slaves. By 1801 Toussaint ruled the whole island of Hispaniola. Napoleon then sent an army to subdue the rebels. Toussaint was arrested and died in prison, but the people of Haiti won independence in 1804.

Napoleon made himself emperor of France in 1804. He ruled until 1814 when he was forced to abdicate.

After the chaos of the French Revolution, an ambitious soldier gained power in France. He was the successful general Napoleon Bonaparte, who came from Corsica.

Napoleon seized power on 9 November 1799 and set up a three-man government called a Consulate. He was First Consul and really ruled as a dictator.

Napoleon proved to be as clever a minister as he had been a general . He reorganized the government and set up a new system of laws, known as the *Code Napoléon*. In 1804 he persuaded the French senate to give him the title of emperor.

But Napoleon was ambitious, and he set out to conquer the whole of Europe. He nearly succeeded, but after years of warfare he was finally defeated at the Battle of Leipzig in 1814, and was forced to abdicate.

The 'Hundred Days' lasted from 20 March 1815 to 29 June. This period was Napoleon's last attempt to be the ruler of France.

After his defeat in 1814, Napoleon was exiled to the island of Elba in the Mediterranean. He was allowed to rule the island and keep his title of emperor.

In 1815 Napoleon heard that many people in France were dissatisfied with their new king, Louis XVIII. He decided to return. With 1200 men, Napoleon landed in the south of France. The first troops sent to oppose him greeted him as their hero. He was soon back in Paris, and took power for a hundred days.

Two armies opposed Napoleon. One consisted of British, Dutch, Belgians and Germans, and one of Prussians. They met Napoleon and his army near the village of Waterloo in Belgium, on 18 June. The emperor was defeated and finally exiled to St Helena, in the South Atlantic.

▲ WHEN DID THE GREEKS
FIGHT FOR
INDEPENDENCE?

**Greece fought a war of
independence against Turkey
from 1821 to 1829.**

From 146 BC Greece came
under Roman rule and, later,
that of the Byzantine (East
Roman) Empire. From the
1400s it was under the control
of the Ottoman Turks.

The Greeks began longing
for independence in the late
1700s. In 1770, Greeks in the
Peloponnese staged a revolt
with Russian help, but the
Turks suppressed it harshly.

In 1814 a group called
Philiké Hetairia (the 'Friendly
Band') began training fighters
in the mountains, and in 1821
they started a new revolt. The
Turks, with Egyptian help,
tried to crush the rebellion.

In 1827 Britain, France and
Russia came to the aid of the
Greeks. They destroyed a
Turkish fleet at the Battle of
Navarino (shown here).
Turkey, tied up in a war with
Russia, recognized Greek
independence in 1832. Greece
gained extra land in the early
1900s.

▲ WHEN DID SOUTH
AMERICA GAIN
INDEPENDENCE?

**Spain's colonies won their
independence between 1809
and 1825. Brazil freed itself
from Portugal in 1822.
Guyana won its
independence in 1966, and
Surinam in 1975.**

In 1808, Napoleon invaded
Spain and deposed its king.
This started the fight for
independence by Spain's
South American colonies.

The main leader of the
revolution was a wealthy man
named Simón Bolívar. In 1810
he began a campaign to free
Venezuela, which lasted nine
years. Eventually he won
independence for five
countries – Colombia,
Ecuador, Peru, Venezuela and
Upper Peru, which was
renamed Bolivia after him.

Further south, the wars of
independence were led by José
de San Martín, who helped to
liberate Argentina, Chile and
Peru. Bernardo O'Higgins
joined San Martín in freeing
Chile. Brazil did not have to
fight for its freedom.

▼ WHO WROTE THE COMMUNIST MANIFESTO AND WHEN WAS IT PUBLISHED?

The *Communist Manifesto* was published in London in February 1848. It was written by two Germans, Karl Marx and Friedrich Engels.

Marx was a young philosopher and journalist whose socialist views made it impossible for him to work in his native Germany. He sought refuge in Paris. There he met Engels, a young economist.

The two moved to Brussels, where they wrote the *Communist Manifesto*. This 24-page document was designed to present the views and policies of a new organization, the International Communist Federation.

Marx and Engels believed that the poverty and suffering experienced by many people were caused by the capitalist system of society. In this system wealth is controlled by a few people who make profits from industry and business. Marx and Engels felt that there would be more progress if the workers were in control.

▼ WHEN DID ROME BECOME THE CAPITAL OF ITALY?

Although modern Italy became a unified kingdom in 1861, Rome was not part of it until 1870.

Rome has always occupied a special place in Italy. It is the home of the popes, whose headquarters are at the Vatican. Rome was also the capital of the Papal States. These lands were ruled directly by the popes.

During the revolutions of 1848, the French sent troops to Rome to protect the pope. The Italian patriot Giuseppe Garibaldi (shown here) tried to capture the city in 1862 but failed. The Italian government then tried to take over Rome but was foiled by the French.

In 1870 France was at war with Prussia and had to withdraw its troops from Rome. This enabled the Italians to take over the city unopposed. Pope Pius IX refused to agree to the loss of his possessions and regarded himself as a prisoner in the Vatican.

▲ WHEN WAS THE 'YEAR OF REVOLUTIONS'?

A series of uprisings in Europe in 1848 led to it being called the 'Year of Revolutions'.

The revolutions came at a time of bad harvests, famine and unemployment. The growing interest in socialism and communism led many people to think that they must change their governments if things were to be improved.

The first uprising (shown here) was in France. The people of Paris wanted an increase in the number of citizens allowed to vote. When King Louis Philippe failed to act, they forced him to leave the throne, and proclaimed the second French Republic. The Austrians were inspired by this and ousted their foreign minister, Prince Metternich.

Similar uprisings in Hungary and Sardinia won their people new constitutions, and many Italian cities drove out the Austrian troops who occupied them. There were also riots in Germany and demonstrations in Britain.

The United States bought extra land on three occasions, in 1808, 1853 and 1867.

The first purchase was the Louisiana Territory, a vast area of land west of the Mississippi River. It had been French, but France had given it to Spain in 1762.

The United States used the Mississippi as a highway, and was anxious to have its rivermouth port of New Orleans. In 1801 the president of the USA heard that Napoleon had forced the Spaniards to return Louisiana to France. He began to negotiate with the French, but without success.

In 1803, France and Britain were at war. Napoleon realized that the French might have difficulty in holding on to Louisiana during the war. He offered the Louisiana Territory to the Americans for $15,000,000. The United States borrowed the purchase money from English and Dutch banks.

The second purchase was the Gadsden Purchase of 1853. As a result of war with Mexico in 1848, the United States acquired a large area that was originally Spanish. But in one area the frontier was not clear. To avoid disputes over it, the USA bought a strip of land from Mexico. The deal was negotiated by James Gadsden, US envoy to Mexico, for $10,000,000.

The third purchase was Alaska, which the USA bought from Russia in 1867 for $7,200,000. The Russians were anxious to dispose of the land which they used only for fur-hunting.

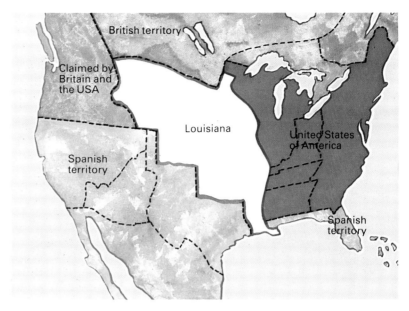

The gold rush started at the end of 1848 and reached its height during 1849.

James Wilson Marshall was a carpenter. He was hired to build a sawmill beside the American River, near Coloma in California. There, on 24 January 1848, he found nuggets of gold. The news quickly spread. Soon, Marshall's employer, John A. Sutter, found himself besieged by a horde of gold-hungry prospectors.

At first the prospectors came from California's population of 26,000. But after President James Polk announced the news, people from all over the world flocked to California. Sixty shiploads sailed from the eastern USA around Cape Horn. These were the first of the 'Forty-Niners', as the 1849 prospectors were called. They arrived in February, but even more came overland as soon as the winter was over. By the end of 1849 California's population topped 107,000.

The American Civil War began on 12 April 1861, and lasted until 26 May 1865. More than 500,000 men died in the war.

The basic cause of the US Civil War was slavery. The southern states used slave labour to work in the cotton plantations. At that time there were 34 states. In 15 of these, most black people were slaves. In the 19 states to the north and west, black people were free.

In 1860 Abraham Lincoln, who opposed slavery, was elected president. At once seven southern states withdrew and set up a new nation, the Confederate States of America. They feared that if slavery were abolished they would face economic disaster. Lincoln took action to stop this break-up of the Union, and war began.

The war led to the abolition of slavery and a victory for the North. But it left great bitterness between North and South that has still not completely disappeared.

The Battle of Gettysburg was a turning point in the American Civil War. It lasted from 1 July to 3 July 1863.

Gettysburg is a little town in Pennsylvania, in the North. The Confederate commander, General Robert E. Lee, led an army of 75,000 men into the North. He wanted to take the fighting out of the ravaged South and perhaps force the North to start peace negotiations.

The armies manoeuvred for position on 1 July. Ninety thousand Union troops established their positions in the hills south of Gettysburg. On 2 July Lee's Confederate troops tried hard to capture the hills, but failed.

On 3 July Confederate troops under General George E. Pickett stormed the hills, but were too weak to hold them. Lee had to retreat, having lost 20,000 dead and wounded. He never had the strength to mount another major attack on the North.

The battle was fought on 25 June 1876. Sioux Indians wiped out a US cavalry column led by Colonel George A. Custer.

Trouble with the Indians began in 1874 when the US government broke a treaty. They sent a force of miners and soldiers into the Black Hills of South Dakota, a region sacred to the Indians. The Indians refused to sell the land, so the government decided to drive them out.

During the campaign Custer and 650 men were ordered to advance into Montana to look for an Indian village, but not to fight a major battle.

Custer found the village on the Little Bighorn River and decided to attack. He split his forces into three columns. Custer's own column fell into a Sioux ambush led by Chief Sitting Bull. Custer and his men were killed. People have argued ever since about whether Custer disobeyed orders or not.

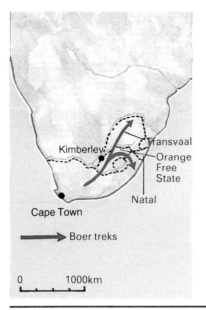

Cape Town

Kimberley

Transvaal

Orange Free State

Natal

→ Boer treks

0   1000km

The Great Trek was a mass migration by Boer settlers in South Africa in 1836 and 1837.

The Dutch were the first European settlers in South Africa. They were known as *Boers*, which means 'farmers'. The British took over the colony in 1814 after the Napoleonic Wars.

The Boers did not like the British policies. These included making English the official language of the colony, and the freeing of slaves. So the Boers decided to find a new home where they could live as they pleased.

In 1836 the Boers began a massive *trek* (journey or migration) to fresh lands further from the sea. They settled in the lands which are now known as Natal, the Orange Free State and the Transvaal. The Transvaal was so-called because it lay across the Vaal River. Britain later took over Natal but recognized the other two Boer colonies as independent lands.

▶ WHEN WAS THE ZULU EMPIRE FOUNDED?

The Zulus formed an empire in Natal in the 1820s. It lasted until 1879.

The Zulus settled in what is now northern Natal, probably in the late 1600s. They began to grow in importance under the rule of Dingiswayo in the early 1800s.

Dingiswayo began training a disciplined military force. Under his guidance the Zulu warriors were organized into *impis* (regiments), and carried shields and *assegais* (light spears).

Dingiswayo's successor, Chaka, continued building the Zulus into a military force. He conquered Natal and incorporated other tribes into his empire and army. Chaka's successor, Dingaan, came into conflict with the Boers.

In 1873 Cetewayo became king. He was capable, cruel and a tyrant. He clashed with the British and in 1879 a British force set out to defeat him. The Zulus won a victory at Isandhlwana but were finally defeated at Ulundi.

▶ WHEN DID THE INDIAN MUTINY TAKE PLACE?

The Indian Mutiny was a revolt by Indian soldiers in the Bengal army against their British officers in 1857-8.

There were several causes for the mutiny. Many Indians resented changes carried out by their British rulers, and also the British takeover of their territories.

The immediate cause was the issue of new gun cartridges that had to have the ends bitten off before they were fired. The cartridges were greased, and a rumour spread that the grease was a mixture of pork fat or cow fat. This shocked both the Hindu and Muslim Indians. To Hindus the cow is a sacred animal, and Muslims do not touch pork.

The revolt broke out in May 1857. Indian mutineers captured garrisons at Delhi and Kanpur, and massacred the British. Supported by Sikhs, British troops put down the mutiny fiercely. Afterwards, the British stopped trying to change Indian ways of life.

The Crimean War lasted from 1854 to 1856. It was fought by Britain, France, Sardinia and Turkey against Russia. The Crimea is a Russian peninsula on the Black Sea.

Fighting between Turkey and Russia began in 1853. One of the causes was Russia's claim to protect Christians in Palestine, which was ruled by Turkey. Russia also wanted free passage for its warships through the Turkish-held Dardanelles Strait. This links the Black Sea to the Mediterranean.

Britain and France joined the war because they thought that Russia was seizing too much of Turkey's European territory. They invaded the Crimea to attack the Russian naval base at Sevastopol.

Both sides were badly organized. More British soldiers died from disease than fighting until nursing pioneer Florence Nightingale set up proper medical care. Neither side gained much from the war.

Until 1867 Japan was ruled by military governors called shoguns. Then the emperor took power and began to modernize the country.

Japan kept itself isolated from the rest of the world until a naval force arrived from the United States in 1853-4. The Americans were protesting against the bad treatment of US sailors who had been shipwrecked on Japanese islands. Japan signed a trade treaty with the United States and other countries.

In 1867 the Japanese emperor, Mutsuhito, gained power. He took the name *Meiji*, which means 'Enlightened Rule'. The Meiji government set out to modernize Japan. They abolished old customs and set up a new legal system. The Japanese built railways and a telegraph system, and started modern industries. Some Japanese people even took up Western dress and customs.

Japan and Russia went to war in 1904 over rival claims to Manchuria and Korea. Japan's biggest victory was the naval battle of Tsushima Strait.

The Japanese began trading in Korea during the 1880s. Korea was then controlled by China. In 1894 Japan and China went to war, and Japan won control of Korea.

Japan also had eyes on the Liaotung Peninsula, in Manchuria, which Russia wanted. The Japanese offered to give up Liaotung in return for Korea, where Russia was trying to gain a foothold. When the Russians ignored their offer, the Japanese attacked. They declared war two days later.

In 1904, a peace conference was set up by the president of the United States. Japan was given the Liaotung Peninsula, half of Sakhalin Island (between Russia and Japan), and rights in Korea and Manchuria. Two years later Japan took over all of Korea.

▲WHEN WAS THE SECOND FRENCH EMPIRE FOUNDED?

The Second French Empire was set up by Napoleon's nephew Napoleon III in 1852.

After Napoleon's downfall, the French monarchy was restored. When Charles X became king he tried to make the monarchy as powerful as it had been before the Revolution. This caused a new revolt in Paris in 1830. Charles abdicated and the throne was offered to a distant relative, Louis Philippe.

Louis Philippe reigned for 18 years. In 1848, when his government opposed a reform of the voting system, the people of Paris rebelled again and fighting broke out. Louis Philippe decided to abdicate. He went into exile in England and a new republic was proclaimed. Louis Napoleon, nephew of Napoleon I, became its first president.

Within four years the republic also came to an end. Louis Napoleon (shown here) set up a second Empire with himself as Emperor.

▲WHEN WAS GERMANY UNIFIED?

The German *Reich* (Empire) was formed in January 1871 as a result of the Franco-Prussian War.

Prussia was ruled by King Wilhelm I and his Chancellor, Otto von Bismarck. They wanted to unite the many states of Germany into one country under Prussian leadership.

Bismarck knew that a war with France would make the German states band together. France and Prussia fell out when the crown of Spain was offered to a relative of Wilhelm. Bismarck gave an account of the negotiations to the Press that seemed very insulting to the French.

France declared war on 16 July 1870. As Bismarck had expected, the German states at once agreed to unite. The French were not ready for war, and were defeated. Prussian troops swept into France. Wilhelm was proclaimed *Kaiser* (emperor) of Germany at Versailles, as shown in the picture.

▲WHEN WAS THE PARIS COMMUNE SET UP?

The Paris Commune was a revolutionary council set up after the Franco-Prussian War in 1871.

The Franco-Prussian War ended with the defeat of the main French army and the emperor, Napoleon III. Two days later, members of the French Assembly proclaimed the Third French Republic.

To make peace with Germany, France had to pay a huge sum of money, give up Alsace and Lorraine, and allow German troops to march in triumph through Paris.

Many Parisians feared that the new government would not be republican enough. The working people of the city rose in revolt. They formed a central committee, the Commune, to run Paris and lead a new revolution. But government soldiers fought their way into Paris. After six weeks of fighting, and great bloodshed, the Commune was overthrown. The picture shows Parisians defending the Commune against government troops.

**The Manchu Dynasty came
to power in China in 1644. It
was overthrown in 1911.**

In their last years of power the
Manchus had many problems.
From 1842 onwards, several
Western nations made unfair
trade treaties with China.
There were also rebellions in
China. The most serious of
these was the Taiping
Rebellion of 1851-64. In a
disastrous war with Japan, in
1894-5, China also lost control
of Korea and Taiwan.

The Manchus were led by
the powerful Empress-
Dowager Tz'u Hsi, who ruled
on behalf of her son Kuang
Hsu. They resisted change as
long as they could. After 1900

the Manchus began to make
sweeping reforms.

In 1908 Kuang Hsu and the
Empress-Dowager died. A
two-year-old boy, Pu-yi,
became emperor. Discontent
with the Manchus grew

rapidly. In 1911 an uprising
swept away the rule of the
emperor. A republic was set up
with a doctor, Sun Yat-sen, as
president. Sun Yat-sen is seen
here with Mrs Sun and
Chinese army officers in 1911.

**Italy used planes in the
Tripolitan War of 1911. Other
countries began to use
warplanes in World War I.**

In 1911 Italy took Libya from
Turkey in the Tripolitan War

and used planes to drop bombs.

In World War I, which
followed in 1914, both sides
used aircraft. At first they used
them for reconnaissance but
soon began dropping small
bombs and shooting at ground
targets.

At first aircraft were used by
armies and navies. Britain

formed the first air force, the
Royal Air Force, in 1918.

The French first used air
power in 1793. They put an
observer in a balloon to watch
enemy troop movements
during a war with Austria. The
Austrians also used unmanned
balloons to bomb Venice
during a war in 1849.

▶ WHEN DID THE TSAR OF RUSSIA AGREE TO SWEEPING REFORMS?

Tsar Nicholas II agreed to the formation of a Duma (parliament) in 1905, following an uprising.

The uprising came as a result of Japan's defeat of Russia in the war of 1904-5. For some years there had been demonstrations calling for a democratic government, which the tsar refused to grant.

Russia's defeat in the war sparked off even bigger demonstrations. Matters came to a head on 22 January 1905, when a procession of workers and their families marched to the Winter Palace in St Petersburg to present a petition. Police opened fire on the procession, killing 70 people and wounding 240. This incident, shown here, is called 'Bloody Sunday'.

Strikes, riots and mutinies of soldiers and sailors followed. The Tsar had to agree to an elected parliament and other reforms. But these reforms were not enough to prevent later revolution.

◀ WHEN DID THE EASTER RISING TAKE PLACE IN IRELAND?

The rebellion began on Easter Monday, 24 April 1916 and lasted a week.

The Irish had been campaigning for independence from Britain for many years. It was finally agreed by Parliament in London, but was postponed because of World War I.

Some Irish people were not prepared to wait until the war ended. They formed a group called the Irish Volunteers. Some of the Volunteers came under the control of the Irish Republican Brotherhood, which decided on rebellion. They hoped for weapons from Britain's enemy, Germany.

The leaders of the Brotherhood decided on an Easter revolt, but the weapons they were expecting failed to appear. About 1000 people seized the General Post Office and other buildings in Dublin. They surrendered after days of fighting. Fifteen of their leaders were shot under martial law.

▶ WHEN DID PASSIVE RESISTANCE BECOME A POLITICAL FORCE?

Passive resistance became a political force in South Africa in 1906. Later it was extended to India.

Mohandas Karamchand Gandhi was an Indian lawyer and patriot. He adopted the idea of passive resistance when he was working in South Africa and suffered racial discrimination. Gandhi later changed the name of passive resistance to *satyagraha*, which he defined as a 'force which is born of truth and love or non-violence'. The aim of *satyagraha* was to bring about change without violence.

The government of the Transvaal in South Africa passed a law in 1906 requiring every Indian there to be fingerprinted. In an eight-year campaign the Indians refused to obey the law, and the government repealed it.

In 1915 Gandhi returned to India. He applied his ideas of *satyagraha* there in the struggle for independence against Britain.

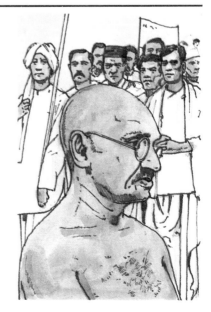

The Bolsheviks seized power on the night of 6-7 November, 1917.

This coup is known as the 'October Revolution' because the date was 25-26 October according to the calendar then in use in Russia. This was the second revolution of 1917. The first was in March (though it is called the February Revolution). It was partly caused by the heavy defeats Russia was suffering in World War I against Germany.

The revolution began with strikes and demonstrations in which the troops joined. Tsar Nicholas II abdicated. A provisional government was formed, headed by a lawyer named Alexander Kerensky.

The Bolsheviks were a revolutionary group who thought the new government was as muddled as that of the tsar. They wanted to transform Russia on socialist lines. Their leader, Vladimir Lenin, ordered his Red Guards to seize the headquarters of the provisional government. From then on government was in the hands of *soviets* (councils) of revolutionaries. The picture shows Lenin talking at a political meeting.

The Fascist dictator Benito Mussolini ruled Italy from 1922 to 1943. The Nazi dictator Adolf Hitler ruled Germany from 1933 to 1945.

Italy was in a state of chaos after World War I ended in 1918. There were riots, strikes, inflation, a rising crime rate and unemployment.

Mussolini formed political clubs whose symbol was the fasces, an axe surrounded by rods. It had been the symbol of power in ancient Rome. The members became known as Fascists. Their aim was to seize power. In 1922 they converged on Rome, where Mussolini formed a government. Once in power, he became a dictator. Germany, defeated in World War I, was in an even more disorganized state. Hitler, an agitator and orator, set up a National Socialist Party to which he rallied all the discontented people of the country. Its followers were known as Nazis.

In the 1930 elections the Nazis became the second biggest party in the Reichstag, the German parliament. In 1933 the president, Paul von Hindenburg, offered Hitler the post of chancellor (premier). Within two years Hitler had murdered his rivals and made himself dictator.

241

▲ WHEN DID THE SPANISH CIVIL WAR TAKE PLACE?

▲ WHEN DID THE SPANISH CIVIL WAR TAKE PLACE?

The Spanish Civil War began in 1936 and lasted until 1939. It was a revolt against Spain's left-wing government.

Spain had been dogged by political unrest for many years. The election of a left wing government in February, 1936, brought matters to a head.

In July the army suddenly announced a revolution. It began in Morocco, where Spain had troops, and quickly spread to the mainland. It was headed by the army commander in the Canary Islands, General Francisco Franco. The army was supported by other right-wing groups and by the Roman Catholic Church.

Franco received help from Germany and Italy, while the government had aid from Russia. Fighting was bitter, and more than 600,000 people died. Franco's forces won.

► WHEN DID WORLD WAR II START?

World War II began with the German invasion of Poland on 1 September 1939.

Germany had been threatening Poland for some time. The German dictator, Adolf Hitler, wanted the so-called Free City of Danzig (Gdansk) to be united with Germany. He also wanted a link across the Polish Corridor, which allowed Poland access to the sea but cut off the main part of Germany from East Prussia.

Britain and France had pledged support for Poland. On 3 September, after Poland was invaded, they declared war. They were joined by Australia, India and New Zealand. South Africa and Canada quickly followed.

In the first year of war Germany overran Poland, Denmark, Norway, Luxembourg, the Netherlands, Belgium and France. Italy joined in on Germany's side. Germany and Italy then overwhelmed Yugoslavia and Greece. Germany also attacked Russia in June, 1941.

▲ WHAT HAPPENED AT PEARL HARBOR?

On the morning of 7 December 1941, Japanese bombers attacked the United States naval base (shown here) at Pearl Harbor, Hawaii. They destroyed six warships, damaged 12 others and destroyed 174 aircraft.

The Japanese attacked while their officials were negotiating in Washington about causes of dispute between Japan and the United States. The basic cause of conflict was Japan's occupation of the French colony of Indochina (now Vietnam, Laos and Cambodia) in 1940. The US government banned the sale of oil and rubber to Japan.

The Americans were caught off guard at Pearl Harbor. A telegram from Washington, warning that the Japanese might take some action, did not arrive until the attack was over. The Pearl Harbor attack took the United States into the war against Japan and its allies, Germany and Italy.

The Battle of Stalingrad lasted from August 1942 to January 1943, during World War II.

The battle began as a German attempt to capture Stalingrad (now called Volgograd), a city on the Volga River. Their plan was to seize the city and sweep north to take Moscow.

The Germans slowly forced their way into the city. But the Russians resisted and fought stubbornly for every street and house. Just enough Russian reinforcements were sent into Stalingrad to keep the defence going. At the same time they assembled a huge army just north of the city.

On 19 November the Russian army attacked, and in four days surrounded the enemy. The Germans surrendered on 31 January, by which time they had lost about 350,000 men.

D-Day was the Allied landing in Normandy, France, during World War II. It took place on 6 June 1944.

The Normandy invasion was the main western attack on Germany by Britain, the USA and their allies. Three million men, 9000 ships and 11,000 aircraft took part. After the invasion, the Germans began to retreat. The Russians also attacked from the east. Germany surrendered on 7 May 1945.

The Yalta Conference of 1945 was a meeting of the 'Big Three' Allied war leaders. They were Winston S. Churchill of Britain, Franklin D. Roosevelt of the United States and Joseph Stalin of the Soviet Union.

The talks took place at the Crimean seaside resort of Yalta. By this time the end of the war was in sight. The Germans, fighting furiously, were being driven back by the Russians in the east and by the other allies in the west.

The purpose of the conference was to decide on the Allies' future policy towards Germany. Britain and the USA made a number of concessions to the Russians. They agreed to split Germany into British, Russian, French and American zones of occupation. The Russian zone is now East Germany.

243

Dr Fidel Castro, a young lawyer, led the revolution. He took power in Cuba in January, 1959.

Most African countries gained their independence from Europe between the 1950s and 1970s.

European colonial powers carved up Africa among themselves during the 1800s. By 1914 only two countries were independent – Ethiopia and Liberia – though South Africa had gained almost complete freedom in 1910. Ethiopia was ruled by Italy from 1935 to 1941.

The move towards independence began as soon as World War II ended in 1945. Egypt had already become independent in 1922. Its neighbour Libya, an Italian colony, was the first to gain freedom after the war, in 1951. Other countries to gain independence in the 1950s were Morocco, Sudan, Tunisia, Ghana and Guinea.

The main independence move came in the 1960s when 32 former colonies attained their freedom. They included almost all the French possessions in Africa.

By the early 1980s only a few African territories did not have independence. They included Namibia (South-West Africa), which the United Nations had put under South African rule, and some offshore islands. The Canary Islands ranked as Spanish provinces. Madeira remained a Portuguese district. Réunion was an overseas department of France, and St Helena remained British.

A military dictatorship led by a former army sergeant, Fulgencio Batista, held power in Cuba from 1934 to 1944 and from 1952 to 1959. Though some people prospered under his rule, most Cubans lived in great poverty.

Castro tried to start a revolution in 1953. He was captured and jailed but was released in 1955. In 1956 he returned to Cuba from exile and began a guerrilla war.

The guerrillas grew in strength until they became too much for Batista, who fled the country on 1 January 1959. Castro, shown here, set up a revolutionary government.

Cuba had strong links with the United States, which had helped to free it from Spanish rule in 1898. But relations cooled after Castro took over American businesses in Cuba. Castro then turned to the Soviet Union for military and economic help.

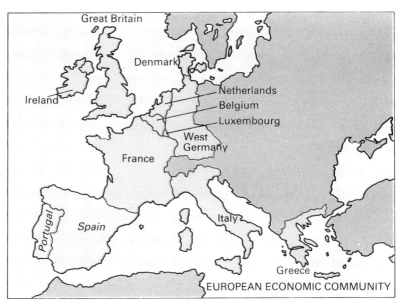

EUROPEAN ECONOMIC COMMUNITY

Egypt became a republic in 1953, following a revolt by army officers.

Egypt was part of the Ottoman Empire until 1914, when the British took control. It became an independent kingdom in 1922, but British troops stayed until 1936. After that some remained to guard the Suez Canal. This waterway was partly owned by Britain.

Egypt's king, Farouk, was an incompetent ruler who spent his life in luxury and dissipation. In 1952 a group of army officers forced him to resign in favour of his baby son, Fuad II. The commander-in-chief of the army, Muhammad Neguib, became prime minister. A year later the republic was set up with Neguib as president.

In 1954 Neguib was forced to resign. He was succeeded by Gamal Abdel Nasser (seen here), who had led the 1952 revolt. In 1956 Nasser nationalized the Suez Canal. Britain and France tried to take it back by force but were stopped by the United Nations.

The European Economic Community was founded when France, Italy and four other countries signed the Treaty of Rome in 1957.

The other four countries were West Germany and the 'Benelux' group – Belgium, the Netherlands and Luxembourg. The six nations had already been co-operating in the European Coal and Steel Community, set up in 1952.

The six removed trade barriers among themselves and agreed to charge the same duties on goods imported from outside the Community. They also set up a Parliament and a Court of Justice.

In 1973 Britain, the Republic of Ireland and Denmark joined the E.E.C. Greece was admitted in 1981.

Norway planned to join the EEC in 1973, but its people voted against it. Spain and Portugal applied to join in the early 1980s, while Greenland (part of Denmark) voted to pull out.

The Vietnam War, between North and South Vietnam, ended in 1975.

Vietnam was under French rule from 1883 until World War II, when Japan took it over. After the war, the northern Vietnamese set up a communist government. From 1946 France fought the Communists. This war ended in 1954 with the partition of Vietnam into North and South Vietnam.

By 1957, North and South Vietnam were at war. Other countries sent troops. The USA, which supported the South, had over half a million troops there by 1969. South Vietnam surrendered to the North on 30 April 1975.

245

◄ WHERE WAS SILK FIRST PRODUCED?

Silk was first made in China. Threads from silkworm cocoons were spun on spinning wheels, then woven into fine cloth.

The Chinese found out how to make silk over 5000 years ago. They guarded the secret, for silk was a rare fabric and very costly. Traders made the long journey along the 'Silk Road' to buy Chinese silk, travelling from as far as India and the Middle East.

In AD 552 two Persian monks smuggled the secret of silk-making out of China. They hid silkworm eggs inside hollow bamboo canes, and also took seeds of the mulberry tree, whose leaves silkworms eat.

In time, people in Europe learned how to rear silkworms (the larvae of the silk moth) and to make silk. Silk was used to make fine, soft robes for rulers and nobles. To make silk, the delicate thread used by the silkworm to spin its cocoon must be unwound. As much as 300 metres may be unwound from one cocoon.

► WHERE WAS THE POTTER'S WHEEL INVENTED?

Pottery was one of the earliest inventions. At first, pots were shaped by hand out of wet clay. Turning pots on a wheel came later.

The wheel was invented in Sumeria, Babylon and elsewhere in the Near East around 3000 BC. Clay pots had already been made for over 5000 years, but they were crude and often broke.

Making pots is a skilful craft. The potter needs skill not only in spinning the wheel to shape the pot, but also in firing the pot in a kiln to harden it. The first potters learned also how to glaze (coat) pots with various substances to make the pots stronger and more decorative.

The invention of the potter's wheel led to one of the first industries – pottery. A skilful potter could make enough pots to exchange them for food and other goods, or sell them for money.

◄ WHERE WERE THE FIRST OLYMPIC GAMES HELD?

Every four years, from 776 BC, the Greeks held a great festival. Artists, writers and athletes gathered to honour the great god Zeus. The contests were held at Olympia, and became known as the Olympic Games.

The first Olympic Games were not just sporting contests. There were plays and recitals by poets, as well as races. To the Greeks, the Games expressed the union of mind and body, striving for victory to honour Zeus, the king of the gods.

The events lasted for three days. Athletes ran, wrestled, rode horses and drove chariots. The Games began with the Olympic oath and ended with prizes and feasting.

The Olympic Games continued until AD 393. They were then forgotten until 1896, when they were revived at Athens on the suggestion of a Frenchman, Baron Pierre de Coubertin. They continue to be held every four years.

► WHERE DID THE GREEKS FOUND COLONIES?

The rulers of ancient Greece encouraged people to set off and found new colonies overseas. So Greek civilization spread far beyond its birthplace.

By the 8th century BC, Greece could no longer feed its growing population. The rulers of the Greek city-states feared discontent. So they were happy to see some of their citizens leave home to found new Greek colonies, where there was land for all.

Some Greek colonists went east to the Black Sea. But most journeyed west to Italy, Sicily and southern France. A few went as far as Africa, including Egypt.

Each Greek colony became a 'little Greece' in a strange land. The Greek settlers traded for goods with the cities where they had once lived. In this way Greek skills and Greek ideas were carried to new cities all around the Mediterranean coast.

France
Spain
Italy
Greece
Black Sea
Asia Minor
Sicily
Mediterranean Sea
North Africa

◄ WHEN DID PEOPLE FIRST USE MONEY?

Today we use money to buy things. But when trade began thousands of years ago, there was no money. So people exchanged goods. The invention of money made trade much simpler.

The first metal coins were minted (made) in about 800 BC. Before then, all trade had been done by barter – that is, by exchanging goods. For example, a tool-maker might barter tools in exchange for meat or clothing.

As civilization developed, trade became more complex. Barter was a clumsy method. A trader needed small, easily-carried tokens to exchange, but the tokens had to be valuable. So the first coins were made of metal, in particular gold and silver.

Gold coins have real value. Paper money, on the other hand, is merely a token. The paper itself is worthless. Paper money was invented in China, and was in use there by AD 800.

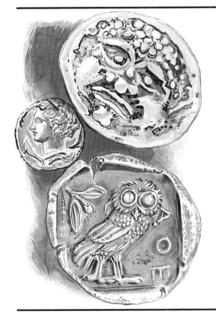

► WHERE WERE ROADS FIRST PAVED?

When people first began to travel, they followed rough tracks and trails. In bad weather, it was safer to stay at home. Paved roads were not thought of until wheeled carts came into use.

The earliest paved roads were made in Babylon some 4000 years ago. As people began living in towns and trading with their neighbours, they needed better transport. A cart could not cross wild country, for fear of breaking an axle or sinking into mud or sand.

Many ancient cities had paved roads, and we can still see their remains today. But undoubtedly the greatest road-builders of the past were the Romans. Their roads ran straight from town to town.

Roman roads were built by army engineers. They were made of stones and gravel, and cambered (sloped) so that rain would drain away to the sides. Roman armies marched swiftly along these fine roads to keep the peace within the Roman Empire.

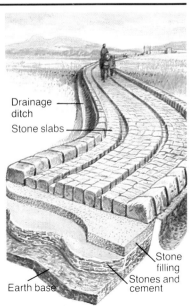

Drainage ditch
Stone slabs
Stone filling
Stones and cement
Earth base

247

The first farmers tilled the soil with hand ploughs rather like garden hoes. It was in Mesopotamia, around 4000 BC, that farmers began using oxen to pull ploughs.

The plough was probably invented before the wheel. It began as a rough wooden tool, dragged up and down a field to scratch the surface of the soil. The farmer sowed seeds in the channel made by the plough.

Around 500 BC, a much improved plough appeared. It had a blade, or share, tipped with iron. And it was made in such a way that the blade turned the soil completely over, making a furrow.

In the Middle East, a small plough worked perfectly well. But larger ploughs were needed to tackle the heavy, hilly soils of northern Europe. Some ploughs were so heavy that they needed a team of up to eight oxen to pull them. Because the oxen could not turn sharply, fields became very large. Each field was divided into long strips, with drainage ditches in between.

The first farmers worked with their hands, using simple tools. Training animals to pull ploughs and carts, as well as work machines, made the farmer's life much easier.

An ox is much stronger than a human. It can pull a heavier plough, and do more work in a day. The use of oxen to help with farm work dates from about 4000 BC in Mesopotamia, in the 'fertile crescent' where farming began.

The animals that could be tamed in this way were herd animals such as cattle, asses, horses and camels. Oxen were harnessed with a wooden yoke across their necks. The yoke was not suitable for horses, however, and so horses were kept only for riding until much later, when the horse-collar harness was invented.

In the Middle East, animals were used to provide the power for simple machines, such as water pumps for irrigating fields. Animals were used everywhere to carry loads.

Once people had more than just one or two possessions, they needed a way of keeping property safe. The earliest locks were made in Egypt in about 2000 BC. They were clumsy, but they worked.

The locks invented by the ancient Egyptians were made of wood. The idea was simple. A door was kept shut by a bolt slid across the door and into a slot in the door frame. The bolt had several holes drilled in

it. When it was slid shut, pins in the lock dropped down into the holes. The bolt was then held fast.

To open the lock, the pins had to be lifted free. This was done with a key which was pushed into a hole in the bolt. Only the right key, with the right number of pegs cut into it, would fit.

The Egyptians took great trouble to secure the rich tombs of the pharaohs against thieves. Even so, many tombs were plundered and stripped of their treasures.

Iron must be heated in a furnace before it can be shaped to make tools. The secret of 'smelting' iron was discovered in the Near East around 1500 BC.

As early as 4000 BC, people had learned to make tools and weapons from copper, which is a fairly soft metal. Copper can be hammered into shape when cold. In Sumeria, smiths found that copper and tin could be mixed to make bronze.

Iron is much stronger than copper or bronze. To smelt it, a very hot furnace is required. Ancient iron tools have been found at Ur of the Chaldees and inside Egyptian tombs. By 1200 BC iron had replaced copper and bronze.

Iron was thought to be magical, and the smiths who forged iron swords and spears were believed to have supernatural power. The Greeks valued iron as highly as gold. The Chinese, who invented efficient bellows to make furnaces very hot, made fine iron.

War in ancient times was fought at close range. But then, as now, the 'arms race' was on. The first soldiers to use iron weapons were the Assyrians. They became the most feared of all.

The first real armies were those of Assyria and Egypt, some 3000 years ago. Before then, wars were fought mainly by small groups of warriors. Egypt had many soldiers, but few wore any kind of protective clothing. Egyptian archers used reed arrows tipped with stone or copper.

Iron, the new metal, was harder and sharper. The Assyrians discovered how to use it in warfare. They made iron heads for their spears and arrows. For defence, the Assyrian soldiers wore long coats of iron chain-mail.

Iron weapons were much stronger than weapons made of copper or bronze. Sword, spear, shield and armour could be made of iron, making the 'iron warrior' much more formidable than his foes.

The Chinese invented the rocket. From this simple firework have come today's space rockets and missiles.

The first rockets were tubes filled with gunpowder (a mixture of potassium nitrate, charcoal and sulphur). The Chinese discovered thousands of years ago that gunpowder explodes when burned. Packed into a tube, the exploding gunpowder pushed out a stream of hot gas, sending the tube flying off in the opposite direction.

The Chinese let off fireworks for fun, but also fired rockets as weapons of war. In the Middle Ages, the invention spread to Europe. During the wars of the early 1800s the British army used rocket batteries to bombard Copenhagen in 1807 and during the battle of Leipzig in 1813.

The forerunner of the modern long-range rocket was the German V2. This was used during World War II.

▼ WHERE DID HOUSES
FIRST HAVE CENTRAL
HEATING?

Until the 20th century, most people in cold countries kept warm beside open fires. We think of central heating as a modern invention. In fact, the Romans had central heating 2000 years ago.

The Romans were excellent builders. Their houses had proper drains and their towns had good water supplies. A wealthy Roman's house usually had underfloor heating too.

The heat came from a furnace. The floor was built on brick pillars so that hot air from the furnace could flow freely beneath it and up through pipes to rooms above. This system was known as a hypocaust. At the public baths, the hypocaust heated water for the hot pools and steam rooms. There Romans would meet to relax and enjoy a bath, and maybe a massage.

The Romans built central-heating systems throughout their Empire. But after the Romans, the secret of the hypocaust was forgotten.

▼ WHERE DID ALEXANDER
LEAD HIS ARMY?

Alexander, King of Macedonia, was a famous warrior. He was called 'the Great' because he led his army to victory after victory.

Alexander was born in 356 BC. Macedonia was then a small kingdom in Greece. Becoming king at the age of 20, Alexander set out on an astonishing quest for power.

First, he conquered the other city-states of Greece.

▲ WHERE DID THE ROMANS
BUILD HUGE AQUEDUCTS?

An aqueduct is a bridge or channel built to carry drinking water into a city. The Romans built aqueducts so well that some still exist today.

Every Roman town needed a reliable water supply. Sometimes it was necessary to build an aqueduct to bring water from a nearby lake or river. The aqueduct was either a conduit (channel) or a huge bridge carrying a canal on top.

Persian Empire and defeated it. He invaded Egypt and founded the city of Alexandria.

Even then, his ambition was not satisfied. He led his army into India, but his troops were weary of conquest. They refused to march further, and Alexander had to turn back.

In 12 years, Alexander was never defeated. He was only 33 when he died. After his death, his vast empire broke up. After Alexander, no other general could rule such a conquest.

Near Nîmes in France is an aqueduct built by the Roman general Agrippa. It has three storeys, or tiers, raised on arches. The longest aqueduct was over 85 kilometres long. One of the most famous was called the Aqua Appia. It was built in 312 BC to carry water into Rome, and was over 16 kilometres long. Nearby ran the road called the Via Appia, or Appian Way. Both were built by the Roman military engineer Appius Claudius Caecus.

The Roman Empire was the greatest of ancient times. Rome's rule stretched from Britain in the west to the Black Sea in the east. Its Empire lasted for 500 years.

Rome began as a small kingdom in what is now Italy. The Romans first conquered Italy (by 200 BC), then the other Mediterranean lands and North Africa. They eventually ruled most of western and central Europe.

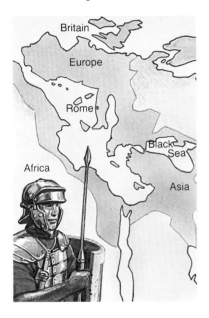

Augustus became the first Roman emperor in 27 BC. Roman rule brought peace to the conquered lands. But the Roman armies were faced with attacks from barbarians living beyond the Empire.

In AD 476 the barbarians captured Rome. By then the Empire was weak and divided. Only in the East, with its capital at Constantinople, did the Roman Empire survive. The Eastern Empire lasted until Constantinople fell to the Turks in 1453.

A university is a place of 'all learning'. New knowledge in the Middle Ages led to the setting up of great centres of learning throughout Europe. Many of these universities are still in existence today.

By the 1300s, knowledge was growing rapidly. For centuries education had been left to the Church. Now, all over Europe, universities came into being.

Great universities were founded in cities such as Paris, Bologna, Oxford, Cambridge and Prague. The only subjects taught at first were law, theology (religion) and medicine. One of the first medical schools was founded in the 9th century at the university of Salerno in Italy.

Each university was granted a royal charter. This gave it privileges and the right to award degrees to its students. Scholars from all over Europe taught at the universities. They taught in Latin, the 'universal language'. Today there are universities in many countries, teaching a variety of subjects.

In 1947 a goatherd came across some ancient scrolls in a cave close to the Dead Sea. These scrolls contain parts of the Bible written perhaps 200 years before the birth of Christ.

The Dead Sea Scrolls caused great interest among scholars. Reading and preserving the scrolls required much patience and careful work. The scrolls had been rolled inside jars for

safe-keeping, and they had to be unrolled with great care.

Almost every book of the Old Testament appears, at least in fragments, in the scrolls. The oldest passages from the Book of Leviticus, were written in an early Canaanite form of Hebrew.

The scrolls were probably stored in the caves by Jews at the time when Palestine was ruled by Rome. The hot, dry desert air helped to preserve the fragile scrolls. From them we have learned much about how the Bible came to be written.

▶ WHERE DID MUHAMMAD FLEE?

The religion of Islam was founded by the Prophet Muhammad. In AD 622 he had to flee from his home in Mecca to Medina.

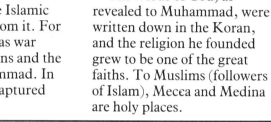

Muhammad was born in about AD 570 in Mecca, in present-day Saudi Arabia. At the age of 40 he set out to call people to a belief in one God.

Muhammad was persecuted when he began preaching. With a few followers, he was forced to flee from Mecca to Medina. His flight is known as the Hegira, and the Islamic calendar is dated from it. For some years there was war between the Meccans and the followers of Muhammad. In 630, Muhammad captured Mecca.

The words of God, as revealed to Muhammad, were written down in the Koran, and the religion he founded grew to be one of the great faiths. To Muslims (followers of Islam), Mecca and Medina are holy places.

▶ WHICH EUROPEAN CITY WAS THE CAPITAL OF AN ISLAMIC EMPIRE?

The Moors were a Muslim people of North Africa. They created a large empire, which included part of Spain, and made Seville their capital. The Moors took Islamic art, science and learning to Europe.

The Moors originally lived on the Barbary coast of North Africa. They were converted to Islam in AD 707. At this time Islam was growing fast, and the Moors took part in this expansion.

They invaded Spain, and remained powerful there for hundreds of years. They made Seville, their capital city, a centre of Islamic culture. Islamic civilization was more advanced than that of medieval Europe, especially in the fields of science and medicine.

Christian leaders fought against the Moors. Gradually, the power of the Moors weakened. In 1238 they retired to Granada, the last Moorish kingdom in Europe, and were eventually driven out in 1492.

◀ WHERE WAS CATHAY?

Before the 13th century, Europeans knew little of Asia. To them, Cathay (China) was an unknown land. No Europeans had been there until the Polo family made their journeys.

Chinese civilization was the oldest on Earth, but the Chinese cared little about the world outside. In Europe, only a few fantastic stories of 'Cathay' were known.

In 1260, the brothers Niccolo and Maffeo Polo set out from Venice to trade in the East. They returned in 1269 with tales of their visit to Cathay, where they had met its Mongol ruler, Kublai Khan.

In 1271 they left Venice once more. With them went Niccolo's son, Marco. The overland journey to China took four years. The Polos did not return to Venice until 1295. Marco travelled throughout China in the service of Kublai Khan. When he returned, Marco wrote a book about his travels. From it, Europeans discovered that they had much to learn from the Chinese.

WHERE DID EUROPE GET SPICES FROM IN THE MIDDLE AGES?

For people in medieval Europe, winter was a hard time. There was little food for farm animals, so most were killed in autumn. Spices were used to preserve and flavour meat during the winter. These spices came from Asia.

The need to disguise the bad taste of rotten meat led Europeans to explore the oceans. This is strange, but true, for the spices the Europeans needed came from the Spice Islands, in what are now the East Indies.

The journey overland was long, with the result that spices were very costly. In the 1400s, Europeans searched for new sea routes to the Indies.

When Columbus landed in the New World in 1492, he hoped he had reached the Spice Islands. He was wrong. But the quest for spices had led to the discovery of a vast new continent.

WHERE WAS THE FIRST BOOK PRINTED?

The Chinese were the first people to print books on paper. They used wood blocks for this. Much later, the mechanical printing press was invented.

The earliest known printed book was made around AD 868. It is called the *Diamond Sutra* and was hand-printed, using wooden blocks. This printing method is slow. Even so, it is faster than copying books by hand. In Europe, at that time, all books were copied by hand – usually by monks. Books were so precious that they were often chained to reading stands.

In the 1400s, a German known as Johannes Gutenberg invented a printing machine. This used separate pieces of metal type for each letter. The letters were arranged in order to make up a whole page of words. This was then printed by a screw-type press. The printing press made it possible to print books in much larger numbers.

WHERE DID THE LONGBOW PROVE TO BE DECISIVE IN WARFARE?

In the Middle Ages, the longbow was the main 'long-range' weapon. Often it was the archers who decided the outcome of a battle.

In 1337, England and France went to war. The war lasted more than a hundred years. In 1346, the English army won the battle of Crécy. The English success owed much to their skill with the longbow. In 1415, English and Welsh archers won another battle, at Agincourt.

The longbow was powerful and accurate. With it, an archer could bring down a knight on horseback. The longbow could be shot more rapidly than its rival, the crossbow. Medieval kings encouraged archery as a sport, to ensure that there would be a ready supply of trained bowmen for use in war.

Archers were also carried on warships. Many longbows have been found in the wreck of the English ship *Mary Rose*, which sank in 1545.

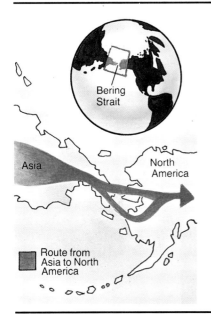

◀ WHERE DID THE AMERICAN INDIANS COME FROM?

When Columbus discovered America he thought he had reached the Indies, in Asia. So he called the people 'Indians'. Columbus was wrong. But the American Indians had in fact come from Asia thousands of years earlier.

The American Indians look rather like the Mongols who still live in eastern Asia. The Indians crossed a 'land bridge' to reach North America. Today, the two continents are separated by a channel of sea called the Bering Strait.

The Indians began settling in America about 25,000 years ago. They lived by hunting and farming. There were many groups, or tribes, and each had its own customs and beliefs.

The Indians had to travel on foot, since the horses which had once lived in America had died out before the Indians arrived. It was the Spanish who re-introduced horses to America in the 1500s.

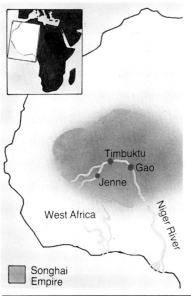

◀ WHERE WAS THE SONGHAI EMPIRE?

In the 1500s there was a rich and powerful empire in West Africa. This was the empire of the Songhai, who were soldiers, farmers and traders.

The Songhai Empire included lands in the countries we now call Mali, Niger and Nigeria. The Songhai people controlled the trade and fishing along the great Niger River. From around AD 800, they played an important part in West African events. The Songhai kings challenged the Islamic rulers of the Mali Empire farther north. For many years there was war.

The Songhai grew rich on the salt and gold trades. They controlled the caravan routes to the north. Their downfall came in the late 1500s. Already weakened by squabbles between its princes, Songhai was attacked by Moroccan armies. The Moroccans had firearms and, with the help of these new weapons, captured the important Songhai towns of Gao and Timbuktu.

◀ WHERE WAS EL DORADO SUPPOSED TO BE?

***El Dorado* is Spanish for 'the golden one'. Early explorers in South America heard strange tales of a land so rich that its ruler bathed in gold dust.**

We now use the expression 'El Dorado' to mean an imaginary country full of riches. But the tales the early Spanish adventurers heard, as they explored South America in the 1500s, told of a man, not just a country.

El Dorado was said to be the chief of a tribe living in a marvellous city called Omoa. Each year, as part of a great sacred festival, the chief bathed in gold dust, for the land was so rich that gold was as plentiful as water.

El Dorado was supposed to live somewhere in what is now Colombia. None of the Spanish explorers who went in search of his fabulous land ever discovered it. But they did find plenty of gold elsewhere in South America.

▶ WHERE DID THE PILGRIM FATHERS LAND?

In November, 1620, a small ship landed in North America. It was called the *Mayflower*. On board were some 35 settlers from England, remembered today as the Pilgrim Fathers.

The Europe from which the Pilgrim Fathers came was torn by religious quarrels. The Pilgrim Fathers wanted peace to set up a Church of their own, so they decided to risk the perilous two-month voyage across the ocean to America.

The Pilgrim Fathers planned to sail in two ships. But when one proved unsafe, all the passengers crowded aboard the *Mayflower*. The sea voyage was stormy but they reached America and settled where Plymouth, Massachusetts, now stands.

Half of the settlers died during the first winter. But the colony survived to harvest its first crops in November 1621. This is remembered in the USA today as Thanksgiving Day, on 24 November.

▶ WHERE DID A TEA PARTY START A REVOLUTION?

The colonists of America were tired of old ways. They wanted to govern themselves. When Britain tried to tax its colonies in America, the colonists protested. The American Revolution followed.

By the mid 1700s there were 13 British colonies in America. The colonies made their own local laws but the British government kept control of money and trade.

In 1763, the British also gained control of French territory in North America. To raise money for stationing troops there, the British government tried to tax the colonists. One of the taxes was on tea.

The Americans protested. In 1773 a group of colonists crept on to a ship in Boston harbour. Disguised as Indians, they threw its cargo of tea into the water. The 'Boston Tea Party' began a revolution, leading to American independence in 1783.

▶ WHERE DID THE OPIUM WAR BREAK OUT?

The war of 1840-42 between Great Britain and China is called the Opium War. It started when the Chinese government tried to stop Europeans from importing the illegal drug opium into China.

For hundreds of years China had tried to keep out foreign traders, but Europeans were eager to profit from the trade in opium, a drug which was smoked in pipes.

The Chinese government tried to end this trade, and destroyed the British merchants' stocks of opium. The British declared war and attacked China.

The Opium War ended in 1842 with the Treaty of Nanking. This opened five ports in China to British trade, and handed over Hong Kong to Britain. China was also forced to pay damages to the British merchants.

This began a period of foreign domination of China, which was to be the cause of the later Boxer Rebellion.

▶ WHERE DID AMERICAN SLAVES FOUND A FREE COUNTRY?

During the 1700s many Africans were taken to work as slaves in America. In 1822 a homeland for freed slaves was set up in Africa. Its name was Liberia.

In America, rich white people owned many black slaves. But others fought to end the evil of slavery. This struggle eventually led to the US Civil War (1861-65).

A few black slaves won their freedom before the Civil War, but they were homeless. They decided to return to Africa, the land from which their ancestors had been taken in the slave ships.

Liberia, the land of freedom, was founded in 1822. Its capital, Monrovia, was named after the US President James Monroe.

Today, Liberia is an independent republic. Many of its citizens can trace their ancestry back to those first settlers who made the return journey from America to Africa.

◀ WHERE DID THE BOXER REBELLION TAKE PLACE?

In the 1890s powerful European countries controlled much of China's trade. The Chinese uprising against this unfair control is known as the Boxer Rebellion.

The 'Boxers' were members of a patriotic secret society called the 'Society of the Righteous and Harmonious Fists'. They were angered to see China falling more and more under foreign influence. In 1900 the Boxers rose in rebellion to drive out the foreigners. The Empress Dowager, Tzu-hsi, encouraged the rebels.

In the capital, Peking, the Europeans took refuge inside their embassies. The siege of Peking lasted 55 days before an international army fought its way into the city to rescue the Europeans.

After the Boxer Rebellion, the Europeans demanded that China pay compensation. The Boxers had failed; but they had shown how weak the Chinese emperors had become. In 1911 China became a republic.

▶ WHERE DID TANKS FIRST PLAY A PART IN WARFARE?

World War I was a war of terrible machines. Trench warfare killed thousands of soldiers. In 1916 a strange new weapon crawled into battle – the tank.

The generals could not understand the new warfare. As whole armies became bogged down in the muddy trenches of Europe's battlefields, they looked for a breakthrough. Cavalry had been made out of date by barbed wire and machine guns. A new weapon was needed.

In the summer of 1916, during the battle of the Somme, the British introduced the first tanks. They were armoured tractors, crawling on caterpillar tracks, firing cannon and machine guns. Not even a trench could halt them. They were sent into battle singly, to help soldiers on foot. Only a few people saw that the tank's future lay in mass onslaughts. This was proved in World War II when German tank armies swept across much of Europe in a few weeks.

◄ WHERE DID THE LEAGUE OF NATIONS MEET?

After the slaughter of World War I, many nations sought a lasting peace. The League of Nations was set up in 1920 with the aim of settling quarrels peacefully. The League met at Geneva, in Switzerland, but it was doomed to fail.

The League of Nations was meant to act as a world council, but it had no real powers. The leader who did the most to bring the League into existence was Woodrow Wilson, the President of the USA. Unfortunately, Wilson could not persuade the USA to join the League. Other states, such as Germany, left the League as soon as their own behaviour was criticized.

The League could not prevent the world slipping into another war in 1939. It had failed. In 1945, the United Nations Organization was set up, with similar aims. The UN has been more successful, but still lacks the power to be a true 'world government'.

► WHERE WERE THE FIRST ATOMIC BOMBS DROPPED?

World War II was nearly over by 1945, but Japan fought on. To end the war, a terrible new weapon was used: the atomic bomb.

During World War II, both sides worked to make an atomic bomb. Scientists from many countries gathered in the United States. There the first atom bomb was tested on 16 July, 1945.

By 1945, Germany was defeated but Japan was still fighting. To land armies in Japan would have been slow and costly. So the Allies decided to use their new weapon. On 6 August, 1945, an atomic bomb was dropped on the Japanese city of Hiroshima. On 9 August, a second bomb was dropped on Nagasaki.

Both cities were destroyed. Over 100,000 people were killed and an equal number were injured. The war was over, but the world now feared the terrible destructive power of the atomic bomb.

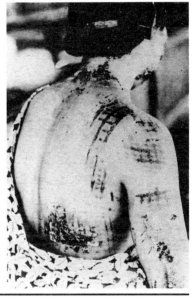

◄ WHERE WAS THE SIX-DAY WAR FOUGHT?

The state of Israel came into being in 1948. Since then, Israel has fought several wars with neighbouring Arab countries. In 1967, the Israelis won a war in just six days.

Israel was founded in what had been Palestine. The Jews had long dreamed of a homeland, a reborn Israel. But the Arabs living in Palestine and neighbouring states opposed this idea.

After World War II, many Jewish people went to live in Palestine. The homeland was declared and in 1948 the state of Israel came into existence. At once there was war between Israel and its neighbours.

Israel has fought many wars since 1948. In 1967, Israel fought both Egypt and Jordan. The Israeli armies, helped by air attacks, won a rapid victory in six days. Israel captured the west bank of the River Jordan and seized much Egyptian territory in Gaza and Sinai.

▼ WHY WERE THE EARLY
CHRISTIANS PERSECUTED?

WHY WERE THE EARLY CHRISTIANS PERSECUTED?

At the time of Christ, Rome ruled the world. Christianity seemed a threat to Rome, so the early Christians risked death for their faith.

Persecution of Christians began under the Roman Emperor Nero. He blamed the Christians for the fire that destroyed much of Rome in AD 64, and many were killed.

To escape arrest, Christians met secretly in underground catacombs, or burial

chambers. Persecution was at its height in AD 250 when the Emperor Decius declared himself to be a god. The Romans worshipped many gods. To believe in only one god was treason. Christians were burned alive or thrown to wild animals in the arena.

Despite the dangers, the new religion grew stronger. Finally, in AD 312, the Roman Emperor Constantine became a Christian. The Christians were able to worship freely and Rome became the centre of the Church.

WHY DID THE CHINESE BUILD THE GREAT WALL?

Ancient China was a rich, proud empire. To keep out enemies, the Chinese emperors built a great wall across the north of China. It became one of the wonders of the world.

The Great Wall of China is 2400 kilometres long. Work on it began in 221 BC, linking a chain of forts along China's northern frontier. A road ran along the wall and signals could be sent quickly along it by patrolling soldiers.

Beyond the wall, to the north, lived fierce nomad tribes, such as the Mongols. For centuries, the wall kept out these terrifying barbarians. But in the end the Mongols did conquer China and made it part of their vast empire.

WHY WERE THE VIKINGS BOLD SEA VOYAGERS?

In their fast wooden long-ships, Vikings crossed unknown seas to explore new lands.

The Vikings came from Scandinavia between AD 800 and 1100. They were farmers, but they were also fierce warriors and bold seamen. Their ships were strong and seaworthy. In them, Vikings sailed to Iceland and Greenland. One band, led by Leif Ericsson, crossed the Atlantic Ocean and founded a colony in North America. Another group, the Rus, settled in Kiev and gave their name to Russia.

Viking raids terrorized much of Europe. But in time, the Vikings gave up their roving and began to lead more peaceful lives.

▲ WHY WERE MEDIEVAL CASTLES BUILT?

In the Middle Ages, kings and lords built castles to defend their lands from enemies. Peasants from nearby villages took refuge inside the castles when war broke out.

The medieval castle developed from the wooden fort. At the centre of the castle was a tall tower, or keep. This was surrounded by high towers, thick stone walls and deep moats or ditches. The moats were filled with water. From the walls, soldiers could fire arrows at the enemy.

The windows were very narrow to stop missiles from entering the castle from outside. The attackers would lay siege to the castle, hoping to starve the defenders into surrender.

▼ WHY DID THE CRUSADERS FIGHT THE SARACENS?

For 200 years Muslims and Christians fought for the Holy Land of Palestine.

The Holy Land was sacred to both Muslims and Christians. In 1096, Pope Urban II called for a Crusade, or 'war of the Cross' to free the Holy Land from the Muslim Saracens.

The Crusaders came from all over Christendom, but failed to defeat the Saracens. The famous English king Richard the Lion Heart went to the Holy Land to fight and there was even a children's crusade in 1212.

The Crusaders brought home to Europe many new ideas from their wars in the East.

Muslim empire
Christian areas
Crusader routes
Muslim advance into Europe

Poitiers
Rome
Acre — Palestine
Jerusalem
Mecca

▼ WHY DID LUTHER DISAGREE WITH THE CHURCH?

The medieval Church was very powerful. Martin Luther, a German monk, dared to challenge it. His protest started the Reformation.

In Luther's day (he was born in 1483), the Church had fallen into bad ways. Some priests sold pardons for sins to anyone who could pay. The relics of dead saints, such as hair and bones, were also sold.

Luther thought this was

wrong. He pinned up a list of 95 arguments, setting out what he thought was wrong with the Church. For this rebellion, he was eventually excommunicated (cast out) of the Church.

However, others agreed with Luther. They set up breakaway 'Protestant' churches and refused to obey the Pope in Rome. In England, King Henry VIII made himself head of the Church. The movement begun by Luther is called the Reformation.

▶ WHY WERE THE FIRST AMERICANS CALLED INDIANS?

When Christopher Columbus set sail in 1492 he hoped to reach Asia and the rich spice islands of the Indies. Instead he found a New World and a new people, whom he called 'Indians'.

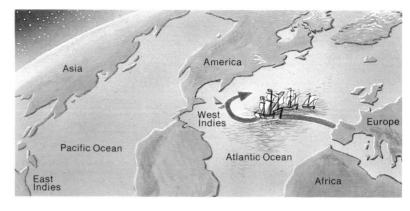

Columbus guessed that the Earth was round. By sailing west, he expected to reach the Indies faster than by sailing east, around Africa. He did not know that a huge continent, America, was in the way. So, when his ships reached the West Indies, he thought he must be in Asia and that the people living on the islands must be Indians. Many Indians were killed or enslaved by the Europeans who followed Columbus.

◀ WHY DID CHARLES I OF SPAIN BOAST: 'IN MY EMPIRE THE SUN NEVER SETS'?

King Charles I ruled Spain from 1516 to 1556. During his reign, Spain seized a huge empire in the New World. America's gold made Spain the greatest power in Europe.

As well as being King of Spain, Charles was also Holy Roman Emperor. He thought of himself as ruler of all Catholic Europe. He faced serious problems. Europe was being attacked by the Turks from the East, and was divided by religious quarrels.

But in the New World of America, Spain discovered vast riches. In 1519 Hernan Cortes and 500 *conquistadores* (conquerors) captured the Aztec Empire of Mexico. A few years later, Francisco Pizarro conquered the Incas of Peru. Treasure fleets bore gold and silver home across the sea to Spain.

In Europe's struggle for new lands overseas, Spain won a head start.

▶ WHY DID PEOPLE BEGIN TO WORK IN FACTORIES?

Until the 1700s most people lived and worked in the countryside. Then came a great change, the Industrial Revolution. People left their villages and went to work in factories in new, crowded towns.

Why did this change take place? One reason was the invention of the steam engine and other machines. Goods could be made faster by machine than by hand. Roads, canals and railways made travel much faster too. Jobs such as cloth weaving, which people had done at home, were taken over by machines.

Factories were built to house the machinery. And towns sprang up to house the workers who were needed to run the factories. Life for the workers was hard and dangerous. Britain was the first country to have an Industrial Revolution. Europe and America quickly followed, and by the mid-1800s factories were common.

▶ WHAT CAUSED THE FRENCH REVOLUTION?

In 1789 the French people rose against their rulers. They wanted freedom and equal rights for all.

France supported the American colonists in their fight for freedom from British rule. But France itself was divided. The king had great power, and the rich nobles and Church owned most of the land. The middle classes and the poor paid heavy taxes, but they had little power.

In 1789 the French parliament met for the first time in 164 years to discuss reforms. But the 'Three Estates' or groups (Nobles, Church, and Middle Classes and Peasants) could not agree. Fighting broke out in Paris when a mob attacked the Bastille prison. In 1793 the king was executed and France became a republic.

◀ WHY WAS ITALY UNIFIED?

In Roman times, Italy was one country. Later, it split up into small city-states. In the 1860s Italy threw off foreign rule and again became one nation.

The Italian city-states were once rich and powerful. But their quarrels made them weak, leaving them open to foreign conquest.

Napoleon Bonaparte tried to make himself king of a united Italy, but failed. The Austrians became masters of Italy. But the Italians dreamed of unity, and found a skilful statesman in Count Cavour and a bold general in Giuseppe Garibaldi.

In 1861 Garibaldi's one thousand 'redshirts' drove the Austrian forces out of southern Italy, and the struggle was over. Victor Emmanuel of Piedmont-Sardinia became the first king of a united Italy.

Only two states remained ouside the new kingdom. Venice joined Italy in 1866 and the Papal States, around Rome, joined in 1870.

▶ WHY DID EUROPEAN NATIONS COLONIZE AFRICA?

Until the 1800s Africa was the 'Dark Continent'. Few Europeans knew anything about it. As explorers began to uncover Africa's secrets, Europe took more interest in the huge con-tinent's minerals and land. A scramble for colonies took place.

The journeys of Livingstone and Stanley in the 1860s and 1870s revealed Africa's vast wealth. The European nations of France, Britain, Belgium, Germany, Spain, Italy and Portugal rushed to seize as much land in Africa as they could. In 1885 they agreed to share Africa between them, and by 1902 Liberia was the only free African country.

Some European settlers, like the South African Boers, came to farm the new land. Others wanted minerals, such as gold and diamonds.

European officials were sent out to govern the colonies. The Africans lost their land and were often ill-treated.

**At the outbreak of World
War I, Russia was a poor,
backward country. The
war brought defeat and
discontent. In 1917 came
revolution.**

In 1917 Russia was a huge,
undeveloped country, ruled
by a weak Czar (emperor).
There was much unrest, and
the government could do
little. The army was defeated
in the war with Germany.
The people were starving.
There had already been one
attempt at revolution, in 1905.

Czar Nicholas II refused to

**People called World War I
the Great War, the 'war to
end wars'. They were
shocked at the numbers of
people killed and injured.**

It was a mechanized war, the
first in which machine guns,
aircraft, submarines and
poison gas showed their
terrible power. In 1914 when
the fighting began, generals

on both sides expected quick
victories. Instead, the
German and Allied armies
became bogged down in
trench battles. Millions of
men died trying to gain a few
metres of muddy ground.

Cities were bombed from
the air. The war spread
overseas. Over eight million
troops were killed. More than
20 million more people died
from hunger and disease. By
1918 both sides were
exhausted.

modernize his vast empire. In
1917 he was forced to
abdicate, but the new democratic government was weak.
Power was seized by the
Communists, led by Lenin,
who set up a revolutionary
government.

The Czar and his family
were executed. To mark the
change in Russia's history,
the capital was moved from
Petrograd (now Leningrad) to
Moscow. Russia became the
world's first Communist
state.

**In modern times, China
has seen civil war and
revolution. In 1934 the
founder of Communist
China, Mao Tse-tung, led
the Communists on an
epic 'Long March'.**

China's civil war was fought
between the Nationalist
government of Chiang Kai-
shek and the Communists.
Near to defeat, the Com-

munists had to retreat north
to Yenan in 1934. This
became known as the 'Long
March'.

In 1937 the two opposing
armies united to fight off the
Japanese. But in 1945 civil
war began again. This time
the Communists were vic-
torious. By 1949 they
controlled all mainland China.

The leader of the new
China was Mao Tse-tung, one
of the heroes of the Long
March. He ruled China until
his death in 1976.

After World War II Germany was in ruins. It was divided into East and West. The old capital, Berlin, was divided by a wall to stop East Germans fleeing to the West.

The most important problem today is how to settle international disputes peacefully. The United Nations was set up in 1945 with this as its chief aim.

During the 1930s the League of Nations could not stop ruthless dictators like Adolf Hitler. During World War II (1939 to 1945), the Allies fighting against Germany and Japan called themselves the 'United Nations'. When peace returned in 1945, they formed a new world organization called the United Nations. It had 51 members.

Today the UN has more than 150 members. It is not a 'world government', since its powers are limited. But it tries to persuade countries to solve problems peacefully, rather than by war.

The victorious Allies divided Germany into zones. The Russians turned the eastern half into Communist East Germany. Many Germans fled to the west into the free Federal Republic of West Germany.

Berlin stands in East German territory. It, too, is

The land of Palestine (Israel) is the ancient home of both Arabs and Jews. In 1948 a new Jewish 'homeland' was created.

Ever since the Romans occupied Palestine, Jews had dreamed of a new Israel. After Turkish rule of the area ended in 1918, both Arabs and Jews had claims to Palestine.

Jewish settlers began to emigrate to Palestine from all over Europe, where they had lived for centuries. Many more arrived after World War II.

In 1948 the United Nations decided that Palestine should be divided between Arabs and Jews. The state of Israel was created as a national homeland for the Jews. Since that time there has been conflict between the two peoples, and many Palestinian Arabs have fled to neigh-bouring countries.

now divided. Many people fled from East Berlin into the western part of the city, so in 1961 the East Germans built a wall across the city to seal the border.

The grim Berlin Wall is a constant reminder of the 'cold war' between East and West. Special crossing points are open only at certain times. People trying to escape to the West face armed guards and barbed wire. Those who are unsuccessful may be captured or shot.

The samurai were the knights of medieval Japan. They were proud and brave, and would fight to the death for their lord. The samurai's fantastic armour struck fear into their foes.

During the Middle Ages, Japan was torn by civil war. During this time, samurai formed an army of highly-trained warriors. They fought on horseback and their favourite weapons were long swords. They were also expert bowmen.

The samurai despised cowards. They would never surrender. When gunpowder muskets first appeared, they called them 'cowards' weapons'. Yet, in the end, it was musket fire that defeated the samurai with their swords and armour.

For 800 years the samurai held on to their special place in Japanese life. Even when they were no longer required in battle, they remained powerful as the upholders of Japan's ancient customs.

In the Middle Ages, knights were specially trained soldiers. They wore armour and fought on horseback. A knight swore an oath to serve his king. In return, the king gave land to the knight.

The king needed loyal warriors to fight his wars and also to help him rule the land. His knights were the pride of his army. In return for their service, the knights received payment in the form of lands. This arrangement, called feudalism, lasted for hundreds of years.

Some knights were 'dubbed' (made a knight) on the field of battle. But most trained from boyhood, serving first as a page and then as a squire to an older knight.

Knights were supposed to uphold the law, and be honourable. So the idea of a special knightly code of honour arose. This was called 'chivalry'.

The most famous knights were the legendary Knights of the Round Table.

To train for battle, and to show off their skill, knights took part in mock fights. These were known as jousts. Such contests took place in front of an audience at open-air tournaments. Jousting often took place at celebrations such as coronations.

Jousting was a mock fight between two knights. They fought in an enclosure known as the 'lists'. The knights wore armour and rode horses. They charged at one another, trying to knock each other off their horses with lances. The fight often continued on foot, with the knights using swords and clubs.

At a tournament, crowds gathered to watch jousts and other mock battles. Sometimes the knights fought so fiercely that they killed or wounded one another. So special rules were introduced to make jousting safer, and the knights had to use blunt weapons.

WHAT WAS THE RENAISSANCE?

The word *Renaissance* means 'rebirth'. It describes the time in Europe's history when people rediscovered the art and learning of the past, and added new, exciting ideas of their own.

After the fall of the Roman Empire (about AD 500), much of the ancient learning was forgotten. During the Middle Ages, learning was closely tied to religion. Few people could read or write.

Around 1500, new ideas began to emerge. Artists such as Leonardo da Vinci looked back to ancient Greece and Rome for inspiration. Scientists, such as Copernicus, studied the world and disagreed with the teachings of the Church about it. The time was ripe for change. There were wealthy merchants ready to back new ventures. Also, there were new ways of spreading knowledge, such as Gutenberg's newly-invented printing press.

WHAT WAS THE NEW WORLD?

To Europeans of the 1400s, 'the world' meant Europe, Africa and Asia. But as European sailors began to venture farther from home, they discovered a New World – the continent of America.

Viking rovers actually landed in North America around AD 1000. But almost 500 years passed before the next European explorers arrived. Ships were small and clumsy and sailors feared to sail out of sight of land. They had no compasses or maps.

In 1453 the Turks captured Constantinople. This stopped European merchants reaching Asia overland. So they set out to find a new sea route to the East. When Christopher Columbus left Spain in 1492, he hoped to find a westerly passage to the rich spice islands of the Indies.

Columbus believed that the world was round. But he did not imagine that beyond the Atlantic Ocean he would land on the shores of a New World, the vast continent of America.

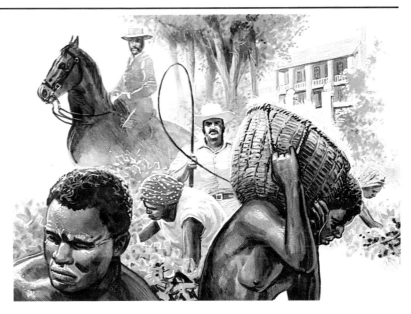

WHAT WAS THE SLAVE TRADE?

Slavery is an ancient and evil trade. The ancient Greeks and Egyptians, for example, made slaves of people captured in war. After Europeans settled in America, slaves captured in Africa were shipped across the sea to work in the American plantations.

The Arabs had traded in African slaves for centuries before Europeans joined in during the 1500s. Slave ships from Africa crossed the Atlantic Ocean, packed with men, women and children.

Many slaves died during the dreadful voyages. In America the slaves were sold in slave markets. Some worked as house servants, but most worked on cotton and sugar plantations. Many were ill-treated by their masters. Britain eventually banned the slave trade in 1807. But the black slaves in the southern United States did not gain their freedom until the American Civil War of 1861–65.

267

▼ WHAT WAS THE INDUSTRIAL REVOLUTION?

In history, a revolution is a time of great change. In the late 1700s and early 1800s, a new age began – the Age of Machines. It was also the Age of Industry, when millions of people began to work in mills, mines and factories.

Improved transport made these changes possible. Canals and railways carried goods from the new factories to the ports. Inside the

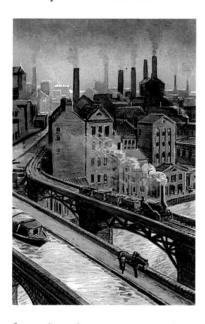

factories, the steam engine's mighty power was harnessed to drive machinery. Coal was the fuel, iron was the material and steam was the power that made the Industrial Revolution.

The new railways carried people faster than ever before. New iron ships steamed the oceans. Within a few years villages grew into towns.

The Industrial Revolution made Europe and America rich and powerful. Factory owners made fortunes. But factory workers often had to live in overcrowded slums.

▼ WHAT CAUSED WORLD WAR I?

The Great War of 1914–18 was the most terrible the world had seen. Many nations took part, and millions of people died. The war was caused by rivalry in Europe. But it actually began with a murder.

In 1914 the Austrian Archduke Ferdinand was shot dead by a rebel while visiting Sarajevo in Serbia (now part of Yugoslavia). This murder started a chain of events that led to war in Europe within two months.

On one side were Germany, Austria and Turkey. On the other were Britain, France and Russia, joined later by the USA. Most people thought the war would end quickly. But new weapons, such as the machine gun, were so deadly that neither side could break through. Armies became bogged down in trench warfare. For the first time ever, civilians were bombed from the air. The war dragged on until 1918, when Germany surrendered.

▼ WHAT WAS THE WALL STREET CRASH?

In the 1930s the world was swept into a disastrous money crisis. Money lost its value. Businesses collapsed and trade slumped. The crisis began on Wall Street, in New York.

Wall Street was the home of the US Stock Market, where stocks and shares were traded. In October 1929 the market 'crashed'.

Before the collapse, people

had been buying shares recklessly. Prices rose high above their true value. Suddenly, a panic began, and everyone started selling.

Banks were ruined. Many businesses and factories closed. The Wall Street Crash brought on the Great Depression – a slump in world trade which lasted for several years. Millions of people lost their jobs during the slump. Soup kitchens, like the one shown in the photograph, were set up to provide food for unemployed people.

▼ WHAT IS NATO?

'NATO' stands for North Atlantic Treaty Organization. It is a military alliance set up in 1949 by the USA and its allies in Western Europe. Its headquarters are in Brussels, Belgium.

When World War II ended, Europe was in ruins. It was also divided in two, for the eastern half was controlled by the USSR. The Western European nations feared that the USSR might try to attack them, so they set up an alliance for self-defence.

The USA and Canada are also members of the North Atlantic Treaty Organization. NATO now has 15 members.

NATO has its own commander, and each country contributes part of its armed forces. Troops, aircraft and ships of NATO carry out manoeuvres together to develop co-operation between the nations.

The countries of Eastern Europe belong to a similar alliance. This is known as the Warsaw Pact.

Iceland

NATO countries

Warsaw Pact countries

Norway

United Kingdom

Denmark

USSR

Netherlands
Belgium
Luxembourg
West Germany

Poland
East Germany
Czechoslovakia

France

Hungary

Portugal

Romania

Bulgaria

Italy

Turkey

Greece

▲ WHAT IS THE 'COLD WAR'?

World War II ended in 1945, but the victorious Allies were soon quarrelling. The USA and the USSR were suspicious of one another. They began an 'arms race' and disagreed on many things. This is the so-called 'cold war'.

In 1945 Europe was divided by the 'iron curtain', separating the Communist East from the non-Communist West. The USSR set up Communist governments in the countries it had freed from Nazi rule.

The struggle between the West (or 'Free World') and the East (Communists) went on in many parts of the world. The Korean War (1950–53) became a trial of strength between the two sides. So, too was the Vietnam War (1945–76). Today, the same mistrust that began the cold war threatens the world with destruction, because of the build-up of nuclear weapons on both sides.

▼ WHAT IS THE 'THIRD WORLD'?

The richest countries in the world are those with modern farms and factories, such as the USA. Next come nations such as Brazil, which have rich resources still to be tapped. Then there are the poorest nations, which have few natural resources. These are the countries of the 'Third World'.

Most Third World countries are in Africa and Asia. When the United Nations was set up in 1945, one of its aims was to help poor countries. Many of these countries were then colonies, ruled by Europeans. Today, almost all are independent.

Few Third World countries can grow enough food to feed their growing populations or earn enough money by trade to build homes, schools and hospitals quickly enough.

Some help for the Third World comes from UN experts, who can advise on new farming methods and train people in new skills.

WORLD HISTORY

▼ WHO LIVED AT UR?

Ur was one of the city states built by the ancient Sumerians. Its ruins lie in southern Iraq.

The Sumerians founded Ur during the 3000s BC. The River Euphrates flowed nearby.

The early settlement at Ur was wiped out by a flood. It is remembered in the Bible as the Great Flood.

A highly civilized group of Sumerian people settled at Ur after the Flood. They included sculptors, potters, metalworkers and builders.

A royal graveyard, containing gold, silver and bronze objects dating from about 2700 BC was excavated in the 1920s.

The kings and queens of Ur were buried with a large retinue of their poisoned courtiers who hoped to serve them in the next world.

▼ WHO WAS SARGON OF AKKAD?

Sargon was a king who reigned from about 2630 to 2305 BC. He founded the world's first major empire.

Sargon was vizier (chief minister) to one of the kings who ruled in Sumer (modern Iraq). He took over the throne and founded the city of Agade (or Akkad), somewhere in north Babylonia.

In time he conquered all the other kings of Sumer, extending his rule south to the Persian Gulf, west to the Mediterranean and north into what is now Turkey.

The people of this empire were called Akkadians.

Under Sargon's successors the Akkadians developed the art of writing. They also designed the first helmets to be used in warfare, made out of copper and leather.

▼ WHO WERE THE HITTITES?

The Hittites had an empire based on what is now central Turkey. It lasted for about 700 years, from the 1900s to the 1200s BC.

The Hittites were related to the peoples of Europe and northern India. They crossed the Caucasus mountains from east-central Europe to conquer Anatolia (modern Turkey). Their capital was the city of Hattusas near modern Ankara.

After they became powerful around 1500 BC the Hittites spread south along the Mediterranean coast.

They wrote on clay tablets, both in hieroglyphics (picture writing) and in cuneiform (wedge-shaped) script. Hittite kings also served as high priests. They had a legal system. The Hittites were among the first people to use iron.

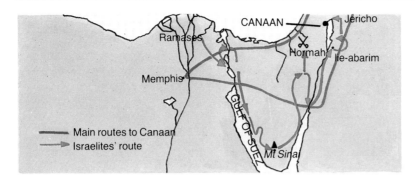

Main routes to Canaan
Israelites' route

▲ WHO WAS MOSES?

Moses was the Hebrew prophet who led the people of Israel from bondage in Egypt to Canaan.

The story of Moses is told in four books of the Bible – *Exodus*, *Leviticus*, *Numbers*, and *Deuteronomy*. This is the only direct reference to him.

However, an Egyptian inscription of about 1200 BC mentions Israel, and an Egyptian historian, Manetheo, writing in the 200s BC, told how certain Hebrews were expelled from Egypt. 'Moses' used to be an Egyptian name.

According to the Bible account, the Israelites were an oppressed group in Egypt, which provided slave labour. Moses became their leader and led them out of Egypt towards Canaan (Palestine), probably during the 1200s BC.

For many years the Israelites were nomads (wanderers). They did not reach Canaan until after Moses's death.

▶ WHO WERE THE ASSYRIANS?

The Assyrians lived in the northern part of what is now Iraq. They flourished from about 2900 BC to 600 BC.

The Assyrians lived in a highland area on the Tigris River. Their chief cities were Assur and Nineveh. Their buildings were made of sun-baked bricks, but their temples and palaces had stone foundations and elaborate stone wall-carvings.

The Assyrian state was built up around its army, the first large force to be equipped with iron weapons. The Assyrians had an empire stretching from Egypt to the Persian Gulf.

They extracted silver from mines in what is now southern Turkey, and Assur soon became a thriving trade centre between east and west. Small rods of silver were used in exchange for goods (especially fabrics, horses and camels).

The Assyrians worshipped Ashur, god of war. In 600 BC Assyria was conquered by the Medes and Babylonians.

▶ WHO WAS KING NEBUCHADREZZAR?

Nebuchadrezzar was king of Babylon from 605 to 562 BC. In the Bible his name is spelt Nebuchadnezzar.

A few months before he succeeded his father Nebuchadrezzar took Syria and Palestine from Egypt in a battle at Carchemish, now in Southern Turkey.

The Egyptians encouraged the defeated peoples to rebel, so Nebuchadrezzar had to mount a series of fresh campaigns. He overran the little Hebrew kingdom of Judah, sacked its capital, Jerusalem, and took many captives to Babylon.

Babylon was already a big and wealthy city when Nebuchadrezzar became king, and he added many fine buildings to it, including the Ishtar Gate (right).

To please his wife, Amytis, who disliked the flat plain of Babylon, Nebuchadrezzar built a huge terraced garden, famed as the Hanging Gardens of Babylon and one of the Seven Wonders of the World.

◀WHICH KING FIRST UNITED EGYPT?

Menes, the ruler of Upper Egypt, conquered the Nile Delta area (Lower Egypt) in about 2850 BC.

The kingdom of Upper Egypt extended south from where Cairo is now to the first cataract (steep rapids) on the Nile, the site of present-day Aswan.

Menes wore a white, cone-shaped crown. The rulers of Lower Egypt, the swampy area of the delta, wore a red crown. After his conquest, Menes wore a double crown, the white crown inside the red one.

Menes was a personal name. He took a different name as a ruler, and appears in lists of early kings as Narmer, Lord of the Two Lands.

The king built a capital city for his double kingdom at Memphis, south-west of Cairo. Its citadel was surrounded by a white wall.

Egyptian history tells us that Menes/Narmer reigned for 62 years and that his wife's name was Neith-hetep. Soon after he died – killed by a hippopotamus – he was declared a god.

▶ WHO SENT A TRADING EXPEDITION TO THE LAND OF PUNT?

Many Egyptian rulers sent traders to the Land of Punt, but the two most famous expeditions were sent by Mentohotep III and Queen Hatshepsut.

The Land of Punt lay on the Red Sea Coast, now occupied by part of Ethiopia, Djibouti and north Somalia. It was rich in gold, ivory and spices.

Early trading between Egypt and Punt was apparently overland. By about 2000 BC, the third king Mentohotep decided that it would be better to go by sea and sent one ship.

About 500 years later Queen Hatshepsut, who ruled from 1503 to 1482 BC, sent a fleet of five ships to Punt. An inscription in her mortuary temple at Deir el-Bahri, near Luxor, describes the cargo of fragrant woods, incense, eye make-up, apes, dogs, panther-skins and living myrrh trees.

▶ WHO DESIGNED THE FIRST PYRAMID?

The first pyramid was the Step Pyramid at Saqqara in Egypt. It was designed by Imhotep, physician to King Djoser, in the 2500s BC.

Imhotep is notable as the first non-royal person whose name is recorded in history.

He was a man who had many talents. As well as being the court physician, he was a priest, an astronomer, a writer and the king's chief minister.

The Step Pyramid is about 60 metres high. It was the central feature of Djoser's royal tomb. The tomb was more than just a burial place. It provided temples, galleries, courtyards and rooms where religious services could be held to honour the dead king.

The whole Saqqara complex was the first monument to be built entirely of stone: mud bricks were usually used for part or all of the buildings.

The Step Pyramid is so called because its sides form a series of giant steps. Later pyramids had smooth sides.

▼ WHICH PHARAOH
WORSHIPPED ONE GOD?

**Amenhotep IV, who reigned
from 1379 to 1362 BC,
worshipped the Aten, the
Sun's disc.**

Amenhotep IV became
pharaoh (king) on the death of
his father, whose reign was
peaceful and prosperous.

Early in his reign the young
pharaoh adopted the worship
of the Aten. He believed the
Aten was the God of the whole
world, not just of Egypt. He
abolished the worship of
Amun-Rê, a combined god of
the air and god of the Sun, and
a host of other gods and
goddesses. He took the name
Akhenaten after the Aten.

Akhenaten built a new
capital city, Akhetaton,
abandoning Thebes, the city of
his predecessors.

Akhenaten devoted all his
time to religious affairs and
neglected the government of
his country, so by the time he
died, at the age of about 30,
Egypt had lost most of its
empire. Soon Egypt returned
to its old gods, and Thebes
became the capital once more.

▼ WHO WAS
TUTANKHAMUN?

**Tutankhamun was the young
son-in-law of Akhenaten. His
tomb, containing rich
treasures, was found in 1922.**

Tutankhamun's original name
was Tutankhaten. He was
married as a boy to
Akhenaten's third daughter,
Ankhesenpaaten. He was
probably only about ten years
old when he was made pharaoh
in succession to Smenkhkare,
his wife's brother-in-law.

After about two years the
boy-king proclaimed that all
the old gods should be
worshipped again and he
moved back to the old capital
city, Thebes. He also changed
his name to incorporate that of
the god Amun-Rê.

Tutankhamun's tomb,
found in 1922 by the British
archaeologist Howard Carter,
is the only Egyptian royal
tomb that had escaped being
robbed in ancient times. The
King's body still lies in the
tomb, but most of the
treasures are in the Cairo
Museum. Tutankhamun was
only 18 when he died in 1351
BC.

▲ WHO WAS NEFERTITI?

**Nefertiti was the wife of
Akhenaten, the Egyptian
pharaoh who tried to change
his country's religion.**

Nefertiti may have been a
foreign princess, but she and
her husband looked so alike
that she may well have been his
sister. Egyptian kings often
married their sisters.

We know what Nefertiti and
Akhenaten looked like because
several sculpted heads of the
couple were found in the ruins
of Akhenaten's capital,
Akhetaton, a site now called
Tell el-Amarna.

During Akhenaten's reign,
artists were encouraged to
make lifelike portraits rather
than the stylized types that are
typical of art in ancient Egypt.

Nefertiti helped her
husband in his religious
ceremonies and bore him six
daughters. Then she seems to
have fallen out of favour and
lived in retirement or maybe
even in captivity.

Nefertiti's eldest daughter,
Meritaten, married
Akhenaten's successor,
Smenkhkare.

The Jomon people were the earliest known inhabitants of Japan. They lived from about 7000 BC to 250 BC.

'Jomon' means 'cord pattern', and the Jomon people have been given their name because they made pottery with a cord pattern on it.

It seems likely that the Jomon people came to Japan from Siberia. They may be the ancestors of the Ainu, a small group of people living in northern Japan. The Ainu men have bushy hair and beards, unlike most modern Japanese.

The Jomon people lived in semi-underground houses, pits covered with sloping roofs. They used stone tools. They appear to have lived largely by hunting and fishing.

Large middens (rubbish dumps) have been found containing the remains of shellfish with bone fish hooks which were apparently used for deep-sea fishing. So the Jomon people must have had sea-going boats. Bones show that they ate wild boar and deer.

Stone arrowheads used for hunting

▲ WHICH EMPERORS WERE KNOWN AS THE SONS OF HEAVEN?

The title 'Son of Heaven' was given to Chinese emperors from Bronze Age times until the title of emperor was abolished in 1911.

The early rulers of China were both emperors and high priests. The rulers of the Shang Dynasty (family) who ruled from 1766 BC, claimed to be descended from a supreme god named Shang Ti.

The Shang believed that the emperor was their link with heaven and that when he died he would go there to join Shang Ti. During an emperor's lifetime he was also known as the 'One Man'.

For many hundreds of years the Chinese worshipped the spirits of their ancestors; the 'Son of Heaven' was the leader of this religious cult.

The title 'Son of Heaven' may have originated before the Shang Dynasty. But the earlier dynasties, going back to 2697 BC, are largely legendary and nothing definite is known about them.

▲ WHO WAS LAO-TSE?

Lao-tse was a philosopher who lived in China about 2,500 years ago. He founded a religion and way of thinking called Taoism.

According to tradition, Lao-tse was born in 604 BC. His name was actually Lao-tan, but he is called Lao-tse which means 'Master Lao'. At first he lived a quiet, secluded life which grew busier after he became librarian at the court of the Chou dynasty of Chinese rulers.

Lao-tse became known for his wisdom and philosophy and in 517 BC the young Confucius came to ask his advice.

Eventually Lao-tse tired of worldly affairs, and set out on a journey westward in search of rest and contemplation.

On his travels he met a warden at a frontier post with whom he left his writings on Tao, literally 'The Way'. He was last heard of journeying towards the Pass of Hsien-ku, in the western mountains of China.

Taoism advocates a simple, virtuous life, close to nature.

▲ WHO WAS THE BUDDHA?

▲ WHO WAS CONFUCIUS?

▼ WHO WERE THE NOK PEOPLE?

The Nok people lived from about 900 BC in what is now northern Nigeria. They were the earliest people in Black Africa to make sculptures.

The Buddha, which means 'The Enlightened One', was Siddhartha Gautama, the son of an Indian prince who lived in the 500s BC. He spent most of his life preaching.

Confucius was a Chinese philosopher who lived nearly 2,500 years ago. Millions of people have followed his teachings almost as a religion.

Archaeologists first found the Nok sculptures in 1931. They are named after the little village of Nok which lies south-east of the town of Kano.

Tradition says that Siddhartha was born in 563 BC. He was brought up to a life of luxury. When he was 16 he married the Princess Yasodhara, and they had a son, Rahula.

The real name of Confucius was K'ung Ch'iu. He became known as K'ung-fu-tzu, which means Great Master Kung; Confucius is a Latin form of that title.

The art and way of life of these unknown people is called the Nok culture. Traces of it have been found at many other sites in the area north of the junction of the Niger and Benue rivers.

When he was about 29 the prince realised that the world was full of sickness and misery. One night he left home, exchanged his rich clothes with the rags of a beggar and became a wandering monk.

Confucius was born in 551 BC in the town of Ch'ü-fou in Shantung province, where his descendants still live. He became famous as a scholar while still a young man.

The sculptures are made of earthenware. Some are life-size human heads. Others are small models of animals and humans. All the human heads have pierced ears, so the people must have worn jewellery.

For six years he tried to find enlightenment (religious understanding) by fasting and self-denial. He finally realised this was not the way either; he needed something in between riches and starvation.

Many people in China were poor, miserable and badly governed. Confucius believed in treating people as he would want to be treated. His ambition was to obtain a high government post so that he could put his ideas of peace and justice into practice. Eventually the rulers of his own state, Lu, gave him an apparently high post – but he soon found that he had no real power so he resigned to spend his last years teaching. He died at the age of 72.

The Nok people also smelted iron and made stone axes. From the sculptures it seems that they were farmers.

Nobody knows how the Nok culture ended, but the present-day Yoruba tribe may be descended from the Nok.

Sitting under a Bo-tree one day to meditate, enlightenment suddenly came to him. He spent the rest of his life teaching others the way to *Nirvana* or happiness, by following the 'Middle Way'. He died at the age of 80.

▶ WHO WAS JULIUS CAESAR?

Gaius Julius Caesar was a brilliant Roman general and writer who became the ruler of Rome.

Caesar was a member of an aristocratic Roman family. He was born in 100 BC.

In 68 BC Caesar entered a political career, holding a succession of public positions. In 59 BC he was elected consul.

With two other men, Gnaeus Pompeius and Marcus Crassus, Caesar formed a three-man group to rule Rome, called the Triumvirate. After his year of office as consul Caesar went off to conquer Gaul (France). In nine years of campaigning he managed to evict the Germans who ruled Gaul and also to invade Britain twice.

In 49 BC Caesar returned to Rome and made himself dictator. He campaigned in Egypt where he fell in love with its queen, Cleopatra.

Although he ruled Rome wisely, he had enemies who were jealous of his success. In 44 BC they assassinated him.

◀ WHO WAS CLEOPATRA?

Cleopatra VII was the ruler of Egypt from 51 BC to 30 BC. She was beautiful and ruthless.

Cleopatra was the last of the Ptolemy family from Macedonia, who ruled Egypt for 300 years. On the death of her father in 51 BC she became joint ruler with her younger brother Ptolemy XIII who, in accordance with Egyptian tradition, also became her husband. She was then 18.

In 49 BC Ptolemy's guardians ousted Cleopatra from power. Then she met Julius Caesar, in Egypt pursuing his rival Pompey. Caesar put her back on the throne.

Ptolemy XIII having died, Cleopatra married a still younger brother, Ptolemy XIV, but went off to Rome with Caesar, and had his son.

After Caesar's death she returned to Egypt where she fell in love with another Roman general, Marcus Antonius. By him she had twins. When Antonius died, Cleopatra killed herself.

▶ WHO FOUNDED THE ARMENIAN EMPIRE?

The founder of the Armenian Empire was Tigranes the Great, who became king of that country in 95 BC.

Armenia was a region covering the present-day Armenian Soviet Socialist Republic and part of neighbouring Turkey.

Tigranes, sometimes called Dikran, came to the throne when he was about 45. At that time he was the hostage of a neighbouring king but he bought his freedom by handing over part of Armenia.

He began at once to enlarge his kingdom by attacking Parthia where he had been a hostage. In the next few years he overran Syria, northern Mesopotamia (now a good part of Iraq) and Phoenicia, now part of Lebanon and Israel.

Tigranes' expansionist policies brought him into conflict with Rome. An army led by Gnaeus Pompeius defeated him in 66 BC. Tigranes had to surrender and become a Roman vassal. His empire had vanished.

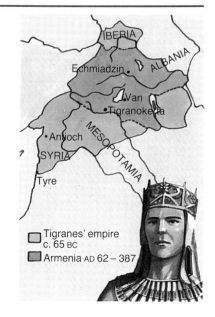

Tigranes' empire c. 65 BC
Armenia AD 62 – 387

◄WHO WAS JESUS OF NAZARETH?

Jesus was a Jewish rabbi (teacher) who founded the Christian religion. Its followers believe that he was the Son of God, sent to Earth to save mankind.

Jesus was born in Bethlehem in Judea, where his mother, Mary, and her husband Joseph, a carpenter, had travelled to register their names in a census. But his hometown was Nazareth in the province of Galilee.

Little is known about Jesus's early life, except that his parents fled to Egypt for a while to escape persecution by the king of Judea, Herod the Great. Herod ruled Judea for the Romans.

Jesus began teaching when he was about 30 years old. He soon had a large following of Jews who hailed him as the Messiah, a saviour whom prophets had said would come to help them.

The Romans and orthodox Jewish religious leaders saw Jesus as a troublemaker and he was tried and crucified in AD 29.

►WHO BECAME THE FIRST POPE?

According to tradition, the first pope, or head of the Christian Church, was Peter, one of the apostles (close followers) of Jesus of Nazareth.

Before he met Jesus, Peter's name was Simon. He was a fisherman. Jesus called him Peter, which means 'rock', saying 'Upon this rock I will build my Church'.

After Jesus was crucified in AD 29 he appeared to his disciples. Peter took the lead in proclaiming that Jesus had conquered death and was undoubtedly the Messiah (Christos in Greek).

Peter travelled, preaching the message of Jesus. Tradition has it that he went to Rome and became Bishop of Rome – the official title of popes ever since. He was martyred in about AD 64 in the reign of Emperor Nero.

A shrine, believed to have marked the grave of Peter, has been found under St Peter's Basilica in the Vatican in Rome.

▼WHO WAS THE FIRST CHRISTIAN MISSIONARY?

The apostle Paul was the first true missionary. He preached Christianity to the Gentiles – that is, to non-Jewish peoples.

Paul was a Jewish tent-maker, named Saul, born in Tarsus in Asia Minor (modern Turkey). Having studied the Jewish religion in Jerusalem, Saul was shocked by the apparent new 'heresy' taught by Jesus, and set to work to wipe it out. As he was travelling from Jerusalem to Damascus he had a vision which convinced him that he was wrong; instead he became an ardent follower of Jesus. He is always regarded as an apostle, though his conversion came after Jesus's death.

Although a Roman citizen (Paul was the Latin form of his name), he did more than anyone else to spread Christianity. He was probably tried and put to death in Rome about AD 67 because of his revolutionary ideas.

ITALY
Rome
MACEDONIA
Troy
ASIA
Antiochia
Iconium
Derbe
Antioch
SYRIA
Ephesus
Sidon
CYPRUS
Athens
GREECE
Corinth
CRETE
MEDITERRANEAN SEA
Syracuse
Malta
Joppa
Jerusalem

■ First journey ■ Third journey
■ Second journey ■ Journey to Rome

▶ WHO WERE THE SCYTHIANS?

The Scythians were a group of nomadic (wandering) tribes living in Scythia, the southern part of what is now the Soviet Union, more than 2,000 years ago.

The original homeland of the Scythians was around the Altai Mountains in Central Asia. They began moving westward about 800 BC, and by 650 BC they had conquered northern Iran and eastern Turkey.

The Medes of Persia drove the Scythians out. They then settled in what is now southern Russia and in the Crimea.

Some Scythians also moved into eastern Europe, as far west as Hungary and Poland. They were finally conquered by Goths in the AD 100s.

The Scythians were bold warriors, skilled archers and horsemen. Their graves contain fine sculptures and utensils in gold, silver and other metals. Some tombs in the Altai Mountains were found to be frozen, their contents preserved as in a modern deep-freeze.

▶ WHO WERE THE THRACIANS?

The Thracians were tribesmen who lived in the eastern part of the Balkan peninsula. Thrace now forms part of Greece, Turkey and Bulgaria.

Some Thracians in ancient times were warlike while others were peaceful farmers. They are first recorded more than 3,500 years ago.

They appear to have been fond of poetry and music. Their culture apparently influenced that of Greece, notably in religion.

The Thracians believed in life after death. They indulged in animal worship and human sacrifice. Among their important gods was Sabazius, who was similar to the Greek god Dionysus, god of vegetation and later god of wine.

The Greeks built many cities along the coast of Thrace. From the 300s BC the land was largely under Greek control. For a time in the 500s BC it was conquered by Persia. Byzantium (now Istanbul) was a Thracian city.

▶ WHO WERE THE CELTS?

The Celts were a group of tribes living in central Europe in the 500s BC. Many migrated west. Their language survives in Welsh, Gaelic and Breton.

Present-day descendants of the Celts are found in Brittany, Cornwall, Ireland, the Isle of Man and Scotland. The Cornish and Manx languages have almost died out. Because the Ancient Britons were Celts, many English place names are of Celtic origin.

In their heyday the Celts were both mighty warriors and good farmers. Many of their settlements were in huge hill forts, whose great earth ramparts can still be seen.

Celtic laws and traditions were not written down but passed on by word of mouth. They were preserved by the mysterious Druids, who were the religious leaders. The Druids held ceremonies among sacred groves of trees where they worshipped several gods, especially the Sun.

Celtic smiths worked in gold, bronze and iron.

Attila was the leader of the Huns, a warlike group of tribes from central Asia which terrorized Europe in the AD 400s.

In AD 434 Attila and his brother Bleda became joint rulers of the Huns, at that time based in Hungary. After 11 years Attila murdered Bleda, so becoming sole ruler. In 447 he began a career of conquest.

He forced the rulers of the Eastern Roman Empire to pay him a large annual fee to leave them alone. He then led a large army of Huns into Gaul (France) and demanded the hand of Honoria, sister of the Western Roman emperor Valentinian III, in marriage. One story says that Honoria asked him to come so that she could escape from someone that she was unwillingly engaged to.

The Romans defeated Attila at Châlons-sur-Marne in 451. He died two years later.

Boudica – often wrongly called Boadicea – was ruler of the Iceni, a Celtic British tribe, in about AD 60.

The queen became leader of the Iceni when her husband Prasutagus died, leaving her alone with her two daughters. Their kingdom was in what is now Norfolk, in East Anglia.

The Roman rulers in Britain maintained that Prasutagus had left his kingdom to the Roman emperor. When

Boudica claimed the throne the Roman procurator (ruler), Decianus Catus, ordered her to be whipped. The soldiers who carried out the order also assaulted Boudica's daughters.

Led by their tall, red-headed queen, the Iceni tribe at once rebelled. They sacked three towns, Camulodunum (Colchester), Verulamium (St Albans) and Londinium (London), slaying 70,000 Romans and their allies.

A strong Roman army quickly crushed the rebellion and Boudica poisoned herself.

A number of Germanic tribes living in northern and central Europe were called barbarians. They included the Alamanni, Franks, Goths, Heruli and Vandals.

The ancient Greeks coined the name 'barbarian' to describe all foreigners who did not speak Greek. They thought that the strangers' unintelligible languages sounded like 'Bar . . . bar . . .'

From this it was only a step to use the term barbarian to describe apparently less cultured peoples. The Greeks and the Romans did this.

The northern frontier of the Roman Empire lay on a line marked by two rivers, the Rhine and the Danube. This frontier was 2,400 km long, and even a Roman army of 400,000 was not enough to defend it against barbarian attacks.

The barbarians finally conquered the Western Roman Empire in AD 476. The Eastern or Byzantine Empire lasted until 1453, when it fell to the Ottoman Turks.

Spanish kingdoms

Territory acquired by Kings of Aragon

NAVARRE Toulouse

ARAGON Barcelona

Madrid CASTILE

Lisbon Portugal

GRANADA

Baleares

◄WHO WERE FERDINAND AND ISABELLA?

Ferdinand inherited the kingdom of Aragon; Isabella became queen of Castile. Their marriage united most of Spain.

When Ferdinand was born in 1452 Spain consisted of the poor Christian kingdoms of Aragon, Castile and Navarre, and the Moorish (Arab) province of Granada.

Ferdinand married Isabella in 1469. Isabella inherited her kingdom in 1474 and

Ferdinand became king of Aragon in 1479.

The couple were fanatical Christians. They started an Inquisition to suppress heresy and harass the Jews. In 1492 their armies drove the Moors from Granada.

The same year they agreed to finance an Italian sailor, Christopher Columbus, to sail under the Spanish flag to find a westward route to the Indies. He discovered America.

So this royal marriage led to the unification of Spain, the discovery of America and the creation of a Spanish empire.

►WHO WAS LEONARDO DA VINCI?

Leonardo was one of the world's most talented people. He was a painter, sculptor, architect, anatomist, scientist, inventor, engineer and musician.

This extraordinary man was born at Vinci, in Italy, in 1452 and died in France in 1519. He was a leading figure of the Renaissance, the rebirth of learning which lasted from the 1400s to about 1600.

He worked for Lorenzo the

Magnificent in Florence, Lodovico Sforza in Milan, Cesare Borgia in Romagna and Francis I in France.

Leonardo began many projects, but finished only a few. His artistic masterpiece is the wall painting of the Last Supper at the Monastery of Santa Maria delle Grazie, Milan.

He is noted for his advanced knowledge of anatomy.

The volumes of notebooks and drawings that he left show that he wrote not only left handed but also in 'mirror writing', possibly so that people would not steal his ideas.

◄WHO WAS LORENZO THE MAGNIFICENT?

Lorenzo was a member of the powerful Medici family which dominated Florence and Tuscany in Italy from the mid-1300s to the 1600s.

At the age of 20 Lorenzo succeeded his father who died in 1469. At that time the city-state of Florence was a republic. Like his father and grandfather Lorenzo had no formal title, apart from *magnifico signore*, magnificent lord.

Lorenzo ruled with the aid of a council but was in fact a dictator. His skill in diplomacy helped to keep Florence strong and his ability to manipulate finances helped to make Florence prosperous.

Il magnifico is best remembered as a patron of the arts – not so much for the glory of his city as for his own private collection. His writings helped to make the Italian spoken in Tuscany the national language of all Italy.

Il Moro, the Moor, was the nickname given to Lodovico Sforza, Duke of Milan, because of his dark hair and his swarthy complexion.

Lodovico, born in 1451, was the younger brother of Galeazzo Maria Sforza, Duke of Milan. Galeazzo was vain and cruel. In 1476 three of his subjects killed him. He was succeeded by his seven-year-old son, Giangaleazzo, with Lodovico as regent.

Not content with his position, Lodovico assumed full power in 1481 and on the death of Giangaleazzo in 1494 he became duke.

However, he feared that Giangaleazzo's friends would rebel against him, so he invited the French to enter Italy and help him.

This move proved his undoing. The French turned on him and drove him from power. Though he was restored to his dukedom by the Swiss, they too turned on him. From 1500 to his death in 1508 he was a prisoner of the French.

Desiderius Erasmus was a Dutch scholar and writer who tried to reform the Roman Catholic Church from within.

Erasmus was made a priest in 1492 but rebelled against the monastic lifestyle. Having studied in Paris for a while, he became a wandering scholar in the early 1500s, dividing his time between England, France, Italy and the Netherlands.

Erasmus campaigned for reform through his mildly humorous writing satirizing the many corrupt practices that were harming the work of the Church.

Most of his work aimed at trying to make theology more accurate and he reformed the text of the New Testament. But he got caught in the middle of quarrels between Protestants and Catholics.

Before he died in 1536 in Switzerland, Erasmus saw the Reformation in full flood, with Protestants breaking from Rome. But Erasmus was a moderate and this was not the kind of reformation that he had intended.

John Calvin was a French theologian, one of the leaders of the Reformation.

Calvin's name was originally Jean Chauvin. In later years he used a Latin version of the name, Calvinus.

He was born at Noyon, in Picardy, in 1509. His father originally wanted him to study theology and become a priest but later persuaded him to become a lawyer instead.

Calvin was converted to Protestantism about 1534 and was exiled from France. He went to Geneva, where he and other Protestants tried to set up a religious government.

The Genevese revolted against this idea, so Calvin retired to teach theology in Strasbourg. However, there was chaos and anarchy in Geneva and he was asked to come back in 1541.

In Geneva Calvin set up a very strict religious and civic government, for a time even abolishing taverns and the use of non-Biblical Christian names. His Protestantism became known as Calvinism.

▲ WHO MET AT THE COUNCIL OF TRENT?

The Council of Trent was a series of conferences at which bishops of the Roman Catholic Church met between 1545 and 1563 at Trento, in northern Italy.

The purpose of the council was to redefine various beliefs of the Church and to reform some bad practices that had grown up.

It was a major move in the Counter-Reformation, the Roman Catholic Church's answer to Protestantism.

The council was called by Pope Paul III. He hoped that representatives of the Protestant Churches would attend but only a few did so – and they would not accept the authority of the council.

The first session, which lasted from 1545 to 1547, was attended by 72 bishops and their advisers. The second, in 1551-52, attracted only 59.

The final session, from 1561 to 1563, was attended by 235 Church leaders including six cardinals, as well as eight ambassadors. The council's decrees were agreed by Pope Pius IV in 1564.

▼ WHO WAS SULEIMAN THE MAGNIFICENT?

Suleiman I was one of the most important sultans of the Ottoman Turkish empire. He ruled from 1520 to 1566.

'The Magnificent' was the title by which Suleiman was known to Europeans, but to his own people he was 'The Lawgiver' because of reforms in law and government which were carried out during his reign.

The magnificent side of Suleiman's character was shown in his drive to extend his empire. He added to it in turn Belgrade, Budapest, Rhodes, Tabriz, Baghdad, Aden and Algiers, with the territories around them.

His major campaigns were against Persia. During one campaign he besieged Vienna.

Suleiman was infatuated by a beautiful Russian slave, Roxalana, whom he took to be his concubine. To please her he had his legitimate sons, Bayazid and Mustafa, put to death so that Roxalana's son, Selim, could succeed him as the next sultan. Sulieman died in 1566 while besieging a fortress in Hungary.

▼ WHO WERE THE JANISSARIES?

The janissaries were a picked body of soldiers who formed the core of the Ottoman Turkish army.

The name janissary comes from the Turkish *yeni çeri*, which means 'new soldiery'. The corps was formed sometime in the 1400s as the first regular Ottoman army.

The earliest janissaries were recruited from children of Christian people under Turkish rule. These children were carefully selected and taken from their parents to be brought up as Muslims.

However, the recruitment of Christian children had stopped by 1700, when the janissaries were merely a corps of picked men, including many Turks.

Although the janissaries were expected to provide their own weapons, they proved to be a formidable fighting force. Their numbers rose from 12,000 to more than 500,000.

The janissaries rebelled several times, deposing sultans and supporting new ones. In 1826 Sultan Mahmud II abolished the corps.

The Habsburgs were a German royal family who ruled in Europe for more than 600 years.

The family took its name from *Habichtsburg* (Hawk's Castle) a fortress built at Aargau near Zürich in Switzerland in 1020.

Count Rudolf IV of Habsburg was elected as Holy Roman Emperor (ruler of the German lands) in 1273, with the title Rudolf I. From then until 1806, when the empire came to an end, most of its rulers were Habsburgs.

The most powerful Habsburg was the Emperor Charles V, who was elected in 1519. He was already King of Spain, Duke of Burgundy and ruler of the Spanish Netherlands (modern Belgium and the Netherlands), Sicily, Naples, Sardinia and the West Indies.

Other lands Charles inherited or acquired later included Austria, Bohemia, Hungary, Peru and Mexico.

By 1556 Charles had had enough. He abdicated and retired to a monastery in Spain, dying in 1558.

Elizabeth was the last Tudor ruler of England. Under her inspired leadership England became a wealthy and powerful nation.

Elizabeth was the daughter of Henry VIII and his second wife, Anne Boleyn. She was brought up to be a fine scholar.

She succeeded her elder sister, Mary I, in 1588. Mary had tried to restore Roman Catholicism in England. Elizabeth led the country back to Protestantism.

She was a skilled diplomat and never married because of the problems that marriage might bring.

England was a rival of Spain for the riches of the New World. Elizabeth kept the two countries from going to war for as long as she could, but when Philip I of Spain sent a large fleet, the Armada, to invade England she personally urged her sailors on to victory.

Poetry, music and drama flourished during her reign, which encouraged talented men like William Shakespeare.

Henry III, king of Navarre, became king of France as Henry IV in 1589. He succeeded his brother-in-law, Henry III of France, who was assassinated.

Henry of Navarre was descended from Louis IX, king of France in 1226-70. His ancestors held the title Duke of Bourbon. He inherited the French throne when the Valois family had no more heirs after Henry III.

Henry IV was leader of the Huguenots, the French Protestants. He adopted the Roman Catholic faith to please the majority of his subjects, observing cynically, 'Paris is worth a Mass'.

Civil war had been raging in France between Huguenots and Catholics. Henry helped to stop the fighting by the Edict of Nantes, which gave the Huguenots equal political rights.

Henry paid off France's debts, and set up a strong army. He was murdered in 1610 by a mad schoolmaster, François Ravaillac.

◄WHO IS KNOWN AS THE FATHER OF MODERN PHILOSOPHY?

Philosophy today is based largely on the work of the French mathematician, scientist and philosopher René Descartes.

Descartes was born in 1596. He had a private income so he was able to devote most of his life to studying and writing.

He believed that it is possible to arrive at the truth by reason alone. His starting point was the Latin phrase *Cogito, ergo sum* 'I think, therefore I am'.

He used this theory to prove that humans are real, that if a person is thinking he must be alive to be doing so. He went on by logical steps to prove that the world and God exist.

Descartes's writings made him many admirers. In 1649 he was invited to visit Queen Christina of Sweden. She wanted him to teach her philosophy. But the bitter cold of a Swedish winter gave him pneumonia from which he died in 1650, aged 53.

► WHICH CARDINAL MADE THE KINGS OF FRANCE SUPREME?

The cardinal was Armand Jean du Plessis, duke of Richelieu, who served as chief minister of Louis XIII from 1624 to 1642.

Richelieu became bishop of Luzon in 1606, when he was 21 – the post was given to his family as a reward for military services. He was made cardinal in 1622 and duke in 1631.

Richelieu ruled France well. He began by curbing the power of the nobles. He then ended the political privileges of the Huguenots, the French Protestants. His actions made the king, acting through his chief minister, the supreme power in France.

In foreign affairs Richelieu determined to curb the power of the Habsburgs, the ruling family in Germany. Although he was a leader of the Roman Catholic Church, he took France into alliance with the Protestant enemies of the Catholic Habsburg emperor.

He founded the French Academy in 1635.

◄WHO BECAME THE LORD PROTECTOR OF ENGLAND?

The title of Lord Protector was given to Oliver Cromwell in 1653, after the English Civil War.

Cromwell was born in 1599. He was a country gentleman, farming his estates, until he was 41.

In 1640 he was elected a member of Parliament. He took part in the quarrel between Parliament and King Charles I and when war broke out between king and Parliament, Cromwell raised a troop of cavalry. His soldiers were known as 'Ironsides'. He was inspired by his deeply-held Puritan faith.

After taking a leading part in the trial and execution of Charles, Cromwell tried to make Parliament efficient, but failed. His supporters in the army then dissolved Parliament and made Cromwell Lord Protector – he refused the title of king.

Though he called two Parliaments Cromwell ruled as a dictator until his death in 1658.

► WHO WAS CATHERINE THE GREAT?

Catherine II was Empress of Russia for 34 years, from 1762 to 1796.

Catherine was a German princess. Her original name was Sophia Augusta Frederica of Anhalt-Zerbst. She was married to the Emperor Peter III of Russia.

Catherine was 16 in 1745 when she married. She was witty and well educated; Peter was weak in body and mind. At that time he was heir to his aunt, the Empress Elizabeth.

Six months after Peter became emperor, Catherine and some army officers deposed him. He died a few weeks later.

Catherine proved to be a good ruler, especially in foreign affairs. Russia acquired the Crimea from the Turks.

At home Catherine improved medical care, education (for women especially) and religious toleration. But she extended serfdom, a form of slavery.

Catherine worked long hours on government business and on her books and plays.

◄ WHO WAS MARIE ANTOINETTE?

Marie Antoinette was an Austrian princess who became queen consort of Louis XVI of France. She was executed during the French Revolution.

The marriage of Louis, then heir to the throne, and Marie Antoinette, an attractive, intelligent girl of 15, took place in 1770. It was arranged to cement an alliance between Austria and France.

Louis was slow thinking and slow moving. His wife was quick, vivacious and energetic. For these reasons Marie Antoinette played a large part in affairs of state at a time when France was in turmoil.

At that time the rich in France were very rich and the poor very poor. Through ignorance Marie Antoinette just did not understand the plight of the poor, who thought that she was extravagant. People mistrusted her because she was Austrian.

In 1793 the revolutionaries tried her for treason, and she was sent to the guillotine.

► WHO WAS FREDERICK THE GREAT?

Frederick II, known as The Great, was King of Prussia, a German country now divided between Russia, Poland and East Germany.

Frederick became king in 1740 when he was 28. He had been trained as a soldier but had spent a lot of his time studying music and philosophy.

Almost at once he became involved in the War of the Austrian Succession, in which several rival claimants tried to take the throne of Austria from Empress Maria Theresa.

Frederick's main motive in the war was to seize the province of Silesia from Austria, which he did. He proved to be a brilliant general.

In the course of later wars he acquired territory from Poland. But the cost of war weakened the economy which he had to build up again during the last years of his reign.

As Frederick was a good flute player he attracted to his court many fine musicians.

◄WHO WAS GARIBALDI?

Giuseppe Garibaldi was one of three patriots who worked to unite Italy and free it from foreign rule.

Garibaldi was born in 1807. He took part in an unsuccessful rebellion in Piedmont in 1834. He fled to South America where he spent the years 1836-48 in guerrilla warfare.

In 1848 he fought in an army trying to defend the newly-formed Roman republic against French and Austrian attacks. After it was defeated he settled in America.

He returned to Italy in 1854. By this time Count Camillo Cavour, premier of Piedmont, and Giuseppe Mazzini, whose patriotism had originally inspired Garibaldi, were working to start a new revolt.

In 1860 Garibaldi led a force of 1089 volunteers, the Redshirts, in a landing on Sicily, which he freed from its Spanish Bourbon rulers. He then conquered the mainland part of the Sicilian kingdom which led to the uniting of Italy. He failed to free Rome, then under the Pope's rule.

◄WHO WAS THE FIRST KING OF A UNITED ITALY?

The king was Victor Emmanuel II, ruler of Piedmont-Sardinia. He was the only non-clerical Italian to rule any part of Italy.

In the early 1800s Italy was divided into seven states. One, the Papal States, was ruled by the Pope. The Kingdom of the Two Sicilies – Sicily and southern Italy – was ruled by a Spanish Bourbon king. The rest was under Austrian control.

In most of these states political opponents of their governments were arrested, tortured and imprisoned.

A series of secret societies was formed to fight foreign domination. Among the main conspirators were Giuseppe Mazzini, and Giuseppe Garibaldi.

Political freedom and unity for Italy were eventually gained largely through the prime minister of Piedmont-Sardinia, Count Camillo Cavour. By uniting revolt with diplomacy, he placed Victor Emmanuel on the throne of a united Italy by 1861.

► WHO WAS 'THE WIDOW AT WINDSOR'?

The widow was Queen Victoria, the British monarch who had the longest reign. She was a widow for 40 years.

Victoria was 18 when she became queen in succession to her uncle, William IV, in 1837. In 1840 she married her first cousin, Prince Albert of Saxe-Coburg-Gotha.

Albert died of typhoid fever in 1861, leaving Victoria desolate. She mourned for much of the rest of her reign.

Victoria and Albert had nine children. At her death Victoria had about 37 great-grandchildren and was related to almost all the royal families of Europe.

Five of her granddaughters married monarchs – the Tsar of Russia and the kings of Greece, Norway, Romania and Spain. A grandson became Kaiser (emperor) of Germany. A great-granddaughter married the king of Sweden.

The kings of Hanover and the Belgians were Victoria's uncles. One cousin married the queen of Portugal, another the Emperor Maximilian of Brazil.

▶ WHO WAS KNOWN AS THE
IRON CHANCELLOR?

**The 'Iron Chancellor' was
Otto von Bismarck, the
Prussian statesman who
united Germany in 1871.**

Bismarck was born in 1815.
He was a *Junker*, a country
squire. He studied law,
became a member of the
Prussian Diet (parliament) and
served as ambassador to Russia
and France. In 1862 he was
appointed prime minister.

Bismarck led Prussia into
three successful wars: in 1864

it defeated Denmark, in 1866
Austria and in 1871 France.
Bismarck is generally thought
to have provoked France into
declaring war in order to unite
the German states.

After France's defeat
Bismarck persuaded the
German princes to offer the
crown to the Prussian king,
William I, who became the first
Kaiser (emperor) of Germany.

William created Bismarck a
prince and Chancellor of the
new Germany. He was known
as the 'Iron Chancellor' because
he said problems should be
solved by 'blood and iron'.

▶ WHO WAS ABRAHAM
LINCOLN?

**Abraham Lincoln was the
16th president of the United
States. He kept the country
together during the civil war
of 1861-65.**

Lincoln was a farmer's son. He
worked in a village store, then
as a surveyor and as a
postmaster. Meanwhile he
studied to become a lawyer.

He served first in the Illinois
legislature (State Parliament)
and then as a Congressman.
He became an opponent of

slavery. He did not want to
abolish it but he did not want it
to spread either, particularly in
the new territories of Kansas
and Nebraska.

In 1860 Lincoln was elected
president. Knowing his views
on slavery, seven Southern
states broke away from the
Union. Four more followed.

This led to civil war.
Lincoln worked hard for
victory over the rebel states
and to ensure their return to
the Union. Five days after the
fighting ended in April 1865
Lincoln was shot dead at a
theatre.

◀ WHO WAS THE EMPRESS-
DOWAGER?

**The Empress-Dowager was
Tz'u-hsi of China who lived
from 1835 to 1908 and ruled
for many years.**

Tz'u-hsi was a wife of the
Emperor Hsien-feng and
mother of Emperor T'ung-
chih. She was regent for her
son who died in 1875.

He was followed on the
throne by his cousin, Ch'ing
Kuang-hsu, then aged three.
Tz'u-hsi, still in control of
China, remained so until 1889.

Because the Empress-
Dowager disliked change she
fought against any attempts to
modernize China. But when
the Emperor assumed power
he listened to the advice of
reformers. In a series of
decrees he announced changes
in schooling, the civil service,
the armed forces and the
construction of railways.

Horrified, Tz'u-hsi seized
power again. She had the
young emperor imprisoned
and stopped all reforms. It was
in vain: three years after her
death China became a
republic.

◄WHO FORMED THE FIRST TRADE UNIONS?

The earliest trade unions were probably the trade clubs formed by workers in various trades, such as carpenters and shoemakers, in the 1600s.

Associations of workers in a number of trades existed from medieval times. But the early groups were guilds of craftsmen rather than unions of less skilled workers.

Before the 1700s people tended to work at home or in very small groups.

Trade unions as we know them today grew up when men, women and children worked in factories created during the Industrial Revolution.

In Europe most governments passed laws in the late 1700s which banned associations of workers. In the United States unions were not made illegal, but they made little progress.

Modern trade unions, for unskilled and semi-skilled workers as well as craftsmen, grew up during the second half of the 19th century.

◄WHO WERE THE SUFFRAGETTES?

The name 'suffragettes' was given to women who took militant action in support of women's suffrage – that is, the right to vote.

Campaigns for women's suffrage began in many countries during the 1800s. Campaigning in the United States began in earnest in 1848, and by 1869 Wyoming had given women the right to vote. In 1920 the US gave all women the vote.

At the start of campaigning in Britain in 1865 it met with stiff opposition. But militancy did not begin until 1905 when two women rose to ask questions about the vote at a Liberal Party meeting and were ejected brutally.

Thereafter the suffragettes damaged property in Britain, went to prison, and while in prison went on hunger strike. Some women over 30 received the vote in 1918 and all women over 21 did so in 1928.

France and Italy did not grant women's suffrage until after World War II.

◄WHO CREATED THE RED ARMY?

The Red Army was the army of the Bolshevik (Communist) government which took power in Russia in 1917. It was organized by Leon Trotsky.

Trotsky, born in 1879, was one of the Bolshevik leaders who seized power. His original name was Lev Davidovich Bronstein but he took a new name as a revolutionary leader.

Trotsky was second only in importance to Vladimir Lenin,

the head of the Bolshevik government.

The Red Army was formed in January 1918. It consisted at first only of volunteer workers and peasants but it lacked good officers. Trotsky recruited officers of the old tsarist army.

Soon afterwards a number of anti-Communist groups tried to set up rival governments. These, called Whites, were crushed by the Red Army.

After Lenin's death Trotsky was sent into exile. Lenin's successor, Joseph Stalin, had Trotsky assassinated in Mexico City in 1940.

▶ WHO FOUNDED THE SOVIET UNION?

The founder of the Soviet Union – more correctly, the Union of Soviet Socialist Republics – was Vladimir Lenin.

Lenin was born Vladimir Ilyich Ulyanov in 1870 but he later took the name Lenin.

Lenin opposed the monarchy in Russia after his elder brother was executed for plotting to kill the tsar. His Communist views caused him to be exiled to Siberia in 1895.

When he was released in 1900 he left Russia and began plotting revolution.

The revolution began in March 1917 while Lenin was still abroad. He hurried home, won the support of many soldiers, sailors and workers, and overthrew the new Liberal-Democratic government of Russia in November 1917.

By 1921 Lenin had eliminated all opposition and had made Russia the Communist state it is today. He retired after a stroke in 1922 and died in 1924.

▶ WHO WAS KNOWN AS THE MAHATMA?

Mahatma, which is a Sanskrit word meaning 'great soul', was the term of affection applied by Indians to Mohandas Karamchand Gandhi, who worked to free his land from British rule.

Gandhi was born in 1869. He studied law in London then went to South Africa to work. There he led many campaigns on behalf of Indians who were suffering from discrimination.

He devised a system of non-violent civil disobedience which he called *satyagraha*.

Gandhi returned to India in 1915. He was a small, frail man who wore traditional Indian dress and lived simply and frugally. In spite of his weak appearance he led a long campaign for Indian independence which was finally achieved in 1947.

He tried to stop the feud between Hindus and Muslims, but he was assassinated in 1948 by one of his own Hindu people who disliked Gandhi's tolerance of all religions.

▶ WHO FOUNDED MODERN TURKEY?

The Republic of Turkey was founded by the general and statesman Kemal Atatürk.

His name was originally Mustafa. While at the army staff college in Istanbul his skill in mathematics earned him the name 'Kemal', which means perfection.

When Mustafa Kemal was born in 1881, Turkey, then called the Ottoman Empire, was ruled by a sultan. During World War I it sided with Germany and was defeated.

After the war, in which he had risen to the rank of general, Kemal organized a nationalist movement to resist foreign control. The nationalists then overthrew the sultan and proclaimed a republic, with Kemal as its president.

Kemal modernized his country, liberating women, improving education and introducing the Western alphabet instead of Arabic. In 1934 he took the surname Atatürk, Father of Turks. He died in 1938.

▶ WHO WAS BENITO
MUSSOLINI?

Mussolini was a Fascist who ruled Italy as a dictator from 1922 to 1943. He was known as Il Duce (The Leader).

Mussolini was born in 1883. He was first a teacher, then a journalist and political agitator.

In 1919 he founded the Fascist Party, named after the axe-like symbol of power in ancient Rome. The party was strongly nationalistic and opposed to Communism.

The Fascists used armed gangs, the Blackshirts, to attack the opposition, especially all Left-wing organizations. They became so powerful that in 1922 Mussolini was asked to form a government.

To increase Italy's power he conquered Ethiopia in 1935-36. In 1939 he seized Albania. His closest ally was the German dictator Adolf Hitler, who led Italy unwillingly into World War II. After Italy was heavily defeated, Mussolini was overthrown and shot.

▶ WHO WAS STALIN?

Joseph Stalin was dictator of the Union of Soviet Socialist Republics. He led Russia to victory in World War II but had millions of Russians 'liquidated'.

Stalin lived from 1879 to 1953. His name was Iosif Dzhugashvili, but he took the name Stalin, meaning 'steel', in 1913.

After the Revolution Stalin became secretary of the Communist Party. When Lenin died in 1924 Stalin made himself leader.

In a series of five-year plans Stalin's government reorganized farming and industry and did away with private businesses. People lived in fear of the secret police. Any potential opponents were killed in a series of purges in 1935-37.

In 1939 Stalin signed a pact with Hitler, agreeing to carve up Poland and not to go to war. But two years later Hitler invaded Russia. At the end of the war Stalin set up Communist rule in six eastern European countries.

◀ WHO WAS TITO?

Tito led Yugoslavia's resistance to the Germans in World War II and became his country's Communist president.

Tito was born in 1892, a peasant's son, named Josip Broz. He fought in the Austrian army in World War I until he was captured by the Russians. In Russia he became a Communist.

In 1920 he returned to his homeland, Croatia, now part of the new country of Yugoslavia, and there organized a Communist party.

During the war, Tito – a name he adopted in 1934 – led a group of Communist resistance fighters known as the Partisans.

Unlike the other eastern Europe Communist countries, Yugoslavia under Tito stayed independent of Moscow, despite all threats.

Both during the war and after, Tito proved he was a born organizer, capable of taking the right decisions in difficult circumstances. He died in 1980.

Hitler ruled Germany as a dictator from 1933 to 1945. He started World War II.

Hitler was born in Austria in 1889. He wanted to be an artist but was not talented enough. In World War I he was decorated for bravery.

After the war he formed the National Socialist Party, 'Nazis' for short. In 1933 he was made chancellor (prime minister).

Within six months Hitler had eliminated all rival political parties, and soon after had his rivals among the Nazis put to death. Hitler was master of Germany, known as *Der Führer* (The Leader).

Hitler began persecuting the Jews, rearmed Germany and set out to conquer Europe. In turn he seized Austria, Czechoslovakia and most of Western Europe. It took the combined forces of Britain, Russia and the United States to crush him. He committed suicide in 1945.

Churchill was a soldier, statesman and writer who became Britain's leader during World War II.

Churchill's full name was Winston Leonard Spencer-Churchill. He was the grandson of the seventh Duke of Marlborough.

He began his career as a soldier and by the time he was 24 he had taken part in three campaigns and written a book.

In 1901 Churchill was elected a Conservative MP. Three years later he changed parties to become a Liberal. During World War I and after he held many high posts in government, served as a soldier again for a time and became a Conservative again.

From 1929 to 1939 Churchill was out of office but with the start of World War II he was back in government. From 1940 to 1945, when he was Prime Minister, his speeches and courage inspired the country. He held the office again from 1951 to 1955. He died in 1965.

Mao Zedong – Mao Tse-tung in the older form of his name – ruled China for 27 years.

In 1921 revolutionary leader Mao helped to found the Chinese Communist Party. In 1928 the Nationalists who ruled China launched an attack on Jiangxi province where the Communists had their base.

In 1934 Mao led his Communist 'Red Army' to safety in Shaanxi province, in what is called the Long March.

In 1937 the Communists and their rivals formed an alliance against the Japanese who had invaded China. But they fell out again in 1946. By 1949 the Communists had won and Mao ruled China.

He quickly organized his people towards modernizing the country. He achieved cultural and economic changes that surprised the world – the 'Great Leap Forward' of 1958 and the 'Cultural Revolution' of 1966.

From 1959 to his death in 1976 Mao was chairman of the Communist party.

◀WHO UNIFIED SAUDI ARABIA?

Arabia was conquered and unified by Ibn Saud who lived from about 1880 to 1953.

The family of Saud ruled a large part of Arabia in the early 1800s, but by 1891 the family was in exile in Kuwait. Some of Arabia belonged to the Ottoman (Turkish) empire and the rest was small kingdoms.

In 1902 a young Saudi leader, 'Abd al-'Aziz ibn 'Abd al-Rahman ibn Faisal al Sa'ud, began the reconquest of his family's former lands. With 200 men he seized Riyadh, the present capital, and the territory around it.

In 1913 Ibn Saud, as he became known, seized the Persian Gulf coastline between Qatar and Kuwait from the Turks. By 1922 he ruled the whole of central Arabia, the Nedj, and took the title Sultan of Nedj.

In 1926 Ibn Saud conquered Hejaz (the Red Sea coast) and in 1932 he proclaimed his lands to be one kingdom under the name of Saudi Arabia. Money from oil made it rich.

◀WHO FORMED THE AFRICAN NATIONAL CONGRESS?

The African National Congress was formed by a group of African leaders in 1912 at a conference held at Bloemfontein, South Africa.

The leaders were tribal chiefs, lawyers, clergymen and businessmen from all over South Africa, who were trying to improve the status of Black Africans in South Africa.

The congress made little progress until the 1940s, when the Reverend James Calata, then secretary-general, reorganized it into a strong nationalist party.

In 1952 a campaign of passive resistance to apartheid (racial segregation) laws was launched. More than 8,000 Africans were jailed. One of its leaders, Chief Albert Luthuli, was awarded the 1960 Nobel Peace Prize.

In 1960 the South African government banned the African National Congress but Nelson Mandela (left) led it until he was jailed for life on terrorism charges in 1963.

◀WHO WAS HO CHI MINH?

Ho Chi Minh founded the Communist state of North Vietnam which he ruled until his death in 1969.

Ho was born in 1890 and named Nguyen That Thanh. He took the name Ho Chi Minh, which means 'He Who Shines', in 1941.

Ho went to Europe in 1911 and while there helped to found the French Communist party.

Indochina was occupied by the Japanese during World War II. In 1945, with Chinese backing, Ho entered Vietnam and proclaimed a Communist republic. From 1946 to 1954 Ho's troops fought the French. Vietnam was divided in two, with the north under Ho's Communist rule.

In 1957 Communist guerrillas, the Viet Cong, began fighting against the repressive government of South Vietnam. Ho backed them, and a full-scale war ensued with the United States supporting the south. Ho died before the war ended in a Communist victory.

► WHO WAS MARTIN LUTHER KING?

King was a Black Baptist minister and civil rights leader who tried to gain equal rights for Blacks. He was killed in 1968.

Martin Luther King, Jr. was the son of a Baptist minister. He began his equal rights campaign in 1955 when he led a boycott of buses in his home town, Montgomery, Alabama because the bus company made Blacks occupy rear seats.

The campaign succeeded.

King always emphasized non-violence and racial brotherhood, but he was subjected to violence himself: bombs were thrown at his home, he was stoned in Chicago and stabbed in New York City. But he carried on and was awarded the 1964 Nobel Peace Prize.

In 1967 King spent five days in jail for demonstrating.

For 1968 King planned a 'Poor People's March', but before it could take place a white ex-convict gunned him down at a strike in Memphis, Tennessee.

► WHO ARE THE PALESTINIANS?

Palestinians are people of Palestine, the historic land now covered by Israel, the West Bank part of Jordan and the Gaza Strip, and especially Arab refugees from this region.

The United Nations divided Palestine in 1947 into two countries, one for Jews and one for Arabs. Before partition took place in May 1948 Arabs and Jews fought fiercely, and a stream of Arab refugees began to pour out of Palestine.

The flood of refugees grew following two massacres in April 1948, one of Arabs by Jews, one of Jews by Arabs.

Neighbouring Arab countries tried to destroy the new Jewish state, Israel, in May 1948 but failed. Meanwhile the number of refugees rose to 700,000. Many set up camps in the Gaza Strip.

The Palestine Liberation Organization (PLO) was set up in 1964 to fight for Arab rights in Palestine. The number of Palestinian refugees had risen to over 2,000,000 by 1984.

► WHICH RELIGION DO SUNNIS AND SHI-ITES BELONG TO?

Sunnis and Shi-ites form the principal divisions of Islam. The groups split in the AD 600s.

The Sunni Muslims are the main body of Islam. They are followers of *sunna* (the way) of the Prophet Muhammad. About nine-tenths of the world's 513,000,000 Muslims are Sunnis.

The Shi-ites broke away from the larger group of Muslims over a question of leadership. In 656 Ali became caliph (ruler) of the Arab empire. He was a cousin of Muhammad who had married the Prophet's daughter.

But several Muslims, including Mu'awiya the governor of Syria, refused to accept Ali as caliph. There was some warfare, which lasted until Ali was assassinated by another sect, the Kharijites.

Ali's supporters were called the Shi'at Ali, the party of Ali. From being a political group they became a separate religious sect. Their main support is in Iran and Iraq.

SCIENCE

Everything is made of tiny particles called atoms. Every atom is made of even smaller particles. In the centre is the nucleus. Around it move very tiny particles called electrons.

An atom is about a hundred-millionth of a centimetre across, and it is mostly empty space! The nucleus is 10,000 times smaller than the atom, and the electrons are ten times smaller still.

The electrons move in orbits in the space around the nucleus. The nucleus is made of small particles called protons and neutrons. The simplest atom is a hydrogen atom. It contains one electron moving around a nucleus of one proton. The biggest normal atom is a uranium atom. It has 92 electrons and its nucleus is made of 92 protons and 146 neutrons.

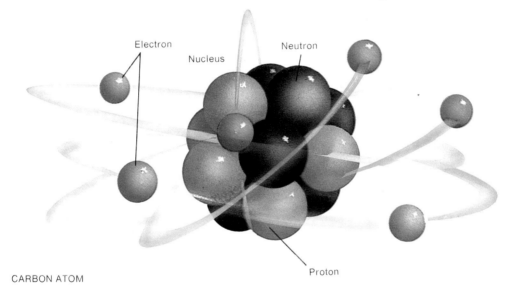

Electron Nucleus Neutron

Proton

CARBON ATOM

An electron is a very tiny piece of electricity. The amount of electricity that an electron has is the smallest amount that it is possible to have.

When an electric current flows through a wire, electrons leave the atoms in the wire and move to other atoms. To light a torch bulb, more than a million million million electrons have to flow through the wire in the bulb every second.

The electrons that move around the nucleus of an atom give it a kind of electrical shell.

The electrons each have a negative electric charge. This electric charge produces an electric field, and the field repels other negative electric fields. If one atom approaches another, the electric fields around their electron shells repel each other and prevent them from touching.

The protons in the nucleus of an atom each have a positive electric charge. Normally, an atom has the same number of electrons and protons. The neutrons have no charge. The electrons' negative charges balance the protons' positive charges, so that the atom has no electric charge as a whole.

Atoms can easily lose or gain electrons, but not protons or neutrons, which are protected by the electron shells around the nucleus. The atoms of the substances in batteries have gained or lost electrons. The battery makes electrons flow through the wires connected to it to bring its atoms back to normal.

▼ WHAT IS A MOLECULE?

Almost everything is made of molecules. Molecules are tiny particles that are too small to be seen except in the most powerful microscopes. A molecule is in fact a group of atoms.

In a pure substance like pure water, every molecule is made of the same number of the same atoms. Each water molecule has two hydrogen atoms and one oxygen atom.

In molecules, the atoms are linked by bonds. These bonds are electrical forces that hold the atoms close but not touching one another. The bonds form by an exchange of electrons between the atoms in the molecule.

A molecule may have as few as two atoms. The oxygen gas in the air consists of oxygen molecules each containing two oxygen atoms. Some substances are made of molecules containing thousands of atoms in chains or complex shapes.

▼ WHAT IS A COMPOUND?

A compound is a substance in which the molecules are made of atoms of different elements. Water is a compound because its molecules contain hydrogen and oxygen atoms. It is a compound of hydrogen and oxygen. It is not the same as a mixture of hydrogen and oxygen. In such a mixture, there are separate hydrogen molecules and oxygen molecules.

Compounds include salt, which is a compound of sodium and chlorine, and sugar, which is a compound of carbon, hydrogen and oxygen.

The bonds between the atoms in the molecules of compounds cannot easily be broken. A compound therefore cannot easily be changed into its elements. Electricity is needed to break down water or salt into their elements, for example.

There are many natural compounds, as well as new ones produced by scientists.

▲ WHAT IS AN ELEMENT?

Everything is made of elements. The hydrogen and oxygen in water are both elements. In an element, all the atoms are the same. Other elements include carbon, mercury, chlorine, nitrogen, iron, aluminium, copper, silver and gold. Fewer than 100 different elements exist naturally in the whole universe.

All the atoms in an element are the same because the nucleus of each atom contains the same number of protons. A carbon atom contains six protons, and this number is called the element's atomic number.

If the number of protons changes, then the element becomes a different element. However, the number of electrons and neutrons in the atom can change slightly without the element changing. The forces that hold the protons in the nucleus are very strong indeed. It takes a lot of energy to change the number of protons.

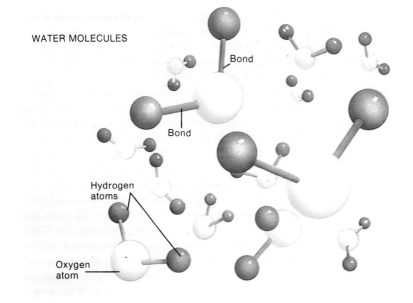

WATER MOLECULES

Bond

Bond

Hydrogen atoms

Oxygen atom

▼ WHAT IS A SOLID?

A solid is a substance or a material that does not flow. Solids include ice, steel, wood, paper, cloth, salt and sugar. A piece of a solid may bend, stretch or contract in size, but it does not otherwise change its shape.

A solid is made of atoms or molecules that are arranged in rows or patterns. The atoms or molecules are pulled together by forces between them. If the forces are strong,

SOLID

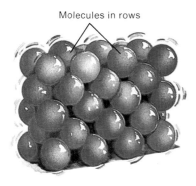

Molecules in rows

then the solid is hard and tough. If they are weak, then the solid is soft or may break easily.

The atoms or molecules constantly vibrate to and fro over a short distance. The amount of vibration depends on how hot or cold the solid is. The hotter it is, the more they vibrate.

At a certain temperature, the atoms or molecules begin to break away from one another. The solid melts and becomes a liquid. This temperature is called the melting point of the solid.

▼ WHAT IS A LIQUID?

A liquid can flow and change its shape. Liquids include water, milk, mercury, petrol and oil. When a certain amount of liquid is placed in a container, it takes the shape of the container but its volume remains the same.

In a liquid, the atoms or molecules are in small groups that move about on their own. This is why a liquid can flow and take up any shape, and

LIQUID

Groups of molecules

why a piece of a solid can move through a liquid.

As a liquid gets hotter, the groups of atoms or molecules move faster. They begin to break up into single atoms or molecules and leave the liquid. A gas is formed. At the boiling point, the liquid boils and all of it turns into gas.

When a liquid gets colder, the groups of atoms or molecules slow down. At the freezing point, they settle into rows and the liquid becomes a solid. The boiling point of water is 100°C and the freezing point is 0°C.

▼ WHAT IS A GAS?

A gas is a substance that flows and increases in size until it fills a container. The air is a mixture of gases. It has no container and spreads out over the entire world. As well as oxygen and other gases in the air, gases include steam, chlorine, hydrogen and helium.

In a gas, the atoms or molecules are not linked together. They move about singly in all directions at great

GAS

Single molecules

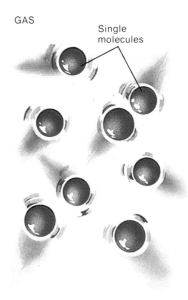

speed. This is why a gas rapidly takes up all the space in a container and fills it. If there are more atoms or molecules, they are closer together and the pressure of the gas is greater.

As a gas gets colder, its atoms or molecules slow down. At the boiling point, they form groups and the gas condenses to a liquid. Steam condenses to water at 100°C.

A vapour is a form of gas that exists below the boiling point. It forms above a liquid as single atoms or molecules escape from the liquid.

►WI
MOD

Man
the fi
Galil
from
impo
disco
Gree
Dark
After
Galil
scien
and n

Galile
use a

► WHAT IS WATER MADE OF?

Water is made of hydrogen and oxygen. In water molecules, hydrogen atoms and oxygen atoms are linked together. They do not normally come apart.

Water can be changed into hydrogen gas and oxygen gas by passing an electric current through it. In fact, water does not conduct electricity very well, so a little acid is usually added.

In the water molecules, the hydrogen and oxygen atoms are bound together because they have formed a bond with electrons. The electric current causes these electrons to return to the atoms, breaking the bonds in the molecules. Separate hydrogen atoms and oxygen atoms are formed, and they link up to give hydrogen molecules and oxygen molecules. As they do so, bubbles of hydrogen gas and oxygen gas form on the electrodes in the water.

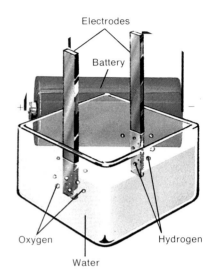

Electrodes

Battery

Oxygen

Hydrogen

Water

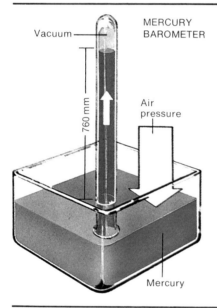

Vacuum

MERCURY BAROMETER

760 mm

Air pressure

Mercury

◄ WHAT IS MERCURY?

Mercury is the only liquid metal. All other metals, like iron, copper or aluminium, are solid. However, mercury becomes solid if it gets cold enough. But it has to be very cold, at least − 39 C or colder.

Mercury is unusual only because its freezing point of − 39 C is the lowest of any metal. This is also lower than the normal range of temperature at which we live.

Mercury is therefore a good liquid to use in thermometers. Mercury thermometers can measure temperatures from − 39 C up to 356 C, the boiling point of mercury.

Mercury is also used in mercury barometers, which measure the pressure of the atmosphere. The pressure of the air forces mercury to a certain height in a tube with a vacuum at the top. The height depends on the air pressure, which can be measured in millimetres of mercury. Normal atmospheric pressure equals 760mm of mercury.

► WHAT IS AIR MADE OF?

Air is made of the gases oxygen, nitrogen and argon. The air always contains the same amounts of these gases. Unless the air is dry, it also contains some water vapour.

The approximate proportions of the gases in pure air at sea-level are nitrogen 78%, oxygen 21% and argon 1%. There are also very small amounts of carbon dioxide, neon and helium.

The air also contains varying amounts of water vapour and gases that come from burning fuel, as well as dust particles floating in the air. The amounts of these gases and dust depend on the location.

In the upper air, above a height of 100 kilometres, there is much less nitrogen and more oxygen.

Life on Earth depends on the oxygen and nitrogen in the air because plants and animals need these elements to grow. Argon has no effect on living things.

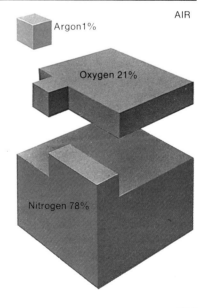

AIR

Argon 1%

Oxygen 21%

Nitrogen 78%

◀ WHO FIRST PROVED THAT ATOMS EXIST?

Philosophers in ancient Greece first thought of atoms. But they could not prove that all things are actually made of atoms. In 1803, the British scientist John Dalton was able to prove that this is true, even though atoms were too small to be seen with the microscopes made at that time.

Dalton knew that all substances are made of elements. Water is made of hydrogen and oxygen, for example. Also, any amount of a pure substance always contains the same elements in the same proportions. Dalton showed that this is because atoms of the elements are linked in these proportions in a pure substance. In water, there are always two hydrogen atoms for every oxygen atom. Dalton also showed that atoms of different elements have different weights.

▶ WHO WAS CHARLES DARWIN?

Charles Darwin was a British scientist who lived from 1809 to 1882. He first showed that all living things evolve. This happens because when an animal is born, it may be very slightly different from its parents. Thus over many generations, the animal may change its form and slowly evolve into a different kind of animal. This is called evolution. Darwin's theory of evolution was published in 1859.

Darwin got much of his evidence for evolution during a five-year voyage around the world. He saw many different kinds of animals and came to believe that one kind of animal evolves into another. But he could not explain why this should happen. After the voyage, Darwin spent more than 20 years working out how evolution occurs. His theory suggested that evolution is the result of natural selection. This means that new kinds of animals evolve because they are better fitted to survive in their surroundings than other kinds, which may gradually die out.

His theory also showed why there are many different kinds of animals in the world. They have evolved from other kinds of animals in the past. Different kinds of plants have evolved too and also human beings, probably from ape-like creatures.

One important piece of evidence was the group of finches that Darwin discovered on the Galapagos Islands in South America. These birds are alike but have different kinds of beaks. Darwin suggested that all had evolved from one kind of finch that flew to the islands in the past. As they bred and spread over the islands, the finches found new kinds of food, and they evolved into several different kinds of finches adapted to eat the different foods available to them. Some now eat seeds, some cones or nuts and others feed on insects.

WHO DISCOVERED THE LAWS OF HEREDITY?

Heredity makes children resemble both their parents in certain ways. Animals and plants pass on their features too. The person who discovered how heredity works was a monk called Gregor Mendel. He lived in Czechoslovakia from 1822 to 1884. Mendel discovered the laws of heredity by planting peas in his monastery's garden and studying the plants that grew.

Mendel was a monk who devoted years of study to heredity. He grew many generations of peas, crossing one kind with another to see which features were passed on to the next generation.

He found that the kinds of peas which grew depended on the combinations of features in the parent plants. He was then able to produce laws that explain how heredity works. However, Mendel was ignored and his laws were not believed until about 50 years later.

WHO LINKED ELECTRICITY AND MAGNETISM?

The Danish scientist Hans Oersted discovered that electricity produces magnetism in 1820. He placed a compass needle near a wire. When an electric current flowed in the wire, the needle moved because the current made the wire magnetic.

Oersted's discovery of a link between electricity and magnetism was very important. Soon afterwards, the British scientist Michael

Faraday used it to make the first electric motor. Electricity fed to the motor produces a magnetic field that makes magnets turn inside the motor. Faraday later invented the electric generator, in which electricity is made by turning coils of wire in a magnetic field. Transformers change electricity into magnetism and back again.

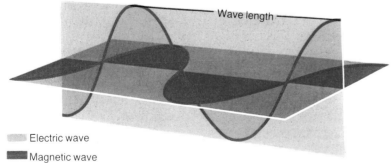

Electric wave

Magnetic wave

WHO DISCOVERED THE NATURE OF LIGHT?

Light is made of electricity and magnetism. This was discovered by the British scientist James Clerk

Maxwell. It took him nearly 20 years to work out the nature of light. He succeeded in 1873.

Maxwell was fascinated by light. Twelve years earlier, he

made the first colour photograph, which was of a tartan ribbon.

Maxwell knew that electricity and magnetism were linked, and worked out that if rays consisting of electric and magnetic fields could exist, they would travel at the speed of light. He therefore suggested that light is an electromagnetic radiation. If so, Maxwell said that other kinds of electromagnetic radiation must also exist. Another kind – radio – was discovered in 1888, after Maxwell's death.

◄WHO CLASSIFIED THE ELEMENTS?

There are just over a hundred elements of which everything is made. They fall into several groups of elements that are alike. The first person to realize this was the Russian scientist Dmitri Mendeleyev. In 1869, he published a table of the elements showing them in their groups.

Mendeleyev's table is still used to classify the elements. When Mendeleyev published it, 63 elements were known. Mendeleyev placed similar elements in the same groups in the table but gaps resulted. Instead of changing the table to remove the gaps, Mendeleyev said that the gaps represented elements that had not been discovered. From their position in the table, he predicted what three of these elements would be. All three were discovered shortly after and they were exactly as Mendeleyev had forecast.

►WHO MADE MORE THAN 1000 INVENTIONS?

Thomas Edison made almost 1300 inventions in his lifetime. Edison lived in the United States from 1847 to 1931. His most famous invention was the phonograph in 1877. The phonograph recorded sound in the same way as the gramophone but the records were cylinders instead of flat discs. Edison made the very first recording, which was of himself reciting 'Mary had a little lamb'.

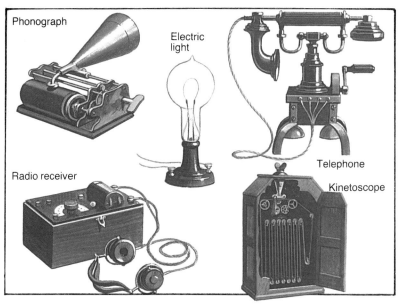

Phonograph

Electric light

Radio receiver

Telephone

Kinetoscope

Edison did not make all his inventions single-handed. After several early successes, he set up a team of scientists to work for him. This was the first research laboratory, and Edison directed investigations into any field that might produce a useful invention.

In addition to sound recording, Edison made or contributed to several other important inventions. He invented an electric light bulb in 1879. However, the British scientist Joseph Swan also invented one at the same time, so both men share the credit for it. The telephone was invented by Alexander Graham Bell in 1876, but Edison quickly improved it into a practical instrument that people could use. In 1881, Edison built a power station to supply electricity to homes. This and another power station in Britain were the world's first power stations.

Edison was one of several inventors who developed motion pictures. His research team had the idea of placing the pictures on a strip of film and the first public film show took place at Edison's laboratories in 1891. Edison's contribution to radio was to discover the Edison effect, which causes an electric current to flow through a vacuum in an electronic valve or tube. The effect was discovered in 1883 and later used by others to make valves for the first radio sets. The Edison effect is also used in the picture tube of a television set.

▲ WHO DISCOVERED RADIOACTIVITY?

▲ WHO REVOLUTIONIZED PHYSICS IN 1900?

▲ WHO DISCOVERED RADIUM?

Radioactivity consists of invisible rays. They were discovered in 1896 by the French scientist Antoine Becquerel. He detected the rays coming from a mineral containing uranium, which is now used as a nuclear fuel. Radioactivity is also called radiation and it can be harmful. The radiation sign above is used to warn people of radioactivity.

Becquerel discovered radioactivity by accident. He placed a piece of uranium mineral on a photographic plate, which was wrapped in black paper so that it would not be exposed to the light. Luckily, Becquerel did not use the plate but decided to develop it. He found that it was strongly fogged as if light had got to it. Becquerel realized that invisible rays from the mineral had penetrated the paper and caused the plate to fog. Marie Curie later named this radioactivity.

Physics is the branch of science that studies energy. In 1900, the German scientist Max Planck produced a new theory called the quantum theory. Before that time, scientists could not understand several effects of energy. Because the quantum theory could answer many important questions on energy, it totally changed physics.

The quantum theory explained that energy in the form of light and other rays or waves is made up of minute particles of energy. A particle of energy is called a 'quantum' of energy. A quantum of light is also known as a 'photon'. Using this theory, scientists were later able to explain how atoms can receive and produce energy. The quantum theory also explains how electricity is produced from light in photoelectric or solar cells.

Marie Curie, who was born in Poland but lived in France, discovered radium with her husband Pierre Curie. They thought that a mineral called pitchblende contained an unknown element. It took them four years to produce the element, because the mineral had a very small amount of it. They called the new element radium, and it is used to treat the dangerous illness cancer.

Pitchblende is radioactive and the Curies thought that this was due to radium. They had to treat eight tons of pitchblende to get just one gram of radium. The extraction process did not remove the radioactivity and the new element turned out to be very highly radioactive. This showed that radioactive rays come directly from the atoms in radioactive elements. The discovery later led to the production of nuclear energy from radioactive elements.

Until early in this century, scientists believed that atoms were the smallest things that could exist. Then in 1911, the British physicist Ernest Rutherford discovered that atoms are made up of even tinier particles. Six years later, Rutherford first split the atom by knocking some particles out of atoms of nitrogen gas.

Rutherford investigated atoms by firing alpha rays at them. In 1911, he found that rays were deflected by a hard particle in the centre of the atom. This was the nucleus of the atom. The nucleus turned out to contain even smaller particles called protons. Rutherford later split nitrogen atoms by firing alpha rays to knock out some protons from the nuclei. This gave oxygen atoms, the first time one element was changed into another.

Relativity is the name of a theory that Albert Einstein first published in 1905. Einstein worked on relativity for many years and published a second theory later. Relativity is about the nature of time and space, and also mass and energy. Einstein's way of looking at these things was totally different to any that had gone before. His explanations made possible many new discoveries, one of which was nuclear power.

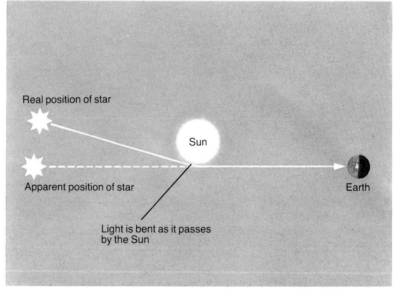

Real position of star

Apparent position of star

Sun

Light is bent as it passes by the Sun

Earth

Einstein's theories of relativity produced several astonishing conclusions. One of them is that mass can be turned directly into energy, a small amount of matter giving a huge quantity of energy. This was shown to be true when nuclear energy was discovered. Another conclusion is that objects get heavier and time slows down as they move. The effect is only noticeable at extremely high speeds, and it has been observed in fast-moving nuclear particles. At the speed of light, mass would become infinite and time would stop. This means that no object (such as a spaceship) can travel at or beyond the speed of light.

Another conclusion of relativity is that the force of gravity distorts space. From this Einstein said that a strong field of gravity such as that of the Sun or a star would bend light rays, and he predicted how much bending would occur. The bending of light rays was later observed in an eclipse of the Sun, and the amount was exactly that which Einstein had forecast.

Albert Einstein was born in Germany in 1879 and lived there and in Switzerland and the United States, where he died in 1955. He is generally considered to be one of the three greatest physicists to have lived, the others being Archimedes and Isaac Newton.

► WHO DISCOVERED VITAMINS?

Vitamins are substances that we need for health. Illness results if any are missing from food. The need for vitamins was discovered by accident in 1896. The Dutch scientist Christiaan Eijkman found that chickens became ill if they were fed on polished rice. The reason was that polished rice lacks vitamins.

The outer covering of rice grains contains a vitamin necessary for health and polishing removes it. Eijkman did not realize this, and the discovery that we need small amounts of such substances was made by the British scientist Frederick Hopkins in 1906. He suggested that diseases such as rickets and scurvy could be cured in human beings by giving them the necessary substances. This was later found to be true and the name vitamin was given to the substances required. A number of vitamins are now known.

Vitamin A	
Thiamine B$_1$	
Riboflavin B$_2$	
Niacin	
Pyridoxine	
Pantothenic acid	
Folic acid	
Vitamin B$_{12}$	
Vitamin C	
Vitamin D	
Vitamin E	MANY FOODS

◄ WHO INVENTED THE TRANSISTOR?

Three American scientists invented the transistor in 1948. They were William Shockley, John Bardeen and Walter Brattain. Transistors replaced valves in electronic machines, being much smaller and more reliable. They made portable radio and television sets possible.

Transistors are made of pieces of silicon or other substances and amplify electric currents passing through them.

Transistors can be connected together to produce small but complex electric circuits that handle signals such as those used in radio and television. In the 1950s, integrated circuits began to be made. They consist of single components containing several interconnected transistors that form a circuit. Microchips are kinds of integrated circuits containing many thousands of transistors.

◄ WHO DISCOVERED THE STRUCTURE OF DNA?

DNA is a substance inside all the cells of living things. It governs heredity so that one generation can produce another. In 1953, the British scientist Francis Crick and the American scientist James Watson discovered the structure of DNA. This explained how heredity works.

DNA molecules in cells can make copies of themselves. In this way, new cells are produced that are exactly like the old cells. When a living thing is born, its cells are copies of its parents' cells and it inherits their features. Crick and Watson found that DNA molecules consist of groups of atoms arranged in two long intertwined strands called a double helix. The strands can form new DNA molecules in which the pattern of atoms is exactly the same. All the features of a living thing come from its DNA structure.

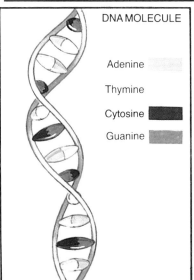

DNA MOLECULE

Adenine
Thymine
Cytosine
Guanine

AN EARLY EUROPEAN PRINTING PRESS

The first books were printed in China and Korea in about AD 700. The earliest ones known are scrolls in which the writing was printed with wooden blocks. It took a long time for printing to reach Europe. There books were first printed in Germany in about 1450.

Paper and ink were also invented in China. Printing books became possible with the invention of movable type – separate blocks of wood each with a letter or symbol that could be put together to print writing. Type made of porcelain was invented in China in about 1050, and then metal type was invented in Korea.

In Europe, Johann Gutenberg of Mainz, in Germany, began to use metal type and a printing press to print books in about 1450. The first full-length printed book was the Gutenberg Bible of about 1454. Only 21 copies of this book now exist.

Books were written out by hand before printing began, so were rare and expensive. With the invention of printing, books became cheaper and plentiful. People were able to read much more and knowledge spread rapidly.

PASCAL'S CALCULATOR

The first instrument to help people make calculations was the abacus. This has beads that are moved along wires in a frame to represent numbers. It developed in Babylonia in about 3000 BC. The first calculating machine was invented in France in 1642. It could add and subtract numbers automatically.

The first calculating machine was built by the French scientist Blaise Pascal at the age of 19. Numbers were fed into the calculator by operating wheels. These wheels turned gears inside the calculator. The gears then moved dials with numbers so that the result showed in a set of windows. The calculator worked well but it could only add and subtract numbers. The first calculating machine that could also multiply and divide was invented by the German scientist Gottfried Leibnitz, in 1694.

Mechanical calculating machines based on the same principles as these first calculators were used until the 1970s. Electronic calculators then became widespread.

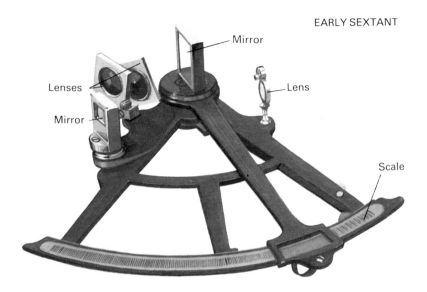

EARLY SEXTANT

Mirror

Lenses

Mirror

Lens

Scale

▲ WHEN WAS THE
SEXTANT FIRST USED?

The sextant is an instrument that navigators use to find their position. With a sextant, they can observe the Sun or a star in the sky to work out where they are on the Earth.

The sextant was invented by John Hadley of Britain and Thomas Godfrey of the United States in 1731. It made navigation easier, and sea travel became safer.

The sextant measures how high the Sun or a star such as

the Pole Star is above the horizon. The navigator looks through lenses and mirrors fixed to the sextant, and views the Sun or star and the horizon. A scale on the sextant then gives the height of the Sun or star. From this and the time of the observation, the navigator can work out the position.

Accurate clocks were also developed during the 1700s. By using them with the sextant, navigators on ships at sea were able to find their correct position for the first time.

The sextant was first thought of by Sir Isaac Newton. He suggested that a simple observing instrument called a quadrant could be improved by fixing a telescope to it.

► WHEN WAS COAL GAS
FIRST USED?

Coal gas was first made in Britain in 1727. In 1760, George Dixon used the gas for the first time to light a room in his house at Durham. The gas light was much brighter than the light of oil lamps or candles. However, after a gas explosion, Dixon stopped his experiments.

Coal gas is made by heating coal in closed ovens. The process was rather dangerous. William Murdock and other British scientists found safe ways of using gas for lighting homes. Gas lighting made a big difference to people's lives. In 1807, gas began to be used for street lighting in London, making the city a safer place. From 1805, it was also used to light factories so that they

could continue producing goods at night. Gas lighting also allowed people to gain education after work at evening classes.

From 1802 onwards, beginning in Germany, coal gas was also used for heating

homes and as a fuel for cookers. It later became a valuable source of chemicals for industry.

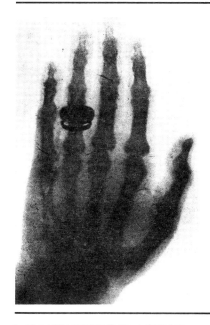

◀ WHEN WERE X-RAYS DISCOVERED?

X-rays were discovered in 1895 by the German scientist Wilhelm Roentgen. He found them by accident. Roentgen was experimenting with a cathode-ray tube, an early form of the tube used today in television sets. One day he noticed that some crystals in the room glowed with light when the tube was switched on. This was because the tube produced X-rays.

Roentgen covered the cathode-ray tube with cardboard and found that the crystals still glowed. He took the crystals into the next room and still the crystals glowed. Roentgen realized that the tube was producing invisible rays that could penetrate even walls.

Roentgen knew of no other rays like this. He called them X-rays because in science 'X' is often used to stand for something that is unknown. Roentgen soon discovered that X-ray photographs show the bones inside the body.

▶ WHEN WERE PLASTICS INVENTED?

The first plastic was a material called Parkesine. It was invented by a British scientist called Alexander Parkes. He discovered the plastic in about 1860 when seeking a substitute for horn obtained from animals. It was used to make objects such as door-knobs.

Parkesine was made from cellulose and camphor, which are natural materials obtained from plants. An American inventor called John Hyatt discovered the same plastic in 1868 when seeking a substitute for ivory. He called it celluloid, the name it has today. Another early plastic made from cellulose was artificial silk, invented by the British scientist Joseph Swan in 1883.

The first plastic to be made from chemicals was Bakelite, which was invented by the Belgian chemist Leo Baekeland in 1907. This was the first material that was totally artificial.

◀ WHEN WERE TELEPHONES FIRST USED?

The telephone was invented in the United States by Alexander Graham Bell (shown here) in 1876. The first telephones were used in Boston in 1877, and the first public call box was installed in Connecticut in 1880. The first automatic telephone exchange opened at La Porte, Indiana, in 1892.

Other people in the United States also invented telephones, notably Antonio Meucci in 1854 and Elisha Grey in 1876. However, Bell was judged to be the inventor of the telephone in court actions contesting his claim to have invented it.

Bell invented the telephone when trying to find a way of helping deaf people to hear. His telephone gave the clearest speech. However, no one was interested in it until the Emperor of Brazil tried the telephone and exclaimed 'My God – it talks!'. The telephone then became an immediate success.

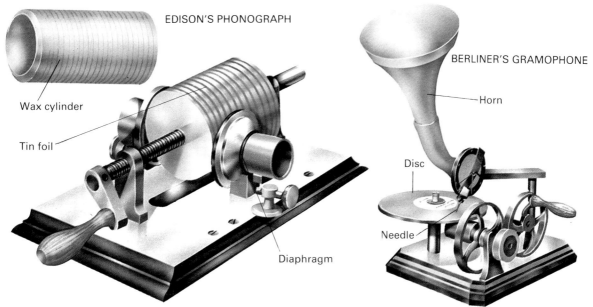

EDISON'S PHONOGRAPH

Wax cylinder

Tin foil

Diaphragm

BERLINER'S GRAMOPHONE

Horn

Disc

Needle

▲ WHEN WAS THE RECORD PLAYER INVENTED?

The record player was invented by the American inventor Thomas Edison in 1877. It was called a phonograph and played cylinders instead of discs. The first recording was of Edison himself reciting *Mary Had A Little Lamb*. **The gramophone, which plays flat discs and not cylinders, was invented by a German, Emile Berliner, in 1887.**

Edison used a cylinder with a layer of soft tin-foil. He spoke into the machine, causing a diaphragm (plate) connected to a needle to vibrate. The cylinder rotated so that the vibrating needle cut a groove in the tin-foil. To play back the recording of his voice, the cylinder was turned and the needle placed in the groove. The needle then vibrated the diaphragm, which gave out the sound.

Edison's phonograph could not reproduce music or speech very well. An improved instrument using wax cylinders was produced by Edison and others in 1888, and a large horn was used to amplify the weak sound given by the diaphragm.

The gramophone, which plays discs instead of cylinders, first appeared in 1889 in Germany. It was not until 1898 that copies of discs were made in quantities. Before then, the performers had to record a song or piece of music over and over again to make enough records to sell to the public.

▶ WHEN DID RADIO BROADCASTING BEGIN?

The first radio broadcast to contain speech and music was made on 24 December 1906 in the United States. The broadcast was given by the Canadian inventor Reginald Fessenden. The first radio station began operating in New York in 1907.

Radio waves were discovered by the German scientist Heinrich Hertz in 1887. The Italian inventor Guglielmo

Marconi began experimenting with radio in 1894. He first sent messages consisting of morse signals in 1895. In 1901 he succeeded in transmitting signals across the Atlantic Ocean (see photograph).

Reginald Fessenden began experiments in sound radio broadcasting in 1900. In the first broadcast of 1906, Fessenden talked, sang, recited and played the violin. The first radio station opened the following year. At first it only broadcast records of popular music.

▼WHEN WAS TELEVISION INVENTED?

The first television picture was produced by the British inventor John Logie Baird in 1924. It was a still picture of a cross that he transmitted a distance of three metres. Baird's system is not the electronic television system that we use today. Electronic television was invented in the United States in 1927 by Philo Farnsworth.

Baird invented a mechanical system of television in which the picture was formed by a spinning disc. In 1925, Baird produced the first colour pictures, first television recording and the first international transmission.

However, the mechanical system gave a small, fuzzy picture. Electronic television was developed in the United States by the engineer Vladimir Zworykin (shown here) during the 1930s. It soon replaced the mechanical system. The first public television service of the kind we have today began in Britain in 1936.

▼WHEN WAS NUCLEAR POWER FIRST PRODUCED?

Nuclear power was first produced by the Italian scientist Enrico Fermi in the United States in 1942. Fermi built the first nuclear reactor at Chicago. In the reactor, uranium was used to produce heat. This kind of reactor is used in nuclear power stations today.

To produce nuclear power, atoms of uranium or some other element must break apart. This process is called nuclear fission and it produces immense energy. Nuclear fission was discovered in 1939, just before World War II.

Scientists worked hard in America during the war to make a reactor in which nuclear fission could be controlled. Fermi succeeded in 1942. Uncontrolled nuclear power is also produced in the atomic bomb. The first such bomb was tested in the United States in 1945. Two bombs were then dropped on the cities of Hiroshima and Nagasaki in Japan.

▼WHEN WAS RADAR INVENTED?

Radar was invented during the 1930s. Scientists in several countries worked on radar at this time. The first successful radar system was produced in Britain in about 1935.

During World War II, radar stations around the coast of Britain helped to warn of the arrival of enemy aircraft. Without radar, it is possible that Germany might have defeated Britain.

Radar works by sending out radio signals that bounce off distant objects. The radar set detects the signals that return and produces a picture indicating the position of the objects.

British and American scientists worked together to invent methods of using very short radio waves called microwaves. With microwaves, small but very accurate radar sets could be installed in ships and aircraft, as well as on land. They gave Britain and America superiority over German and Japanese forces.

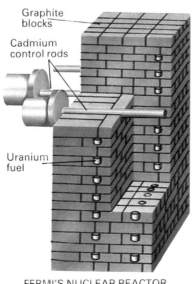

Graphite blocks

Cadmium control rods

Uranium fuel

FERMI'S NUCLEAR REACTOR

HOW DOES A DISHWASHER WORK?

You load the dirty crockery and cutlery into the dishwasher. It first sprays the dishes with hot water to wash away all the grease and dirt. Then it heats the crockery and cutlery to dry it.

A dishwashing machine has a control dial to set a programme of washing and rinsing. This depends on the kind of crockery and cutlery being washed and on how dirty they are. First, the machine's heater warms the washing water to about 70°C, much hotter than the hands can bear. Then spinning bars spray jets of hot water over the utensils to clean them.

The water may contain detergents to dissolve grease and wetting agents to help rinse away the dirt. The dishwasher's control unit adds these substances to the water when they are needed, and times the washing programme. Finally, the dishwasher's heater may be used to dry the utensils.

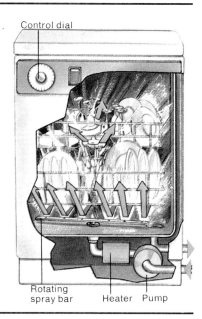

Control dial

Rotating spray bar   Heater   Pump

HOW DO SCALES WORK?

The scales used to weigh food in the kitchen are called spring balances. When the pan is loaded, it squeezes a spring inside the balance. This makes a pointer turn and shows the weight. When the food is taken off the pan, the spring pushes or pulls the pointer back again.

Bathroom scales work in the same way as kitchen scales. They have a much stronger spring because they weigh people, who may be heavy.

Inside the scales, a rack and pinion gear is connected to the pointer or dial. As the pan is pushed down, it moves the gear and the pointer or dial turns to indicate the weight. The pan rests on a spring so that the distance it moves depends on the weight pushing it down.

Electronic scales have a device that produces an electric signal when they are loaded. This signal goes to a small computer that calculates the weight and lights up the display on the scales.

Pointer

Dial   Rack and pinion gear   Spring

HOW DOES A MICROWAVE OVEN WORK?

A microwave oven does not have burning flames or red-hot plates like gas and electric cookers. You put the food into a metal box and press a switch. Inside the box, invisible heat rays bombard the food and cook it very quickly.

A microwave oven gets its name from the rays that cook the food, which are called microwaves. They are like radio waves, and the rays heat up objects in the same way as the Sun's rays warm us. However, microwaves penetrate into the food, so that it cooks on the inside as well as outside. In an ordinary oven, it takes time for the heat to get to the inside of the food. Microwaves heat up the inside immediately, which is why a microwave oven cooks or heats up food so quickly.

Some microwave ovens contain small computers that automatically cook the food at the correct temperature for the right length of time.

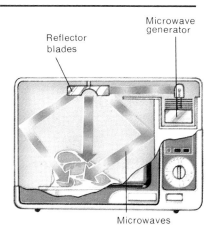

Microwave generator

Reflector blades

Microwaves

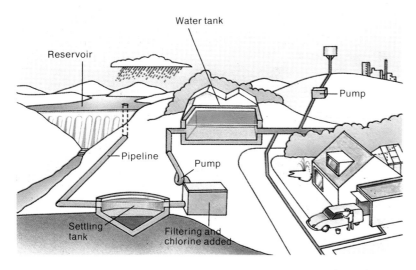

Reservoir

Water tank

Pump

Pipeline

Pump

Settling tank

Filtering and chlorine added

Water comes to a house through underground pipes. It usually comes from a large reservoir fed by a river or stream. Then it may go to a big tank on high ground above the homes in a region so that the water then flows down to the houses there.

Reservoirs are formed by building dams across river valleys so that huge lakes of water pile up behind them.

Water also comes directly from lakes and rivers or from wells dug deep in the ground. In all cases, the water is rainwater. It either falls on high ground and then flows into rivers and lakes, or it soaks away underground and fills wells.

From the reservoirs, lakes, rivers or wells, the water goes to water works to be purified. The pure water is then pumped to water tanks or water towers to be stored. Then it flows through pipes to homes by gravity, or it is pumped to houses.

The water we take from reservoirs, lakes, rivers and wells is not always fit to drink. Before it reaches homes, it goes to water works to be purified. There chemicals are added to kill germs and to remove dirt from the water. The water also goes through filters to make it clean.

The first stage in purifying water is to remove particles of dirt and bacteria. This is done by adding chemicals that make them clump together and settle on the bottom of the purification tanks. The water is filtered again by passing it through beds of sand to trap any dirt particles and bacteria that remain. Then the water may be treated to kill any disease germs, for example by adding chlorine.

Other chemicals may be added to improve the water. Fluoride is sometimes added to water to help strengthen teeth. Water softeners stop the water from producing a deposit that clogs up pipes.

Things get dirty because particles of dust and dirt stick to them. Soapy water dissolves the grease that makes dust and dirt stick to the clothes. The particles float away into the water, and the things are cleaned.

Ordinary water does not remove dirt from things because grease and water do not mix. Soap is made of long thin molecules that attach

themselves to water molecules at one end and to grease molecules at the other end. In this way, the soap molecules link the water and grease molecules so that the grease dissolves and is washed away with the water.

Detergents like washing-up liquid work in exactly the same way as soap.

Soap is made by boiling caustic soda with animal fats such as tallow, and vegetable oils such as coconut oil. Most soap is also perfumed and coloured.

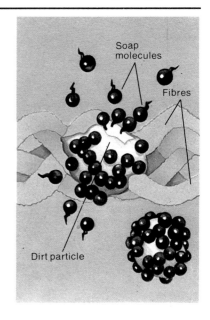

Soap molecules

Fibres

Dirt particle

► HOW
WORK?

**A hot ir
creases
irons ar
electric
is an ele
electric
A stean
to make
damp.
remove
wrinkle
could n

An elect
control 1

► HOW DO DRAINS AND SEWERS WORK?

Drains and sewers carry waste water away from homes. Rainwater drains carry rainwater to soak away in the ground. Waste water from kitchens, bathrooms and toilets goes through pipes under the ground to be purified.

Houses in the country often have a septic tank. This is a large underground tank in the garden into which waste water is piped. The water is purified

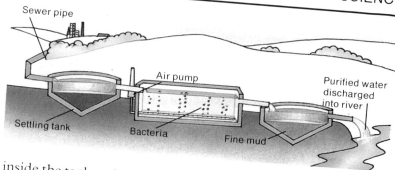

Sewer pipe

Air pump

Purified water discharged into river

Settling tank

Bacteria

Fine mud

inside the tank and soaks away in the ground.

In cities and towns, waste water goes into sewer pipes under the streets. These pipes take the waste to sewage disposal plants, where the waste water goes through

settling tanks and filters to remove solid wastes.

The water may also be treated in tanks with air and bacteria that consume the impurities in the water. The water is then clean enough to be piped to a river or the sea.

Gas
pres

Cup lid

Stopper

Container

Vacuum

◄ HOW DO VACUUM FLASKS KEEP THINGS HOT?

A vacuum flask can keep drinks hot for several hours. This is because the flask stops as much heat escaping from the drink as possible. As the drink loses very little heat, it keeps hot for a long time.

A vacuum flask is designed to prevent heat loss in several ways. The silver walls of the container inside the flask reflect heat rays back into the container. In addition, there

is a vacuum between the walls of the container to stop heat flowing through the walls. The container is surrounded by an outer shell made of insulating materials that slow down the rate of heat loss. In this way, heat leaks out of the flask very slowly.

A vacuum flask is not only used for keeping things hot. Because heat does not flow out of the flask quickly, it does not easily enter the flask either. For this reason, things like iced drinks or liquid air can be kept cold in a vacuum flask.

► HOW
CLEANI

**A vacu
air at (
does so
and di
are tra
the cle
contai
which
suck ir

The va
have bi
and dir
carpet
suck th

► HOW DOES A PRESSURE COOKER WORK?

A pressure cooker is like a large saucepan with a tight-fitting lid. A little water is put in the cooker with the food. When the cooker is heated, the water boils and produces steam inside the cooker. This steam makes the food cook very quickly.

The reason that food cooks quickly inside a pressure cooker is that it gets very hot. When the water boils inside

the cooker, the steam that is produced cannot get out. It builds up a high pressure inside the cooker.

Steam that is at a high pressure is hotter than ordinary steam that comes out of a kettle. The greater the pressure, the hotter the steam and the faster the food cooks. On the lid of the cooker is a valve that lets some steam out when the pressure reaches a certain level. The valve can be set to raise or lower the steam pressure inside the cooker. In this way, the temperature can be changed.

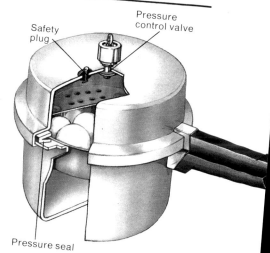

Pressure control valve

Safety plug

Pressure seal

337

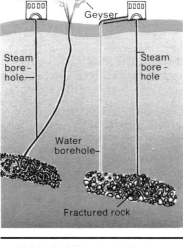

It is very hot inside the Earth, and in some parts of the world it is very hot near the surface. Hot water or steam may come up through vents in the rock, or through holes drilled down to the hot region. This hot water is used to warm homes, and the steam goes to power stations to make electricity.

Heat that is tapped from below ground is called geothermal power. It is used mostly in Iceland, Italy, New Zealand, Japan and the United States. These are volcanic regions where hot water and steam rise to the surface at hot springs and geysers. Other countries are looking for geothermal power.

As well as drilling down to them, it is also possible to tap the heat of hot dry rocks. Pumping water down a bore-hole to the rock fractures it and turns the water to steam. The steam then rises up a second borehole.

▶ HOW DOES A WINDMILL WORK?

Big windmills with blades like huge aircraft pro-pellors are being built to produce electricity to supply cities and towns. The blades turn a shaft that is connected to an electric generator on top of the windmill. Small windmills are used to pump water or to generate electricity for farms.

Small windmills have a vane behind the sails to catch the wind if it changes direction and turn the sails into the wind. Large windmills have an automatic control system that turns the head of the windmill into the wind.

The largest windmills have blades that are 60 metres long, and are mounted on towers about 100 metres high. The blades need to be very large and high to catch as much wind as possible. In this way, more of the energy that is in the wind is turned into elec-tricity. In the future, rows of huge windmills may line the coast in windy regions.

Wind-power generator at Gedser, Denmark

◀ HOW DO WE USE SOLAR POWER?

We can use the Sun's warmth to provide free heat. Solar panels on the roofs of houses trap the Sun's rays. They warm water flowing through the panels. In this way solar power helps to produce hot water for washing and heating.

Solar panels are covered with glass to trap the Sun's rays. Inside they are painted black to absorb as much heat as possible. Water runs through pipes in the panels and is warmed by the Sun's heat. The warm water goes to a tank, and it may return to the solar panels to be heated some more. In this way, the Sun's heat is used to warm the hot water supply of a house. Solar power may not be enough to heat the water fully, but it is a free source of energy and therefore reduces heating costs.

Houses may have heat exchangers and heat storage tanks so that the heat can be stored.

▼ HOW IS HYDRO-ELECTRIC POWER MADE?

Hydro-electric power is a kind of electricity. It is made in power stations at waterfalls or high dams. Water falling down pipes to the power station drives generators. The electricity they produce goes to homes and factories. It is no different from the electricity produced by other kinds of power stations.

Hydro-electric power stations can only work where water falls a long way. This is so that the water gains enough power to drive the electricity generators in the power station. A high dam may therefore be built to store up the water in a large reservoir above the power station. The station contains turbines in which the stream of falling water drives paddle-shaped blades round. A shaft connected to the blades then powers the generators as in ordinary power stations.

Hydro-electric stations continue to work at night, when little electricity is needed. To prevent this waste of power, the turbines in some hydro-electric power stations are fed with power at night to act as pumps. They pump water up to the reservoir above the station. The station then uses this water to generate power during the day.

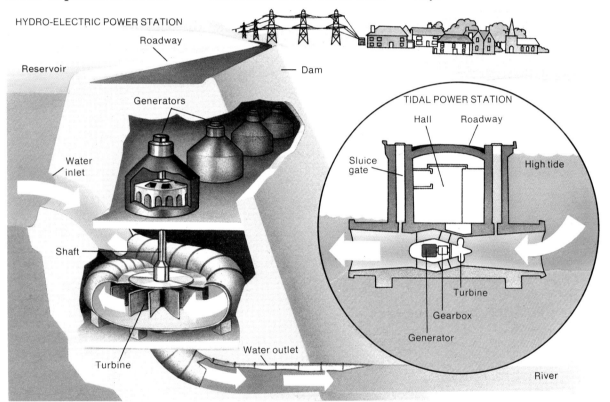

HYDRO-ELECTRIC POWER STATION
Roadway
Reservoir
Dam
Generators
Water inlet
Shaft
Turbine
Water outlet

TIDAL POWER STATION
Hall   Roadway
Sluice gate
High tide
Turbine
Gearbox
Generator
River

▲ HOW DO WE GET POWER FROM THE SEA?

We can get power from the sea by using the tides. As the tides rise and fall, water flows in and out of river mouths. The water can be used to drive electricity generators in a barrage (a kind of dam) built across the river. There is a tidal power station at the mouth of the River Rance in France.

Like hydro-electric power stations, tidal power stations do not use any fuel. They are therefore very cheap to run, but they cost a lot to build. Tidal power stations do not produce much power when the tide is changing. So, at times of low power demand, a tidal power station may use power to pump water into the river mouth from the sea so that it can be used later when power is required.

Tidal power stations can only be built where there is a large rise and fall in water level caused by the tides. This occurs in narrow river estuaries, straits and bays. Not many sites are suitable for tidal power stations, so it is unlikely that many will be built to follow the Rance tidal station in France, the world's first. Possible sites include the Severn estuary in England and the Bay of Fundy in Canada, where the tides can rise and fall by 16 metres.

Cement is usually made from limestone and clay, but chalk and sand may also be used. These materials are fed into a big machine that crushes them into small pieces and mixes them. Then the mixture is heated in a kiln. When it cools, it is ground into cement powder.

The principal minerals in cement are lime, which comes mainly from limestone, and silica and alumina, which are provided by clay. Some iron ore is also used. After crushing and blending, the various ingredients are fed into a rotating kiln and heated to about 1500°C for several hours. This heating produces a clinker that is then ground to a powder with a mineral called gypsum. This is added to regulate the time that the cement takes to harden. Adding water to the cement powder makes the minerals combine together, producing a firm bond as the cement hardens.

Concrete is made by mixing gravel or small stones, sand and cement together with water. These materials are placed in a revolving concrete mixer, or they can be mixed together with a spade. The concrete is a paste that sets to form a hard material. It is used in building to make floors and walls, as well as roads, bridges and dams.

Most concrete is made in a concrete mixer, which revolves to turn the ingredients over and over so that they mix thoroughly. The mixer is up-ended and the concrete poured out. It is then carried or piped into a mould, where the concrete sets hard in the shape of the mould. Slabs, blocks and pipes are made in this way, and constructions can be built in any shape required by using concrete. However, concrete is not very strong and has to be strengthened, often by placing steel bars in the concrete to reinforce it.

Skyscrapers are tall buildings that tower in the air. First, holes are dug in the ground so that the skyscraper is firmly fixed in place by its underground foundations. Then a high frame is built up from the foundations. Finally, walls and floors are fixed to the frame.

The foundations of a skyscraper are laid by drilling holes in the ground and filling them with concrete. If the ground is firm, the foundations are wide so that they will spread the weight of the building and they do not go very deep. If the ground is not very firm, deep shafts of concrete are driven into the ground to anchor the skyscraper firmly.

Then a frame of steel girders or concrete beams is erected, often with a pillar-like concrete core containing lift shafts and stairs. The frame and core take all the weight of the building so that the walls do not have to support the floors above.

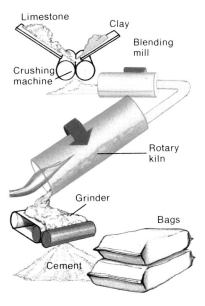

Precast concrete frame

Wall unit

▶ HOW ARE TALL
BUILDINGS AND CHIMNEYS
DEMOLISHED?

Demolition experts who
knock down high buildings
and chimneys must make
sure that they will not fall
on other buildings nearby.
Sometimes, they have to
take the building or
chimney apart piece by
piece. But to save time,
they may be able to blow it
up instead.

To make a building collapse
so that it falls straight down
without tipping over, experts
place explosives throughout
the building. When the
charges are fired, all the walls
collapse at the same time.
Before demolishing the
building, the beams
supporting it are weakened so

that none of the walls fall
outwards. A chimney can be
made to fall in a particular
direction by first making a
hole in one side of the base

while supporting the chimney
with posts. By setting fire to
the posts or knocking them
away, the chimney will topple
over in this direction.

▼ HOW ARE TUNNELS
BUILT?

Many tunnels are dug with
tunnelling machines

called moles. These are
like huge drills that cut a
shaft through the ground.
At the head of the mole,
rotating cutters dig out

the rock or soil, which is
carried away along a
conveyor belt. Powerful
jacks act like springs to
force the mole forward as
it removes the rock and
soil ahead.

As the mole edges forward
through the ground,
engineers fix lining panels
into place to form the walls of
the tunnel. For power and
safety, the mole is driven by
electric motors and hydraulic
jacks, which are fed with
high-pressure fluid along
lines from the surface.

In good conditions, a mole
can burrow through the
ground at five metres an hour
for a train-sized tunnel.
Progress may be slow when
the soil is waterlogged, as the
water or soft soil tends to flow
into the tunnel. To prevent
this happening, the head of
the mole is contained in a
sealed compartment.

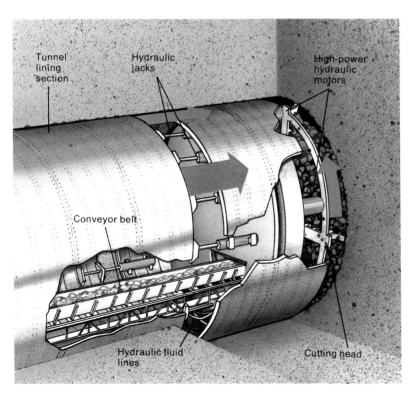

Tunnel lining section

Hydraulic jacks

High-power hydraulic motors

Conveyor belt

Hydraulic fluid lines

Cutting head

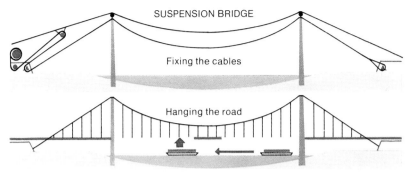

SUSPENSION BRIDGE

Fixing the cables

Hanging the road

▲ HOW ARE BRIDGES BUILT?

Most bridges rest on supports called piers. A wall is built in the river to keep out the water, and the piers are fixed in the bed of the river. Then the bridge is built on the piers. When it is finished, some of the piers may be taken away. Suspension bridges are built by fixing cables across a river from high towers on each side. The road is then hung from the main cables.

Long bridges need to be supported between the piers that hold them up. Arches carry a bridge by transferring its weight to the supports at each end of the arches. Frames of girders may be built above or below the road or railway to strengthen the bridge.

Cantilever bridges are made in two sections, each supported on a pier near each end of the bridge. The sections meet in the middle of the bridge, giving a long span.

▶ HOW DOES A ROAD DRILL WORK?

Road drills are used to break through the road surface and dig up the road. The drill has a strong blade like a chisel that strikes the road many times a second. It is driven by compressed air piped to the drill from a compressor.

Road drills are also called pneumatic drills because they work on compressed air. As the air enters the drill, the diaphragm valve first lets the air into the base of the piston, forcing it upwards. This action causes the valve to rock and send air to the top of the piston, which moves down and strikes the blade of the road drill.

The air then leaves through the exhaust, and the valve rocks back to admit more air to the base of the piston again. The whole action is then repeated.

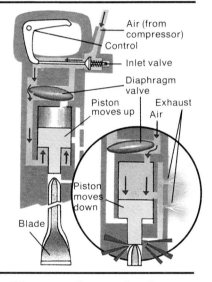

Air (from compressor)
Control
Inlet valve
Diaphragm valve
Piston moves up
Exhaust Air
Piston moves down
Blade

◀ HOW ARE ROADS BUILT?

To build a road, engineers first make the ground level. Then they construct a base of stones or gravel, on which they put a layer of concrete or macadam (crushed rock mixed with clay or tar). Finally a layer of tar called bitumen or asphalt is usually spread on top. The road builders also make drains at the side of the road to carry away rainwater.

Motorways have to be hard-wearing to carry heavy traffic. They are often made of concrete, usually with a surface of tough bitumen. Roads in towns do not carry such heavy traffic, and are generally made of gravel and macadam and surfaced with asphalt and chippings. These roads can be easily dug up to get to the service pipes beneath. These include drains to carry off rainwater, electricity and telephone cables, and pipes containing water and gas. Beneath these pipes are sewers which carry wastes from buildings to sewage disposal plants or to a river or the sea.

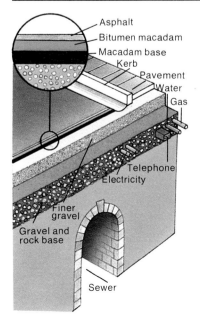

Asphalt
Bitumen macadam
Macadam base
Kerb
Pavement
Water
Gas
Telephone
Electricity
Finer gravel
Gravel and rock base
Sewer

▶ HOW DO ROBOTS WORK?

Most robots consist of a mechanical arm with a gripper like a pair of tongs at one end. Inside the arm are hydraulic motors that can move the arm and gripper in any direction. The arm is connected to a box of controls that operate the motors to make the robot perform a particular action.

The controls of the robot are able to move its arm and gripper to exactly the same positions every time the robot performs a certain task.

The robot is first taught the various movements that it must make. A human operator uses the controls to make the robot perform the action. The controls contain a memory like a computer memory that remembers all the arm and gripper positions. They can then direct the robot to carry out this action over and over again with perfect precision. A new action can be fed into the memory to make the robot carry out a different task.

▲ WHAT ARE ROBOTS USED FOR?

Robots are mainly used to do jobs that involve carrying out the same action over and over again. These are jobs like painting and welding, and loading and unloading parts in factories and taking them from one place to another.

Robots are used in industries such as car manufacture because they can repeat the same task as many times as required without making a mistake. The jobs they do are fairly simple, like spraying paint in the same pattern over each car body that comes to them, or welding the same parts of the body together.

As robots improve, they will even be able to check the jobs that they are doing. Some robots already have vision and touch sensors. They make parts for products and assemble them.

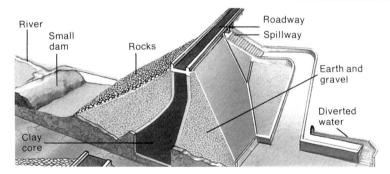

River
Small dam
Rocks
Roadway
Spillway
Earth and gravel
Diverted water
Clay core

▲ HOW ARE DAMS BUILT?

A dam is a huge barrier built across a valley so that river water piles up behind it to form a lake. Many dams are constructed by heaping up **earth and rock, while others are made of concrete or stone blocks. While the dam is being built, the river is diverted around the site. A small dam or wall is built to send the water to one side.**

An earth-fill dam is made with a solid core of clay surrounded by earth and gravel and covered with rocks. A central wall may be needed to stop water seeping through the dam. Like some dams made of concrete or stone, they are so big that their weight keeps them in place.

Buttress dams are thin dams built with supports called buttresses to hold them up. Arch dams have high narrow walls that are curved. The water presses the dam into the sides of the valley, and this stops it from giving way.

▶ HOW IS LEATHER MADE?

Real leather is made from the hides or skins of animals. Cattle hides are used to make most leather. Other animals that provide leather include pigs, sheep, goats and also sharks and snakes. To make leather, the hair or fur is removed and then the hides or skins are tanned to stop them from rotting.

Hair or fur is removed from the hides or skins by soaking them in lime solution and scraping them. Most leather is then tanned in solutions containing tannin, which is obtained from plants. The tannin combines with the protein in the hide or skin.

Some leather is tanned with chemicals instead. After dyeing, the leather is treated with oil or grease to make it flexible.

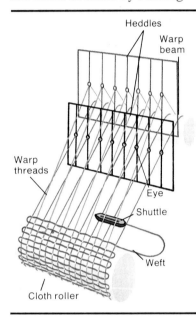

Heddles
Warp beam
Warp threads
Eye
Shuttle
Weft
Cloth roller

◀ HOW IS CLOTH WOVEN?

Much cloth is made by weaving threads together. A loom is used for weaving. Lines of threads called warp threads move up and down in the loom. In between each movement, a shuttle pulls another thread called the weft between the warp threads. This action weaves the warp and weft threads together.

The warp threads are wound on a roller called the warp beam. They then pass through holes called eyes in frames of wires called heddles. The frames move up and down as the shuttle passes to and fro. In this way, the weft thread passes alternately above and below the warp threads, weaving a pattern. To get different patterns, the warp threads move up and down in different arrangements. A roller pulls the warp threads through the loom, and the cloth winds on to the roller as it turns. Power looms and hand looms work in basically the same way.

▶ HOW DOES A ZIP FASTENER WORK?

Metal zips have lines of tiny teeth, while plastic zips contain small loops on each side. When you pull the slide of the zip fastener up, it pushes the teeth or loops together.

Beneath each tooth in a metal zip fastener is a small space. The slide is narrow at the bottom so that it forces the teeth together as you pull up the zip. The teeth on one side fit between the teeth on the other side. As they come together, each tooth slots into the space under the tooth above and the zip stays closed. As the slide moves down, a divider at the top of the slide pulls the teeth apart.

Top pieces and a bottom piece at the ends of the fastener stop the slide coming off, though some zips are designed to separate completely by pulling one line of teeth out of the bottom piece. Plastic zips have two spiral coils instead of lines of teeth, but they work in the same way.

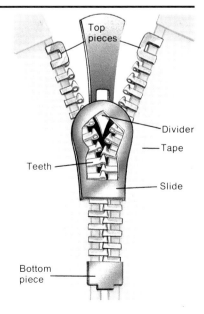

Top pieces
Divider
Tape
Teeth
Slide
Bottom piece

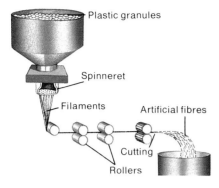

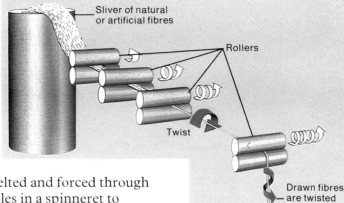

▲ HOW ARE TEXTILE FIBRES SPUN?

Textiles like cloth are made with thread or yarn, which come from fibres. Natural fibres are plant or animal hairs, while artificial fibres are made of plastic. The fibres are combed loosely together to form a strip of fibres called a sliver. Then the sliver is rolled and twisted to make the thread or yarn.

Artificial fibres are made from plastic granules, which are melted and forced through holes in a spinneret to produce filaments. These are drawn through rollers and then cut to make fibres.

To spin thread, a sliver of either artificial or natural fibres (such as cotton or wool) is drawn through rollers. These rotate faster and faster to pull out the fibres in the sliver. The fibres are also twisted and link together to produce the thread or yarn. This goes to a spinning frame, where the thread is twisted again as it is wound on to a bobbin. The thread is then ready to be woven into cloth.

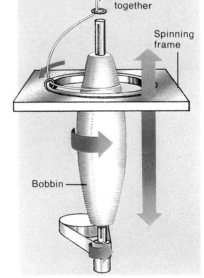

▶ HOW IS POTTERY MADE?

Pottery includes containers like bowls and mugs and objects like tiles that are all made of clay. The pots and other articles are first formed in soft wet clay. Then the pottery is heated in a kiln.

Many potters use a wheel that is powered by a foot treadle to shape clay. They control the wheel with one foot as they shape the pot between their thumbs and fingers. Handles and spouts are made separately and stuck to the pot using very soft clay. Other kinds of pottery are made by cutting or moulding the clay into shape.

Before the pottery is fired in the kiln, it is dried. Then a glaze may be added. When the glaze is fired, it produces a shiny coating on the pottery. Often, the glaze is added after the pot is fired, so that a second firing is required to glaze the pottery. The glaze may also give the pottery a certain colour, or the pottery may be painted before or after glazing.

The finest pottery is called porcelain or china. It is white, but some light shines through the porcelain. One of the main ingredients of porcelain is kaolin, or China clay.

Pottery is also made in great quantities in factories. Machines press and mould the clay into shape. Glazing and decorating may also be done automatically.

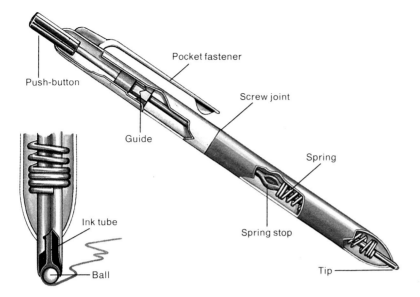

◀ HOW IS INK MADE?

The kind of ink used with fountain pens is often made by mixing water with coloured pigments or dyes. It takes some time to dry because the water has to evaporate and leave the pigment or dye on the paper. The kind of ink in colouring pens and ballpoint pens contains dyes or pigments mixed with liquids that dry very quickly.

Pigments are coloured powders that lie on the surface of the paper. Dyes are coloured materials that penetrate the surface and colour the paper itself.

Inks used for printing are made by mixing pigments with special oils or varnishes that help to bind the pigment to the paper. Carbon black is a black pigment that is often used to make black printing ink. It is a fine black powder similar to soot. Coloured pigments used in printing inks and the dyes in other kinds of inks are made from chemicals.

▲ HOW DOES A BALLPOINT PEN WORK?

Inside a ballpoint pen is a thin tube of ink. At the tip of the tube is an opening with a tiny ball in it. When you write, the ball spins as the tip moves over the paper. The ink sticks to the ball and then flows onto the paper.

The ink that is used in a ballpoint pen is special ink that dries as soon as it meets the air. This means that the writing will not smudge. In addition, the ink dries on the ball at the tip of the pen as soon as it is lifted from the paper. The dry ink seals the opening at the tip of the pen, and the ink inside cannot flow out or dry up inside.

Many ballpoint pens have push-button actions that push the ink tube forward for writing and retract it when the pen is not in use. The push-button operates a guide that rotates to force the tube up or down, and a spring holds it in position.

▶ HOW DOES AN ERASER WORK?

You can remove pencil marks from paper with an eraser or rubber. The pencil puts a layer of graphite particles on the surface of the paper. The particles are sticky, and attach themselves to the rubber as it moves over the paper.

A soft rubber stays clean because its surface rubs away as it is used. To remove deep pencil marks and also ink marks, a hard rubber can be

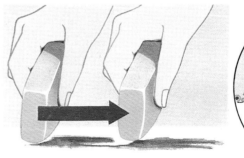

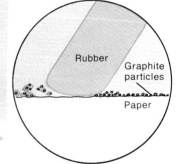

used. This does not pick up the pencil or ink markings. Instead, it rubs away the top surface of the paper.

Typists can correct mistakes in typing in other ways. A special white paint that dries quickly can be spread over the mistake to blot it out. Then the typist goes back and types the correct letter or word in the same place. Typists can also use a white paper or ribbon that types white letters over a mistake so that it disappears.

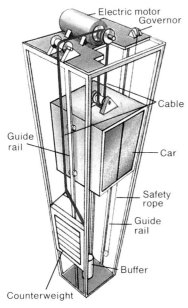

The car of the lift that carries people up and down hangs from one end of a cable. An electric motor turns a drive pulley that winds the cable up and down. At the other end of the cable is a big weight called a counter-weight. This is as heavy as the car and balances it.

The counterweight balances the weight of the car so that the motor has to raise and lower only the weight of the people inside the lift. The car runs between guide rails up and down the shaft. Controls inside the lift car operate the motor to take the car to any floor, and other motors open and close the doors.

A safety device called a governor stops a lift from falling if the cable breaks. A safety rope connected to the car turns the governor, and if it moves too quickly the governor operates a switch that makes the car grip the guide rails and stop. Even if this does not work, a buffer at the bottom of the lift shaft will break the car's fall.

Escalators are the moving stairs that carry people up and down in places like big shops. They move as fast as four metres a second. The steps of the escalator are connected by an endless chain that goes round and round without stopping. At the end, the steps go underneath the escalator and back to the beginning.

The steps of the escalator have wheels which run on rails under the steps. In the sloping part of the escalator, the rails are situated beside each other so that the steps are raised one above or below the other like a staircase.

Near the top and bottom, the steps level out so that people can walk on or off the escalator. Here, the rails move apart so that the tops of the steps line up with each other. The motor that drives the chain connecting the steps together also drives the handrail through a set of gears.

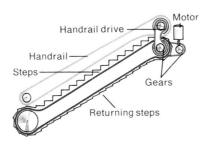

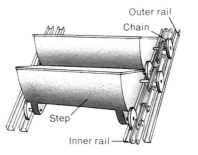

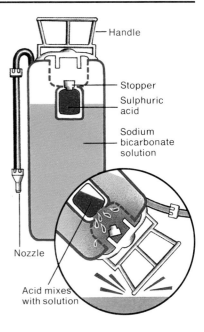

To put out a fire, the ex-tinguisher sprays out liquid or a vapour or foam. This cools the fire and also covers it to stop air from getting to the fire. One common type of fire extinguisher sprays water. Gas produced inside the extinguisher forces the water out.

Inside a water-filled ex-tinguisher is a bottle of sulphuric acid and a solution of sodium bicarbonate. To use this extinguisher, you turn it upside down or strike a knob. This action either opens or breaks the bottle of acid, and it mixes with the bi-carbonate solution. Immedi-ately, a large amount of carbon dioxide gas is released inside the extinguisher, forcing the solution out of the nozzle in a powerful jet.

To fight fires caused by electrical faults or burning chemicals, water is not used. Instead, firemen have ex-tinguishers that spray a heavy vapour or a smothering foam.

To play a brass instrument such as a trumpet, you put your lips onto the mouthpiece. Then you close your lips tightly and blow air through the middle of them. Your lips vibrate, and this vibration sets the air in the trumpet vibrating and gives a sound. Other brass instruments include the trombone, horn, tuba, bugle and euphonium.

To get different notes on most brass instruments, you press keys or valves. This opens or closes sections of tubing in the instrument, making the length of the column of air inside the instrument get longer or shorter. This makes the note get lower or higher in pitch. However, there are usually only three keys or valves, and pressing all combinations of these gives only seven notes. A trombone has a slide that the player moves in and out to get notes, but it too cannot produce more than seven notes.

To get more notes, the brass player tightens his or her lips. Without using the valves or slide, a brass player can get a set of notes called harmonics. These are the notes played in bugle calls, because a bugle has no valves. Good players can get very high notes in this way.

To get the notes that lie in between the harmonics, the player uses the keys, valves or slide. Hitting the right note on a brass instrument is a combination of the right lip pressure and the correct key, valve or slide position.

To get a sound from a woodwind instrument like the clarinet, you put the mouthpiece into your mouth and blow. This sets the column of air inside the instrument vibrating and a note comes out. You also finger the keys on the instrument to open and close holes along the side, and get different notes.

Not all woodwind instruments are made of wood. The saxophone is made of metal, and so too are many flutes. The various instruments also have different kinds of mouthpieces. In the piccolo and flute, the player blows air across a hole in the side of the instrument. This makes the edges of the hole vibrate, which set the air column in the tube of the instrument sounding. The recorder is similar, but the player blows into a mouthpiece which sends the air across the edge of a hole in the tube.

The other woodwind instruments have mouthpieces that contain stiff reeds. Blowing into the mouthpiece sets the reed vibrating and this makes the air column in the instrument sound. The clarinet and saxophone have a single reed, whereas the oboe, English horn and bassoon contain a double reed.

To get different notes, the fingers open and close holes in the instrument or operate keys that move pads over the holes up or down. This action changes the length of the air column vibrating inside the instrument.

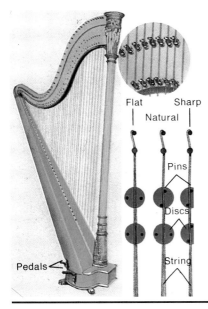

Flat — Sharp
Natural
Pins
Discs
String
Pedals

◀ WHY DOES A HARPIST USE PEDALS?

If you watch an orchestra in action, you will see the harpist pressing pedals on the harp as well as playing the strings. Moving the pedals up and down gives the harpist more notes. The pedals turn small discs with pins that grip the strings.

The kind of harp played in orchestras does not have enough strings to play all the notes that are needed. It can only play a scale of notes that is rather like the white notes on the piano.

To get the other notes (like the black notes), the harpist has to press the pedals. The discs turn so that the pins make the lengths of string vibrate shorter or longer, giving sharp or flat notes.

There are seven pedals, one for each note of the scale from A to G. Moving the D pedal to sharp, for example, changes all the D strings to D sharp. To help find the right notes, some of the strings have colours.

▶ HOW DO STRING INSTRUMENTS MAKE A SOUND?

String instruments have tight strings that make a sound. When you play the guitar, you pluck the strings with your fingers. The other main string instruments are the violin, viola, cello and double bass. These instruments are usually played with a bow.

All string instruments give a sound when the strings vibrate. Plucking the strings sets them vibrating for a short time. When a bow is moved across a string, the rough surface of the hairs in the bow keeps it vibrating. Plucking harder or pushing the bow down make the vibration stronger and the sound gets louder.

The sound that the strings make is not very loud. The vibration of the strings sets the hollow body of the instrument vibrating too, making the sound louder.

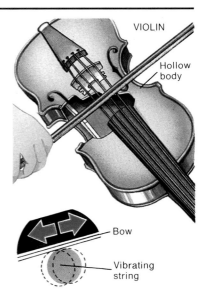

VIOLIN
Hollow body
Bow
Vibrating string

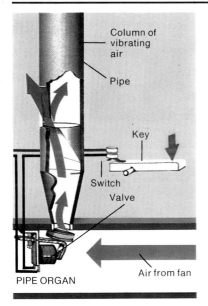

Column of vibrating air
Pipe
Key
Switch
Valve
Air from fan
PIPE ORGAN

◀ HOW DOES AN ORGAN MAKE SOUNDS?

When the organist presses the keys on a pipe organ, air is blown into some of the pipes of the organ. Each pipe gives out a different note. Pipe organs are the organs seen in churches. Electric organs produce sounds from loudspeakers.

In a pipe organ, the flow of air is usually produced by an electric fan. When a key is pressed, it operates a valve to let the air into a set of pipes. The air flows over the edge of a hole cut in a pipe or over a brass reed in the pipe. These vibrate and set the column of air in the pipe vibrating so that it makes a sound.

Pipes of different sizes give different notes. The organist pushes buttons called stops to send the air to particular sets of pipes to get different sounds. In electric organs, the keys are like switches that turn on electronic sound generators. These generate electric signals that go to a loudspeaker.

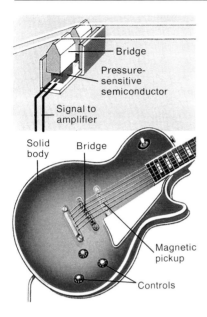

▲ HOW DOES AN ELECTRIC GUITAR WORK?

An electric guitar has strings like an ordinary guitar. However, the strings do not produce the sound. When a string is played, it makes a pickup under the strings give an electric signal. The signal goes to an amplifier and a loudspeaker, which produces the sound.

Because the strings do not produce the sound, an electric guitar can be solid. The strings are made of metal.

In guitars with magnetic pickups, the metal strings vibrate above magnets in the pickup. This causes the magnetic fields of the magnets to vary, producing an electric signal in coils surrounding the magnets.

A pressure-sensitive pickup is fixed to the strings at the bridge of some guitars. It vibrates as the strings vibrate and produces an electric signal. The strength of the signal depends on how hard the strings are played, so that the guitarist can make the music louder or softer.

▶ HOW IS AN ACOUSTIC GUITAR MADE?

An acoustic guitar is made of wood, and the best guitars are made by hand. The body of the guitar is hollow. Supports send the vibration of the strings throughout the body and make it sound too. This sound comes from the body through the sound hole under the strings.

Six strings made of metal or gut are fixed to the bridge of the guitar. These are threaded through pegs in the machine head, and the nuts tighten up the strings until they are in tune.

The neck of the guitar is made of solid wood across which metal strips called frets are fixed. The frets form the

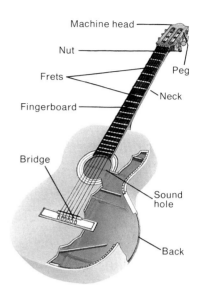

fingerboard, which the guitarist uses to press the strings against the frets and get the notes required. An acoustic guitar can be turned into an electric guitar by attaching a pickup to it.

▶ HOW DOES A SYNTHESIZER WORK?

A synthesizer produces electronic music. You can use the controls to make many different sounds. This is because the synthesizer can create electric signals that make these sounds come from a loudspeaker connected to the synthesizer.

The synthesizer can imitate other instruments or make a wide range of sounds of its own. Most synthesizers are played with keyboards, but you first have to set the controls to get the particular sound you want.

The controls operate the electronic circuits inside the synthesizer. The circuits produce electric signals that vary in strength in the same way that sound waves vary in strength. The signals go to an

amplifier, and then to a loudspeaker. The signals make the loudspeaker cone vibrate, and it produces sound waves with the right kind of sound.

Instead of a keyboard, a computer can be used to operate a synthesizer. The computer is first programmed with the music.

▶ HOW DOES A PIANO WORK?

When you press piano keys, hammers move forward and strike the strings. The hammers have heads of felt, and the strings are made of taut wire. The hammers make the strings vibrate to produce sound. Dampers move against the strings when you take your fingers off the keys, and the strings stop sounding.

Connected to each key of the piano is a mechanism called the action. It consists of a set of wooden levers. When the key is pressed down, it raises a jack that moves the hammer to strike the string.

At the same time, the damper moves away from the string so that it is free to vibrate the sound. A check keeps the hammer near the string so that it is ready to strike the string again quickly if the key is pressed again without being released first. When the key is released, the jack moves down and the hammer falls away from the string sounding.

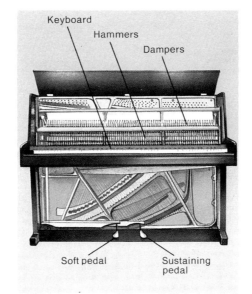

Keyboard
Hammers
Dampers
Soft pedal
Sustaining pedal

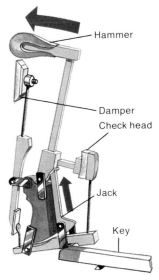

Hammer
Damper
Check head
Jack
Key

▲ WHAT DO THE PEDALS ON A PIANO DO?

Most pianos have two pedals. The left pedal makes the music softer. The right pedal makes the sounds of the notes carry on when you take your fingers off the keys. It is called the sustaining pedal.

The soft pedal works in various ways. It often moves the hammers for the middle and lower notes slightly to one side. These notes each have two or three strings. Pressing the soft pedal makes the hammers strike only one string, making the sound softer.

On other pianos, all the hammers are moved nearer the strings. When the keys are pressed, the hammers do not have to move so far to strike them. They therefore hit the strings with less force and give less sound. When the sustaining pedal is pressed, all the dampers move away from the strings. The strings continue to sound until the notes die away.

◀ HOW DO DRUMS MAKE A SOUND?

A skin is stretched over the frame of the drum. When you hit the drum, the skin vibrates and gives a sound. It also sets the frame and the air inside the frame vibrating too, and their sounds mix with the sound of the skin.

The kind of sound a drum makes depends on how you hit it. Using a drumstick gives a harsh crack, while using your hands or a soft mallet gives more of a thump. The sound also depends on the size of the drum. A bigger skin gives a deeper or more booming sound and a smaller skin a higher tone.

A snare drum has two skins with a set of wires that can be fixed against the lower skin. The wires rattle against the lower skin when the upper skin is struck, giving a bright edge to the sound.

Timpani or kettledrums are played in orchestras. These drums can produce different notes by tightening or loosening the skin.

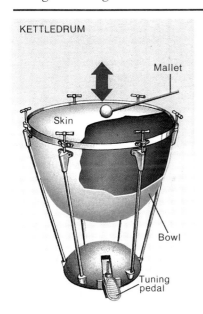

KETTLEDRUM

Mallet
Skin
Bowl
Tuning pedal

369

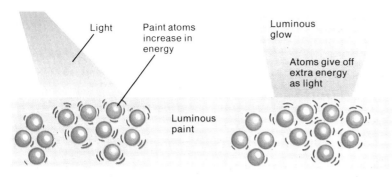

Light — Paint atoms increase in energy — Luminous paint

Luminous glow — Atoms give off extra energy as light

▲ WHY DO LUMINOUS PAINTS GLOW IN THE DARK?

Luminous paints glow in the dark. This is because they absorb light energy when they are in the light. As soon as it is dark, they give out this energy as a **bright glow. The glow fades when all the energy stored in the paint is used up.**

When any material is lit, the atoms in its molecules gain energy. But they lose this extra energy immediately by reflecting the light back. Luminous materials do not reflect all the light energy right away. They keep some energy and lose it gradually. This extra energy shows up as a glow in the dark.

Some materials seem to glow brightly in daylight. This is because they gain energy from the daylight like luminous paint, but immediately give off all the extra energy as light of one colour. This is why the colour looks bright. These materials are called fluorescent.

▶ HOW ARE STATUES MADE?

A sculptor may carve a statue from a block of stone or of wood. Using a hammer and chisel, he or she chips away at the block to form the statue. Metal statues are first made in clay, and a mould is made. The statue is cast by pouring molten metal into the mould and leaving it to set.

A sculptor who carves a statue has to take great care not to cut away too much stone or wood from the block. Then the final statue may be delicately polished to make the surface smooth and shiny.

Making a metal statue can be easier because the sculptor first works in clay. Instead of cutting away, he or she builds up the statue in clay. The figure can then be altered by taking some of the clay away or adding more. To support the clay figure, the sculptor builds it on a frame. The clay figure is then used to make a mould to produce the metal statue.

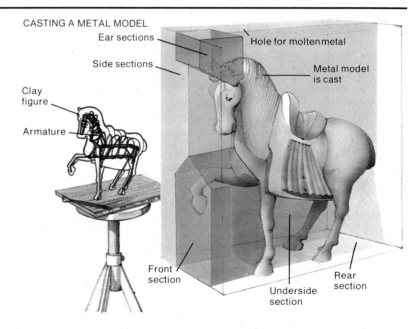

CASTING A METAL MODEL

Ear sections — Side sections — Clay figure — Armature — Front section — Hole for molten metal — Metal model is cast — Underside section — Rear section

▲ HOW ARE STATUES AND MODELS CAST?

First a clay figure is made, then a mould is made by covering the figure in plaster. The figure is removed, and the middle of the plaster mould is almost filled with a core of material. Then molten metal is poured between the mould and the core.

The 'lost-wax' process is often used to cast metal statues. Hot wax is poured into a plaster mould of the clay figure. It sets to form a hollow copy of the figure.

The wax copy is then placed in a casting box and surrounded inside and out with fine sand. The sand fits around the wax impression to form another mould. Then liquid metal is poured through a hole into the mould. It melts the wax, which runs out of the mould, and then sets to produce a hollow metal statue or model.

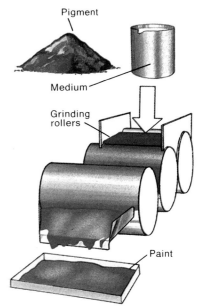

▲ HOW IS A MOSAIC MADE?

A mosaic is a picture or pattern made in a floor or on a wall. Thousands of tiny pieces of coloured materials are fitted together. The design is worked out first, then the pieces are fixed in wet cement.

Mosaics are usually made with pieces of tile. The pieces are cut to the right size first and coloured if necessary. Mosaics can also be made with glass, and small pebbles can be set in attractive patterns.

The design of the pattern or picture is first drawn on paper. Then it is scratched out in a layer of wet cement on the floor or wall. The pieces, which are called tesserae, are then fixed in place. When the cement is dry, the gaps between the tesserae are filled with a cement called grout.

To speed up this process, some mosaics are laid in sections made of tesserae fixed to a soft backing material.

▲ WHAT ARE PAINTS MADE OF?

Paints are made of coloured powders called pigments and a liquid such as oil. The liquid sets hard when it is brushed onto a surface and colours it. Water colours are mixtures of pigments with a little water. The pigment stays on the paper when the water dries out.

Paints are made by grinding the pigments and a liquid medium between rollers. More of the medium and pigment may then be added to give the paint the right thickness and depth of colour.

Oil paints and paints that protect surfaces often contain varnish as the medium. The varnish may come from natural oils or synthetic resins made like plastics.

Other paints contain solvents that evaporate, leaving the pigment in a film of resin. Emulsion paints contain synthetic resins that mix with water. As the paint dries, it leaves the resin behind on the surface.

▼ WHAT IS AN ETCHING?

An etching is a print made from a metal plate. The picture is drawn on a metal plate. Ink is applied to the plate and paper is rolled over it to make a print.

The etching plate is coated with a layer of a special varnish. Then the artist uses an etching tool with a sharp point to draw the picture on the plate. The point scrapes away the varnish, exposing the metal beneath.

Next, the plate is put into a bath of acid. The layer of varnish protects the plate, except where the tool has removed the coating. There it eats away the metal and forms grooves in the plate. On inking the plate, ink is left in the grooves. As the paper is rolled over the plate, it lifts the ink to print the picture.

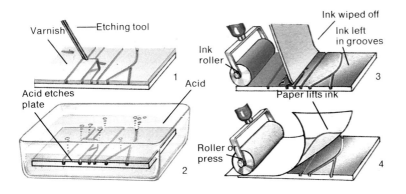

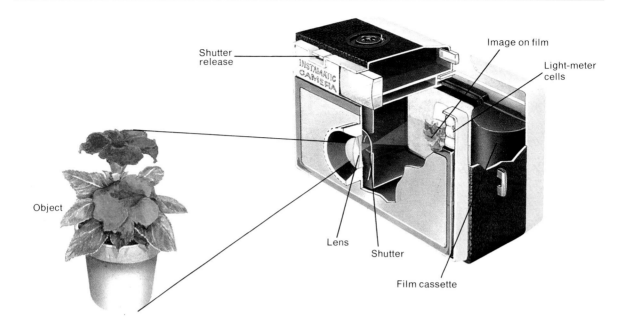

Shutter release

Image on film

Light-meter cells

Object

Lens

Shutter

Film cassette

▲ HOW DOES PHOTOGRAPHY WORK?

When you take a photograph, light enters the camera and makes a picture on the film. The light changes the film so that the picture shows up when the film is developed. This is done by placing the film in chemicals known as developers.

Black-and-white films contain a layer of a compound of silver. Colour films have several layers. Where light strikes the silver compound, it partly changes it to silver. When the film is developed, the parts exposed to light are completely changed to silver. The parts that were not exposed still contain silver compound, which is removed. The silver forms a thin black layer in the film, giving a negative image of the picture. In this, the light parts are dark and the dark parts are light. A print, in which the dark parts are dark and the light parts are light, is then made from the negative.

▲ HOW DOES A CAMERA TAKE PICTURES?

The lens on the front of a camera makes a picture appear on the film inside the camera. By looking into the viewfinder, you can see the picture that the camera will take. You then press the shutter release to take the photo.

The light rays that come from an object in front of the camera are refracted (bent) by the lens to project an image of the object on to the film. The image is upside down and back to front, but the picture is seen the right way when a print or slide is made. When the shutter release is pressed, the shutter opens for a fraction of a second and exposes the film. The exposure is so short that moving objects appear to be still.

The lens may also have an aperture that opens or closes to let more or less light through the lens. The aperture is opened if the scene being photographed is not brightly lit.

▲ HOW DOES A LIGHT METER WORK?

A light meter tells you the brightness of the scene being photographed. Light from the scene goes into the light meter. It is then changed to a small electric current. This works a dial that shows you how to set the camera's shutter speed and aperture to take a good photograph.

A light meter contains light-sensitive cells that convert light rays into electricity. Alternatively, the cells change the strength of an electric current flowing through the cells from a small battery in the camera. Either way, a stronger electric current is produced when more light enters the meter. The current moves a needle so that you can check the brightness of the scene being photographed.

From the position of the needle, you can see how to set the shutter and the aperture in order to make the correct exposure and get a good photograph.

▶ HOW DOES A FLASH WORK?

The bulbs in a flash-cube contain metal wire or foil and a small tube of powder. When the shutter release is pressed, it makes a spring strike the tube and fire the powder. This heats the wire or foil in the bulb, making it burn brightly and produce a flash of light.

A flash-bulb contains oxygen, so that the wire or foil burns with a very bright light. The light is slightly yellow and this is why flash-bulbs for daylight colour film are blue. The blue container changes the colour of the flash to the white colour of sunlight.

Some flash-bulbs are fired by electricity. A switch inside the camera makes the bulb flash at exactly the same moment as the shutter opens. It does this by connecting a battery to the flash-bulb.

Unlike a flash-bulb, an electronic flash can be used again and again. The flash contains a tube that gives out a bright flash of white light when a strong electric charge passes through it.

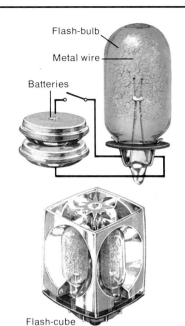

Flash-bulb

Metal wire

Batteries

Flash-cube

▼ HOW ARE COLOUR SLIDES MADE?

A colour film has three layers that take yellow, red and blue pictures of a scene. A colour slide or print contains three layers that are yellow, red and blue. When you look at a colour print or slide, these three colours combine in various ways to give a full-colour picture.

A colour film is made of three layers of light-sensitive emulsion containing silver compounds. The three layers are sensitive to different colours in the light. The film also contains a transparent yellow band which helps to separate the colours in the light. When a colour film is developed to make a colour slide, as shown here, the silver produced in the exposed parts of the three layers is replaced by yellow, red and blue dyes, and the yellow band is removed. When the slide is viewed, white light passes through it to the eyes. The yellow, red and blue images combine to give a full-colour picture. For example, the yellow and blue layers combine to give green. Black is given by all three layers, and white is seen if all the layers are clear. A colour print also contains three layers of yellow, red and blue, like a colour slide.

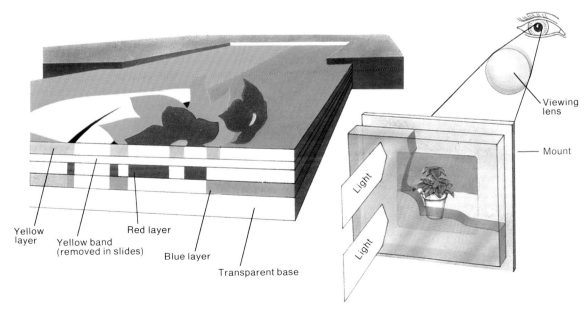

Yellow layer

Yellow band (removed in slides)

Red layer

Blue layer

Transparent base

Light

Light

Viewing lens

Mount

▼ HOW DOES A FILM PROJECTOR WORK?

A film is a long strip of still pictures. As it passes through the projector, each picture is lit up and a lens projects an image of the picture on the screen. The pictures are projected so quickly that they appear to be moving.

A cinema film is projected at a rate of 24 frames (still pictures) per second. Home projectors are slower. The film has a row of sprocket holes along one or both edges. Sprockets in the projector pull the film into the film gate. The film then stops for a moment and light from a lamp passes through the frame. The lens projects the picture on the screen. The sprockets then turn and advance the film to show the next frame. As the film moves, the blade of a rotating shutter passes between the lamp and the film so that the movement of the film does not show on the screen.

In sound films, light from the lamp passes through the sound track and strikes a light-sensitive cell, which produces an electric signal. The signal varies in strength as the sound track passes. It goes to an amplifier and loud-speaker, which gives the sound.

In some sound films, the sound is recorded on a magnetic strip along the film like a tape recording.

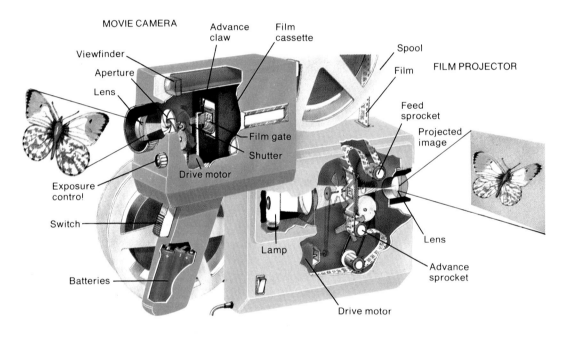

▲ HOW DOES A MOVIE CAMERA WORK?

A movie camera has a film like an ordinary camera. But instead of taking just one picture at a time, it takes many pictures every second. As the film moves past the lens in the camera, a shutter continually opens and closes to give a long line of pictures on the film. Then the film is developed and shown on a screen.

Many movie cameras take a cassette of film. The cassette contains a long strip of film that lasts several minutes. It has an opening through which the film passes into the film gate. A claw mechanism pulls on the sprocket holes in the film to advance it frame by frame. The film stops in the film gate as the claw moves back, and the shutter opens briefly to expose the film. The aperture of the lens may be set by an automatic exposure control. The shutter then closes as the claw advances the film.

In many movie cameras, the shutter consists of a rotating half disc. To make slow motion films, the speed of the film is increased so that more frames are exposed every second. However, the projector always runs at the same speed. The film takes longer to pass through the projector than the camera, which slows down the action. Slowing the camera speed down speeds up the action.

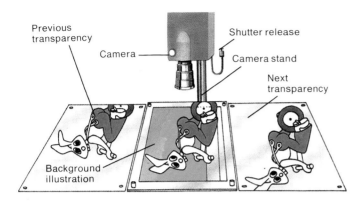

Previous transparency
Camera
Shutter release
Camera stand
Next transparency
Background illustration

In a cartoon film, drawings seem to move. In fact you are seeing 24 different drawings every second, which gives the illusion of movement. Each of the drawings is photographed separately with a special movie camera.

Each frame of the cartoon is photographed on an animation stand. The drawing is placed on a table and the camera is mounted on a frame above. So that artists need not paint the whole of every frame, parts of the picture are painted on separate transparent sheets. Then these are placed on top of a background illustration to build up each frame.

Cartoon makers also use computers to produce the drawings. The artist draws on an electronic board with a special pen. The computer then fills in the colour.

Sound waves make a microphone produce an electric signal. This signal goes to an amplifier and loudspeaker.

Inside the microphone, the sound waves strike a thin plate called a diaphragm. The diaphragm vibrates at the same rate as the sound waves. It is connected to a device that produces an electric signal varying in strength at the same rate as the vibrations.

In a crystal microphone, a piezoelectric crystal generates the signal by responding to pressure placed on it by the diaphragm. Moving-coil microphones contain small coils of wire suspended between the poles of a magnet. The diaphragm vibrates the coils to give a signal.

Ribbon microphones are similar but have a metal ribbon instead of coils. Condenser and carbon microphones are fed with an electric current, and vibration of a condenser or carbon granules varies the current to create a signal.

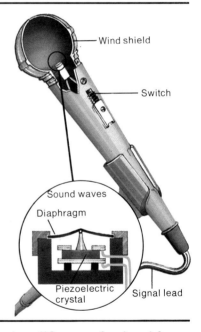

Wind shield
Switch
Sound waves
Diaphragm
Piezoelectric crystal
Signal lead

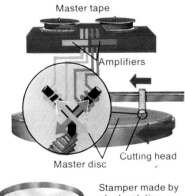

Master tape
Amplifiers
Master disc
Cutting head
Stamper made by electroplating master disc
Master disc

Most records are first recorded on tape in a recording studio and a master disc is made from the tape. Moulds called stampers are then made from the master disc. The records are produced by pressing a piece of plastic between the stampers.

The master tape made in the studio has two sound tracks.

Amplifiers send a signal from each track to the cutting head of a disc cutter. The head cuts a groove in the lacquer coating of a master disc by using the two signals to form the walls of the groove. A stamper is then made by electroplating the master disc and peeling away the layer of metal formed. This has ridges where the record has grooves.

To manufacture the final record, a piece of plastic is pressed between two stampers.

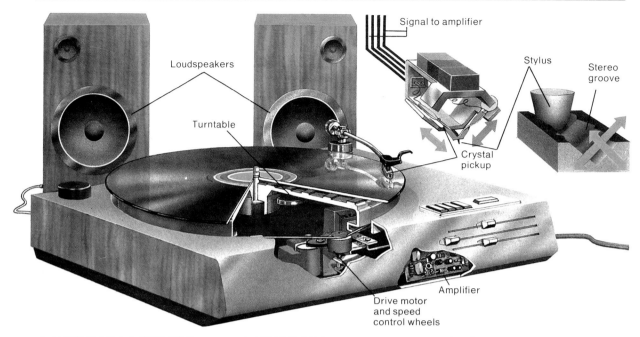

Signal to amplifier

Loudspeakers

Stylus

Stereo groove

Turntable

Crystal pickup

Amplifier

Drive motor and speed control wheels

▲ HOW DOES A RECORD PLAYER WORK?

When you play a record, you place the needle on the pickup of the record player in the groove of the record. As the record turns, the tiny curves in the groove make the needle vibrate. This causes the pickup to produce an electric signal. The signal goes to an amplifier and a loudspeaker to give the music.

There are two kinds of pickups for record players. Crystal pickups contain a piezoelectric crystal. The crystal is connected to the needle, or stylus. As the stylus vibrates in the groove, it continually twists the crystal, making it produce an electric signal.

Magnetic pickups contain tiny coils of wire that vibrate between the poles of magnets and generate a signal. Some record players contain an amplifier and a loudspeaker. With others, these have to be connected to the record player.

▲ HOW DOES A LOUDSPEAKER PRODUCE SOUNDS?

A loudspeaker makes the sounds that come from record and cassette players, radio and television sets. Inside the loudspeaker is a cone of a material such as plastic. It is connected to a coil or wire and a magnet. When an electric signal is fed to the loudspeaker, the magnet makes the coil move. The cone vibrates and the sound comes out.

When the electric signal is fed to the coil, it produces a varying magnetic field. A magnet placed around it attracts and repels the coil, which in turn vibrates the loudspeaker cone. The cone and its coil and magnet are known as a drive unit. Many loudspeakers have several drive units. Large units produce deep sounds and small units give high sounds.

In an electrostatic loudspeaker a plate is made to vibrate by electrostatic forces and not by magnetic fields.

▲ HOW DOES STEREO WORK?

When you hear a stereo record or cassette, the sound comes from two loudspeakers. The sounds appear to be spread out between them. This is because the music is recorded on the tape or record in two parts called tracks. One goes to the left-hand speaker and the other to the right-hand speaker.

When the master tape is made in the studio, the sound is recorded in two tracks along the tape. One is a left-hand track and the other a right-hand track. The sounds are divided between the two tracks. An instrument that is only on the left-hand track comes from the left-hand speaker, while a singer recorded on both tracks comes from both speakers.

On a record, the two tracks are recorded in the two walls of the groove. The pickup has two crystals or coils that produce two signals which go to the loudspeakers.

▼ HOW DOES A TAPE
RECORDER WORK?

A tape recorder works by changing sound waves into magnetism. The sound is recorded as a magnetic pattern along the recording tape. When the tape is played, the magnetic pattern is turned back into sound.

A microphone is usually connected to the tape recorder, although many cassette recorders contain their own microphone. It turns the sound into an electric signal, which is amplified by the recorder's amplifier and then fed to the record head. The head is a coil of wire wound around an iron ring with a gap in it. The signal causes the head to produce a varying magnetic field. As the tape passes the head, it is magnetized by it. To play the tape, it is moved over the head again and the passing magnetic field makes the coil give out an electric signal. The signal then goes to an amplifier and loudspeaker connected to the head.

In many recorders, the same head is used to record and to play tapes. High-quality machines have separate heads for record and playback. When a tape is being recorded, another head erases any recording that is already on the tape. It produces a magnetic field that removes any magnetism from the tape.

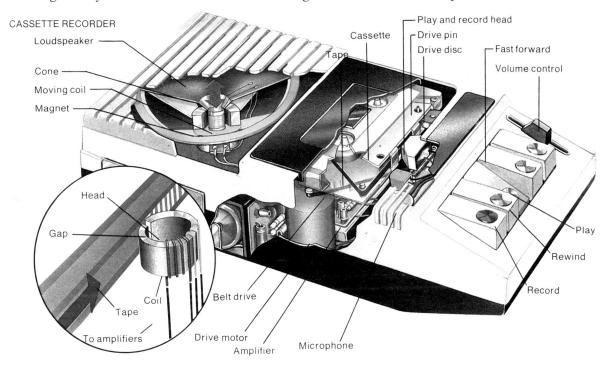

CASSETTE RECORDER

Loudspeaker — Cone — Moving coil — Magnet — Head — Gap — Coil — Tape — To amplifiers — Belt drive — Drive motor — Amplifier — Microphone — Tape — Cassette — Play and record head — Drive pin — Drive disc — Fast forward — Volume control — Play — Rewind — Record

▲ HOW ARE CASSETTES
MADE?

Like a record, music cassettes are produced from a master tape made in a recording studio. It is played back very fast and the speeded-up sounds are recorded on tape also travelling at a high speed. This tape is then used to make cassettes.

Recording tape at high speed enables copies of tapes to be made very quickly. Both the copy of the master tape and the tape used to make the cassettes are speeded up by the same amount. Then when the cassette tape is played at its normal speed, the original music will be heard.

A cassette has two sides. The music of one side is recorded along the top of the tape, and the other side is recorded along the bottom. The head of the cassette player lines up with the top of the tape. To hear the other side, the cassette is turned over.

Both sides of the cassette are recorded at once. The copy of the master tape used to make cassettes has both sides recorded on it: one playing forwards and one playing backwards. When the cassette is turned over to play the other side, the music comes out forwards.

As a cassette is put into a player, the centres of the reels fit over spindles that turn the reels.

You can talk on the radio by using the citizen's band radio. You have a small radio set that is both a transmitter and a receiver. As you speak, the set sends out radio waves over a few kilometres. Anyone receiving your transmission can listen and then reply. You then receive the radio waves that they transmit.

To prevent radio stations from interfering with each other, each one is allocated a different frequency for transmission. The frequencies are grouped in bands, each of which has a different kind of use.

In many countries, the citizen's band is allocated for private use. The sets operate on several channels within the band, and the signals are weak so that they do not carry very far. In this way, many people can use the citizen's band without interfering with one another. Citizen's band radio is popular with car and lorry drivers.

The radio waves that carry television pictures move in a straight line from the transmitter to the aerial. They can go only as far as the distance from the transmitter to the horizon. Waves carrying radio broadcasts can move over the horizon. Some radio transmissions can travel around the world.

Low-frequency (long-wave) radio waves can travel over the horizon and pass around mountains. Depending on their power, these signals can cross continents and oceans.

High-frequency (short-wave) signals do not bend in this way. They travel in straight lines, but are reflected back to Earth from the upper atmosphere. In this way, they can bounce around the world. Television signals, which are very high frequency signals, are sent to communications satellites in orbit. They cut through the atmosphere, and the satellite transmits them back to the Earth below.

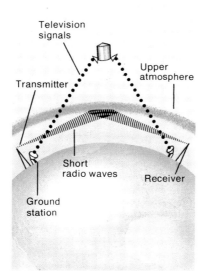

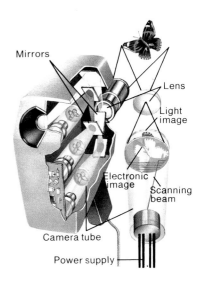

A television camera produces an image on a light-sensitive tube. This tube turns the light in the image into an electric signal. When the signal goes to a television set, the picture appears on the screen.

The lens of a television camera projects an image of the scene before it into the camera tube. In colour television cameras, there are three tubes that respond to the red, blue and green light in the image.

Coloured mirrors or prisms split the image into three colours. Each image falls on a light-sensitive plate, producing a pattern of electrons that form an electronic image on a target behind the plate. A beam of electrons scans the target in a sequence of lines. The intensity of the electron image makes the beam vary in strength. It produces a vision signal that varies according to the brightness of each part of the image that is scanned.

▼ HOW DOES RADIO WORK?

When you switch on a radio, it picks up invisible radio waves. The waves come through the air from a transmitter. At the radio station, music or speech is changed into an electric signal. This signal goes to the transmitter and is changed into radio waves. The aerial of your radio picks up the radio waves. The radio changes the waves back into sound.

The transmitter of a radio station sends out a carrier wave at a particular frequency. The frequency is measured in hertz (Hz). The carrier wave is produced by sending an electric signal that alternates at this frequency to the transmitter. The frequency is so rapid that it causes electrons in the metal atoms of the transmitter to vibrate and give out radio waves at the frequency.

However, the carrier signal is first combined with a sound signal from the microphones at the radio station's studio. This causes the carrier wave to vary in such a way that it carries the sound as variations in its strength or frequency. The carrier wave strikes the radio aerial and loosens the electrons in its atoms to produce a weak electric signal at the same frequency.

The tuner in the radio detects this frequency, and removes the carrier signal to give the sound signal.

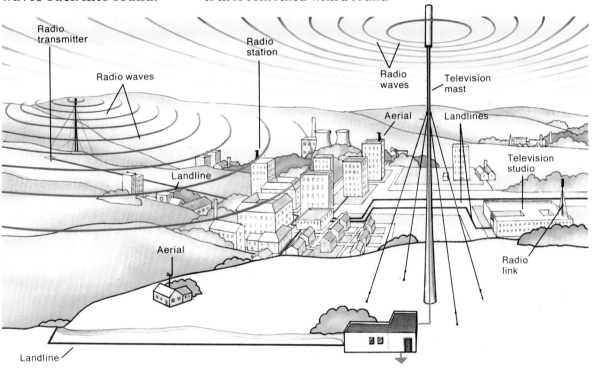

▲ HOW DO TELEVISION PICTURES GET TO HOMES?

At the television studio, the cameras produce electric signals. These picture signals then go to the television transmitter near your home. The transmitter turns the signals into radio waves that spread out through the air. The aerial on your set picks up the waves, and the television set turns them back into pictures.

The signals from the studio usually travel along cables called landlines to the transmitter. Radio links may also be used to send the signals to distant transmitters.

Large television masts serve big cities. However, the radio waves that carry the picture signals do not travel very far. Country areas are therefore served by local repeater transmitters. Each home usually has its own aerial on or inside the roof, or on the set.

The pictures and the sound of a television transmission are carried by a carrier wave in the same way as radio. Television programmes can even be transmitted from satellites in space to homes. Large dish-shaped aerials are needed to pick up the transmissions. Television also reaches many homes by cable. In this case, the sound and picture signals are not transmitted by radio, but are sent through a cable directly to homes.

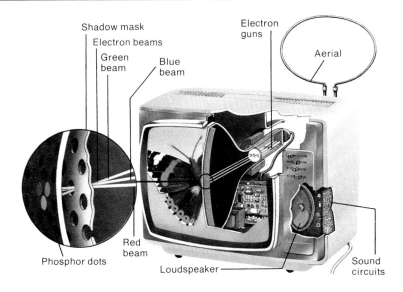

Shadow mask
Electron beams
Green beam
Blue beam
Electron guns
Aerial
Phosphor dots
Red beam
Loudspeaker
Sound circuits

◄ HOW DOES COLOUR
TELEVISION WORK?

If you look closely at a colour television picture, you will see that it is made up of tiny red, green and blue dots or stripes. These three colours mix together when you look at the screen from a distance to give a full-colour picture.

A colour camera produces three vision signals corresponding to the red, green and blue light in the scene. A colour set receives these three signals and sends them to three electron guns. Three electron beams scan the screen, one for each colour.

The whole screen is made up of a mosaic of dots or stripes of phosphor that glow red, green and blue when struck by the electron beams. To make sure that each beam produces the right colour, the beams pass through holes in a shadow mask behind the screen. The angles of the beams and the holes are arranged so that each beam can only pass through to strike phosphors of the correct colour.

▲ HOW DOES A TELEVISION SET WORK?

The television aerial picks up a signal from the transmitter. The signal goes to the tube in the set. Inside the tube, a beam of electrons (tiny electric particles) is fired in lines across the screen. The screen lights up in lines that make up a picture.

The signal received by the aerial is a copy of the vision signal produced by the camera. This signal goes to the controls of an electron gun that fires a beam of electrons at the screen. Where the beam strikes the back of the screen, it produces a dot of light.

The beam scans the screen in the same sequence of lines as in the camera, and builds up a picture on the screen. A new picture is produced 25 or 30 times a second, so that the image appears to move. The sound is produced in the same way as in a radio set.

► HOW DOES A VIDEO RECORDER WORK?

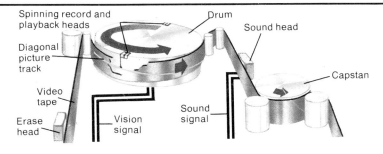

Spinning record and playback heads
Diagonal picture track
Video tape
Erase head
Vision signal
Drum
Sound head
Capstan
Sound signal

You can record a television programme on a video cassette using a video recorder. The video cassette contains tape like a tape cassette. It records the electric signal coming from the television aerial.

A video recorder records vision or video signals as magnetic patterns in a track along the tape. It has record and replay heads similar to those in sound tape recorders,

but the tape has to move much faster over the head than with sound recording.

In fact, the tape does not move quickly; instead, the head does. There are two heads mounted in a rotating drum, around which the tape

moves. The heads spin rapidly as the drum passes along the tape, recording the vision signal in a series of diagonal tracks across the tape. The sound is recorded in a straight track along one edge of the tape.

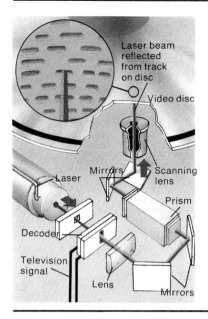

A video disc is like a gramophone record except that it has pictures recorded on it as well as sound. To see the film on the disc, you play it on a video disc player connected to a television set.

You cannot make your own video recordings on a video disc player. You can only play what is recorded on the disc.

There are several different video disc systems. One has a spiral groove in the record and a pickup with a stylus that rests in the groove. The picture signal is recorded as a sequence of electric charges that is detected by an electrode in the stylus.

A similar system does away with the groove by guiding an electrode over a spiral track of pits stamped in the surface of the disc.

A third system, shown here, uses a laser beam to scan a spiral track. As the record spins, the reflected beam varies in intensity and goes to a decoder that produces the vision signal.

An aqualung is used by a diver to swim freely underwater. The diver carries a cylinder of compressed air on his or her back. Air from the cylinder goes to a mouthpiece. This allows the diver to breathe air in from the cylinder.

For the diver to be able to breathe easily, the pressure of the air must be equal to the pressure of the water around the diver. A flexible diaphragm moves in and out to regulate the air pressure as the diver breathes.

On breathing in, the air pressure in the mouthpiece falls slightly and water pressure forces the diaphragm inwards. The diaphragm operates a lever to open the inlet valve on the air hose connected to the cylinder and air flows to the diver.

On breathing out, the air pressure moves the diaphragm back, cutting off the air supply. Valves open to let this air escape.

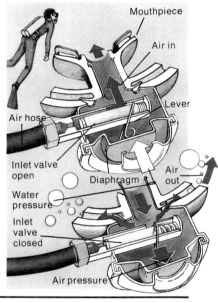

When a parachute opens, it billows out above the parachutist. The large canopy of the parachute pulls against the air and slows the fall. The parachutist can pull on lines attached to the canopy to try and land in a particular place.

The parachute is packed carefully with a pilot chute that pulls out the main canopy. The canopy may have gaps that allow the air through in a controlled flow. The air resistance of the canopy cancels out the weight of the parachutist. The parachutist then falls at a constant speed and strikes the ground at about four metres per second. This is the same as jumping off a wall just over one metre high. As the parachutist lands, he or she pulls a quick-release catch. Some parachutes are shaped like squares and have lines of cells that blow out to form a simple wing. The parachutist has more control with this type.

▶ HOW DO MAGNETS WORK?

Inside a magnet are lots of very tiny magnets. These are not separate objects, but very small parts of the magnet that each act like a tiny magnet. In a magnet, these tiny magnetic parts line up in rows.

The magnetic parts are called domains. An unmagnetized material contains domains, but their magnetism points in different directions, so that the magnetism of each domain is cancelled out by other domains, so the material has no overall magnetism.

But when a strong magnetic field is used to magnetize the material, it lines up the magnetism of each domain so that its magnetic effect acts in the same direction.

When a magnet is cut or broken, each piece is still magnetic because its domains are still lined up. The magnetism of the domains is caused by the electrons in the atoms of the material. They produce a magnetic effect as they spin around the nucleus (centre) of each atom.

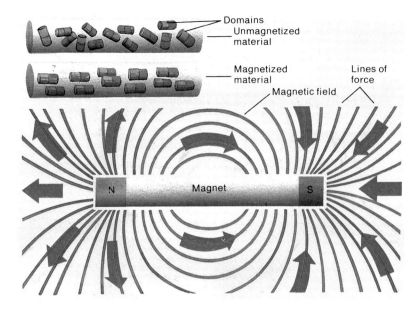

Domains
Unmagnetized material

Magnetized material

Lines of force

Magnetic field

N   Magnet   S

▲ WHAT IS A MAGNETIC FIELD?

Every magnet has a magnetic field. This is the invisible force that makes the magnet pick up steel pins and other objects. It also makes magnets pull or push on each other.

Every magnet has a north pole (N) and a south pole (S). You can find which pole is which by suspending a magnet from a string. It turns until the north pole faces north and the south pole faces south.

Invisible lines of magnetic force curve out between the two poles. These lines make up the magnetic field of the magnet. When two magnets approach, their magnetic fields act on each other. The magnets attract one another only if a north pole meets a south pole. If the two poles are the same, the magnets repel one another.

The Earth has a magnetic field that extends from the poles all over the globe. It causes a magnetic compass to turn and point towards the poles.

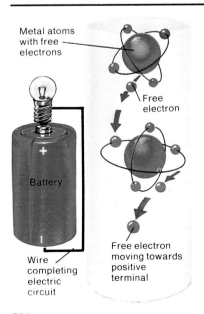

Metal atoms with free electrons

Free electron

Battery

Free electron moving towards positive terminal

Wire completing electric circuit

◀ HOW DOES ELECTRICITY FLOW ALONG A WIRE?

When electricity flows in a wire, tiny particles called electrons move through the wire. Each electron has a very small electric charge. As the electrons arrive, they produce electricity. To make a bulb in a room light up, about two million million million electrons flow every second.

The electrons come from a source of electricity like batteries or the generators in power stations. Each electron has a negative electric charge. The electrons leave the negative terminal and flow through the wire to the positive terminal to complete an electric circuit.

Electricity only flows through metals like copper and steel. This is because the electrons in the outer part of the atoms of these metals are free to move. These free electrons drift from one metal atom to the next. This makes an electric charge flow rapidly along the wire.

HOW DOES A CAR
BATTERY WORK?

A car battery does not run out of electricity, since it can be recharged. The battery contains plates bathed in acid. The acid changes the material in the plates and makes them produce electricity. Feeding electricity back into the battery changes the plates back to the first material.

The plates of a car battery are arranged in pairs. One plate in each pair is made of spongy lead and the other is lead oxide. The pairs are suspended in dilute sulphuric acid. Separator plates keep them apart, and dividers group the plates into cells within the battery.

Each cell gives 2 volts. The

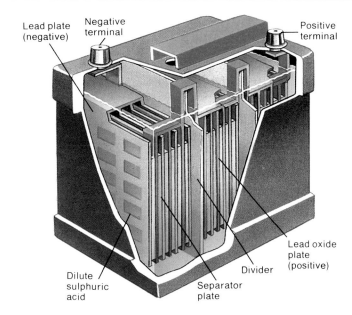

Lead plate (negative) · Negative terminal · Positive terminal · Lead oxide plate (positive) · Divider · Separator plate · Dilute sulphuric acid

lead plates of one cell are connected to the lead oxide plates of the next, and so on. This gives a total output of 12 volts if there are 6 cells. To produce current, the sulphuric acid attacks the plates. It changes both the

lead and the lead oxide into electrons are produced at the lead plate and flow to the lead oxide plate, creating an electric current.

HOW DOES AN ELECTRIC
MOTOR WORK?

When you switch on an electric motor, it makes something rotate. This could be the wheels of a toy train, for example. The electric current makes a wire coil inside the motor become magnetic. A magnet then makes the coil turn, and this powers a shaft.

The electric current flows from a battery through a coil suspended between the poles of a magnet. The coil produces a magnetic field whose poles move towards the poles of the magnet. The north pole of the coil is attracted towards the magnet's south pole. The south pole of the coil's field similarly moves towards the magnet's north pole. As a result, the coil rotates.

As its poles pass the magnet's poles, the electric current suddenly reverses and flows in the opposite direction. The commutator causes this to happen. As the current reverses, so does the coil's magnetic field. The south pole becomes a north pole and vice-versa, so that the coil is now repelled by the poles of the magnet to which it was previously attracted.

In this way, the coil keeps moving. The commutator reverses the current flow every half turn.

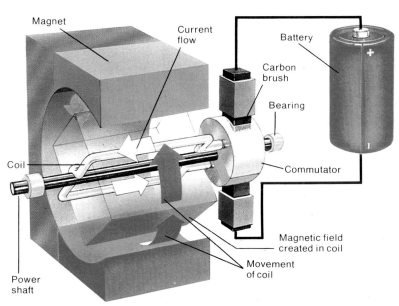

Magnet · Current flow · Battery · Carbon brush · Bearing · Commutator · Magnetic field created in coil · Movement of coil · Coil · Power shaft

**A transformer changes
the voltage of an electric
current. Inside the transformer, the current enters
a coil and the coil
produces a magnetic field.
The field makes another
current flow in another
coil in the transformer.**

A transformer increases or
decreases the voltage of an
alternating current. This kind
of current reverses its
direction of flow many times a
second.

Transformers are used to
produce electricity at very
high voltage for long distance
transmission. This voltage is
then lowered in more transformers before reaching
homes.

The current enters the

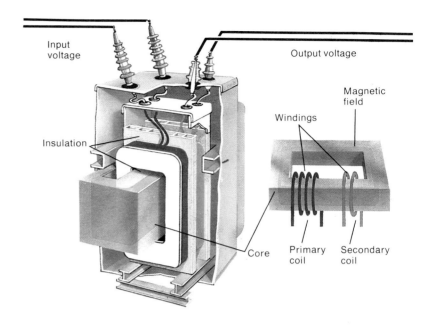

primary coil of the
transformer, which generates
a magnetic field in an iron
core inside the coil. The field
continually reverses as the
current does so. It cuts

through a secondary coil
around the core, producing
another alternating current in
the coil.

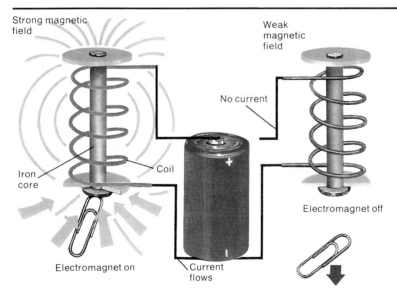

**An electromagnet is a kind
of magnet worked by elec-
tricity. Its magnetism can
be switched on and off. It
contains a coil of wire
wound around an iron bar.
When an electric current**

**flows through the coil, the
bar becomes strongly
magnetic.**

The iron core inside the coil
of an electromagnet produces
a much stronger magnetic
field than the coil alone. This
is because the coil magnetizes
the iron the instant that the

current is switched on.
However, the iron core does
not keep this magnetism when
the electromagnet is switched
off. It is demagnetized
immediately.

Large electromagnets on
cranes are used to raise and
transport loads of scrap iron.
The electromagnet picks up
the iron when it is switched
on, and the crane moves it to
the required place. Then the
current is switched off and the
scrap iron falls to the ground.

Electromagnets are used to
produce strong magnetic
fields in many electrical
machines, including electric
motors and generators. They
can also produce varying
magnetic fields, depending on
the strength of the current fed
to them. Electromagnets are
therefore used in making
electrical meters to measure
things, and in tape recorders
and loudspeakers.

**Electrical machines like
radio and television sets
contain transistors. The
transistors increase small
electric currents. They can
also switch the currents on
or off.**

A transistor is made up of
three layers of a material
called a semiconductor. The
thin central layer is called the
base, and the two thick outer
layers are the emitter and the
collector.

A current flows from the
emitter to the collector, but is
stopped by the base. A low
electric signal is fed to the
base to alter its electrical
nature. If this signal
increases, the base lets
through more current. If it
decreases, the base restricts
the flow of current.

The flow of current
through the transistor therefore varies in the same way as
the base signal fed to the transistor. As the current is
greater than the signal, the
transistor amplifies the signal.
If the base signal is zero, no
current flows through

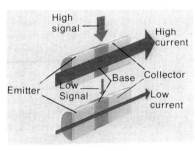

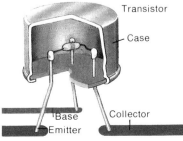

**Inside an electronic
machine, such as a
calculator, are microchips
containing many
thousands of parts like
transistors. Because there
are so many parts, they
have to be small. The
electrons that make up the
current are very tiny, so
the parts can be made very
small too.**

A tiny microchip may contain
hundreds of thousands of
transistors and other
electronic components. This
great number is necessary
because the microchip has to
carry out very many
electronic operations very
quickly to do calculations. If
the parts are small and close
together, the electric currents
can flow between the various
components very rapidly.

As all the components can
be made of silicon, they are
manufactured as small as
possible inside a single chip of
silicon – the microchip.

**Microchips are made
from very thin slices of a
material called silicon.
The tiny electronic parts
inside the microchip are
formed on the surface of a
slice. Several layers of
silicon are added in tiny
but very complicated
patterns.**

Each layer of components is
formed on the surface of the
silicon by etching. A pattern
outlining the shapes of the
components is reduced by a
photographic method and
projected on the surface. It
produces a mask with holes in
the shape of the pattern.

The silicon is then treated
with materials that penetrate
the holes in the mask and alter
the electrical nature of the
silicon beneath. In this way,
the surface is covered with a
layer of tiny regions having
different electrical properties.

This process is repeated
several times, forming the
components of the chip and
their connections.

▶ HOW DOES A DIGITAL WATCH WORK?

A digital watch shows the time in numbers. At the heart of the watch is a quartz crystal which vibrates an exact number of times every second. Every time it vibrates, it produces an electric signal. The other parts of the watch count the signals and change the numbers in the display to show the right time.

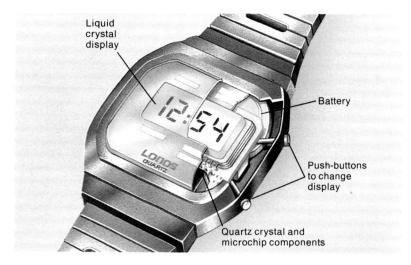

Liquid crystal display

Battery

Push-buttons to change display

Quartz crystal and microchip components

The quartz crystal gives out an electric signal when it is stretched or compressed. An electric current is fed from the batteries in the watch to make the crystal vibrate at an exact frequency.

The quartz crystal gives out an electric signal at this frequency, and it goes to the microchip components in the watch. These count the signals produced by the quartz crystal, and every second send another signal to

the digital display to change the time that is shown.

The microchip can also count up the seconds to display minutes and hours and to show the date, even working out the change from one month to the next.

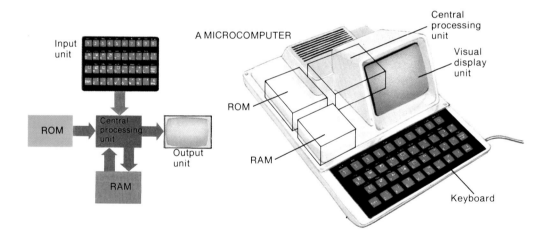

Input unit

A MICROCOMPUTER

Central processing unit

Visual display unit

ROM

ROM

Central processing unit

Output unit

RAM

RAM

Keyboard

▲ HOW DOES A COMPUTER OPERATE?

To make a computer work, you have to give it a program. This tells the computer what to do to perform a particular task, like adding up. Then you give it information (data) such as numbers that it needs to start, and the computer works out the answer.

Every computer, no matter how large or small, contains four basic units. These are the input, memory, central processing and output units.

The input unit is often a keyboard. It is used to feed a new program of instructions into the computer, and also data or information such as numbers. Both the program and data are held in a part of the memory unit called the RAM. They may also be fed

to the RAM from a magnetic tape or disc that stores programs and data.

Another part of the memory unit called the ROM contains instructions that operate the central processing unit. This unit then follows the program and works out results from the data.

Finally, the central processor sends the results to the output unit, which may be a screen or printer.

Binary   Decimal

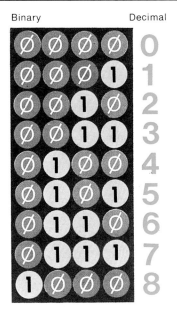

**Computers work by using
only two numbers – 0 and
1. A computer changes
numbers and words into
codes made up of 0s and
1s. It makes calculations
with these codes.**

The codes of 0s and 1s used
by computers are known as
binary numbers. All the
program instructions and the
data are fed into computers in
the form of decimal numbers,
letters, symbols and signs.
Each of these has a particular
binary number that is
produced by the input unit.
They consist not of figures,
but of electric pulses.

When a pulse arrives at any
point in the computer, it
represents a 1. If no pulse
arrives, there is a 0. The codes
are stored in the computer's
memory as on-off sequences
of electric charge or
magnetism.

The central processor
calculates by combining the
pulse sequences in various
ways, producing a binary
number that is decoded to
give the result.

**The most powerful super-
computers can do about
100 million calculations
every second! However,
each one is a simple piece
of arithmetic, like adding
two numbers together.
The computer splits up a
difficult problem into
many of these simple
pieces of arithmetic.**

One of the most difficult
problems is forecasting the
weather. To work out how the
atmosphere is going to behave
tomorrow takes many
millions of calculations. Only
a supercomputer can do this
before the weather actually
happens.

A computer can work this
fast because it breaks all its
calculations down into codes
of electric signals. The
electric pulses that make up
the codes move through the
tiny circuits in the computer's
microchips in extremely short
times. The computer's central
processor arranges the pulses
to form new codes and carry
out the calculations millions
of times a second.

**Some computers can
speak to people. They have
a voice unit that can
produce a certain number
of words. Each word has
its own electric code. A
microchip in the
computer produces the
codes which go to the voice
unit.**

The voice unit of a computer
contains a voice synthesizer.
To get the words into the
synthesizer, a person speaks
the words into a machine that
converts the sounds into
digital signals. These are
sequences of electric pulses
like the binary codes that
make computers work. The
signals are then stored in the
synthesizer's memory unit.

When the computer speaks,
it takes the codes of the words
required from the memory. It
then changes the codes into
electric signals that go to an
amplifier and loudspeaker to
produce the words.

Speaking computers are
used to give information to
people. They can also read
books to blind people.

**Nuclear power stations
contain nuclear reactors
which use uranium fuel.
The uranium gets very hot
and a coolant (a liquid or
gas) moves through the
reactor to be heated. Then
the hot coolant goes to a
boiler to make steam,
which powers electricity
generators.**

Inside the fuel rods in the
reactor core, uranium nuclei
split as neutron particles
strike them. The smaller
nuclei and other particles
produced move off at great
speed, producing heat. To
prevent this chain reaction
speeding up so that all the
uranium atoms split too
quickly, control rods are
lowered into the reactor.
They soak up neutrons so that
the rate of splitting slows. If
the reactor begins to overheat,
the control rods automatically
drop into the reactor to stop it
working.

The coolant is usually
water or carbon dioxide gas.
It passes through a heat
exchanger in the boiler,
making water flowing around
the heat exchanger boil. In
some nuclear reactors, the
reactor boils water to steam
directly in the core. The
steam is then piped to steam
turbines, which in turn drive
electricity generators. The
steam is condensed back into
water, which returns to the
boiler or reactor.

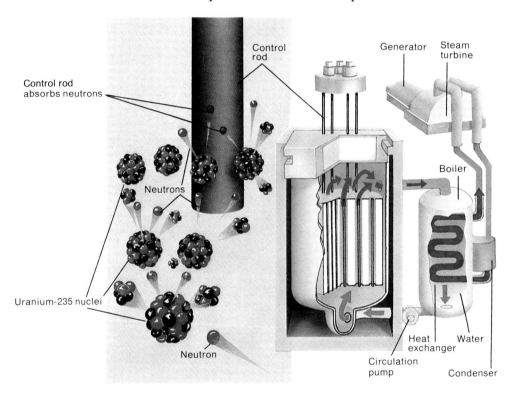

**▲ WHY IS NUCLEAR
ENERGY SO POWERFUL?**

**Nuclear energy is
produced by the tiny
particles in the nuclei
(centres) of atoms. These
particles are held together
by very strong forces.
Breaking the nuclei
releases these forces,
giving great power.**

In a reactor, a nuclear
reaction is controlled to give
useful energy. The nuclear
fuel is a rare form of uranium
metal called uranium-235.

When the nucleus of a
uranium-235 atom is struck
by a neutron, it breaks into
two smaller nuclei and several
more neutrons. These
neutrons may then strike
other uranium nuclei, causing
them to split and give out yet
more neutrons. In this way,
more and more uranium
nuclei split.

The reactor's control rods
absorb most of the extra
neutrons produced to keep
the nuclear reaction going at a
steady rate. As the nuclei split
apart, the very strong forces
holding the nuclear particles
together are released. They
make the neutrons and
smaller nuclei move at
immense speed, producing
great heat. In this way, some
of the mass of the uranium is
turned into energy.
Conversion of a little mass
produces a lot of energy.

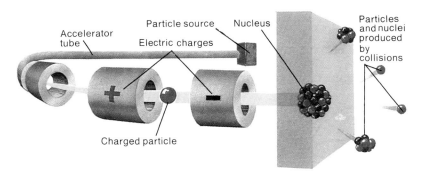

Accelerator tube — Particle source — Electric charges — Charged particle — Nucleus — Particles and nuclei produced by collisions

▲ HOW CAN ATOMS BE SPLIT?

Everything is made of tiny particles called atoms which cannot be broken apart. If they could, everything would fall apart.

However, scientists can split atoms to find out about the particles inside them.

Scientists split atoms in large machines called particle accelerators. These machines use powerful electric charges to send a beam of particles along a tube. These are particles like protons that have an electric charge. The charges on the tube push or pull the particles, accelerating them to a very high speed.

The beam is then directed to a target. The particles collide with atoms in the target and split the nucleus in some of the atoms. The nucleus breaks into more particles and smaller nuclei, which move into a detector. The detector identifies the particles coming from the broken nucleus.

▶ HOW DO WE KNOW HOW OLD FOSSILS ARE?

Fossils are the remains of prehistoric animals and plants. They are thousands or millions of years old. A fossil, or the rock in which it is found, is very slightly radioactive. Scientists can tell how old fossils are by measuring this radioactivity.

Over a certain time, the radioactivity of a material decreases steadily to zero. It may take thousands or millions of years for a material to lose its radioactivity.

Plants and animals contain very small amounts of radioactive elements. Their radioactivity begins to decrease as soon as they die. Measuring this radioactivity therefore gives their age.

Radioactive minerals in rocks begin to lose their radioactivity as soon as they are formed. Because rocks form around plant and animal remains, finding the age of the rock is another method of discovering the age of the fossils in it.

◀ WHAT MAKES SOME MATERIALS RADIOACTIVE?

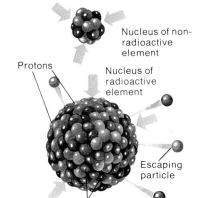

Nucleus of non-radioactive element — Protons — Nucleus of radioactive element — Escaping particle — Neutrons

Some materials give out invisible rays called radioactivity. Some of the rays are like X-rays. Others are streams of tiny particles. They come from atoms in the material that break apart.

At the centre of every atom is a nucleus. It is made up of very small particles called protons and neutrons packed tightly together. If the material contains elements that have many protons and neutrons in the nucleus, it may be radioactive.

The particles do not like being packed together in large numbers, so some may leave the nucleus, making the element radioactive.

Two kinds of particles may be produced. Alpha particles are each made up of two protons and two neutrons. Beta particles are electrons produced by the break-up of neutrons.

A laser produces a very thin but very powerful beam of coloured light. Inside the laser is a material like a crystal. It is fed with light or other kinds of energy, which it releases as very bright light.

The material that produces the light from a laser is called an active material. The first lasers had a ruby crystal. Now special glass rods and tubes of dyes and gases are also used.

The active material receives energy from a pumping source. The energy that it pumps in may be electricity or light. This energy is absorbed by the atoms, which are raised to a high-energy state. Then all the atoms lose this extra energy at the same moment by producing light of exactly the same colour.

The material has a mirror at one end so that the light emerges in a thin beam from the other end. Some lasers produce invisible infra-red rays instead of light.

Light moves at a speed of nearly 300,000 kilometres per second. It takes light just over a second to reach us from the Moon and eight minutes to travel to the Earth from the Sun. It takes years for light to get to us from the stars.

The speed of light in space is 299,792.5 kilometres per second. It travels at a slightly slower speed through air, water and other transparent materials.

Other kinds of rays similar to light also travel at the same speed. They include radio and television signals, infra-red or heat rays, ultraviolet rays and X-rays.

The speed of light is thought to be the fastest possible speed at which anything can travel. Because a spaceship could not travel faster than light, no matter how powerful it was, it would take many years to travel to even the nearest star.

phosphors. In the sorting machine, an ultraviolet lamp causes the pattern to light up. The code is 'read' by the machine, which sends the letter to the correct compartment for delivery.

In ultraviolet light, inks and paints look very different from their appearance in ordinary light, and this can show up a forgery..

Some ultraviolet light reaches us from the Sun. This tans us and also produces vitamin D in the skin, which prevents a bone disease called rickets.

Address code

By air mail
Par avion
Aerogramme

Letter directed into correct slot

Ultraviolet lamp

Signal to sorting machine

Ultraviolet light is a form of light that is invisible. However, if it strikes certain materials called phosphors, it makes them glow. It is used to sort letters by machine, and to identify forged documents and paintings.

Letters arriving at a postal sorting office are given address codes in the form of patterns marked in pale or invisible inks containing

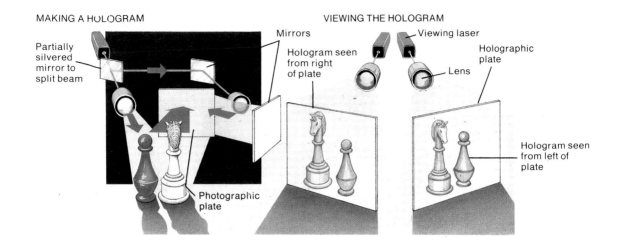

MAKING A HOLOGRAM

Partially silvered mirror to split beam

Mirrors

Photographic plate

VIEWING THE HOLOGRAM

Hologram seen from right of plate

Viewing laser

Holographic plate

Lens

Hologram seen from left of plate

WHAT ARE HOLOGRAMS?

Holograms are amazing pictures that appear to have depth just like real objects. For example, if you look at a hologram of the front of a cube and then move to one side, you will see the sides of the cube just as if you were walking around it! Holograms are made with lasers.

To make a hologram, the object is lit by light from a laser. This light reflects from the object and strikes a photographic plate placed nearby. At the same time, the laser beam is split so that it also reflects from mirrors and strikes the plate directly.

The plate is then developed. A black-and-white pattern appears on it, producing a holographic plate. When one side of this plate is lit up by a laser beam and it is viewed from the other side, an image of the object appears behind the plate.

The image is in three dimensions, just like the real object, but in the colour of the laser light. Projection holograms can be projected by lasers to appear in front of the holographic plate. There are also special holograms that can be seen by daylight.

HOW ARE X-RAYS PRODUCED?

When you have an X-ray, a machine sends a quick burst of X-rays through a part of your body such as your mouth or chest. The X-rays are invisible and you feel nothing. The rays then strike a piece of photographic film. When it is developed, an image of the inside of your mouth or chest appears on the film.

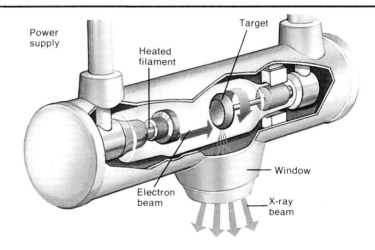

Power supply

Heated filament

Target

Electron beam

Window

X-ray beam

The X-ray machine contains a filament that is heated to produce a stream of electrons. A high-voltage power supply fed to the X-ray machine accelerates the electrons in a beam towards a metal target.

As the electrons are stopped by the target, they give out X-rays.

The X-ray beam leaves the machine through a window, and goes through the patient's body. The rays pass through flesh more easily than teeth or bones, which cast X-ray shadows. A film pack is placed next to the part of the body to be examined, and the X-rays penetrate the wrapping and expose the film.

Alternatively, the rays produce an image on a fluorescent screen, which is rather like a television screen.

▶ WHY DO THINGS LOOK NEARER UNDERWATER?

If you try to pick up an object in a tank or pool of water, you'll find that it is deeper than it looks. The reason for this is that light rays from the object bend as they leave the water.

Rays of light from an object travel up through the water to the surface. As they move from the water into the air, the rays bend towards the surface of the water. The light rays then travel to the eyes.

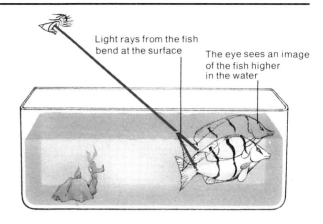

Light rays from the fish bend at the surface

The eye sees an image of the fish higher in the water

However, our eyes always assume that light travels from anything we see in a straight line without bending. We see the object in the position it would have if light travelled in a straight line to the eyes. It therefore appears to be higher in the water.

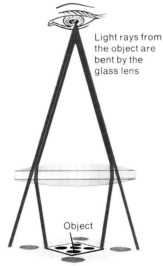

Light rays from the object are bent by the glass lens

Object

The eye sees an enlarged image

◀ HOW DOES A MAGNIFYING GLASS WORK?

Light rays from an object pass through the magnifying glass to reach your eyes. The glass bends the rays, which reach your eyes as if they were coming from a bigger object.

The magnifying glass is a lens. Refraction causes light rays passing through a lens to bend at the surfaces between the air and the glass. The glass is a convex lens, which bends light rays from all points on the object towards each other. However, the eye believes that the rays have come from the object in a straight line without bending. This causes an enlarged image of the object to appear behind the glass.

A magnifying glass can also project an image on a piece of paper. You can make an image of the Sun appear and burn the paper. This is because the glass bends all the Sun's rays passing through it so that they meet on the paper and form an image.

▶ HOW DOES A MIRROR WORK?

When you look in a mirror, light rays go from you and strike the mirror. The rays bounce off the mirror and come back to your eyes. You see an exact image of yourself, but it is reversed.

A mirror is made of glass with a shiny coating on the back. The light rays pass through the glass and are reflected from the coating.

Light rays are reflected

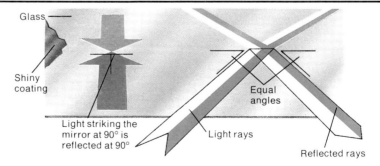

Glass

Shiny coating

Light striking the mirror at 90° is reflected at 90°

Equal angles

Light rays

Reflected rays

back by a flat mirror at the same angle as they strike the mirror. This makes an image seen in a flat mirror appear to be the same size and shape as the object.

However, the image is always reversed. This is because light rays from the right side are reflected back on this side. In the image, you see the object's right side to your right. But if you were to see the real object in the same position as the image, its right side would be to your left.

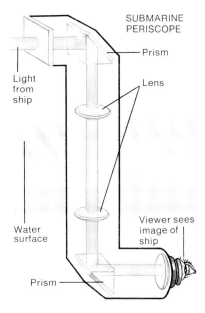

SUBMARINE
PERISCOPE

— Prism

Light
from
ship

— Lens

Water
surface

Viewer sees
image of
ship

Prism —

▲ HOW DOES A PERISCOPE
WORK?

You can use a periscope to
see something from a
higher level as if you were
taller. A simple periscope
has two sloping mirrors,
one above the other. Light
from an object strikes the
top mirror, which reflects
it to the bottom mirror.
This mirror reflects the
light into your eyes, and
you see an image of the
object.

A submarine has a periscope
so that it can observe ships on
the surface when it is
submerged. This periscope
works in the same way as a
simple periscope, but has
prisms instead of mirrors to
give a high-quality image. It
also has lenses to produce a
magnified view of a ship on
the surface.

Periscopes have many other
uses. They enable people to
look into parts of a machine or
building that are sealed off or
are dangerous to enter. In an
emergency, an engineer can
inspect a nuclear reactor or
the hold of an aircraft with a
periscope, for example.

▼ HOW MUCH CAN A
MICROSCOPE MAGNIFY?

You can see objects highly
magnified in an optical
microscope. The most
powerful microscope can
make an object look as
much as 2500 times bigger
than it really is. Electron
microscopes can make
things look even bigger
still.

At the bottom of the microscope, a mirror and condenser
shine a beam of light through
the object. The object is
usually held between two thin
plates of glass.

The focusing knob is then
turned to bring the objective
lens very close to the object.
This lens makes light rays
from the object meet. They
form a magnified image of the
object inside the tube of the
microscope. The light rays go
on to the eyepiece lens, which
magnifies the image more.

The magnifying power is
given by multiplying together
the powers of the objective
and eyepiece lenses. A
microscope may have several
lenses to give different magnifications.

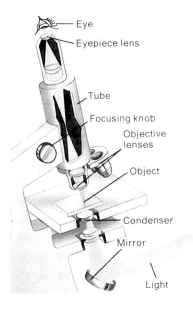

— Eye
— Eyepiece lens

— Tube

— Focusing knob

Objective
lenses

— Object

— Condenser

Mirror

Light

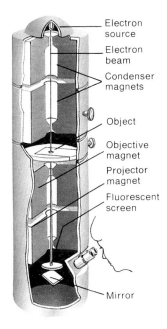

Electron
source

Electron
beam

Condenser
magnets

Object

Objective
magnet

Projector
magnet

Fluorescent
screen

Mirror

▲ HOW DOES AN ELECTRON
MICROSCOPE WORK?

The electron microscope
can magnify objects by as
much as a million times.
Instead of using light rays,
it works with beams of
tiny particles called
electrons. The image is
seen on a screen or may be
photographed.

Optical microscopes cannot
magnify more than about
2500 times because the light
rays cannot produce a sharp
image. Electron microscopes
use beams of electrons instead
of light rays. Electrons have a
much shorter wavelength
than light, which enables
much greater magnifications
to be achieved.

The electron microscope
works like an optical
microscope with a condenser
and objective and eyepiece
(projector) lenses. The lenses
are powerful magnets or
electrodes. They produce an
electron image using a beam
of electrons passed through
the object. The projector
forms this image on a
fluorescent screen.

▲ HOW DO SOME OBJECTS FLOAT ON WATER?

If you are very careful, you can lower a needle on to some water and it will float on the surface. The surface of the water has an invisible 'skin' over it. The needle is held by this skin so that it appears to float on the water.

In the water, the water molecules pull at each other with a strong force. This binds the molecules together so that the water remains a liquid.

The molecules at the surface pull more strongly because there are no water molecules pulling from above them. This forms a kind of surface barrier because the surface molecules also pull on the molecules of any object at the surface.

If the object is light, like a needle, then the pull of the surface water molecules stops it from sinking. This pull is called surface tension. It enables some insects, such as the pond skaters shown here, to walk across the surface of water.

▼ HOW DO PULLEYS WORK?

You can lift very heavy loads with a pulley. You pull on the rope, and the pulley wheels go round. The pulley is fixed to the ceiling or a support and lifts the load.

The weight of the load that can be raised with a pulley depends on the number of wheels and the way in which they are connected together. If the pulley has one rope, with a six-wheel pulley you can lift a load six times greater than you could without it.

The reason for this is that the amount of rope that you pull is six times as long as the distance that the load is raised. This increases the amount of force you apply to the load by six times and you can lift the load.

However, it does not increase the amount of effort or work involved. Work depends on the distance you move a load as well as its weight. Moving 80 kilograms by one metre requires the same work as lifting ten kilograms by eight metres.

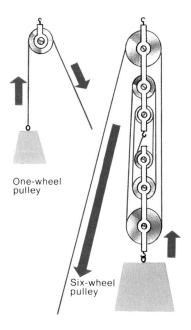

One-wheel pulley

Six-wheel pulley

Only about a tenth of the ice shows above the water

▲ HOW CAN ICE FLOAT IN WATER?

Ice floats on water because a piece of ice is lighter than the same amount of water. The ice is not very much lighter than the water, so it floats low in the water.

When water freezes to ice, the water molecules line up in rows. But as they do so, the molecules move apart slightly. The ice increases in size as it forms and this gives ice a lower density than water, making it float in water.

The force between the molecules is very strong, and nothing can resist the expansion that occurs as the ice forms. This is why water pipes sometimes burst in winter. The ice expands and cracks the pipe. Then when the weather gets warmer, the ice melts and water pours from the cracked pipe.
It is unusual for a liquid to expand on freezing, but it is a good thing that water does so. The layer of ice that may form over lakes and the sea in winter prevents the water beneath from freezing.

Hydraulic machines operate brakes on vehicles, presses and hammers for shaping metal objects, and lifting and digging machines. The hydraulic systems in these machines work with fluid at high pressure.

Hydraulic systems are used in machines that have to create a very powerful force over a short distance. For example, a hydraulic jack raises a large vehicle just off the ground.

A hydraulic system contains two pistons that move up and down in cylinders. The cylinders beneath the pistons are filled with a hydraulic fluid such as oil, and the cylinders are connected by a pipe. When

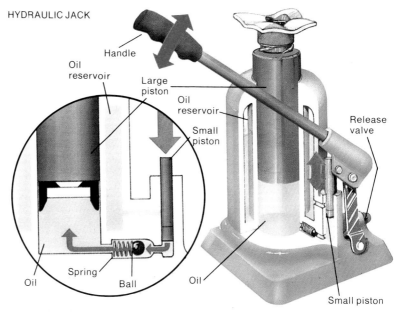

HYDRAULIC JACK

one piston is pushed down, it increases the pressure of the fluid throughout the system. The increased fluid pressure then raises the piston in the other cylinder.

The first piston is smaller than the second. But as the

fluid pressure is the same in both cylinders, the second piston rises with more force because it is bigger. However, to produce this pressure, the first piston has to move down a greater distance than the second piston is raised.

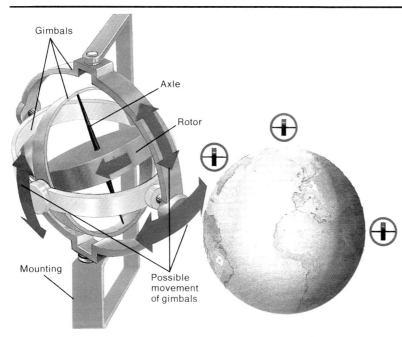

The disc or rotor of the gyro-compass is powered by an electric motor so that it spins non-stop. The axle of the rotor always points in the same direction and it can be set to point north.

The rotor is mounted in gimbals that do not force it to turn. As the ship or aircraft changes direction, the gimbals turn so that the axle of the rotor still points north. This movement is transmitted to the compass card, which also turns to show the direction of true north.

Another kind of gyro-compass automatically sets itself north-south. It works like a gyroscope, which turns at right-angles to the direction in which the axle moves. In the gyrocompass, the rotor turns in response to any movement of the axle away from true north and brings it back to true north.

A gyrocompass shows the direction of north like a magnetic compass. But instead of using magne- **tism, it contains a spinning disc like a gyroscope. The axle of the disc always points north. A card marked with directions shows which way north lies.**

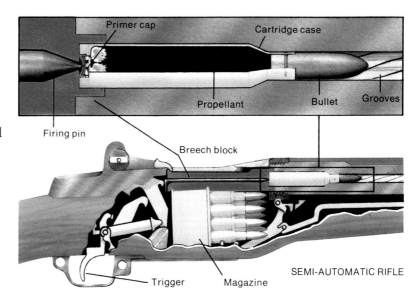

SEMI-AUTOMATIC RIFLE

Labels: Primer cap, Cartridge case, Firing pin, Propellant, Bullet, Grooves, Breech block, Trigger, Magazine

▶ HOW DO EXPLOSIVES WORK?

When an explosive goes off, the chemicals in the explosive suddenly produce lots of gas and heat. The hot gases expand in size very quickly. This gives the explosion its force and makes a wave of high pressure move out through the air.

High explosives like gelignite produce large amounts of hot gas very quickly to give a powerful instant explosion. The chemical reaction that occurs moves through the explosive at speeds of up to 7.5 kilometres a second.

High explosives are set off with detonators. These are small explosive charges that fit into the main explosive. A wire connects the detonator to a battery or other source of power. To set off the explosion, a current is sent to the detonator. It heats a wire inside the detonator and the detonator explodes, setting off the main charge. Low explosives like gunpowder do not need detonators.

▲ HOW DOES A RIFLE WORK?

Pulling the trigger of a rifle releases a spring. This makes a firing pin strike the base of a cartridge. The cartridge contains explosive and a bullet. The firing pin sets off the explosive, and the gas produced by the explosion makes the bullet fly out of the rifle.

In the cap of the cartridge is a primer that detonates to set off the charge of propellant in the cartridge case. Spiral grooves around the inside of the barrel cause the bullet to spin as it leaves the rifle. The spin stabilizes the flight of the bullet so that it points forward and does not tumble.

Automatic rifles contain a chamber of cartridges called a magazine. The force of the explosion throws the cartridge case from the breech block. It then raises another cartridge from the magazine into the firing position and fires it.

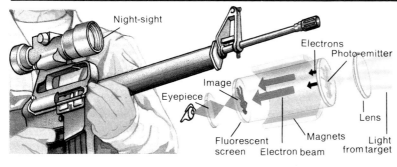

Labels: Night-sight, Electrons, Photo-emitter, Image, Eyepiece, Lens, Fluorescent screen, Electron beam, Magnets, Light from target

▲ HOW DOES THE NIGHT-SIGHT ON A GUN WORK?

Marksmen can see a target even at night. This is because there is always a little light even if it looks totally dark. The night-sight picks up this light
from the target and makes an image of it appear on a small screen.

At the front of the night-sight is a lens. It focuses the very weak light rays coming from the target onto a metal disc called a photo-emitter. This

disc produces electrons where it is struck by light rays. The electrons travel down the tube of the night-sight, and are focused into a beam by magnets around the tube. The beam strikes a fluorescent screen at the end of the tube, causing it to light up with an image of the target.

The marksman views it through the eyepiece of the night-sight to aim his rifle at the target. This kind of night-sight can brighten a target by fifty times, so that it becomes visible in total darkness.

▶ HOW DOES AN ATOMIC BOMB WORK?

An atomic bomb makes a huge explosion powerful enough to destroy a city. It contains pieces of uranium or plutonium instead of ordinary explosive. When the bomb is dropped, the pieces are fired together inside the bomb and it explodes.

When the pieces of uranium or plutonium meet, the nuclei of the atoms begin to break apart. A nuclear chain reaction occurs like that in a nuclear reactor (see page 64). However, the reaction is not controlled and a huge amount of energy is released.

To start the chain reaction, a critical mass of uranium or plutonium is formed. Stray neutrons in the mass start the chain reaction, and the mass contains enough atoms to keep the reaction going.

Instead of firing separate pieces of uranium or plutonium together to form the critical mass, a hollow sphere may be crushed into a solid lump by explosives.

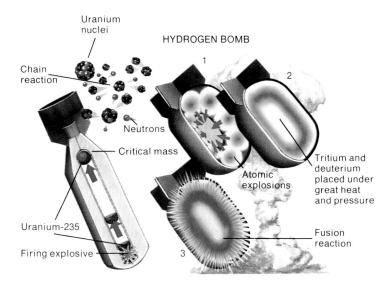

ATOMIC BOMB

Uranium nuclei

HYDROGEN BOMB

Chain reaction

1

2

Neutrons

Critical mass

Tritium and deuterium placed under great heat and pressure

Atomic explosions

Uranium-235

Fusion reaction

Firing explosive

3

▲ HOW DOES A HYDROGEN BOMB WORK?

A hydrogen bomb is so powerful that it needs atomic bombs to set it off. These atomic explosions cause an even more powerful nuclear explosion in a layer of hydrogen around the atomic bombs.

Around the atomic triggers of a hydrogen bomb are materials that produce forms of hydrogen called deuterium and tritium. The atomic explosions cause this fuel to be placed under enormous heat and pressure. A nuclear reaction called fusion then occurs.

The nuclei of the deuterium and tritium are forced together and they form nuclei of helium. This causes a loss of mass because the helium nuclei have less mass than the nuclei from which they form. The lost mass is converted into an enormous amount of energy and the bomb explodes.

▶ HOW DOES A MISSILE GET TO ITS TARGET?

A missile is a rocket with an explosive warhead. When the missile reaches its target the warhead explodes. The missile may chase the target if it is moving. The guidance system in the missile detects heat coming from its engine or uses radar. Other missiles are guided from the ground.

A radar system may track both the missile and its target. A computer reads the radar

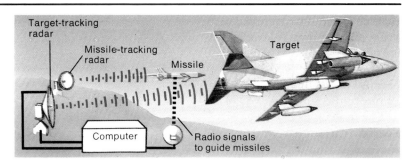

Target-tracking radar

Missile-tracking radar

Missile

Target

Computer

Radio signals to guide missiles

signals and controls the missile's guidance system to guide it to the target by radio.

Missiles may also be guided by operators linked to the missile by a long wire or by radio. Some missiles are able to follow a laser beam directed at the target by the operator.

Large missiles that are intended to destroy cities or missile sites fly on a set course.

Some missiles have computers containing maps of the land below. They can 'see' where they are going and keep to the right course.

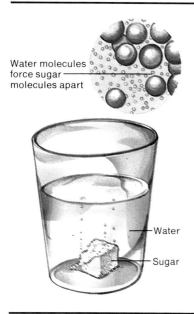

Water molecules force sugar molecules apart

Water

Sugar

◀ WHY DOES SUGAR DISSOLVE IN WATER?

If you put some sugar in water and stir it, it disappears. However, the water tastes of sugar. The sugar dissolves, or enters the water. This is because it breaks up into tiny particles that spread out through the water.

Inside sugar crystals, molecules of sugar are lined up neatly in rows. As the sugar is placed in the water, water molecules invade the crystals. The water molecules come between the sugar molecules and force them apart. The sugar molecules move out among the water molecules as the sugar dissolves in the water. Heating the water makes the sugar dissolve quickly because it makes the molecules move faster.

In many substances, the forces that hold their molecules together are too strong to allow water molecules to force them apart. These substances therefore do not dissolve in water.

▶ WHY DOES A BOAT FLOAT ON WATER?

A boat can float on water even if it is made of metal, which is heavier than water. This is because the boat pushes aside some of the water. The water pushes back on the boat, and supports its weight. This makes it float.

The support that a boat gets from the water is called up-thrust. The amount of up-thrust is equal to the weight of the water that the boat pushes aside or displaces. If the upthrust produced is equal to the weight of the boat, then it will float. The boat must therefore displace a large amount of water in order to float. This is why boats are hollow and broad in shape.

If the boat were made of solid metal or was narrow so that it was much smaller in size but the same weight, it would not displace as much water. The amount of upthrust produced would be not enough to support the weight of the boat and it would sink.

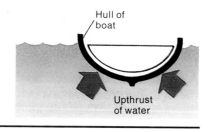

Hull of boat

Upthrust of water

◀ WHY DOES WATER FLOW MORE EASILY THAN SYRUP?

Syrup flows very slowly from an upturned tin or jar because it sticks to the sides of the container. Water does not stick as much as syrup, so it flows more easily.

The molecules of syrup pull on each other with a strong force. They also pull strongly at the molecules in the sides of the container. These forces or bonds between the molecules act to slow down the movement of the syrup.

The bonds between water molecules are not as strong as the bonds between syrup molecules. With water, movement is not slowed as much as with syrup, so water flows more easily.

Syrup flows faster if it is warmed. This happens because the heat causes the syrup molecules to move about within the syrup more quickly. The extra movement weakens the bonds between the molecules in the syrup, and as a result the warm syrup flows faster than cold syrup.

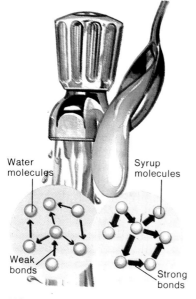

Water molecules

Syrup molecules

Weak bonds

Strong bonds

▶ WHY DOES WATER FREEZE IN WINTER?

It may get so cold in winter that the temperature falls to freezing point (0°C) or lower. When water gets this cold, it freezes.

Water is made up of molecules that move about. This is why water is liquid and flows easily. The speed of movement depends on the temperature of the water. The hotter it is, the faster the molecules move. As the temperature falls, the molecules gradually get slower and slower.

At freezing point, their movement becomes so slow that each molecule begins to exert a pulling force on the molecules around it, and they begin to line up in rows. The molecules do not stop moving, but each one now vibrates around one position instead of moving about freely. As the molecules take up their positions, the water changes from being a liquid and becomes a solid. That is, it turns into ice.

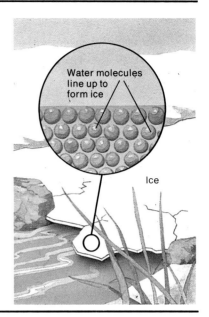

Water molecules line up to form ice

Ice

◀ WHY DOES A PUDDLE DRY UP IN SUNSHINE?

The warmth of the sunshine makes some of the water turn into water vapour. Water vapour is an invisible gas which mingles with the air. Slowly, all the water turns into water vapour, and the puddle dries up.

When water turns into water vapour, it is said to evaporate. This happens because the molecules of water are constantly moving within the water. At the surface, some molecules escape from the water and enter the air. In this way, water vapour is formed. Evaporation continues in this way if a wind is blowing to carry away the water vapour, or if it is warm and dry.

Usually, the molecules continue to escape and the water turns completely to water vapour. However, the air may become so laden with water vapour that no more water molecules can escape from the surface. The air becomes very humid, and puddles do not dry up.

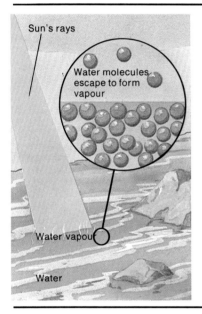

Sun's rays

Water molecules escape to form vapour

Water vapour

Water

▶ WHY IS ICE SLIPPERY?

If you try to pick up a piece of ice, it usually slips out of your fingers. This is because the warmth of your fingers melts the surface of the ice and turns it into water. A film of water therefore forms between your fingers and the ice, making the ice feel slippery.

If the ice is very cold, it feels sticky instead of slippery. This is because the warmth of your fingers first melts the surface of the ice, but the ice is so cold that this water immediately freezes again, making your fingers stick to the ice.

Ice skaters are able to skate on ice for a different reason. The weight of the skater's body throws great pressure on the ice as the skates pass over the ice. This pressure causes the ice to melt beneath the skates, so that the skater in fact slides on a film of water between the skates and the ice. This film immediately freezes to ice again after the skater has passed.

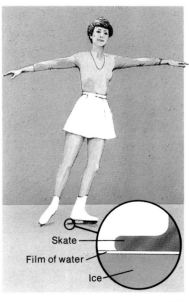

Skate

Film of water

Ice

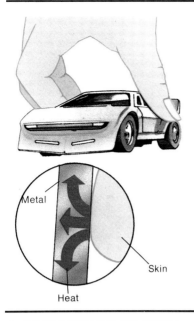

Metal

Skin

Heat

◄ WHY DOES METAL FEEL COLD?

When you touch something made of metal, it feels cold. The reason for this is that some heat flows from your fingers into the surface of the metal. Because the skin on your fingers loses heat, it goes cold and the metal feels cold.

Metal objects feel cold in a cool climate because metal is a good conductor of heat. This means that heat flows through metal easily. Heat therefore leaves the skin of your fingers and flows into the metal. It does this because your fingers are warmer than the metal. The heat moves on through the metal, so that the surface of the metal does not get as warm as the skin on your fingers. Heat continues to flow from your fingers into the metal, and it feels cold.

Wood or cloth are poor conductors of heat. The surface of an object made of wood or cloth quickly warms up as you touch it, and it does not feel cold.

▶ WHY DOES WOOD BURN BUT NOT IRON?

For anything to burn, it needs the oxygen gas that is in the air. When wood burns, it takes in oxygen. Together, the wood and oxygen give out heat and form ash. The wood has to be heated to make it take in oxygen. When it is hot enough, it catches fire and begins to burn. Iron does not take in oxygen like this when it is heated. It therefore does not catch fire and burn.

Things like wood burn because the oxygen molecules in the air split apart the molecules in the wood, forming molecules of ash and also gases, including carbon dioxide. To do this, the wood and oxygen molecules need a certain amount of energy so that they will move or vibrate faster and overcome the forces that keep them apart. This energy comes from heat.

Iron molecules do not split as wood molecules do, no matter how hot the iron is heated.

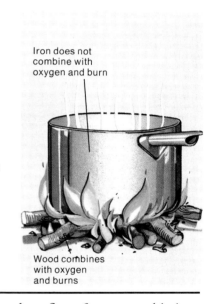

Iron does not combine with oxygen and burn

Wood combines with oxygen and burns

◄ WHY DO CLOTHES KEEP YOU WARM?

Clothes may feel cold when you first put them on. But they soon warm up and then keep you warm throughout the day. This is because your body produces heat. The clothes stop most of this heat from leaving your body.

Clothes are good insulators. This means that they do not conduct heat very well. The heat of your skin first warms the clothes, and then little heat flows from your skin into them. Some heat does get through, particularly if the outer surface of the garments is cold. This is why you put on more clothes or thicker garments to keep warm on a cold day.

The main reason why clothes are good insulators is that they contain air. Air is trapped between the fibres in the cloth. Also, a layer of air is caught between the clothes and your skin. Air is a poor conductor of heat, and so clothes keep your body heat in.

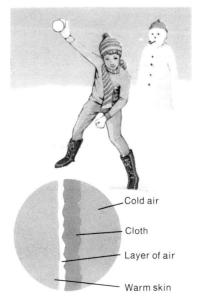

Cold air

Cloth

Layer of air

Warm skin

▼ WHY IS A FLAME HOT?

When a candle or a fire is lit, it burns with a hot flame. It has to be heated with a match or a lighter to catch fire. As the burning continues, the candle or the fuel in the fire takes up oxygen in the air. As it does so, it gives out heat and the flame continues to be hot.

In anything that is hot, the molecules are moving or vibrating quickly. The hotter it is, the faster the molecules

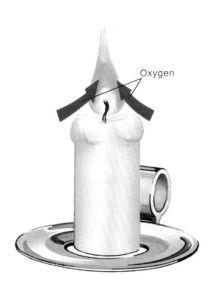

Oxygen

move or vibrate. In a flame, oxygen in the air is combining with a fuel, for example wood. The molecules of wood and of oxygen each break apart and then come together to form new molecules of ash and also of invisible gases like carbon dioxide, which escape into the air. As they do so, energy is given out by the old molecules and taken up by the new molecules. However, the new molecules do not take up as much energy as that given out. The extra energy makes them move faster and causes heat to be produced as the wood burns.

▼ WHY DO MATCHES LIGHT WHEN YOU STRIKE THEM?

When you strike a match, you rub the head of the match against the rough surface on the side of the matchbox. This makes the head of the match get hot. The head contains substances that burst into flame when they get hot. This is why the match lights.

As the head of the match moves over the rough surface, the molecules in the head and

the surface collide with each other and move faster. This makes the head of the match hotter. In the head are substances that catch fire without much heating. The heat produced by striking the match is enough to make the head burst into flame.

In safety matches, the side of the matchbox contains a substance that is needed to make the head of the match catch fire. These matches therefore do not light when struck on any other surface.

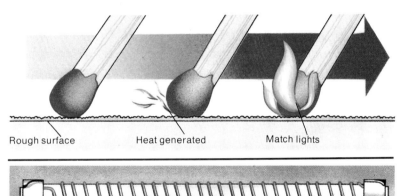

Rough surface   Heat generated   Match lights

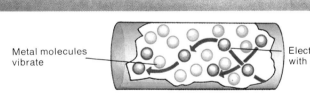

Metal molecules vibrate   Electrons collide with molecules

▲ WHY DOES AN ELECTRIC FIRE GLOW RED?

When you switch on an electric fire, electricity flows through the wire in the bars. This makes the bars get hot. If anything gets hot enough, it gives out light. First it glows red, then yellow and finally white if it gets really hot. Electric fires get hot enough to glow red.

An electric current consists of a flow of tiny particles called electrons. As the electrons

pass through the wire in the bars of an electric fire, they collide with the molecules of metal in the wire. This makes the molecules vibrate faster and the metal gets hotter. In this way, the energy of the electricity is changed into heat energy.

At high temperatures, things give out light energy as well as heat energy. At very high temperatures, the light has a lot of energy and is white. But at the lower temperature of an electric fire, the light has less energy and the bars of the fire glow red.

TRANSPORT

▶ WHEN WAS THE STEAM
LOCOMOTIVE INVENTED?

The steam engine was invented in the 1700s. It was used to drive pumps. Then a clever engineer saw that the power of steam could be used to turn wheels, to make a 'locomotive'.

Richard Trevithick, a Cornish mining engineer, built a 'horseless carriage' driven by a steam engine in 1801. It ran on the roads. Later, in 1804, he made another, which ran on metal rails.

George Stephenson and other engineers took up this idea. Stephenson built a steam locomotive for the first public railway in 1825. In 1829 he won a competition for the best

STEPHENSON'S *ROCKET*

engine with his locomotive 'Rocket'. This locomotive managed a top speed of 57 kilometres an hour. Its success started the railway age, and its design was widely copied. The locomotive was driven by two cylinders powered by steam

from a multi-tube boiler.

In 1830 Stephenson's locomotives opened the Liverpool and Manchester Railway. This was the first public railway meant from the start to be used only by steam trains.

▶ WHEN WAS THE FIRST
PUBLIC RAILWAY
OPENED?

The first public railway in the world was the Stockton and Darlington line in north-east England. It opened in 1825, and its trains were hauled by the first steam railway-locomotive.

Railways had been used to move coal for many years. But the wagons were horse-drawn. The invention of the steam locomotive brought a completely new form of transport.

George Stephenson persuaded the owners of the Stockton and Darlington railway to use his new steam

engine instead of horses. He drove the first train himself. The locomotive was called *Locomotion*, and the first passenger coach was called *Experiment*. It looked like a horse-drawn carriage, with

railway wheels instead of coach wheels.

On the first trains, passengers often sat in open wagons. Smoke and sparks from the locomotive's chimney made it an uncomfortable ride.

In the 1800s settlers headed west across the vast new land of America. They dreamed of a railroad across the continent. In 1869 that dream came true.

Railways began to be built in America soon after the start of the railway age. The first public steam railroad in the USA was opened in 1830.

The first US railroads were short, joining the towns of the eastern states. Crossing the Wild West was a far more difficult task. Work on the transcontinental railroad began in 1863. The Union Pacific headed west from Iowa, while the Central Pacific started laying track eastwards from California.

The railroads had to cross rivers, deserts, mountains, swamps and ravines. Often hostile Indians fought to stop the 'iron horse' from crossing their hunting grounds.

The photograph shows the two tracks meeting in Utah, in 1869. The completed railroad was 2775 kilometres long. New towns sprang up beside the track. Trains carried settlers west to California, and eastwards to the big cities.

In 1932 the first diesel railway-locomotive went into service. Diesel trains quickly took over from steam trains after that.

The diesel engine was invented by the German engineer Rudolf Diesel in 1894. It is a form of internal combustion engine which burns less fuel than other types of engine. In 1932 the German railways started using diesel locomotives. By the 1950s diesels were common on other railways, especially in the USA.

The largest diesel locomotives haul heavy trains on the US railroads. Often several engines are needed to pull one train. The diesel engine is usually connected to an electricity generator, which produces electric power to work the motors turning the wheels of the locomotive.

Diesel locomotives can reach speeds of over 200 kilometres an hour, but the world's fastest trains are electric (up to 330 kilometres an hour). Electric trains, which take current from the rails or overhead wires, are common. However, diesel still rules the rails in North America.

▲ WHEN WAS THE FIRST AIRCRAFT FLIGHT MADE?

People flew in a balloon in 1783. It was not until 1903 that an aircraft (a heavier-than-air flying machine) first flew. Yet within a few years, aircraft were crossing the oceans.

After the Montgolfier brothers proved that people could fly in balloons (1783), it seemed that the problems of flight had been solved. Unfortunately, balloons can only go where the wind takes them. People tried putting sails, oars and steam engines into balloons to beat this problem. They also tried airships and gliders.

On 17 December 1903, the long wait ended. Two Americans, Orville and Wilbur Wright, tested a petrol-engined aircraft called the *Flyer*. It took off and flew, with Orville as pilot, for 40 metres at Kitty Hawk in North Carolina, USA.

► WHEN WERE THE FIRST METAL PLANES BUILT?

Early planes were made of wood and canvas to keep down weight. Not until the 1930s did metal planes take to the skies.

Most of the planes that fought in World War I were biplanes (double-winged). They looked rather like box kites, with their wings held together by wooden struts and wires.

The monoplane has a single set of wings. It is better for high-speed flight because its shape is more streamlined (smooth). One of the first monoplane fighters was the Russian Polikarpov 1-16 of 1933.

The German designer Hugo Junkers began building all-metal aircraft, the most famous of which was the Junkers Ju-52 (1932). The new metal aircraft had bodies shaped like smooth tapering tubes. Light but strong alloys (mixtures of metals) were used to build them. Today almost all aircraft are built of metal, specially made to withstand the heat and stress of high speeds.

JUNKERS JU-52

▲ WHEN DID THE FIRST AIRLINERS FLY?

Passenger air-travel began after World War I. The aircraft were unwanted warplanes, slow and uncomfortable. But by the 1930s larger, faster and more comfortable airliners had appeared.

In the 1920s an air journey was often cold and bumpy. Long flights took days, for the plane had to land several times to refuel. The first 'modern' airliner was the all-metal American Boeing 247 of 1933. It carried ten passengers.

One of the largest 1930s airliners, however, was an old-fashioned biplane, the HP 42. This British airliner flew slowly, but comfortably, from London to Africa and India. Another famous airliner was the Douglas DC-3 of the 1940s. It carried 21 passengers.

Flying boats were also popular in the 1930s. They crossed the great oceans, landing on the water rather than on concrete runways.

GLOSTER-WHITTLE E28/39

The fastest a propeller-driven plane can fly is around 750 kilometres an hour. In 1939 a new age of speed began, with the first flight by a jet plane.

A British engineer named Frank Whittle had worked on the theory of jet flight since the early 1930s. He wanted to build an engine which, because it needed no propeller, would work well in the thin air at great heights.

Germany was also at work on the jet engine. In 1939 the Heinkel He 179 made the world's first jet flight. The Germans also built the first jet warplane, the Me 262. It was a twin-jet fighter-bomber.

Whittle's own engine was first flown in 1941. The plane was the Gloster E28/39. Jets came too late to play much part in World War II.

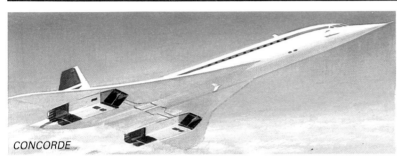
CONCORDE

FW-61 HELICOPTER

Inventors drew plans for flying machines very like helicopters in the 1400s. But it was not until 1936 that the first practical helicopter took to the air.

A helicopter has no wings. It lifts itself off the ground by means of a large rotor, or propeller. Once aloft, the rotor is tilted slightly forward to make the helicopter fly forwards. Helicopters can fly backwards too, and even hover in one spot in mid-air.

The famous Italian artist and inventor Leonardo da Vinci drew a helicopter. But his machine never flew. The first successful helicopter was the German FW-61 of 1936. It had two rotors. A Russian, Igor Sikorsky, did much to advance helicopter design, and Sikorsky helicopters were used during World War II. After the war, the use of helicopters increased enormously.

Aircraft first broke the so-called 'sound barrier' in the 1940s. Today *Concorde* carries passengers at over twice the speed of sound.

At sea level, sound travels at about 1200 kilometres an hour. Higher up, the speed is slower, around 950 kilometres an hour. When a plane reaches this speed, it makes a shock wave in the air. This wave can be heard as a 'sonic boom'.

Only a jet or rocket plane can reach such high speeds. The American Bell X-1 was the first piloted plane to break the 'sound barrier' and prove that supersonic flight was not really dangerous.

In the 1960s two supersonic airliners were built. The Russian Tupolev Tu-144 first flew in 1968, but did not prove a success. The *Concorde*, built by Britain and France, flew a year later and went into regular airline service in 1976. *Concorde* is smaller than a jumbo jet, but much faster, crossing the Atlantic at over 2000 kilometres an hour.

▶ WHEN WERE THE FIRST
SHIPS BUILT?

People probably used logs to float across rivers. These were the first boats. Ships large enough to sail the open sea were first made in Egypt 5000 years ago.

Logs tied together made a raft. A log hollowed out made a canoe. Reeds tied in bundles would also float. We know that the Ancient Egyptians made reed boats, because pictures of them have been found in tombs. But such craft (shown in the picture) were only safe for river travel.

The Egyptians made larger boats, with sails and oars, to explore the open sea. Other peoples living on the shores of the Mediterranean Sea also built boats. They built long, slender galleys for war and broad, slower-moving cargo ships for trade. Oars were used to drive the ship along when there was not enough wind.

The sailors kept in sight of land. They had no maps or compasses to navigate with.

▶ WHEN WERE FULLY
RIGGED SHIPS USED?

Most early ships had one large sail. By the 1400s ships had three masts carrying several sails. These were the first 'fully-rigged' ships.

A ship's rig is its arrangement of sails. The first sea-going vessels usually had a single square sail, although some had a triangular or 'lateen' sail instead.

As ships grew larger, extra sails were added. Square and triangular sails were found to

CARRACK

work well together. By the 1400s the three-masted carrack had appeared. This was the first fully-rigged ship. It was steered by a stern rudder, replacing the older steering oar.

After the carrack came the galleon. As ship design improved, extra sails were added for greater speed. By the 1800s the fastest clippers could sail at 39 kilometres an hour (21 knots).

▶ WHEN WERE
SUBMARINES FIRST
BUILT?

Since ancient times, sailors have dreamed of travelling beneath the sea. But not until 1801 did an inventor make a submarine craft. It took years to develop the submarines of today.

Amazingly, a kind of submarine was tried as early as 1620, though it was little more than a watertight barrel. In 1775 an American one-man submarine called *Turtle* tried to sink a British warship. But the honour of building the first submarine goes to Robert Fulton of the USA, whose *Nautilus* of 1801 could stay under water for four hours.

However, it was not until the 1890s that navies finally accepted submarines, thanks to the work of another American, John Holland. His submarine set the model for the craft used in World Wars I and II. It had petrol engines for surface travel and electric motors for moving beneath the waves.

TURTLE SUBMARINE

For thousands of years sailing ships ruled the seas. Their greatest days came in the 1700s and early 1800s. This was the age of the great wooden battleships and the graceful China clippers.

By the 1500s the shape of the sailing ship had become settled. For the next 300 years it did not change very much. However, there were many improvements.

The greatest warships of the days of sail were 100-gun and 74-gun battleships. These wooden ships had cannon ranged along their sides. In battle, they sailed alongside one another, firing broadsides of cannon balls. Ships like these fought at the battle of Trafalgar in 1805.

In the 1840s came the last and most elegant of all sailing ships – the clipper (shown in the picture). Its task was to carry tea from China to the USA and Britain. It was built for speed, and could sail 650 kilometres in a day. To reach

port first (and so get the highest prices for their cargo), the tea clippers sometimes raced one another across the oceans. As well as tea, clippers also carried wool from Australia.

Although fast, the clippers (like all sailing ships) relied on favourable winds. In time, these graceful ships gave way to the steamship, which could keep up the same speed, day and night, whatever the wind.

CLERMONT

Just as sailing ships reached their peak, they were challenged by a new rival – the steamer. The first steamships took to the seas in the early 1800s. Soon they ruled the waves.

A steam-powered river boat called the *Pyroscaphe* was built in France in 1783. But the first practical steamboats were the US *Clermont* of 1807 and the

Scottish *Comet* of 1812. Both had steam engines driving paddle wheels.

In 1819 a small steamer called *Savannah* sailed across the Atlantic, although it only used its engine for part of the way.

In the 1840s the screw propeller began to replace the paddle wheel on steamships. I. K. Brunel's steamship *Great Eastern* (1858) had both screws and paddles. It was built to sail all the way to Australia without taking on extra coal for its boilers.

▼ WHY DO CITY RAILWAYS RUN UNDERGROUND?

Many major cities have an underground railway network. The trains carry office workers, shoppers and so on between their homes and the city centre, by-passing the crowded streets above.

Underground railways are the only practical way of moving large numbers of people, most of whom are travelling at the same time of day. City centres

would be completely choked if every commuter went by car or bus. Trains have only a few seats and a lot of standing room, so that a large number of people can squash in. At peak hours there may be a train every $1\frac{1}{2}$ minutes.

Building a railway underground is extremely costly, so most lines run on the surface outside city centres. Modern planners try to develop mass transit systems. Trains run from the centre to the main suburbs and feeder bus services take people the rest of the way.

▼ WHY DO RAILWAYS USE BRIDGES AND TUNNELS?

Bridges carry railways across roads, rivers or valleys. Tunnels take them through hillsides. In both cases, they avoid time-consuming detours.

Locomotives run most cheaply and efficiently on flat, straight track without curves or gradients. But this does not happen very often.

When they meet an obstacle such as a steep hill, railway

▲ WHY DO RAILWAY TRACKS NEED REGULAR MAINTENANCE?

Regular maintenance of railway track is very important. Even the slightest crack in a rail could cause a serious accident.

Until recently, railwaymen would walk each stretch of track, tapping the rails to detect any faults and checking their alignment by eye. Nowadays, most of this work is done by machine.

engineers have to decide whether to divert the line round it or to tunnel through it. Going round is probably cheaper, but will add to the journey time and so increase running costs. Tunnelling requires costly special equipment, but the result is a straight track. Trains do not have to slow down for curves and can therefore keep a higher speed.

Some natural features, such as the Alps, cannot be avoided. There is no choice but to build a tunnel.

Track-measurement cars, which run independently or as part of a regular train, look for faults. Other machines tamp (pack down) the ballast, check and correct alignment and replace sections of track.

One of the weakest and most dangerous points is the joint between two rails. Rails used to be short (no more than 30 metres), but since about 1960, welded rails have been laid on most lines. These are up to 400 metres long and when laid are welded (joined together) to form a rail several kilometres long.

414

▶ WHY ARE RAILWAY SIGNALS SO IMPORTANT?

Signals control the movement of trains. They keep them away from each other, and they also help to keep them running efficiently and on time.

The block is the basis of a signalling system. A block is a stretch of line in one direction. No more than one train may be in a block at one time. A stop signal controls entry into the block. If it is red, the driver may not proceed. A distant signal some way before the start of the block warns the driver of what the stop signal will show, so that if necessary he can start to slow down.

Keeping trains apart ensures two things: safety and efficiency. Electronic controls prevent a signalman putting two trains on a collision course. At busy stations and junctions, signals often give the speed at which the train is to go and direct the driver to a particular platform.

▲ WHY ARE SOME RAILWAYS ELECTRIFIED?

In most European countries, the busiest lines are electrified. Electric trains are cheap to operate, but the trackside equipment they need is expensive.

The advantages of electric trains are that the locomotives cost less to build and run than diesels. They take their power from outside, from the national grid, rather than creating it themselves, as diesels do. And electricity is cheaper than oil.

The big disadvantage is the cost of electrification. Overhead wires have to be installed along the entire line, and often bridges have to be raised. Electric locomotives are also less versatile: they can only run on electrified lines, whereas diesels can go anywhere. On the whole, heavily-used inter-city lines are worth electrifying, especially if the improved service makes trains competitive with planes. Some commuter lines are also electrified.

▼ WHY DO TRAINS RUN ON RAILS?

The wheels of every rail vehicle (such as locomotive, passenger carriage and freight wagon) sit on the rails. A flange, or lip, on the inside edge of each wheel holds it to the rail.

Steel wheels and steel rails are a very efficient combination. Because there is not much friction between them, a locomotive can pull ten times as much as a road vehicle of the same power.

Rails alone could not support the weight of a train. The rails are laid on steel or concrete sleepers. These sit on a bed of ballast, or stones, packed onto the roadbed.

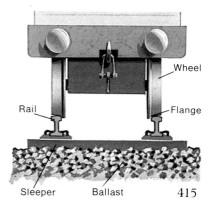

**Until the 1930s, most
aircraft were biplanes.
They had two sets of
wings, one above the
other. Struts and wires
ran between the wings,
holding them together.**

When they built the first
planes at the start of this
century, the pioneers of flight
had no previous experience to
rely on. Cantilever wings,
supported only by the plane's
fuselage, were not to be
developed for several decades.

Early aircraft wings were
braced by a network of
external struts and wires.
These gave biplanes one of
their main advantages, for it
was possible to make com-
paratively thin wings which
were efficient aero-
dynamically. In addition,
wingspan (the distance from
one wing-tip to the other) was
shorter than on monoplanes,
which have one set of wings.

The system of struts was
also a disadvantage, for struts
greatly increase drag. Drag is
the resistance the air makes as
a plane moves through it.
Although drag was reduced
by streamlining the struts and
wires, it always remained
greater than on an equivalent
single-wing plane. Biplanes
were also quite complex to
manufacture and maintain.

On early aircraft, whether
monoplanes or biplanes, the
pilot sat in a tiny open cockpit
well wrapped up against the
weather. The first plane flew
in 1903. Within ten years, air-
mail flights had begun. Planes
were used in World War I and
by the early 1920s there were
regular passenger services.

**A plane's propeller uses
the power produced in the
engine to drive the
aircraft forwards.**

Propellers consist of three or
four blades fixed to a hub.
The blades act as aerofoils. As
they turn, the air that passes
over their top surface moves
more quickly than air that
passes underneath. As a result
there is reduced pressure in
front and increased pressure
behind. This produces thrust.

Most propellers are variable-
pitch: the angle of the blades
on the hub can be altered to
suit the plane's speed.

Propeller craft are still
cheaper than jets at speeds up
to about 800 kilometres per
hour. Light planes are driven
by piston engines, but larger
propeller craft have turbo-
props. In turbo-props air is
compressed in a compressor,
mixed with fuel and ignited in
a combustion chamber. The
exhaust gases drive a turbine
that in turn drives both the
compressor and the
propellers.

▼ WHY ARE PASSENGER
AIRSHIPS NO LONGER
USED?

Airships were a popular means of long-distance travel in the 1920s and 1930s. But a series of accidents put them out of favour.

Airships work on the same principle as balloons. Most passenger airships were rigid: their envelope was surrounded by a rigid aluminium framework. Inside the envelope were gas bags filled with hydrogen or helium. To climb, ballast (normally water or sand) was released. To descend, gas was allowed to escape from the bags. Passengers and cargo travelled in a gondola beneath the envelope.

Four major airships crashed in the 1930s and many people died. Since then, airships have hardly been used at all. Now, however, there are plans to build cargo-carrying airships. These would be cheaper to build than ordinary planes and less costly to use.

▲ WHY DO HOT-AIR
BALLOONS FLY?

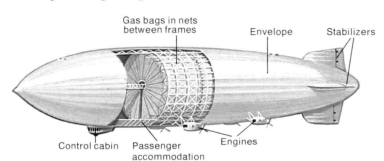

Gas bags in nets between frames · Envelope · Stabilizers · Control cabin · Passenger accommodation · Engines

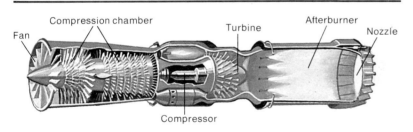

Compression chamber · Fan · Turbine · Afterburner · Nozzle · Compressor

▲ WHY DO SOME AIRCRAFT
HAVE JET ENGINES?

Jet engines burn a mixture of compressed air and fuel. The exhaust gases stream out of the back of the engine and provide thrust to move the plane.

Most modern jet engines are turbo-jets. A fan at the front of the engine sucks air back to the compressor, which is driven by a turbine.

The compressor consists of a series of blades that compress the air (raise it to a very high pressure) and force it into the combustion chamber. Here it is mixed with fuel. The exhaust gases from the mixture drive the turbine that drives the compressor. The gases then stream out of the engine through a nozzle.

It is the thrust of the hot gases rushing out of the jet that propels the plane. An afterburner between the turbine and the nozzle acts as a second combustion chamber, increasing thrust. Vanes fitted to the exhaust nozzle provide reverse thrust.

Hot-air balloons use the difference in weight between hot air inside the balloon and colder air outside to obtain lift.

Ballooning is based on the theory of displacement. A container filled with hot air, or with a gas such as hydrogen or helium, will stay airborne. This is because the weight of the air it displaces is not less than the weight of the gas or hot air.

A hot-air balloon consists of a wicker basket in which the pilot and crew stand, a gas burner and a large airtight nylon envelope with a big opening at the base. To ascend, you turn on the burner, which heats the air inside the balloon in only a few minutes. To descend, you allow the air inside the balloon to cool. This takes quite a long time, and so the burner may be turned off for a while before the balloon starts to descend. On landing you open a ripping panel to deflate the balloon quickly and prevent the wind dragging it.

▼ WHY DO YACHTS HAVE DIFFERENT TYPES OF SAIL?

Yachts travel by wind-power. Different sails are used in order to capture the wind and make full use of it.

The standard sails on a small yacht are the mainsail and the jib. The mainsail is a large triangular sail hoisted tight to the mast. Its bottom edge is fixed to a flexible boom. The boom follows each change of wind direction so that the wind always fills the mainsail completely. The jib billows out from the bows (front) of the yacht to catch the wind.

Many yachts also have a foresail (also hoisted from the mast), a cruising chute, used to catch the wind when it is behind the boat, and a spinnaker, which has a similar purpose.

Together, the jib and mainsail create an aerofoil shape that helps to propel the boat. Sails are continually adjusted to make best use of the wind.

▼ WHY DO BOATS HAVE KEELS?

The keel is the lowest part of a boat's bottom. It runs the whole length of the boat, and the rest of the vessel is built up from it.

The original purpose of a keel was structural. On wooden ships, the ribs (long wooden planks that formed the framework for the sides) were fixed into the keel. So too were the stempost (at the bows) and the sternpost. The keel itself was a long piece of timber, or several pieces joined together.

Modern sailing boats have fixed or drop keels. Fixed keels are ballasted to help overcome wind-pressure and keep the boat upright. Small yachts and dinghies have drop keels. In a following wind (blowing in the boat's direction of travel), the keel is raised to reduce resistance and increase speed. In a side wind it is lowered to resist drift and help the wind propel the boat.

▼ WHY ARE THERE DIFFERENT TYPES OF MERCHANT SHIP?

Ships are built to do different types of work. Cargo vessels vary according to the cargo they carry.

Ships are expensive to build and run. To make a profit, shipowners have to specialize. An oil tanker, for instance, is built to carry oil and nothing else. The engine room, bridge and crew quarters are situated at the stern, which leaves the rest of the ship for huge oil tanks.

Container ships are designed to carry as many containers as possible, both in the hold and on deck. Some general cargo vessels are still at work. Their holds can take virtually any type of freight.

Roll-on/roll-off ferries are an efficient way of carrying cars and their passengers. The cars are driven directly on board.

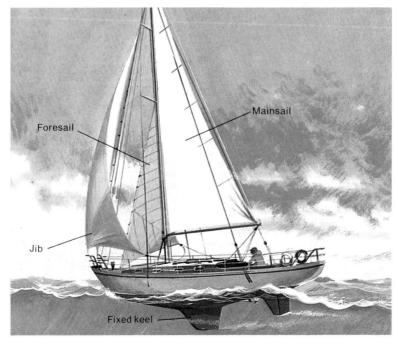

Oil tanker

General cargo vessel

Roll-on/roll-off ferry

Container ship

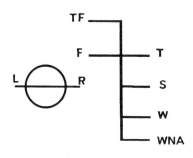

WHY DO SHIPS HAVE LOAD-LINES?

Load-lines must be painted amidships on every merchant vessel. They are a safety measure that shows how much cargo a ship may carry.

The circle on the left is known as the Plimsoll Line. Samuel Plimsoll was a 19th-century social reformer who fought for greater safety at sea.

The horizontal line through the centre shows the depth to which a vessel may be loaded in summer in salt water. The initials *LR* stand for Lloyd's Register, the London organization in charge of enforcing these regulations.

The marks on the right show the maximum loading depth in different conditions, from bottom to top: Winter North Atlantic (WNA), Winter (W), Summer (S) and Tropical (T). The rougher the sea, the less cargo a ship may carry. TF and F stand for Tropical Fresh and Fresh. Fresh water is much less buoyant than salt, and so a vessel can safely be loaded to a greater depth at an inland port. Maritime charts show in which parts of the world each load-line applies.

WHY WERE SUBMARINES INVENTED?

A vessel that can travel underwater is extremely useful in wartime. It can attack enemy ships and can also be used to land men and equipment in secret.

At the end of the 19th century submarines with their own weapon, the torpedo, were developed.

Submarines played a very important role in both world wars. They attacked enemy ships and prevented them from reaching home with food and equipment.

Many submarines are nuclear-powered. The first, the American *Nautilus*, was launched in 1954. They can stay submerged for a very long time and are armed with long-range missiles that can be launched underwater. They are now a vital part of a country's defence system.

Undersea craft used for civilian purposes are called submersibles.

WHY DO CANALS HAVE LOCKS?

A lock is like a step. It raises or lowers barges on the canal from one level to another.

Canals are artificial waterways. When they run through hilly country, they have to change level at a lock.

A barge travelling upstream enters the lock through a pair of lock gates, which close behind it. Sluices at the other end of the lock are opened to let in water, and gradually the water-level in the lock rises. When it is the same level as the canal beyond the lock, the farther gates are opened and the barge moves forward.

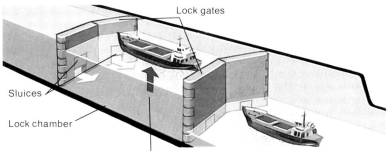

Lock gates

Sluices

Lock chamber

Water-level rises as sluices let water in

The world's longest railway is the Trans-Siberian Railway that runs across the Soviet Union.

The Trans-Siberian Railway was built to link European Russia with the Pacific Ocean in the Far East. The railway's name means 'across Siberia'. Its track runs right across Siberia, the northern part of Asia. This Siberian stretch of track measures 7407 kilometres from Chelyabinsk near the Ural Mountains to the port of Vladivostok on the Pacific Ocean.

You could take an even longer trip by joining the train at Moscow in European Russia. The distance from Moscow to Nakodhka, at the end of the line, is 9438

kilometres. This is the world's longest train journey. It involves 97 stops and lasts eight days.

In 1938, work started on making a short-cut to bypass a long southern loop around Lake Baikal. Laying this

northern stretch of track involved shifting colossal quantities of earth and building 3700 bridges. The new line was complete by 1983. It will shorten the journey across Siberia by 500 kilometres.

The Orient Express was a famous luxury passenger train that used to travel across Europe from west to east and back. Its name comes from *Orient*, another word for 'east'.

The Orient Express brought great style to rail travel in Europe. The train had a library, smoking-room, ladies' boudoir, dining-car and sleeping-cars.

People sat in red-plush armchairs. They washed in bathrooms with mosaic floors and ate in a tapestry-lined dining-car with an embossed leather ceiling.

The route of the train has changed several times since the name Orient Express was first used in 1883. At times wars and other problems have made

it impossible for trains to travel across all Europe.

At one time passengers could travel direct from Paris to the Turkish city of Istanbul, where Europe meets Asia. The train passed through Milan in Italy, Belgrade in Yugoslavia, and Sofia in Bulgaria. Today's

nearest equivalent runs from Paris to Vienna in Austria and Bucharest in Romania.

In the early 1980s the Venice Simplon Orient Express began running between London and Venice. It brought back the luxury travel of the old-style Oriental Express.

▲ WHERE IS THE LONGEST ROAD?

▲ WHERE DO PEOPLE USE RICKSHAWS?

▲ WHICH CITY HAD THE FIRST UNDERGROUND RAILWAY?

The world's longest road is the Pan-American Highway. It runs from north-western North America to the far south of South America.

The Pan-American Highway extends from Alaska to Chile. In fact it is not a single road, but a system of routes linking the countries of North and Central America and those of the west coast of South America.

The highway system remains incomplete. A stretch of swampy tropical forest, called the Darién Gap, separates Panama from Colombia and so cuts off the route between Central and South America.

American nations began planning a Pan-American road link in the 1920s. They had built most of the system by the early 1950s. South American countries paid for the parts of the highway within their own borders. The United States helped to pay for the section between Texas and Panama.

People use rickshaws as taxis in East and South-East Asia. They are light vehicles, often pulled or pedalled by a man, and usually carrying one passenger.

The name rickshaw comes from *jinrikisha*, which is made up of three Japanese words: *jin* (man), *riki* (power) and *sha* (vehicle).

Rickshaws were supposedly invented by a missionary to Japan in about 1870. A rickshaw has a chair-like body. It is covered with a movable hood and is mounted on springs. Early models had two large wheels with wire spokes, and two shafts. A passenger sat in the back and the rickshaw driver stood between the shafts, with which he pulled the rickshaw along. Pulling the rickshaw required great physical effort.

The use of rickshaws spread to China, India and Africa. Rickshaws with built-in cycles or motorcycle engines have mostly taken the place of the type that was pulled along.

London was the world's first city to have an underground railway. The first part of this system was opened in 1863.

London needed an underground railway system by the 1860s. The city was growing fast and its streets were becoming crowded with slow, horse-drawn traffic.

Because London stands on soft clay, it was fairly easy to drive tunnels under the city. The workers dug down from street level to make the first shallow, underground track. This was built for steam trains.

Later, engineers cut new tunnels at deeper levels for railway lines served by electric passenger-trains. The London underground railway now has a number of interlinked lines that cover 410 kilometres.

Today, many cities have underground railways. They include Paris, Milan, New York and Moscow.

421

Different types of plane travel at a variety of altitudes, or heights. How high a plane flies depends largely on what it was designed for, and on regulations laid down by authorities that control air traffic.

Small, propeller-driven planes mostly fly at fairly low levels – high enough to avoid dangers such as mountains and tall structures, but below the flight paths that are used by jet airliners.

Jet airliners often fly at a height of about 9000 metres. *Concorde*, a supersonic airliner, flies even higher. Flying high helps planes to keep above rough weather. But air-traffic controllers assign flight levels to planes to prevent them colliding.

Some military planes can reach amazing altitudes. The American Lockheed SR-71 spy plane can fly 30.5 kilometres high, and a Russian 'Foxbat' (MiG-25) has soared to an incredible height of 37.7 kilometres.

MiG-25 'Foxbat'

In 1981 an airport at Jeddah in western Saudi Arabia became the world's largest. Two years later, Saudi Arabia completed an even larger airport, shown here in the picture, at the capital, Riyadh.

King Abdul-Aziz International Airport at Jeddah was built mainly to receive the nearly two million Muslim pilgrims who visit Mecca each year.

The airport site covers 116.6 square kilometres. There are two main runways and four terminals. The Haj terminal, the world's largest roofed building, covers 1.5 square kilometres. In style it resembles a cluster of nomads' tents, but it has marble walls and glass-fibre roofs.

In 1983, the even larger King Khaled Airport opened at Riyadh. This also has two runways and four terminals. There is a royal pavilion, as well as covered parking for 7700 cars, and buildings for the people who live and work there.

The busiest air routes are those between certain cities in North America, and over parts of Europe.

A good indication of where the most air traffic occurs is the number of people passing through different airports. Chicago International Airport handles the most flights. Nearly a quarter of a million people arrived at or left the airport in 1980. Over 43 million people passed through it. Most were taking flights to or from other American cities.

The next busiest airport is Hartsfield International Airport at Atlanta, Georgia. A new terminal, opened in 1980, allows it to cope with up to 60 million people a year.

The busiest international airport is Heathrow Airport, London. By the early 1980s Heathrow handled more than 28 million passengers a year.

On average, more than two and a half times as many people fly in North America as in the next busiest areas: Europe and Russia.

The worst accident in the history of air travel happened at Tenerife, one of the Canary Islands off north-west Africa. More than 500 people died when two jumbo jets collided there before take-off in 1977.

The disaster took place at Los Rodeos Airport on 27 March, 1977. The airport was crowded with planes which had been diverted there after a terrorists' bomb had exploded at a big airport on a nearby island.

A Dutch KLM Boeing-747 and a Pan-Am Boeing-747 were taxiing for take-off in mist and drizzle. The Dutch plane struck the Pan-Am plane and both burst into flames. All the 248 people aboard the Dutch plane died, and 335 perished on the other aircraft. There were over 60 survivors.

Pilot error, poor visibility and lack of radar at the airport helped to cause this terrible disaster. Nobody had noticed when one plane moved into the other's path.

The 'black box' is the popular name for a flight recorder, a device carried in aircraft. Its purpose is to reveal the cause of faults if these develop in flight.

Flight recorders show how aircraft systems behave. They give information about a plane's heading, height, air speed, rate of descent and so on. On some recorders, the information appears as lines engraved on a strip of metal foil. This is housed in a crashproof, fireproof, floatable box. In a crash the box is hurled clear and recovered later. There are also digital recorders which record the information in binary code.

Besides a flight recorder, airliners carry a cockpit voice recorder to record aircrew conversations. Between them, the flight recorder and voice recorder help experts to learn what caused a crash, even if all aboard were killed. Such information helps designers to produce safer planes.

Engineers can position aircraft engines anywhere where they will work without unbalancing the plane in flight.

All aircraft engines must be placed where pipes can feed fuel to them from storage tanks. Piston engines, turbo-jets and turbo-props must all be able to suck in air from the front and force out air or hot gases from the back, to thrust a plane forward.

Piston engines and turbo-prop engines spin airscrews (propellers) that push or pull a plane along. 'Puller' airscrews project forward from engines mounted in the nose or wings. A few planes have pusher airscrews jutting backwards from wing-mounted engines. There are even push-pull twin-engined aircraft, with airscrews at both ends.

Airliners have turbo-jets built into or slung below the wings, or on the rear fuselage. Fast warplanes have turbo-jets in or alongside the fuselage.

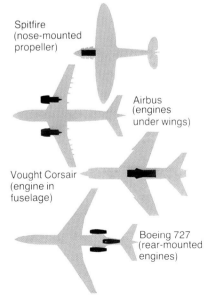

Spitfire (nose-mounted propeller)

Airbus (engines under wings)

Vought Corsair (engine in fuselage)

Boeing 727 (rear-mounted engines)

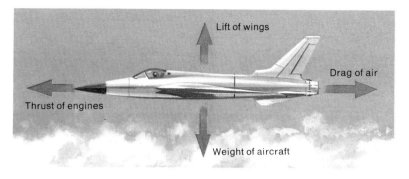

Lift of wings

Drag of air

Thrust of engines

Weight of aircraft

▲ HOW DO AIRCRAFT FLY?

To fly, aircraft need power, which they get from their engines. They also need lift to raise them from the ground and keep them in the air. Lift is provided by the wings.

Aircraft wings are aerofoils. They have a rounded upper surface and a flat underside. Their front edge is rounded and the back edge is tapered. As the plane moves through the air, the front edges of the wings split the air in two. One half moves over the rounded top edge, the other under the flat bottom edge. The air on top moves faster than the air underneath because it has further to travel. This reduces the pressure above the wing and creates lift.

At take-off, the aircraft's engines provide the power to generate lift. When the plane is flying at a constant speed, the lift from the wings equals the weight of the plane. The forward thrust of the engines balances the resistance, or drag, set up by the air.

▼ HOW IS AIR-TRAFFIC CONTROL ORGANIZED?

Air-traffic controllers make sure that planes take off and land safely and with as little delay as possible. They tell pilots exactly where to fly so that collisions with other planes are avoided.

When a plane is about 2700 metres away from an airport and 600 metres above it, it enters the terminal control area. Working from the traffic control centre, which looks out on the runways, an air-traffic controller guides the pilot down, telling him at which speed and height to fly.

Radar provides air-traffic controllers with continuously updated information about the exact position, destination and identity of every plane, and about weather conditions.

The controller makes the final decision about which plane should land where.

Planes waiting to land are often 'stacked' – they circle the airport in a vertical queue. As a plane approaches the air-field, radio beams guide it to the runway. Air-traffic controllers are also responsible for aircraft taking off, and they often control planes throughout their flight from one city to the next.

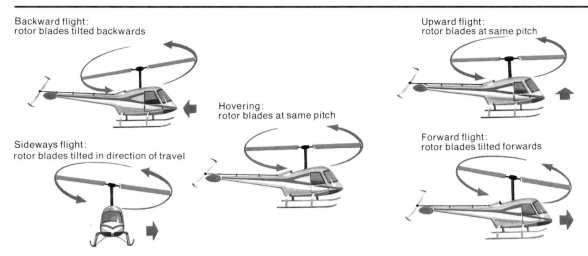

Backward flight:
rotor blades tilted backwards

Upward flight:
rotor blades at same pitch

Hovering:
rotor blades at same pitch

Sideways flight:
rotor blades tilted in direction of travel

Forward flight:
rotor blades tilted forwards

▲ HOW DO HELICOPTERS FLY?

Helicopters can fly in any direction, and even hover. The rotor blades control the direction.

The helicopter's engine drives the rotor. The blades of the rotor are aerofoils, and they generate lift when they rotate. When a helicopter hovers, the blades all rotate at the same pitch. The weight of the craft balances the upward pull of the rotor.

To climb, the angle of attack of the blades must be increased. The angle of attack is the angle at which the leading edges of the blades meet the air. To move forwards, the blades are tilted forwards. This increases their angle of attack at the rear of the helicopter but decreases it at the front, so pushing the craft forwards. Similar adjustments can make the helicopter fly in any direction.

The spinning of the rotor makes the helicopter itself rotate in the opposite direction. In most helicopters a tail rotor cancels this out.

▼ HOW DO PLANES TAKE OFF AND LAND VERTICALLY?

Vertical take-off planes go straight up into the air. They use the thrust developed by their jets to lift themselves or to land.

In normal jet planes, the jet engine is positioned horizontally. Air is sucked in at one end and mixed with fuel in a compression chamber. The exhaust gases stream out at the other end, thrusting the plane forwards. Vertical take-off and landing (VTOL) planes make use of the same process, but their jets are positioned vertically. The exhaust is directed downwards and the resulting thrust is vertical.

VTOL craft are useful for military purposes, but less so for carrying passengers on commercial flights. Extremely powerful engines are needed for vertical take-off, and these leave less room for passengers and freight. VTOL craft are also very noisy. Some types of VTOL planes have separate engines to provide lift, or swivelling jets that can be positioned vertically or horizontally.

Forward flight:
jet nozzles point backwards

Take-off, landing and hovering:
jet nozzles point downwards

Climbing:
jet nozzles point diagonally

425

detailed work. Sometimes a scale model is built and tested in a tank.

Now the ship starts to take shape. Sections of the hull are built in the shipyard and are brought to the building berth for assembly. Some ships are assembled from amidships in each direction. On others, workers begin at the stern and work towards the bows. Some parts, such as the propeller and the anchor, are made in another place.

The launch, when the ship slides into the water, is an occasion of great ceremony. The fitting-out takes place afterwards. This involves installing the engine, the plumbing, electrical and navigational equipment, life-boats and so on. The ship is also furnished and decorated.

▲ HOW ARE SHIPS BUILT?

Ships are built in two main stages. First the shell is built. Then comes the fitting-out, when the machinery and equipment are installed.

Months of planning are necessary before the construction work can begin. First, a general design is agreed. Then detailed working drawings of every single part are made. Often a computer does a lot of the

▼ HOW DO TRAWLERS FISH?

Trawlers fish with a large bag-like net called a trawl. They use it to catch fish such as cod, plaice, sole, hake and halibut.

The trawl may be over 100 metres long. It is let out on

long warps, or ropes, from the stern to enormous depths, sometimes 1500 metres or more. The fish are swept in at the wide, open end and then get trapped at the narrower, closed end. Floats and large wooden weights called otter boards keep the mouth of the net open. When the net is full, powered winches haul it on

board through a ramp at the stern.

Many modern trawlers are large factory vessels on which the fish are automatically gutted, filleted and frozen. There may even be a quality control laboratory.

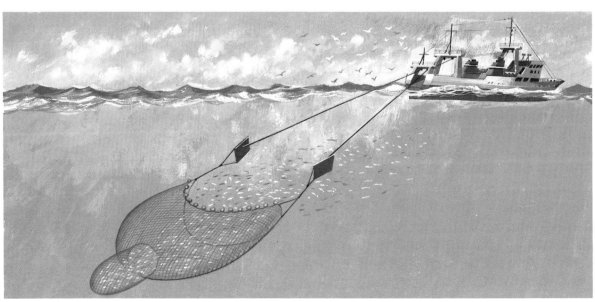

The propeller drives the ship through the water. Power is created by the ship's engines. It is transmitted to the propeller. The turning propeller converts the power into thrust for pushing the ship through the water.

Marine propellers usually have between four and seven blades, made of manganese bronze. As they turn, they speed up the movement of the water passing through them. The speeded-up water drives the ship forwards.

There are fixed and variable-pitch propellers. On fixed propellers, the angle of the blades cannot be changed.

This means that the ship operates best only at her normal cruising speed. On variable-pitch propellers, the blade angle can be altered to suit the speed required and different weather conditions.

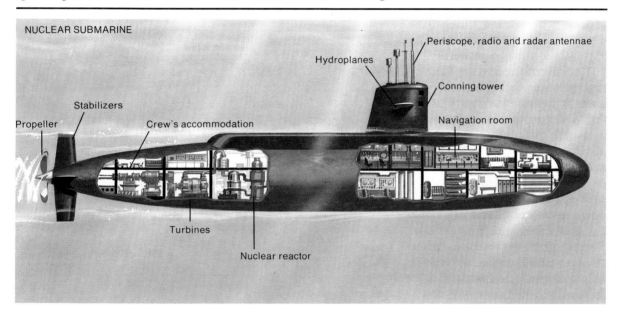

NUCLEAR SUBMARINE

Hydroplanes

Periscope, radio and radar antennae

Conning tower

Navigation room

Stabilizers

Propeller

Crew's accommodation

Turbines

Nuclear reactor

Submarines use small fins called hydroplanes to dive and surface. Ordinary submarines are powered by electric motors and diesel engines. Nuclear submarines produce their power in a nuclear reactor.

When the submarine wants to dive, its ballast tanks are flooded with sea water, and the hydroplanes are set to direct the craft downwards.

Once it is submerged, the hydroplanes are readjusted to control the angle of the dive. When the submarine has reached the right depth, the hydroplanes are set to horizontal, and small auxiliary ballast tanks are flooded.

The opposite happens when the vessel surfaces. The hydroplanes are set to direct the craft up. When it is close to the surface, compressed air is used to blow water out of the main ballast tanks. As the conning tower, which contains the periscope and is used for observation, breaks the surface, fresh air is sucked in to finish emptying the tanks.

Ordinary submarines use battery-powered electric motors while they are underwater and diesel engines when cruising on the surface. The diesel engines also recharge the batteries.

Nuclear subs use heat from a nuclear reactor on board to drive a steam turbine. The turbine also generates the electricity the vessel needs. Nuclear submarines can submerge for a long time.

▶ WHAT DOES A DREDGER DO?

Dredgers remove mud, sand or shingle from the beds of rivers, lakes, canals or harbours. This work keeps waterways open and can be a way of gathering building materials and mining tin and gold.

Exactly what a dredger does depends upon how it is designed.

Bucket dredgers use an endless chain of buckets to scoop up silt. They tip this into a chute that lets it slide down into a barge moored beside the dredger.

Dipper dredgers scoop up material in a huge mechanical shovel that can be swung around and lowered from a boom. Grab dredgers work in a similar way, but use a scoop with jaws that can be closed and opened.

Suction dredgers are like giant vacuum cleaners. Their powerful pumps suck up mud or sand through pipes.

▶ WHAT IS A SUPER-TANKER?

Supertankers are giant oil tankers. They are built to carry huge loads of crude oil from oil-fields around the world to industrial regions such as north-west Europe.

By the 1980s supertankers included the largest vessels of any kind. Biggest of all was the *Seawise Giant* which can carry a total load of over 560,000 tons. This monster is roughly as long as four soccer pitches laid end to end, and wider than six tennis courts placed side by side. Yet a handful of crew can manage the ship.

People built supertankers because they were cheap to run. It costs less to shift a huge load in one ship than to divide that load among several ships.

But huge size brings some drawbacks. Supertankers cannot stop or turn quickly. If one runs aground its spilt oil pollutes huge areas.

▶ WHAT ARE BARGES USED FOR?

Most barges are flat-bottomed boats used for carrying heavy loads on inland waterways.

Barges mainly carry building materials like cement, wooden planks and sand. They also carry food, like grain and sugar, or fuels like coal and oil. Some roll-on roll-off barges can take over 300 lorries.

Many barges have no engines of their own. Some are towed by horses or electric engines that run on rails along the banks of rivers or canals. Others are pushed or pulled by tugs. One tug can pull a number of barges at once.

Moving heavy loads by barge may be slower than shifting them by road or rail but it is also less expensive.

The name *barge* is also used to describe a large motorboat carrying a high-ranking naval officer, or an elegantly decorated and roomy pleasure boat.

432

WHAT IS A PADDLE STEAMER?

In this kind of steamship the engine turns one or more paddle wheels. Each paddle wheel has spokes that end in broad blades. These beat the water and push it backward to thrust the steamer forward.

Some paddle steamers have two paddle wheels, one at each side. Others have only one paddle wheel fitted to the ship's stern. The side wheels are usually covered by curved paddle boxes that may be decorated.

Many tugs and excursion vessels once had side paddles. These helped the boats to make sharp turns near piers.

In the United States, big stern-wheel paddle steamers once took thousands of passengers up and down the Mississippi River. Such ships had shallow hulls but carried heavy loads.

Most paddle steamers have been replaced by diesel-engine ships with screws instead of paddles.

WHAT IS A HYDROFOIL?

This looks like an ordinary craft until it picks up speed. Then it rises on underwater wings called foils. Hydrofoils are used mostly as ferries making short, fast trips.

Foils increase a hydrofoil's speed because they reduce the friction caused by the hull rubbing against the water.

Most hydrofoils have one of four main types of foil. Ladder foils are arranged like rungs on a ladder: the faster the vessel moves, the more the foils show up above the surface. Depth-effect foils are single wings that ride just under the surface and work well in calm, shallow water. Submerged foils are small foils that ride deeper down at angles that can be controlled. They work well in rough seas.

Most modern hydrofoils have surface-piercing foils. These are shaped like a shallow V and they keep the craft stable as it turns sharply or speeds through steep waves.

WHAT IS A SUBMERSIBLE USED FOR?

These small, powered craft are designed for underwater work or exploration.

Since the 1950s inventors have developed many kinds of submersible.

The first to be produced was the French *Soucoupe*, or diving saucer. Its crew could study sea-bed life to a depth of 300 metres.

Later came the *Aluminaut*. This American submersible's crew of three could operate grappling arms to rescue sunken objects lying as much as 4600 metres deep.

Nowadays manned and robot submersibles do valuable work on undersea oil and gas pipes and other installations.

Some unmanned submersibles have built-in cameras, sonar equipment, power tools and lights. An observer and a pilot at the surface can guide this type of submersible by remote control as it works 600 metres below.

OUT IN SPACE

▼ WHY DO THE PLANETS
REVOLVE ROUND THE SUN?

If the planets did not move, the Sun's pull would drag them inwards. But if they moved too quickly, they would fly off into space. The closer a planet is to the Sun, the faster it must move.

The planets all move in the same direction. They were probably formed from the same spinning cloud of material that produced the Sun. At birth, the Sun would have been spinning on its axis in a few hours. The cloud's pull slowed it down to its present 25-day period.

Apart from Venus and Uranus, all the planets spin in an anti-clockwise direction too. Venus spins very slowly backwards, while the axis of Uranus is tilted right over, so that it spins on its side.

▼ WHY IS THERE LIFE ON
THE EARTH?

All life, from human beings to bacteria, will die if it becomes too hot or too cold, or if there is no air to breathe. No other planet in the Solar System has the right conditions for Earth-like life.

Known life is based on microscopic cells containing countless carbon atoms. But cells need substances containing elements such as hydrogen, oxygen and nitrogen if they are to survive. Although all the planets contain these basic elements, the Earth is the only planet with large amounts of water and oxygen. Both are essential for life.

The Sun's deadly rays are also filtered out by ozone (a kind of oxygen) in the upper atmosphere.

▼ WHY CAN'T WE SEE
OTHER SOLAR SYSTEMS?

The nearest star is over a quarter of a million times as far away as the Sun. At this distance, even a large planet would be invisible in the biggest telescope. But some stars appear to 'wobble' slightly in the sky. This may be caused by the gravitational pull of a planet.

Most astronomers believe that a star in the constellation Cygnus known as *61 Cygni* has a planet revolving around it. Accurate measurements show that it is being pulled from side to side by an invisible companion, which must have about ten times the mass of Jupiter. It cannot be a faint star, because no star can be as small as this. It could not become hot enough to shine.

Mercury Venus Earth Mars Jupiter Saturn Uranus Neptune Pluto

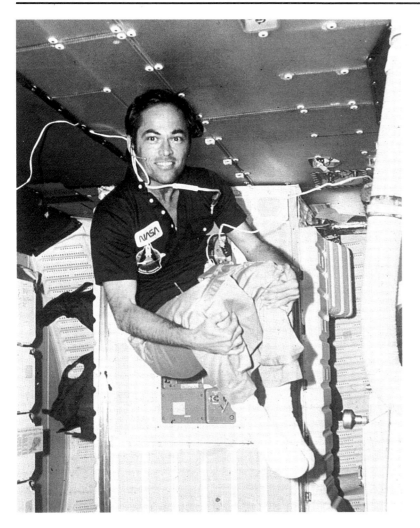

A planet is a dark body orbiting a star. It can only be seen by the starlight it reflects. All the planets in the Solar System reflect light from the Sun. A moon (or satellite) also shines by reflection, but it revolves around a planet.

Of the nine planets, only Mercury and Venus have no known satellites. Spacecraft have helped to discover 14 around Jupiter and 23 around Saturn. Saturn has the largest satellite in the Solar System, Titan, which is 5120 kilometres across. It is larger than both Mercury and Pluto.

Most satellites are much smaller than their planet, although the Moon is a quarter of the Earth's diameter and Pluto is only twice as large as its moon Charon. Mars has two tiny moons, Phobos and Deimos, 23 kilometres and 13 kilometres across. Titan, and the four largest satellites of Jupiter, can be spotted with good binoculars.

Weight is the force you feel when the floor, or a chair, stops you from falling towards the centre of the Earth. If a hole opened in the ground, you would be weightless while falling down it. This is known as 'free fall'. Flying through space, everything is in free fall.

An astronaut floats inside his cabin because he is moving at the same speed as the spacecraft. He will feel weight only if the motors fire, because the spacecraft will change speed or accelerate.

At take-off there is tremendous acceleration, and the astronaut is pushed down hard onto his couch. He feels several times heavier than he did when standing on the Earth's surface.

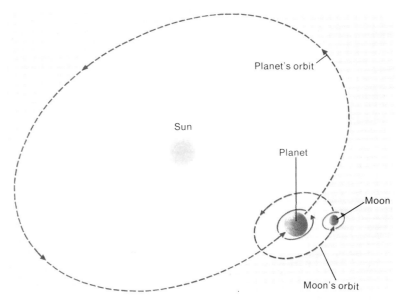

Sun

Planet's orbit

Planet

Moon

Moon's orbit

435

If iron is left outside exposed to the weather, it turns rusty. The rocks on the surface of Mars contain iron which has turned into a kind of rust. This red, dusty material covers the planet's surface and is sometimes blown into huge dust storms.

▲ WHY IS MARS A DEAD WORLD?

The two *Viking* spacecraft which reached the planet in 1976 and examined its surface did not find any signs of life. They also discovered that the temperature is always below freezing point, and the atmosphere is thin and unbreathable.

All known living things contain cells made up of carbon atoms. The *Viking* landers did not find in the Martian soil any cells of the kind familiar to scientists, whereas the Earth's soil is teeming with them. Perhaps Mars has cells of a different type, or perhaps the spacecraft could have landed in more favourable places?

Mars may once have been warmer than it is now. From Earth, we can see channels in the surface which could have been carved by running water, and microscopic life-forms might have survived. But most people are convinced that Mars is a dead world.

Rust, or iron oxide, is a compound made of iron and oxygen combined together. There is now no oxygen left in Mars' atmosphere, since it also combined with other materials, forming water (with hydrogen) and probably carbon dioxide (with carbon). There are some 'rusty' rocks to be seen in various places on the Earth. One of these is the Grand Canyon in Arizona, USA.

On Mars, the dust is so fine that it hangs in the thin air as a permanent haze, causing the sky to be pink rather than dark blue. Sometimes the surface of Mars disappears from our sight for days or weeks beneath thick clouds of dust raised by the Martian winds.

▶ WHICH PLANET SPINS THE FASTEST?

Jupiter, which is the largest of the planets in the Solar System, spins on its axis in the shortest time, only 9 hours and 50 minutes. The next fastest planet is its giant neighbour Saturn, with a 'day' of 10 hours and 16 minutes.

Jupiter is much less solid than the Earth, and this causes different parts of its surface to rotate in different times. The Great Red Spot takes about five minutes longer to go round once than do objects near Jupiter's equator. The white oval cloud shown in the photograph, which has been seen and recorded for many years, also has its own different period of rotation.

When an object spins, an effect known as centrifugal force makes it begin to fly apart. This force causes Jupiter's equatorial regions to bulge outwards by about 5000 kilometres. If it did not rotate, Jupiter would be a perfect sphere.

The atmosphere of Venus is about 90 times as thick as our own. Although it is always cloudy, enough sunlight breaks through to heat the ground during its four-year 'day'. This thick atmosphere acts like a blanket, holding in the heat, so that the midday temperature is 480°C, as hot as an oven turned fully on.

This is often called the 'greenhouse effect', since the air inside a greenhouse heats up for the same reason. Sunlight can pass through the glass, but when it has been absorbed by the ground inside, it is turned into heat radiation. This is blocked by the glass and cannot escape. Like the atmosphere of Venus (and of the Earth) it is a heat trap.

The atmosphere of Venus contains a lot of carbon dioxide, a gas which holds in heat very well. More carbon dioxide in our own atmosphere would raise the surface temperature of the Earth to a dangerous level.

The innermost planet, Mercury, seems to swing out first on one side and then on the other side of the Sun. These appearances are known as 'elongations'. At eastern elongation (to the left of the Sun, as seen from the northern hemisphere) it is low in the western sky after sunset. At western elongation, it rises in the dawn sky. At these times, it looks like a star.

Mercury takes about 116 days to return to the same elongation, so there are three morning and three evening elongations each year.

Spring evening elongations and autumn morning elongations are the easiest to see, but Mercury is never very obvious to observers in Britain and northern Europe.

Mercury sometimes passes in front of the Sun. The next 'transit' of this type will occur on 13 November 1986.

The surface of the Sun is about four times as hot as a furnace. The lens or cornea in your eye acts like a burning-glass. If you look straight at the Sun, the lens will be destroyed for life.

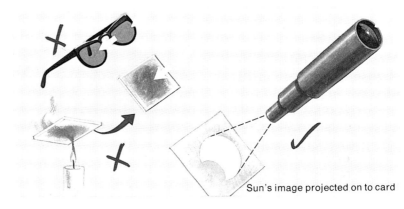

Sun's image projected on to card

Some people suggest looking at the Sun through smoked glass. Don't! The Sun may look dim, but the dangerous heat rays can pass through. Whenever there is an eclipse of the Sun, some people are blinded because they take foolish risks of this sort.

To observe the Sun, you should project its image through binoculars or a telescope onto a sheet of white card. Sunspots can then be seen easily and safely by a group of people together.

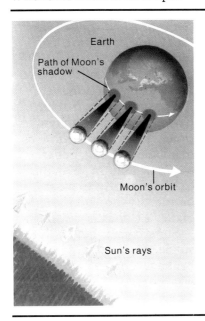

Earth

Path of Moon's shadow

Moon's orbit

Sun's rays

The Sun is about 400 times the diameter of the Moon, but it is also 400 times as far away from the Earth. This means that both bodies look about the same size in the sky. If the Moon passes in front of the Sun, it can block out the brilliant disc, so that the faint surrounding 'corona' can be seen.

A solar eclipse can be seen only at New Moon, when the Moon is between the Earth and the Sun. But the line-up must be exact, or else only a partial eclipse will be seen, and the beautiful corona will not appear.

The diameter of the Moon's shadow on the Earth's surface, within which a *total* eclipse can be seen, is never more than a few hundred kilometres wide. This is why people wishing to see an eclipse must be prepared to travel a long way to see one. On average, a total eclipse is seen from the same site every 350 years.

The Earth's atmosphere is like a pale red filter, and makes all the light coming from space turn slightly reddish. But an object which is very low in the sky has to shine through much more air than one high in the sky. This means that its light passes through more of this red filter, and its tint is deeper.

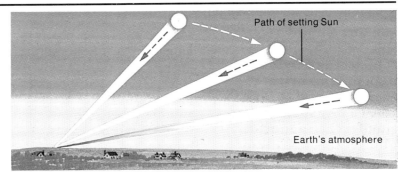

Path of setting Sun

Earth's atmosphere

Since red light passes through air more easily than any other colour does, photographs of the Earth's surface taken from aircraft or satellites are often taken using a red filter.

The same is true of the thin atmosphere of Mars. Photographs taken with a red filter show the planet's surface details well, whereas pictures taken with a blue filter show the hazy atmosphere of Mars and any thin clouds that may be present.

▶ WHY DOES THE SUN KEEP SHINING?

Even the tiniest object you can see with a microscope contains millions of atoms. Each atom contains much tinier particles still. Inside the Sun, atoms are being pulled to pieces and put together again in a different way. This gives out heat, and keeps the Sun shining.

The Sun is made up of 90 per cent hydrogen atoms, about nine per cent helium atoms (on the Earth, helium is a very light gas used to lift balloons), and one per cent other elements such as oxygen and nitrogen. In its centre, at a temperature of about 20 million degrees, hydrogen atoms are broken down and reassembled as helium atoms. Four hydrogen atoms (H) are required to make one helium atom (He). In this process, a burst of energy is given out.

The Sun's hydrogen will last for thousands of millions of years from now, at least as long as it has already existed.

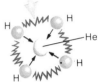

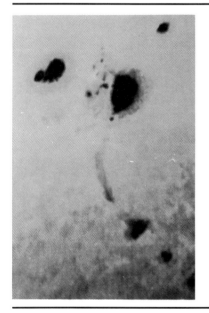

◀ WHY ARE THERE SPOTS ON THE SUN?

Sunspots are huge cool patches on the Sun's surface, caused by a very strong magnetic pull from the layers below. This magnetism acts rather like a cooling wind. Since they are cooler than the surrounding surface, sunspots appear dark.

Sunspots often occur in pairs or complicated groups, and may last for just a few days, or for many weeks. The middle of a spot is coolest and darkest, and is called the 'umbra'. Surrounding this is a lighter region called the 'penumbra'. The umbra is about 1000°C cooler than the Sun's surface, but it is still much hotter than some dim stars.

The Sun shows a regular change of sunspot activity. Every 11 years (as in 1969 and 1980) sunspots are especially common. A very big group of sunspots may measure ten times the Earth's diameter from one side to the other. One this size was seen in 1982.

▶ HOW BIG IS THE SUN?

The Sun measures 1,392,530 kilometres across, or 109 times the diameter of the Earth. Over a million Earths could be squashed into the Sun's globe. If the Sun were the size of a football, the Earth would be only two millimetres across.

Although the Sun is enormous compared with the planets, it is much smaller than many stars. The bright reddish star Betelgeuse in the constellation of Orion, is larger than the orbit of the planet Mars, or about 300 times the diameter of the Sun!

However, astronomers think that the Sun will eventually grow much larger than it is now. Its core will become so hot that the fierce radiation of energy will blast its outer layers into a glowing cloud, swallowing up the inner planets. It will become a 'red giant'.

443

WHY ARE STARS
INVISIBLE IN THE DAYTIME?

The stars are always in the sky, but the bright blue sky hides them. When the Sun sets, the blue fades away and the stars can be seen. This blue is caused by the atmosphere. In space, or on the airless Moon, the sky is always black and stars are always visible.

A powerful telescope can reveal some of the brighter stars even when the Sun is above the horizon. And the planet Venus is sometimes bright enough to be seen in broad daylight with the naked eye.

Some keen-eyed people have also seen Jupiter and Mars in the daytime! But the sky must be very transparent, without the slightest haze, and you must know exactly where to look.

When one of these planets is visible at dawn, it is interesting to see how long it can be kept in view, with the naked eye or binoculars, as the Sun rises and the sky turns to day.

▶ WHY DO STARS TWINKLE?

Out in space, stars do not twinkle. But when their light passes through the Earth's atmosphere, it is made to flicker by the hot and cold ripples of air. You can see this effect by looking at a distant view over a hot road in summer, or across a bonfire.

Astronomers call this effect 'bad seeing'. If the stars twinkle violently, their image

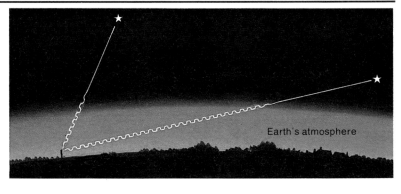

Earth's atmosphere

in the telescope will be a large blur instead of a tiny point, and small detail on the Moon or a planet will be invisible. Most bad seeing is caused by air currents several kilometres high. Large telescopes on mountaintops escape the worst of the unsteadiness, but bad seeing will also occur if the nearby ground is giving off heat waves.

◀ WHY ARE SOME STARS
BRIGHTER THAN OTHERS?

There are two reasons. Some stars give out more light, like a large electric bulb compared with a torch. Also, some stars are much closer to the Earth than others are, and even a dim nearby star may appear brighter than a very luminous distant one.

This distance effect can be seen by looking down a lamp-lit road at night. The distant street lamps look much fainter than the closer ones do. Astronomers call a star's brightness its 'magnitude'. The *apparent* magnitude is its brightness as we see it in the sky. The brightest stars are about magnitude 0, while the faintest visible with the naked eye are about magnitude 6. A star's real brightness, or luminosity, is called its *absolute* magnitude.

Some stars are many thousands of times as luminous as the Sun, but they may be too far away to be detected without a large telescope.

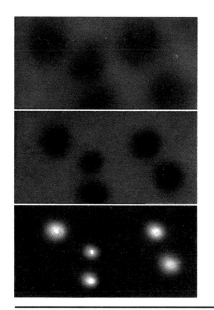

◀ HOW ARE STARS FORMED?

Stars begin their lives as very thin clouds of hydrogen gas, as shown in the top picture. As each cloud shrinks, the centre grows very hot due to the atoms of gas being squeezed together. Eventually, the clouds become so hot that they begin to shine as stars (bottom picture).

To begin with, the cloud which became the Sun was larger than the whole Solar System! Stars are usually formed in clusters, like the famous Pleiades, which were born about 100 million years ago inside a cloud or nebula several light-years across. The Sun was probably born in a cluster, but its companion stars have drifted away and cannot be identified.

Star-formation is still going on in our galaxy, since there are plenty of nebulae. But some other galaxies have very little gas left, and there are no new-born stars in their populations.

▶ HOW DO STARS DIE?

A star shines by turning its hydrogen into another element called helium. This change gives out heat, and keeps the star hot. When its hydrogen fuel runs down, the star begins to die.

Not all stars live for the same length of time. Small stars, dimmer than the Sun, use their fuel so slowly that they may have shone steadily ever since the Galaxy was formed, over 10,000 million years ago.

But very hot and brilliant stars, which contain a lot of hydrogen, may burn out in a few million years. Then they explode as a supernova, leaving wreckage like the Crab Nebula, shown here.

Others gradually blow their surfaces outwards like a red-hot cloud in the 'red-giant' stage. In the far future, the Sun may become a red giant.

▶ WHY DOES THE MILKY WAY LOOK PATCHY?

The Milky Way is our view of countless thousands of distant stars in the Galaxy. In some parts of the Milky Way, the stars are close together and the Galaxy shines more brightly. Elsewhere, it is hidden from view by huge dark clouds or nebulae that lie between us and the stars.

The Sun lies well away from the centre of the Galaxy, which is in the direction of the

constellation Sagittarius. The Milky Way is especially brilliant here, since the space in this direction is crowded with stars.

If we look in the opposite direction, towards Auriga, the Milky Way appears much fainter. The constellations Cygnus and Crux contain prominent dark nebulae in the Milky Way.

445

APOLLO MOON-ROCKET (SATURN 5)

- Spacecraft

Fuel tanks

Third stage

Engines

Fuel tanks

Second stage

Engines

Fuel tanks

First stage

Engines

USA

To escape from the Earth, a rocket must travel at 11 km per second. A single craft could not carry enough fuel to reach this speed: it would be too heavy to leave the ground! So a spacecraft has separate stages, which jump clear as the lower ones use up their fuel.

Normally, a three-stage rocket is powerful enough to launch an interplanetary probe. For example, the *Apollo* Moon-rocket at lift-off weighed about 3000 tonnes (as much as a hundred juggernauts), but over 2000 tonnes of this was fuel for the huge first stage, which took it only about 90 kilometres off the ground. Once this had fallen back to Earth, the craft had enough fuel left to take it all the way to the Moon and back.

Smaller rocket engines may need more stages. The Indian satellite *Rohini*, launched in 1980, required a four-stage rocket powered by solid fuel.

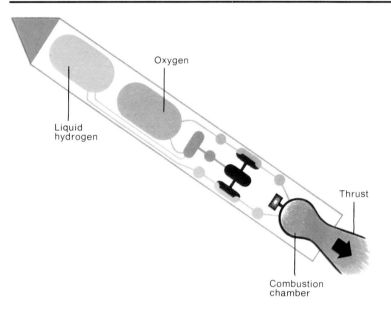

Liquid hydrogen

Oxygen

Thrust

Combustion chamber

On the Earth, we usually move by pushing or pulling against something fixed. But in space there is nothing to push or pull against, so movement must be by reaction. A bullet fired from a gun kicks the firer backwards: hot gas leaving a rocket kicks the spacecraft forward.

Gunpowder rockets can work only in the atmosphere, since the gunpowder fuel needs air in order to burn. A space rocket has to use two fuels that react explosively when they are mixed together. One of these fuels is usually oxygen, stored as a bitterly cold liquid, turning into gas as it passes out through a valve. The other fuel is usually kerosene or liquid hydrogen.

The famous Saturn rocket, which sent men to the Moon and launched the USA's interplanetary probes, uses kerosene as the first-stage fuel, and hydrogen for the other stages.

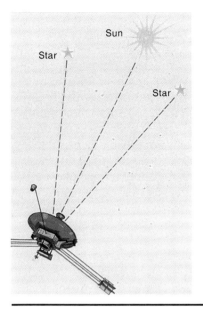

◀ HOW DOES A
SPACEPROBE NAVIGATE?

As a space vehicle travels through space, the Sun appears to move across the stars, just as a traveller on the Earth sees nearby buildings appear to move across more distant ones. A computer calculates where the Sun and stars should be, if the spacecraft is on course.

These observations are made by special telescopes fixed to the craft, but a system of inertial guidance is also used. If a large wheel is set spinning rapidly, it is very hard to move its axis. Like a spinning top, it wants to remain in the same plane. Three wheels, spinning at right angles to each other, keep a platform inside the spacecraft fixed in the same plane, so that course alterations can be measured when the motors fire.

The wheels used in the *Voyager* spacecraft were made so accurately that they would keep spinning for 36 hours if their motors were switched off!

▶ HOW DOES A SATELLITE
STAY IN ORBIT?

If we imagine a fantastically powerful gun on the top of a very high mountain, firing bullets at different speeds, three things could happen. The bullet could land on the ground far below (1); it could fly off into space (2); or it could curve exactly round the Earth and become a satellite (3).

To stay in orbit near the Earth, a satellite must travel at about 8 kilometres per second (28,000 kilometres per hour). Once it has gone into orbit, it will remain circling almost indefinitely. However, if it is less than about 200 kilometres above the Earth, the slight dragging effect of the Earth's outer atmosphere will cause it to lose speed and height, and after a few years it may burn up like a meteor.

A large satellite is braked more easily than a small one. The three-man *Skylab*, launched in 1973, fell to destruction from its orbit after only seven years.

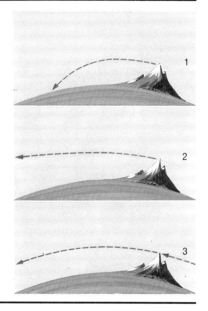

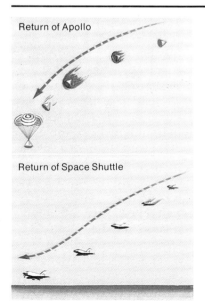

Return of Apollo

Return of Space Shuttle

◀ HOW DOES A
SPACECRAFT RETURN TO
EARTH?

All spacecraft must find a way of slowing down from a speed of many kilometres per second to give the crew, or cargo, a soft touch-down. The landing is usually done by parachute, but the Space Shuttle glides down.

The return of the *Apollo* craft was an example of high-speed atmospheric braking. It hit the atmosphere at a speed of 11 kilometres per second, the outer skin turning white-hot with friction. In a few minutes, the speed had dropped to 100 kilometres per hour, and it landed gently in the ocean by parachute.

The Shuttle, on the other hand, fires its engines in reverse to slow its orbital speed and it coasts down into the atmosphere at about 7 kilometres per second. It gets rid of this speed by banking and rolling along a path that takes it halfway round the world, landing at about 345 kilometres per hour.

▼ HOW DO ASTRONAUTS BREATHE IN SPACE?

Our air contains several different gases. The most important one is oxygen, since this is what we must breathe in order to live. So astronauts have to take an oxygen supply into space, both in their cabin and in their spacesuits.

The Earth's atmosphere contains about 78% nitrogen, a harmless gas which dilutes the oxygen. A pure oxygen atmosphere in a spacecraft can be dangerous, because a single spark could cause an explosion. This happened when three American astronauts were testing an *Apollo* module, and they died in the resulting fire. Soviet spacecraft use a mixture of oxygen and nitrogen.

Another problem is how to get rid of the waste carbon dioxide that is breathed out. This could suffocate the astronauts if it builds up. It can be absorbed by chemicals, but on a very long flight it would be essential to extract and recycle the oxygen so that it could be used again.

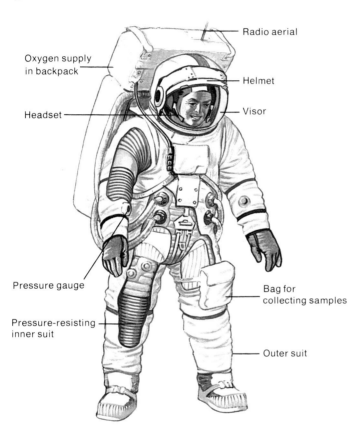

Oxygen supply in backpack

Headset

Pressure gauge

Pressure-resisting inner suit

Radio aerial

Helmet

Visor

Bag for collecting samples

Outer suit

▲ HOW DO ASTRONAUTS SPEAK TO EACH OTHER?

If they are outside the spacecraft or on the Moon's surface, they have to speak by radio, since sound cannot travel in empty space. However, if they are in the atmosphere of the cabin, they can talk normally to each other.

Communication between astronauts and the Earth can be a complicated matter, since our spinning planet regularly carries a single receiving station out of range of the spacecraft. So it is necessary to have several stations spread across the Earth's surface, so that one of them is always in contact with the spacecraft. Communication blackouts happen when a spacecraft is entering the Earth's atmosphere at high speed. The fierce heat strips the oxygen and nitrogen atoms, creating an electrical barrier.

◀ WHY ARE SPACESUITS PRESSURIZED?

When deep-sea fishes are brought to the surface, their eyes puff out because the pressure of the deep sea is no longer pushing on them. We do not realize it, but the atmosphere presses on us with great force. Even if we could breathe out in space, we would swell up and die an agonizing death.

The atmosphere at the Earth's surface produces a pressure equal to the weight of a large lorry on each square metre. We do not notice this, since it is equal both inside and outside our bodies. But if the air inside a metal can is forced out by boiling water inside it, the can collapses under this pressure.

An unprotected astronaut would not only die by swelling up. His blood would also start to boil. The temperature at which a liquid boils depends on the atmospheric pressure. At a height of nine kilometres (the height of Mount Everest) water boils at 74°C. Above about 19 kilometres, blood boils below body temperature. At zero pressure, the astronaut's blood would instantly turn to a deadly foam.

The term 'space walk' is not very accurate. A person can walk only if he is on the surface of a planet, where gravity pulls his feet down onto the ground. In space, an astronaut can only float alongside his spacecraft.

The first space walk was made in March 1965 by one of the crew of a Soviet *Voskhod* satellite, A. Leonov. He remained outside for 24 minutes. Like all space-walkers, he was tied by a safety line. One of the most important walks was made in 1973, when the crew of the American satellite *Skylab* had to repair a damaged heat shield that made the craft dangerously hot.

All spacecraft use electricity. They may have batteries which are kept charged from the Sun's energy. These craft always have large solar panels which collect the Sun's heat. Electricity can also be 'manufactured' specially.

Solar panel

Spacecraft which are going to have to operate for many years usually depend on solar panels, since the Sun is such a reliable and constant source of energy. But it cannot help a space probe travelling towards the outer planets, where sunlight is weak. The *Voyager* craft use small nuclear-power packs, which will last them at least as far as the planets Uranus and Neptune.

Another source of electricity is the fuel cell, in which hydrogen and oxygen combine with each other to produce electricity and water.

The water by-product is useful for manned spacecraft, but the reaction can be dangerous. An exploded fuel cell wrecked the *Apollo 13* Moon mission.

The speed of light is very accurately known: it is 299,792 kilometres per second in space. If a light beam is aimed towards the Moon and reflected back, the distance to the Moon can be worked out.

This method requires a large telescope. Its mirror is used rather like a searchlight's reflector to transmit light pulses towards special reflecting panels left by astronauts on the Moon. Although the total journey only takes 2½ seconds, electronic timers can calculate the length of time to an accuracy of a few millionths of a second. By making many measurements, the Moon's distance is known to within a few metres.

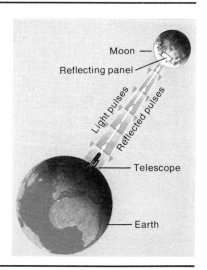

The first man-made object to hit the Moon was the Soviet probe *Luna 2*, in September 1959. The far side was photographed by *Luna 3* (shown here) in the same year. The first close-up photographs of the Moon's surface were taken by the American spaceprobe *Ranger 7* in 1964.

The first soft landings on the Moon were made in 1966, by spacecraft with automatic instruments. American space scientists considered their *Surveyor* landers only as a preparation for the later manned landings. But the Russians have continued sending unmanned probes: first the *Luna* landers, which have launched rock samples back to the Earth for detailed examination, and later the *Lunokhod* mobile devices.

Several different kinds of unmanned spacecraft have been sent to the Moon. Some went into orbit around it and took detailed photographs. Others have landed on the surface and tested the conditions there, sending messages by radio to the Earth.

The Soviet 'lunar rover' or *Lunokhod* is the most advanced unmanned vehicle. Weighing about a tonne, it has television cameras to let the operators see where it is going. It can start and stop at will, turn corners, and take samples of the lunar dust.

Two *Lunokhods* have so far been sent to the Moon by *Luna* space vehicles, while three others *(Lunas 16, 20, and 24)* have returned to the Earth, carrying surface samples. *Luna 24* dug to a depth of two metres. The upper part of the spacecraft is fired from the Moon's surface, finally landing on the Earth by parachute.

Lunar rover

Lunar module

▲ HOW DID APOLLO GET TO THE MOON?

Apollo, **which made the first manned landing in 1969, had to travel in stages. First, it was shot up into Earth orbit; then it flew to the Moon and went into lunar orbit. The lunar module then descended to the surface, leaving the command module awaiting its return.**

Of the 3000 tonnes of spacecraft that left the launching pad, only the 15-tonne lunar module reached the Moon, and over ten tonnes of that was fuel. Apart from the launch itself, and the final splashdown in the Pacific, the most vital moments were when the lunar module landed, and when it rejoined the command module in lunar orbit.

The illustration shows the lunar module in the background. The lower stage remained on the Moon, while the upper part, carrying the two astronauts, blasted free.

▲ HOW DID THE APOLLO ASTRONAUTS EXPLORE THE MOON?

The astronauts' most important task was to collect samples of the lunar rocks and soil. In the first three missions, they explored by foot. In the last three, they used a lunar rover.

They also set up various experiments to be operated from the Earth. These included seismometers, to measure the tremors of the surface; devices to detect atomic particles from the Sun; cosmic dust detectors; and the special reflectors for measuring the lunar distance. These and other devices were set out on the surface around the central power package, a nuclear plutonium reactor capable of producing electricity for many years.

In the illustration, the astronauts are seen pushing tubes into the ground to collect samples. The six missions collected about 400 kilograms of rock.

▲ HOW DID THE LUNAR ROVER WORK?

The lunar rover was a four-wheeled buggy driven by electric batteries. Its top speed was about 12 kilometres per hour, and it had enough power to travel about 65 kilometres before its batteries ran down. The last three *Apollo* flights took a rover.

The rover could carry two astronauts and about 180 kilograms of cargo, including rock samples. It had several cameras fitted to its frame. A colour television camera sent live pictures back to the Earth via the umbrella-like aerial. The wheels had metal treads to give them a good grip on the dusty surface, and both front and rear wheels could be steered, so that it could be turned very sharply.

The astronauts had to unpack it from the lunar lander, where it was stored folded up during the journey from the Earth.

The first close-up photographs of Mars were taken by *Mariner 4* in 1965, but better ones were taken by *Mariner 9*, which went into orbit around Mars in 1971. In 1976, two *Viking* spacecraft landed on the surface and took detailed photographs and measurements.

Both *Viking* craft landed in Mars' northern hemisphere, *Viking 1* at latitude 23°, and *Viking 2* at latitude 48°. Even at *Viking 1*'s site, the temperature never rose above −27°C, and at night it fell to −65°C.

Each craft picked up soil samples and tested them for

living organisms, but nothing similar to Earth-like germs or bacteria was found. The landscape was a desert covered with boulders and the sky, instead of being dark blue as expected, was turned pink by a dust haze. *Viking 2* continued to transmit information until March 1980, while *Viking 1* operated until November 1982.

Two series of spacecraft have visited the planet Jupiter and beyond. *Pioneer 10* passed close to Jupiter in 1973. The following year, *Pioneer 11* also examined Jupiter and went on to pass Saturn in 1979. In the same year, *Voyagers 1* and *2* passed Jupiter, and they have now visited Saturn. *Voyager 2* is expected to pass Uranus in 1986.

These deep-space craft have sent back photographs of the outer planets that are truly amazing, when we consider how far away they are and how long they have had to keep working. In addition to cameras, they also carry instruments to examine the chemical elements of the planets, their magnetic fields, and the particles sent out by

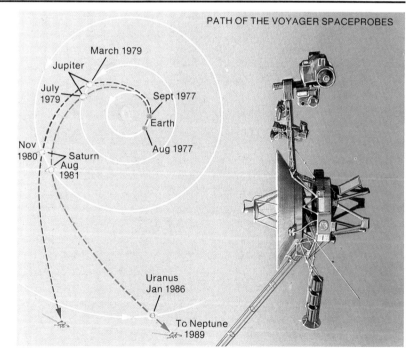

PATH OF THE VOYAGER SPACEPROBES

the Sun. Both craft carry their own computer, although their instruments are operated by commands sent from tracking stations on the Earth.

It is fortunate for us that the outer planets are lined up nicely for a 'tour'. If Jupiter and Saturn happened to be on opposite sides of the Sun, separate probes would have had to be sent to the two planets. Also, *Voyager* probes used Jupiter's tremendous gravitational pull to 'sling' them towards Saturn.

▼ HOW IS THE SPACE SHUTTLE LAUNCHED?

The Shuttle is launched into space attached to two booster rockets and a huge fuel tank. As it reaches a height of about 43 kilometres, the two booster rockets parachute back to Earth. To return, the

Shuttle fires its engines to head Earthwards, and glides down.

Everything about the Shuttle is re-usable, except for the giant fuel tank. This is jettisoned after the craft reaches orbit, falling back into the Indian Ocean. Once this has been detached, the

Shuttle's only rocket power comes from small engines that fire for about $2\frac{1}{2}$ minutes to begin its descent. To get rid of its speed of about 8 kilometres per second, it is taken through a series of steep turns as it enters the upper atmosphere, where the outer skin is heated by friction to about 2000°C.

Booster rockets jettisoned

Launch

Fuel tank jettisoned

Cargo bay opened

Re-entry

Landing

▲ HOW IS THE SPACE SHUTTLE USED?

The Space Shuttle is a 'workhorse'. Its job is to carry astronauts, or cargo, or both, into orbit around the Earth. It can carry six passengers, and has a cargo bay 18.3 metres long and 4.6 metres in diameter.

One of the Shuttle's most important uses will be to carry Spacelab into orbit. Spacelab is a portable workshop or laboratory which fits into the cargo bay. Different teams will equip their own Spacelab, and book a flight. The workshop remains in the Shuttle until it is time to descend once more.

Another very important task for the Shuttle will be to carry the big Space Telescope into orbit.

▶ HOW WILL THE SPACE TELESCOPE WORK?

The Space Telescope, which should be launched into orbit by the Space Shuttle, will have a mirror measuring 2.4 metres across. It will be about ten times as powerful as any telescope now in existence.

The Space Telescope will be completely automated. It will be pointed to different objects by radio messages from the ground, and the photographs it takes will be transmitted down to the Earth by radio.

It will have an enormous advantage over ground-based instruments: the sky will always be clear, and its images will be much sharper. It may even help to detect large planets orbiting around nearby stars. It will certainly bring into view remote galaxies that are undetectable with our present instruments. Knowledge of the universe is certain to take a tremendous jump forward.

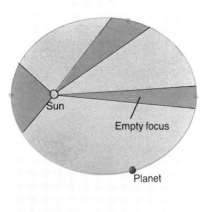

Sun

Empty focus

Planet

◀ WHO DISCOVERED HOW PLANETS MOVE?

Johannes Kepler (1571-1630), discovered the true shape of the planets' orbits around the Sun, which are not circles but ellipses. An ellipse has two points within it, each one called a 'focus'. The Sun is situated at one focus, the other one being empty.

Kepler, who was born in south-west Germany, made his great discovery by using Tycho's observations of the planet Mars. Since he first believed that the planets must move in circles, he spent years trying to make circular orbits 'fit' the observations before abandoning them for ellipses. He also discovered two other laws. One relates each planet's distance from the Sun to the length of its year, and the other states that an imaginary line joining the Sun and a planet will sweep over equal areas in equal times (see illustration), since a planet moves more quickly when at its closest to the Sun.

▶ WHO DISCOVERED JUPITER'S MOONS?

Galileo Galilei, who is almost always referred to by his Christian name alone, lived at a very important time for astronomy and science. During his lifetime (1564-1642), the first telescopes were brought into use, and he was one of the first people to point a telescope to the sky, making several very important discoveries.

The Greek philosopher Aristotle had made statements about the natural world which people had, up to the 16th century AD, accepted without question. For example, he had declared that a heavy stone would fall to the ground more quickly than would a light one. There is a legend that Galileo put this to the test, dropping two from the top of the Leaning Tower of Pisa and proved Aristotle wrong, for they both reached the ground at the same time. Although probably untrue, the story highlights Galileo's reputation for a lively and enquiring mind, heralding the modern 'scientific' age.

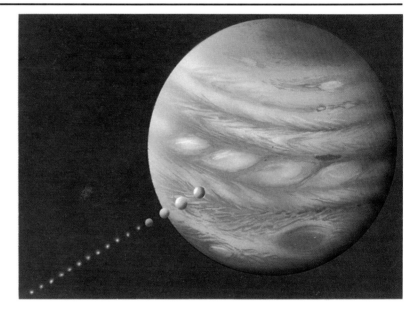

When news of the telescope's invention reached Italy in 1609, Galileo immediately made himself one, even grinding the lenses, and began making astronomical observations. He saw spots on the Sun, mountains and craters on the Moon, and far more stars than he could see with the naked eye. Turning his instrument to the planets, he saw that Venus shows phases like the Moon and that Jupiter has four bright satellites. He called the satellites the 'Medicean stars', in honour of the Medicis, the ruling family of Florence, where he made these observations.

The phases of Venus proved that it must revolve around the Sun and not the Earth; and the fact that Jupiter had satellites was further proof that astronomical bodies could revolve around objects other than the Earth. However, the Bible was then interpreted as stating that the Earth is the centre of the universe. Galileo, on publishing his discoveries, was accused of heresy, and passed his last years in virtual exile in his villa near Florence.

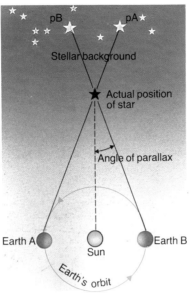

WHO DISCOVERED URANUS?

William Herschel was one of the greatest astronomical observers of all time. He built the largest telescopes of the age, and discovered the planet Uranus, as well as thousands of new objects inside our own galaxy and other galaxies far away.

Herschel (1738-1822) came to England from his native Hanover to teach music, and began observing in 1774, in his spare time. His discovery of Uranus in 1781 earned him a grant from King George III, permitting him to become a full-time astronomer. He built one telescope with a tube 12 metres long in order to probe as far as possible into space. His main aim was to understand how the stars, star clusters, and clouds of glowing gas revealed by his instruments were distributed in space.

During his researches he discovered more than 800 double stars. He found that some pairs of stars, called binary stars, revolve around each other, taking decades or centuries to do so.

WHO FIRST MEASURED THE DISTANCE TO THE STARS?

Friedrich Wilhelm Bessel (1784-1846), a Prussian astronomer, was the first person to measure the distance from the Earth to a star other than the Sun. This was done in 1838, when he stated that a dim star in the constellation Cygnus lies about 55,000 million kilometres or six light years away.

Bessel achieved this amazing result by using 'parallax'. He observed the star, 61 Cygni, on two nights 6 months apart, so that the Earth was at opposite ends of its orbit. In 6 months the star seemed to move from pA to pB. By measuring the angle of shift (parallax) and the distance from the Earth to the Sun, the distance to 61 Cygni could be calculated.

In 1844, Bessel found that the brightest star in the sky, Sirius, exhibits a very slight and leisurely 'wobble'. He suggested that it was being attracted by an invisible companion revolving around it. This faint star was not seen until after Bessel's death.

WHO WAS HALE?

George Ellery Hale (1868-1938), who began his career as a solar astronomer, is now famous for having planned and built the huge 5-metre aperture telescope on Mount Palomar, California. Completed in 1948, after his death, it remained the world's largest until a 6-metre one was built in the Crimea (Soviet Union) in 1976.

Hale lived at a time when interest in the faint and distant objects of the universe was rapidly increasing. To make them out, telescopes with the largest possible aperture were needed, to collect more light. Four times in his life he built the largest telescope in the world, and all four are still in constant use today. Before the 5-metre he built the 2½-metre and 1½-metre telescopes of the Mount Wilson Observatory, California, all of which use mirrors; and the 1-metre telescope at Yerkes Observatory, Wisconsin, which uses a lens, and has been in operation since 1897.

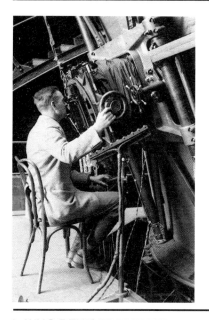

The American astronomer Edwin Hubble was the first person to measure the distance to galaxies beyond our own Milky Way. He also suggested that the more distant galaxies are flying away from each other at a greater rate than nearby ones. This is Hubble's Law.

Hubble started his distance measurements by using the largest available telescope (the 2½-metre on Mount Wilson, California) to make out separate stars in the Andromeda galaxy. By measuring how bright they appeared, he could judge how far away they must be. Because of uncertainties about star brightnesses, he obtained a result of 800,000 light-years instead of two million.

Hubble's Law, which states that the speed of a galaxy's flight away from the observer is related to its distance, forms the cornerstone of modern cosmology, for it suggests that all the galaxies were once close together.

►WHO DEVISED THE BIG BANG THEORY?

Abbé Lemaître (1896-1966), a Belgian astronomer, took up the idea suggested by Hubble's observation that galaxies are flying apart. He originated the 'big bang' theory, in which all the material from which the galaxies were formed existed in a single mass or 'cosmic egg', which exploded.

Lemaître's theory is so widely accepted now that it is hard to believe it attracted so little interest when he published it in 1927. The reason is that Hubble's measurements, on which the calculations were based, put the galaxies too close together, which meant that the 'big bang' would have happened only 2000 million years or so ago, making the Universe younger than the Earth!

The breakthrough came during the Second World War. Astronomer Walter Baade (1893-1960) was able to make accurate measurements of galactic distances, and found that the observable universe is much larger than Hubble had

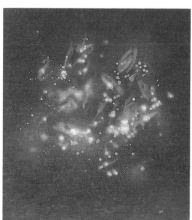
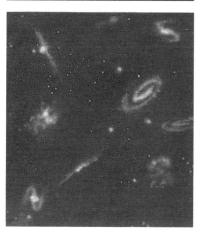
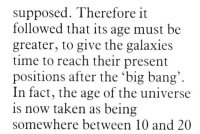

supposed. Therefore it followed that its age must be greater, to give the galaxies time to reach their present positions after the 'big bang'. In fact, the age of the universe is now taken as being somewhere between 10 and 20 thousand million years, far longer than Lemaître's estimate. In that time, if the theory is correct, material thrown out in the explosion has condensed first into galaxy-sized masses, and then into stars within each galaxy.

▼ WHO DISCOVERED WHAT STARS ARE MADE OF?

William Huggins (1824-1910) was one of the first astronomers to study the stars using a spectroscope. This is a device which splits light up into its different colours, giving a spectrum. Each element in the universe, when heated, emits light of a certain colour. Therefore, the spectroscope can identify elements in stars.

Huggins was a wealthy amateur, living near London. He made use of the newly-invented photographic process to take photographs of the spectra of bright stars, and compared these with the spectra of elements such as iron, photographed in his observatory, to see if they were present in the stars.

Huggins was one of the first 'astrophysicists' – people who try to understand what stars are made of, and how they shine. He was also able to prove that some stars are flying towards or away from the Sun, by determining changes in their spectra due to this motion.

▼ WHO WAS LAIKA?

Laika, a small Eskimo dog, was the first living thing to be sent into orbit around the Earth. She was launched from the Soviet Union in *Sputnik 2* on 3 November 1957. Previously, animals and insects had been launched to high altitudes in rockets, but for only a few minutes.

Laika was launched into an orbit whose altitude ranged from 160 to 1700 kilometres. She was sealed inside a cylindrical chamber about 60 centimetres in diameter, which contained a stock of food and instruments for measuring her heartbeat, breathing, and blood pressure. The reason for the experiment was to see how the strain of take-off and a long period of 'weightlessness' would affect a living creature, before sending a man aloft.

Sputnik 2 fell to its doom on 13 April 1958, but Laika was reported to have been humanely killed long before this. Another animal space pioneer, Ham the chimpanzee, was launched in a brief 'space hop' from Cape Canaveral on 31 January 1961.

▼ WHO DISCOVERED QUASARS?

Maarten Schmidt was born in the Netherlands in 1929, and is now Director of the Hale Observatories, California. In 1963 he discovered that the curious 'quasars', or 'quasi-stellar objects', which had baffled astronomers for years, were not stars within our galaxy, but very powerful energy sources at the limit of the observable universe.

These objects had puzzled astronomers because their spectra (the pattern of colours of light they sent out) were different to anything observed elsewhere. Schmidt realised that they were moving away from the Earth at speeds of thousands of kilometres a second, since speed affects the appearance of a spectrum – the so-called 'red shift'.

Following Hubble's Law, Schmidt concluded that the quasars must be more distant than any known galaxies. Physicists have suggested that they are galaxies whose centres are collapsing into a 'black hole', giving out huge amounts of energy.

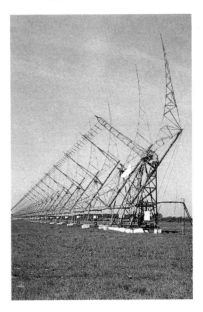

A meteor, or shooting star, is a streak of light caused when an object no bigger than a pebble hurtles into the Earth's atmosphere from space and burns up. On most clear, moonless nights a meteor is seen every few minutes, but sometimes a hundred or more are seen every hour.

These particles, known as meteoroids, have been orbiting the Sun for millions of years like separate tiny planets. They are invisible because they are so small. Some may be fragments left over after the planets were formed. Others may have been thrown out by comets; these usually travel in swarms, causing a meteor 'shower'.

To reach the ground as a meteorite, a meteoroid must have a mass of several kilograms. This is because a lot of material is burned off during its dive through the atmosphere at a speed of up to 50 kilometres a second.

A meteorite is the solid remains of a meteoroid that was large enough to survive its drop through the atmosphere. The largest known meteorite lies where it fell in Hoba West, Namibia, south-west Africa. It is over two metres across and weighs as much as 60 medium-size cars.

We can be sure that much larger bodies have struck the Earth. About 90 ring-shaped features in different parts of the world could have been caused by huge impacts back in prehistoric times. For example, a three-kilometre diameter crater in Brazil was probably caused by an impact about 220 million years ago.

The best-known example of a meteorite crater is in Arizona. This $1\frac{1}{4}$-kilometre crater (shown here) was probably formed when a meteorite the size of a department store hit the Earth 25,000 years ago.

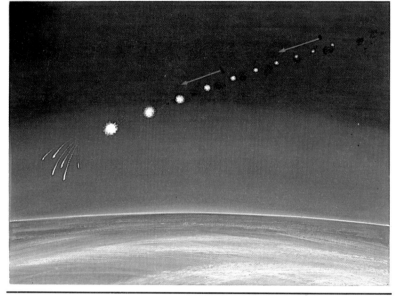

▶ WHAT IS AN ASTEROID?

An asteroid, or 'minor planet', is a small body orbiting the Sun. The largest asteroid, Ceres (shown here compared in size to Italy), is only 1000 kilometres across. Others are much smaller.

Over 2700 asteroids are now known. There is a zone between the orbits of Mars and Jupiter where most are found. But some can pass inside the Earth's orbit, and others go beyond Saturn.

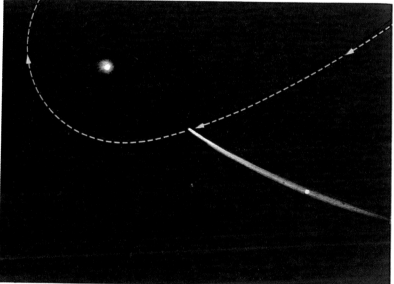

◀ WHAT IS A COMET?

A comet is an icy body just a few kilometres across, orbiting the Sun. Particles the size of dust and sand are mixed with the ice. When the comet passes near the Sun, the heat turns the ice to gas and the dust pours out into space, making the comet look hazy and perhaps giving it a long tail as well.

Most known comets move in very elongated orbits, perhaps carrying them from the chilly zone beyond Jupiter to the hot regions of Venus and Mercury.

Comets are brightest when closest to the Sun, at *perihelion*. When farthest from the Sun, at *aphelion*, most comets are too faint to be seen from the Earth at all.

A comet grows enormously as it approaches perihelion, and tails are often millions of kilometres long. However, the dust is scattered so thinly that individual dust particles may be several kilometres apart.

▲ WHAT WOULD HAPPEN IF A COMET HIT THE EARTH?

Although a bright comet looks huge and impressive, the solid part is no bigger than a minor planet. So the chances of a serious collision are tiny, perhaps once in a hundred-million years.

Even if a comet's nucleus did hit the Earth, it would not do as much harm as a collision with an asteroid of similar size. Comets seem to contain a lot of frozen liquid and dusty rock. But many asteroids contain solid rock and metal, so the impact would be more violent.

However, a comet's nucleus would blast a crater perhaps a hundred kilometres across, and spread destruction over a far wider area.

The Earth has passed through a comet's tail on many occasions. In 1910 the tail of Halley's Comet swept across our planet (as shown in the diagram), but it was so thin that no damage was caused.

ARTS, SPORT AND ENTERTAINMENT

▲ WHY DO HUMAN BEINGS MAKE MUSIC?

Music is one of the most important ways of giving expression to our thoughts and feelings. Even if no words are sung, it can still be a dramatic way of expressing our emotions. It is quite possible that our prehistoric ancestors made use of music as a way of communicating even before they knew how to speak or write.

Music is a way of blending sounds that are made up of three basic parts – rhythm, harmony and melody. These ingredients may be used on their own, or they may be combined in endless ways. Music may be as simple as a lullaby or as complex as an opera with dozens of singers and instruments all blending together to create sounds of enormous richness and power.

Music can be produced by voices, clapping hands and stamping feet or by musical instruments.

▼ WHY DID HAYDN WRITE THE 'FAREWELL' SYMPHONY?

Franz Josef Haydn (1732–1809) wrote this symphony as a gentle hint to his employer, a member of the noble Hungarian Esterhazy family, that he and the orchestra needed a rest and a vacation. As the music drew to a close, one musician after another set down his instrument and stole away until there were only two violins left.

Haydn is often referred to as the 'father of the symphony' Although he did not invent this form of music he was the first person to arrange the instruments of an orchestra into four main groups – strings, woodwinds, brass and percussion. He created a big balanced sound in which all instruments had an important part.

Haydn's influence on other musicians of the 18th and 19th centuries was immense. The composer Mozart was a close friend of his and the young Beethoven once studied as his pupil.

Haydn's musical output was enormous. As well as 104 symphonies he also composed innumerable operas, oratorios, masses, concertos, piano sonatas and music for string quartets. One of Haydn's most famous pieces is *The Creation*.

WHY DO BALLERINAS WEAR BLOCKED SHOES?

Blocked shoes, with square solid toes, are used by ballerinas who dance on the tips of their toes, a position known as on *pointe*. The peculiar shape of these shoes makes it easier for them to balance.

It takes considerable skill for a ballerina to do *pointe* work. Girls usually have at least two years of experience before they begin. The first exercises are performed with the help of the barre. Later the dancers train in the centre of the studio floor. Traditionally, only ballerinas dance on *pointe*. Male dancers do not perform this movement.

Originally, all ballet dancers were men. It was not until 1681 that women began to appear regularly on the public stage in Paris. At this time ballet was greatly encouraged by the interest shown by Louis XIV of France. He recognized it as a form of high art and founded the Royal Academy of Dance to train dancers.

WHY DOES AN ORCHESTRA NEED A CONDUCTOR?

Really big orchestras may have a hundred players or more. It takes the control of a skilled conductor to make sure everyone plays in time with each other.

Today, a typically large orchestra has about 90 instruments divided into four sections: the strings, the woodwinds, brass and percussion.

Each instrument usually plays only a part of the entire musical piece, resting from time to time while other instruments take up the music. It is the conductor's task to guide the players in and out of the music at the right moments.

A conductor also rehearses the orchestra before the concert, preparing it to play the music in a way that satisfies him or her. The conductor will teach the orchestra to interpret the music. In the end, it is the conductor who controls the overall sound that the orchestra produces.

WHY DOES AN OBOE PLAY BEFORE THE REST OF AN ORCHESTRA?

The sound of an oboe has a very steady pitch. For this reason, it is the instrument to which all others in an orchestra tune. Before a performance the oboe can be heard playing an A note. It is followed soon after by what sounds like a general groaning and honking noise as the rest of the orchestra gets into tune.

The oboe is a woodwind instrument. Like all woodwinds (except the flute) the sound is produced by blowing through a reed.

Inside the hollow shaft of the oboe a column of air is set vibrating and a sound is created. Holes up and down the various sections of the oboe can be covered with the fingers or with pads. As they are opened and closed, the length of the column of air alters. The longer the column, the deeper the note. The shorter it is, the higher the note that is played.

▶ WHY DO SNAKES 'DANCE' FOR SNAKE CHARMERS?

Snakes do not really dance to the music of snake charmers. Their slow, swaying motion is only a way of following the movements of the charmers while they prepare themselves to strike.

Cobras, the snakes most favoured by Indian charmers, do not respond to the music of a pipe. In fact they are deaf to high-pitched sounds. It is the closeness of the charmer and his slow movements that excite a snake and provoke it to rear up into a ready-to-strike position with the hood at its neck flared. Fortunately cobras are rather slow to strike and the charmers know when to stop before the snakes have time to lunge.

Indian cobras are very dangerous however. Their venom is a powerful poison and every year several thousand people die from their bites, usually after the cobras crawl into homes at dusk searching for rats.

◀ WHERE DID PUPPETS COME FROM?

Puppets were known long ago in ancient Greece and Egypt. They were always a very popular form of entertainment and were used to tell legends and folk tales.

In Italy in the 16th century, puppet shows were regular events. The puppeteers travelled far and wide to give performances at fairs and market places. Popular puppet characters soon began to appear. In Italy a hero called Pulcinello was based on a character who was popular in theatres of the time. In England, Pulcinello became known as Punch and by 1800 Punch and Judy shows were found all around the country.

There were also other kinds of puppets. Larger versions that were held on stout rods, and whose heads and arms were moved by smaller rods, were also known. Marionettes consist of an entire human or animal 'body' supported by thin strings from above by puppeteers.

▶ WHY IS BULLFIGHTING FOUND MAINLY IN SPAIN?

The native wild bulls of Spain were an especially ferocious breed that would fiercely attack humans. Their descendants today supply the bull-rings and make this sport a favourite of Spain and the Spanish-speaking world.

As long ago as Roman times Spanish wild bulls were hunted by men with axes and lances who 'played' with the beasts before killing them.

Modern bullfighting descends from this custom. Today it has more to do with the skill of the matador than with the killing of a bull. The art of a bullfight, or *corrida* as it is known, is the matador's ability to control the bull with his cape. He must be graceful and daring in his movements and be able to thrill the crowd by working as near to the bull's horns as possible.

Even the best matadors are often gored by bulls, and perhaps as many as a third of the greatest have been killed in the ring.

WHY DO PEOPLE READ HOROSCOPES?

The movements of the major heavenly bodies are believed to shape human affairs and to influence human character. Horoscopes help us to understand how these movements affect our everyday lives. For this reason, many people are fascinated by horoscopes and read them every day to find out more about themselves and their future.

A horoscope is the chart used by astrologers. It shows the position of the Sun, Moon and the planets, and also the signs of the Zodiac. A horoscope is divided into sections, or houses, that stand for wealth, happiness, health, friendship, death and so on. As the planets move through the heavens, they travel from one house to the next, influencing each in turn.

Astrologers plot a person's horoscope from the time of birth in order to understand their nature, and to learn about their future.

WHY ARE THERE 52 CARDS IN A PACK?

The number of cards in a modern deck may have links with the lunar year. There are as many cards as there are weeks in the year. The total sum of the cards, counting aces as one, Jacks as 11, Queens as 12 and Kings as 13, is about the same as the number of days in the year.

The exact origin of playing cards is unknown. Most likely the Chinese were the first to use them, since they were the first people to use paper and paper money. The earliest reference to cards comes from the 10th century, during the time of the Liao Dynasty.

Cards appeared in Italy during the 13th century. Early Italian packs had 78 cards. By the 16th century, French packs had become the most widely used in Europe. They were divided into two red suits of hearts and diamonds and two black suits of spades and clubs. Games played with cards include whist, bridge and poker.

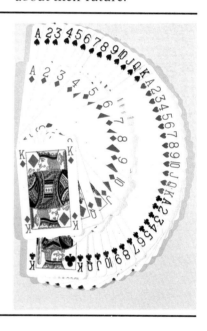

HOW DO VENTRILOQUISTS 'THROW' THEIR VOICES?

Ventriloquists do not 'throw' their voices; they simply talk without moving their lips. An audience may be fooled into thinking they are not speaking at all and that the voice is coming from somewhere else.

The true secret of a ventriloquist is to fool the audience that not a word is being spoken by him. This is done by forming the words in a normal way but then breathing out very slowly and muffling the sounds by tightening one's throat. The lips must not move at all.

It always helps a ventriloquist if there is another object near him which might just be the source of the voice. A dummy doll, for example, makes a perfect device. Usually the spectators' imaginations will fool them into believing that the dummy is speaking. This is even more likely if its mouth also moves.

WHY ARE THE OLYMPIC GAMES HELD EVERY FOUR YEARS?

When the Olympic Games were revived in 1896, 1500 years after last being held, it was decided to stage them every four years, exactly as had been done in ancient Greek times.

The first recorded Olympic Games were held in 776 BC at Olympia, from where they take their name. They grew out of a religious ceremony held there that involved a sprinting race. According to legend, a Cretan named Herakles proclaimed that the race and ceremony were to be held there every four years.

In time the games became the most magnificent sports festival of the ancient world. Competitors came from far and wide and from many kingdoms and states. It was the custom to arrange a formal truce so that everyone could compete, friend and enemy alike. Today the games serve once again as a kind of truce, as well as bringing nations together.

WHY ARE VERY LONG RACES KNOWN AS MARATHON EVENTS?

The highlight of long-distance racing in the Olympics is the marathon. It takes its name from a legendary run made by a Greek soldier in 490 BC. He raced from the plain of Marathon to Athens to announce the news of a great victory over an army of invading Persians.

In 1896, at the first modern Olympics in Athens, it was decided to stage a long road-race. Most of the 16 runners in the first marathon were Greek, but they were untrained and inexperienced and most of them soon collapsed with exhaustion. The winner, a Greek called Spiros Louis, was finally joined by members of the Greek royal family who jogged alongside him on the last lap to the finish line. His victory was a sensation.

Since 1908, the marathon has been fixed at 42.2 kilometres, a distance regularly run in about two and a half hours nowadays.

WHY ARE PROFESSIONAL SPORTSMEN DIFFERENT FROM AMATEURS?

Professionals think of the sports in which they compete as full-time work from which to make a living. Amateurs compete more for love of the sport than for money.

Professional footballers, boxers, tennis players and so on all receive money for their skills. This comes partly as salary and partly from advertising earnings. In the case of amateurs, there are strict rules laid down by athletic associations. These limit what athletes may earn, either from their own performance or by acting as coaches and trainers.

But competition is expensive and amateurs may be helped with training facilities, equipment, food, medical expenses, lodging and transport. They may accept scholarships to colleges which help to support them while they train. Amateurs receive trophies, cups or medals when they win.

▼ WHY DO RUNNERS USE
STARTING BLOCKS?

Starting blocks allow a sprinter to drive forward smoothly and powerfully, and to reach top speed much more quickly than if a standing start was used. The blocks are only needed in sprint races.

Starting blocks were first used in 1927 by the American running coach George Bresnahan. His were made from wood or metal and could be adjusted to support a runner's feet at different angles and distances apart. At Olympia in Greece there are signs of grooves in the track where racers in ancient times might have obtained a good toehold to keep from slipping as the races began.

Until 1884, sprinters started in standing or leaning positions. That year, a Scottish runner began to use a crouched position with one foot in front of the other and both hands touching the ground. From this coiled crouch a runner could spring forward into full racing speed.

▼ WHY DO RUNNERS START
FROM DIFFERENT
POSITIONS IN SOME TRACK
RACES?

When track races are run in lanes, the runners on the outside cover more distance than those on the inside as they come round bends. To ensure that everyone travels the same distance, the runners start at staggered intervals.

Although the 100-metre dash is run in lanes, the race is on the straight and a staggered

start is not needed. Longer races of several laps, where the runners have plenty of time to bunch up on the inside lane, also do not need staggered starts.

It is in the 200-metre and 400-metre sprints, in which all the runners travel flat out in different lanes, that staggered starting positions are needed. These races take the runners round several bends. Unless they start well ahead, those on the outside would end up running much farther than runners on the inside.

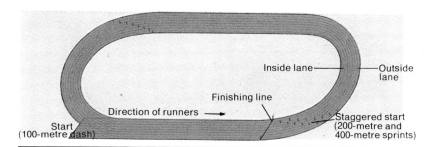

Inside lane—

Outside lane

Finishing line

Direction of runners →

Start (100-metre dash)

Staggered start (200-metre and 400-metre sprints)

▲ WHY CAN SOME RACES
BE WON BY WALKING?

Walking races are also to be found in the Olympics. The rules are strict, for at no point do they allow the contestants to break into a run to beat their rivals.

Race-walking is also known as heel-and-toe racing, as the racers must never break contact with the ground. One foot must always be in touch. The legs must also be held straight as if walking and not be bent, as when running.

The method for race-walking is nothing like normal walking. The hips are rolled rhythmically, the legs are pulled or jerked up and down very rapidly, and the shoulders and arms are swung in very exaggerated pumping movements. The overall effect is very comical to watch. It is something like a penguin's waddle, yet it allows racers to move along at up to 16 kilometres per hour.

Walking races are very long. In the Olympics the events cover 20-kilometre and 50-kilometre distances.

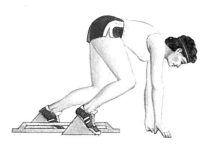

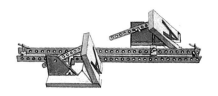

479

▼ WHY IS DISCUS-THROWING STILL A SPORT?

Throwing the discus was a popular sport in ancient Greece. It was often pictured on vases and praised by poets such as Homer. As a recognition of its past importance, it was revived at the first modern Olympics in 1896.

The discus is shaped like a dinner plate with a thick center that tapers to a thin outer rim. It weighs two kilograms (about 4½ pounds).

▼ WHY ARE POLE-VAULTERS NOT HURT WHEN THEY LAND?

A fall from a height of more than 5 metres (16 feet) on to one's back or shoulders could break bones. To avoid this, pole-vaulters land in special pits filled with soft rubber pieces or inflated airbags.

Pole-vaulters make a long approach-run to the hurdle to build up speed. As they approach the uprights, they plant one end of the light-

▼ WHY ARE THERE BARRIERS IN SOME RACES?

Races in which runners meet barriers across the track are known as hurdles if they are short sprints, and steeplechases if they are long-distance events. The barriers test a runner's ability to clear obstacles without breaking stride or losing speed.

The steeplechase is a 3000-metre event in which each lap of the course has four barriers

cantabrian

The discus is thrown from inside a large boundary circle surrounded by a wire cage on three sides so that a wild shot cannot hit the crowd. The thrower faces backwards as he starts, then whirls rapidly through 1½ turns before releasing the discus. Because of its odd shape, the discus is laid flat against the thrower's palm and held in place by his fingertips. As a result, it is not the accuracy of the throw that counts but the distance that is achieved. Present world records are well over 67 metres (220 feet).

weight fibreglass pole in a sunken take-off box. In a single continuous motion they hurl themselves upwards, swinging feet first towards the bar. As the vaulters continue to pull their feet upward, the right leg crosses over the left leg. The chest is now next to the cross-bar. At the last moment they push the pole away and twist over the cross-bar.

Pole-vaulting arose from the countryside tradition of using poles to jump wide ditches and streams.

and one water jump. The runners either hurdle the barriers or step on to them and leap from the top. The water jump is a barrier followed by a long pool of water. Here, the runners all spring from the top of the barrier to take the next step in the water.

Hurdles races are either 110-metre or 400-metre sprints in which there are ten barriers in all. The obstacles are just over 9 metres apart in the 110-metre race, and 25 metres apart in the 400-metre race.

▼ WHY IS GYMNASTICS AN OLYMPIC SPORT?

Gymnastics was a highly popular activity in ancient Greece. Interest in the sport was revived in the 19th century and it was included in the first modern Olympics in 1896. Women's gymnastics was restricted to only one event until 1952.

Gymnastics consists of a series of various physical exercises that are performed on equipment such as the

horizontal bar, parallel bars, rings, balance beam, pommel horse and vault horse.

In addition there are floor exercises which are performed to music. At the highest levels of competition, these exercises resemble dancers' movements in their graceful style.

For many years the Soviet Union and Eastern European countries have reigned supreme at the Olympics, although since the 1960s the Japanese have produced outstanding performances.

▼ WHY IS REAL TENNIS DIFFERENT FROM TENNIS?

Real tennis, or royal tennis, was first played in the Middle Ages. It is played on an indoor court divided in two by a net. The sloping roof of the court may be used as a surface against which to hit the ball. The game of modern tennis, or lawn tennis, was devised in England in 1873. This game is played on level grass courts or hard-surface courts.

Lawn tennis is highly popular throughout the world. It is a game for two or four players. They use rackets of wood or metal to hit a cloth-covered ball across a long, low net that divides the large open court in half. A singles court for two players is 9 yards (8.23 metres) wide, a doubles court for four players is 12 yards (10.97 metres) wide.

The object of the game is for the players to hit the ball to their opponents so that they cannot return it properly. In this way points are scored.

▼ WHY DO MOST GOLFERS HAVE HANDICAPS?

A handicap is a way of scoring so that a good player can be fairly matched with a weaker player. Each golfer is given minus points, depending on the average number of strokes he or she needs to complete the game. Better golfers take fewer strokes so they have lower handicaps. Weak golfers have higher handicaps because they take more strokes.

The aim of golf is for each player to hit the ball from the starting point, or tee, into a small hole with the least number of strokes. The golfer uses a selection of different clubs. The distance between the tee and the hole can be from 100 to 600 yards (90–550 metres). A complete game has 18 holes.

Golf is an ancient Scottish game dating from well before the 15th century. The oldest club still running is the Royal and Ancient Golf Club at St Andrews in Scotland, which was founded in 1754.

481

► WHY IS A YELLOW JERSEY WORN DURING THE TOUR DE FRANCE?

The annual *Tour de France* is the richest and most famous cycle race in the world. It lasts three weeks and is divided into 20 different stages. The winner of each stage wears a much-prized yellow jersey during the next stage of the race.

The *Tour de France* was first held in 1903. It begins each summer in a different French town but always ends in Paris. During the race, the cyclists travel 4,000 kilometres in stages of about 200 kilometres a day. The route varies every year but it takes the race from one side of France to the other. About 12 teams enter the race and each one is heavily sponsored.

► WHY DO RACING DRIVERS WEAR FLAME-PROOF CLOTHES?

In a racing accident the greatest danger always is that a fuel tank will rupture and catch fire. Drivers wear flame-proof overalls, boots and gloves that give them about a minute of protection in a burning wreck. They also have a special oxygen supply to their helmets so that they can avoid breathing poisonous fumes from spilled or burning fuel.

The cars driven by Formula One racing drivers are very compactly built. The narrow cockpit is surrounded by fuel tanks. However, the tanks are lined with special self-sealing material that is designed to close any small puncture that may occur in an accident.

The main danger facing all drivers is not that they will be killed in a crash, but that they may be trapped alive in the wreckage while spilled fuel explodes into flames. Their clothes are designed to protect them from the flames while they escape or are rescued.

◄ WHY ARE COLOURED BELTS WORN IN KARATE?

A karate fighter's level of skill is shown by the colour of the belt he or she wears. Masters wear black belts. Students wear brown, blue, green and orange belts, down to white belts for beginners. Students move upwards from one grade to the next by taking formal exams.

Karate, an oriental form of unarmed combat, was first practised in the Ryukyu Islands in the 17th century. Early in the 20th century it spread to Japan and from there throughout the world.

Karate fighters train to focus the entire muscle power of their body into one blow of great force. Hands, fists, elbows and feet are all used to deliver karate blows.

The training for this form of combat is very hard. It involves strengthening the parts of the body that deliver blows as well as practising breathing exercises.

▼ WHY ARE SUMO WRESTLERS GIANTS?

Sumo wrestlers are enormous men. The best fighters stand well over 1.83 metres high and may weigh 130 kilograms or more. The bigger a wrestler is, the greater are his chances of becoming a champion.

Sumo wrestling is enormously popular in Japan. It takes place in a small sand ring surrounded only by a line of small markers. The object of a fight is for one wrestler either to down his opponent by forcing him to the ground or to drive him physically out of the ring.

The wrestlers fight barefoot and almost naked except for a massive belt-like loin-cloth. Their hair is long and tied up in a traditional knot.

A match is usually very short. It begins with a sudden clash as the two giants hurl themselves together. Each wrestler seeks to throw the other off balance and fling him from the ring. Most matches last under a minute.

▼ WHY DO ICE-HOCKEY PLAYERS WEAR MASKS AND PADS?

Goalkeepers are the only players who wear full face masks during ice-hockey games. They give protection from flying pucks and slashing sticks.

The pucks are not only solid rubber but are made rock-hard by being stored in refrigerators before a game. The pucks rocket towards the goal-mouth at speeds up to 160 kilometres per hour.

▼ WHY DO BOXERS WEAR GLOVES?

Padded gloves protect a fighter's hands. They also spare his opponent from the worst cuts and injuries.

In ancient Greek and Roman times, boxers wore weighted

leather gloves when they fought. These offered their hands a certain amount of protection but they also made their blows extremely damaging.

The sport had become slightly less savage by the time the first organized bouts were held in Britain in the 18th century. A bare-knuckle style of fighting was used then. Padded gloves were not commonly used until the late 19th century.

At the 1968 Olympics a new kind of soft leather glove without a surface seam was introduced. Even this small change made a great difference. It reduced serious cuts around the eyes from 46 during the 1964 Games to less than ten in the 1968 Games.

All six players on a hockey team wear pads when they take to the ice to protect their shoulders and knees. This protection is vital because a fall on to the ice at high speed can produce serious injuries. Pucks, sticks and skates can also become lethal instruments in a hard-played match.

The use of protective headgear became common after the death of a professional Canadian player in the 1960s, who hit his head on the ice after a heavy fall.

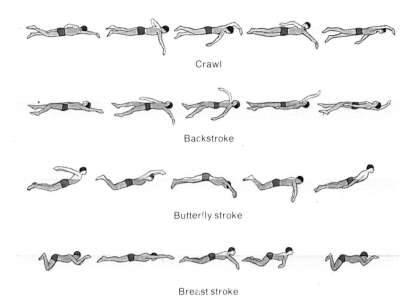

Crawl

Backstroke

Butterfly stroke

Breast stroke

▲ WHY ARE SOME STYLES OF SWIMMING FASTER THAN OTHERS?

Water forms a barrier to the human body as it tries to move through it. Some styles of swimming reduce resistance to the water more than others. This makes them faster.

The most efficient way of travelling through water is a stroke called the crawl. With this stroke, the body cuts through the shallowest amount of water. The crawl is the fastest of all swimming styles and is used by record-setting champions. The crawl was developed in Australia, early in the 20th century, from a stroke used by the people of the South Seas.

Other major styles of swimming include the backstroke, the butterfly stroke and the breast stroke. Breast stroke was used in Europe as long ago as the 16th century. With all of these strokes, the body of a swimmer enters more deeply into the water than with the crawl. Therefore they are slower strokes.

◀ WHY DO SURFBOARDS TRAVEL SO SWIFTLY?

Surfboards skim the surface at speeds much faster than the water may be moving.

Surfing began among the islanders of the South Seas, who used it as a way of skimming over calm lagoons.

They lay on their boards and sculled with their hands or paddled with their feet. More experienced riders began to stand up and balance on waves. They controlled their speed and direction by shifting the weight of their bodies back and forward along the board.

Surfing first became a popular sport in Hawaii, Australia and the west coast of America, where the long Pacific swells made the wave conditions ideal.

▶ WHY IS SOCCER SO WIDELY PLAYED?

Football is the world's most popular sport, and is played in every continent. The high point of international football is the World Cup, which is held every four years.

The rules of soccer were laid down in Britain in the 1860s when the Football Association was formed to control the sport. It is really a simple game in which two teams of 11 players try to score by kicking a ball into the opposing team's goal-mouth.

Players control the ball with their feet or head, but they are not allowed to touch it with their arms and hands. Only the goalkeeper may handle the ball, and then only inside the penalty area in front of his own goal-mouth. A game is 90 minutes long with a break at half-time.

▶ WHY ARE CAMERAS SO
IMPORTANT IN TRACK
RACES?

The finish of a race, whether a sprint or a long-distance event, can be such a close-run thing that it is next to impossible for the human eye to tell which runner came first. Fast-action cameras, able to take dozens of pictures a second, can record the instant a runner bursts across the finish line. They make it possible for judges to declare the winner.

Major races must be correctly judged. This is especially true of short events such as 100-metre sprints. Here the difference between the winner and the runner-up may be a matter of only a few fractions of a second. A new world record can be set when only a tenth of a second has been shaved off the existing time.

In order to record such close results, cameras are placed directly along the finish line. They are triggered when the line is crossed, and can detect a difference of centimetres.

▶ WHY ARE SKIS SO LONG?

Long skis are easier to control than short ones. On a steep slope, most of the ski simply slides over the surface. It is the edge of the ski which bites into the snow and allows a skier to change direction and speed. The greater the surface of ski that is in contact with the ground, the easier it is to control.

Skis are made of plastic, metal or, less often nowadays, of wood. They are very flexible so they can ride easily over the bumps and hollows of a hill. A strong set of bindings holds a skier's boot in place and makes it possible to travel at speeds well over 100 kilometres per hour.

Cross-country skis are used for walking rather than sliding. They are very narrow.

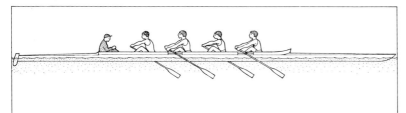

▲ WHY DO ROWING TEAMS
OFTEN CARRY
PASSENGERS?

Rowing teams of four and eight people are often steered by a coxswain, who at first glance seems to be **a passenger. He or she has the very important job of steering the boat and setting the pace of the strokes made by the rowing teams.**

Rowing events are usually held in the sheltered waters of rivers and lakes. Racing boats are so light and low-sided that even a small wave could swamp them. They are narrow and very long, and designed to cut quickly through the water.

The rowers sit in single file on sliding seats with their feet braced against stretchers. Each person uses a single oar. These are set in a line on alternate sides of the boat.

►WHEN WERE MUSICAL INSTRUMENTS FIRST PLAYED?

Musical instruments have been played since prehistoric times. The earliest instruments were objects such as conches (seashells) and bone pipes, which people could use just as they found them.

Later, instruments were made from materials such as wood and pottery. People found that string can make a musical note when stretched tight, so they made the first musical bow.

In early times, music accompanied dancing and religious ceremonies. People of the ancient civilizations of Mesopotamia, Egypt, India, China and Greece then started to listen to music purely as a way of enjoying themselves.

The picture shows musicians of ancient Egypt. The woman on the left is playing a harp. Next to her is a girl playing a lute. The women on the right are playing a double pipe and a lyre.

▲WHEN DID THE FIRST ORCHESTRAS APPEAR?

An orchestra is a large group of musicians. The first orchestras appeared at the beginning of the 17th century, as part of Italian opera.

Early orchestras varied in the instruments they included. Which ones were used seems to have been determined simply by which musicians were available. The orchestra for Monteverdi's opera *Orfeo*, of 1607, included nearly all the instruments known at that time, except drums.

In 18th-century Germany, composers began to write music for four basic groups of instruments in the orchestra. These were the *woodwinds* (such as flutes, oboes and bassoons), *brass* (horns and trumpets), *percussion* (kettledrums) and *strings* (violins, violas, cellos and double bass). These groups of instruments are still the basis of the modern 20th-century symphony orchestra.

◄WHEN WAS MUSIC FIRST WRITTEN DOWN?

Forms of written music existed in the ancient civilizations of Egypt, Mesopotamia and Greece. Exactly when music was first written down is difficult to say. Our knowlege depends on whether copies of the music survive, or whether there are surviving references to it in pictures and literature.

We know that the Greek philosopher Pythagoras (6th century BC) brought a knowledge of musical theory back to Greece after studying in Egypt and Mesopotamia. There is also an example of what experts believe is the musical notation (written music) of a Sumerian hymn dating from between 5000 and 3000 years ago. No one has yet deciphered it.

The first written music which survives in a complete form dates from the 9th century. The sheet of music shown here dates from the Middle Ages.

▲WHEN WAS OPERA
FIRST PERFORMED?

▲WHEN DID MODERN
DANCE APPEAR?

▼WHEN WAS JAZZ FIRST
PLAYED?

The style of music known as jazz emerged at the start of the 20th century. It began in the southern states of the USA, but no one knows exactly when or how it started.

In the southern states of the USA, black slaves had kept the musical traditions of their West African ancestors. They also had their own style of religious songs and music, known as spirituals. Jazz was influenced by both these styles of music.

By the start of the 1900s a distinct type of music had developed in New Orleans, in Louisiana. It was played by black musicians. The early leaders of this 'jazz' music were all trumpeters. They included Joe 'King' Oliver and Louis Armstrong.

In 1917 musicians from New Orleans moved north. Some settled in Chicago. By the early 1920s Chicago was the new centre of jazz. From there it developed into an international style of music.

The beginning of opera is usually dated around 1600 in Italy, when stage plays set to music were first performed.

Works of drama performed to music existed long ago, for example in the Mystery, Miracle and Morality plays of the Middle Ages. These were forms of sacred drama. They arose from traditions begun in the Christian Church as early as the 4th century. There were also types of entertainment for the aristocracy which combined simple plots, poetry and music.

The first full stage play set to music, in which the characters sing, was produced in 1597. Its music has not survived. The first two surviving operas were performed in 1600 in Italy. Both had specially designed costumes, scenery, lighting and stage machinery. Monteverdi was the first great opera composer. His opera *Orfeo* was first performed in 1607.

Modern dance developed at the beginning of the 20th century. There were two styles – one in Europe, and one in America.

The pioneers of modern dance were dissatisfied with classical ballet. They criticized its themes of romantic fairytales and legend, and thought that it did not explore new ideas.

European modern dance explored ideas about the body in relation to space. American modern dance drew inspiration from other cultures. Choreographers invented new ballets. Their themes were based on ancient ritual and myth, as well as modern subjects. The themes were the heart of their dances, instead of being just an aid to the techniques of movement.

One of the early American leaders was Isadora Duncan, shown here. She began to experiment at the beginning of this century. She took her ideas, costume and style of dance from the ancient Greeks.

◀WHEN WERE THE FIRST
SCULPTURES MADE?

The earliest sculptures that have been found are as much as 30,000 years old, dating from the Stone Age. They are tiny figures representing women, which have come to be known as the 'Venuses'.

Stone-Age Venuses have been found all over Europe and Western Asia, from the Pyrenees to Lake Baikal in the USSR. Stone-Age sculptors also made figures of animals. These included mammoths, rhinoceroses, horses, cave bears and various kinds of cat.

Stone-Age sculptors worked in a variety of materials. They used ivory from mammoth tusks, as well as bone and stone such as limestone and sandstone. They also made terracotta figures from a mixture of clay, powdered bone and some kind of fat, possibly animal fat.

The stone sculpture in the picture shows two people embracing. It was made in Jordan 12,000 years ago.

▶WHEN WERE THE FIRST WATERCOLOURS PAINTED?

The use of watercolour in painting has a long history. We know that watercolour paint was used on papyrus rolls in ancient Egypt, and in the earliest paintings of China.

Watercolour is a paint ground in gum (usually gum arabic), which can be dissolved in water. It is usually applied with a brush.

Drawings in watercolour and ink have been the basis of Chinese art since the beginning of the T'ang Dynasty in AD 618. During this period the traditions and techniques of Chinese landscape painting were developing.

Chinese pictures were usually painted on silk, or sometimes paper, mainly in the form of scrolls. These could be hung on a wall or rolled up for storing away. Some paintings were also made on walls or folding screens and panels. The figure shown here was painted by Hsiang Kun in the 2nd century AD.

◀WHEN WAS PERSPECTIVE FIRST USED IN EUROPEAN PAINTING?

Perspective is a method of drawing a picture so as to give an impression of realistic depth and distance. The laws of perspective were worked out and first used in the 15th century in Italy.

The Italian architect Brunelleschi worked out the principles of perspective. These are based on the fact that objects seem smaller the closer they are to the horizon. Brunelleschi's friend Masaccio first applied these ideas to painting in a fresco (wall painting) finished in 1427. The use of perspective gave a totally new approach to painting. It was followed by European artists for 500 years.

The picture shows the dramatic use of perspective. It is a detail from *The Flagellation*, a painting made by Piero della Francesca in about 1460. Piero carefully worked out the perspective of the building and figures.

Japanese colour prints in the style known as *ukiyo-e* were first seen in Europe in the second half of the 19th century. They have influenced many European artists since then.

Ukiyo-e is a style of art which arose in the 16th and 17th centuries to appeal to popular tastes. It continued until the mid-19th century. Some of the works best known in Europe are the landscape prints of Hokusai.

Early *ukiyo-e* prints showed city life and theatre scenes. Later, illustrations of warrior legends became very popular. From 1765 onwards, prints of birds, animals, flowers and landscapes were produced.

The print shown here is by Kunisada. It shows Japanese gods dancing in front of Amaterasu, the Sun goddess.

The painter Picasso came into contact with African art in 1906-7. It totally altered his ideas of how to paint solid objects on a flat surface. In 1907 he started to paint *Les Demoiselles d'Avignon* ('The Young Ladies of Avignon'), shown here. From this developed the style known as Cubism, which completely changed the course of 20th-century art.

For 500 years artists had shown their subjects realistically, from a single viewpoint, using the laws of perspective. Picasso saw that African sculpture had the key to how artists could escape from this rigid approach.

African sculptors express ideas about their subjects instead of showing them in a realistic way. The human head and body are often broken down and shown in an abstract, symbolic way.

Picasso and other Cubist painters abandoned the use of traditional perspective. They began to paint works in which an object is seen from several viewpoints as a fragmented single image.

▲WHEN WAS POLO FIRST PLAYED?

Polo is a game played on horseback with a mallet and ball. It is the oldest of all the sports which use horses. We know that people played polo in Persia (Iran) in the 1st century AD, and it is believed that the Persians invented it.

Polo started as a game used in training cavalry units of the king's guard and other mounted troops. It then became a national sport known as *chaugan*, meaning 'mallet', or 'stick'. *Chaugan* was played a great deal by the men and women of Persian noble families.

The game spread to Arabia, Tibet, China and Japan. Muslims took it to India in the 13th century AD. It was in India that polo was first played by Europeans – by some British tea-planters who formed the first European polo club in 1859. The game quickly became very popular among the British in India. It was first played in England in 1870, and in America in 1876.

▲WHEN WERE BALL GAMES FIRST PLAYED?

Ball games are one of the oldest games played by people. There is evidence in early art that they have been played since prehistoric times.

The ancient Egyptians, the Greeks and the Romans are all known to have enjoyed ball games. They are mentioned in early writings and shown in art, for example on Egyptian monuments.

The Greeks believed that ball play was particularly useful for developing grace and suppleness in the body. The Romans had an area for ball games in Roman baths, and wealthy Romans even had private ball courts in their villas. They used balls made of leather.

Many of the earliest games we know about consisted of no more than throwing the ball from player to player. There were few rules. But we know that team games and competitions of various kinds were also played by the ancient Greeks, particularly the Spartans.

▲WHEN WAS BASKETBALL FIRST PLAYED?

Basketball was played for the first time in December 1891, in America. It was invented by James Naismith at an International Young Men's Christian Association training school.

Naismith was asked to devise a new game to inspire the students. They were bored with their daily physical education class. He used ideas from games such as hockey, football and soccer, blended them with his own ideas, and invented basketball.

The bored students at the YMCA quickly became interested. News of the game spread rapidly to other parts of America. During the next ten years it was introduced into Canada, France, Britain, China, India and Japan.

The first goals were two peach baskets. The iron hoop and net was introduced two years later. People had to climb a ladder to get the ball from the net. Cutting a hole in the net so that the ball could drop through came later.

Kendo

Judo

Karate

▲WHEN DID THE MARTIAL
ARTS FIRST DEVELOP?

The martial arts are methods of self-defence and combat. They began in Japan and evolved into sports at the end of the 19th century and beginning of the 20th century. They are based on techniques which are centuries old, such as those of *jiujitsu*.

Jiujitsu is a way of fighting hand to hand, using as few weapons as possible. It was developed by the warrior class, or *samurai*, in Japan from the 17th century onwards. *Jiujitsu* involves methods of hitting, kicking, throwing, choking and holding an opponent.

Typical martial arts are judo, karate, aikido, sumo and kendo. Judo is a form of jacket wrestling based on *jiujitsu* methods. It was started in 1882 by Jigoro Kano, who founded the first school of judo. Sumo (belt wrestling) also began with the *samurai*.

Karate is a way of fighting without weapons. It was developed over several centuries, probably by people who were forbidden to carry weapons. It became a sport in the 1920s.

Aikido is a system of self-defence designed to subdue the opponent. Kendo, a form of fencing, began in the 18th century as sword-fighting practice. Light bamboo swords were used so that the *samurai* could fence without injuring each other.

▼WHEN DID THE FIRST
MOTOR RACES TAKE
PLACE?

The first motor race was in 1895 in France. The winner was Emile Levassor, who drove a French Panhard. He did more than 48 hours driving at an average speed of 24 kilometres an hour.

There had been informal contests between 'horseless carriages' from the 1880s onwards, as this was a way of proving how safe and fast the motor cars were. The first formal motor race took place in France in June 1895, run from Paris to Bordeaux and back. Soon after, there were races from Paris to Vienna, and from Paris to Berlin.

These races were dangerous events. Dogs and farm carts had to be avoided on bad roads. The driver's vision was sometimes totally obscured by clouds of dust. But these harsh tests of the cars also led to better cars being made.

An international series of races began in 1900, arranged by an American called James Gordon Bennett. They were followed by the Grand Prix series, begun in 1906 by French car makers. These still take place every year.

▶ WHAT IS A MIME?

A mime is a silent play, or acting without words. Actors show what they mean by gestures and facial expressions instead of spoken words. Actors who work like this are also called mimes.

In ancient Greece and Rome mimes were comic plays about absurd characters like stupid old men or ridiculous slaves.

Much later, actors played similar parts in Italian comedies of the kind called *commedia dell' arte*. The actors spoke, but also mimed emotions. Italian characters such as Harlequin found their way into English pantomime where at first all acting was mimed.

Modern mime acting began in the 1800s in France. The first great French mime was Jean-Baptiste-Gaspard Deburau, who died in 1846. Today, famous mimes such as Marcel Marceau imitate actions such as climbing stairs, cleaning windows or chasing a butterfly.

◀ WHAT IS A MYSTERY PLAY?

Mystery plays were plays about Bible stories or saints' lives. They were performed outdoors in the Middle Ages.

'Mystery' comes from the Latin word *ministerium*, meaning 'religious service'. The first mystery plays were acted by priests at services in churches.

Later, tradesmen, craftsmen and other groups put on plays outside churches.

In England, each trade or craft put on an appropriate play. For instance shipwrights, sailors and fishermen acted the story of Noah's Ark. Some mystery plays were acted on platforms. Others took place on wagons drawn through the streets.

A group of plays would be performed at festivals such as Easter or Christmas. Between them, the plays told all the important Bible stories. They taught people religious ideas in a lively, enjoyable way.

▶ WHAT IS KABUKI?

Kabuki **is the name for a type of play performed in Japan. Its name means 'the art of singing and dancing'. Kabuki plays contain plenty of both.**

Many kabuki plays are about a string of exciting events, some of them magical. Actors wear elaborate costumes and their faces are heavily painted. Heroes are white but villains are reddish.

The actors, all men, often fight pretended duels, and mime actions such as drinking tea from invisible cups. Music is played all through each drama and the actors sing, rather like opera singers.

Each kabuki stage is wide, with runways that jut out into the audience. Much of the scenery is very solid and there are excitingly realistic stage effects. These may include, for instance, a village on fire.

A property man dressed in black moves scenery about on the stage during the play, but no one takes any notice of him.

WHAT IS A FLYING BUTTRESS?

A flying buttress is a special kind of side-support helping to hold up a tall building with an arched roof. Many Gothic churches have flying buttresses.

Each flying buttress consists of a bar, an arch, or half an arch, that juts out from the upper part of a wall or pillar. This holds up an arched roof called a vault. The vault puts an outward strain on the wall or pillar. The flying buttress is supported by a buttress forming a solid stone or brick wall. This juts out sideways from the building's main wall, or a supporting pillar. Together, the flying buttress and buttress take the strain of the vault.

Pinnacles on top of the buttresses give them more weight, helping them resist the thrust from the side.

As church architects began to use flying buttresses, they could build high churches with slim walls instead of very much thicker walls.

WHAT IS GOTHIC ARCHITECTURE?

Gothic architecture is a style of building. It was used for many churches and some other buildings raised in Europe from about AD 1140 to 1500.

A church built in the Gothic style tends to be very tall with pointed arches for the roof and windows. The main roof is supported by arched ribs held up by pillars, not by solid walls.

Between the pillars, tall stained-glass windows largely take the place of walls. Flying buttresses rest on stone supports outside the church and help to hold up its roof. Building in this style saved stone and made the inside of a church light and airy.

Many churches have a spire soaring high above the roof. Inside and out there may be carved stone figures of holy people mentioned in the Bible.

Critics who disliked the Gothic style named it after the Goths. These were uncivilized tribes who once invaded Roman Italy.

WHAT IS ART NOUVEAU?

***Art nouveau* means 'new art'. It was a new style of art and architecture that started in Europe in the 1880s and spread to America.**

Many art nouveau artists and architects used designs with lines that curved like the stems of plants, flickering flames, or curling waves.

The English artist Aubrey Beardsley made delicate black-and-white ink drawings. Scotland's Charles Rennie Mackintosh designed sturdy furniture with simple shapes.

The Spanish architect Antoni Gaudí gave weird snaky shapes to the outsides of buildings. Victor Horta of Belgium designed a strange, writhing stairway and the stained-glass doors shown here.

Émile Gallé in France, Karl Koepping, in Germany, and Louis Tiffany, in the United States, made glass vases and other objects with delicate shapes and beautiful colours.

▶ WHAT IS A PENTATHLON?

A pentathlon is a five-part competition for athletes. Its name comes from the Greek words *pente*, meaning five, and *athlon*, meaning contest. In a pentathlon each contestant must take part in five different events. The winner is the one with the highest score.

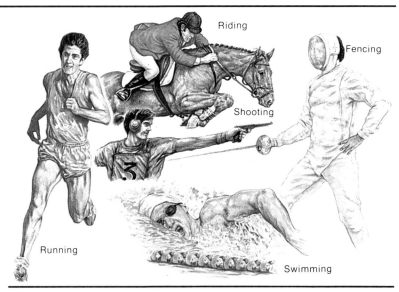

Riding

Fencing

Shooting

Running

Swimming

In ancient Greece and Rome the chosen events were ones thought to test all the strengths and skills of an athlete. These events were wrestling, foot racing, jumping, throwing the javelin and throwing the discus. The javelin was a light spear and the discus was a flat plate made of stone or metal. The athletes had to compete in all events in one day.

In 1912 the old Greek-style pentathlon was brought into the modern Olympic Games. But instead of wrestling, men ran a 1500-metre race.

At the same time, the Olympic Games started the brand-new modern or military pentathlon. This tests the abilities a messenger might have needed in the days of cavalry warfare. Its five events are riding, fencing, swimming, shooting and running 4000 metres.

The Olympic Games dropped the Greek-style pentathlon for men in 1924. In 1964 the Games brought in the women's pentathlon. Athletes competed in a high jump, long jump, 200-metre race, 80-metre race over hurdles, and the shot-put (throwing a heavy metal ball).

Later, women raced over 800 metres instead of 80, and over 100 metres of hurdles.

▼ WHAT IS THE WORLD SERIES?

This is a series of baseball games held in the United States each October. It decides the top baseball team.

The two rival teams are the year's champions of the top two American baseball leagues, the National League and the American League.

As in all baseball games, each team has nine players and most action happens on a diamond-shaped infield with a base at each corner. A pitcher throws a ball to a batter who tries to hit it and run to a base before he is made out by a fielder. A batter who safely reaches all bases scores a run.

A team's innings (turn to bat) ends when three batters are put out. Each game is won by the team scoring the most runs in nine innings.

In the World Series, the teams play the best of seven games. The winners are the first team to win four. Winners of the World Series become world champions.

▼ WHAT IS FIGURE SKATING?

This is one of the three main ice-skating sports. (The other two are speed skating and ice dancing.) Figure skating involves skating patterns called figures on ice.

Figure-skating contests have two main parts. These are school figures and free skating. School figures are based on a figure-of-eight

pattern, and may be skated on both skates or only one. They include about 70 variations. Skaters must try to make both circles of a figure-of-eight the same size, and there are rules for how to hold the body.

Free skating is freer than school figures. Skaters can leap, spin and make other smoothly-linked movements.

In pairs skating, a man and woman skate together. The man sometimes lifts the woman high in the air. For figure skating, skaters need specially shaped skates fixed to high, laced boots that fit very snugly.

▼ WHAT IS FORMULA ONE MOTOR RACING?

This is the world's top-rank type of motor racing. All the most important of the Grand Prix races are those between Formula One racing cars.

A Formula One racing car is low and wedge-shaped. The driver lies in a cockpit in front of the engine. This has a capacity of no more than 3 litres, or 1.5 litres if turbo-

charged or super-charged. It may not have more than 12 cylinders. The five- or six-speed gearbox lets the driver get the most power possible, whatever the speed of the car.

The car runs on broad, treadless tyres. These keep their grip with help from a wing-like aerofoil jutting up behind the engine.

Formula One cars can reach 320 kilometres an hour. The races are about 320 kilometres long. They are run on circuits with straight, fast stretches, and bends where drivers must brake and accelerate hard.

▼ WHAT IS THE FASTEST BALL GAME?

This is one of several games played with a small, hard ball known as a *pelota* (the Spanish for ball). The fastest pelota game is known in Spanish as *pelota vasca*, meaning 'Basque pelota'. Its Basque name is *jaï alaï* or 'merry festival'. Jaï alaï may have begun in thirteenth-century Italy.

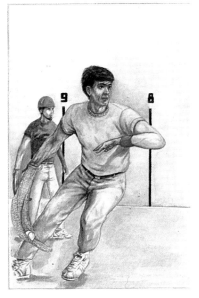

Jaï alaï players wear a long, basket-like *cesta* strapped to one arm. They use the cesta's curved hollow end to catch and throw the small, hard rubber ball called a pelota. There are two rival teams, each with one, two or three players.

They play on a *cancha*, or court, with high walls on three sides. A server hits the ball on the front wall. Opponents must catch it and throw it back before it hits the floor twice.

The ball moves tremendously fast. One pelota reached a measured speed of over 300 kilometres an hour.

► WHO WAS OMAR KHAYYAM?

Omar Khayyam was a Persian poet, astronomer and a brilliant scholar who lived in the 11th century AD. He is most famous as a poet, and a collection of his work, called the *Rubaiyat*, was translated into English by the 19th century poet, Edward Fitzgerald.

Omar Khayyam was born in the city of Nishapur (now called Neyshabur) in Persia (present-day Iran).

Because he was such a talented scholar, he was appointed to the job of royal astronomer, and asked to modernise the Persian calendar. Later, he worked with other astronomers to build an observatory in the city of Isfahan. In his own day, he was famous as a writer on science, history, law, medicine and, especially, mathematics.

He was not thought of as an important poet. In fact, not all scholars agree that the *Rubaiyat* is really his. In any case, it was not published until 200 years after his death.

◄ WHO WROTE *THE TALE OF GENJI*?

The Tale of Genji is an 11th century book from Japan which is sometimes said to be the very first novel ever written. Its author was a woman – Murasaki Shikibu.

Whether or not *The Tale of Genji* is the first ever novel, it is the first important one.

It was written at a time when it was common for the ladies at the court of the Japanese emperor to write diaries. Murasaki herself wrote one

before she wrote *The Tale of Genji*. She also wrote a short story which included some poetry – *Izumi Shikibu nikki*. She wrote *The Tale of Genji* in about 1010. It was an immediate success.

The story is of the life and loves of Prince Genji. He loves several women, and each one reacts differently to him. The book was popular for centuries afterwards – which was not always a good thing. Many writers felt they had to produce very similar books, rather than something new and different.

► WHO TOLD STORIES FOR 1001 NIGHTS?

There was once a princess in Arabia who saved herself from death by telling stories for 1001 nights.

The story tells of a cruel king named Shahryar who had his wife put to death, and then married a new wife every day and had her put to death too. Eventually he married Sharazad, the daughter of his chief minister, who planned to put an end to all this killing.

On her wedding night, she began to tell the king a story. But when she reached the most exciting part of it, she stopped, and said if he wanted to hear the end he would have to let her live another day. This went on for 1001 nights, until the king gave up his plan. Among the stories that Sharazad told were those of *Sindbad the Sailor* and *Aladdin*. The stories are traditional, and come from many parts of the Middle and Far East. The first written copy was made in Arabic in about 1000 AD. The stories are known as the 'Arabian Nights' Entertainment'.

The Divine Comedy – which many scholars think is one of the most important pieces of literature produced in medieval Europe – was written by the poet Dante Aligheri in his own language, Italian.

Dante was born in Florence in 1265, but after getting involved in the politics of the city was forced to leave. After much travelling he settled in the city of Ravenna.

One of the most important aspects of *The Divine Comedy* is that it was written in a modern language. Scholars at the time thought that any serious poetry should be written in Latin.

The poem is in three parts. In the first, the poet – Dante himself – describes a journey through Hell (the *Inferno*) with the poet Virgil as his guide. Next – still in the company of Virgil – he visits Purgatory.

In the final part – this time with Beatrice, a woman he idealised – he visits Heaven, and even glimpses God.

Petrarch was a scholar and poet who had an enormous influence on European poetry from the fourteenth century onwards.

Petrarch's full name was Francesco Petrarca. He lived from 1304 to 1374. Although he was an Italian, he spent much of his life in France.

He wrote more than 400 poems of his own – 366 of which are in a collection called *The Book of Songs*. Many of these are written to a woman called Laura. We do not know if she was a real person, or just Petrarch's ideal woman. He was especially important because he set out firm rules for writing poetry, including the number of lines to be used.

As well as writing poetry, Petrarch spent much of his life researching Latin poetry – though he himself had followed Dante's example and written in Italian. It is thanks to Petrarch's work that the poetry of the Romans Livy and Cicero was rediscovered. Without him, they might have been forgotten altogether.

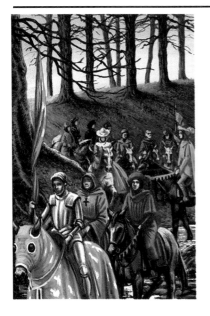

The Canterbury Tales are a collection of stories in verse which are supposed to have been told by the different members of a party of 14th century pilgrims on their way from London to Canterbury. In fact, all the stories are the work of the English poet Geoffrey Chaucer.

Chaucer lived between 1342 and 1400. He had a varied life – he served as a soldier and worked as a diplomat and a civil servant as well as being a poet. *The Canterbury Tales* is his best known work, but not his only one. His romance about the Trojan war – *Troilus and Criseyde* – is still read today but nothing he wrote has remained as popular as *The Canterbury Tales* – which in fact Chaucer never finished.

The stories are designed to reflect the characters of the tellers – they range from the bawdy miller's tale to the knight's story of honour and chivalry. Today, modern English versions of his work are still widely read.

◀WHO WAS DON QUIXOTE?

Don Quixote was the hero of a 17th century novel written by the Spanish author, Miguel de Cervantes.

Cervantes lived between 1547 and 1616. He had an adventurous life – serving first as a soldier (when he was captured by the Turks and kept prisoner) and later as a government servant.

His 'hero', Don Quixote, has adventures of a very different kind. For poor Don Quixote is described as an eccentric old man who decides to become a knight and take on deeds of daring, as in the days of old. So he puts on a suit of rusty old armour, mounts his old horse and sets out with his faithful companion, Sancho Panza (mounted on a donkey).

Being old and short-sighted, Don Quixote makes many mistakes and misunderstands a great many situations. One of the best known stories in the book tells how he mistakes a row of windmills for giants, and sets about fighting them! At the end, Don Quixote settles down quietly at home.

◀WHO MADE THE FIRST COLLECTIONS OF FAIRY TALES?

Many of the fairy tales we know today are so old that we have no idea who first made them up – but we do know that the first collection of European traditional stories was made by the French writer, Charles Perrault, in 1697. Two collectors of fairy tales were the German brothers, Jacob Carl and Wilhelm Carl Grimm.

Perrault's collection of stories was made specifically for children – his own children, in fact. He called them *Tales of the Past* and among the stories he recorded were many that are still favourites today – such as *Puss in Boots* and *Bluebeard*.

The Brothers Grimm (as they became known) were much more serious, scientific collectors of folklore. They tried to record stories just as they heard them. Their work, aimed at adults as well as children, took place between 1812 and 1822. Among their tales were *Hansel and Gretel* (left) and *Tom Thumb*.

◀WHO WAS ROBINSON CRUSOE?

Robinson Crusoe was the name of the hero of an adventure story about a shipwrecked sailor. It was written by the Englishman Daniel Defoe in 1719.

The story tells how Robinson Crusoe was cast up on a desert island, the only survivor of a shipwreck. It goes on to describe how he managed to live alone for many years, and later how he befriended a local man, whom he called Friday.

The idea of a poor castaway having to fend for himself on a desert island has always been popular. Defoe got the idea for the story from real-life tales of shipwrecked sailors – in particular the story of a man named Alexander Selkirk, very like Robinson Crusoe, who was well-known in Defoe's day.

Robinson Crusoe was not Defoe's only work. He was a journalist, who wrote political pamphlets (which sometimes got him into trouble) and the author of several other novels, including *Moll Flanders*, and *A Journal of the Plague Year*.

► WHO WROTE *GULLIVER'S TRAVELS*?

Gulliver's Travels is a satirical story about the adventures of a ship's doctor named Lemuel Gulliver. It was written by Jonathan Swift – a clergyman and scholar who lived from 1667 to 1745.

Swift was born in Ireland and educated at Trinity College Dublin. After spending the early part of his adult life in England, he eventually became Dean of St Patrick's Cathedral, Dublin. His writing is bitterly satirical and he was often very unpopular. Even *Gulliver's Travels*, though it is often told as an enjoyable story for children, was written he said, 'to vex the world'. It is in fact a disguised attack on the unpleasant aspects of life and politics in his own day.

Apart from the familiar story of Gulliver's capture by the tiny people of Lilliput, the book tells of other adventures, including a trip to Brobdingnag, a land of giants, and to a land where horse-like creatures rule.

► WHO WAS CANDIDE?

Candide is the name of the hero of a satirical novel by the French writer Voltaire, who lived from 1694 to 1778.

Voltaire's real name was Francois Marie Arouet. He spent much of his life fighting tyranny, attacking those he thought were wrong with cruel satire.

Candide is his best known work. It tells the story of a young man who, influenced by his tutor Pangloss, is convinced that we live in 'the best of all possible worlds'. Voltaire attacked this philosophy of optimism by describing how Candide, after being involved in many horrific adventures, involving rape, murder, war and an earthquake, eventually abandons this belief and comes to the conclusion that the best we can do is go and 'cultivate our own gardens'.

Voltaire himself was at one point a prisoner in the famous Bastille in Paris, and later he lived in exile in England. He eventually settled in Switzerland.

► WHO CREATED FRANKENSTEIN'S MONSTER?

The story of the scientist Frankenstein, and the monster he made out of parts of other humans, was written by Mary Shelley, and was published in 1818.

Mary Shelley was born in 1797 and died in 1851.

When she was only 17, she fell in love with the poet Percy Bysshe Shelley. Although he was already married, the couple ran away together to Switzerland, where they lived for a while with the poet Lord Byron. When Shelley's wife died in 1816, Mary was able to marry Shelley, but he died only six years later in a sailing accident.

She spent much of her life editing her husband's work. She continued to write herself, published a collection of stories and kept a journal. But *Frankenstein* is her most famous work. It tells how the monster made by Frankenstein saw so much cruelty and evil in the world that he turned against it.

◄ WHO WAS ALESSANDRO MANZONI?

Alessandro Manzoni was a 19th century Italian writer, whose novel, *I Promessi Sposi*, is one of the most important works in Italian literature.

Manzoni was born in 1785 and died in 1873. He was a devout Roman Catholic, and this had a deep effect on his view of the world and therefore on his writing. In his own time he was known as a poet, but today he is remembered for his great novel, *I Promessi Sposi*. This is set in 17th century Lombardy and tells how a wicked local tyrant, Don Rodrigo, tries to prevent a young peasant couple, Renzo and Lucia, from marrying, but without success.

Manzoni wove historical events into the story in a way that was quite new in Italian literature. The kind of language he wrote in was also important. It was a very pure form of the Tuscan dialect, which became the model for Italian writing for the next hundred years.

► WHO WAS MOBY DICK?

Moby Dick was a great white whale, whose story was written by the American, Herman Melville.

The story of Moby Dick is really the story of Captain Ahab, an old seafarer who spends his life trying to capture the great whale. Ahab has lost a leg in his hunt for Moby Dick, and finding him is an obsession. At the end of the story, Ahab's ship is lost and there is only one survivor.

Much of *Moby Dick* tells of the dangers and difficulties of whaling in the 19th century – before the days of factory ships – when the only way to catch a whale was for men to go out from the whaling ships in small boats in the icy sea and harpoon it.

Melville, who lived from 1819 to 1891, knew much about whaling, for he had been out on the ships himself and had had many adventures – including being shipwrecked and taking part in a mutiny. Today we remember him mainly for *Moby Dick*, though he wrote other stories.

◄ WHO WAS VICTOR HUGO?

Victor Hugo was a French poet, dramatist and novelist who is remembered today for two great novels – *The Hunchback of Notre Dame* and *Les Misérables*.

Victor Hugo was born in 1802 and spent much of his childhood travelling with his father, an army officer.

His career as writer started in about 1822, when he began to write plays. *The Hunchback of Notre Dame*, a novel set in medieval Paris, appeared in 1831. Hugo was involved in politics which, in 1851, led to him having to leave France and live in exile for nearly 20 years.

Throughout this time, when he lived mainly in Jersey, he went on writing, and produced two books of poetry – *The Contemplations* and *The Legend of the Centuries* – as well as his greatest novel, *Les Misérables*. This tells the story of Jean Valjean, an escaped convict who tries to lead an honest and useful life.

At the end of his life, Hugo returned to France, where he died in 1885.

▶ WHO WERE THE THREE MUSKETEERS?

The Three Musketeers were the creations of the 19th century French writer, Alexandre Dumas. The musketeers, Porthos, Athos and Aramis, together with their friend d'Artagnan, were supposed to have been adventurers in 17th century France.

Dumas lived from 1803 to 1870. We know him as Dumas *père*, since his son was also a writer. Dumas *père*'s father

(himself the son of a nobleman and a black woman from the Caribbean) was an army general. Dumas, who could hardly read as a young man, went to Paris and became first a playwright and then a popular historical novelist.

Dumas is remembered today both for *The Three Musketeers* and for his melodramatic *The Count of Monte Cristo* – the tale of mysterious ex-prisoner Edmond Dantes, bent on revenge for his unjust captivity.

◀ WHO WAS HANS CHRISTIAN ANDERSEN?

Hans Christian Andersen was a Danish writer of children's stories, whose work includes such favourites as *The Ugly Duckling* and *The Little Mermaid*.

Hans Andersen was born in 1805 and died in 1875. Although his family were poor, he managed to get into university, and afterwards became a writer.

His first book of children's stories had in it some of his

best known – including *The Tinderbox* and *The Princess and the Pea* (left) – but it was years before he was really successful.

He based his stories on traditional tales, but they were very different from the collections of people such as the Brothers Grimm. Instead of being about ogres and witches, many of Andersen's stories such as *The Constant Tin Soldier* and *The Little Fir Tree*, reflect his own rather sad and lonely life.

We know from his letters that he was a sensitive and witty man.

▶ WHO WAS HONORÉ DE BALZAC?

Honoré de Balzac was a French writer whose best known work is a series of about 100 novels and short stories to which he gave the overall title of *The Human Comedy*.

Balzac was born in Tours in 1799. In 1816 he left for Paris where he studied law for three years before deciding to become a writer. He spent much of his life investing in risky ventures and had to write

hard to pay his debts.

His novels, which are about provincial and Parisian life, include characters from many walks of life and cover themes such as fatherly love, greed and envy as well as dealing with many other aspects of life and politics in France.

The Human Comedy is a complicated work, with more than 2000 characters in it, many appearing in more than one novel. The best-known titles include *Old Goriot* and *Cousin Bette*. Balzac died in 1850. The picture shows a statue of Balzac by Rodin.

▲ WHO WAS PHIDEAS?

Phideas was a sculptor in Ancient Greece. Although almost nothing of his work survives today, his fame has lasted until modern times.

In his own day, people said that Phideas had seen the gods and through him, ordinary people could glimpse them.

It is thought that Phideas lived from about 490 to 430 BC. The ruler of Athens, Pericles, put him in charge of an important building programme which included the sculptures of the Parthenon. Phideas made a huge gold and ivory statue of the goddess Athena which, at about 10 metres tall, was the largest statue ever erected in Athens.

A later, bronze statue of Athena was even taller – but because he put his own portrait as well as Pericles's on her shield, he was accused of irreverence and sent into exile.

He also made an ivory and gold Zeus at Olympia (where the remains of Phideas's workshop have been found) and possibly some of the surviving marbles from the Parthenon.

▲ WHO WAS GIOTTO?

Giotto was an Italian artist of the early part of the era we call the Renaissance. He was the most important painter of his time, and was one of the first painters to present lifelike people in realistic backgrounds.

Giotto lived from 1266 to 1337. Like other artists of his time, he did much of his work as frescoes on chapel walls.

Among his most famous pictures are a series of frescoes in Padua, showing the life of Christ. The characters look very lifelike – something quite new in Giotto's day.

He lived and worked in many parts of Italy, at one time in Florence, and then as court painter for the ruler of Naples. By 1334 he was back in Florence as overseer of works for the cathedral and fortifications that were being built.

Giotto was the first in a long line of Italian painters to use a realistic style – although other painters of his own day continued to use a traditional style. The picture is the *Madonna in Maestà*.

▲ WHO WAS PIERO DELLA FRANCESCA?

Piero della Francesca was one of the most important artists of the Italian Renaissance. He is best known for his clear, lifelike pictures, though in his own day he was more famous for his scientific work and he did not have much influence on other painters of his time.

He was born in 1420, and died in 1492. Like other Renaissance artists, he had wide interests.

He was especially concerned with geometry, which he used to help him work out the basic patterns for his pictures and get the perspective right.

His work was often in the form of frescoes, and among the best known of these are those showing the Legend of the Holy Cross in the church of St Francis at Arrezo. Here he shows both ordinary people – peasants sitting at the feet of St Francis – and magnificent figures, such as the Queen of Sheba.

The picture shows part of an altarpiece, *The Baptism of Christ*.

◀ WHO MADE THE FIRST OIL PAINTINGS?

Strictly speaking, we do not know who made the first oil paintings, since the technique goes back to the Middle Ages. But we do know that the Flemish painters Hubert and Jan van Eyck were the first to make the most of the possibilities the method offers in terms of depth and shades of colour.

We know little of Hubert's work, but much more of Jan's, since he left many signed and dated pictures. Because Hubert died first, in 1426, people tend to think he was the elder brother.

Among Jan van Eyck's early works is a painting of the Virgin Mary in a church.

Perhaps his most famous picture is of a man named Arnolfini and his wife, at their wedding. Another – of a man in a red turban – may have been a self-portrait. We are not sure exactly what new method the van Eycks brought to oil painting, but they were famous in their own time for using an entirely new technique.

▶ WHO WAS MICHELANGELO?

Michelangelo is often said to be one of the greatest artists Europe has ever produced. He was certainly one of the most important figures in the Italian Renaissance. His best known work includes some magnificent sculpture as well as the frescoes that cover the ceiling and part of the walls of the Sistine Chapel, in the Vatican in Rome.

His full name was Michelangelo Buonarroti. He was born in 1475 into an aristocratic family. At first his parents tried to stop him from becoming an artist because they did not think it was a suitable profession for someone of his class, but eventually he managed to overcome their opposition. He attended a school for artists run by Bertoldo di Giovanni in the Medici Gardens in Florence.

Following a period in Bologna, Michelangelo went to Rome in 1496, where he produced one of his greatest works – his famous *Pietà*, a statue of the Virgin Mary, still

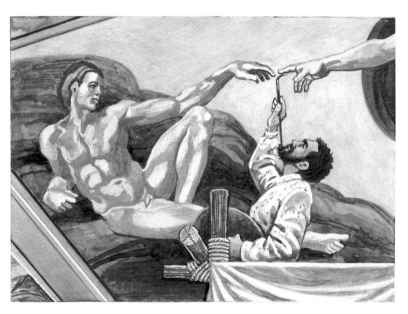

looking like a young girl, with the body of the dead Christ in her arms.

Following this he returned to Florence, where he produced another masterpiece – his statue of the young Biblical king, David.

In 1505 the then Pope, Julius II, asked him to return to Rome to make a tomb. Michelangelo never managed to finish this – he quarrelled with the Pope and went back to Florence. But by 1508 he was in Rome again, painting the frescoes in the Sistine Chapel. When this work was

finished, it covered the whole of the vault and part of the upper walls.

He wanted assistants to help him, but it was hard to find anyone good enough. In the end, he did almost all of it by himself in an extraordinarily short time.

Having started the mammoth task in 1508, he completed it by 1512. Many other great works followed, before Michelangelo died in 1564.

► WHO WAS BERNINI?

Gianlorenzo Bernini was one of the most important sculptors of 17th century Italy. His style was the very ornate fashion which we now call 'Baroque'. Much of his work was done for the great church of St Peter, in the Vatican, Rome.

Bernini was born in 1598. His father – also known as Bernini – was himself a famous sculptor, which meant that from an early age the young Bernini was able to meet the famous and influential people who could find him work.

In 1639 he became the most important artist in the court of Pope Urban VIII, as well as chief architect of St Peter's. Unfortunately he had to leave this work when the Pope died as his successor, Pope Innocent X did not like his style. However, the next Pope, Alexander VII gave him back his job.

Bernini's work was not confined to sacred places. His most famous sculpture (shown in the picture) is the Fountain of the Four Rivers in the Piazza Navona in Rome. The story goes that he had to compete for this job with his arch rival, Francesco Borromini.

It is said that Bernini secured the commission by underhand means – he gave a silver model of the design to the Pope's sister-in-law. The legend goes on to say that Bernini managed to insult Borromini's own work in his design of the fountain. He shows the Nile river god shielding his eyes so that he does not have to look at the church opposite (which Borromini designed) and another god, representing the River Plate, appears so sure that the church is unstable that he has his hands raised to protect himself from falling masonry! In fact, the church was built after the fountain, so this part of the story cannot be true.

By the end of his life, Bernini's rich, ornate work could be seen in many chapels and churches throughout Rome.

He died in 1680.

◄ WHO WAS RODIN?

Auguste Rodin was a French sculptor whose work, often large figures cast in bronze, includes such well-known pieces as *The Thinker* and *The Kiss*.

Rodin was born in Paris in 1840. He studied under various sculptors and worked for a while as a mason.

A trip to Italy in 1875 introduced him to the work of Michelangelo, which impressed him deeply. In 1878 he held an exhibition of his work in which his figures were so lifelike that he was accused of casting them from live models.

He was always a controversial artist – his statue of Balzac, for example, was rejected by the organisation that commissioned it because of the way it was dressed. The forceful bronze in the picture is called *The Hand of God*.

Rodin especially enjoyed the idea of conveying a feeling of movement in his work – many of his models were dancers. He died in 1917, leaving much of his work to his nation.

▲ WHO WERE KNOWN AS THE POST-IMPRESSIONISTS?

The Post-Impressionists is the name given to the group of artists, working mainly in France, whose work followed the Impressionist movement of the 19th century. The name, given to the work of Seurat, Gauguin, Van Gogh and Cézanne, comes from the title of an exhibition held in London in 1910 and called _Manet and the Post-Impressionists_.

Although these artist have been grouped together by the name Post-Impressionist, their work is very different. Seurat painted very static scenes of town and suburban life, using dots and dabs of pure colour, while Gauguin chose to paint in the strong, bright, flat colours, which he associated with the South Sea islands where he lived for many years.

Van Gogh was Dutch, but worked mostly in the south of France. The picture shows part of Cézanne's _Landscape with Poplars_. His work had a strong influence on later artists, including Picasso.

▲ WHO WERE KNOWN AS THE WILD BEASTS?

The group of artists known as _Les Fauves_ (The Wild Beasts) worked in France at the beginning of the 20th century. They included Henri Matisse and André Derain and several other artists.

The group got its name from a critic named Louis Vauxelles who, on seeing their work on the walls of the gallery where they were exhibiting, pointed to a sculpture in the middle of the room and exclaimed: 'Donatello among the wild beasts!' In fact he was referring to the behaviour of the artists rather than their work.

But although they exhibited together (this was in 1905) they were not a definite movement in painting in the way that the Impressionists and Post-Impressionists were.

Nevertheless, they did important work, and influenced many painters who came after them. Collectively their work was the beginning of modern abstract art.

Part of Matisse's _Algerian Woman_ is shown in the picture.

▲ WHO WAS PICASSO?

Pablo Ruiz y Picasso was a Spanish artist who must be the best known of all 20th century painters. Throughout his long life he painted in several different styles, and greatly influenced other painters of his day.

Picasso was born in 1881 in Malaga, Spain. When he started work, the great painters of the Impressionist movement were still alive. His early pictures – done mainly in blue – showed the poverty he saw around him in Barcelona.

Later he moved to Paris where he worked with Georges Braque on pictures showing figures as fragments of geometric shapes – the style we know as cubism.

He became more deeply involved with politics, especially during the Spanish Civil War. One of Picasso's most famous pictures is _Guernica_, which depicts the destruction of a Spanish town. His work was suppressed by the Nazis in World War II.

Picasso died in the south of France in 1973.

◄FOR WHOM DID VIVALDI COMPOSE HIS MUSIC?

Antonio Vivaldi, the Italian composer who lived from 1678 to 1741, composed most of his music for the pupils of a girls' orphanage in Venice.

The orphanage was the Conservatorio della Pietà (known as the Pietà). His job was to teach the violin, but because the choir and orchestra were so good, he composed music for them.

When Vivaldi started work in 1703, he was on good terms with the governors of the Pietà, but in 1713 he upset them by taking time off work to travel about Italy, writing and producing operas.

Eventually he left his job, though he did go on composing for the Pietà. His most famous work includes the four *Four Seasons* concertos – but he wrote hundreds of other pieces. Many of these were written rather fast to fulfil his contract with the Pietà, and critics have accused him – rather unfairly – of having written the same concerto 400 times!

◄WHO WAS JOHANN SEBASTIAN BACH?

Johann Sebastian Bach was the most famous member of a family of musicians from the German town of Eisenach.

Bach was born in 1685. He was taught music first by his father, who was a professional musician, and then, when his father died, by his brother Johann Christoph.

After working for a while as an organist, Bach became musical director to a prince – Leopold of Kothen – in 1717.

During this time, he composed some of his most famous work – the *Brandenburg Concertos*.

Because he was trained as a church organist, and continued to work as one, Bach inevitably wrote a lot of church music. His music for church choirs includes 200 cantatas, as well as a *Mass in B Minor*. He also wrote three settings of the Passion story, the most famous of which is his St Matthew Passion.

Bach suffered a tragedy when, in 1747, he lost his sight. He died very soon afterwards, in 1750.

►WHO WAS MOZART?

Wolfgang Amadeus Mozart lived only 35 years, but in that time he became one of the world's most famous composers.

Mozart was born in Salzburg, in Austria in 1756. He began composing at the age of five and could play the harpsichord and violin so well that even as a very young child his father took him on a tour of Europe, playing before royalty.

As a young man, Mozart settled in Vienna, but in spite of being so talented he was always in financial difficulties.

Mozart's work included many concertos for a variety of instruments, including the piano, horn and bassoon. He also wrote symphonies and several great operas, including *The Marriage of Figaro*, *The Magic Flute*, *Don Giovanni* and *Così fan tutte*.

He died very suddenly after a short illness. Rumour had it that he had been poisoned, but it is more likely that he had a weak heart. He died so poor that only the gravedigger attended his funeral.

▶ WHO WAS BEETHOVEN?

Ludwig van Beethoven has been called the greatest composer who has ever lived – yet he was deaf for much of his life.

Beethoven lived from 1770 to 1827. He was born in Bonn in Germany. He was not a child prodigy, but at the age of 17 he was good enough to go to Vienna to study under Mozart.

Later, he studied with Josef Haydn, but we know he was not satisfied and took extra lessons in secret!

By the age of 32, he knew he was going deaf. Deeply depressed, he had to give up playing, but was able to go on composing because he could still hear the sound of the music in his head. He used to go for long walks, carrying a sketch book in which he wrote down his musical ideas.

He is remembered for many great works – including masterpieces such as the *Moonlight Sonata*, the *Emperor Concerto* and his famous Ninth Symphony, in which he introduced choral music for the first time in a symphony.

▶ WHO WAS TCHAIKOVSKY?

The Russian composer Peter Ilich Tchaikovsky is probably best known as the composer of ballet music, though he wrote many other pieces.

Tchaikovsky was born in 1840 in Votkinsk in Russia. He entered the St Petersburg (now Leningrad) Conservatory of Music in 1862 and from 1865 worked at the Moscow Conservatory. At first his work was unpopular.

In 1877 Tchaikovsky made a disastrous marriage which only lasted a few weeks and left him extremely depressed. In the same year, however, he was offered an income from a wealthy widow, Nadezhda von Meck, who gave him an allowance on condition that they never met! It was at this point that he began to compose most of his major works.

Tchaikovsky's most popular compositions include the ballets *Sleeping Beauty* and *Swan Lake*, the *Romeo and Juliet* Overture, the opera *Eugene Onegin* and his Sixth (*Pathétique*) Symphony.

He died of cholera in 1893.

◀ WHO WAS STRAVINSKY?

Igor Stravinsky was a Russian composer who is best known for the dramatic ballet music he wrote for the impressario Diaghilev.

Stravinsky was born in 1882 in a town in Russia then named Oranienbaum – now Lomonosov. In 1909 he spent a season working in Paris with Diaghilev and his company, the *Ballets Russes*. Stravinsky wrote several scores for the ballet, including *The Firebird* (shown in the picture),

Petrushka (a ballet based on a story of rivalry among the characters in a puppet show) and *The Rite of Spring*.

The last composition was very controversial. The first audience that heard it made so much noise that the music could hardly be heard! But today it is recognised as one of Stravinsky's best works.

During World War I, Stravinsky and his family lived in Switzerland. At the outbreak of World War II he emigrated to the United States where he lived and worked until his death in 1971.

◄WHO WROTE THE FIRST TRAGEDIES?

Tragedy is a kind of drama that grew up in Ancient Greece. Among the early writers of tragedy, the best-known are Aeschylus, Sophocles and Euripides.

Aeschylus lived from 525 to 456 BC. Only seven of his 90 plays survive – we do not, for example, have the first play for which he won a prize in 484 BC. He wrote a new kind of play – using two actors. Until that time, there had been just one actor and a chorus.

Sophocles (496-406 BC) brought in more changes – a third speaker, a less important part for the chorus and a new kind of trilogy (group of three plays) in which each play was complete in itself. We still have seven – including his most famous, *Oedipus Rex*.

Euripides (484-406 BC) was the last of the three. His plays are despairing and often violent, but in later life he started writing tragi-comedies with happy endings. This started a new trend in Greek drama.

◄WHO ARE COLUMBINE AND HARLEQUIN?

Columbine and Harlequin are two main characters in the *Commedia dell'arte* – a form of traditional theatre that started in Italy at the end of the Renaissance and which was popular all over Europe until the 18th century.

Commedia dell'arte was based on very simple plots – usually involving young lovers whose parents do not want them to marry, and a group of witty and intelligent servants, who help them. Each character had a special mask and costume. Into this action, entertainment such as acrobatics, juggling and music were added. The characters of Harlequin and Columbine developed from the French form of this theatre.

Originally they were Arlecchino and Columbina – two of the servants who help the lovers. Arlecchino was at first dressed in rags, but over the years his costume developed into the one we know today. Columbina was shown as a young girl – often loved by Arlecchino.

◄WHO WAS ENGLAND'S GREATEST DRAMATIST?

England's greatest dramatist was also one of the world's greatest – William Shakespeare, the author of 35 plays, whose work remains the most important drama ever written in English.

Shakespeare was born in 1564, in Stratford-on-Avon in Warwickshire. He was educated there and married, but eventually left and went to London, where he became involved with the theatre. He joined a company named the Chamberlain's Men, later called The King's Men, based at the Globe Theatre.

Here he became an actor and a director, writing plays for the company to perform, and probably producing them too. His plays cover a wide variety of subject matter and include histories, light comedies such as *A Midsummer Night's Dream* (left) and dark tragedies such as *Hamlet* and *King Lear*.

As well as writing plays, he was also a poet, and published a collection of sonnets in 1609. He died in 1616.

▶ WHO WAS MOLIÈRE?

Molière – whose real name was Jean-Baptiste Poquelin – was a French writer and great comic dramatist. Among his best known works are *Tartuffe*, *Le Misanthrope* and *Le Bourgeois Gentilhomme*.

Molière was born in 1622 in Paris. As a young man, he set up a theatrical company financed in part by an actress, Madeleine Béjart. The company was not an immediate success and Molière ended up in jail twice for debt.

But eventually things did begin to go well and, in 1658, they played before the King.

Molière became well-known as a playwright – but his work often offended the church. One of his best known works is *Tartuffe*, about a hypocritical religious man who is eventually unmasked. This was banned for five years, but when it was eventually shown, it was a great success.

Molière was a brilliant comic actor, and took part in his own plays. In 1673 he was taken ill while actually on stage, and taken home to die.

▶ WHO SOLD HIS SOUL TO THE DEVIL?

There is a German legend, dating back to the 16th century, about a magician named Faust who sold his soul to the devil in return for knowledge and power. The story has been written many times, but one of the most important versions of it is a dramatic poem by the German writer, Johann Wolfgang von Goethe.

Goethe was born in 1749. As well as being a playwright, he was a critic, journalist, theatre manager, painter, poet and scientist.

His version of the Faust legend was published in two parts – the first in 1808, the second in 1832, the year of his death. He tackled the story in a different way from earlier versions (such as that by the English playwright, Christopher Marlowe) since he saves Faust instead of sending him to hell.

Goethe – a brilliant scholar himself – could not accept that a thirst for knowledge could lead to damnation.

▶ WHO WAS KNOWN AS 'THE DIVINE SARAH'?

'The Divine Sarah' was the name critics gave to the great French actress Sarah Bernhardt.

Sarah Bernhardt, born Henriette Bernard in 1844, spent much of her childhood in a convent and had almost decided to become a nun, but instead one of her mother's friends persuaded her to take up acting.

After finishing training, she slowly built up her reputation until, after a very successful tour in London with France's national theatre company, the *Comédie Francaise*, she set up her own company in 1880.

She became particularly famous for her role as Marguerite Gautier, the heroine of *La Dame aux Camelias*, by Dumas.

In 1905, she injured her knee, and over the next ten years it grew gradually worse until she had the leg amputated. But she continued to act in any part she could do seated. She died in 1923.

Anton Chekhov was a Russian playwright and writer of short stories. Among his best-known works are the plays *Uncle Vanya* and *The Seagull*. His plays are often about the decline of the Russian land-owning class.

Chekhov was born in 1860 in the seaside town of Taganrog. As a young man he trained as a doctor in Moscow, and supported himself and his family by writing comic sketches for magazines. He later built up a reputation as a dramatist and short-story writer.

Eventually he was able to afford an estate south of Moscow, where he lived with his sister until he realised he had tuberculosis and would have to move to the coast for his health. He went to live in Yalta on the Black Sea, and also spent some time in France.

Two of his best-known plays – *The Cherry Orchard* and *The Three Sisters* – were written at this time.

He died in 1904.

Elenora Duse (right) was an Italian actress who was famous for the way she played leading roles in plays by the Norwegian dramatist, Henrik Ibsen.

Eleonora Duse was born in a railway carriage in Italy in 1858. Her family were involved in the theatre, and she first appeared on stage at the age of four – taking leading roles from the age of 14. She first became famous after playing the part of Thérèse Raquin, in a play based on Zola's novel.

Eleonora Duse retired in 1909 because of ill-health, and died in 1923.

Her style was quite different from that of Sarah Bernhardt, who was almost the same age. Instead of projecting her own personality she worked hard at trying to understand the character of the part she was acting. This was particularly important to her when she played in dramas by the young poet Gabriele D'Annunzio, with whom she was in love, and also in Ibsen's plays.

Henrik Ibsen was a Norwegian dramatist who is known as the father of modern drama because he introduced social problems into his plays in a realistic manner.

Henrik Ibsen was born in 1828 in the sea-port of Skein. After training as a chemist, he worked first in Bergen and then in the capital of Norway, Christiana (now called Oslo), writing and directing plays. He left Norway in 1862, and stayed away for 27 years – living mainly in Rome, but also in Munich and Dresden.

These were the years in which he wrote many of his best known plays – starting with *Brand* and *Peer Gynt* and going on to *The Pillars of Society*, *Ghosts*, *The Wild Duck*, *A Doll's House* and several others which examine moral issues.

On his return to Norway near the end of his life, Ibsen wrote two of his most famous plays – *John Gabriel Borkman* and *Hedda Gabler*.

Ibsen died in 1906.

▲ WHO WAS ANNA PAVLOVA?

▲ WHO WAS VASLAV NIJINSKY?

▲ WHO WAS BERTHOLD BRECHT?

Anna Pavlova was a great Russian ballerina who was famous for her solo performances, especially one called *The Dying Swan*.

She was born in 1882 in St Petersburg – now called Leningrad. As a child, she was lucky enough to be accepted by one of the most famous ballet schools of the time, the Imperial School of Ballet in St Petersburg. Later she joined the Mariinsky Theatre Company and became prima ballerina.

She became internationally famous in 1909, when she travelled with the impressario Diaghilev and a company made up of dancers from the Mariinsky and Bolshoi theatres – the *Ballets Russes*.

Next, she performed in London, where she was a huge success. In 1913, she decided she wanted more independence, set up her own company with her husband and ran it for the rest of her life.

She died in 1931, of pneumonia.

Vaslav Nijinsky was one of the greatest-ever male ballet dancers – known for his amazingly high leaps (elevation) and his extremely expressive and dramatic interpretations. He was also a great choreographer, producing controversial new ballets.

Nijinsky was born in 1890, in Kiev in the Ukraine. Both his parents were dancers.

He entered the Imperial School of Ballet in St Petersburg, where he was a star before he finished training. When he joined the Mariinsky Theatre, he partnered some of the greatest ballerinas of the day.

Like Anna Pavlova, he went to Paris in 1909 with Diaghilev's Ballets Russes. He was a resounding success.

As a choreographer he broke away from the classical style of dancing.

In 1919, after a nervous breakdown which was said to be caused by schizophrenia, he left the stage. He died in London in 1950.

Berthold Brecht was a German playwright who had an important influence on 20th century drama. He developed a theory of drama whereby the audience was made to criticise, instead of identifying with, the characters.

Brecht was born in Bavaria in 1898.

After his first successful play – *Baal* – his plays became more socialist. One such play was *The Threepenny Opera*, which, with its music by Kurt Weill, was a huge success.

With the rise of Hitler, Brecht was forced to leave Germany. He went first to Scandinavia and then to the United States. It was while he was there that he wrote his most famous work, *The Caucasian Chalk Circle*.

He left the United States in 1947, because of political pressure. From then, until his death in 1956, he worked mainly in East Berlin, where he had his own company, the *Berliner Ensemble*.

HOW PEOPLE LIVE

▼ WHAT IS A MERMAID?   ▼ WHAT IS A UNICORN?   ▼ WHAT IS A DRAGON?

Mermaids were mythical beasts said to live in the sea. The upper half of a mermaid's body was that of a woman but the lower half was that of a fish, with scales and a tail.

Many people believed that mermaids were as real as any other animal. They were said to love singing and to have magic powers.

People thought mermaids were usually dangerous, and used their beautiful voices to lure sailors to death by drowning. But many tales tell of men who gained power over a mermaid by stealing her mirror or comb, and then married her and took her to live on dry land.

Some people have mistaken a distant seal or sea cow for a mermaid. Maybe this is how the idea of mermaids began.

The unicorn was a mythical beast said to look like a horse. It had a long, straight, spiral horn jutting from its forehead.

In Greek and Roman myths, the unicorn had hind legs like

an antelope's and a tail like that of a lion. The body was white, the head was red, and the eyes were blue. The horn had a white base, black middle and red tip.

In the Middle Ages the unicorn stood for purity. Christian artists often pictured a unicorn with holy people like the Virgin Mary.

Zoologists think that the idea of the unicorn arose when someone saw an oryx far off. From a distance, this big desert antelope sometimes seems to have one long horn instead of two horns.

Dragons are mythical beasts. Many were supposed to have a snake's body and a bat's wings. They breathed fire.

In fact different people had different notions of what

dragons looked like. To the ancient Greeks a dragon was a huge snake. Chinese dragons had legs with clawed feet, but no wings.

Greeks and Romans believed that dragons could be wise and good, but Jews and Christians always thought dragons were evil and dangerous. A Christian legend tells how St George used a magic sword to kill a dragon about to eat a princess.

The Komodo dragons that live on a few Indonesian islands are really no more than very large lizards.

▼ WHAT IS A FLYING SAUCER?

'Flying saucer' is a name often used for any kind of strange object seen in the sky. People also describe such objects as unidentified flying objects, or UFOs for short.

Flying saucers got their name because many were supposed to look like giant saucers. Thousands have been sighted around the world. Many stood still; others dashed across the sky faster than a

plane. This has led some people to think that flying saucers are spaceships from other worlds.

Scientists have rather less exciting explanations. They have found that most flying saucers were really ordinary objects such as weather balloons, planets, meteors or aircraft seen in unusual light.

A few people claim they actually watched a flying saucer land, and met strange beings who came out of it. But doctors usually find that all this happened only in the watcher's own imagination.

▼ WHAT IS THE LOCH NESS MONSTER?

This is supposed to be a huge water animal. It is said to live in northern Scotland in a long, deep lake called Loch Ness.

Many visitors to Loch Ness say they have seen the monster rising from the lake. Some have even photographed objects that might be parts of it. The photographs seem to show a beast about nine metres long. It appears to have a long,

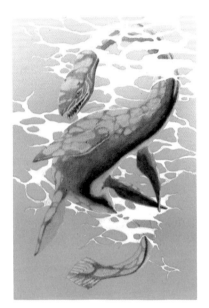

snaky neck, a big barrel-shaped body, and flippers.

Giant reptiles like this once swam in many seas; they are known as plesiosaurs. But all are thought to have died out 65 million years ago.

Many people who thought they saw the monster may have been mistaken. Otters, fish, and even waves, sometimes look like a strange, large animal.

Boats with echo-sounders have shown something large that moves deep down in the lake. Perhaps Loch Ness *does* have a prehistoric monster.

▲ WHAT WAS THE MINOTAUR?

The Minotaur was a mythical monster with a bull's head and a man's body. It was supposed to live on the island of Crete in the Mediterranean Sea.

Greek legend tells that the Minotaur was the child of a white bull and the queen of Crete. The Cretan king, Minos, kept the beast in the Labyrinth. This building was shaped as a maze, from which no one could find the way out. Each year seven youths and seven maidens from the Greek city of Athens were put in the Labyrinth for the bull-man to eat.

One year, an Athenian prince called Theseus killed the Minotaur. Theseus then escaped from the Labyrinth by following a thread given to him by Ariadne, the daughter of the Cretan king.

Archaeologists have dug up ancient palace ruins on Crete. They found many corridors and wall paintings of people playing daring games with bulls. Perhaps these led to the Minotaur legend.

515

▲ WHAT IS A SYNAGOGUE?

A synagogue is a Jewish place of worship and learning. The word means 'to bring together'. Judaists (people belonging to the religion of Judaism) have been meeting in synagogues for more than two thousand years.

Synagogues need not be built in any particular way, as most churches are. But all hold an ever-burning lamp, which stands for the everlasting faith of the Jewish people.

There is also a closet called the holy ark. This holds the Scrolls of the Law (the Jewish Scripture), read out to the worshippers. The services are led by a person who stands on a platform or *bimah*. Any Jew may do this, but most synagogues have a cantor who chants religious music and leads the people in prayer.

The person responsible for religious services and teaching is a rabbi. Rabbis are learned people, and their tasks include explaining the Jewish Scriptures.

▼ WHAT IS A MOSQUE?

A mosque is a place of worship for Muslims. They believe in the faith called Islam. The word *mosque* comes from the Arabic for 'temple'.

A mosque may be a room or a splendid group of large buildings. Many mosques have towers called minarets, from where *muezzins* or criers call people to worship at the hours of prayer.

Muslims remove their shoes and wash in a courtyard. Then they kneel facing a *mihrab* or prayer niche. This shows the direction of Mecca, the holiest city of Islam. Prayers are led by an *imam* who stands in a *mimbar*, or pulpit.

Early mosques were little more than fenced yards. Now many have a gleaming dome, graceful minarets, and a *maktab*, or school. Mosques are often decorated with beautiful patterns but there are no pictures of people or other living things. Islam forbids Muslims to copy what they believe God created.

▲ WHAT IS THE KORAN?

This is the holy book of Islam. Its name means 'a recitation'. Muslims believe that the angel Gabriel told its words to the Prophet Muhammad before he died in AD 632.

The Koran contains 114 *suras*, or chapters, made up of verses that rhyme and are written in Arabic. The world's hundreds of millions of Muslims believe these verses bring a message from Allah, as they call God.

The Koran says that Allah is the only God. It declares that God made the universe, and it calls on all people to submit to God's will. *Islam* means 'submission'.

The book tells how to lead a good daily life. People must pray every day, give to the poor and be brave, just and humble. The Koran says that one day all will come before God to be judged.

The Koran says that Abraham, Moses and Jesus were God's messengers, or prophets, and that the last prophet was Muhammad.

A Buddhist is a follower of Siddhartha Gautama, a long-dead Indian prince known by his title 'Buddha', which means 'Enlightened One'. There are over 200 million Buddhists.

Buddhists believe people suffer because they want what they do not have. Buddhists think the way to escape sorrow is to free yourself from selfish desires.

Buddhists try to have the right beliefs and right hopes, say the right words, do the right things, live the right way of life, make the right effort, think the right thoughts and concentrate in the right way. They try not to be carried away by their feelings or do wrong, but to love their enemies.

Many become monks, living in monasteries and begging for food. All hope to understand their own inner lives and to reach perfect freedom of mind and peace. Buddhists call this condition *nirvana*.

This is a ceremony for Jewish boys. Its name means 'a son of the commandment'. The boys who take part are those thought old enough to obey the commandments of the Jewish religion.

Before the ceremony, each boy receives special instruction in what he must learn and do. The bar mitzvah ceremony is held in a synagogue, usually on the Saturday after the boy's thirteenth birthday. He has to read from a scroll bearing the words of the Torah, the Jewish Law. Then he takes on the religious duties of an adult.

After the ceremony the boy's family invite friends and relatives to a feast. All give the boy presents. At one time boys used to make a speech to show that they knew the Bible and Jewish teachings.

To many Jewish families, the bar mitzvah is almost as important as a wedding. Many Jewish girls take part in a similar ceremony, called a *bas mitzvah*.

Prayer wheels are metal or wooden cylinders containing rolls of paper with printed prayers. They are used by some Buddhists, especially in Tibet.

Each wheel is free to spin around on a rod. Some prayer wheels stand on a table, but others are held in the hand by a handle. When the hand makes a circling movement, a weight hung from the cylinder makes it revolve.

A prayer wheel may contain a number of prayers printed on the roll of paper which is placed inside the cylinder. Each time the wheel is turned, this is supposed to count as saying the prayer as many times as it is printed on the roll. In fact the prayers represent mystical sounds called *mantras*.

Mantras are part of a strange group of magical signs and sounds that found their way into Buddhism in Tibet.

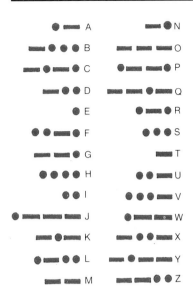

●━ A	━● N
━●●● B	━━━ O
━●━● C	●━━● P
━●● D	━━●━ Q
● E	●━● R
●●━● F	●●● S
━━● G	━ T
●●●● H	●●━ U
●● I	●●●━ V
●━━━ J	●━━ W
━●━ K	━●●━ X
●━●● L	━●━━ Y
━━ M	━━●● Z

◀ WHAT IS MORSE CODE?

This is a code using dots and dashes to stand for letters and numbers. It was once the main way of sending telegraph signals along wires or by radio. The code was invented in 1837 by the American inventor Samuel Morse.

In Morse code, different letters, numbers and punctuation marks are given as different groups of dots and dashes. Dots are sent as short signals, dashes as long signals.

Signals are made by pressing the key of a sending device which alters a continuous electrical or radio signal and produces rapid sounds in a receiver.

The longer you press the key, the longer the signal. One dot lasts half as long as a short dash. A short dash lasts half as long as a long dash. Each gap between the dots and dashes making up a letter lasts as long as one dot. Each gap between the letters of a word lasts as long as three dots.

◀ WHAT IS SEMAPHORE USED FOR?

Semaphore is a method of using flags or mechanical arms or lights to signal messages. Its name comes from two Greek words meaning 'signal carrier'.

Semaphore signalling was invented as a way of sending signals between people who could see one another but were out of earshot. Sailors use semaphore to signal from ship to ship when they are afraid their radio signals

might be overheard by an enemy.

A signaller holds two flags or lights at arm's length and moves his arms to different positions, like the hands on a clock. Each position stands for a different letter. To show numbers, the signaller gives a special numeral signal. This is followed by a letter of the alphabet corresponding to each number.

Semaphore markers on a railway line may form part of the points mechanism. They show train drivers how the points have been set.

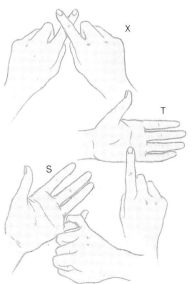

◀ WHAT IS DEAF-AND-DUMB LANGUAGE?

Deaf-and-dumb language is a way of 'talking' with the fingers and hands instead of the mouth. People who are unable to speak or hear can use it to hold conversations.

There are two main kinds of deaf-and-dumb sign language. One method uses one hand, the other uses both hands. In both methods, different finger positions stand for different letters of

the alphabet. Each method involves spelling out words one letter at a time. Talking in deaf-and-dumb sign language is much slower than speaking. Deaf-and-dumb people can talk faster if they also use other gestures and facial expressions as short cuts.

Deaf-and-dumb language is used less than it once was. This is because people who are born deaf can now be taught to speak. Many deaf people also now use hearing aids or learn to lip-read spoken sound by watching the shapes of the speaker's lips.

Braille is a code of raised dots. Blind people can read Braille by running their fingers over the dots on a page. The code was invented in the 1820s by a blind French student called Louis Braille.

Braille is based on a block of six dots which is two dots wide and three dots high. By leaving out different dots, Braille produced 63 different dot patterns standing for different letters, punctuation marks, numbers and even musical notes.

Ten patterns made from the top four dots stand for the first ten letters of the alphabet. Adding a special number sign turns each of these into a number. Adding a bottom left-hand dot to the patterns for A to J makes the letters K to T. Adding a bottom right-hand dot to the patterns for K to O makes the letters U to Z. Other groups of dots build simple words or sounds of speech. People can also type Braille with a special typewriter.

Esperanto is a language invented to make it easy for people of all nations to understand one another. Esperanto was introduced in 1887 in a book written by its Polish inventor, Ludwik Zamenhof.

The Esperanto alphabet uses letters from the Roman alphabet, but not Q, W, X or Y. Some letters have two sounds. The second sound is shown by a mark over the letter.

Esperanto words come mostly from words whose main parts are shared by important European languages. But all nouns end in 'o' and adjectives end in 'a'.

There are no muddling exceptions to the rules of grammar as there are in other languages. This makes Esperanto easy to study. People can learn to speak Esperanto up to twenty times faster than it takes them to learn to speak some other languages. The picture shows the first French taxi-driver to speak Esperanto.

***Micro* means 'small'. Microfilm is used to store bulky information in a small space. It bears extremely tiny photographic copies of printed pages or other kinds of information.**

Microfilm is often used for making copies of books and newspapers, for use in schools or libraries. This adds enormously to the amount of information that can be kept.

Businesses store microfilm copies of business records that would otherwise take up too much office space.

A special camera is used to photograph each page of a book on a tiny panel on a roll of film. As many as a thousand pages can be stored on a microfiche – a sheet of microfilm no bigger than a person's hand.

To read the film, you place it in a machine (seen here) that greatly enlarges the words on the microfilm. To find a special panel on a strip of film you wind on the film.

▲ WHAT IS A SARI?

This is a straight length of woven fabric worn by many Indian women. They drape it loosely around the entire body so that one end serves as a skirt and the other covers the shoulders or the head.

Each sari measures from 5.5 to 8 metres long. A sari is the only piece of clothing that poorer women wear. Most other women wear one over a half-slip.

They wrap the lower end of the sari several times around the waist to form a full skirt with pleats at the front. Then they drape the upper end of the sari loosely over the chest or the shoulders. Usually they also wear a blouse or a rather similar upper garment called a *choli*.

Peasants who work in the fields often wear plain cloth saris coloured white or blue. But many wealthy Indian women have expensive saris of silk with borders of gold thread. Saris have been worn for thousands of years.

▲ WHAT IS A KIMONO USED FOR?

The name *kimono* simply means a 'wearing thing'. Kimonos are loose robes worn by Japanese men and women, mostly indoors. The Japanese have been wearing clothes like this for hundreds of years.

Each kimono, including its sleeves, is cut out of a single piece of material. This is shaped to make a loose robe with a flowing skirt and wide sleeves.

A kimono is usually worn with a sash called an *obi* tied around the waist. The kimono may be made of cotton or silk. Some of the most splendid ones are made of rich silk crêpe with embroidered patterns, and sashes of patterned brocade.

Kimonos are comfortable as well as beautiful. Many Japanese men and women wear light, simple cotton kimonos indoors. Dressy kimonos are very expensive and worn only on special occasions.

▲ WHAT IS A KILT?

A kilt is a knee-length pleated skirt traditionally worn by men from the Scottish Highlands and Ireland. Nowadays they wear their kilts only on special occasions.

Each kilt is pleated at the back from the waist, but the front is plain. Scottish kilts are made of tartans. These are woollen fabrics with usually a red or green background that is criss-crossed by stripes of various colours. Different patterns represent different Highland clans or districts. The traditional Irish kilts are a plain saffron colour.

Most patterned kilts have permanent pleats folded so that the pattern shows up when seen from any angle. Highland regiments have box-pleated kilts with one main stripe showing down each pleat. In front of the kilt, a Highlander may wear a *sporran*, a fur-covered pouch. The men of ancient Egypt wore white linen kilts.

▲ WHAT IS APARTHEID?

▲ WHAT ARE GUERRILLAS?

▲ WHAT ARE MERCENARIES?

This Afrikaans word means 'apartness'. South Africa's white rulers used it to describe their policy for the separate development of the white and non-white peoples of South Africa.

Strict apartheid laws keep whites and non-whites apart. Non-whites are forbidden to marry whites or do the same jobs or live in the same places as whites. Many blacks now live in tribal reserves, or their own nation-states.

South Africa's government said apartheid would help the non-whites to be better off by helping themselves. But many people feel that this cannot happen while most wealth and power belongs to the whites, who are far fewer than the blacks and coloureds.

By the 1980s, though, South Africa had relaxed certain apartheid rules. For instance, people of any colour became freer to watch or play some sports together. Also it became easier for blacks to work and travel in cities.

Guerrillas are fighters who make hit-and-run raids on enemy forces during a war. They tend to fight in small groups, not as part of a main army, and might not wear uniforms. The word *guerrilla* is Spanish for 'little war'.

Bands of guerrillas often fight behind enemy lines. They make sudden attacks against enemy outposts, ambush convoys of enemy lorries, or blow up enemy trains. Guerrillas often find food and hiding places with help from friendly people who live in the area.

By choosing when and where to attack, a small band of guerrillas can make trouble for a far larger enemy force. Thousands of troops may fail to discover a handful of guerrillas if these can hide in a forest, a mountain range or a large city.

Guerrillas have fought in many wars this century in Europe, Africa, Asia and Central America.

Mercenaries are soldiers prepared to fight in any war for any side that pays them. The word *mercenary* comes from a Latin word meaning 'wages'. Some fight just for money, others more for adventure.

More than two thousand years ago, hired soldiers fought for the Persians, Greeks and Romans. About seven hundred years ago the warring kings and princes of Europe hired German and Swiss mercenaries. The mercenary Swiss Guard still protects the Vatican in Rome.

The most famous mercenary fighting unit has long been France's Foreign Legion. Its officers are almost all French, but many of its legionnaires are volunteers from other countries. Some are wanted criminals. The Legion takes anyone young and fit enough to fight unless it knows he is a murderer. Since 1960 some European mercenaries have fought in several African wars.

521

WHEN WERE THE FIRST NEWSPAPERS PUBLISHED?

People began reading newspapers in the 1600s. Until then, news had travelled slowly by word of mouth.

In the Middle Ages, news of a foreign war, or the king's death, often took days to reach distant parts of the country. Town criers shouted out the news to townsfolk.

In the 1500s, after the invention of printing machinery, people began reading pamphlets and newsletters. The first newspaper to be printed regularly was called the *Corante*. It came out in London in 1621 and contained news from France, Italy, Spain and other countries.

Newspapers quickly became popular. In 1643 the first paper with pictures appeared. Its title was the *Civic Mercury*. By the 1700s, newspapers carried news of world events, business, shipping, farm prices, theatre and gossip. Some of today's famous daily newspapers, such as *The Times*, began at this time.

WHEN DID THE FIRST ALPHABET APPEAR?

Stone-Age people wrote in pictures. The first alphabet, with letters standing for sounds, appeared about 3500 years ago.

In simple picture-writing, a sign stands for an object – for example a bird. In time, picture-writing also came to stand for ideas, so a bird-sign might mean 'flying'. The people of ancient Egypt wrote in picture-signs called hieroglyphs.

To write in picture-signs, you need thousands of different pictures or characters. If signs stand for sounds, instead of things, it is easy to group them together to make words.

The Phoenicians, living in the eastern Mediterranean some 3500 years ago, were the first to invent an alphabet of sound-signs. Their alphabet was borrowed and improved by first the Greeks and then the Romans. Our word 'alphabet' comes from the Greek words for the first two letters in their alphabet, *alpha* and *beta*.

PHOENICIAN	ANCIENT GREEK	MODERN ENGLISH
ᚴ ᚷ	A	A
9 9	B	B
1	Γ	C G
ᐁ ᐃ	Δ	D
ᖑ ᖕ	E	E
Y	F	F
ᔦ ᔦ	Z	Z
ᕈ ᕼ	H	H
⊗	Θ	
ᒿ	I	I J
ᕝ ᕝᕓ	K	K
ᒡ ᒪ	Λ	L
ᙢ ᙢ	M	M
ᒥ ᔭ	N	N
ᖳ ᖌ ᖏ	Ξ	X
O O	O	O
ᒣ ᒧ	Π	P
ᖧᐁᖧ	ᐁ	Q
ᖴᖴᖴ	Q	
ᐁ	P	R
W	Σ	S
X	T	T
	Υ	U V
	Φ	W
	X	
	Ψ	Y
	Ω	

WHEN WAS INK FIRST MADE?

Writing was first done not with a pen and ink, but with a stick, making marks in wet clay. Writing on paper with ink began some 4500 years ago.

The ancient Chinese and Egyptians used ink. They mixed soot or lampblack with gum to make a hard stick. The ink stick was mixed with water before being used. To make different coloured inks, the Chinese and Egyptians used minerals, berries, plant juices and crushed insects.

The Chinese used brushes to write in ink and were the first to print with ink, using wooden blocks. When Gutenberg began printing in Europe in the 1400s, the ink was made by mixing varnish or boiled linseed oil with lampblack.

Quick-drying inks appeared in the 1700s. Today most printing inks are made by chemical processes. Different kinds of ink are used to print onto cloth, plastic, paper and other materials.

Coins and other forms of money had been in use for hundreds of years before banknotes appeared. China was the first to print paper money. Notes were not used in Europe until the 1600s.

Shells, stones, beads, teeth, even cattle, were used as money in ancient times. The first proper coins were made from gold and silver. The Greeks were the first people to issue coins that were checked for weight. These looked much the same as the coins we carry today. Modern coins, however, are made of cheaper metals than gold and silver.

Paper money came later, first in China, and then in Europe during the 1600s. The first European banknotes were issued by the Bank of Stockholm in Sweden in 1661. Paper money was lighter to carry than gold coins.

At first many people did not trust the new notes. In time they realized that a banknote was just as valuable as the sum in gold that it represented.

The first bankers were goldsmiths in the Middle Ages. But borrowing and lending money has been part of human affairs for much longer.

Ever since coins first appeared, some 2500 years ago, people have traded in money. The word 'bank' comes from the Italian *banco*, meaning 'bench'. Money-changers and merchants did business from benches in the market place.

Goldsmiths looked after their gold in strongrooms. They let other people store their money there for safety. The paper receipts that the goldsmiths gave their customers came to be used as money – just like coins.

The bankers of Europe helped explorers and merchant adventurers by lending them money to buy ships and trade goods. The first big national bank was the Bank of England, which was started in 1694. The Bank of France began under Napoleon in 1800.

The ancient Chinese had a kind of postal system for sending messages. But postage stamps came into use only in 1840. Stamps made it easier and cheaper for people to send letters.

By the 1700s most European countries had some sort of postal service. In the USA too there were thousands of post offices by the 1830s. Letters were carried on horseback and by stagecoach.

In Britain, Rowland Hill saw that it would save time and money if letters could be sent any distance for a fixed charge. The simplest method was for the sender to buy a postage stamp and stick it on the letter. In 1840 the 'penny post' was used for the first time.

Soon countries all over the world were issuing stamps. Most people could afford to post a letter, and it was not long before people also began to collect the stamps themselves. The development of railways greatly speeded up the sending of mail.

▶ WHERE DO ABORIGINES LIVE?

Aborigines are a country's earliest inhabitants. The best-known aborigines are those of Australia.

Australian Aborigines have dark-brown skin and wavy hair. Their ancestors may have migrated from South-East Asia about 40,000 years ago.

Aborigines lived in small wandering bands and made simple shelters at resting places. They used weapons and tools made from wood and stone to hunt and gather food. One of their weapons was the boomerang. This is a throwing weapon made from wood. One type is cleverly designed to return to the thrower.

Australian Aborigines had their own music, art and religion. At times they would gather for a corroboree, a festival of music and dancing.

There were about 300,000 Aborigines in Australia when Europeans first arrived there two hundred years ago. Many Aborigines were persecuted by European settlers, and now only about 110,000 remain.

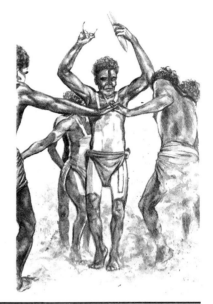

◀ WHERE DO MAORIS LIVE?

The Maoris are the native people of New Zealand. Indeed the word *Maori* means 'native'.

Maoris mostly have light-brown skin, brown or black hair and eyes, a broad face with high cheekbones, and a straight nose. They tend to be tall and strongly built.

Maoris speak a Polynesian language. Hundreds of years ago their ancestors sailed from far-off Pacific islands in huge canoes. They were the first people to discover and settle in New Zealand.

When British settlers arrived in the early 1800s, Maoris were Stone-Age farmers, hunters and fishermen. They were skilled carvers, tattooists and weavers, and sang songs and war chants.

Maoris could be fierce warriors. At times their tribes fought British settlers. But later both groups made peace and intermarried. Maoris now lead a modern way of life but they keep up their customs. The Maoris shown here are wearing traditional dress.

▶ WHERE DO THE TUAREG LIVE?

The Tuareg are nomads of northern Africa. Some roam the Sahara Desert. Others live on its southern edge.

The Tuareg belong to the Berber peoples, who lived in North Africa long before the Arabs arrived. They speak the old Tuareg language and use an ancient kind of writing. The Tuareg are Muslims. In contrast to many Muslims, the Tuareg men, not the women, veil their faces.

There are two Tuareg classes: nobles and vassals. Nobles own camels, goats, sheep and farms set in oases. Vassals mind the nobles' livestock. Negro serfs grow crops on the nobles' farms.

Tuareg are independent and proud. They once raided and traded far across the Sahara. They also fought against the French Foreign Legion. But many Tuareg have now left the desert to find more fertile land to the south. Their old ways of life are vanishing fast.

◄ WHERE DO PYGMIES LIVE?

Pygmies are very small people, mostly living a primitive life. Groups live in remote parts of Africa, the Andaman Islands of the Indian Ocean, Malaysia and the Philippines. Their numbers are few and becoming fewer still.

The best-known pygmies are the African pygmies, known as Negrillos. These live in the hot, steamy forests of Central Africa. Negrillos look very like small Negroes. A full-grown Negrillo is no taller than a 10-year-old Negro boy of normal height.

African pygmies gather wild plants, catch fish, and use poisoned arrows to shoot animals such as monkeys and antelopes. They do not grow crops or keep farm animals.

Negrillos wear few clothes, but make bags and pottery and build simple huts. They are wanderers, but each small group has its own territory. Negrillos trade meat for iron tools and food grown by Negro tribes in the forest.

► WHERE DO ESKIMOS LIVE?

Eskimos live in the cold polar regions of North America and north-east Asia. They are related to the Chinese and Japanese. Their ancestors probably migrated across the Arctic thousands of years ago.

Eskimos are well built to survive long cold, Arctic winters. Their short, stocky bodies store heat better than those of tall, thin people.

Eskimos have learnt how to cope with the cold. They make warm fur coats and build turf-roofed homes, half hidden underground. In winter, hunters far out on the ice build snow houses called igloos.

Eskimos are skilled at fishing and hunting seals and whales. Their hunting boats are slim, skin-covered canoes called *kayaks*. On land, teams of dogs haul sleds that carry equipment and dead game. But old ways of life are dying. Many Eskimos now live in wooden houses in towns.

◄ WHERE DO LAPPS LIVE?

Lapps live mostly in the region of northern Europe called Lapland. This covers parts of northern Sweden, Finland, and the USSR.

Lapps are short, strongly built people. They have straight black hair, low foreheads, and high cheek bones. Many have flat noses and thin lips. Lapps have their own language. They wear colourful clothes of wool and reindeer skins.

Different groups live in different places. Mountain Lapps lead a wandering life with their reindeer herds. Each family shares one tent.

River Lapps live a more settled life along river banks. Besides reindeer, they keep cattle and sheep. River Lapps hunt and fish, and some grow a few crops. Sea Lapps live in wood and turf huts built on the coast. Most work as fishermen.

The Lapps' ancestors lived in Central Asia. They reached Lapland thousands of years ago. Some Lapps now move out of Lapland and marry people to the south.

◄ WHERE HAVE ANCIENT TEMPLES BEEN DISMANTLED AND REBUILT?

When the High Dam was built at Aswan on the River Nile, a great lake formed behind it. To prevent the water engulfing them, two temples at Abu Simbel were dismantled and rebuilt on higher ground.

The Egyptian Pharaoh Ramses II had the temples built at Abu Simbel about 3200 years ago. They were carved out of the face of a cliff beside the River Nile. The Great Temple had 14 rooms and stretched 60 metres into the cliff. Four huge stone seated figures of Ramses II flanked the entrance. Six huge figures guarded the other temple.

In the 1960s, the new Aswan High Dam blocked the Nile and its waters rose. To save the temples, workmen cut them into huge blocks weighing 20 to 30 tonnes each. They raised these to the nearby hilltop, then fitted them together again. About 50 nations gave money to pay for this colossal project.

◄ WHERE IS THE VALLEY OF THE KINGS?

This is a narrow rocky gorge in southern Egypt. Ancient Egyptians buried many of their kings in the valley.

The Valley of the Kings lies on the west bank of the River Nile, near the ancient Egyptian city of Thebes. Here, in the desert, people have discovered more than 60 tombs. They were made more than 3200 years ago.

Each tomb consists of corridors and rooms cut deep into solid rock. Sculptors and artists carved and painted religious signs and writing on the walls. When a king died, people laid his body here inside a great stone coffin. They also left rich treasures for his use in an after-life.

Tombs had secret doors and deep pits to keep out robbers. In time, though, thieves plundered almost every tomb. Only one tomb remained intact. It belonged to Tutankhamun, a young, unimportant king, yet its splendour astonished the archaeologists who found it.

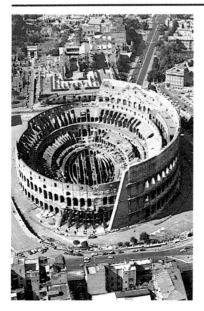

◄ WHERE IS THE BIGGEST ROMAN AMPHITHEATRE?

The biggest ancient Roman amphitheatre is the Colosseum in Rome, Italy. Amphitheatres were early sports stadiums. They had a central arena surrounded by seats. Indeed, their name means 'theatre on both sides'.

The remains of the Colosseum still stand, near the centre of Rome. Its outer walls are 49 metres high, and it measures 187 metres in length and 157 metres in width.

More than 86,000 spectators could sit or stand on tiers raised on arches. They looked down on a big oval central arena. Engineers could flood this for sea-battles. But the Romans used it mostly for fights to the death between trained fighters called gladiators, or between people and wild animals.

The Romans built the Colosseum by AD 80. Its name came later from a colossus (a huge statue) of the Emperor Nero. The Emperor Hadrian had this placed at the entrance.

INDEX